MATHEMATICS OF BUSINESS AND FINANCE

First Edition

Larry Daisley, *Seneca College*

Thambyrajah Kugathasan, *Seneca College*

Diane Huysmans, *Fanshawe College*

Vretta

ISBN 978-0-9866606-0-3
Textbook printed in Canada.

Authors: Larry Daisley, Thambyrajah Kugathasan, Diane Huysmans
Instructional Design: Charles Anifowose
Textbook editor: Lakshmi Kugathasan
Solution manual and test bank editors: Sami Khan, Phoebe Wu
PowerPoint presentations: Anita Joshua
Design and illustrations: Jisha James
Typesetting: Patience Kyereboah
Online lessons voice talent: Scott Fox, Ashley Grecco, Jeremy Ryan
Copyrights researcher: Venessa Edwards

Financial designation problems: Kaplan-Schweser course materials for Certified Financial Analyst designation
Pre-programmed financial calculator: Texas Instruments BAII Plus
Turning Technologies' Student Response System (Clickers) integrated into In-Class Powerpoint Presentations
Expert advice: World Financial Group, TD Canada Trust
The online resources use Cloud Learning™ technologies.

Preface

Mathematics of Business and Finance is a crucial introductory subject for college students as it provides them with the foundation required to succeed in their academic and professional lives. While critical to students' success, this subject is often perceived as intimidating. We created this blended resource to change this perception, also aiming to solve common challenges such as high student dropout rates, low grades, and student absenteeism.

We have worked closely with professors and students from different colleges to meticulously identify different learning methods which cater to the varied learning styles of students. Using these insights, we have created highly intuitive mathematical pedagogies that simplify concepts, making it possible for students to master the skills they need to excel in this subject.

Blended learning, commonly known as hybrid learning, is a method of combining different learning environments, such as face-to-face, web-based, and mobile learning. The goal of blended learning is to enhance the learning experience by catering to different learning styles, including visual, auditory, tactile, and sociological, which are present in the diverse groups of students.

To provide students with an outstanding learning experience, we recommend that they complete the highly interactive and engaging online lessons as a pre-study before attending class. In class, professors will reinforce the concepts using real-world application-based problems from this textbook or with help from the animated PowerPoint presentations. After class, students can use the online lab system, which contains algorithmically generated problems in varying levels of difficulty, to assess their understanding of the subject.

Our aim is to inspire and empower every learner in the world and we hope that you thoroughly enjoy discovering this resource and the value it will bring to students.

Larry, Kuga, Diane, and Vretta's Mathematics of Business and Finance team

Brief Contents

Contents

Chapter 8

Chapter 9

Chapter 11

Chapter 12

List of Exhibits, Tables, and Cases

Exhibits

Tables

Cases

Resources

Textbook

Language The language used in this textbook is simple and straight-forward, while maintaining the levels of sophistication required to thoroughly prepare students for the next stage in their academic and professional careers.

Pedagogies and Learning Methods Numerous pedagogies and learning methods that have been developed and proven over 30 years are incorporated into the textbook. These pedagogies have succeeded in simplifying critical mathematical concepts and significantly improving retention of concepts. The different learning methods to solve problems have also proven to cater to the varied student learning styles.

Calculator The textbook uses the pre-programmed Texas Instruments BAII Plus financial calculator to solve problems in conjunction with algebraic methods wherever required. The calculator instructions are designed using the actual images of the calculator keys, making it very easy for students to follow the sequence of operations.

Exercises The textbook has over 1500 exercises, review exercises, self-test exercises, and comprehensive cases, as well as over 300 solved examples. Problems are designed to test students on real-world, practical applications and are presented in increasing levels of difficulty, with the most difficult problems being indicated by a dot (•). The problems are categorized into pairs of similar questions to provide professors with an opportunity to solve the even-numbered problems in class and assign the odd-numbered problems as home work.

Financial Designation Problems The textbook contains problems that are used to prepare students for the first level of the Certified Financial Analyst (CFA) professional designation exam. This will provide students with exposure to the financial career choices that will be available to them in the future. These problems are identified by a '**CFA Prep.**' icon. CFA Prep.

Solution Manual

All problems in the end-of-section exercises, review exercises, self-test exercises, and cases have been solved using detailed step-by-step methods, including the financial calculator method as demonstrated in the solved examples. The solution manual is available online for professors.

PowerPoint Presentations

The animated PowerPoint presentations are available for professors to use in class. They contain both the algebraic and calculator methods of solving problems. The PowerPoint presentations are designed to work with clickers in class to gauge student understanding of concepts.

Test Bank

A comprehensive test bank, of over 350 problems in varying levels of difficulty, that covers all concepts in the textbook is provided for professors to use as a database for exercises, quizzes, cases, group projects, or assignments.

Online Lessons

The online lessons are created as a pre-study component for students. They contain pedagogies that are highly interactive and engaging, and which teach concepts in a very logical and intuitive way. These lessons are not PowerPoint presentations but are interactive movies that have been created to enrich and enhance the learning experience. Every frame is locked to ensure that students go through the lessons sequentially as they are designed to build on learning concepts in succession. The system automatically records students' progress and performance. Once students complete a lesson, the frame unlocks itself, allowing students to navigate back and forth through the lesson. Professors, on the other hand, have administrative access which allows them to navigate through the online lessons without any restrictions.

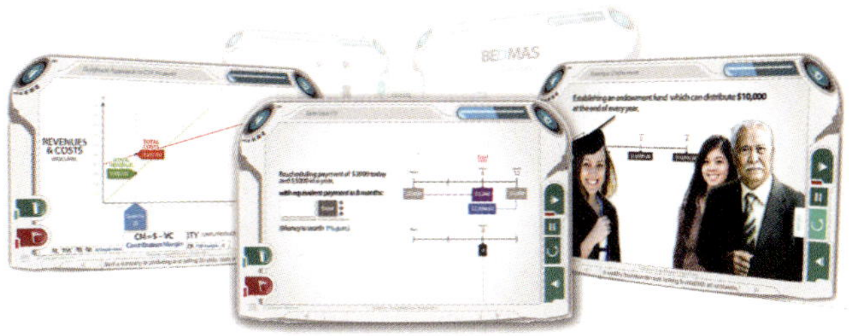

Online Labs

The online lab assessment system contains a rich comprehensive test-bank of real-world problems that are algorithmically generated and that provide students with dynamic feedback on their responses. The labs can also be customized based on course requirements. A few of the customizable features include, previewing and selecting questions, setting the number of questions, setting and modifying start and due dates, opening, closing and re-opening labs, creating new labs and quizzes, and determining the weighting and number of attempts for each question.

Administrative Tools

The following administrative tools will provide professors with the ability to monitor overall class performance and individual student performance on online lessons and labs.

Performance Dashboard for Professors

The lesson performance dashboard provides professors with the average completion percentage per chapter, including a lesson-by-lesson percentage completed visualization for the entire class. The lab performance dashboard provides them with the average percentage mark on each lab for the class. Professors can also download or export individual grades for lessons and labs to a spreadsheet or to the college's course management system.

Performance Dashboard for Students

The lesson performance dashboard provides students with their chapter completion mark, including a lesson-by-lesson percentage completed visualization. The lab performance dashboard provides them with their lab percentage marks.

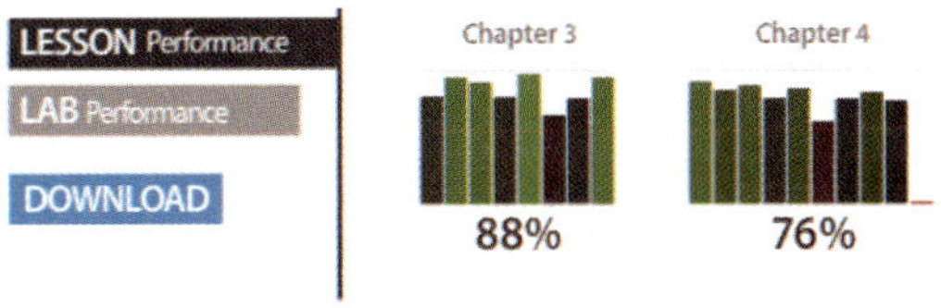

Lab Management System The lab management system is provided for administrators or subject leaders to create new labs, quizzes and case studies, preview and select questions, set the number of questions, set and modify start and due dates, open, close and re-open labs, and determine the weighting and number of attempts for each question.

MATHEMATICS OF BUSINESS AND FINANCE

First Edition

Larry Daisley, *Seneca College*

Thambyrajah Kugathasan, *Seneca College*

Diane Huysmans, *Fanshawe College*

Vretta

Arithmetic is the most elementary branch of mathematics. It includes calculations such as addition, subtraction, multiplication, division, etc. We use arithmetic throughout our lives for everyday tasks such as counting, buying, selling, estimating expenses, and checking bank balances. Arithmetic also forms the basis for all advanced technology, science, engineering, and business studies. In this chapter you will review the basic skills that are necessary for business and finance applications.

1 Review of Basic Arithmetic

LEARNING OBJECTIVES

- Understand place value of numbers and rounding of numbers, decimals, and percentages to required place values.
- Determine the lowest common multiple or denominator (LCM or LCD) and highest common factor (HCF).
- Identify types of fractions and perform computations using fractions.
- Apply basic arithmetic operations in their proper order.
- Calculate the simple arithmetic average and weighted average for a set of values.

(^ ÷ × + −)

CHAPTER OUTLINE

1.1 | Place Value of Numbers and Rounding Numbers

Place Value of Whole Numbers

Place value is the value of a digit as determined by its position in a number, such as ones, tens, hundreds, etc.

The **position** of each digit in a whole number determines the **place value** for the digit. Exhibit 1.1(a) illustrates the place value of the ten digits in the whole number: 3,867,254,129. In this example, 4 is in the 'thousands' place value and represents 4000, whereas 7 is in the 'millions' place value and represents 7,000,000.

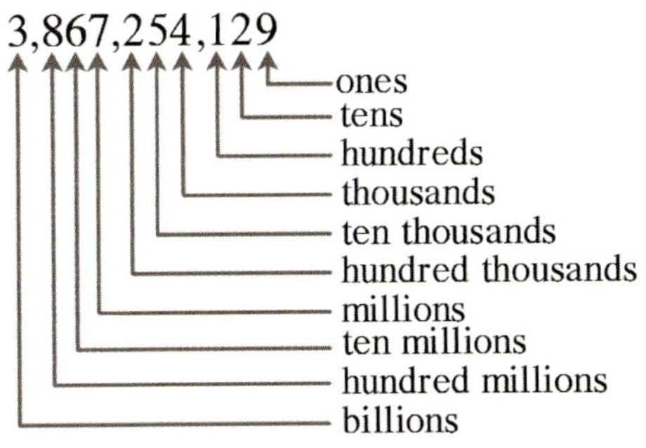

Exhibit 1.1(a): Place Value of a Ten-Digit Whole Number

We read and write numbers, from left to right. A comma (or alternatively, a space) separates every three digits into groups, starting from the place value for 'ones', thereby making it easier to read a whole number.

The place value of 'ones' is 10^0 (= 1) and each place has a value 10 times the place value to its right, as shown in Table 1.1(a) below:

Table 1.1(a) Place Value Chart of Whole Numbers

10^9	10^8	10^7	10^6	10^5	10^4	10^3	10^2	10^1	10^0
1,000,000,000	100,000,000	10,000,000	1,000,000	100,000	10,000	1000	100	10	1
Billion	**Hundred million**	**Ten million**	**Million**	**Hundred thousand**	**Ten thousand**	**Thousand**	**Hundred**	**Ten**	**One**

The vertical red lines denote the positions of the commas that separate the groups of three numbers, starting from the place value for 'ones'. The above 10-digit number written as 3,867,254,129 is called the ***standard form of writing numbers***.

3	8	6	7	2	5	4	1	2	9

This can be written in ***expanded form*** as follows:

- 3,000,000,000 + 800,000,000 + 60,000,000 + 7,000,000 + 200,000 + 50,000 + 4,000 + 100 + 20 + 9

Or

- 3 billion + 800 million + 60 million + 7 million + 200 thousand + 50 thousand + 4 thousand + 1 hundred + 2 tens + 9 ones

This can also be written in ***word form*** as follows:

- Three billion, eight hundred sixty-seven million, two hundred fifty-four thousand, one hundred twenty-nine.

The word 'and' does not appear in the word form of whole numbers.

Place Value of Decimal Numbers

The position of each digit in a decimal number determines the place value of the digit. Exhibit 1.1(b) illustrates the place value of the five-digit decimal number: 0.35796.

The place value of each digit is found by decreasing powers of 10, as shown in Table 1.1(b) below:

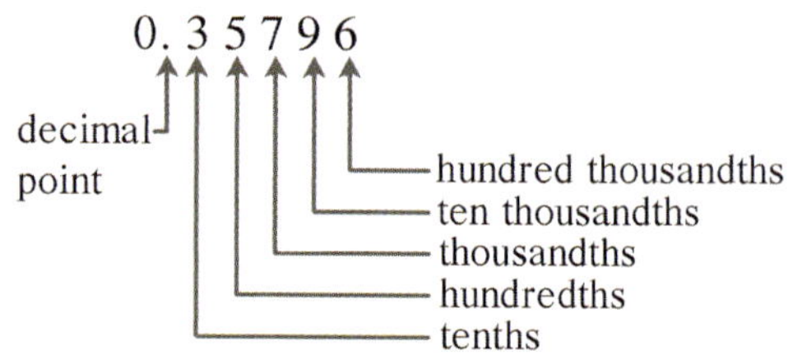

Exhibit 1.1(b): Place Value of a Five-Digit Decimal Number

Table 1.1(b)

Place Value Chart of Decimal Numbers

$10^{-1} = \frac{1}{10}$	$10^{-2} = \frac{1}{100}$	$10^{-3} = \frac{1}{1000}$	$10^{-4} = \frac{1}{10,000}$	$10^{-5} = \frac{1}{100,000}$
0.1	0.01	0.001	0.0001	0.00001
Tenth	**Hundredth**	**Thousandth**	**Ten-thousandth**	**Hundred-thousandth**

Example of the decimal number written in its ***standard form***:

0.	3	5	7	9	6

This can be written in ***expanded form*** as follows:

- 0.3 + 0.05 + 0.007 + 0.0009 + 0.00006

Or

- 3 tenths + 5 hundredths + 7 thousandths + 9 ten-thousandths + 6 hundred-thousandths

This can be written in ***word form*** as follows:

- Zero point three five seven nine six.

Decimal numbers can be expressed in their word form in 3 ways.

For example '.85' can be expressed as: 'point eight five', 'point eighty-five', or 'eighty-five hundredths'.

Example 1.1(a)

Place Value of a Digit

What is the place value of the digit 5 in each of the following and what amount does it represent?

(i) 675,342 (ii) 35,721,890 (iii) 5,916,203,847 (iv) 243.4759

Solution

	(i) 675,342	(ii) 35,721,890	(iii) 5,916,203,847	(iv) 243.4759
Place Value	Thousands	Millions	Billions	Thousandths
Amount it Represents	5000	5,000,000	5,000,000,000	0.005

Example 1.1(b)

Identifying the Digit of a Number Given its Place Value

In 320,948.751, identify the digit that occupies the following place values:

(i) Hundred thousands (ii) Ten thousands (iii) Thousands (iv) Hundredths

Solution

(i) 3 (ii) 2 (iii) 0 (iv) 5

Example 1.1(c)

Writing Numbers in Expanded and Word Forms

Write the following numbers in expanded and word forms:

(i) 9,865,323 (ii) 43,583,621 (iii) 8,213,505,235 (iv) 478.25

Solution

(i) Number: **9,865,323**
Expanded form: 9,000,000 + 800,000 + 60,000 + 5,000 + 300 + 20 + 3
Word form: Nine million, eight hundred sixty-five thousand, three hundred twenty-three

(ii) Number: **43,583,621**
Expanded form: 40,000,000 + 3,000,000 + 500,000 + 80,000 + 3,000 + 600 + 20 + 1
Word form: Forty-three million, five hundred eighty-three thousand, six hundred twenty-one

(iii) Number: **8,213,505,235**
Expanded form: 8,000,000,000 + 200,000,000 + 10,000,000 + 3,000,000 + 500,000 + 5,000 + 200 + 30 + 5
Word form: Eight billion, two hundred thirteen million, five hundred five thousand, two hundred thirty-five

(iv) Number: **478.25**
Expanded form: 400 + 70 + 8 + 0.20 + 0.05
Word form: Four hundred seventy-eight point two five

Example 1.1(d)

Writing Numbers in Standard Form given Word Form

Write the following in standard form:

(i) Thirty-five thousand, eight hundred twenty-five

(ii) Three million, three hundred forty-two thousand, six hundred seventeen

(iii) Half of a million

(iv) Three-quarters of a billion

Solution

(i) 35,825

(ii) 3,342,617

(iii) Half of a million is $\frac{1}{2} \times 1,000,000 = 500,000$

(iv) Three-quarters of a billion is $\frac{3}{4} \times 1,000,000,000 = 750,000,000$

Rounding Whole Numbers and Decimals

Rounding numbers makes them easier to work with and easier to remember. Rounding changes some of the digits in a number but keeps its value close to the original. It is used in reporting large quantities or values that change often, such as in population, income, expenses, etc.

For example, the population of Canada is approximately 33 million or, Henry's car expense for this month is approximately $700.

Rounding of numbers also makes arithmetic operations faster and easier when it is not required to find the exact answer.

For example, if you are required to estimate the area of a rectangular plot of land that measures 114 m by 97 m, you would have to multiply 114×97 which will give you 11,058 m^2. However, you can get a quick estimate by rounding the measurements 114 to 110 and 97 to 100. This will give you an area of $110 \times 100 = 11,000$ m^2.

Rounding Whole Numbers to the Nearest Ten, Hundred, Thousand, etc.

Rounding whole numbers refers to changing the value of the whole number to the nearest ten, hundred, thousand, etc. It is also referred to as rounding whole numbers to multiples of 10, 100, 1000, etc.

For example,

- Rounding a whole number to the nearest ten is the same as rounding it to a multiple of 10.
- Rounding a whole number to the nearest hundred is the same as rounding it to a multiple of 100.
- Rounding an amount to the nearest \$10 refers to rounding the amount to a multiple of \$10.

Rounding Decimals to the Nearest Whole Number, Tenth, Hundredth, etc.

Rounding decimals refers to changing the value of the decimal number to the nearest whole number, tenth, hundredth, thousandth, etc. It is also referred to as "rounding to a specific number of decimal places", indicating the number of decimal places that will be left when the rounding is complete.

For example,

- Rounding to the nearest whole number is the same as rounding without any decimals.
- Rounding to the nearest tenth is the same as rounding to one decimal place.
- Rounding to the nearest hundredth is the same as rounding to two decimal places.
- Rounding to the nearest cent refers to rounding the amount to the nearest hundredth or to two decimal places.

Rules for Rounding Whole Numbers and Decimals

Step 1: Identify the digit to be rounded (this is the place value for which the rounding is required).

Step 2: If the digit to the immediate right of the required rounding digit is less than 5 (0, 1, 2, 3, 4), do not change the value of the rounding digit.

If the digit to the immediate right of the required rounding digit is 5 or greater than 5 (5, 6, 7, 8, 9), increase the value of the rounding digit by one (round up by one number).

Step 3:
- For rounding whole numbers: after step 2, change the value of all digits that are to the right of the rounding digit to 0.
- For rounding decimals: after step 2, drop all digits that are to the right of the rounding digit.

Example 1.1(e)

Rounding Whole Numbers

Round the following to the indicated place values:

(i) 18,568 to the nearest ten

(ii) \$24,643 to the nearest \$100

Solution

(i) Rounding 18,568 to the nearest ten.

- Identify the rounding digit in the tens place: 18,568 (6 is the digit in the tens place).
- The digit to the immediate right of the rounding digit is 8, which is greater than 5; therefore, increase the value of the rounding digit by one, from 6 to 7, and change

Solution continued

the value of the digits that are to the right of the rounding digit to 0, which will give 18,570.

Therefore, 18,568 rounded to the nearest ten (or multiple of 10) is 18,570.

(ii) Rounding $24,643 to the nearest $100.

- Identify the rounding digit in the hundreds place: 24,643 (6 is the digit in the hundreds place).
- The digit to the immediate right of the rounding digit is 4, which is less than 5; therefore, do not change the value of the rounding digit, but change the value of the digits that are to the right of the rounding digit to 0, which will give 24,600.

Therefore, $24,643 rounded to the nearest $100 (or multiple of 100) is 24,600.

Example 1.1(f)

Rounding Numbers (Visual Method)

Round the following to the indicated place value

(i) 627 to the nearest ten (multiples of 10)

(ii) 16.5 to a whole number

Solution

We can visualize these numbers on a number line to determine which number is nearest.

(i) 627 to the nearest ten (multiples of 10)

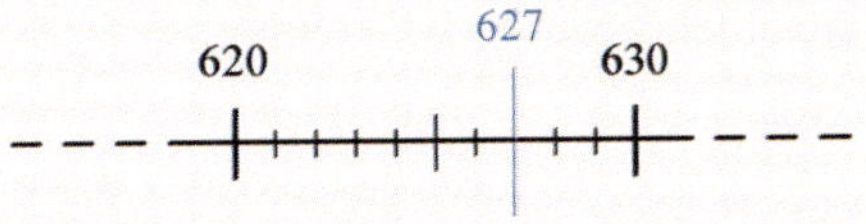

627 is closer to 630, than to 620.

Therefore, 627 rounded to the nearest ten is 630.

(ii) 16.5 to a whole number

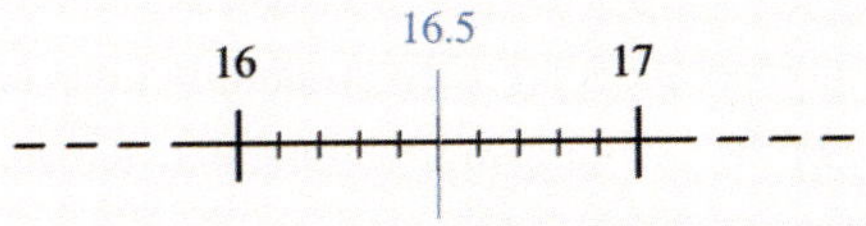

16.5 is exactly in between 16 and 17. By convention, if a number is exactly in the middle, we round it up. Therefore, 16.5 rounded to a whole number is 17.

Example 1.1(g)

Rounding Decimal Numbers

Round the following decimal numbers to the indicated place value:

(i) 268.143 to the nearest hundredth

(ii) $489.677 to the nearest cent

(iii) $39.9985 to the nearest cent

Solution

(i) Rounding 268.143 to the nearest hundredth

- Identify the rounding digit in the hundredths place: 268.143 (4 is the digit in the hundredths place).
- The digit to the immediate right of the rounding digit is less than 5; therefore do not change the value of the rounding digit. Drop all of the digits to the right of the rounding digit, which will give 268.14.

Therefore, 268.143 rounded to the nearest hundredth (or to two decimal places) is 268.14.

Solution *continued*

(ii) Rounding $489.677 to the nearest cent

- Identify the rounding digit in the hundredths place: $489.677 (7 is the digit in the hundredths place).
- The digit to the immediate right of the rounding digit is greater than 5; therefore, increase the value of the rounding digit by one, from 7 to 8, and drop all digits that are on the right side of the rounding digit, which will give $489.68.

Therefore, $489.677 rounded to the nearest cent (or to two decimal places) is $489.68.

(iii) Rounding $39.9985 to the nearest cent

- Identify the rounding digit in the hundredths place: $39.9985 (9 is the digit in the hundredths place).
- The digit to the immediate right of the rounding digit is greater than 5; therefore, increase the value of the rounding digit by one, from 9 to 10, carrying the one to the tenths place, then to the ones, then to the tens to increase 3 to 4. Finally, drop all digits that are on the right side of the hundredths place.

Therefore, $39.9985 rounded to the nearest cent (or to two decimal places) is $40.00.

Example 1.1(h)

Rounding Percentages

Round the following percentages to the number of decimal places as indicated:

(i) 12.834% to one decimal place.

(ii) 67.386% to two decimal places.

(iii) 25.325% to two decimal places.

Solution

(i) Rounding 12.834% to one decimal place.

- Identify the rounding digit in the tenths place: 12.834% (8 is the digit in the tenths place).
- The digit to the immediate right of the rounding digit is less than 5; therefore, do not change the value of the rounding digit. Drop all of the digits to the right of the rounding digit, which will give 12.8%.

Therefore, 12.834% rounded to one decimal place (or nearest tenth) is 12.8%.

(ii) Rounding 67.386% to two decimal places.

- Identify the rounding digit in the hundredths place: 67.386% (8 is the rounding digit in the hundredths place).
- The digit to the immediate right of the rounding digit is greater than 5; therefore, increase the value of the rounding digit by one, from 8 to 9, and drop all the digits that are to the right of the rounding digit which will give 67.39%.

Therefore, 67.386% rounded to two decimal places (or nearest hundredth) is 67.39%.

(iii) Rounding 25.325% to two decimal places.

- Identify the rounding digit in the hundredths place: 25.325% (2 is the rounding digit in the hundredths place).
- The digit to the immediate right of the rounding digit is equal to 5; therefore, increase the value of the rounding digit by one, from 2 to 3, and drop all the digits that are to the right of the rounding digit which will give 25.33%.

Therefore, 25.325% rounded to two decimal places (or nearest hundredth) is 25.33%.

Example 1.1(i)

Rounding a Set of Percentages which Add Up to 100%

Stephanie spends 40.18% of her salary on rent, 20.61% on food, 15.62% on travel, 10.15% on entertainment, 5.5% on pet food, and saves the remaining 7.94%. Express these percentages rounded to the nearest percentage without decimals.

Solution

These percentages rounded to the nearest percentage without decimals (percentage with whole numbers) would be:

Rent: 40%, Food: 21%, Travel: 16%, Entertainment: 10%, Pet food: 6%, and Savings: 8%.

However, the sum of these percentages would give you:

$$40\% + 21\% + 16\% + 10\% + 6\% + 8\% = 101\%$$

We have to round these numbers to give us a total of only 100%, so 1% has to be reduced from one of these rounded numbers such that it does not have a significant effect.

Changing the largest percentage will result in a smaller effect than changing the other percentages. If 40% is reduced to 39%, the change is $\frac{39\% - 40\%}{40\%} \approx -2.5\%$ but if 6% is reduced to 5%, the change is $\frac{5\% - 6\%}{6\%} \approx -16.67\%$. Changing 40% has a smaller effect than changing the 6% value.

Therefore, the percentages rounded to the nearest whole numbers are best represented as:

Rent: 39%, Food: 21%, Travel: 16%, Entertainment: 10%, Pet food: 6%, and Savings: 8%

$$39\% + 21\% + 16\% + 10\% + 6\% + 8\% = 100\%$$

Note: *When the final answer must be expressed as a percentage or when using percentages in calculations, rounding should not be done during intermediate calculations. Instead rounding to the required decimal places should only be done at the end of all calculations.*

In business and finance applications, final answers are generally rounded to the nearest hundredth (2 decimal places) for value of money (e.g., $1234.56) and percentages (e.g., 4.86%).

1.1 | Exercises

1. Write the following numbers in (a) expanded form and (b) word form:
   i. 5,249,346 ii. 95,275,385 iii. 1,146,045,787 iv. 297.50

2. Write the following numbers in (a) expanded form and (b) word form:
   i. 9,265,335 ii. 30,673,984 iii. 3,405,553,978 iv. 119.75

3. Write the following in standard form:
   a. Sixty-five thousand, two hundred forty-four point thirty-four
   b. Twelve million, four hundred fifty-two thousand, eight hundred thirty-two
   c. One-eighth of a million d. Half of a billion

4. Write the following in standard form:
   a. Eight hundred thirty-three thousand, six hundred forty-one point eighty-two
   b. Thirty-two million, six hundred eighty-four thousand, two hundred fifty-six
   c. Three-quarters of a million d. One-tenth of a billion

5. Write the following in standard form:
   a. Eighty-nine million, six hundred thirteen thousand, five hundred twenty-two, point one three
   b. Sixteen million, two hundred seventeen thousamd, five hundred sixty-seven
   c. Half of a million
   d. Three-quarters of a trillion

6. Write the following in standard form:
   a. Nine hundred fifty thousand, six hundred fifty, point zero five.
   b. Sixty-five thousand, eight hundred, point fifty-six
   c. One-quarter of a billion
   d. Half of a thousand

7. Round the following to the indicated place values:
   a. 1645 to the nearest ten
   b. 9558 to the nearest thousand
   c. $25,972 to the nearest $1000
   d. $895 to the nearest $10

8. Round the following to the indicated place values:
   a. 9157 to the nearest hundred
   b. 53,562 to the nearest ten
   c. $7915 to the nearest $100
   d. $1095 to the nearest $10

9. Round the following to the indicated place values:
   a. 132.1356 to the nearest tenth
   b. 2.8525 to the nearest whole number
   c. $85.4273 to the nearest cent
   d. $34.9861 to the nearest cent

10. Round the following to the indicated place values:
   a. 14.3575 to the nearest thousandth
   b. 142.9852 to the nearest whole number
   c. 86.6246 to the nearest cent
   c. 4.0573 to the nearest cent

11. Round the following percentages to (a) the nearest whole percentage (without decimals), to (b) 1 decimal place:
   (i) 5.567% (ii) 29.875% (iii) 75.253% (iv) 115.796%

12. Round the following percentages to (a) the nearest whole percentage (without decimals), to (b) 1 decimal place:
   (i) 56.596% (ii) 140.265% (iii) 8.955% (iv) 19.555%

13. Round the percentages in Problem 11 to the nearest percentage with 2 decimal places.

14. Round the percentages in Problem 12 to the nearest percentage with 2 decimal places.

15. Estimate the following by first rounding the numbers to the nearest ten:
   a. $745 + 1045$
   b. $428 + 255$
   c. $326 + 1555$
   d. $2449 - 2255$
   e. $946 - 452$
   f. $855 - 251$

16. Estimate the following by first rounding the numbers to the nearest ten:
   a. $357 + 245$
   b. $451 + 625$
   c. $3255 + 2105$
   d. $495 - 357$
   e. $868 - 745$
   f. $1858 - 255$

17. Estimate the values in Problem 15 by rounding to the nearest hundred.

18. Estimate the values in Problem 16 by rounding to the nearest hundred.

19. Estimate the following by first rounding the numbers to the nearest ten:
   a. 58×75
   b. 472×48
   c. 95×71
   d. $85 \div 9$
   e. $396 \div 24$
   f. $145 \div 26$

20. Estimate the following by first rounding the numbers to the nearest ten:
    a. 63×59 b. 35×97 c. 246×45 d. $78 \div 19$ e. $245 \div 45$ f. $38 \div 8$

21. A prepaid phone card to Singapore costs $5 for 3 hours. Find the cost per minute rounded to the nearest cent.

22. A prepaid phone card to China costs $2.50 for 1 hour. Find the cost per minute rounded to the nearest cent.

23. 55.25% of the employees of a large software company are engineers, 35.40% are project managers and team leads, 2.40% are senior managers, and the rest are administrative staff. Express these percentages rounded to the nearest percentage without decimals.

24. Amy invested 4.20% of her savings in bonds, 32.65% in stocks, 25.55% in mutual funds, and the balance in her brother's business. Express these percentages rounded to the nearest percentage without decimals.

1.2 | Factors and Multiples

Factors of a number are whole numbers that can divide the number with no remainder.

- For example, factors of 12 are 1, 2, 3, 4, 6, and 12. We can express factors of a number by showing how the product of two factors results in the number.

$$12 = 1 \times 12$$
$$12 = 2 \times 6$$
$$12 = 2 \times 2 \times 3$$
$$12 = 3 \times 4$$

Multiples of a number are whole numbers that can be divided by the number with no remainder. Multiples of a number can be expressed as the product of the number and a whole number.

- For example, multiples of 10:

  10, (10+10), (10+10+10), (10+10+10+10), (10+10+10+10+10) ...

  10, 20, 30, 40, 50

  10, (10×2), (10×3), (10×4), (10×5)

  Therefore, multiples of 10 are 10, 20, 30, 40, 50 ...

Prime Numbers and Composite Numbers

A **prime number** is a whole number that has only two factors: 1 and the number itself; i.e., prime numbers can be divided only by 1 and the number itself.

- For example, 7 is a prime number because it only has two factors: 1 and 7.

Example 1.2(a) **Identifying Prime Numbers**

Identify all the prime numbers less than 25.

Solution The prime numbers less than 25 are 2, 3, 5, 7, 11, 13, 17, 19, and 23.

A **composite number** is a whole number that has at least one factor other than 1 and the number itself; i.e., all whole numbers that are not prime numbers are composite numbers.

0 and 1 are neither prime numbers nor composite numbers.

- For example, 8 is a composite number because it has more than 2 factors: 1, 2, 4, and 8.

Example 1.2(b)

Identifying Composite Numbers

Identify all the composite numbers less than 25.

Solution

All the composite numbers less than 25 are

4, 6, 8, 9, 10, 12, 14, 15, 16, 18, 20, 21, 22, and 24.

Example 1.2(c)

Finding Factors of Prime Numbers

Find all the factors of 13.

Solution

1 and 13 are the only factors of 13.

Example 1.2(d)

Finding all Factors of Composite Numbers

Find all the factors of:

(i) 12

(ii) 20

Solution

(i) The factors of 12 are 1, 2, 3, 4, 6, and 12.

(ii) The factors of 20 are 1, 2, 4, 5, 10, and 20.

Example 1.2(e)

Finding the Prime Factors of Composite Numbers

Find all the prime factors of 24.

Solution

All the factors of 24 are: 2, 3, 4, 6, 8, 12, and 24.

In the above factors, only 2 and 3 are prime numbers.

Therefore, the prime factors of 24 are 2 and 3.

Least or Lowest Common Multiple (LCM)

The **Lowest Common Multiple (LCM)** of two or more whole numbers is the smallest multiple that is common to those numbers.The LCM can be determined from one of the following methods:

Method 1

(1) First, select the largest number and check to see if it is divisible by all the other numbers. If it divides, then the largest number is the LCM.

(2) If the largest number does not divide the other numbers then find a multiple of the largest number that is divisible by all the other numbers.

(3) If none of the multiples of the largest number are divisible by all the other numbers (i.e., if the numbers have no common factors), then the LCM of the numbers is the product of all the numbers.

Method 2

(1) Find the prime factors of each of the numbers and list the different prime numbers (using a factor tree as shown in the example that follows).

(2) Count the number of times each different prime number appears in each of the factorizations.

(3) Find the largest of these counts for each prime number.

(4) List that prime number as many times as you counted for it in step 3.
The LCM is the product of all the prime numbers listed.

Example 1.2(f)

Finding the Lowest Common Multiple

Find the LCM of the following:

(i) 3, 6, and 18

(ii) 9 and 15

(iii) 3, 5, and 8

Solution

(i) 3, 6, and 18

Method 1

(1) The largest number, 18, is divisible by both 6 and 3.
Therefore, 18 is the LCM of 3, 6, and 18.

Method 2

1	3	6 → 2×3	18 → 2×9 → $2 \times 3 \times 3$
2	Number of 3's = 1	Number of 2's = 1 Number of 3's = 1	Number of 2's = 1 Number of 3's = 2
3	Largest count of prime number of 2's = 1 Largest count of prime number of 3's = 2		
4	LCM = $2 \times 3 \times 3 = 18$		

(ii) 9 and 15

Method 1

(1) The largest number, 15, is ***not*** divisible by 9.

(2) Multiples of 15 are 15, 30, 45…
45 is divisible by 9.
Therefore, 45 is the LCM of 9 and 15.

Method 2

1	9 → 3×3	15 → 3×5
2	Number of 3's = 2	Number of 3's = 1 Number of 5's = 1
3	Largest count of prime number of 3's = 2 Largest count of prime number of 5's = 1	
4	LCM = $3 \times 3 \times 5 = 45$	

- If the last digit of the number is 0, 2, 4, 6, or 8, then the number is divisible by 2.
- If the sum of digits of the numbers is divisible by 3, then the number is divisible by 3.
- If the last digit of the number is 0 or 5, then the number is divisible by 5.

(iii) 3, 5, and 8

Method 1

(1) The largest number, 8, is ***not*** divisible by 3 and 5.

(2) Multiples of 8 are 16, 24, 32, 40, 48, 56, 64…
None of the multiples listed above are divisible by 3 and 5.

(3) Since 3, 5, and 8 have no common factors, the LCM is the product of all the numbers: $3 \times 5 \times 8 = 120$.
Therefore, 120 is the LCM of 3, 5, and 8.

Solution *continued*

Method 2

1	3	5	8 → 2×4 → $2 \times 2 \times 2$
2	Number of 3's = 1	Number of 5's = 1	Number of 2's = 3
3	Largest count of prime number of 2's = 3 Largest count of prime number of 3's = 1 Largest count of prime number of 5's = 1		
4	$\text{LCM} = 2 \times 2 \times 2 \times 3 \times 5 = 120$		

Least or Lowest Common Denominator (LCD)

The **Lowest Common Denominator (LCD)** of a set of two or more fractions is the smallest whole number that is divisible by each of the denominators. It is the least common multiple (LCM) of the denominators of the fractions.

In performing addition and subtraction of fractions, it is necessary to find the equivalent fraction using the least common denominator. The best choice for a common denominator is the LCD, because it makes any further simplification easier.

Example 1.2(g) **Finding the Lowest Common Denominator**

Find the LCD of $\frac{4}{9}$ and $\frac{7}{15}$.

Solution

The LCD of the fractions $\frac{4}{9}$ and $\frac{7}{15}$ is the same as the LCM of the denominators 9 and 15. It is the same as in Example 1.2(f)(ii). Therefore, the LCD of $\frac{4}{9}$ and $\frac{7}{15}$ is 45.

Highest Common Factor (HCF)

The factors that are common for two or more numbers are called **common factors** of those numbers.

The **Highest Common Factor (HCF)** of two or more numbers is the largest common number that divides the numbers with no remainder. In other words, the HCF is the largest of all the common factors. HCF is useful when simplifying fractions. For this purpose, HCF is also known as the Greatest Common Divisor (GCD).

Example 1.2(h) **Finding the Common Factors**

Find the common factors of 12 and 18.

Solution

The factors of 12 are 1, 2, 3, 4, 6, 12.

The factors of 18 are 1, 2, 3, 6, 9, 18.

The common factors are: 2, 3, and 6.

1 is a factor that is common to all numbers but is not included in the list of common factors.

Example 1.2(i) **Finding the Highest Common Factor**

Find the HCF of 72, 126, and 216.

Solution

The factors of 72 are 1, 2, 3, 4, 6, 8, 9, 12, 18, 24, 36, 72.

The factors of 126 are 1, 2, 3, 6, 7, 9, 14, 18, 21, 42, 63, 126.

The factors of 216 are 1, 2, 3, 4, 6, 8, 9, 12, 18, 24, 27, 36, 54, 72, 108, 216.

The common factors are 2, 3, 6, 9, and 18.

Therefore, the HCF is 18.

1.2 | Exercises

1. Find all the prime numbers and composite numbers of each range of numbers given below (excluding both numbers):
   a. Between 1 and 10 b. Between 14 and 28 c. Between 32 and 42 d. Between 44 and 58
2. Find all the prime numbers and composite numbers of each range of numbers given below (excluding both numbers):
   a. Between 10 and 22 b. Between 28 and 38 c. Between 42 and 55 d. Between 54 and 72
3. Find all the prime factors of the following composite numbers:
   a. 36 b. 28 c. 54 d. 65
4. Find all the prime factors of the following composite numbers:
   a. 20 b. 34 c. 46 d. 21
5. Find the Lowest Common Multiple (LCM) of the following:
   a. 5 and 15 b. 6 and 8 c. 4, 6, and 18 d. 4, 10, and 12
6. Find the Lowest Common Multiple (LCM) of the following:
   a. 7 and 21 b. 6 and 9 c. 2, 15, and 30 d. 3, 7, and 14
7. Find the Lowest Common Denominator (LCD) of the following:
   a. $\frac{2}{7}$ and $\frac{3}{14}$ b. $\frac{8}{3}$ and $\frac{4}{11}$ c. $\frac{3}{4}, \frac{6}{15}$, and $\frac{8}{5}$ d. $\frac{1}{2}, \frac{13}{3}$, and $\frac{6}{7}$
8. Find the Lowest Common Denominator (LCD) of the following:
   a. $\frac{1}{3}$ and $\frac{32}{21}$ b. $\frac{7}{8}$ and $\frac{5}{12}$ c. $\frac{1}{6}, \frac{11}{4}$, and $\frac{3}{5}$ d. $\frac{2}{5}, \frac{4}{13}$, and $\frac{3}{11}$
9. Find the (a) factors, (b) common factors, and (c) highest common factors (HCF) of the following:
   i. 36 and 84 ii. 48 and 160 iii. 76, 114, and 152 iv. 96, 144, and 216
10. Find the (a) factors, (b) common factors, and (c) highest common factors (HCF) of the following:
    i. 13 and 91 ii. 93 and 124 iii. 33, 143, and 176 iv. 85, 102, and 204

1.3 | Fractions

Definition of Fractions and Types of Fractions

A **fraction** is a rational number written as one integer divided by another non-zero integer. It is usually written as a pair of numbers, with the top number being called the numerator and the bottom number the denominator. A fraction line (horizontal bar) separates the numerator and the denominator. Use of fractions is another method of representing numbers.

division sign →	$\frac{3}{8}$	← numerator ← denominator

For example, $\frac{3}{8}$ (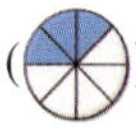) is a fraction. It is read as "three divided by eight", "three-eighths", or "three over eight", which all indicate that 3 is the numerator and 8 the denominator.

A **proper fraction** is a fraction in which the absolute value of the numerator is less than the absolute value of the denominator; i.e., the absolute value of the entire fraction is less than 1. For example,

- $\frac{3}{8}$ () is a proper fraction.
- $\frac{-2}{5}$ in absolute value is $\frac{2}{5}$ (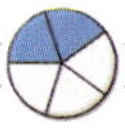) which is a proper fraction.
  Therefore, $\frac{-2}{5}$ is a proper fraction.
  (Note: the larger the denominator, the smaller the size of each piece)

The absolute value of a number refers to the positive sign of that number.

For example, the absolute value of −2 is 2.

i.e. |−2| = 2.

An **improper fraction** is a fraction in which the absolute value of the numerator is greater than the absolute value of the denominator; i.e., the absolute value of the entire fraction is more than 1.

For example,

- For example, $\frac{7}{4}$ () and $\frac{-3}{2}$ (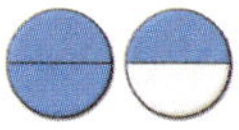) are improper fractions.
  (seven quarters) (negative three halves)

A **mixed number** consists of both a whole number and a fraction, written side-by-side, which implies that the whole number and proper fraction are added.

- For example, $3\frac{5}{8}$ implies $3 + \frac{5}{8}$

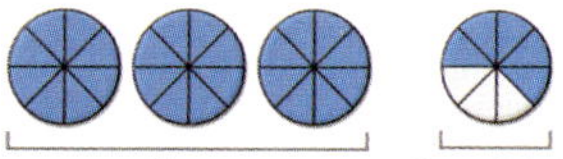

A **complex fraction** is a fraction in which one or more fractions are found in the numerator or denominator.

- For example, $\frac{1}{\left(\frac{3}{4}\right)}$, $\frac{\left(\frac{2}{3}\right)}{6}$, and $\frac{3\frac{5}{6}}{\left(\frac{1}{8}\right)}$ are complex fractions

Reciprocal of a Fraction

When the numerator and denominator of a fraction are interchanged, the resulting fraction is called the reciprocal of the original fraction.

- For example, the reciprocal of $\frac{4}{7}$ is $\frac{7}{4}$

Note: The reciprocal of a fraction is not its equivalent fraction.

Whole Number as a Fraction

Any whole number can be written as a fraction by dividing it by 1 (i.e., 1 is the denominator).

- For example, $7 = \frac{7}{1}$

Converting a Mixed Number into an Improper Fraction

Follow these steps to convert a mixed number into an improper fraction:

- Multiply the whole number by the denominator of the fraction and add this value to the numerator of the fraction.

- The resulting answer will be the numerator of the improper fraction.
- The denominator of the improper fraction is the same as the denominator of the original fraction in the mixed number.
- For example, $3\frac{5}{8} = \dfrac{3(8)+5}{8} = \dfrac{29}{8}$

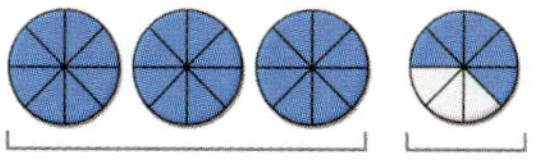

$3 \times 8 = 24$ pieces   5 pieces

Thus, there is a total of 29 pieces, each piece being one-eighth in size.

Converting an Improper Fraction into a Mixed Number

Follow these steps to convert an improper fraction into a mixed number:

- Divide the numerator by the denominator.
- The quotient becomes the whole number and the remainder becomes the numerator of the fraction.
- The denominator is the same as the denominator of the original improper fraction.
- For example, $\dfrac{29}{8} = 3\frac{5}{8}$ Because,

$$\begin{array}{r} 3 \\ 8\overline{)29} \\ 24 \\ \hline 5 \end{array}$$

3 ← Quotient: whole number of the fraction

5 ← Remainder: numerator of the fraction

Converting a Fraction into an Equivalent Fraction

When both the numerator and denominator of a fraction are either multiplied by the same number or divided by the same number, the result is a new fraction called an equivalent fraction. Equivalent fractions imply that the old and new fractions have the same value.

For example, to find 2 equivalent fractions of $\dfrac{2}{5}$ 

$\dfrac{2}{5} = \dfrac{2 \times 2}{5 \times 2}$ Multiplying both numerator and denominator by 2, we obtain,

$= \dfrac{4}{10}$ 

$\dfrac{2}{5} = \dfrac{2 \times 3}{5 \times 3}$ Multiplying both numerator and denominator by 3, we obtain,

$= \dfrac{6}{15}$ 

Therefore, $\dfrac{4}{10}$ and $\dfrac{6}{15}$ are equivalent fractions of $\dfrac{2}{5}$

Consider another example to find 2 equivalent fractions of $\dfrac{36}{60}$:

$\dfrac{36}{60} = \dfrac{36 \div 2}{60 \div 2}$ Dividing both numerator and denominator by 2, we obtain,

$= \dfrac{18}{30}$

$\dfrac{36}{60} = \dfrac{36 \div 4}{60 \div 4}$ Dividing both numerator and denominator by 4, we obtain,

$= \dfrac{9}{15}$

Therefore, $\dfrac{18}{30}$ and $\dfrac{9}{15}$ are equivalent fractions of $\dfrac{36}{60}$

Converting a Fraction into its Decimal Form

A proper or improper fraction can be converted to its decimal form by dividing the numerator by the denominator.

- For example, $\frac{2}{5} = 0.4$, $\frac{13}{8} = 1.625$

A mixed number can be converted to its decimal form by first converting it to an improper fraction then dividing the numerator.

- For example, $3\frac{5}{2} = \frac{3(2)+5}{2} = \frac{11}{2} = 5.5$

$$11\frac{3}{7} = \frac{11(7)+3}{7} = \frac{80}{7} = 11.428571...$$

Reducing or Simplifying a Fraction

Dividing both the numerator and denominator of a fraction by the same number, which results in an equivalent fraction, is called **reducing** or **simplifying** the fraction.

For example, we can simplify $\frac{16}{20}$ as shown:

$$\frac{16}{20} = \frac{16 \div 2}{20 \div 2} = \frac{8}{10}$$ Dividing both numerator and denominator by 2, we obtain,

$$\frac{16}{20} = \frac{16 \div 4}{20 \div 4} = \frac{4}{5}$$ Dividing both numerator and denominator by 4, we obtain,

Therefore, $\frac{8}{10}$ and $\frac{4}{5}$ are reduced fractions of $\frac{16}{20}$

Fraction in Lowest (or Simplest) Terms

A fraction in which the numerator and denominator have no factors in common (other than 1) is said to be a **fraction in its lowest (or simplest) terms**. Any fraction can be **fully reduced** to its lowest terms by dividing both the numerator and denominator by the highest common factor (HCF).

Example 1.3(a) **Reducing Fractions to their Lowest Terms**

Reduce the fraction $\frac{40}{45}$ to its lowest terms.

Solution

The factors of 40 are 1, 2, 4, 5, 8, 10, 20, 40.

The factors of 45 are 1, 3, 5, 9, 15, 45.

The HCF is 5.

Therefore, dividing the numerator and denominator by the HCF, 5, results in the fraction in its lowest terms:

$$\frac{40}{45} = \frac{40 \div 5}{45 \div 5} = \frac{8}{9}$$

Basic Arithmetic Operations with Fractions

It is best to convert a mixed number into an improper fraction before performing any basic arithmetic operations.

Comparing Fractions

Fractions can easily be compared when they have the same denominator. If they do not have the same denominator, find the LCD of the fractions, then convert them into equivalent fractions with that LCD as their denominator.

Example 1.3(b)

Comparing Fractions

Which of the fractions, $\frac{5}{12}$ or $\frac{3}{8}$ is greater?

Solution

We first find the LCD of the fractions, which is the same as the LCM of the denominators.

The LCM of 12 and 8 is 24.

Now convert each of the fractions to its equivalent fraction with 24 as the denominator.

Multiply the denominator by 2 to obtain the LCD of 24 and multiply the numerator by 2 to as well to maintain an equivalent fraction.

$$\frac{5}{12} = \frac{5 \times 2}{12 \times 2} = \frac{10}{24}$$

Similarly, to convert $\frac{3}{8}$ to an equivalent fraction with 24 as denominator.

$$\frac{3}{8} = \frac{3 \times 3}{8 \times 3} = \frac{9}{24}$$

Since the denominators are the same, we can now compare the numerators of the above to identify the greater fraction.

$10 > 9$, which implies that $\frac{10}{24} > \frac{9}{24}$; therefore, $\frac{5}{12} > \frac{3}{8}$

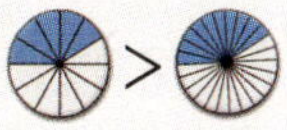

Adding Fractions

Addition of fractions requires that the denominators of every fraction be the same. To make them the same, first find the LCD and change each fraction to its equivalent fraction having the same denominator. Now, add the numerators of each of the equivalent fractions. The resulting fraction will have the common denominator, and its numerator will be the result of adding the numerators of the equivalent fractions.

Example 1.3(c)

Adding Fractions

Add $3\frac{5}{6}$ and $\frac{4}{9}$

Solution

$$3\frac{5}{6} + \frac{4}{9} = \frac{(3 \times 6) + 5}{6} + \frac{4}{9}$$

$$= \frac{23}{6} + \frac{4}{9}$$

Finding the equivalent fraction using the LCD of 18, we obtain,

$$= \frac{69}{18} + \frac{8}{18} = \frac{77}{18}$$

Converting the improper fraction to a mixed number, we obtain,

$$= 4\frac{5}{18}$$

Subtracting Fractions

The process for subtraction of fractions is the same as that of addition of fractions. First, find a common denominator, then change each fraction to its equivalent fraction with the common denominator. The resulting fraction will have that denominator, and its numerator will be the result of subtracting the numerators of the original fractions.

Example 1.3(d)

Subtracting Fractions

Subtract $\frac{2}{3}$ from $12\frac{1}{2}$

Solution

$$12\tfrac{1}{2} - \frac{2}{3} = \frac{(12 \times 2) + 1}{2} - \frac{2}{3}$$

$$= \frac{25}{2} - \frac{2}{3}$$

Finding the equivalent fraction using the LCD of 6, we obtain,

$$= \frac{75}{6} - \frac{4}{6} = \frac{71}{6}$$

Converting the improper fraction to a mixed number, we obtain,

$$= 11\tfrac{5}{6}$$

Multiplying Fractions

When multiplying two or more fractions, simply multiply the numerators to get the new numerator and multiply the denominators to get the new denominator.

Example 1.3(e)

Multiplying Fractions

Multiply

i. $\frac{3}{2} \times \frac{4}{11}$

ii. $\frac{9}{13} \times 4$

iii. $\frac{7}{12} \times \frac{4}{21}$

iv. $15 \times \frac{2}{5}$

Solution

i. $\frac{3}{2} \times \frac{4}{11} = \frac{3}{{}_1\cancel{2}} \times \frac{\cancel{4}^{2}}{11} = \frac{3}{1} \times \frac{2}{11} = \frac{6}{11}$

ii. $\frac{9}{13} \times 4 = \frac{9}{13} \times \frac{4}{1} = \frac{36}{13}$

iii. $\frac{7}{12} \times \frac{4}{21} = \frac{\overset{1}{\cancel{7}}}{\underset{3}{\cancel{12}}} \times \frac{\overset{1}{\cancel{4}}}{\underset{3}{\cancel{21}}} = \frac{1}{3} \times \frac{1}{3} = \frac{1}{9}$

iv. $15 \times \frac{2}{5} = \frac{\overset{3}{\cancel{15}}}{1} \times \frac{2}{\underset{1}{\cancel{5}}} = \frac{3}{1} \times \frac{2}{1} = \frac{6}{1} = 6$

Dividing Fractions

The division of fractions is done by multiplying the numerator by the receiprocal of the denominator.

When a fraction is inverted, the resulting fraction is called the 'reciprocal' of the original fraction.

- For example, $\frac{\left(\frac{5}{3}\right)}{\left(\frac{7}{9}\right)} = \frac{5}{3} \div \frac{7}{9} = \frac{5}{3} \times \frac{9}{7} = \frac{45}{21} = \frac{15}{7}$

Note: Dividing by $\frac{7}{9}$ is the same as of multiplying by the reciprocal of $\frac{7}{9}$ which is $\frac{9}{7}$.

When a fraction is a mixed number, convert it to an improper fraction and continue with the arithmetic operation.

- For example, $\frac{2\frac{1}{4}}{5\frac{5}{8}} = \frac{\left(\frac{9}{4}\right)}{\left(\frac{45}{8}\right)} = \frac{9}{4} \div \frac{45}{8} = \frac{\overset{1}{\cancel{9}}}{\underset{1}{\cancel{4}}} \times \frac{\overset{2}{\cancel{8}}}{\underset{5}{\cancel{45}}} = \frac{2}{5}$

Example 1.3(f) **Dividing Fractions**

Divide $\frac{3}{20}$ by $1\frac{4}{5}$

Solution

$$\frac{3}{20} \div 1\frac{4}{5}$$

$$= \frac{3}{20} \div \frac{9}{5}$$

Multiplying $\frac{3}{20}$ by the reciprocal of $\frac{9}{5}$, we obtain,

$$= \frac{3}{20} \times \frac{5}{9} = \frac{\cancel{3}^{1}}{_{4}\cancel{20}} \times \frac{\cancel{5}^{1}}{\cancel{9}_{3}} = \frac{1}{12}$$

Converting a Complex Fraction into Proper or Improper Fraction

A complex fraction can be converted to a proper or improper fraction by dividing the numerator by the denominator and then simplifying the expression.

- For example, $\frac{\left(\frac{7}{2}\right)}{5} = \frac{7}{2} \div 5$
  $= \frac{7}{2} \times \frac{1}{5} = \frac{7}{10}$
- $\frac{8}{\left(\frac{9}{2}\right)} = 8 \div \left(\frac{9}{2}\right)$
  $= 8 \times \left(\frac{2}{9}\right) = \frac{16}{9}$

1.3 | Exercises

1. Convert the following mixed numbers into improper fractions:
   a. $1\frac{1}{2}$ b. $12\frac{3}{4}$ c. $7\frac{3}{5}$ d. $9\frac{2}{3}$
2. Convert the following mixed numbers into improper fractions:
   a. $5\frac{2}{3}$ b. $15\frac{6}{7}$ c. $6\frac{4}{5}$ d. $4\frac{3}{4}$
3. Convert the following improper fractions into mixed numbers:
   a. $\frac{12}{7}$ b. $\frac{17}{8}$ c. $\frac{31}{9}$ d. $\frac{14}{5}$
4. Convert the following improper fractions into mixed numbers:
   a. $\frac{23}{12}$ b. $\frac{35}{6}$ c. $\frac{46}{5}$ d. $\frac{34}{3}$
5. Find the missing values:
   a. $\frac{2}{3} = \frac{?}{12} = \frac{12}{?}$ b. $\frac{15}{25} = \frac{3}{?} = \frac{?}{35}$ c. $\frac{22}{12} = \frac{?}{6} = \frac{55}{?}$ d. $\frac{75}{45} = \frac{25}{?} = \frac{?}{18}$
6. Find the missing values:
   a. $\frac{5}{8} = \frac{20}{?} = \frac{?}{24}$ b. $\frac{12}{9} = \frac{?}{18} = \frac{4}{?}$ c. $\frac{36}{42} = \frac{?}{14} = \frac{30}{?}$ d. $\frac{9}{4} = \frac{27}{?} = \frac{?}{20}$
7. Reduce the following to their lowest fractions:
   a. $\frac{80}{12}$ b. $\frac{156}{18}$ c. $\frac{68}{10}$ d. $\frac{36}{144}$

8. Reduce the following to their lowest fractions:

a. $\frac{70}{15}$ b. $\frac{225}{30}$ c. $\frac{124}{48}$ d. $\frac{75}{345}$

9. Which of the following fractions is greater:

a. $\frac{8}{7}$ or $\frac{13}{12}$? b. $\frac{5}{13}$ or $\frac{16}{39}$?

10. Which of the following fractions is smaller:

a. $\frac{2}{5}$ or $\frac{3}{8}$? b. $\frac{12}{15}$ or $\frac{35}{45}$?

11. Perform the addition, reducing to the lowest fraction:

a. $5\frac{2}{3} + 1\frac{5}{12}$ b. $\frac{7}{9} + \frac{5}{6}$ c. $\frac{11}{20} + \frac{8}{10}$

12. Perform the addition, reducing to the lowest fraction:

a. $16\frac{1}{8} + 1\frac{1}{2}$ b. $\frac{1}{3} + \frac{3}{8}$ c. $\frac{9}{12} + \frac{4}{5}$

13. Perform the subtraction, reducing to the lowest fraction:

a. $18\frac{5}{7} - 2\frac{2}{5}$ b. $\frac{21}{13} - \frac{1}{3}$ c. $\frac{35}{18} - \frac{3}{6}$

14. Perform the subtraction, reducing to the lowest fraction:

a. $12\frac{4}{3} - 5\frac{1}{3}$ b. $\frac{9}{10} - \frac{1}{2}$ c. $\frac{21}{25} - \frac{7}{8}$

15. Perform the multiplication, reducing to the lowest fraction:

a. $11\frac{4}{3} \times 1\frac{1}{74}$ b. $\frac{4}{5} \times \frac{23}{9}$ c. $\frac{6}{9} \times \frac{19}{12}$

16. Perform the multiplication, reducing to the lowest fraction:

a. $9\frac{3}{5} \times 1\frac{29}{96}$ b. $\frac{3}{8} \times \frac{5}{11}$ c. $3 \times \frac{7}{9}$

17. Perform the division, reducing to the lowest fraction:

a. $10\frac{1}{4} \div 2\frac{27}{48}$ b. $\frac{8}{12} \div \frac{2}{4}$ c. $\frac{1}{7} \div \frac{3}{5}$

18. Perform the division, reducing to the lowest fraction:

a. $23\frac{1}{2} \div 8\frac{13}{16}$ b. $\frac{10}{15} \div \frac{3}{7}$ c. $\frac{3}{8} \div 4$

For problems 19 to 26, express the answer in mixed fractions.

19. Find the total weight of three items that weigh $3\frac{2}{3}$ kg, $4\frac{1}{2}$ kg, and $5\frac{3}{8}$ kg.

20. I used $2\frac{1}{5}$ litres of paint for my bedroom, $1\frac{1}{4}$ litres for my study room, and $7\frac{1}{3}$ litres for my living room. How many litres of paint have I used for the three rooms?

21. Henry is $8\frac{1}{4}$ years old. Amanda is $2\frac{5}{12}$ years old. How many years younger is Amanda than Henry?

22. I purchased $12\frac{1}{3}$ hectares of land and sold $4\frac{2}{5}$ hectares. How many hectares are remaining now?

23. A car can travel $8\frac{1}{4}$ km with 1 litre of gas. How many kilometres can it travel using $45\frac{3}{5}$ litres of gas?

24. I can walk $5\frac{3}{8}$ km in 1 hour. How far can I walk in $4\frac{1}{3}$ hours?

25. Cheng can walk $5\frac{1}{4}$ km in $1\frac{1}{2}$ hours. How many kilometres can he walk in 1 hour?

26. $2\frac{3}{4}$ litres of juice weighs $4\frac{2}{3}$ kg. Find the weight (in kilograms) of 1 litre of juice.

1.4 | Order of Operations (BEDMAS)

When arithmetic expressions contain multiple operations with brackets, exponents, divisions, multiplications, additions, and subtractions, the arithmetic operation is performed in the following sequence:

1. Perform all operations within the **brackets**. If there is more than one bracket, start with the innermost bracket and move outwards to complete all the brackets.
2. Perform operations with **exponents**.
3. Perform the necessary **divisions** and **multiplications** in the order in which they appear from left to right.
4. Complete the operation by performing the necessary **additions** and **subtractions** in the order in which they appear.

The order of operations: Brackets, Exponents, Divisions, Multiplications, Additions, Subtractions can be remembered by the acronym, BEDMAS.

Example 1.4(a) **Computing Arithmetic Expressions by Following the Order of Operations.**

Compute the following arithmetic expressions:

(i) $6 + 4 \times 50 \div (8 - 3)^2 - 1$

(ii) $12 + 3^2 [(8 \times 5) / 5] - 7 + 2$

Solution

Order of arithmetic operations:
Brackets
Exponents
Divisions
Multiplications
Additions
Subtractions

(i) $6 + 4 \times 50 \div (8 - 3)^2 - 1$

$= 6 + 4 \times 50 \div \mathbf{(8 - 3)}^2 - 1$	Work on the operations in the bracket
$= 6 + 4 \times 50 \div \mathbf{(5)^2} - 1$	Perform the operation with the exponent
$= 6 + \mathbf{4 \times 50} \div 25 - 1$	Perform multiplication
$= 6 + \mathbf{200 \div 25} - 1$	Perform division
$= \mathbf{6 + 8} - 1$	Perform addition
$= \mathbf{14 - 1}$	Perform subtraction
$= 13$	

(ii) $12 + 3^2 [(8 \times 5) / 5] - 7 + 2$

$= 12 + 3^2 [\mathbf{(8 \times 5)} / 5] - 7 + 2$	Work on the operations in the inner bracket
$= 12 + 3^2 \mathbf{(40 / 5)} - 7 + 2$	Work on the operations in the outer bracket
$= 12 + \mathbf{3^2} (8) - 7 + 2$	Perform the operation with the exponent
$= 12 + \mathbf{9 (8)} - 7 + 2$	Perform multiplication
$= \mathbf{12 + 72 - 7 + 2}$	Perform addition and subtraction
$= 79$	

Signed Numbers

When signed numbers (e.g., -10, -55) are multiplied or divided, the result will be a number with a sign.

Multiplying two signed numbers
(+) (+) = (+)
(−) (−) = (+)
(+) (−) = (−)
(−) (+) = (−)

The following are rules to be followed while multiplying or dividing two signed numbers:

a. When both numbers are positive, the final answer will be positive.

■ For example,

(i) $(+5)(+4) = +20$ (ii) $\frac{+12}{+3} = +4$

Dividing two signed numbers

$\frac{(+)}{(+)} = (+)$

$\frac{(-)}{(-)} = (+)$

$\frac{(-)}{(+)} = (-)$

$\frac{(+)}{(-)} = (-)$

b. When both numbers are negative, the final answer will be positive.

- For example,

  (i) $(-5)(-4) = +20$ (ii) $\frac{-12}{-3} = +4$

c. When only one of the numbers is negative, the final answer will be negative.

- For example,

  (i) $(+5)(-4) = -20$ (ii) $(-5)(+4) = -20$

  (iii) $\frac{+12}{-3} = -4$ (iv) $\frac{-12}{+3} = -4$

  (vi) $\frac{-25}{+15} = \frac{-5}{3}$ *or* $-\frac{5}{3}$ (v) $\frac{+30}{-4} = \frac{+15}{-2} = \frac{-15}{2}$ *or* $-\frac{15}{2}$

Note: When multiplying or dividing more than 2 signed numbers, group them into pairs and determine the sign using the signed number rules.

For example,

(i) $\underbrace{(-3)(-2)}\underbrace{(+4)(-1)}(-5)$

$= \underbrace{(6)(-4)}(-5)$

$= \underbrace{(-24)(-5)} = 120$

(ii) $\frac{\overbrace{(-15)(+8)}(-50)}{\underbrace{(-25)(14)}}$

$= \frac{-(15\times 8)(-50)}{-(25\times 14)} = \frac{+15\times 8\times 50}{-25\times 14}$

$= -\frac{15\times 8\times \cancel{50}^{2}}{{}_{1}\cancel{25}\times 14} = -\frac{15\times 8\times \cancel{2}^{1}}{\cancel{14}_{7}}$

$= -\frac{15\times 8}{7} = -\frac{120}{7}$

Exponential Notation

Exponents provide a shorter way of representing the products of repeated numbers.

For example, when 2 is multiplied 5 times, in standard notation, it is represented as:

$$2\times 2\times 2\times 2\times 2$$

However, when 2 is multiplied 100 times, it would be tedious to represent it using the standard notation. The shorter way to represent this repeated multiplication is by using exponents.

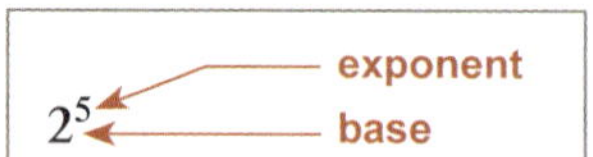

When 2 is multiplied 5 times, it is represented as 2^5 using exponents.

Similarly if 'a' is multiplied 'n' times it would be represented as a^n, where 'n' is a positive integer.

$$\underbrace{a\times a\times a\times a\times a\times \ldots\times a}_{n \text{ factors of } a} = a^n$$

To convert an exponential notation to a standard notation, expand the notation to show the repeated multiplication. The number in the exponent shows the number of times the base is multiplied.

- For example, $8^4 = 8\times 8\times 8\times 8$

  $8^3 = 8\times 8\times 8$

  $8^2 = 8\times 8$

When the exponent is 1, the result is the number itself.

- For example, $8^1 = 8$. This is represented by the formula $\boldsymbol{a^1 = a}$.

When the exponent is 0, the result is 1.

- For example, $3^0 = 1$. This is represented by the formula $\boldsymbol{a^0 = 1}$.

When the exponent is negative, it is represented by $a^{-n} = \frac{1}{a^n}$, where $'n'$ is a positive integer.

Negative exponent means dividing by that many number of factors instead of multiplying.

$$a^n = a \times a \times a \times a \times a \times \ldots \times a \quad \text{(multiplication of } 'n' \text{ factors of } 'a')$$

$$a^{-n} = \frac{1}{a^n} = \frac{1}{a \times a \times a \times a \times a \times \ldots \times a} \quad \text{(division of } 'n' \text{ factors of } 'a')$$

Therefore, a^n and a^{-n} are reciprocals.

For example,

$$8^{-1} = \frac{1}{8^1} = \frac{1}{8}$$

$$8^{-2} = \frac{1}{8^2} = \frac{1}{8 \times 8}$$

$$8^{-3} = \frac{1}{8^3} = \frac{1}{8 \times 8 \times 8}$$

Standard Notation		Exponential Notation
$8 \times 8 \times 8 \times 8$	=	8^4
$8 \times 8 \times 8$	=	8^3
8×8	=	8^2

Factors are divided by 8 ↓   Exponents are reduced by 1 ↓

If this pattern is continued further

$$8 = 8^1$$

$$1 = 8^0$$

$$\frac{1}{8} = 8^{-1}$$

$$\frac{1}{8 \times 8} = 8^{-2}$$

$$\frac{1}{8 \times 8 \times 8} = 8^{-3}$$

A positive number with a negative exponent will not result in a negative answer.

Fractions with Exponents

When a fraction has a **positive exponent**, the number in the exponent indicates the number of times the numerator is multiplied by itself and the number of times the denominator is multiplied by itself.

- For example, $\left(\frac{2}{5}\right)^3 = \left(\frac{2}{5}\right)\left(\frac{2}{5}\right)\left(\frac{2}{5}\right) = \frac{2 \times 2 \times 2}{5 \times 5 \times 5}$

- $\frac{2^4}{3^5} = \frac{2 \times 2 \times 2 \times 2}{3 \times 3 \times 3 \times 3 \times 3}$

When a fraction has a **negative exponent**, change the fraction to its reciprocal and drop the sign. After this change, the number in the exponent indicates the number of times the numerator and denominator is multiplied.

$$\left(\frac{a}{b}\right)^{-n} = \left(\frac{b}{a}\right)^n$$

- For example, $\left(\frac{2}{5}\right)^{-3} = \left(\frac{5}{2}\right)^3 = \left(\frac{5}{2}\right)\left(\frac{5}{2}\right)\left(\frac{5}{2}\right) = \frac{5 \times 5 \times 5}{2 \times 2 \times 2}$

Note: The reciprocal of $\frac{2}{5}$ *is* $\frac{5}{2}$

Calculator Method to Find the Exponent

The exponent key on different calculators can be identified by symbols such as y^x, x^y, ^, etc.

The sequence of operations to calculate the exponents also depends on the calculator. In this section, you will learn to calculate exponents using Texas Instruments BA II Plus calculator.

Example 1.4(b) **Calculating exponents using Texas Instruments BA II Plus calculator**

Calculate (i) 16^4 (ii) 5^{-4} (iii) $(1.04)^4 - 1$ (iv) $1 - (1.005)^{-4}$

Solution

(i) 16^4

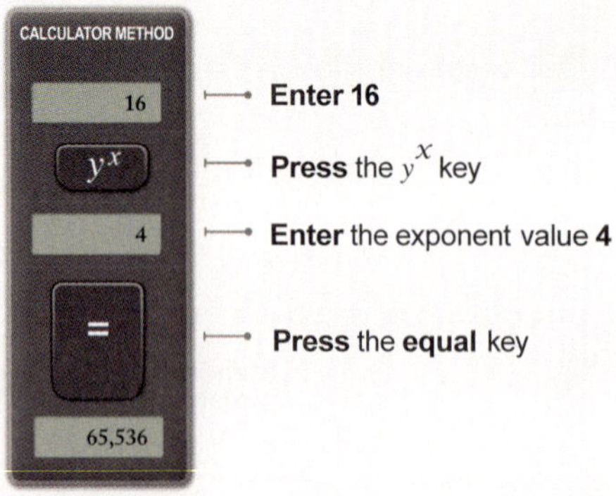

(ii) 5^{-4}

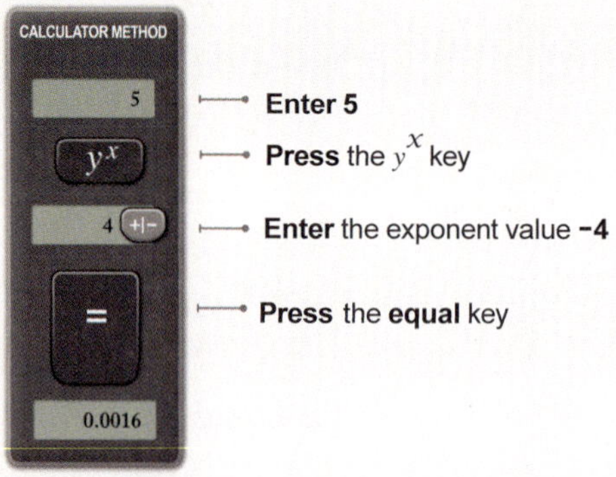

(iii) $(1.04)^4 - 1$

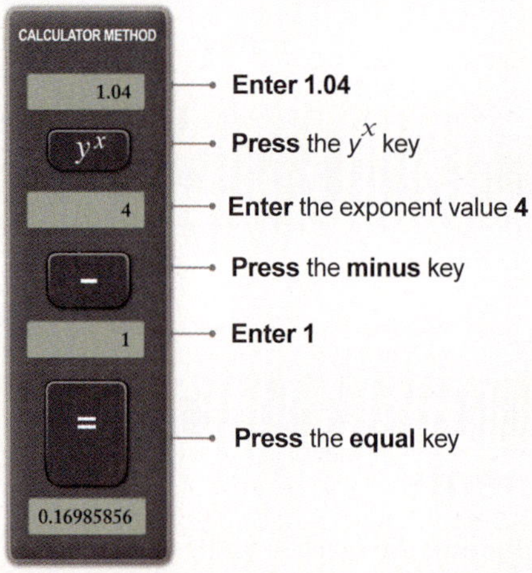

(iv) $1 - (1.005)^{-4}$

Solve using BEDMAS order of operations

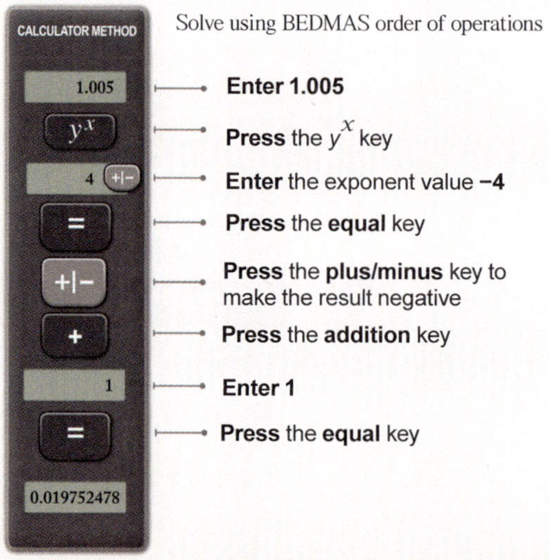

1.4 | Exercises

Evaluate the following:

1. a. $45 - (5 + 7)^2$ b. $18 - 8 \div 2 + 6$
2. a. $32 + (9 - 5)^3$ b. $4 \times 6 \div 2 - 5$
3. a. $128 \div (-16) \div (-2)$ b. $4(-3^2) + 4$
4. a. $200 \div (-10) \div 5$ b. $20(5 - 2^2) + 5$
5. a. $11^2 - 4 \times 54 \div (5 - 2)^3 - 3$ b. $31 - [(15 \div 3) \times 32 \div 2^2(26 \div 13)]$
6. a. $(-1)(-3)(2)(-5)(-6)$ b. $(-5)(-3)(12)(-3)(-1)$
7. a. $[(1 + 12)(1 - 5)]^2 \div (5 + 3 \times 2^2 - 4)$ b. $(-8)(2)(3)(-4)(-1)$
8. a. $3(7^2 + 2 \times 15 \div 3) - (1 + 3 \times 4)^2$ b. $(12)(1)(-7)(4)(-2)$
9. $\dfrac{8 \times 7 - 16 + 3^2 \times 2}{2^5 - (59 - 7^2) \div 2 \times 6}$

10. $\dfrac{-52+(56\div 8)\times 9+6^2}{3\times(6\times 4\div 8)+157-11^2}$

11. $\dfrac{6+(8^2-5)-(6^2+13)}{60\div 12+\left[5^2-(-2)\times(-11)\right]}$

12. $\dfrac{32\div(-8)-9+(127-5^3)\times 2^3}{[(-54)\div 6+33]\div[(-8)\times(-3)]}$

13. $\dfrac{[(-6)\times 7+(-12)\div(-4)+3]\div 6}{[(-24)\div 8+4]\div[14-16+3]}$

14. $\dfrac{8\{9-(-2)-7[4+(-1)]\}}{-12+4[-4-(-3)]\div 7}$

15. $\dfrac{16+4(3)}{10-4+1}+\dfrac{(16+4)3}{10-(4+1)}$

16. $\dfrac{2(6)+4}{24-(7+3)}+\dfrac{2(6+4)}{24-7+3}$

17. $14-3\{[(6-9)(-4)+12](-2)\}$

18. $5(-4)-3\{(-9+6)+(-3)-4[2(-1)-7]\}$

19. Evaluate the following exponents:

a. $\left(\dfrac{1}{4}\right)^2$ b. $\left(\dfrac{3}{5}\right)^{-3}$ c. 12^5 d. 17^{-5}

20. Evaluate the following exponents:

a. $\left(\dfrac{2}{8}\right)^4$ b. $\left(\dfrac{1}{5}\right)^{-5}$ c. 6^6 d. 11^{-3}

Evaluate problems 21 to 30 and round your answer to 2 decimal places:

21. a. $4500\left(1+0.005\times\dfrac{240}{365}\right)$ b. $1500\left(1+0.04\times\dfrac{7}{12}\right)$

22. a. $600\left(1+0.002\times\dfrac{180}{365}\right)$ b. $960\left(1+0.05\times\dfrac{3}{12}\right)$

23. a. $\dfrac{2500}{\left(1+0.001\times\dfrac{150}{365}\right)}$ b. $\dfrac{1800}{\left(1+0.05\times\dfrac{5}{12}\right)}$

24. a. $\dfrac{1250}{\left(1+0.02\times\dfrac{160}{365}\right)}$ b. $\dfrac{2700}{\left(1+0.04\times\dfrac{7}{12}\right)}$

25. a. $\dfrac{3000\left[(1.06)^5-1\right]}{0.06}$ b. $\dfrac{1400\left[(1.03)^{20}-1\right]}{0.03}$

26. a. $\dfrac{800\left[(1.04)^{10}-1\right]}{0.04}$ b. $\dfrac{750\left[(1.02)^{25}-1\right]}{0.02}$

27. a. $5400(1.005)^8$ b. $2400(1.02)^{-10}$

28. a. $1275(1.03)^7$ b. $4650(1.04)^{-6}$

29. a. $\dfrac{2400\left[1-(1.02)^{-8}\right]}{0.02}$ b. $\dfrac{400\left[1-(1.05)^{-12}\right]}{0.05}$

30. a. $\dfrac{950\left[1-(1.03)^{-15}\right]}{0.03}$ b. $\dfrac{1200\left[1-(1.04)^{-20}\right]}{0.04}$

1.5 Averages

Simple Arithmetic Average

The simple arithmetic average of numbers is also often called the arithmetic mean (or mean) of numbers. It is the sum of all the values of the terms divided by the number of terms added. The answer will always be larger than the lowest value amongst the terms and smaller than the highest value amongst the terms.

Changing the order of the numbers does not change the average of the numbers and the average of a list of integers is not necessarily an integer.

Example 1.5(a) **Calculating the Arithmetic Average of Numbers**

Calculate the arithmetic average of 45, 65, 85, and 90.

Solution

$$\textit{Arithmetic average} = \frac{45+65+85+90}{4} = \frac{285}{4} = 71.25$$

Note: *The answer is larger than the lowest value of 45 and smaller than the highest value of 90.*

A summation method is easily generalized for any number of terms as follows:

Formula 1.5(a) **Arithmetic Average**

$$\textit{Arithmetic Average} = \frac{\textit{Sum of all values}}{\textit{Number of terms}} = \frac{x_1 + x_2 + x_3 + \ldots + x_n}{n} = \frac{\sum_{i=1}^{n} x_i}{n}$$

Where 'x_1' refers to the 1st term, 'x_2' refers to the 2nd term, etc., and 'x_n' refers to the nth term, where 'n' refers to the total number of terms.

Example 1.5(b) **Calculating the Arithmetic Average of Numbers**

The following are the earnings of a worker for the last 5 days: $150, $225, $350, $270, and $325. Find his average earning per day.

Solution

$$\textit{Average earnings per day} = \frac{\sum_{i=1}^{5} x_i}{n} = \frac{150+225+350+270+325}{5} = \frac{1320}{5} = \$264.00$$

Therefore, his average earning per day is $264.00.

Example 1.5(c) **Calculating a Missing Number Given the Average of Other Numbers**

The average of 6 numbers is 50. If five of the numbers are 40, 25, 75, 30, and 50, what is the 6th number?

Solution

Let x represent the 6th number

$$\frac{40 + 25 + 75 + 30 + 50 + x}{6} = 50$$

$$40 + 25 + 75 + 30 + 50 + x = 6 \times 50$$

$$220 + x = 6 \times 50$$

$$= 300$$

$$x = 300 - 220 = 80$$

Therefore, the 6th number is 80.

Or

The average of 6 numbers = 50

Therefore, the sum of 6 numbers = 50 × 6 = 300

The sum of 5 numbers = 40 + 25 + 75 + 30 + 50 = 220

Therefore, the 6th number is 300 − 220 = 80

Example 1.5(d)

Calculating Average of all Numbers Given the Average of Two Sets of Numbers

If the average of 3 numbers is 45 and the average of 4 other numbers is 55, find the average of all the 7 numbers rounded to 2 decimal places..

Solution

If the average of 3 numbers is 45, then the sum of the 3 numbers would be $45 \times 3 = 135$.

Similarly, the sum of the other 4 numbers would be to $55 \times 4 = 220$.

Now, the average of all the 7 numbers would be the sum of the 7 numbers divided by 7.

$$\frac{135 + 220}{7} = 50.714285... = 50.71$$

Therefore, the average of the 7 numbers is 50.71.

Weighted Average

The weighted average is often called the weighted arithmetic mean. It is similar to an arithmetic average, but instead of each of the data points contributing equally to the final average, some data points contribute more than the others.

When all the values of the terms are not of equal importance, each quantity to be averaged is assigned a different weight. These weightings determine the relative importance of each value.

If all the weightings are equal, then the weighted average is the same as the arithmetic average.

For example, a student's final evaluation in a subject is often based on different components, such as quizzes, assignments, tests, exams, etc. Each component will be assigned a value by the teacher, which will help determine the student's final grade earned for the subject.

Quizzes and assignments may be worth a smaller percentage of the total grade, compared to major tests and exams which may carry additional weight in the final grade earned. This means that the tests and exams carry more importance in determining a student's grade in the subject, although the successful completion of the other components will allow the student to earn the highest grade.

The weighted average is calculated as follows:tt

If $w_1, w_2, w_3, \dots w_n$ are the weightings assigned for the terms and $x_1, x_2, x_3, \dots x_n$ are the values of the terms in that order, then,

Formula 1.5(b)

Weighted Average

$$Weighted\ Average = \frac{w_1x_1 + w_2x_2 + w_3x_3 + \dots + w_nx_n}{w_1 + w_2 + w_3 + \dots + w_n} = \frac{\sum_{i=1}^{n} w_ix_i}{\sum_{i=1}^{n} w_i}$$

Example 1.5(e)

Calculating the Weighted Average

The final average of a subject is determined by 3 tests and a final examination. Each test is worth 20% and the final exam is worth 40%. A student received 70, 60, and 80 marks out of 100 for the tests and 95 marks out of 100 for the final exam. Calculate the student's final average for this subject based on:

(i) The weighted average.

(ii) The simple arithmetic average.

Which method is most suitable for this situation and why?

Solution The weighted average:

Terms	Value of terms (x_i)	Weight of terms (w_i)	$w_i x_i$
Test 1	$\frac{70}{100}$	$w_1 = 20\%$	$0.70 \times 20\% = 14\%$
Test 2	$\frac{60}{100}$	$w_2 = 20\%$	$0.60 \times 20\% = 12\%$
Test 3	$\frac{80}{100}$	$w_3 = 20\%$	$0.80 \times 20\% = 16\%$
Final examination	$\frac{95}{100}$	$w_4 = 40\%$	$0.95 \times 40\% = 38\%$
		$\Sigma w_i = 100\%$	$\Sigma w_i x_i = 80\%$

Using Formula 1.5(b),

$$\textit{Weighted Average} = \frac{\sum_{i=1}^{n} w_i x_i}{\sum_{i=1}^{n} w_i} = \frac{80\%}{100\%} = \frac{0.80}{1} = 80.00\%$$

(iii) The simple arithmetic average:

$$\textit{Arithmetic average} = \frac{\left(\frac{70}{100} + \frac{60}{100} + \frac{80}{100} + \frac{95}{100}\right)}{4} = \frac{\left(\frac{305}{100}\right)}{4} = \frac{305}{400} \times 100\% = 76.25\%$$

The simple arithmetic average does not reflect the importance given to the final examination.

The weighted average of 80.00% reflects the greater importance given to the final exam and is most suitable for this situation.

Example 1.5(f)

Calculating the Grade Point Average

Jean, a 1st semester student at National College of Business, received the following 1st semester marks along with the credit earned per subject.

Subject	Percentage Mark	Credit Hours Earned
English	81%	2
Business Mathematics	97%	3
Marketing	79%	3
Computer Applications	68%	2
Accounting	72%	3
Business Management	75%	4

He planned to transfer to Hollings College of Business that required him to submit a Grade Point Average (GPA) of his performance. They use students' GPA to assess their overall academic achievement in college. When calculating the GPA, the percentage mark for each course must first be converted into a grade point, and then the grade points for all courses are averaged, weighted by credit hour. They provide the following grade point conversion chart to calculate his GPA.

Percentage Mark	Grade Point
80% to 100%	4.0
70% to 79%	3.3
60% to 69%	2.7
50% to 59%	1.7
40% to 49%	1.2

Based on the above information, calculate his GPA.

Solution

Subject	Percentage Mark	Grade Point (x_i)	Credit Hours Earned (w_i)	Grade Point × Credit Hours Earned $w_i x_i$
English	81%	4.0	2	$2 \times 4.0 = 8$
Business Mathematics	97%	4.0	3	$3 \times 4.0 = 12$
Marketing	79%	3.3	3	$3 \times 3.3 = 9.9$
Computer Applications	68%	2.7	2	$2 \times 2.7 = 5.4$
Accounting	72%	3.3	3	$3 \times 3.3 = 9.9$
Business Management	75%	3.3	4	$4 \times 3.3 = 13.2$
			$\sum w_i = 17$	$\sum w_i x_i = 58.4$

Using Formula 1.5(b),

$$Weighted\ Average = \frac{\sum_{i=1}^{n} w_i x_i}{\sum_{i=1}^{n} w_i} = \frac{58.4}{17} = 3.435294... = 3.44$$

Therefore, his GPA is 3.44.

Example 1.5(g)

Calculating the Weighted Average on the Return on Investments

An investment banker assured a wealthy businesswoman Angel that she will receive a 8% return on her investments in a year if she invested her money with them. Angel agreed and invested her savings with the banker.

The banker created a portfolio of investments for her by investing 30% of it in high-tech stocks, 10% in oil stocks, 25% in software company startups, and the balance in a savings account. At the end of the year, hi-tech stocks grew by 18%, oil stocks dropped by 4%, the investment in software company startups grew by 32% and the amount in the savings account grew by 5.5%.

Did Angel's money grow by the amount that was assured to her?

Solution

Investment	Return (x_i)	Investment (w_i)	$w_i x_i$
Hi-tech stocks	18%	30%	$0.30 \times 18\% = 5.4\%$
Oil stocks	−4%	10%	$0.10 \times (-4\%) = -0.4\%$
Software companies	32%	25%	$0.25 \times 32\% = 8\%$
Savings account	5.5%	35%	$0.35 \times 5.5\% = 1.925\%$
		$\sum w = 100\%$	$\sum w_i x_i = 14.925\%$

Using Formula 1.5(b),

$$Weighted\ Average = \frac{\sum_{i=1}^{n} w_i x_i}{\sum_{i=1}^{n} w_i} = \frac{14.925\%}{100\%} = 14.93\%$$

Therefore, Angel's investment grew by 14.93% which was less than the return assured to her.

1.5 | Exercises

1. Calculate the arithmetic average of the following:
   a. 12, 18, 26, and 32.
   b. 35.50, 86.25, 75.75, and 12.50

2. Calculate the arithmetic average of the following:
   a. 50, 45, 72, and 86.
   b. 120.70, 118.25, 110.75, and 95.50

3. The number of hours Yara worked each of the last 4 weeks were: 40 hours, 35 hours, 37.5 hours, and 36 hours. Find the average number of hours she worked per week.

4. The following are the times it took Alexus to reach her office on 4 different days: 45 minutes, 55 minutes, 30 minutes, and 47 minutes. What is the average time it took her to get to work?

5. The average of 5 numbers is 120. If four of the numbers are 118, 130, 125, and 110, what is the fifth number?

6. The average interest rate charged by 4 banks for a loan is 5.5%. If three of the banks offered interest rates of 6.25%, 4%, and 6.5%, calculate the interest rate charged by the fourth bank.

7. If the average of 4 numbers is 60 and the average of 2 other numbers is 50. Find the average of all the 6 numbers.

8. Jade scored an average mark of 85.5% in 3 subjects and an average mark of 91% in 4 other subjects. Find the average score of all the 7 subjects.

9. A footwear retailer sold 10 pairs of sneakers for $50 each, 14 pairs of leather shoes for $150 each, 3 pairs of boots for $225 each, and 6 pairs of sandals for $25 each. Calculate the average price of shoes sold based on:
   a. Weighted average.
   b. Simple arithmetic average.

   Which method is most suitable for this situation and why?

10. A call center has 4 categories of employees, each paid a particular wage. Managers are paid $25 an hour, clerks are paid $16 an hour, technicians are paid $20 an hour, and administrative assistants are paid $14 an hour. The call center has 3 managers, 22 clerks, 4 technicians, and 6 administrative assistants. Calculate the average pay per employee based on:
    a. Simple arithmetic average.
    b. Weighted average (category of employees).

11. The manager of a sporting goods store was given the following data regarding the sales made for the month of March.

Product	Price per unit	Items sold
Snow boards	$450.00	30
Skis	$175.00	18
Roller blades	$230.00	22
Basket balls	$65.00	43

    What was the average price per unit sold in March?

12. Anthony managed his own portfolio of investments. If he invested 40% of his savings in low-risk stocks, 30% in medium-risk stocks, and the balance in high-risk stocks, what would be the average return on his investment if the growth on low-, medium-, and high-risk stocks were 4%, 6%, and 9% respectively?

1 | Review Exercises

Answers to odd-numbered problems are available at the end of the textbook

1. Find the answers to the following and round to 2 decimal places:
   a. $75.45 \div 12$ b. $845 \div 365$
   c. $29.25 \div 4$ d. $48{,}000 \div 26$

2. Find the answers to the following and round to 2 decimal places:
   a. $125.71 \div 4$ b. $775 \div 365$
   c. $56{,}000 \div 52$ d. $142.75 \div 12$

3. Find the answers to the following and round to the nearest cent:
   a. $\$28.39 \times 1.50$ b. $\$37.48 \times 2.00$
   c. $\$40.75 \times 2.25$ d. $\$25.56 \times 19.50$

4. Find the answers to the following and round to the nearest cent:
   a. $\$37.50 \times 1.50$ b. $\$37.45 \times 12.25$
   c. $\$91.38 \times 6.50$ d. $\$2.25 \times 9.75$

5. Find the lowest common multiple (LCM) of the following:
   a. 44, 60 b. 9, 36, 64 c. 90, 165

6. Find the lowest common multiple (LCM) of the following:
   a. 24, 40 b. 9, 12, 15 c. 80, 120

7. Find the highest common factor (HCF) of the following:
   a. 15, 25 b. 6, 8, 10 c. 25, 125, 200

8. Find the highest common factor (HCF) of the following:
   a. 14, 49 b. 12, 18, 20 c. 30, 75, 180

For problems 9 to 12 express your answer as a mixed number.

9. I worked $6\frac{1}{3}$, $5\frac{1}{2}$, $7\frac{1}{4}$, and $5\frac{2}{5}$ hours during the last 4 days. Find the total number of hours worked during the 4 days.

10. Emily worked $3\frac{2}{3}$, $4\frac{1}{4}$, $1\frac{3}{5}$, and $2\frac{1}{2}$ hours overtime during the last 4 days. Find the number of overtime hours she worked during the 4 days.

11. A flight from Toronto to Singapore takes $19\frac{2}{3}$ hours. $11\frac{3}{4}$ hours after the flight leaves Toronto, how long until it reaches Singapore?

12. Hanna lost $4\frac{1}{8}$ kg last month when she was ill, but gained $3\frac{1}{3}$ kg this month during her recovery period. How much weight did she lose over the two months?

13. Evaluate the following:
    a. $(5 + 4)^2 - 4^3 \div 8 + 3$
    b. $(6 \times 3 - 8)^2 \div (2^3 \times 5 - 3 \times 5)$

14. Evaluate the following:
    a. $16 \div 4 \times 2 - (7 - 5)^2$
    b. $(2^3 - 3)^2 - 5 \times 20 \div (3^3 - 2)$

15. Evaluate the following and round the final answer to 2 decimal places:
    a. $150{,}000(1 + 0.0575)^{-9}$
    b. $\dfrac{800[(1.005)^{48} - 1]}{0.005}$

16. Evaluate the following and round the final answer to 2 decimal places:
    a. $80{,}000(1 + 0.0375)^{-24}$
    b. $\dfrac{250[(1.0025)^{120} - 1]}{0.0025}$

17. The average monthly salary of 5 employees is \$4500. Four of the employees' monthly salaries are \$4230, \$3730, \$3970, and \$5420. Find the monthly salary of the 5th employee.

18. The average age of 6 employees is 35 years. The ages of 5 employees are 28, 32, 40, 38, and 27. Find the age of the 6th employee.

19. A store sold 20 shirts at \$20 each, 35 shirts at \$25 each, and 40 shirts at \$30 each. Calculate the weighted average selling price per shirt.

20. In a company, 15 employees are paid \$16 per hour, 11 employees are paid \$22 per hour, and 14 employees are paid \$25 per hour. Calculate the weighted average hourly rate of the employees rounded to the nearest cent.

1 | Self-Test Exercises

Answers to all problems are available at the end of the textbook

1. Peter earns \$37.56 per hour. Last week he worked 32.50 hours. Calculate his pay rounded to the nearest cent.

2. Estimate by rounding each number to the nearest thousand:

   66,541 + 7891 + 19,725 – 13,978 – 2495

3. Find the lowest common multiple (LCM) of the following:

   a. 18, 24 b. 4, 10, 16 c. 18, 36, 64

4. Find the highest common factor (HCF) of the following:

   a. 16, 20 b. 14, 35, 70 c. 24, 36, 48

5. Rainfall for the last 3 months of the summer were $15\frac{7}{8}$ cm, $18\frac{2}{3}$ cm, and $9\frac{3}{4}$ cm. Calculate the total rainfall incentimetres.

6. A recipe requires $8\frac{3}{8}$ cups of white flour and $2\frac{3}{8}$ cups of wheat flour. How many more cups of white flour than wheat flour are required for this recipe?

7. Evaluate the following:

   a. $4(8 \times 3^2 - 4^3) \div (10 + 2 \times 3)$

   b. $100 \div (2 + 3)^2 - 3^2 \div 3$

8. Evaluate the following and round the final answer to 2 decimal places:

   a. $\frac{1500\left[1-(1.02)^{-60}\right]}{0.02}$

   b. $2500\left(1+\frac{0.09}{4}\right)^2\left(1+\frac{0.06}{2}\right)^3$

9. The average sales amount for a store for the first 3 months is \$42,525 and that for the next 9 months is \$37,775. Find the av erage sales for the 12-month period.

10. Benedict invested in 250 shares of Company A at \$15 per share, 300 shares of Company B at \$25 per share, and 150 shares of Company C at \$35 per share. Calculate the weighted average price per share.

1 | Summary of Formulas

Arithmetic average | 1.5 (a)

$$\textit{Arithmetic Average} = \frac{\textit{Sum of all values}}{\textit{Number of terms}} = \frac{x_1 + x_2 + x_3 + \ldots + x_n}{n} = \frac{\sum_{i=1}^{n} x_i}{n}$$

Weighted average | 1.5 (b)

$$\textit{Weighted Average} = \frac{w_1 x_1 + w_2 x_2 + w_3 x_3 + \ldots + w_n x_n}{w_1 + w_2 + w_3 + \ldots + w_n} = \frac{\sum_{i=1}^{n} w_i x_i}{\sum_{i=1}^{n} w_i}$$

Algebra is a branch of mathematics that introduces the concept of using variables to represent numbers. These variables, together with numbers, are used to express statements and equations using rules of operations. Algebra provides a framework to derive formulas to solve general problems, rather than finding a solution to a particular problem. Algebra will help you develop logical thinking and problem solving skills in a systematic and analytical way. The study of algebra is required in any occupational field, including business.

2 Review of Basic Algebra

LEARNING OBJECTIVES

- Understand exponents and evaluate exponents using rules of exponents.
- Define and perform basic calculations using properties of common and natural logarithms.
- Perform basic operations on algebraic expressions.
- Setup basic linear equations with one variable.
- Solve linear equations with one variable using various arithmetic operations.
- Create, rearrange, and use equations to solve for unknown variables.

$$x(x^2+5y^3)$$

CHAPTER OUTLINE

2.1 | Algebraic Expressions

Algebra is a branch of mathematics that is used to analyze and solve day-to-day business and finance problems. It deals with different relations and operations by using letters and symbols to represent numbers, values, etc.

Algebraic expressions consist of one or more terms with a combination of variables, numbers, and operation signs. In order to solve most problems in business and finance mathematics, the use of equations and formulas is necessary. These equations and formulas are formed using algebraic expressions.

In arithmetic, we use only numbers in expressions.

- For example, $25 + 15$, $75 - 22$, 8×9, $\frac{9}{5}$

In algebra, we use both numbers and variables (letters and symbols that represent various numbers) in expressions.

- For example, $2x + 5$, $30 - 5y$, $6(2a + 5)$, $\frac{b+3}{2}$

When a certain letter of the alphabet is used to represent a varying quantity, it is called a **variable**; i.e., a variable is used to represent something that can change in an algebraic expression. Sometimes, a letter may represent a specific quantity that does not change in value. This is called a **constant**.

- For example,
  - If 'x' represents a person's age, then 'x' is a variable as the value of 'x' changes from year to year.
  - If 'a' represents a person's date of birth, then 'a' is a constant as the value of 'a' is always the same.
  - The constant *pi* can be expressed as, $\pi = 3.14159265...$

In algebra, we use variables, numbers, and operation signs to translate word problems into equations.

- For example,
  - If the sum of two numbers is 100, it can be represented by the equation: $x + y = 100$.
  - If $x = 40$, then $y = 60$.
  - If $x = 10$, then $y = 90$.

Note: In algebraic expressions involving multiplication, the number and the variable(s) are written together without the operation sign for multiplication.

- For example,
  - $5a$ means $5 \times a$, or $5(a)$, or $5 \cdot a$
  - xy means $x \times y$, or $x\ (y)$, or $x \cdot y$

The following key words will help in translating word problems into algebraic expressions and equations:

Table 2.1 **Arithmetic Operations and their Meanings**

Keyword	Meaning
Addition (+)	add, sum, plus, more than, increased by, appreciate, rise
Subtraction (−)	subtract, difference, minus, less than, decreased by, depreciate, fall
Multiplication (×), (•)	multiply, product, times, of
Division (÷)	divide, ratio, divided by, quotient
Equal (=)	is, was, gives, given by

For example,

In words	In algebraic expression
1. Ten more than a number	$x + 10$
2. A number more than ten	$10 + x$
3. A number less than twenty	$20 - x$
4. Twenty less than a number	$x - 20$
5. Product of five and a number	$5x$
6. Divide 20 by a number	$\frac{20}{x}$
7. Divide a number by 20	$\frac{x}{20}$
8. Half of a number	$\frac{1}{2}x = \frac{x}{2}$
9. Twice a number	$2x$
10. Ten more than the product of two numbers	$xy + 10$
11. 'x' less than 'y'	$y - x$
12. 'y' less than 'x'	$x - y$
13. Seventy decreased by 3 times a number	$70 - 3x$
14. 'm' subtracted from 'n'	$n - m$

Terminology used in Algebraic Expressions

A **variable** is a letter that represents one or more numbers. For example, 'x', 'y', and 'a'.

A **term** is a number, variable, or a combination of numbers and variables which are multiplied and/or divided together. Terms are seperated by addition and subtraction operators.

- For example, 5, x, $5x$, $2xy$, $4ab$, $\frac{xy}{3}$, $\frac{4x}{y}$

- For example,
  - $5x + 1$ has 2 terms.
  - $7x^2y^2 - 4x + 3$ has 3 terms
  - $\frac{x}{4} - y^2 + \frac{x}{y}$ has 3 terms

An **expression** is a combination of terms. It usually refers to a statement of relations between variables.

- Examples of expressions with one variable:
  - $(2x + 5)$
  - $(9x - 3)$
- Examples of expressions with two variables:
  - $(5x - 7y + 5)$
  - $(xy + 3x - 7)$

A **coefficient** is the numerical factor in front of the variable in a term.

- For example,
  - In the expression $2x + 3y + 5$, the coefficient of the first term, $2x$, is $+2$ and the coefficient of the second term, $3y$, is $+3$.
  - In the expression $5xy - 2x$, the coefficient of the first term, $5xy$, is $+5$ and the coefficient of the second term, $-2x$, is -2.

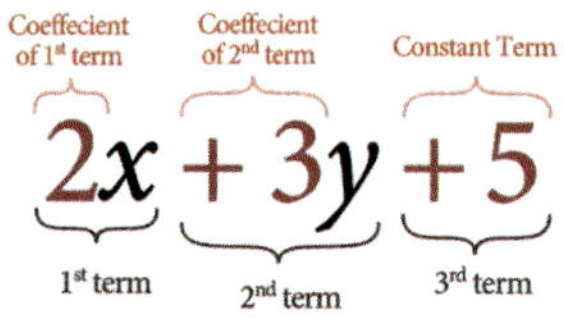

A **constant term** is a term that has only a number without any variables.

- For example, in the expression $2x + 3y + 5$, the third term, $+5$, is a constant term.

Like terms are terms that have the same variables and exponents.

- For example,
  - $5x$ and $9x$ are like terms.
  - $30a^2$, $-4a^2$, and $9a^2$ are like terms.

Unlike terms are terms that have different variables or the same variables with different exponents.

- For example,
  - $12y$ and $3y^2$ are unlike terms.
  - x^2, x, and 1 are unlike terms

Factors refer to each of the combinations of variables and/or numbers multiplied together in a term.

- For example,
  - 5 and x are factors of the term $5x$.
  - 3, x, and y are factors of the term $3xy$.

Monomial is an algebraic expression that has only one term.

- For example, 8, $7x$, $4y$, and $2xy$ are monomials.

Binomial is a polynomial with exactly 2 terms.

- For example, the following are binomials:
  - $4x - 3y$
  - $x - 5$
  - $4xy + 7x$

Trinomial is a polynomial with 3 terms.

- For example, the following are trinomials:
  - $2x + 3y + 5$
  - $xy + x - 2$
  - $2x + xy + 3z$

Polynomial is an algebraic expression that has two or more terms.

- For example,
  - $8x^2 - 5x + 3$ is a polynomial with 3 terms where,

First term: $8x^2$,	Second term: $-5x$,	Third term: 3
Coefficient of first term: 8	Coefficient of second term: -5	This is a constant term

Evaluating Algebraic Expressions

In an algebraic expression, when we replace all the variables with numbers and simplify the expression, it is referred to as evaluating the algebraic expression. The simplified answer is the value of the expression.

Example 2.1(a)

Evaluating Algebraic Expressions

Evaluate the following:

(i) $2x + y$, where $x = 10$ and $y = 5$

(ii) $\frac{3xy + 3x}{2y + 5}$, where $x = 3$ and $y = 2$

Solution

(i) $2x + y$, where $x = 10$ and $y = 5$

Substituting 10 for 'x' and 5 for 'y' in the expression, we obtain,

$$2x + y = 2\,(10) + 5 = 20 + 5 = 25$$

Note that $2x$ means $2 \times x$.

(ii) $\frac{3xy + 3x}{2y + 5}$, where $x = 3$ and $y = 2$

Solution continued

Substituting 3 for 'x' and 2 for 'y' in the expression, we obtain,

$$\frac{3(3)(2)+3(3)}{2(2)+5} = \frac{18+9}{4+5} = \frac{27}{9} = 3$$

Example 2.1(b) **Evaluating Algebraic Expressions Involving Exponents**

(i) Evaluate $\frac{(5x)^2 \times 4y}{50}$, where $x = 2$ and $y = 3$

(ii) Evaluate $2(x^2 + 3x) - 5y$, where $x = 4$ and $y = -3$

Solution

(i) Evaluate $\frac{(5x)^2 \times 4y}{50}$, where $x = 2$ and $y = 3$

Substituting 2 for 'x' and 3 for 'y' in the expression, we obtain,

$$\frac{[5(2)]^2 \times 4(3)}{50} = \frac{10^2 \times 12}{50} = \frac{100 \times 12}{50} = 24$$

Remember to follow BEDMAS.

(ii) Evaluate $2(x^2 + 3x) - 5y$, where $x = 4$ and $y = -3$

Substituting 4 for 'x' and -3 for 'y' in the expression, we obtain,

$2[(4)^2 + 3(4)] - 5(-3) = 2(16+12) + 15 = 56 + 15 = 71$

Basic Arithmetic Operations with Algebraic Expressions

All arithmetic operations can be applied to algebraic expressions.

Addition and Subtraction

When adding or subtracting algebraic expressions, first collect the like terms and group them, then add or subtract the coefficients of the like terms.

Example 2.1(c) **Addition and Subtraction of Algebraic Expressions**

(i) Add $(3x + 7)$ and $(5x + 3)$

(ii) Add $(4y^2 - 8y - 9)$ and $(2y^2 + 6y - 2)$

(iii) Subtract $(x^2 + 5x - 7)$ from $(2x^2 - 2x + 3)$

(iv) Subtract $(5y^2 + 8y - 6)$ from $(-2y^2 - 7y + 5)$

Solution

While grouping like terms, the sign of the term moves with the term.

When a bracket is preceded by a positive sign (+), then drop the bracket.

When a bracket is preceded by a negative sign, drop the bracket and change the sign of every term.

(i) $(3x + 7) + (5x + 3)$

$= 3x + 7 + 5x + 3$ — Grouping like terms, we obtain,

$= 3x + 5x + 7 + 3$ — Adding like terms, we obtain,

$= 8x + 10$

(ii) $(4y^2 - 8y - 9) + (2y^2 + 6y - 2)$

$= 4y^2 - 8y - 9 + 2y^2 + 6y - 2$ — Grouping like terms, we obtain,

$= 4y^2 + 2y^2 - 8y + 6y - 9 - 2$ — Adding and subtracting like terms, we obtain,

$= 6y^2 - 2y - 11$

(iii) $(2x^2 - 2x + 3) - (x^2 + 5x - 7)$ — Expanding by distributing the negative sign to terms within the bracket, we obtain,

$= 2x^2 - 2x + 3 - x^2 - 5x + 7$ — Grouping like terms, we obtain,

$= 2x^2 - x^2 - 2x - 5x + 3 + 7$ — Adding and subtracting like terms, we obtain,

$= x^2 - 7x + 10$

Solution continued

(iv) $(-2y^2 - 7y + 5) - (5y^2 + 8y - 6)$ Expanding by distributing the negative sign to terms within the bracket, we obtain,

$= -2y^2 - 7y + 5 - 5y^2 - 8y + 6$ Grouping like terms, we obtain,

$= -2y^2 - 5y^2 - 7y - 8y + 5 + 6$ Adding and subtracting like terms, we obtain,

$= -7y^2 - 15y + 11$

Multiplication

Multiplying a Monomial by a Monomial

When multiplying a monomial by a monomial, multiply the coefficients and multiply all variables. If there are any similar variables, use the exponent notation.

Example 2.1(d) **Multiplying Monomials by Monomials**

(i) Multiply $6x^2y$ and $5xy$

(ii) Multiply $(3a^3)$, $(-4ab)$, and $(2b^2)$

Solution

(i) $(6x^2y)(5xy)$ Grouping coefficients and variables, we obtain,

$= (6)(5)(x^2)(x)(y)(y)$ Multiplying, we obtain,

$= 30x^3y^2$

(ii) $(3a^3)(-4ab)(2b^2)$ Grouping coefficients and variables, we obtain,

$= (3)(-4)(2)(a^3)(a)(b)(b^2)$ Multiplying, we obtain,

$= -24a^4b^3$

Multiplying a Polynomial by a Monomial

When multiplying a polynomial by a monomial, multiply **each term** of the polynomial by the monomial.

Example 2.1(e) **Multiplying Polynomials by Monomials**

(i) Multiply $2x^3$ and $(3x^2 + 2x - 5)$

(ii) Expand and simplify $8x(x+3) + 4x(x - 4)$

Solution

(i) $2x^3(3x^2 + 2x - 5)$ Expanding, we obtain,

$= 6x^5 + 4x^4 - 10x^3$

(ii) $8x(x+3) + 4x(x - 4)$ Expanding, we obtain,

$= 8x^2 + 24x + 4x^2 - 16x$ Grouping like terms, we obtain,

$= 8x^2 + 4x^2 + 24x - 16x$ Adding and subtracting like terms, we obtain,

$= 12x^2 + 8x$

Multiplying a Polynomial by a Polynomial

When multiplying a polynomial by a polynomial, each term of one polynomial is multiplied by each term of the other polynomial. Then, group the like terms and simplify using addition and subtraction.

Example 2.1(f) **Multiplying Polynomials by Polynomials**

(i) Multiply $(x^2 + 5)$ and $(x - 4)$

(ii) Multiply $(x^2 + 7)$ and $(2x^2 + 5x + 2)$

(iii) Expand and simplify $(x + 5)(2x - 6) + (3x - 4)(x - 5)$

Solution

(i) $(x^2 + 5)(x - 4)$

$= x^3 - 4x^2 + 5x - 20$

(ii) $(x^2 + 7)(2x^2 + 5x + 2)$ Expanding, we obtain,

$= 2x^4 + 5x^3 + 2x^2 + 14x^2 + 35x + 14$ Adding like terms, we obtain,

$= 2x^4 + 5x^3 + 16x^2 + 35x + 14$

(iii) $(x + 5)(2x - 6) + (3x - 4)(x - 5)$ Expanding, we obtain

$= (2x^2 - 6x + 10x - 30) + (3x^2 - 15x - 4x + 20)$

$= 2x^2 - 6x + 10x - 30 + 3x^2 - 15x - 4x + 20$ Grouping like terms, we obtain,

$= 2x^2 + 3x^2 - 6x + 10x - 15x - 4x - 30 + 20$ Adding and subtracting like terms, we obtain,

$= 5x^2 - 15x - 10$

Division

Dividing a Monomial by Monomial

When dividing a monomial by a monomial, group the constants and each of the variables separately and simplify them.

Example 2.1(g)

Dividing Monomials by Monomials

(i) Divide $8x^2y$ by $6x$

(ii) Divide $9x^2$ by $2x^2$

Solution

(i) $\frac{8x^2y}{6x} = \frac{8}{6} \times \frac{x^2}{x} \times y = \frac{4}{3}xy$

(ii) $\frac{9x^2}{3x^2} = \frac{9}{3} = 3$

Dividing a Polynomial by a Monomial

When dividing a polynomial by a monomial, divide **each term** of the polynomial by the monomial.

Example 2.1(h)

Dividing Polynomials by Monomials

(i) Divide $(9x^3 + 3x^2)$ by $6x$

(ii) Divide $(2x^3 + 4x^4 + 7x)$ and $4x^4$

Solution

(i) $\frac{9x^3 + 3x^2}{6x} = \frac{9x^3}{6x} + \frac{3x^2}{6x} = \frac{3x^2}{2} + \frac{x}{2} = \frac{3x^2 + x}{2}$

(ii) $\frac{2x^3 + 4x^4 + 7x}{4x^4} = \frac{2x^3}{4x^4} + \frac{4x^4}{4x^4} + \frac{7x}{4x^4} = \frac{1}{2x} + 1 + \frac{7}{4x^3}$

Factoring Algebraic Expressions with Common Factors

Factoring algebraic expressions means finding the common factors for both coefficients and the variables in all the terms. Once the factors are found, the expression will become a product of a monomial and a polynomial or a combination of both.

Example 2.1(i)

Factoring Algebraic Expressions

Factor the following:

(i) $12x + 18y$

(ii) $8y^2 + 18y$

(iii) $12xy^3 + 6xy^4 - 9x^3y^5 - 3xy^3$

(iv) $14(2x+y) - 7x(2x+y)$

Solution

(i) $12x + 18y$

$12x = 2 \times 2 \times 3 \times x$

$18y = 2 \times 3 \times 3 \times y$

HCF is $2 \times 3 = 6$

By dividing the original expression by the HCF 6, we obtain,

$6(2x + 3y)$

(ii) $8y^2 + 18y$

$8y^2 = 2 \times 2 \times 2 \times y \times y$

$18y = 2 \times 3 \times 3 \times y$

HCF is $2y$

By dividing the original expression by the HCF $2y$, we obtain,

$2y(4y + 9)$

(iii) $12xy^3 + 6xy^4 - 9x^3y^5 - 3xy^3$

HCF is $3xy^3$

By dividing the original expression by the HCF $3xy^3$, we obtain,

$3xy^3(4 + 2y - 3x^2y^2 + 1)$

(iv) $14(2x+y) - 7x(2x+y)$

HCF is $7(2x+y)$

By dividing the original expression by the HCF $7(2x+y)$, we obtain,

$$\frac{14(2x+y)}{7(2x+y)} - \frac{7x(2x+y)}{7(2x+y)} = 7(2x+y)(2-x)$$

2.1 | Exercises

1. Identify the following terms in the equations:

   a. 2nd term and 3rd term in $3x^2 + 7xy - 4y + 7$

   b. 3rd term and 4th term in $x^2 - 5x - y + 3$

   c. 1st term and 3rd term in $9xy + 7x - 6y + 2$

2. Identify the following terms in the equations:

   a. 1st term and 4th term in $-x^2 + 9xy + y + 7$

   b. 2nd term and 3rd term in $7xy \times 4y + 7$

   c. 1st term and 3rd term in $10x^2 + 5xy - 6x + 7y$

3. State the constant term and the coefficient of all other terms in each of the following expressions:
   a. $5x^2 - 3xy + 5$ b. $-2y^2 + 3x + 1$ c. $-2xy^2 - 2x^2y + 7$ d. $8y^2 - 4$

4. State the constant term and the coefficient of all other terms in each of the following expressions:
   a. $-2y^2 + 3y - 4$ b. $y^5 - 2y^7 - 2$ c. $2x^3 - 3x^2 + 1$ d. $-6x^2 + 6$

5. Simplify:
   a. $13x^2 + 8x - 2x^2 + 9x$ b. $-18y - 5y^2 + 19y - 2y^2$ c. $6x - 3x + 2y^2 + y^2$

6. Simplify:
   a. $7x + 12x^2 - 4x + 5x^2$ b. $-14y - 2y^2 + 7y + 7y^2$ c. $9x^2 - 6x^2 + 7y - 6y$

7. Simplify:
   a. $\dfrac{3x + 5x}{5x}$ b. $\dfrac{12y - 3y}{4y + 2y}$ c. $\dfrac{(16y)(8x)}{(4x)(8y)}$

8. Simplify:
   a. $\dfrac{8x}{x + 5x}$ b. $\dfrac{20y - 5y}{-4y + 7y}$ c. $\dfrac{(20y)(4x)}{(2x)(5y)}$

9. Simplify:
   a. $3[5 - 3(4 - x)] - 2 - 5[3(5x - 4)+8] - 9x$
   b. $6[4(8 - y) - 5(3+3y)] - 21 - 7[3(7+4y)-4] + 198y$

10. Simplify:
   a. $5 - \frac{1}{4}\{x - 8[3 - 5(2x - 3) + 3x] - 3\}$ b. $\frac{1}{5}\{y - 15[2 - 3(3y - 2) - 7y] - 4\} + 7$

11. Simplify:
   a. $y - \{4x - [y - (2y - 9) - x] + 2\}$ b. $(x - 1) - \{[x - (x - 3)] - x\}$

12. Simplify:
   a. $2y + \{-6y - z[3x + (-4x + 3)] + 5\}$ b. $9x - \{3y + [4x - (y - 6x)] - (x + 7y)\}$

13. Simplify:
   a. $5\{-2y + 3[4x - 2(3 + x)]\}$ b. $2y + \{8[3(2y - 5) - (8y + 9) + 6]\}$

14. Simplify:
   a. $4\{-7y + 8[5x - 3(4x + 6)]\}$ b. $7x - \{5[4(3x - 8) - (9x + 10)] + 14\}$

15. Simplify:
   a. $(2y - 1)(y - 4) - (3y + 2)(3y - 1)$ b. $(2x + 3)(2x - 1) - 4(x^2 - 7)$
   c. $(5x - 6)^2 - (x + 5)^2$

16. Simplify:
   a. $(y + 4)(y - 3) + (y - 2)(y - 3)$ b. $4(2x - 1)(x + 3) - 3(x - 2)(3x - 4)$
   c. $(2y - 3)^2 - (y + 3)^2$

17. Simplify:
   a. $\dfrac{-x^2y - xy^2}{xy}$ b. $\dfrac{x^2y - 3xy^2 + 4x^2y + xy}{xy}$ c. $\dfrac{6xy^2}{7} \times \dfrac{21x^2}{y} \times \dfrac{1}{36xy^2}$

18. Simplify:

a. $\frac{x^2y - 3xy^2}{xy}$ b. $\frac{3x^3y^3 + 6x^2y - 3xy^2 + 3xy}{3xy}$ c. $\frac{12x^2y^3}{5} \times \frac{15x^2}{4xy} \times \frac{1}{30x^3y}$

19. Simplify:

a. $\frac{3x+9}{14} \times \frac{7x+21}{x+3}$ b. $\frac{x^2-5x}{2x+10} \times \frac{3x+15}{4x}$ c. $\frac{5xy-15y}{4x-12} \times \frac{3x-9}{4x-12}$

20. Simplify:

a. $\frac{16}{3x^2y+4x} \times \frac{6x^2y+8x}{12}$ b. $\frac{3xy+4y}{8y} \times \frac{12y^2}{3x+4}$ c. $\frac{x^2+xy}{7x-14} \times \frac{14x-28}{x+y}$

21. Evalute the following expressions given $x = 2$ and $y = 3$:

a. $\frac{19x - 5y}{9}$ b. $x^2 + 6x + 8$ c. $\frac{(3x)^2(5y)}{6y}$ d. $-2x^2 + 3x + 8y$

22. Evalute the following expressions given $x = 5$ and $y = 4$:

a. $\frac{7x - 5y}{3}$ b. $-x^2 + 10x + 7$ c. $\frac{(2x)^2(2y)}{5y}$ d. $4x^2 + 10x - 4y$

23. Simplify and evaluate the following expressions:

a. $6y + 4y - 7y$, where $y = 10$ b. $2z - z + 7z$, where $z = 7$

c. $(6x)(3x) - (5x)(4x)$, where $x = 3$ d. $(2x)(0.5x + 4x)(5x + x)$, where $x = 5$

24. Simplify and evaluate the following expressions:

a. $3x + 5x - 8x$ where $x = 4$ b. $3A - A + 6A$, where $A = 10$

c. $(10x \times 4.5x) - (11x \times 4x)$, where $x = 50$ d. $(4x)(12x + 0.25x)(0.5x + x)$, where $x = 3$

25. Identify like terms:

a. $12A + 4B - 7A - B$ b. $6x + 8y - 5x - 3y + 7$

c. $-2x + 8x - 12x + 5y + 7y$ d. $6xy^2 - 2x^2y - 4x^2 + 2xy^2 + 3x^2y + 2x^2 + 4$

26. Identify like terms:

a. $6B + 8A - A - 2B$ b. $14 - 3x + 10y + 4y$

c. $3x + 6x - 20x + 8y + 8y + 5x$ d. $3x^2y - 12xy^2 - 6x^2y - 5xy - 2xy - 4xy^2$

27. Identify like terms, group them, simplify, and evaluate:

a. $3a + 6b - 16c - a + 8b + 4c + 2$, where $a = 3$, $b = 2$, $c = 1$

b. $x^2 - x + 2x^2 - x$, where $x = 5$

28. Identify like terms, group them, simplify, and evaluate:

a. $3x - 60y - 17z - 2x + 62y + 4z + 1$, where $x = 5$, $y = 8$, $z = 2$

b. $-a^2 - 3a + 3a^2 + 4a$, where $a = 15$

29. Factor the following expressions:

a. $6x^2y - 3xy - 9y$ b. $15y^2 - 12y - 3$ c. $6ab - 8bc + 7ac + 3cb$

30. Factor the following expressions:

a. $10ab - 8bc$ b. $8a^3 - 4a^2$ c. $10x^2 - 6x - 4x^2$

31. Factor the following expressions:

a. $6xy - 9yz$ b. $10x^3 - 4x^2$ c. $60y^2 - 40y - 180y^2$

32. Factor the following expressions:

a. $12a^2b - 16ab - 24b$ b. $33x^2 - 3x - 11x^2$ c. $4xy - 12yz + 3xz + 15zy$

33. Factor the following expressions:

    a. $5x(y + 2) + 3(y + 2)$ b. $4y(x - 5) - x^2 + 5x$ c. $xy - 2y + 5x - 10$

34. Factor the following expressions:

    a. $7x(m - 4) + 3(m - 4)$ b. $3y(x - 1) + 2x^2 - 2x$ c. $4x - xy - 20y + 5y^2$

35. Factor the following expressions:

    a. $x^2 + x - xy - y$ b. $2x^2 + 3y + 2x + 3xy$

36. Factor the following expressions:

    a. $x^2 - 4y + 4x - xy$ b. $5x^2y - 10x^2 + y^2 - 2y$

2.2 | Simple Algebraic Equations and Word Problems

An algebraic equation is a mathematical statement that shows the equality between two algebraic expressions or between a number and an algebraic expression.

- For example,
  - Two algebraic expressions: $5x + 7 = x + 19$
  - Algebraic expression and a number: $2x + 5 = 13$

The value of 'x' that satisfies this equation is the solution to that equation.

Examples of Writing Simple Algebraic Equations in One Variable

- Six more than a number, 'n', is 15.
  - $n + 6 = 15$
- In 20 years, A will be 60 years old.
  - $A + 20 = 60$
- Fourteen decreased by twice a number is six.
  - $14 - 2x = 6$
- The product of five and the sum of a number and four is sixty.
  - $5(x + 4) = 60$
- The quotient of six and a number is three.
  - $\frac{6}{n} = 3$

Equivalent Equations

Equations with the same solutions are called equivalent equations.

- For example,
  - $2x + 5 = 13$ (Equation 1)
  - $2x = 8$ (Equation 2)
  - $x = 4$ (Equation 3)

  Equations 1, 2, and 3 are equivalent equations because $x = 4$ satisfies each equation.

Principle of Equations

If $a = b$, then $b = a$

- For example, if, $14 + 9 = x$
  then, $x = 14 + 9$

If 'c' is any number and $a = b$, then,

$$a + c = b + c \quad \text{Addition Principle}$$

$$a - c = b - c \quad \text{Subtraction Principle}$$

$$a \times c = b \times c \quad \text{Multiplication Principle}$$

$$\frac{a}{c} = \frac{b}{c} \quad \text{Division Principle}$$

Performing the same operation on both sides of an equation will result in an equivalent equation.

Steps to Solve Algebraic Equations with one Variable

1. Clear the equation of fractions and/or decimals whenever possible, to make calculations and rearrangements easier.
2. Expand and clear brackets in the equation, if present, by following the order of arithmetic operations (BEDMAS).
3. Use the addition and subtraction principles to collect and group all **variable** terms to the **left side** of the equation, and to collect all **constants** to the right side of the equation.
4. Use the division and multiplication principles to ensure that the coefficient of the variable is +1.
5. You should now have a single variable on the left side, and one or more numbers on the right side. Compute the right side of the equation to find the solution.
6. Verify the answer against the original problem.
7. State your answer.

Example 2.2(a)

Solving Equations Using the Addition Principle

Solve the following and verify the solution:

(i) $x - 11 = 4$

(ii) $x - \frac{2}{3} = \frac{1}{5}$

Solution

(i) $x - 11 = 4$ — Adding 11 to both sides, we obtain,

$$x - 11 + 11 = 4 + 11$$

$$x = 15$$

Verify:

$x - 11 = 4$ — Substituting 15 for x, we obtain,

$$15 - 11 = 4$$

$$4 = 4$$

(ii) $x - \frac{2}{3} = \frac{1}{5}$ — Adding $\frac{2}{3}$ to both sides, we obtain,

$$x - \frac{2}{3} + \frac{2}{3} = \frac{1}{5} + \frac{2}{3}$$

$x = \frac{1}{5} + \frac{2}{3}$ — Using LCD of 15, we obtain,

$$x = \frac{3}{15} + \frac{10}{15}$$

$$x = \frac{13}{15}$$

Solution continued

Verify:

$x - \frac{2}{3} = \frac{1}{5}$ Substituting $\frac{13}{15}$ for x, we obtain,

$\frac{13}{15} - \frac{2}{3} = \frac{1}{5}$ Using LCD of 15, we obtain,

$\frac{13}{15} - \frac{10}{15} = \frac{3}{15}$

$\frac{3}{15} = \frac{3}{15}$

Example 2.2(b) **Solving Equations Using the Subtraction Principle**

(i) $8 + x = 20$

(ii) $x + \frac{2}{5} = \frac{3}{4}$

Solution

(i) $8 + x = 20$ Subtracting 8 from both sides, we obtain,

$8 - 8 + x = 20 - 8$

$x = 12$

(ii) $x + \frac{2}{5} = \frac{3}{4}$ Subtracting $\frac{2}{5}$ from both sides, we obtain,

$x + \frac{2}{5} - \frac{2}{5} = \frac{3}{4} - \frac{2}{5}$

$x = \frac{3}{4} - \frac{2}{5}$ Using LCD of 20, we obtain,

$x = \frac{3}{4} - \frac{2}{5} = \frac{15}{20} - \frac{8}{20} = \frac{7}{20}$

Example 2.2(c) **Solving Equations Using the Multiplication and Division Principles**

(i) $5x = 20$

(ii) $\frac{3}{8}x = 12$

Solution

(i) $5x = 20$ Dividing both sides by 5, we obtain,

$\frac{5x}{5} = \frac{20}{5}$

$x = 4$

(ii) $\frac{3}{8}x = 12$ Multiplying both sides by $\frac{8}{3}$, we obtain,

$\frac{3}{8}x\left(\frac{8}{3}\right) = 12\left(\frac{8}{3}\right)$

$x = 4 \times 8 = 32$

or

$\frac{3}{8}x = 12$ Multiplying both sides by 8, we obtain,

$\frac{3}{8}x(8) = 12(8)$

$3x = 96$ Dividing both sides by 3, we obtain,

$\frac{3x}{3} = \frac{96}{3}$

$x = 32$

Example 2.2(d)

Solving Equations Using All the Principles

(i) $\frac{x}{3} + 5 = 7$

(ii) $8x + 7 - 3x = -6x - 15 + x$

(iii) $2(3x - 7) = 28 - 3(x + 1)$

Solution

(i)

$\frac{x}{3} + 5 = 7$

$\frac{x}{3} + 5 - 5 = 7 - 5$ Subtracting 5 from both sides, we obtain,

$\frac{x}{3} = 2$ Multiplying both sides by 3, we obtain,

$\frac{x}{3} \times 3 = 2 \times 3$

$x = 6$

(ii)

$8x + 7 - 3x = -6x - 15 + x$ Grouping like terms on both sides, we obtain,

$8x - 3x + 7 = -6x + x - 15$

$5x + 7 = -5x - 15$ Adding $5x$ to both sides, we obtain,

$5x + 5x + 7 = -5x + 5x - 15$

$10x + 7 = -15$ Subtracting 7 from both sides, we obtain,

$10x + 7 - 7 = -15 - 7$

$10x = -22$ Dividing both sides by 10, we obtain,

$\frac{10x}{10} = \frac{-22}{10}$

$x = -2.2$

(iii)

$2(3x - 7) = 28 - 3(x + 1)$ Expanding both sides, we obtain,

$6x - 14 = 28 - 3x - 3$ Adding $3x$ to both sides and simplifying, we obtain,

$9x - 14 = 25$ Adding 14 to both sides and simplifying, we obtain,

$9x = 25 + 14$

$9x = 39$ Dividing both sides by 9 and simplifying, we obtain,

$x = \frac{39}{9} = \frac{13}{3}$

Steps to Solve Word Problems

1. Read the entire problem and understand the situation.
2. Identify the given information and the question to be answered.
3. Look for key words. Some words indicate certain mathematical operations.
4. Choose a variable to represent the unknown(s).
5. State what that variable represents, including the unit of measure.
6. Where necessary, draw a simple sketch to identify the information. This helps to think clearly about the scenario.
7. Create an equation (or set of equations) to describe the relationship between the variables and the constants in the question.
8. Rearrange the equation(s) and solve for the unknowns.

Example 2.2(e) **Solving a Word Problem Using Algebraic Equations**

If Harry will be 65 years old in 5 years, how old is he today?

Solution

Let Harry's age today be x years.

Therefore, in 5 years, Harry's age will be, $x + 5 = 65$

Solving for x, $x = 65 - 5$

$= 60$

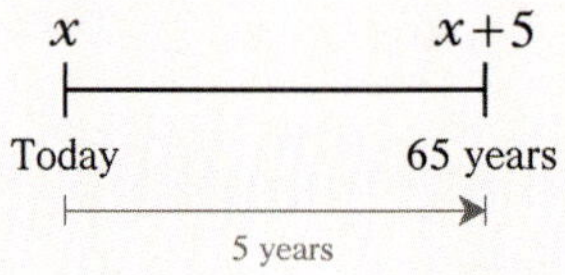

Therefore, Harry is 60 years old today.

Example 2.2(f) **Solving a Word Problem Using Algebraic Equations**

The perimeter of a rectangular garden is 50 metres. The length is 5 meters more than the width. Find the dimensions of the garden (Hint: perimeter = 2 times the length + 2 times the width).

Solution

Let the width be w metres.

Therefore, the length is: $length = (w+5)$ metres

$Perimeter = 2(length) + 2(width)$

$50 = 2(w+5) + 2w$

$50 = 2w + 10 + 2w$

$2w + 10 + 2w = 50$

$4w + 10 = 50$

$4w = 50 - 10$

$4w = 40$

$w = 10$

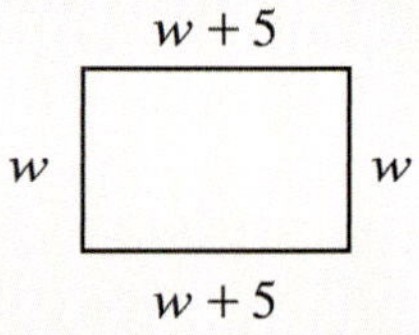

Perimeter = 50m

Therefore, the width of the garden is 10 metres, and the length = 10 + 5 = 15 metres.

2.2 | Exercises

1. Write the algebraic expression for the following:
   a. Three less than twice a number.
   b. Two times a number divided by five.
   c. Twenty-five increased by three times a number.
   d. Six times the total of three and a number.

2. Write the algebraic expression for the following:
   a. A number less than four times a number.
   b. Fifteen divided by three times a number.
   c. Seven times the sum of a number and five.
   d. Twenty increased by twice a number.

3. Write the algebraic equation for the following:
   a. The sum of a number and six is ten.
   b. Six times a number is seventy-two.
   c. A number divided by five is four.
   d. Two-thirds a number is twelve.

4. Write the algebraic equation for the following:
   a. A number decreased by fifteen is five.
   b. Two-fifths a number is six.
   c. The product of a number and four is twenty-eight.
   d. A number divided by three is three.

5. Solve the algebraic equations in Problem 3.

6. Solve the algebraic equations in Problem 4.

For problems 7 to 20, solve for the unknown using principles of equations, and round to 2 decimal places, wherever applicable.

7. a. $x - 20 = 10$ b. $22 = 40 - x$ c. $21 + x = 4$ d. $16 + x = 22$

8. a. $x - 25 = 17$ b. $54 = 23 - x$ c. $50 + x = 45$ d. $12 + x = 38$

9. a. $x - \frac{4}{5} = \frac{3}{5}$ b. $\frac{10}{15} = x - \frac{4}{3}$ c. $x + \frac{2}{5} = \frac{1}{4}$

10. a. $x - \frac{1}{6} = \frac{5}{6}$ b. $7x - 16 = 22$ c. $x + 0.13 = 70$

11. a. $5x = 20$ b. $11x + 4 = 17$ c. $10y - 0.09y = 17$

12. a. $4x = 24$ b. $\frac{8}{2}x = 20$ c. $\frac{x}{7} + 15 = 24$

13. a. $8x + 7 - 3x = -6x - 15 + x$ b. $2(3x - 7) = 28 - 3(x + 1)$
    c. $(4 + 6)(2 + 4x) = 45 - 2.5(x + 3)$

14. a. $x - 2 - 4x = -3x - 8 + 5x$ b. $4(2x - 5) = 32 - 4(x - 2)$
    c. $(5 + 0.5x)(1 + 3) = -1.2(2x + 4) + 25$

15. $\frac{x - 7}{2} + \frac{x + 2}{3} = 41$

16. $\frac{7}{12}(2x - 1) + \frac{3}{4}(x + 1) = 3$

17. a. $\frac{5}{y + 4} = \frac{3}{y - 2}$ b. $\frac{7}{5x - 3} = \frac{5}{4x}$

18. a. $\frac{3}{x + 1} = \frac{2}{x - 3}$ b. $\frac{5}{y + 2} = \frac{3}{y}$

19. a. $15 + 5(x - 10) = 3(x - 1)$ b. $4(y + 7) - 2(y - 4) = 3(y - 2)$

20. a. $2(x - 3) + 3(x - 5) = 4$ b. $8(2y + 4) - 6(3y + 7) = 3y$

21. If three times a number plus twenty is seven times that number, what is the number?

22. Fifteen less than three times a number is twice that number. What is the number?

23. A 25-metre long wire is cut into 2 pieces. One piece is 7 metres longer than the other. Find the length of each piece.

24. A 9-metre long pipe is cut into 2 pieces. One piece is twice the length of the other piece. Find the length of each piece.

25. \$500 is shared between Andy and Becky. Andy's share is \$150 less than Becky's share. Calculate the size of each of their shares.

26. \$200 is shared between Bill and Ann. Ann's share is \$50 more than Bill's share. Calculate the size of each of their shares.

27. Movie tickets that were sold to children were \$3 cheaper than those sold to adults. If a family of 2 adults and 2 children paid \$34 to watch a movie at the cinema, what was the price of the adult tickets, and what was the price of the children tickets?

28. Giri had twice the number of quarters (25 cents) in his bag than dimes (10 cents). If he had a total of 54 coins, how many of them were quarters? What was the total dollar value of these coins?

29. A square garden, with sides of length x, is widened by 4 metres and lengthened by 3 metres. Write the equation for the area (A) of the expanded garden. If each side was originally 10 metres in length, find the new area. (Hint: Area of a Rectangle = Length × Width)

30. A square garden, with sides of length x, has had its width reduced by 4 metres and its length reduced by 2 metres. Write the equation for the Area (A) of the shrunken garden. If each side was originally 20 metres in length, find the new area.

2.3 | Exponents

The concept of exponents was covered in Chapter 1, Section 1.4, where exponents were used to express repeated multiplication or division of the same numbers.

$$\underbrace{a \times a \times a \times a \ldots \times a}_{'n' \text{ factors of } 'a'} = a^n \qquad \frac{1}{\underbrace{a \times a \times a \times a \times a \times \ldots \times a}_{'n' \text{ factors of } 'a'}} = \frac{1}{a^n} = a^{-n}$$

- For example,

$$\underbrace{2 \times 2 \times 2 \times 2 \times 2}_{5 \text{ factors of } 2} \text{ is represented by: } 2^5$$

(exponent: 5; base: 2)

$$\frac{1}{\underbrace{8 \times 8 \times 8}_{3 \text{ factors of } 8}} \text{ is represented by: } \frac{1}{8^3} = 8^{-3}$$

(exponent: −3; base: 8)

The above exponent principle is applied to express repeated multiplication of a variable or an algebraic term.

In algebra, when $'n'$ is a positive integer, the general form of an exponent using variables is represented by:

$$\underbrace{x \times x \times x \times x \times x \ldots x}_{'n' \text{ factors of } 'x'} = x^n \qquad \frac{1}{\underbrace{x \times x \times x}_{'n' \text{ factors of } 'x'}} = \frac{1}{x^n} = x^{-n}$$

Some useful applications of the above with examples are given below:

	Exponential Form	Expanded Form	Example
(i)	$-x^n = -(x)^n$	$= -(x \times x \times x \times x \ldots \times x)$	$-2^5 = -(2 \times 2 \times 2 \times 2 \times 2) = -32$ $-2^4 = -(2 \times 2 \times 2 \times 2) = -16$
(ii)	$(-x)^n$	$= (-x)\,(-x)\,(-x) \ldots (-x)$	$(-2)^5 = (-2)(-2)(-2)(-2)(-2) = -32$ $(-2)^4 = (-2)(-2)(-2)(-2) = 16$
(iii)	$-x^{-n} = -(x)^{-n}$	$= -\frac{1}{x^n}$ $= -\frac{1}{x \times x \times x \times x \ldots \times x}$	$-2^{-5} = -(2)^{-5} = -\frac{1}{2^5}$ $= -\frac{1}{2 \times 2 \times 2 \times 2 \ldots \times 2} = -\frac{1}{32}$
(iv)	$(-x)^{-n}$	$= \frac{1}{(-x)^n}$ $= \frac{1}{(-x) \times (-x) \times (-x) \times (-x) \ldots \times (-x)}$	$(-2)^{-5} = \frac{1}{(-2)^5}$ $= \frac{1}{(-2) \times (-2) \times (-2) \times (-2) \times (-2)}$ $= \frac{1}{-32} = \frac{-1}{32}$ $(-2)^{-4} = \frac{1}{(-2)^4}$ $= \frac{1}{(-2)(-2)(-2)(-2)}$ $= \frac{1}{16}$
(v)	ax^n	$= a(x \times x \times x \times x \ldots \times x)$	$3x^4$, where $x = 2$, $= 3(2)^4 = 3(2 \times 2 \times 2 \times 2) = 48$
(vi)	$(ax)^n$	$= (ax) \times (ax) \times (ax) \times (ax) \ldots \times (ax)$	$(3x)^4$, where $x = 2$, $(3 \times 2)^4 = 6 \times 6 \times 6 \times 6 = 1296$

Note: *The examples above assume that x is a positive number.*

Rules of Exponents and Evaluation of Exponents

'Rules of exponents' is also referred to as 'laws of exponents' or 'properties of exponents'. When the bases of exponents are the same, there are seven basic rules, as follows:

Rule #	Rule	Rule in Exponential form	Example
1	Product Rule	$(x^m)(x^n) = x^{m+n}$	$2^4 \times 2^3 = 2^{(4+3)} = 2^7 = 128$
2	Quotient Rule	$\frac{x^m}{x^n} = x^{m-n}$	$\frac{3^5}{3^3} = 3^{5-3} = 3^2 = 9$
3	Power of a power	$(x^m)^n = x^{mn}$	$(2^4)^2 = 2^{4\times 2} = 2^8 = 256$
4	Power of a product	$(xy)^m = x^m y^m$	$(3\times 5)^4 = 3^4 \times 5^4$ $= 81 \times 625 = 50{,}625$
5	Power of a quotient	$\left(\frac{x}{y}\right)^m = \frac{x^m}{y^m}$	$\left(\frac{3}{5}\right)^4 = \frac{3^4}{5^4} = \frac{81}{625}$
6	1 or −1 as an exponent	$x^1 = x$ and $x^{-1} = \frac{1}{x}$	$x = 7$ and $n = 1$, then $7^1 = 7$ and $7^{-1} = \frac{1}{7}$
7	Negative exponent	$\left(\frac{x}{y}\right)^{-m} = \frac{y^m}{x^m}$	$\left(\frac{2}{3}\right)^{-4} = \left(\frac{3}{2}\right)^4 = \frac{3^4}{2^4} = \frac{81}{16}$
8	Zero (0) as an exponent	* $x^0 = 1$	$x = 9$ and $n = 0$, then $9^0 = 1$
* $\frac{x^n}{x^n} = x^{(n-n)} = x^0$ Also, $\frac{x^n}{x^n} = 1$, therefore, $x^0 = 1$			

The exponent button on the Texas Instruments BA II Plus calculator is the y^x button, as shown in this picture.

***Note:** There are no rules for addition or subtraction of exponents. These operations would have to be done separately.*

For example, $2^3 + 2^5 = (2 \times 2 \times 2) + (2 \times 2 \times 2 \times 2 \times 2) = 8 + 32 = 40$

Example 2.3(a)

Solving Expressions Using the Product Rule and the Quotient Rule

Solve: $(2^2)^3 \times 2^7 \div 2^9$

Solution

$$2^6 \times 2^7 \div 2^9$$

$$2^{(6+7-9)} = 2^4 = 16$$

Example 2.3(b)

Solving Expressions that Have Exponents with Different Bases

Solve: $2^4 \times 3^4$

Solution

$$2^4 \times 3^4 = (2 \times 2 \times 2 \times 2) \times (3 \times 3 \times 3 \times 3) = 16 \times 81 = 1296$$

Example 2.3(c)

Solving Expressions that Have Negative Exponents

Solve: $\left(\frac{5}{4}\right)^{-2} \times \left(\frac{2}{3}\right)^{-3}$

Solution

$$\left(\frac{5}{4}\right)^{-2} \times \left(\frac{2}{3}\right)^{-3} = \left(\frac{4}{5}\right)^2 \times \left(\frac{3}{2}\right)^3 = \frac{4^2}{5^2} \times \frac{3^3}{2^3} = \frac{16}{25} \times \frac{27}{8} = \frac{2}{25} \times \frac{27}{1} = \frac{54}{25}$$

Fractional Exponent

When the exponent, 'n', of a variable is a fraction, we call it a fractional exponent. The fractional exponent, $\frac{1}{n}$, replaces the radical sign, $\sqrt{\ }$.

For example,

$$\text{The square root of } x = \sqrt{x} = x^{\frac{1}{2}}$$

$$\text{The cube root of } x = \sqrt[3]{x} = x^{\frac{1}{3}}$$

$$\text{Similarly, the } n^{\text{th}} \text{ root of } x = \sqrt[n]{x} = x^{\frac{1}{n}}$$

Fractional exponents obey all the rules of exponents.

(i) $x^{\frac{1}{n}} = \sqrt[n]{x}$

For example, if $x = 16$ and $n = 4$,

then, $16^{\frac{1}{4}} = \sqrt[4]{16}$ Read as the 4th root of 16

$= 2$

(ii) $x^{\frac{m}{n}} = \left(x^{\frac{1}{n}}\right)^m = [\sqrt[n]{x}]^m$

This refers to finding the nth root of x, then raising the result to the power of m.

For example, if $x = 16$, $m = 3$, and $n = 4$,

then, $16^{\frac{3}{4}} = \left(16^{\frac{1}{4}}\right)^3 = [\sqrt[4]{16}]^3 = [2]^3 = 8$

Or

$x^{\frac{m}{n}} = (x^m)^{\frac{1}{n}} = \sqrt[n]{x^m}$

This refers to raising 'x' to the power of 'm', then finding the nth root of the result.

For example, if $x = 16$, $m = 3$, and $n = 4$,

then, $16^{\frac{3}{4}} = (16^3)^{\frac{1}{4}} = \sqrt[4]{16^3} = \sqrt[4]{4096} = 8$

Note: *The first method is easier because first finding the nth root results in a small number, which is easy to raise to the power of 'm'.*

(iii) $x^{-\frac{m}{n}} = \frac{1}{x^{\frac{m}{n}}} = \frac{1}{(\sqrt[n]{x})^m}$

For example, if $x = 27$, $m = 4$, and $n = 3$,

then, $27^{-\frac{4}{3}} = \frac{1}{27^{\frac{4}{3}}} = \frac{1}{(\sqrt[3]{27})^4} = \frac{1}{(3)^4} = \frac{1}{81}$

$$x^{\frac{1}{n}} = \sqrt[n]{x}$$

$$x^{\frac{m}{n}} = \sqrt[n]{x^m}$$

$$x^{-\frac{1}{n}} = \frac{1}{x^{\frac{1}{n}}} = \frac{1}{\sqrt[n]{x}}$$

$$x^{-\frac{m}{n}} = \frac{1}{x^{\frac{m}{n}}} = \frac{1}{\sqrt[n]{x^m}}$$

2.3 Exercises

For problems 1 to 6, simplify where possible and then evaluate.

1. a. $5^4 - 4^2$ b. $\frac{3^9 \times 3^2}{3^5}$ c. $\frac{(2^5)^4}{4^6}$ d. $4^0 - 4^4$ e. $\frac{10^6}{10^0}$ f. $\frac{3^7}{27}$

2. a. $10^3 - 7^2$ b. $\frac{2^9 \times 2^1}{2^5}$ c. $\frac{(2^5)^4}{16^3}$ d. $3^0 + 3^4$ e. $\frac{8^5}{8^3}$ f. $\frac{5^6}{125}$

3. a. $\left(\frac{5}{2}\right)^2\left(\frac{5}{2}\right)^3$ b. $-10^4 \times 10^3$ c. $(-5)^2 \times (4)^2$ d. $3^4 \times 3^{(4+2)}$ e. $(2 \times 3^2)^4$ f. $3^{-2} \times 3^3$

4. a. $\left(\frac{5}{3}\right)^3\left(\frac{3}{5}\right)^2$ b. $-2^4 \times 2^2$ c. $(-2)^2 \times (3)^2$ d. $10^4 \times 10^{(3+2)}$ e. $(5 \times 2^2)^3$ f. $12^{-8} \times 12^9$

5. a. $\sqrt[4]{25^2 \times 25^2}$ b. $\sqrt[2]{3^4 \times 2^4}$ c. $(2^6)^{\frac{1}{3}}$ d. $\left(\frac{3^9}{3^3}\right)^{\frac{1}{3}}$ e. $(9)^{\frac{3}{2}}$ f. $-5^3(-25)^3$

6. a. $\sqrt[4]{5^2 \times 25^3}$ b. $\sqrt[6]{9^3 \times 27^4}$ c. $(5^{15})^{\frac{1}{5}}$ d. $\left(\frac{2^{12}}{2^4}\right)^{\frac{1}{4}}$ e. $(16)^{\frac{3}{4}}$ f. $-100^2 \times (-10)^4$

For problems 7 to 12, simplify the expressions and and write your answers with positive exponents..

7. a. $(5x)(4x^2)$ b. $(x^9) \times (x^2) \div x^5$ c. $(x^5)^4 \div x^3$ d. $x^0 \cdot x^4$ e. $\frac{x^6}{x^0}$ f. $\frac{x^7}{x}$

8. a. $(3x)(6x^2)$ b. $x^{10} \times x^{20} \div x^{30}$ c. $(x^5)^4 \div x^{20}$ d. $x^4 \cdot x^0$ e. $\frac{x^0}{x}$ f. $\frac{x^2}{x}$

9. a. $\left(\frac{x}{y}\right)^2\left(\frac{x}{y}\right)^3\left(\frac{x}{y}\right)^2$ b. $\left(\frac{x}{y}\right)^2\left(\frac{x}{y}\right)^3$ c. $-x^4 \times x^3$ d. $(-y)^4(y)^2$ e. $(xy^2)^4$ f. $x^{-5} \times x^7$

10. a. $\left(\frac{x}{y}\right)^4\left(\frac{x}{y}\right)^2\left(\frac{x}{y}\right)^{-8}$ b. $\left(\frac{x}{y}\right)^5\left(\frac{x}{y}\right)^{-3}$ c. $x^6 \times (-x)^5$ d. $(-y)^5 \times (y)^1$ e. $x^0 \times x^{(2 \times 3)}$ f. $(x^3y^2)^5$

11. a. $(x^3)^2(x^2)^3(x^{3-1})$ b. $\sqrt[4]{x^6 x^{10}}$ c. $\sqrt[3]{x^9 x^6}$ d. $(27x^6)^{\frac{1}{3}}$ e. $\left(\frac{x^9}{x^3}\right)^{\frac{1}{3}}$ f. $\frac{(-x)^3(-x)^4}{x^5}$

12. a. $(x^{5-1})(x^3)^2(x^2)^{-3}$ b. $\sqrt[4]{x^8 x^4}$ c. $\sqrt[2]{x^{10} y^{-6}}$ d. $(81x^8)^{\frac{1}{4}}$ e. $\left(\frac{x^{19}}{x^4}\right)^{\frac{1}{4}}$ f. $\frac{(-x)^6(-x)^4}{x^9}$

2.4 | Logarithms

Concept of Logarithm and its Relation to Exponents

We know that multiplication is a faster method for finding the answer to repeated addition.

For example, 5 + 5 + 5 + 5 + 5 + 5 + 5 is the same as 7 × 5.

Similarly, the use of logarithm is a faster method of finding the unknown exponent.

Exponential Form

$$10^3 = 1000$$

$$5^2 = 25$$

Exponent

$$a^x = y$$ ← Number

Base

Read as: base '*a*' raised to the '*x*' is '*y*' or '*a*' to the power of '*x*' is '*y*'.

Logarithmic Form

$$\log_{10} 1000 = 3$$

$$\log_5 25 = 2$$

Number

$$\text{Log}_a y = x$$ ← Logarithm (exponent)

Base

Read as: logarithm of '*y*' to the base '*a*' is '*x*' or log '*y*' to the base '*a*' is '*x*'.

As seen above, a logarithm is the exponent to which the base is raised to get the number.

Any positive number can be used as the base for logarithms.

For example, 100 is the same as 10^2. Here, the base is 10 and the exponent is 2. Therefore, the logarithm of 100 to the base 10 is 2.

$\underbrace{10^2 = 100}_{\text{Exponential form}}$ is the same as $\underbrace{\log_{10} 100 = 2}_{\text{Logarithmic form}}$

Similarly, 125 is the same as 5^3. Here, the base is 5 and the exponent is 3; therefore, the logarithm of 125 to the base 5 is 3.

$\underbrace{5^3 = 125}_{\text{Exponential form}}$ is the same as $\underbrace{\log_5 125 = 3}_{\text{Logarithmic form}}$

Common Logarithms (log)

Common logarithms are based on base '10' and referred to by 'log'.

The base of a logarithm should be a positive number and it is only possible to find logarithms for positive numbers, i.e., there is no logarithm of a negative number.

Common logarithms are always to the base 10. If no base is shown in the common logarithmic expression, it is assumed to have base 10 and is referred to by the symbol 'log'.

Common Logarithmic Form	Exponential Form
$\log_{10} 1000 = 3 = \log 1000 = 3$	$10^3 = 1000$
$\log_{10} 100 = 2 = \log 100 = 2$	$10^2 = 100$
$\log_{10} 10 = 1 = \log 10 = 1$	$10^1 = 10$
$\log_{10} 1 = 0 = \log 1 = 0$	$10^0 = 1$
$\log_{10} y = x = \log y = x$	$10^x = y$

Natural Logarithms (ln)

Natural logarithms are based on base 'e' and referred to by 'ln'.

Natural logarithms are always to the base 'e' where the constant $e = 2.718282...$

'e' is a special number in mathematics (similar to π which is equal to 3.141592...) and is found by $\left(1 + \frac{1}{n}\right)^n$ where 'n' is a large number.

Assume $n = 100{,}000$ then $e = \left(1 + \frac{1}{100{,}000}\right)^{100{,}000} = 2.718282...$

In business and financial calculators, the natural logarithm key, ln, is the only logarithmic key available. The common logarithm key, **log**, is not available. Natural logarithm is referred to by the symbol '**ln**' (pronounced "lawn") which has the base '*e*'.

If the base of a logarithmic expression is 'e' then it is simply expressed by '**ln**'.

To find the natural logarithm of a number with the Texas Instruments BAII Plus calculator, enter the number first then press the 'LN' key.

Natural Logarithmic Form	Exponent Form
$\log_e 1 = \ln 1 = 0$	$e^0 = 1$
$\log_e e = \ln e = 1$	$e^1 = 2.718282...$
$\log_e 10 = \ln 10 = 2.302585...$	$e^{2.302585} = 10$
$\log_e 1.005 = \ln 1.005 = 0.00498754...$	$e^{0.00498754} = 1.005$

The natural logarithm key on the Texas Instruments BA II Plus calculator is the 'LN' button, as shown in this picture.

The rules of logarithms are used to evaluate the exponent 'n' in business and finance mathematics formulas, which you will study in subsequent chapters.

Rules of Logarithms

Common logarithms (log) and natural logarithms (ln) follow the same rules.

Table 2.4

Rule #	Rule	Common Logarithms (log): Rule in Common Logarithmic Form	Common Logarithms (log): Example	Natural Logarithms (ln): Rule in Natural Logarithmic Form	Natural Logarithms (ln): Example
1	Product Rule	$\log(AB) = \log A + \log B$	$\log(50 \times 10) = \log 50 + \log 10$	$\ln(AB) = \ln A + \ln B$	$\ln(50 \times 10) = \ln 50 + \ln 10$
2	Quotient Rule	$\log\left(\frac{A}{B}\right) = \log A - \log B$	$\log\left(\frac{50}{10}\right) = \log 50 - \log 10$	$\ln\left(\frac{A}{B}\right) = \ln A - \ln B$	$\ln\left(\frac{50}{10}\right) = \ln 50 - \ln 10$
3	Power Rule	$\log(A)^n = n \log A$	$\log(50)^2 = 2 \log 50$	$\ln(A)^n = n \ln A$	$\ln(50)^2 = 2 \ln 50$
4	Zero as a power or One as logarithm	$\log(A)^0 = \log 1 = 0$	$\log(50)^0 = \log 1 = 0$	$\ln(A)^0 = \ln 1 = 0$	$\ln(50)^0 = \ln 1 = 0$

We know $x^0 = 1$
Thus, $10^0 = 1$
and $e^0 = 1$

Therefore,
$\log_{10} 1 = 0 \rightarrow \log 1 = 0$
$\ln_e 1 = 0 \rightarrow \ln 1 = 0$

Example 2.4(a)

Solving Equations using Natural Logarithms (ln)

Solve for 'n' in the following equations:

(i) $1024 = 2^n$

(ii) $3749 = 1217(1.005)^n$

Solution

(i)
$$1024 = 2^n$$
Taking ln on both sides, we obtain,
$$\ln 1024 = \ln 2^n$$
Using Power Rule, we obtain,
$$\ln 1024 = n \ln 2$$
$$n = \frac{\ln 1024}{\ln 2} = 10$$

(ii)
$$3749 = 1217(1.005)^n$$
$$\frac{3749}{1217} = (1.005)^n$$
Taking ln on both sides, we obtain,
$$\ln\left(\frac{3749}{1217}\right) = \ln(1.005)^n$$
Using Power Rule, we obtain,
$$\ln\left(\frac{3749}{1217}\right) = n \ln 1.005$$
$$n = \frac{\ln\left(\frac{3749}{1217}\right)}{\ln 1.005} = \frac{1.125100...}{0.004987...} = 225.582147...$$

2.4 | Exercises

1. Express in logarithmic form:

   a. $10^5 = 100{,}000$ b. $2^6 = 64$ c. $3^2 = 9$

   d. $4^5 = 1024$ e. $6^5 = 7776$ f. $9^4 = 6561$

2. Express in logarithmic form:

   a. $10^4 = 10{,}000$ b. $2^3 = 8$ c. $3^3 = 27$

   d. $4^4 = 256$ e. $6^4 = 1296$ f. $8^2 = 64$

3. Express in exponential form:

a. $\log_{10}100 = 2$ b. $\log_2 32 = 5$ c. $\log_3 729 = 6$

d. $\log_4 64 = 3$ e. $\log_5 625 = 4$ f. $\log_6 216 = 3$

4. Express in exponential form:

a. $\log_{10}1000 = 3$ b. $\log_2 4 = 2$ c. $\log_3 243 = 5$

d. $\log_4 4096 = 6$ e. $\log_5 125 = 3$ f. $\log_6 1296 = 4$

5. Calculate the following (rounding to 4 decimal places):

a. ln 2250 b. ln 154 c. ln 27

d. ln 10.05 e. ln 1.005 f. ln 0.675

6. Calculate the following (rounding to 4 decimal places):

a. ln 0.165 b. ln 1.02 c. ln 12.51

d. ln 39 e. ln 276 f. ln 1550

7. Solve for 'n' (rounding to 2 decimal places):

a. $250 = (30)^n$ b. $7500 = (45)^n + 500$ c. $10{,}000 = 2000(1.2)^n$ d. $(1.05)^n = 1.31$

8. Solve for 'n' (rounding to 2 decimal places):

a. $320 = (15)^n$ b. $8000 = (35)^n + 1500$ c. $15{,}000 = 5000\,(1.04)^n$ d. $2.5 = (1.05)^n$

9. Express the following as a sum or difference of two or more natural logarithms:

a. $\ln\left(\frac{3}{7}\right)$ b. $\ln\,(4 \times 9)$ c. $\ln\left(\frac{AB}{C}\right)$ d. $\ln\left(\frac{X}{YZ}\right)$ e. $\ln\left(\frac{3x}{2yz}\right)$

10. Express the following as a sum or difference of two or more natural logarithms:

a. $\ln\left(\frac{40}{13}\right)$ b. $\ln\,(7 \times 8)$ c. $\ln\left(\frac{x}{ab}\right)$ d. $\ln\left(\frac{xy}{c}\right)$ e. $\ln\left(\frac{5x}{2ab}\right)$

11. Express as a single natural logarithm:

a. $\ln 8 + \ln 5$ b. $\ln 15 - \ln 3$ c. $2\ln 5 + 3\ln 3$

d. $5\ln 2 - 2\ln 3$ e. $3\ln a + 2\ln b - 5\ln c$

12. Express as a single natural logarithm:

a. $\ln 25 + \ln 4$ b. $\ln 60 - \ln 15$ c. $2\ln 8 - 3\ln 3$

d. $4\ln 5 - 3\ln 2$ e. $4\ln x - 2\ln y + 3\ln z$

13. Express as a single natural logarithm.

a. $2\ln 5$ b. $3\ln 6$ c. $5\ln\frac{a}{b}$

d. $4\ln\,(a \times b)$ e. $3\ln 2 + 4\ln 3 - 2\ln 4$

14. Express as a single natural logarithm.

a. $5\ln 2$ b. $6\ln 3$ c. $2\ln\frac{x}{y}$

d. $3\ln\,(xy)$ e. $2\ln 3 + 3\ln 2 - 4\ln 2$

15. Solve for 'n' (rounding to 2 decimal places):

a. $n = \ln\left(\frac{4285}{4000}\right)$ b. $n = \ln\left(\frac{3645}{2175}\right)$ c. $n = \frac{\ln\left(\frac{7200}{4725}\right)}{\ln(1.01)}$ d. $n = \frac{\ln(2.5)}{\ln(1.03)}$

16. Solve for 'n' (rounding to 2 decimal places):

a. $n = \ln\left(\frac{6750}{3200}\right)$ b. $n = \ln\left(\frac{75{,}000}{2200}\right)$ c. $n = \frac{\ln\left(\frac{5120}{2250}\right)}{\ln(1.005)}$ d. $n = \frac{\ln(3)}{\ln(1.02)}$

2.5 | Formulas and their Applications

Formulas are similar to equations. In formulas, the relationship among many variables is written as a rule for performing calculations. To solve for one of the variables in a formula, rearrange the formula to isolate the required variable, simplify, and then solve for the required variable. Rearrangement can be performed using the rules that you have learned in the previous sections of this chapter.

To solve for a required variable using a formula, it is important to know what each symbol in the formula represents. For example, consider the formula for simple interest: $I = Prt$. In this simple interest formula, 'I' represents the amount of simple interest, 'P' represents the amount of investment or loan, also known as principal, 'r' represents the interest rate per annum, and 't' represents the time period in years.

To solve for any of the variables, 'I', 'P', 'r', or 't' in this simple interest formula, we can rearrange the variables as shown below:

$$I = Prt \qquad \text{is the same as } Prt = I$$

Solving for 'P':

$$\frac{Prt}{rt} = \frac{I}{rt} \qquad \text{Dividing both sides by '}rt\text{', we obtain}$$

$$P = \frac{I}{rt}$$

Solving for 'r':

$$\frac{Prt}{Pt} = \frac{I}{Pt} \qquad \text{Dividing both sides by '}Pt\text{', we obtain}$$

$$r = \frac{I}{Pt}$$

Solving for 't':

$$\frac{Prt}{Pr} = \frac{I}{Pr} \qquad \text{Dividing both sides by '}Pr\text{', we obtain}$$

$$t = \frac{I}{Pr}$$

Example 2.5(a) **Rearranging to Isolate Variables**

Rearrange and isolate the variable:

(i) 'M' in $S = C + M$

(ii) 'P' in $C + E + P = S$

(iii) 'R' and 'B' in $P = RB$

(iv) 'b' and 'm' in $y = mx + b$

(v) 'P' in $S = P(1 + rt)$

Solution

> If $a = b + c$,
> then $b + c = a$

(i)

$$S = C + M$$

$$M + C = S \qquad \text{Subtracting 'C' on both sides, we obtain,}$$

$$M + C - C = S - C$$

$$M = S - C$$

(ii)

$$C + E + P = S \qquad \text{Subtracting 'C' and 'E' on both sides, we obtain,}$$

$$C + E + P - C - E = S - C - E$$

$$P = S - C - E$$

Solution continued

(iii) $P = RB$

Isolating 'R'

$$RB = P$$

Dividing both sides by 'B', we obtain,

$$\frac{RB}{B} = \frac{P}{B}$$

$$R = \frac{P}{B}$$

Isolating 'B'

$$RB = P$$

Dividing both sides by 'R', we obtain,

$$\frac{RB}{R} = \frac{P}{R}$$

$$B = \frac{P}{R}$$

(iv) $y = mx + b$

Isolating 'b'

$$mx + b = y$$

Subtracting 'mx' from both sides, we obtain, obtain,

$$mx - mx + b = y - mx$$

$$b = y - mx$$

Isolating 'm'

$$mx + b = y$$

Subtracting 'b' from both sides, we

$$mx + b - b = y - b$$

$$mx = y - b$$

Dividing both sides by 'x', we obtain,

$$\frac{mx}{x} = \frac{y - b}{x}$$

$$m = \frac{y - b}{x}$$

(v) $P(1 + rt) = S$

Isolating 'P' by dividing both sides by '(1 + rt)', we obtain,

$$\frac{P(1 + rt)}{(1 + rt)} = \frac{S}{(1 + rt)}$$

$$P = \frac{S}{(1 + rt)}$$

Example 2.5(b)

Solving for Variables Using the Rearranged Simple Interest Formula

In the simple interest formula $I = Prt$, find:

(i) 'I', when $P = \$1000$, $r = 5\% = 0.05$, $t = 3$ years

(ii) 'P', when $I = \$150$, $r = 3\% = 0.03$, $t = 1$ year

(iii) 'r', when $I = \$500$, $P = \$8000$, $t = 2$ years

(iv) 't', when $I = \$40$, $P = \$800$, $r = 5\% = 0.05$

Round your answers to 2 decimal places wherever applicable.

Solution

(i) Substitute the value for 'P', 'r', and 't' in the formula: $I = Prt$

$$I = 1000 \times 0.05 \times 3 = \$150.00$$

(ii) Substitute the value for 'I', 'r', and, 't' in the rearranged formula: $P = \frac{I}{rt}$

$$P = \frac{150}{(0.03 \times 1)} = \$5000.00$$

(iii) Substitute the value for 'I', 'P', and 't' in the rearranged formula: $r = \frac{I}{Pt}$

$$r = \frac{500}{8000 \times 2} = 0.03125 = 3.125\% = 3.13\% \text{ (Rounded to 2 decimal places)}$$

(iv) Substitute the value for 'I', 'P', and 'r' in the rearranged formula: $t = \frac{I}{Pr}$

$$t = \frac{40}{800 \times 0.05} = 1 \text{ year}$$

Formulas to Find the Perimeter (P) and Area (A) of Common Plane Figures

1. Square:

$$P = 4S$$
$$A = S^2$$

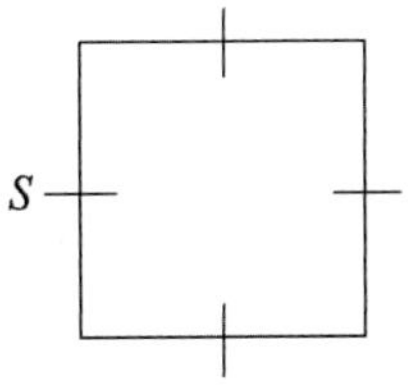

2. Rectangle:

$$P = 2(l + w)$$
$$A = l \times w$$

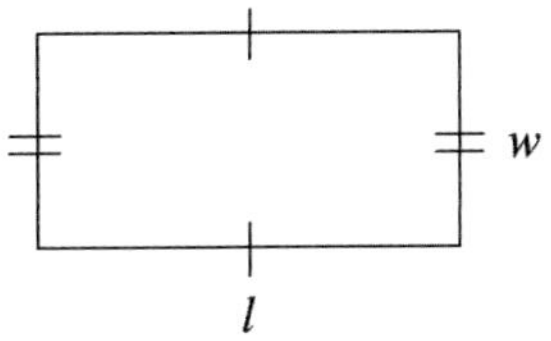

3. Triangle:

$$P = a + b + c$$
$$A = \frac{1}{2} b \times h$$

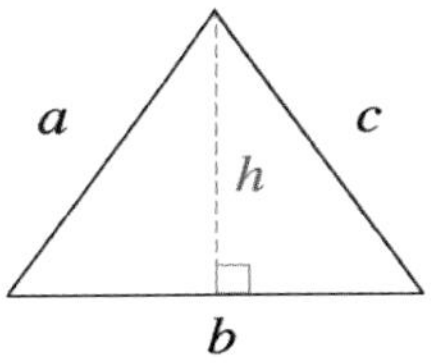

4. Parallelogram:

$$P = 2\,(a + b)$$
$$A = b \times h$$

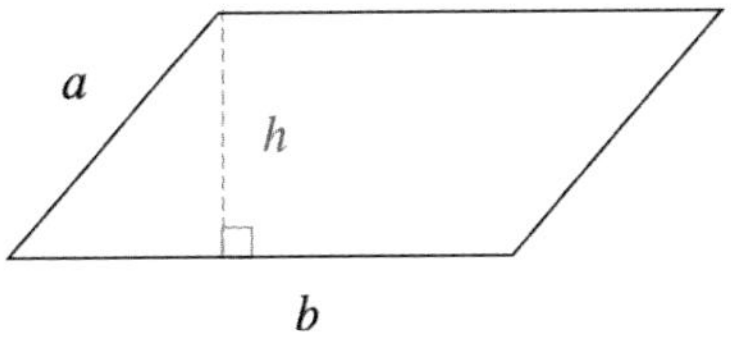

5. Trapezium:

$$P = a + b + c + d$$
$$A = \frac{(a + b)}{2} \times h$$

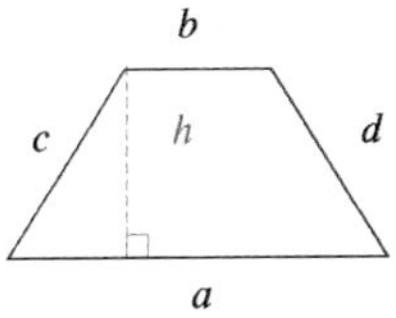

6. Circle:

$$P = \text{Circumference } (C)$$
$$C = 2\pi r$$
$$A = \pi r^2$$

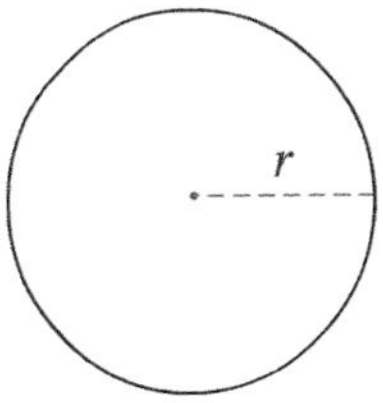

Formulas to Find the Surface Area (SA) and Volume (V) of Common Solid Objects

1. Square Prism

$$SA = 6s^2$$

$$V = s^3$$

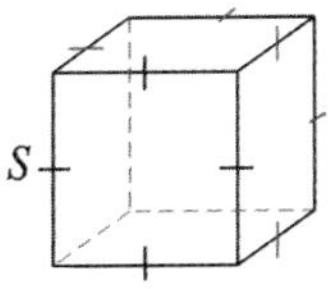

2. Rectangular Prism

$$SA = 2(l \times W + l \times h + w \times h)$$
$$V = l \times W \times h$$

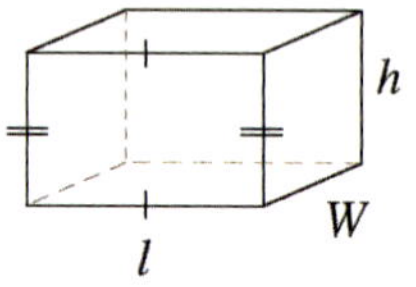

3. Triangular Prism

$$SA = \text{Area of all 5 faces}$$
$$V = B \times h$$

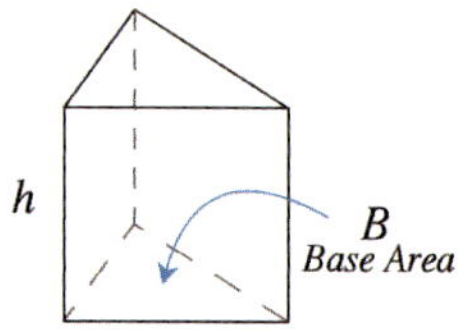

4. Cylinder

$$SA = 2\pi rh + 2\pi r^2$$
$$V = \pi r^2 h$$

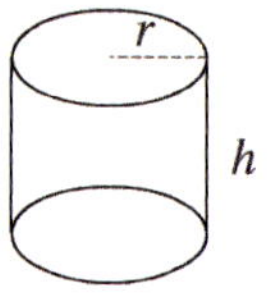

5. Cone

$$SA = \pi r^2 + \pi rs$$
$$V = \frac{1}{3}\pi r^2 h$$

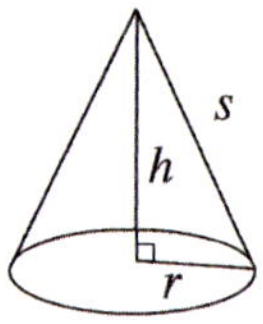

6. Triangular pyramid

$$SA = \text{Area of all 4 faces}$$
$$V = \frac{1}{3} B \times h$$

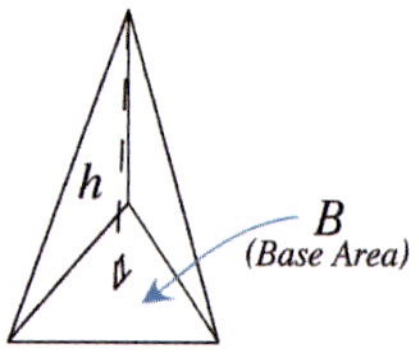

7. Sphere

$$SA = 4\pi r^2$$
$$V = \frac{4}{3}\pi r^3$$

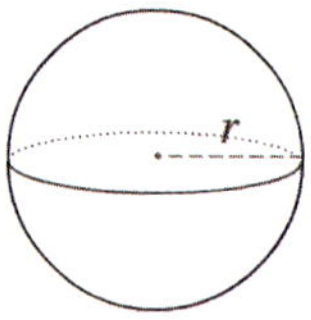

Example 2.5(c)

Calculating the Perimeter and Area of Plane Figures Using Formulas

Find the perimeter and area of the following plane figures:

(i) A triangle with sides of 5 cm, 8 cm, and 10 cm (base) and a height of 4 cm.

(ii) A parallelogram with sides of 9 cm and 6 cm and a perpendicular distance of 5 cm between the 9 cm sides.

Solution

(i) Triangle:

$$P = a + b + c = 5 + 8 + 10 = 23 \text{ cm}$$
$$\text{Area} = \frac{1}{2} b \times h = \frac{1}{2} \times 10 \times 4 = 20 \text{ cm}^2$$

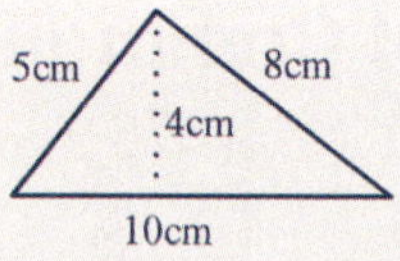

(ii) Parallelogram:

$$P = 2(a + b) = 2(9 + 6) = 30 \text{ cm}$$
$$\text{Area} = b \times h = 9 \times 5 = 45 \text{ cm}^2$$

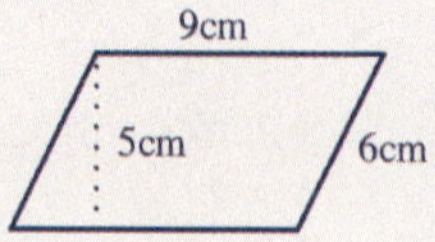

Example 2.5(d) **Calculating Surface Area and Volume of Solid Objects Using Formulas**

Find the surface area and volume of the following solid objects:

(i) A sphere with a radius of 12 cm.

(ii) A cylinder with a height of 15 cm and a base with a radius of 6 cm.

Solution

(i) Sphere:

$SA = 4\pi r^2 = 4\pi(12^2) = 1809.557368... = 1809.56 \text{ cm}^2$

$V = \frac{4}{3}\pi r^3 = \frac{4}{3}\pi(12^3) = 7238.229474... = 7238.23 \text{ cm}^3$

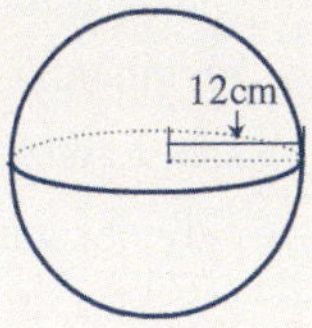

(ii) Cylinder:

$SA = 2\pi rh + 2\pi r^2 = 2\pi(6)(15) + 2\pi(6^2)$

$= 791.681348... = 791.68 \text{ cm}^2$

$V = \pi r^2 h = \pi(6^2)(15) = 1696.460033... = 1696.46 \text{ cm}^3$

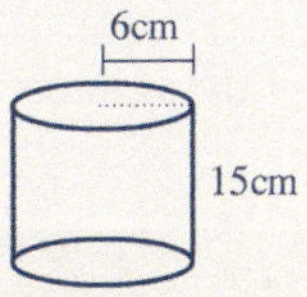

2.5 | Exercises

1. Rearrange and isolate the variables:
   a. 'L' in $N = L(1 - d)$
   b. 'C' in $S = C + M$
   c. 'E' in $C + E + P = S$
   d. 'r' in $C = 2\pi r$
   e. 'r' in $S = P(1 + rt)$

2. Rearrange and isolate the variables:
   a. 'b' in $A = \frac{b - h}{2}$
   b. 'R' in $P = R \times B$
   c. 'C' in $C + E + P = S$
   d. 'd' in $N = L - dL$
   e. 't' in $S = P(1 + rt)$

3. Rearrange and isolate the variables:
   a. 'a' and 'c' in $b = \frac{ac}{1 - a}$
   b. 'a' and 'b' in $c = \frac{a - c}{b}$

4. Rearrange and isolate the variables:
   a. 'a' and 'c' in $b = \frac{c + ac}{a - 2}$
   b. 'a' and 'b' in $c = \frac{ab - b}{4 + a}$

5. In the simple interest formula $I = Prt$, find:
   a. 't', when $I = \$21$, $P = \$700$, $r = 0.01$
   b. 'P', when $I = \$250$, $r = 0.05$, $t = 2.5$
   c. 'r', when $I = \$500$, $P = \$5000$, $t = 0.75$

6. In the trade discount formula $N = L(1 - d)$, find:
   a. 'N', when $L = \$250$, $d = 0.20$
   b. 'L', when $N = \$300$, $d = 0.40$
   c. 'd', when $L = \$900$, $N = \$630$

In problems 7 to 10, find the perimeter and area of the following plane figures:

7. a. A rectangle with sides of 15 m and 20 m.
   b. A circle with a radius of 8 cm.

8. a. A square with sides 8 mm long.
   b. A circle with a radius of 25 cm.

9. a. A triangle with sides of 9 cm, 4 cm, and 6 cm (base) and a height of 5 cm.
   b. A parallelogram with sides of 12 cm and 4 cm and a perpendicular distance of 3.5 cm between the 12 cm parallel sides.

10. a. A triangle with sides of 16 cm, 14 cm, and 5 cm(base) and a height of 13 cm.
    b. A parallelogram with sides of 14 cm and 7 cm and a perpendicular distance of 5.5 cm between the 14 cm parallel sides.

11. Find the surface area and volume of the following solid objects:
    a. A rectangular prism with sides of 40 cm, 80 cm, and 150 cm.
    b. A sphere with a radius of 20 cm.
    c. A cylinder with a height of 15 cm and a base with a diamèter of 12 cm.

12. Find the surface area and volume of the following solid objects:
    a. A rectangular prism with sides of 60 cm, 200 cm, and 30 cm.
    b. A sphere with a diameter of 50 cm.
    c. A cylinder with a height of 51 cm and a base with a radius of 5.0 cm.

13. Find the volume of a cone with a base area of 140 cm^2 and a height of 40 cm.

14. Find the volume of a triangular pyramid with a base area of 270 m^2 and a height of 15 m.

2 | Review Exercises

Answers to odd-numbered problems are available at the end of the textbook

1. Simplify the following expressions then evaluate:
    a. $-4x^2 + 3x - 5 + 7x^2 - 2x + 3$ where $x = 2$
    b. $4x^2 - 5 + 7x - 2x^2 - x - 3$ where $x = -1$
    c. $-y^2 + 4xy + x^2 - 6y^2 - xy - 11x^2$ where $x = 1$ and $y = 2$
    d. $(x - 4)(x + 2) + 3(x + 2)$ where $x = 3$

2. Simplify the following expressions then evaluate:
    a. $3x^2 - x + 2 + x^2 - 5x - 2$ where $x = 3$
    b. $-5y^2 - 7y + 3 + y^2 - 5y + 2$ where $y = -2$
    c. $-4x^2 + 6xy - 6y^2 + 6x^2 - 2xy + 3y^2$ where $x = 2$ and $y = 1$
    d. $(y - 2)(y - 3) + 2(y - 2)$ where $y = 4$

3. Factor the following expressions then evaluate:
    a. $6x^2 - 4x$ where $x = 1$
    b. $3y^3 - 12y^2$ where $y = -2$
    c. $7xy + 14x^2$ where $x = 1$
    d. $9x^3 - 6x^2 + 3x$ where $x = 3$ and $y = 2$

4. Factor the following expressions then evaluate:
    a. $8y^2 - 64y$ where $y = 2$
    b. $16x^2 - 4x^3$ where $x = -1$
    c. $15y^2 + 10xy$ where $x = -1$ and $y = 2$
    d. $16x^3 + 8x^2 - 4x$ where $x = 2$

5. Write in algebraic expressions:
    a. Twelve increased by three times a number.
    b. Difference between a number and five.
    c. Product of three more than a number and the number.
    d. Sum of ten times a number and fifteen.

6. Write in algebraic expressions:
    a. Eight decreased by twice a number.
    b. Six less than the total of a number and ten.
    c. Sum of 15 and half of a number.
    d. Product of two times a number and seven.

7. Write the following in algebraic equation and solve:
    a. The sum of five times a number and seventeen is forty-two.
    b. A number divided by fifteen is forty-five.
    c. The difference between a number and ten is ten.
    d. The product of four times a number and three is thirty-six.

8. Write the following in algebraic equation and solve:
    a. The product of five and a number is seventy-five.
    b. Three more than two times a number is nine.
    c. The sum of two times a number and eight is one hundred.
    d. A number divided by three is seven.

9. Solve for the unknown variable, x, using principle of equations:

   a. $5x - 5 = 10$ b. $\frac{x}{3} + 4 = 10$

   c. $12 - 3x = 3 - 4x$ d. $4(x + 4) = 24$

10. Solve for the unknown variable, x, using principle of equations:

    a. $3x - 5 = -17$ b. $\frac{x}{4} - 2 = 1$

    c. $4x - 2 = 13 - 6x$ d. $3(2x - 5) = 3$

11. Simplify and evaluate:

    a. $(-3)^2 + 2^3$ b. $(-3)^2(2^3)$

    c. $\frac{2^8}{2^4}$ d. $\sqrt[3]{125}$

    e. $\left(\frac{4}{9}\right)^{-\frac{1}{2}}$ f. $\frac{4^9}{4^5 \times 4^2}$

12. Simplify and evaluate:

    a. $(-5)^3 + 3^2$ b. $2^3(-2)^4$

    c. $\frac{3^7}{3^5}$ d. $\sqrt[5]{32}$

    e. $\left(\frac{1}{8}\right)^{-\frac{2}{3}}$ f. $\frac{3^4 \times 3^2}{3^3}$

13. Simplify the expression, and express your answer with a positive exponent:

    a. $(x^4)(3x^3)$ b. $\frac{x^6}{x^2}$

    c. $\left(\frac{x^2}{y}\right)^3\left(\frac{x}{2y^2}\right)^2$ d. $(8x^6)^{\frac{1}{3}}$

    e. $\left(\frac{4x^3}{2y^2}\right)^3$ f. $\left(\frac{x^7}{x^0}\right)^2$

14. Simplify the expression, and express your answer with a positive exponent:

    a. $(x^3)(2x^5)$ b. $\frac{x^9}{x^6}$

    c. $\left(\frac{2x^2}{y}\right)^2\left(\frac{3x}{y^2}\right)^3$ d. $(4x^2)^{\frac{1}{2}}$

    e. $\left(\frac{3x^2}{4y^3}\right)^2$ f. $\left(\frac{x^0}{y^3}\right)^3$

15. Solve for 'n' and express the answer to 2 decimal places:

    a. $2060 = 1225(1.02)^n$ b. $5215 = (1.005)^n + 600$

    c. $2187 = 3^n$ d. $n = \frac{\ln\left(\frac{2775}{1200}\right)}{\ln(1.03)}$

    e. $n = \frac{\ln(3)}{\ln(1.02)}$ f. $n = \frac{\ln(500)}{\ln(2)}$

16. Solve for 'n' and express the answer to 2 decimal places:

    a. $6075 = 4150(1.03)^n$ b. $4815 = (1.04)^n + 900$

    c. $15{,}625 = 5^n$ d. $n = \frac{\ln\left(\frac{4950}{1250}\right)}{\ln(1.005)}$

    e. $n = \frac{\ln(1200)}{\ln(5)}$ f. $n = \frac{\ln\left(\frac{4235}{1615}\right)}{\ln(1.048)}$

17. A sphere has a surface area of 450 cm^2.

    a. Find its radius to 2 decimal places.

    b. Find its volume to the nearest cm^3.

18. A cylinder with a height of 15 cm has a volume of 3000 cm^3.

    a. Find its base radius to 2 decimal places.

    b. Find its surface area to the nearest cm^2.

19. Rearrange the formula $V = \frac{1}{3}\pi r^2 h$ to isolate the variable 'h'. Find 'h', when $r = 11$ cm and $V = 4560$ cm^3. Round your answer to 2 decimal places.

20. Rearrange the formula $V = \frac{1}{3}\pi r^2 h$ to isolate the variable 'r'. Find 'r', when $V = 2280$ cm^3 and $h = 15$ cm. Round your answer to 2 decimal places.

2 | Self-Test Exercises

Answers to all problems are available at the end of the textbook

1. Simplify the following expressions first then evaluate:
   a. $2x^2 + 5x + 1 - 4 - 3x - x^2$ where $x = 2$
   b. $-3x^2 + 2x + 2x^2 - 8x + 10$ where $x = -3$
   c. $9x^2 - 4xy + y^2 - 6y^2 - 3xy + 10x^2$ where $x = 1$ and $y = 2$
   d. $5(2x - 3y) - 2(3x - 2y) + 7$ where $x = 2$ and $y = 1$

2. Factor the following expressions first then evaluate:
   a. $18y^2 - 12y$ where $y = -2$
   b. $15y^3 + 12y^2 + 3y$ where $y = 1$
   c. $14xy - 21x^2$ where $x = 2$ and $y = 1$
   d. $8xy^2 - 6x^2y$ where $x = 1$ and $y = -1$

3. Write in algebraic expressions:
   a. Twenty-five less than three times a number.
   b. A number increased by eighteen.
   c. The difference between twice a number and six.
   d. The quotient of a number and three.

4. Write the following in algebraic equation and solve:
   a. Nine less than twice a number is twenty-one.
   b. Twenty-two is five times a number decreased by 3.
   c. Four times eight is sixteen times a number.
   d. Thirty is a product of six and a number.

5. Solve for the unknown variable x, using principles of equations:
   a. $24 - 5x = 4$
   b. $\frac{x}{3} - 2 = 4$
   c. $8 + 2x = 4 - 5x$
   d. $3(3x - 3) = 33$

6. Simplify and evaluate and express your answer with a positive exponent:
   a. $(-2)^3(-2)^4$
   b. $(-5)^3 + 2^2$
   c. $\frac{(-10)^5}{(-10)^2}$
   d. $\sqrt[3]{27}$
   e. $(216)^{\frac{1}{3}}$
   f. $\frac{5^3 \times 5^4}{5^2}$

7. Simplify the expression and express your answer with a positive exponent:
   a. $(3x^3)^2$
   b. $(4x^2y^3)^2$
   c. $(16x^0y^4)^{\frac{1}{2}}$
   d. $\left(\frac{x^6}{x^2}\right)^{-\frac{1}{2}}$
   e. $(x^{-3}y)^2$
   f. $\frac{x^{-7}x^{-3}}{x^{-10}}$

8. Solve for 'n' and express the answer to 2 decimal places:
   a. $n = \frac{\ln\left(\frac{2200}{1200}\right)}{\ln(1.04)}$
   b. $n = \frac{\ln(1475)}{\ln(10)}$
   c. $n = \frac{\ln(5000)}{\ln(3)}$
   d. $460 = 240(1.05)^n$
   e. $750 = (1.05)^n + 600$
   f. $1296 = 6^n$

9. In the formula $f = (1 + i)^m - 1$, solve for 'f' when,
   a. $i = \frac{0.05}{12}$ and $m = 2$
   b. $i = 0.005$ and $m = 2$

10. In the formula $S = P(1 + rt)$,
    a. Isolate 't'
    b. Find the value of 't' when, $S = \$1200$, $P = \$1000$, and $r = 0.10$

Percentages and percent changes make comparisons easy and are used very often in our daily lives in making business decisions. Due to the simplicity of expression in day-to-day business statements, percentages have turned out to be a widely accepted measure of expressing fractions (ratios) or decimals. Some examples of the use of percentages that you would have come across include interest rates charged by banks on student loans, discounts offered at clothing stores, sales tax charged on items purchased, commission received by a sales representative on sales made, etc. The strong foundation that you will receive in this chapter will help you make intelligent business decisions in your day-to-day lives.

3 Percentages, Percent Changes, and their Applications

LEARNING OBJECTIVES

- Convert percentages to equivalent fractions and decimal values and use different methods to solve percentage problems.
- Understand percent change sign conventions and calculations.
- Understand the concept of payroll and calculate (or use) gross pay based on annual salary, sales commissions, hourly rate, and piecework rate.
- Calculate sales taxes and property taxes in different provinces of Canada.

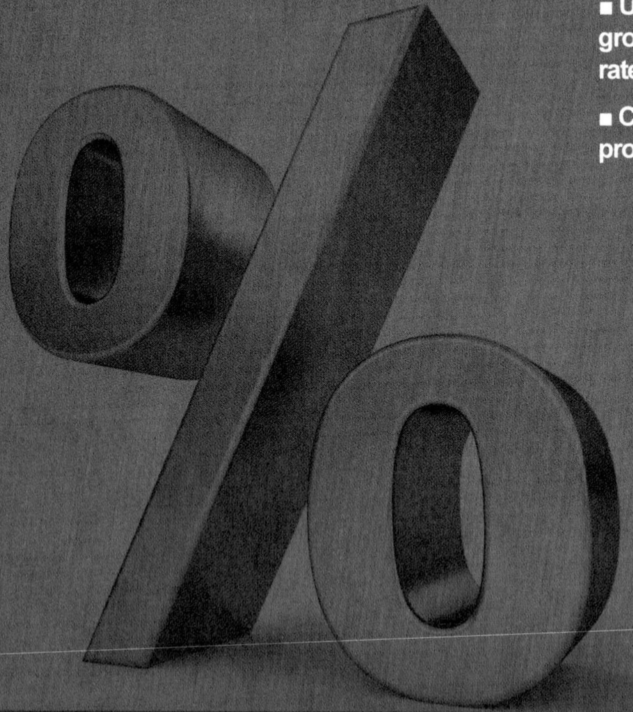

CHAPTER OUTLINE

3.1 | Percentages

Introduction

'Percent' (per cent or per hundred in the literal meaning) is used to express a quantity out of 100 units and is represented by the symbol %.

For example, 'C' out of 100 = $C\%$

A percentage can be defined using:

- Fractional ratio notation, as in, $C\% = \frac{C}{100} = C \times \left(\frac{1}{100}\right)$
- Decimal notation, as in, $C\% = 0.01C$

Percentage is a value expressed out of a hundred.

For example, 5% is equal to 5 out of a hundred.

Relationship Among Percentages, Fractions (Ratios), and Decimals

Although in day-to-day business, the word 'percentage' is commonly used, in actual calculations, fractions (ratios) or decimal equivalents are used. Therefore, it is necessary to know how to convert from one form to the other.

Converting a Percentage to a Fraction (Ratio)

- If the percentage is a whole number, remove the percentage sign, divide by 100 (or multiply by $\frac{1}{100}$), and reduce to lowest terms.

  For example, to convert 60% to a fraction in its lowest terms:

  $60\% = \frac{60}{100}$ Reducing this to the lowest terms, we obtain,

  $= \frac{6}{10} = \frac{3}{5}$

  Therefore, $60\% = \frac{3}{5}$

- If the percentage includes a decimal, change it to a fractional equivalent, and follow the steps as explained above.

  For example, to convert 42.5% to a fraction:

  $42.5\% = \frac{42.5}{100} = \frac{425}{1000}$ Reducing this to the lowest terms, we obtain,

  $= \frac{85}{200} = \frac{17}{40}$

  Therefore, $42.5\% = \frac{17}{40}$

- If the percentage is a fraction (or a combination of a whole number and fraction), convert it to its decimal equivalent or improper fraction and follow the steps as explained above.

  For example, to convert $6\frac{1}{2}\%$ to a fraction:

  $6\frac{1}{2}\% = \frac{6\frac{1}{2}}{100}$ Rewriting the numerator in decimal form, we obtain,

  $= \frac{6.5}{100}$ Eliminating the decimal by multiplying both numerator and denominator by 10, we obtain,

  $= \frac{65}{1000}$ Reducing this to the lowest terms, we obtain,

  $= \frac{13}{200}$

Or

$6\frac{1}{2}\% = \frac{6\frac{1}{2}}{100} = 6\frac{1}{2} \div 100$ Converting the mixed number to an improper fraction, we obtain,

$= \frac{13}{2} \div 100$

$= \frac{13}{2} \times \frac{1}{100} = \frac{13}{200}$ Therefore, $6\frac{1}{2}\% = \frac{13}{200}$

Converting a Percentage to a Decimal

- If the percentage is a whole number or decimal, remove the '%' sign and move the decimal point 2 places to the left. This is the same as dividing the number by 100 and dropping the '%' sign.

  Consider the following examples:

  (i) To convert 45% to a decimal number

  $45\% = 45.0\% = 0.45$

  This is the same as: $45\% = \frac{45}{100} = 0.45$

  Therefore, 45% = 0.45

  (ii) To convert 0.38% to a decimal number

  $0.38\% = 0.38\% = 0.0038$

  This is the same as: $0.38 = \frac{0.38}{100} = 0.0038$

  Therefore, 0.38% = 0.0038

- If the percentage is a fraction or a mixed fraction (combination of a whole number with a fraction), change it to its decimal equivalent and follow the steps as shown above.

  For example, to convert $2\frac{1}{2}\%$ to a decimal number,

  $2\frac{1}{2}\% = 2.5\% = 0.025$

  Therefore, $2\frac{1}{2}\% = 0.025$

Converting a Decimal to a Percentage

- To convert a decimal number or a whole number to a percentage, move the decimal point 2 places to the right and insert the '%' sign. This is the same as multiplying the number by 100 and inserting the '%' sign.

  Consider the following examples:

  (i) To convert 0.35 to a percentage

  $0.35 = 35.0\%$

  This is the same as: $0.35 \times 100\% = 35\%$

  Therefore, 0.35 = 35.00%

  (ii) To convert 5 to a percentage

  $5.00 = 500\%$

  This is the same as: $5 \times 100\% = 500\%$

  Therefore, 5 = 500.00%

Example 3.1(a)

Application Problem

If Darwin earns 3 times the amount that Harry earns, what percentage is Darwin's earning compared to Harry's?

Solution

Here, '3 times' has to be converted to a percentage = $3 \times (100\%) = 300\%$.

Therefore, Darwin's earning is 300% of Harry's.

Note: This also means that Darwin earns 300% − 100% = 200% more than Harry.

Converting a Fraction (Ratio) to a Percentage

- First convert the fraction to a decimal by dividing the numerator by the denominator, then, convert the decimal to a percentage as explained in the previous section.

  For example, to convert $\frac{3}{8}$ to a percentage:

  $\frac{3}{8} = 0.375 = 37.50\%$ Or $\frac{3}{8} = 0.375 \times 100\% = 37.50\%$

  Therefore, $\frac{3}{8} = 37.50\%$

Example 3.1(b)

Converting a Mixed Fraction to a Percentage

Convert $5\frac{1}{2}$ to a percentage.

Solution

First, convert the mixed fraction to a decimal, then convert the decimal to a percentage.

$5\frac{1}{2} = 5.50 = 5.50 \times 100\% = 550.00\%$

Example 3.1(c)

Application Problem

Peter and Angela are two students studying Mathematics of Finance, but in different colleges. Peter managed to secure a score of 46 out of 60 on the final exam, while Angela scored 63 out of 75. Who has scored better on the exam?

Solution

By observation, it is not possible to answer the question because Peter's score is expressed on a base of 60, while Angela's score is on a base of 75. To compare their scores, we need to convert them to their percentage equivalent, as shown below:

$$\text{Peter's score: } \frac{46}{60} = 0.766666... = 76.67\%$$

Angela's score: $\frac{63}{75} = 0.84 = 84.00\%$

Therefore, Angela scored better than Peter on the exam.

Calculations Involving Percentages

There are many methods used in solving percentage problems. Described below are three common methods:

Method 1: Formula Method

Every percentage problem will contain three variables:

Base (B): Whole quantity or value (100%). It is usually followed by the word 'of'.

Portion (P): Portion of the whole quantity or value (portion of the base).

Rate (R): Percentage relationship between base and portion. It usually carries the sign '%' but is used in a decimal or fractional equivalent in calculations.

> $R\%$ converted to a ratio (or decimal) is $\frac{R}{100}$ (or $0.01R$)

The relationship between these variables can be expressed as follows:

$$Portion = Rate \times Base$$

This is given by the formula,

Formula 3.1

Portion

$$P = R \times B$$

Rearranging, we obtain, $R = \frac{P}{B}$ and $B = \frac{P}{R}$

Therefore, if any two of these quantities are known, then the third quantity can be found.

Method 2: Algebraic Method

Solving problems using algebraic methods involve forming an equation for an unknown 'x' and then solving for 'x'. In this method, we assume that the unknown is 'x'.

Method 3: Ratio-Proportion Method

The whole amount or quantity is represented by 100% and is known as the **base**. The **portion** is a part of the base and it forms a percentage of the base. Thus, in the ratio-proportion method, we first identify the base and portion in the problem, then using ratio and proportions, we compare the portion to the base and solve for the unknown.

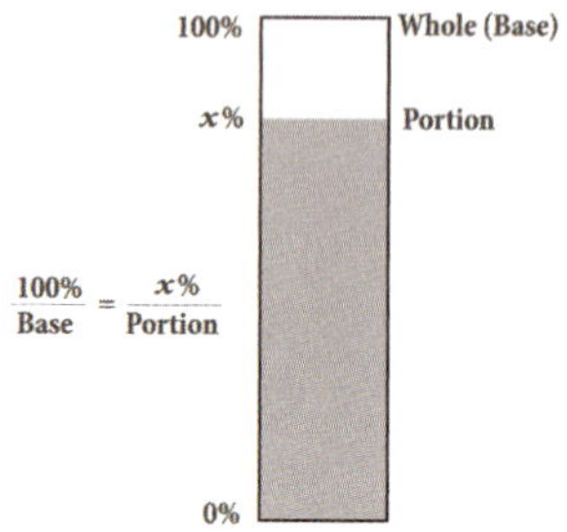

P, *R*, *B* triangle

Here is a triangle that can be used to help in rearranging the formula P = R × B to find R or B.

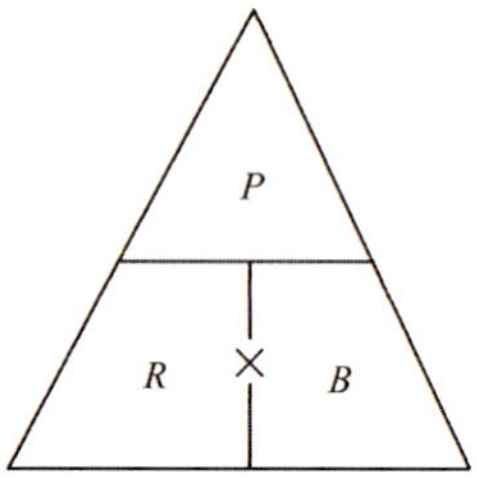

Variables beside each other at the bottom are multiplied ($R \times B$, as shown).

Variables at the bottom are divided by the variable on top: P.

Cover the variable that you want to rearrange to see the new formula.

For example, if you want to solve for 'R', the formula can be found by covering 'R' and reading the remaining variables in the above triangle, to get $R = \frac{P}{B}$.

Example 3.1(d)

Calculating the Portion of a Whole Quantity

What is 75% of $250? (Or, 75% of $250 is how much?)

Solution

Method 1: Using the Formula Method:

$R\% = 75\%$ (value with % sign); i.e., $R = 0.75$

$B = \$250.00$ (value after the word 'of')

$$P = R \times B$$

$$P = 0.75 \times 250 = \$187.50$$

Therefore, 75% of $250 is $187.50.

Method 2: Using the Algebraic Method:

This can be re-written as '*x is 75% of $250*'.

We need to find '*x*'

$$x = 75\% \times 250$$

Expressing the percentage as a fraction, we obtain,

$$= \left(\frac{75}{100}\right) \times 250$$

$$= 0.75 \times 250$$

$$= \$187.50$$

Therefore, 75% of $250 is $187.50.

Clues to remember some arithmetic operations used in problems:

Addition (+): Add, sum, plus, more than, increased by, appreciate, rise

Subtraction (–): Subtract, difference, minus, less than, decreased by, depreciate, fall

Multiplication (×): Multiply, product, times, of

Division (÷ or /): Divide, ratio, divided by, quotient

Equal (=): Is, was, gives, given by

Unknown value: What, how much, (usually denoted by some letter, such as '*x*')

Method 3: Using the Ratio-Proportion Method:

Here, the whole amount of $250 is the base and is represented by 100%. 75% is a portion of the base, as illustrated:

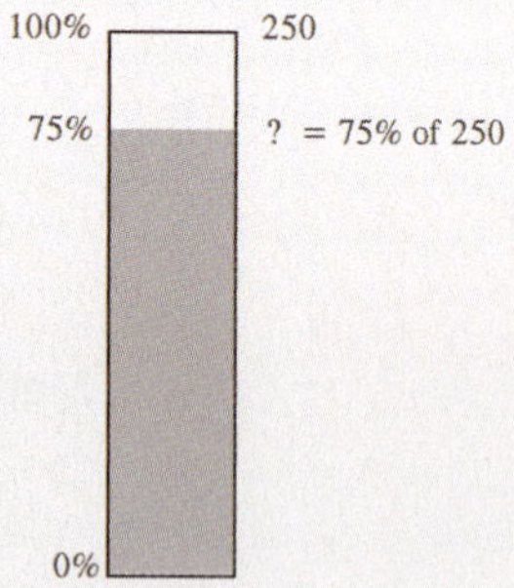

Portion	Base
75%	100%
x	250

$$\frac{75}{x} = \frac{100}{250}$$ Cross-multiplying, we obtain,

$$x = \frac{250 \times 75}{100} = \$187.50$$

Therefore, 75% of $250 is $187.50.

The following examples use the formula method; however, you can solve them using any of the three methods described earlier.

Example 3.1(e)

Calculating Rate When Portion and Base are Known

What percent of \$775 is \$1250? (Or, \$1250 is what percent of \$775?)

Solution

B = \$775.00 (value after the word 'of'), P = \$1250.00 (the other value), R = ?

Using Formula 3.1, $P = R \times B$ Rearranging, we obtain,

$R = \frac{P}{B}$ Substituting values for 'P' and 'B', we obtain,

$$R = \frac{1250}{775}$$

$$R\% = \frac{1250}{775} \times 100\% = 161.290322...\%$$

Therefore, 161.29% of \$775.00 is \$1250.00.

Example 3.1(f)

Calculating Base When Portion and Rate are Known

50% of what number is 200?

Solution

$R\%$ = 50% (value with '%' sign) = 0.50

P = 200 (the other value)

B = ? (value after the word 'of')

Using Formula 3.1, $P = R \times B$ Rearranging, we obtain,

$B = \frac{P}{R}$ Substituting values for 'P' and 'R', we obtain,

$$B = \frac{200}{0.5} = 400$$

Therefore, 50% of 400 is 200.

Example 3.1(g)

Calculating Portion When Rate is More Than 100%

What is 150% of 200?

Solution

$R\% = 150\% = 1.50$, $B = 200$, $P = ?$

Using Formula 3.1, $P = R \times B$

$= 1.50 \times 200 = 300$

Therefore, 150% of 200 is 300.

Example 3.1(h)

Application Problem Based on Repeating Decimals

Sandra owns $25\frac{1}{3}\%$ of a web development company. If the company is valued at \$180,000 what is the value of Sandra's ownership in the company?

Solution

Identify the base, portion, and rate:

B = \$180,000

$R\% = 25\frac{1}{3}\% = 25.333333...\% = 0.253333...$ (Store this value in calculator memory and recall it to multiply)

Solution *continued*

Do not round intermediary steps in calculations. Store the intermediary step value in your calculator and recall it for later calculations.

Using Formula 3.1, $P = R \times B$

$= 0.253333... \times 180{,}000$

$= \$45{,}600.00$

Alternatively, this can be solved by converting the mixed fraction to a proper fraction:

$B = \$180{,}000$

$R\% = 25\frac{1}{3}\%$ Converting the mixed number to an improper fraction, we obtain,

$= \frac{76}{3}\%$ Expressing the percentage as a fraction, we obtain,

$= \frac{76}{3} \times \frac{1}{100} = \frac{76}{300}$

Using Formula 3.1, $P = R \times B$

$= \frac{76}{300} \times 180{,}000$

$= \$45{,}600.00$

Therefore, Sandra's ownership in the company is $45,600.00.

3.1 | Exercises

Compute the missing values in Problems 1 and 2:

1.

	Percentage	Decimal	Fraction in lowest terms
a.	80%	?	?
b.	?	0.25	?
c.	?	?	$\frac{3}{2}$
d.	$6\frac{1}{2}\%$	?	?
e.	?	0.048	?
f.	?	?	$\frac{2}{25}$
g.	$10\frac{3}{5}\%$	?	?
h.	?	2.25	?
i.	?	?	$\frac{1}{400}$
j.	−26%	?	?
k.	?	−0.15	?
l.	?	?	$-\frac{7}{12}$

2.

	Percentage	Decimal	Fraction in lowest terms
a.	2%	?	?
b.	?	0.245	?
c.	?	?	$\frac{5}{12}$
d.	$\frac{1}{2}\%$	?	?
e.	?	0.002	?
f.	?	?	$\frac{97}{365}$
g.	$12\frac{2}{5}\%$	?	?
h.	?	1.075	?
i.	?	?	$\frac{3}{80}$
j.	−7.5%	?	?
k.	?	−0.05	?
l.	?	?	$-\frac{5}{8}$

3. Calculate the following:

   a. 20% of 350
   b. 12.5% of 800
   c. 130% of 40
   d. 0.25% of 75
   e. $\frac{1}{4}\%$ of 200 km
   f. $5\frac{1}{2}\%$ of $1000

4. Calculate the following:

   a. 45% of 180
   b. 2.5% of 960
   c. 285% of 110
   d. 0.755% of 120
   e. $\frac{1}{8}\%$ of 450 km
   f. $12\frac{3}{4}\%$ of $1260

5. Answer the following (round your answers to two decimal places):
   a. What percent of 220 is 100?
   b. What percent of \$90 is \$100?
   c. 280 m is what percent of 2 km?
   d. 15% of what amount is \$27.90?
   e. 120% of what amount is 156?
   f. $8\frac{1}{4}$% of \$200 is how much?
   g. \$16.50 is 0.75% of what amount?
   h. How much is $\frac{1}{4}$% of \$108?

6. Answer the following (round your answers to two decimal places):
   a. What percent of 1100 is 110.50?
   b. What percent of \$110.50 is \$1100?
   c. 180 g is what percent of 3 kg?
   d. 30% of what amount is 708?
   e. 215% of what amount is 258?
   f. $25\frac{3}{4}$% of \$2680 is how much?
   g. \$16.40 is 0.5% of what amount?
   h. How much is $\frac{3}{4}$% of 350 kg?

7. A company that makes games, sets sales targets of \$280,000 per year for each of their sales people. If Amanda, an excellent salesperson achieved 250% of her target this year, calculate the amount of sales she made.

8. If the population of Canada was estimated to be 33,930,830 on January 2010, and the population of Ontario was estimated to be $37\frac{2}{3}$% of Canada's population, calculate the population of Ontario, rounded up to the nearest whole number.

9. When there was a boom in the real-estate market, Lucy sold her property for \$410,440, which was 130% of the amount she paid for it. Calculate the amount she paid for the property.

10. Ronald, an investment banker sold his shares for \$18,568.50 when there was a boom in the stock market. Calculate the amount he paid for the shares if his selling price was 180.65% of the amount he paid for the shares.

11. Evan, a business development representative of a leading pharmaceutical firm, took his client out for a dinner that cost \$180.75 before taxes. If the tax was \$23.50, calculate the tax rate.

12. A leading information technology company donated \$87,790 of its 2010 fiscal revenue of \$17,558,643 towards socially responsible causes. What percent of their revenue did they contribute towards these causes?

13. Neel Plastics Manufacturing Corporation targets to obtain \$120,000 of funding from their investors to purchase new machinery. If they could only obtain 25.5% of their total target, calculate the amount of money that is yet to be received.

14. Pamela and Martha run a business that made a profit of \$12,750. As Pamela invested a higher amount in the business, she received 57.5% of the profits and Martha received the rest. Calculate Martha's share of the profit, in dollars.

15. Dawson purchased a pair of shoes on boxing-day that was discounted by 10% from the original price of \$50. Calculate how much he paid for the pair of shoes.

16. Jamie went to the mall during the holiday season to purchase a wall painting for his mother. He liked a picture that was selling for \$199.99 and which had a seasonal discount of 18% on its selling price. How much would this picture cost Jamie after the discount?

17. The Ministry of Transportation was upset that they overshot their construction budget for a local highway. If their total expenditure was \$1,280,000 for the highway, which was 111% of their budgeted amount, calculate the amount budgeted to build the highway.

18. If Henry's actual business expenditure was \$14,480 in March and \$14,806.50 in April, which were 112% and 122% of his budgeted expenditure for March and April respectively, calculate his total budgeted expenditure for the two months.

• 19. Assume that 300,000 people immigrated to Canada in 2010 out of which 12.25% were from China, 9.75% were from the Philippines, and the rest were from other countries.

a. Calculate the number of people who immigrated to Canada from China.

b. If the combined number of immigrants from China and Philippines constituted 0.195% of the population of Canada, calculate the population of Canada in 2010. (Round your answers up to the nearest whole number.)

• 20. A dinner at a restaurant cost you $27.80 and you tipped the waiter 15% of the cost.

a. What was the value of the tip?

b. If the tip that you gave the waiter was 2% of all the money he made from tips that night, calculate the amount that the waiter earned from tips that night.

• 21. The labour cost for manufacturing a $30,000 car is increased by 5%. If the cost of labour was 30% of the total cost of manufacturing the car, by what amount did the cost of the car increase?

• 22. The material cost for manufacturing a $2000 TV decreased by 10%. If the cost of material was 40% of the total cost of manufacturing the TV, by what amount did the TV cost decrease?

• 23. Tudor and Rani, two sales representatives in a company, were earning $2815 per month and $2875 per month, respectively. After a yearly appraisal, if Tudor's salary increased by 14% and Rani's increased by 11%, who would have the higher salary?

• 24. Reggie's annual salary increased from $42,000 to $46,830 this year and his colleague Gerald's annual salary increased from $39,500 to $44,437.50. Who received a higher rate of increase this year?

3.2 | Percent Change

To find a percent increase or decrease, find the amount of increase or decrease and then determine what percent this is of the initial value.

Introduction

The percentage by which a quantity increases or decreases from its initial value is called **percent change** (%C). The amount of increase or decrease is expressed as a percent change from its initial value.

$$\textit{Amount of Increase or Decrease} = \%C \times \textit{Initial Value}$$

A change could be positive or negative. Some quantities, such as hourly rate of pay generally increases, while some quantities such as price of an item during a sale decreases.

- If the final value is more than the initial value, i.e.,

$$\textit{Initial Value} + \textit{Amount of Increase} = \textit{Final Value}$$

$$V_i + \%C\,(V_i) = V_f$$

Then the following formula can be derived for percent change:

Formula 3.2

Percent Change

$$\%C = \frac{(V_f - V_i)}{V_i} \times 100\%$$

We can derive the equation used to calculate the initial value (V_i) as follows,

$$V_i + \%C\,(V_i) = V_f$$

$$V_i\,(1 + \%C) = V_f$$

$$V_i = \frac{V_f}{1 + \%C}$$

$$\%C \textit{ in decimal form} = 0.01C = c$$

$$V_i = \frac{V_f}{1 + c}$$

- If the final value is less than the initial value,

$$\textit{Initial value} - \textit{Amount of Decrease} = \textit{Final Value}$$

$$V_i - \%C\,(V_i) = V_f$$

and the value of $\%C$ will be negative in Formula 3.2.

Consider an example where Company A's profit increased from \$165,000 to \$170,000 in a year and Company B's profit increased from \$122,000 to \$126,000 in the same year. Which company has shown better relative change in profit?

At first you may calculate the difference in profits and compare it to arrive at the answer. That is, Company A's profit for that year is 170,000 − 165,000 = \$5000.00 and Company B's profit for that year is 126,000 − 122,000 = \$4000.00 and you might say that Company A has grown more than Company B. However this comparison is **incorrect** because we want to find out which company has a better relative change in profit. This brings us to the understanding of 'percent change'.

Using Formula 3.2, $\%C = \dfrac{(V_f - V_i)}{V_i} \times 100\%$

Company A's Percent Change in Profit:

$$\%C_{\text{Company A}} = \frac{170{,}000 - 165{,}000}{165{,}000} \times 100\%$$

$$= \frac{5000}{165{,}000} \times 100\% = 3.03\%$$

Company B's Percent Change in Profit:

$$\%C_{\text{Company B}} = \frac{126{,}000 - 122{,}000}{122{,}000} \times 100\%$$

$$= \frac{4000}{122{,}000} \times 100\% = 3.28\%$$

Thus, even though Company B had a smaller increase in profit than Company A during the year, Company B had a better relative growth compared to Company A.

Similarly, in financial applications, it would be more important to calculate percent changes and associated values instead of relying on a mere difference between two values.

There are many methods used in solving percent change calculations. Described in the following example are three common methods used to solve a percent change problem:

Example 3.2(a)

Calculating Final Value When Percent Change is Positive

If a \$20 hourly rate of pay is increased by 10%, find the new hourly rate.

Solution

Method 1: Using the Algebraic Method

$\%C = +10\% = +0.1, \quad V_i = \$20, \quad V_f = ?$

$$\textit{Initial Value} + \textit{Amount of Increase} = \textit{Final Value}$$

$$V_i + \%C \times V_i = V_f \qquad \text{Substituting values, we obtain,}$$

$$20 + 0.1\,(20) = V_f$$

$$20 + 2 = V_f$$

$$V_f = \$22.00$$

Therefore, the new hourly rate is \$22.00.

When there is an increase in initial value, %C will be positive and the final value will be greater than the initial value.

Method 2: Using the Formula Method

$V_i = \$20, \quad \%C = 10\%, \quad V_f = ?$

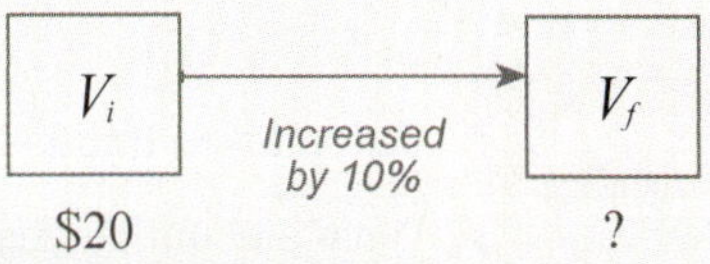

Solution *continued*

Using Formula 3.2,

$$\%C = \frac{(V_f - V_i)}{V_i} \times 100\%$$ Substituting values, we obtain,

$$10\% = \frac{V_f - 20}{20} \times 100\%$$ Eliminating the percentage, we obtain, (Note: 10% = 0.10 and 100% = 1)

$$0.1 = \frac{V_f - 20}{20}$$ Cross-multiplying, we obtain,

$$20(0.1) = V_f - 20$$

$$2 = V_f - 20$$ Adding 20 to both sides, we obtain,

$$V_f = \$22.00$$

Therefore, the new hourly rate is $22.00.

> **Helpful Check:**
> **If the percent change is positive, then the final value must be greater than the initial value.**

Method 3: Using the Texas Instruments BA II Plus Calculator

The Texas Instruments BAII Plus has a percent change worksheet which can be used for solving percent change problems, as shown below:

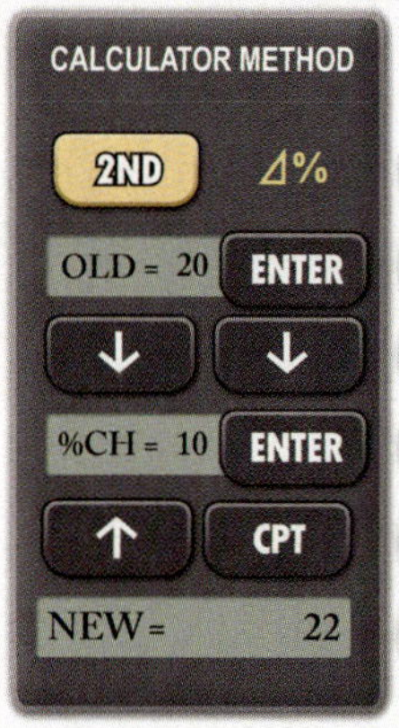

1. Press 2ND then Δ (secondary function of the number 5 key). This opens the percent change worksheet.
2. **Enter** the **initial value** and **press ENTER**.
3. **Press** the **down arrow** key **twice**.
4. **Enter** the percent change directly as **10** (not as 10% or 0.10) then **press ENTER**.
5. **Press** the **up arrow** key then **press CPT**.
6. The calculator will display the final value.

Method 4: Using the Ratio-Proportion Method

In this method, we compare the original value and final value using ratios and proportions to find the unknown.

The original value of $20 represents 100%. This is increased by 10% to a final value of 110%, as illustrated:

Original value	Final value
20	x
100%	110%

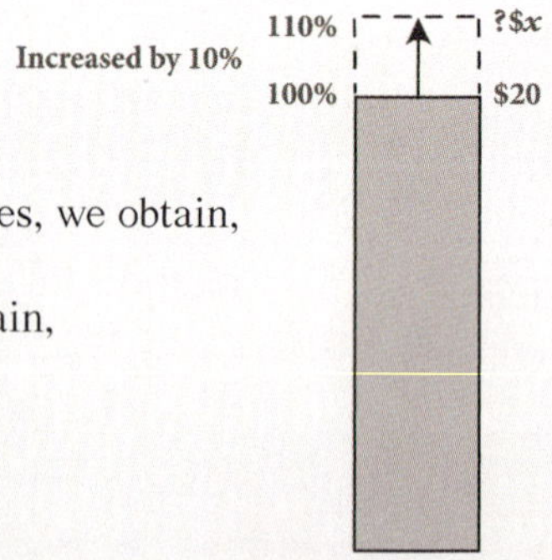

$$\frac{20}{100\%} = \frac{x}{110\%}$$ Eliminating the percentages, we obtain,

$$\frac{20}{1} = \frac{x}{1.1}$$ Cross-multiplying, we obtain,

$$x = \frac{1.1 \times 20}{1}$$

$$x = \$22.00$$

Therefore, $20.00 increased by 10% is $22.00.

The examples that follow use the formula method; however, you can solve them using any of the three methods described in Example 3.2(a).

Example 3.2(b) **Calculating Initial Value when Percent Change is Negative**

What amount decreased by 40% is $400?

Solution $\%C = -40\%, \quad V_f = \$400, \quad V_i = ?$

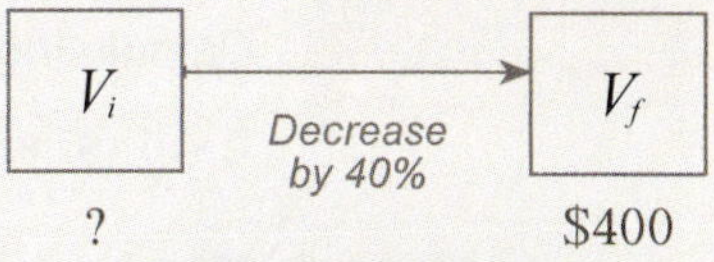

Using Formula 3.2,

$$\%C = \frac{(V_f - V_i)}{V_i} \times 100\%$$

Substituting the values, $$-40\% = \frac{400 - V_i}{V_i} \times 100\%$$

Eliminating the percentages, $$-0.40 = \frac{400 - V_i}{V_i}$$

Cross-multiplying, $$-0.40V_i = 400 - V_i$$

Adding V_i to both sides, $$V_i - 0.40V_i = 400$$

$$0.60V_i = 400$$

$$V_i = 666.666666... = \$666.67$$

Therefore, \$666.67 decreased by 40% is \$400.00.

Helpful Check:
If the percent change is negative, then the final value must be smaller than the initial value.

When there is a decrease from the initial value, %C will be negative and the final value will be smaller than the initial value.

Example 3.2(c)

Calculating Percent Change When Final Value is Higher than Initial Value

\$1000 increased by what percentage gives \$1200?

Solution $V_i = \$1000, \quad V_f = \$1200, \quad \%C = ?$

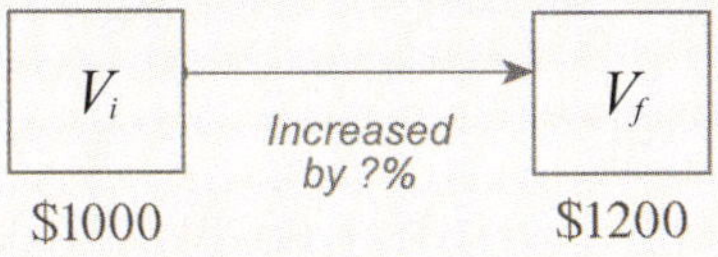

Using Formula 3.2, $$\%C = \frac{(V_f - V_i)}{V_i} \times 100\%$$

Substituting the values, $$\%C = \frac{1200 - 1000}{1000} \times 100\%$$

$$= 20.00\%$$

Therefore, \$1000.00 increased by 20.00% gives \$1200.00.

Example 3.2(d)

Calculating Percent Change When Initial and Final Values are Given as a Percentage

If the Bank of Canada increases its prime lending rate from 2.25% to 3.35%, calculate the percent increase in the prime rate.

Solution $V_i = 2.25\%, \quad V_f = 3.35\%, \quad \%C = ?$

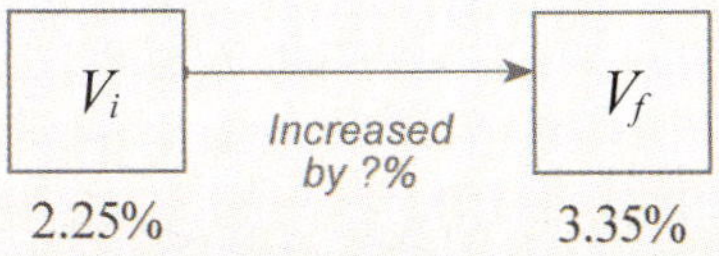

Using Formula 3.2, $$\%C = \frac{(V_f - V_i)}{V_i} \times 100\%$$

Substituting the values, $$\%C = \frac{3.35\% - 2.25\%}{2.25\%} \times 100\%$$

$$= 0.488888... \times 100\% = 48.89\%$$

Therefore, the percent increase in prime rate is 48.89%.

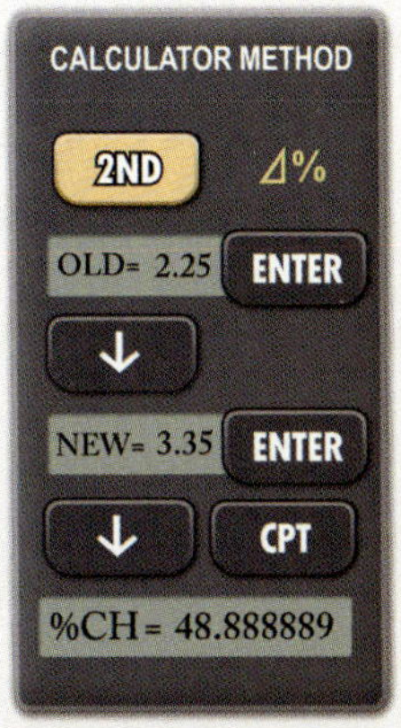

Example 3.2(e)

Calculating Percent Change When the Statement is Reversed

If Ali earns 25% more than Brian, then Brian earns what percent less than Ali?

Solution

Method 1: Using the Algebraic Method

Let Ali's earnings be A and Brian's earnings be B.

$$A = B + 25\% \text{ of } B \qquad (\text{or } A = 125\% \text{ of } B)$$

$$A = 1.25B \qquad \text{Expressing } B \text{ as a fraction of } A \text{, we obtain,}$$

$$B = \frac{1}{1.25}A = 0.80$$

$$B = 0.80A$$

That is, B is 80% of A (which is 20% less than A).

Therefore, if Ali earns 25% more than Brian, then Brian earns 20% less than Ali.

Method 2: Using the Algebraic Method, Assuming a Value for *B*

Given: $A = B + 25\%$ of B

$A = 1.25B$ Assume $B = \$1000$, then A earns \$1250

To find: B earns what% less than A, i.e., \$1000 is what % less than \$1250

$$1000 = 1250 - x\% \text{ of } 1250$$

$$x\% \text{ of } 1250 = 1250 - 1000 = 250$$

$$x\% = \frac{250}{1250} = \frac{1}{5} = \left(\frac{1}{5}\right) \times 100\% = 20\%$$

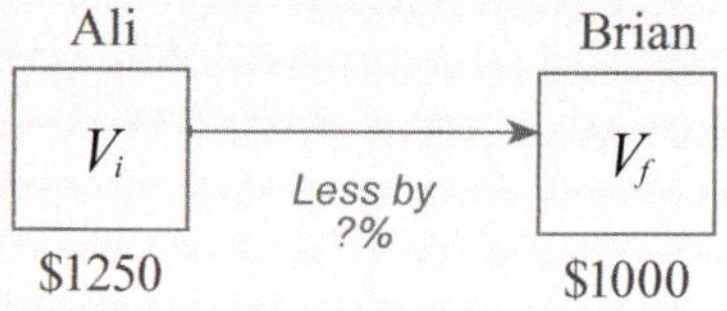

Therefore, if Ali earns 25% more than Brian, then Brian earns 20% less than Ali.

Method 3: Using a Financial Calculator, Assuming a Value for Brian's Earnings

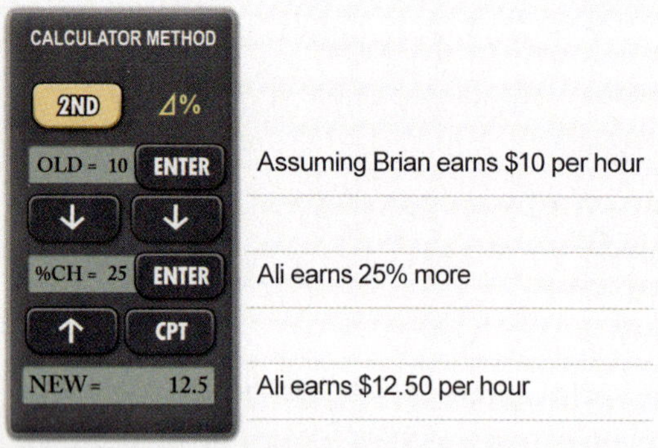

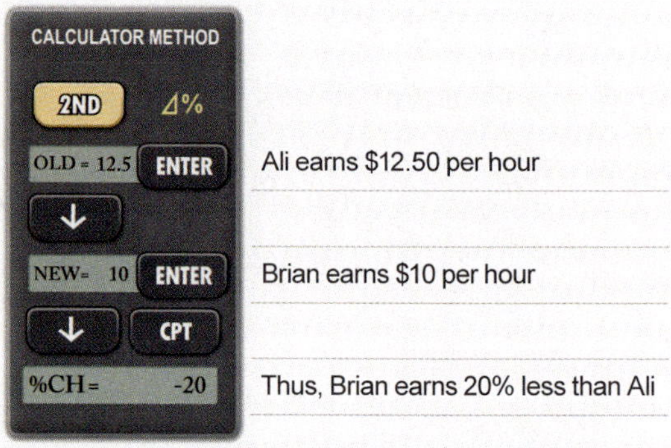

Example 3.2(f)

Calculating Percent Change When the Value of a Currency Increases (Appreciates) or Decreases (Depreciates) Against Another Currency

If the US dollar appreciated 10% relative to the Canadian dollar, by what percent has the Canadian dollar depreciated relative to the US dollar?

Solution

Assume US\$1 = C\$$x$

If the US dollar appreciated by 10%, then,

$$\text{US\$1} = \text{C\$}1.10x$$

Dividing both sides by 1.10, $\text{US\$}\frac{1}{1.10} = \text{C\$}x$

$$\text{US\$}0.909090... = \text{C\$}x$$

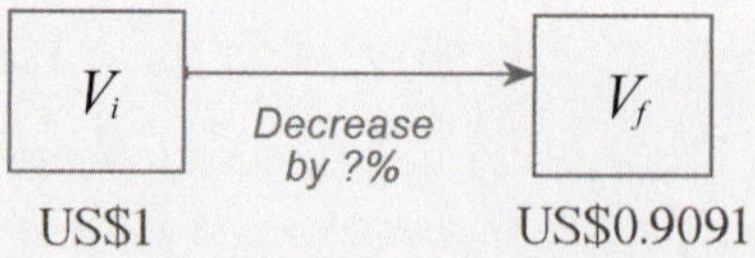

Solution *continued*

Therefore, V_i = US\$1, and V_f = US\$0.909090...

Using Formula 3.2, $$\%C = \frac{(V_f - V_i)}{V_i} \times 100\%$$

Substituting the values, $$\%C = \frac{\text{US\$0.909090...} - \text{US\$1}}{\text{US\$1}}$$

$$= -0.090909... = -9.09\%$$

Therefore, if the US dollar appreciated by 10% relative to the Canadian dollar, then the Canadian dollar depreciated by 9.09% relative to the US dollar.

Percent Change When the Initial Value (V_i) is Negative

In the algebraic equation $$V_i \pm \textit{Amount of Increase} = V_f,$$

where, $$\textit{Amount of Increase} = \%C \times V_i$$

When V_i is increased by an amount, regardless of the value or sign for V_i, add the amount of increase to find V_f : i.e., the 'quantity' added to V_i should be positive.

$$V_i + \textit{Amount of Increase} = V_f$$

When V_i is decreased by an amount, regardless of the value or sign for V_i, subtract the amount of decrease to find V_f : i.e., the 'quantity' that is subtracted from V_i should be positive.

$$V_i - \textit{Amount of Decrease} = V_f$$

Ther efore, the 'quantity' that is added or subtracted should always be a positive quantity. The sign in the formula will determine the increase or decrease.

When the original quantity (V_i) is negative, use the absolute sign for V_i to calculate the amout of increase or decrease. This ensures that the amount of increase or decrease will be a positive answer

Therefore, when V_i is negative,

$$\textit{Amount of Increase or Decrease} = \%C \times \textit{Absolute value of } V_i$$
$$= \%C\,|V_i|$$

If the final value is greater than the initial value,

$$\textit{Initial Value} + \textit{Amount of Increase} = \textit{Final Value}$$
$$V_i + \%C|V_i| = V_f$$

and, $$\%C = \frac{(V_f - V_i)}{|V_i|}$$

If the final value is smaller than the initial value,

$$\textit{Initial Value} - \textit{Amount of Decrease} = \textit{Final Value}$$
$$V_i - \%C\,|V_i| = V_f$$

and the value of $\%C$ will be negative.

The absolute value of a number '*a*' written as |*a*| will always be a positive number (regardless of the sign value for '*a*').

For example, |−5| = 5 and |5| = 5.

Example 3.2(g)

Percent Change When V_i is a Negative Value

The average temperature in Toronto last winter was −4°C. If the average temperature this winter increased by 1.15°C, calculate the percent change in temperature this winter from last year's winter.

Solution

Method 1:

Since V_i is negative, $\textit{Amount of Increase} = \%C\,|V_i|$

$$1.15 = \%C\,|-4|$$
$$1.15 = \%C\,(4)$$

Solution *continued*

Cross-multiplying, $\%C = \frac{1.15}{4} \times 100\%$

$= 28.75\%$ increase

Therefore, the temperature increased by 28.75% this winter from last year's winter.

Method 2:

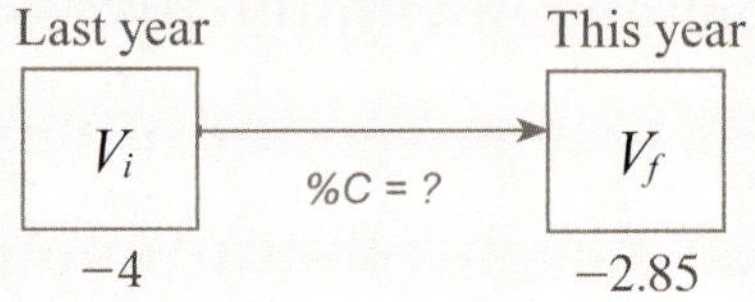

$V_f = -4 + 1.15 = -2.85$

Using Formula 3.2, $\%C = \frac{(V_f - V_i)}{|V_i|} \times 100\%$

Substituting values, $\%C = \frac{-2.85 - (-4)}{|-4|} \times 100\% = \frac{-2.85 + 4}{4} \times 100\%$

$= \frac{1.15}{4} \times 100\%$

$= 28.75\%$ increase

Therefore, the temperature increased by 28.75% this winter from last year's winter.

Example 3.2(h)

Percent Change Comparing Unit Quantities

A jeweler made and sold 500 g of silver chains for \$90. If he reduced the weight of the silver in the chain to 450 g and reduced the price to \$85.50, by what percentage did the unit rate change?

Solution

Unit price of the 500 g silver chain: $\frac{90}{500} = \$0.18$ per gram of silver

Unit price of the 450 g silver chain: $\frac{85.50}{450} = \$0.19$ per gram of silver

There is an increase in the unit price of the chain.

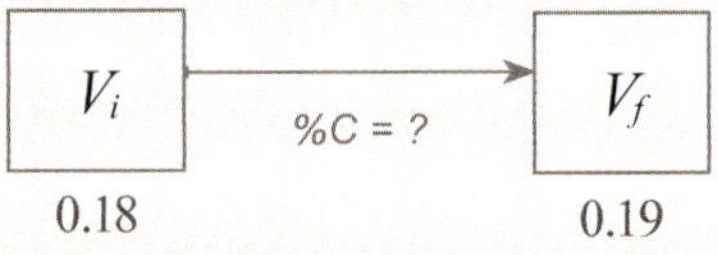

Using Formula 3.2, $\%C = \frac{(V_f - V_i)}{|V_i|}$

Substituing values, $\%C = \frac{0.19 - 0.18}{0.18} \times 100\%$

$= 0.055555... \times 100\% = 5.56\%$ increase

Therefore, the unit rate increased by 5.56%.

3.2 | Exercises

1. Answer the following problems, rounding your answers to two decimal places.
   a. What is 180 increased by 70%?
   b. \$90 decreased by 90% is how much?
   c. How much is \$4500 increased by 150%?
   d. What amount increased by 25.75% is 855.10 kg?
   e. What amount decreased by 10% is \$477?
   f. What amount increased by 180% is 20.65?
   g. \$1200 decreased by what percent is \$300?
   h. 750 kg is what percent less than 1000 kg?

2. Answer the following questions, rounding your answers to two decimal places.
   a. What is 2680 increased by 85%?
   b. \$880.45 decreased by 85% is how much?
   c. How much is \$1850.50 increased by 300%?
   d. What amount increased by $90\frac{1}{2}\%$is 110.49 kg?
   e. What amount increased by 28% is 231.75?
   f. What amount increased by 600% is 24.92?
   g. \$800 increased by what percent is \$1800?
   h. 102 km is what percent more than 85 km?

3. If Harley's salary of \$2000 per month is increased by 5.5%, what is his new salary?

4. Revenues of Python Graphics Corporation rose by 280% from last year. If their revenue last year was \$860,760, calculate their revenue this year.

5. After a discount of $12\frac{1}{2}$%, a publishing company purchased an offset printing press for \$245,000. Calculate the original price of the machine.

6. A clothing retail outlet purchased clothes in bulk from a wholesaler for \$86,394. This was after a discount of $10\frac{3}{4}$ % on the purchase. Calculate the original price of the clothes.

7. The sales tax of 13% increased the cost of a meal at a restaurant to \$34.50. What was the cost of the meal before taxes?

8. After paying income taxes of 45%, Carla's take-home annual income was \$45,000. Calculate her income before deducting income taxes.

9. If calculators that sell in stores for \$30 each in stores are being offered online for \$24 each, calculate the percentage discount offered online.

10. If Lilo's student loan of \$12,000 will increase to \$12,860 by the end of the year, calculate the percent increase of her debt.

11. The average daytime summer temperature in Calgary increased by 3.0°C this year. If the average daytime summer temperature last year was 29°C, calculate the percent change in the average daytime summer temperature this year.

12. The average yearly snowfall in Vancouver increased by 3 cm this year. If the average yearly snowfall last year was 47.5 cm, calculate the percent change in average yearly snowfall this year.

• 13. The average winter temperature in Toronto increased by 2.0°C this year. If the average winter temperature last year was −15°C, calculate the percent change in average winter temperature this year.

• 14. The average winter temperature in Montreal increased by 1.15°C this year. If the average winter temperature last year was −10°C, calculate the percent change in the average winter temperature this year.

15. Gabrielle's portfolio of shares comprised of investments of \$8600 and \$12,400 in the telecommunication and information technology industries, respectively. If the market price of her telecommunication shares dropped by 65% and that of information technology grew by 25%, by what percent did the total value of her investments change?

16. Kemi had her money invested in two types of mutual funds: \$2800 in low-risk funds and \$700 in high-risk funds. If the value of her high-risk funds grew by 30% and that of the low-risk funds dropped by 10%, by what percent did the total value of her investments change?

17. If the current fixed mortgage rate of 5.4% rises to 6.6%, calculate the percent increase in the mortgage rate.

18. Prior to July 01, 2010, first-time home buyers of new houses in Ontario had to pay only 5% in federal sales taxes. However, since July 01, 2010, they have to pay 13% in harmonized sales taxes to the Federal Government when purchasing new houses worth more than \$400,000. What is the percentage increase in sales taxes to a first-time home buyer of a new house worth \$500,000?

• 19. The price of a telecommunication share dropped by \$2.50 at the end of the first year and dropped by a further \$3.45 at the end of the second year. If the price of the share at the end of the second year was \$12.55, calculate the percent change in the price of the share each year from its price at the beginning of each year. What was the percent drop in the price over the two-year period?

• 20. Amtex Computers Inc. sells refurbished laptops online. They were selling a particular model at \$400 at the beginning of the year and reduced the price by \$80 at the end of the first year. At the end of the second year, they increased the price by \$64. Calculate the percentage change in the price of this model at the end of each year from its price at the beginning of each year. If he makes a sale at the end of the second year, calculate the discount offered from the original price of $400.

- 21. If Roger scored 20% more than Judie, by what percent is Judie's score less than Roger's?
- 22. If Harry earns 15% more than Beary per hour, by what percent is Beary's earning less than Harry's?
- 23. If the Canadian dollar appreciated 5% relative to the British pound, by what percent has the British pound depreciated relative to the Canadian dollar?
- 24. If the Australian dollar appreciated 15% relative to the British pound, by what percent has the British pound depreciated relative to the Australian dollar?

25. Sandra posted an advertisement on an auction site to sell her phone for 50% more than what she had paid for it. Since it did not sell withing a month, she decreased the advertised price by 50% and it sold immediately. By what percentage more or less than her purchase price did she sell the phone?

26. If the temperature rose by 12% from the average temperature, then falls by 12%, by what percent did the final temperature increase or decrease from the average temperature?

27. Last month, a 750g box of cereal was sold at a grocery store for $3.00. However, this month, the cereal manufacturer launched the same cereal in a 600g box, which is being sold at $2.50. By what percentage did the unit rate change?

28. A 450 g pack of butter was sold for $3.50. If the manufacturer reduced the size of the pack to 250g and sold it at a reduced price of $2.00, by what percentage did the unit rate change?

- 29. The overall increase in the price of a house from 2008 to 2010 was 4%. If the price increased by 5% from 2008 to 2009 and its value in 2009 was $472,500, calculate the value of the house in 2010.
- 30. The price of a share dropped by 3% from February to March, down to $4.25 in March. If the overall price fell by 5% between February and April, calculate its price in April.

3.3 | Payroll

Introduction

Employees of an organization receive payment from their employers for their services completed and this payment is usually given to them either as a salary or commission, or a combination of both. Employers maintain a record called **payroll** that registers the employees' names, types of payment, and amount of payment made towards them. They also deduct part of the employees' salary to pay towards the employees' taxes, pension, savings, etc. These are called **payroll deductions**. The payment that the employer offers to pay an employee is called **gross pay** and the actual payment received after all deductions is called **net pay**.

In this section we will calculate (or use) the gross pay given to employees based on:

- Annual salary
- Commissions
- Hourly rate
- Piecework rate

Annual Salary

If you are employed by an organization paying you an annual salary, your employer should provide you with the following information:

- Amount of annual salary
- Pay period (frequency of payments)
- Workweek (number of working hours per week)
- Overtime factor (used to calculate overtime rate)

Amount of Annual Salary

Annual: once a year

This is the amount that you will be paid for your service over a period of one year.

For example, Melinda was excited because she received her first job offer from Rubol Corp. for $50,000 per annum. In this case, Rubol Corp. has agreed to pay her a gross annual salary of $50,000.

Pay Period (Frequency of Payments)

In North America, there are four standard pay periods. Depending on where you work and the type of your employment, your pay period may fall into any one of the following categories:

- Monthly (once a month)
- Semi-monthly (twice a month)
- Bi-weekly (every two weeks)
- Weekly (once a week)

Monthly: once a month

- If you are paid **monthly**, you will receive 12 payments through the year as there are 12 months per year.

  For example, you may receive your payment on a particular date of every month.

Semi-monthly: twice a month

- If you are paid **semi-monthly**, you will receive 2 payments per month. You will receive $2 \times 12 = 24$ payments through the year.

  For example, you may receive your payment on the 1st and 15th of every month.

Bi-weekly: once in 2 weeks

- If you are paid **bi-weekly**, you will receive a payment once in two weeks (every other week). You will receive $\frac{52}{2} = 26$ payments through the year. (We assume that there are 52 weeks per year for all calculations; payment for extra days in the year will be adjusted in the last payment of the year.)

  For example, you may receive your payment every other Friday.

A semi-monthly payment is not a bi-weekly payment. With a semi-monthly payments you will receive 24 payments; whereas, with bi-weekly payments you will receive 26 payments.

- If you are paid **weekly**, you will receive a payment every week. As there are 52 weeks per year, you will receive 52 payments through the year.

  For example, you may receive your payment every Friday.

Note: *In the examples and exercises, we will be using 52 weekly pay periods or 26 bi-weekly pay periods per year. However, it is possible to have 53 weekly pay periods or 27 weekly pay periods depending on the year and the payment days. In those circumstances, periodic payment is calculated by dividing the annual salary by the number of pay days.*

Example 3.3(a)

Calculating Payment Per Pay Period Given Annual Salary

Hailey works for a publishing company and has been made an offer of $48,000 per annum. Calculate her gross pay for a pay period, if paid (a) monthly, (b) semi-monthly, (c) bi-weekly, (d) weekly.

Solution

One monthly payment is not equal to four weekly payments.

Monthly pay: $\frac{Annual\ Salary}{12\ pay\ periods} = \frac{48,000}{12}$ = \$4000.00 monthly payments

Semi-monthly pay: $\frac{Annual\ Salary}{24\ pay\ periods} = \frac{48,000}{24}$ = \$2000.00 semi-monthly payments

Bi-weekly pay: $\frac{Annual\ Salary}{26\ pay\ periods} = \frac{48,000}{26}$ = \$1846.15 bi-weekly payments

Weekly pay: $\frac{Annual\ Salary}{52\ pay\ periods} = \frac{48,000}{52}$ = \$923.08 weekly payments

The pay for the pay period is given by the following formula:

Formula 3.3(a)

Pay for Pay Period

$$Pay\ for\ pay\ period = \frac{Annual\ Salary}{Number\ of\ pay\ periods\ per\ year}$$

Example 3.3(b)

Calculating Equivalent Monthly Payment Given Weekly Payment

Rodney is paid \$1500 weekly. Calculate the equivalent monthly payment assuming 52 weeks per year.

Solution

First, calculate the annual salary then calculate the monthly salary.

Since he is paid weekly, his annual salary = $Weekly\ salary \times 52 = 1500 \times 52 =$ \$78,000.00.

$$Monthly\ payment = \frac{Annual\ Salary}{12\ pay\ periods} = \frac{78,000}{12} = \$6500.00$$

Therefore, the equivalent monthly payment is \$6500.00.

Workweek (Number of Working Hours per Week)

Depending on the type of profession/job, the number of hours you work every week may vary; 40 hours, 37.5 hours or 35 hours, are the most common number of working hours per week.

By knowing the number of hours you work per week, you can calculate your hourly rate (the amount you are paid per hour) from the following formula:

Formula 3.3(b)

Hourly Rate of Pay

$$Hourly\ rate\ of\ pay = \frac{Pay\ per\ week}{Number\ of\ working\ hours\ per\ week}$$

From Formula 3.3 (a), Pay per week = $\frac{Annual\ Salary}{52\ pay\ periods}$

Example 3.3(c)

Calculating Hourly Rate of Pay Given Annual Salary

Trevor is being paid \$26,000 per annum at Oxford Editorials. How much is he making per hour assuming that he is required to work 40-hour workweeks?

Solution

$$Pay\ per\ week = \frac{Annual\ Salary}{52\ pay\ periods}$$

$$= \frac{26,000}{52} = \$500$$

$$Hourly\ rate\ of\ pay = \frac{Pay\ per\ week}{Number\ of\ working\ hours\ per\ week}$$

$$= \frac{500}{40} = \$12.50\ \text{per hour}$$

Therefore, he is making \$12.50 per hour.

Example 3.3(d)

Calculating Hourly Rate of Pay Given Monthly Salary

Caroline is being paid \$2385 every month at Ruby Florists. How much is she making per hour assuming that she is required to work 40-hour workweeks?

Solution

Since she is paid monthly, she will receive 12 payments through the year.

$$\begin{aligned} \textit{Annual salary} &= \textit{Monthly salary} \times 12 \\ &= 2385 \times 12 \\ &= \$28{,}620.00 \end{aligned}$$

$$\begin{aligned} \textit{Pay per week} &= \frac{\textit{Annual Salary}}{\textit{52 pay periods}} \\ &= \frac{28{,}620}{52} = \$550.384615... \end{aligned}$$

$$\begin{aligned} \textit{Hourly Rate of pay} &= \frac{\textit{Pay per week}}{\textit{Number of working hours per week}} \\ &= \frac{550.384615...}{40} = \$13.759615... \end{aligned}$$

Therefore, she is making \$13.76 per hour.

Example 3.3(e)

Calculating Semi-Monthly Payment Given Hourly Rate of Pay

Rodney is paid \$25 per hour for the 40-hour workweeks at Japan Travels Inc. Calculate his semi-monthly payment.

Solution

$$\begin{aligned} \textit{Pay per week} &= \textit{Hourly rate of pay} \times \textit{Number of hours worked per week} \\ &= 25 \times 40 = \$1000.00 \end{aligned}$$

$$\begin{aligned} \textit{Annual salary} &= \textit{Weekly pay} \times 52 \\ &= 1000 \times 52 = \$52{,}000.00 \end{aligned}$$

$$\begin{aligned} \textit{Semi-monthly salary} &= \frac{\textit{Annual Salary}}{\textit{24 pay periods}} \\ &= \frac{52{,}000}{24} = \$2166.666666... \end{aligned}$$

Therefore, his semi-monthly payment is \$2166.67.

Overtime Factor (Used to Calculate Overtime Rate)

If you work more than the specified number of hours per week, you will be paid extra for the additional hours worked. This extra pay is calculated using an **overtime rate.** As this is additional work done by you, you would normally receive more than your hourly rate for the work and this depends on the policy of the organization. Some organizations pay $1\frac{1}{2}$ times your hourly rate for every extra hour worked and some pay 2 times your hourly rate. This factor (e.g. $1\frac{1}{2}$ times or 2 times) that employers use is called the **overtime factor.**

Example 3.3(f)

Calculating Overtime Rate of Pay

Sally, a senior instructional designer at McMillan is paid \$60,000 per annum. McMillan has a 40-hour workweek and the overtime rate is double the regular rate (overtime factor of 2). Calculate Sally's overtime rate of pay.

Solution

Calculate her pay per week and the hourly rate of pay.

$$\textit{Pay per week} = \frac{\textit{Annual Salary}}{\textit{52 pay periods}}$$

$$= \frac{60{,}000}{52 \text{ weeks}} = \$1153.846154...$$

$$\textit{Hourly Rate of pay} = \frac{\textit{Pay per week}}{\textit{Number of working hours per week}}$$

$$= \frac{1153.846154...}{40} = \$28.846153...$$

$$\textit{Overtime factor} = 2$$

$$\textit{Overtime rate per hour} = \textit{Overtime factor} \times \textit{Regular hourly rate}$$

$$\textit{Overtime rate per hour} = 2 \times \$28.846153... = \$57.692307...$$

Therefore, for every extra hour that Sally works (over the standard 40 hours), she will be paid $57.69 per hour.

Example 3.3(g)

Calculating Gross Pay Including Overtime Pay

Amanda is paid an annual salary of $48,000 and this is paid to her bi-weekly. The company has a standard 40-hour workweek and an overtime factor of $1\frac{1}{2}$. She worked 95 hours during the last pay period.

(i) Calculate Amanda's bi-weekly pay.

(ii) Calculate her gross pay (total pay without any employer deductions for taxes, Canadian pension fund, etc.) for that period.

Solution

(i) $$\textit{Bi-weekly Pay} = \frac{\textit{Annual Salary}}{\textit{26 pay periods}}$$

$$= \frac{48{,}000}{26} = \$1846.153846...$$

Therefore, Amanda is paid $1846.15 bi-weekly.

(ii)

$$\textit{Hourly Rate of pay} = \frac{\textit{Bi-weekly pay}}{\textit{Number of working hours per week} \times 2}$$

$$= \frac{1846.153846...}{40 \times 2} = \$23.076923...$$

or

$$\textit{Pay per week} = \frac{48{,}000}{52} = 923.076923...$$

$$\textit{Hourly Rate of pay} = \frac{\textit{Pay per week}}{\textit{Number of working hours per week}}$$

$$= \frac{923.076923...}{40} = \$23.076923...$$

$$\textit{Overtime factor} = 1\tfrac{1}{2}$$

$$\textit{Overtime rate per hour} = \textit{Overtime factor} \times \textit{Regular hourly rate}$$

$$\textit{Overtime rate per hour} = 1\tfrac{1}{2} \times \$23.076923... = \$34.615384... \text{ per hour}$$

$$\textit{Number of hours worked overtime} = 95 - (2 \times 40) = 15 \text{ hours}$$

Therefore, her overtime pay for 15 hours = 15 × $34.615384... = $519.230769...

Therefore, her gross pay for the period $= \textit{Bi-weekly pay} + \textit{Overtime pay}$

$$= \$1846.153846... + \$519.230769...$$

$$= \$2365.384615... = \$2365.38$$

Commissions

If your employment is based on commission, your gross pay is usually based on a percentage of sales for a given pay period (e.g. weekly/monthly).

Sales commissions are generally given to encourage sales people to sell more, because the more they sell, the more money they will make.

This payment is called a sales commission and is of different types:

a. Straight commission

b. Graduated commission (variable commission)

c. Base salary + commission

d. Quota then commission

Straight Commission

Straight commission refers to a type of payment where the employee is paid a percentage of the sales amount for the period as a salary.

Example 3.3(h)

Calculating Salary Based on Straight Commission

Arnold's salary is 5% of the sales that he makes for the month. If the sales he makes for the month are \$50,000, then what is Arnold's salary for that month?

Solution

Sales for the month: \$50,000

$$\begin{aligned} \textit{Amount of commission} &= 5\% \text{ of } \$50{,}000 \\ &= 0.05 \times 50{,}000 \\ &= \$2500.00 \end{aligned}$$

Therefore, Arnold's salary for the month will be \$2500.00.

Graduated Commission (Variable Commission)

Graduated commission refers to a type of payment where the employee's commission increases gradually as his or her sales increase.

Example 3.3(i)

Calculating Salary Based on Graduated Commission

Melissa is paid 2% sales commission for the first \$10,000 of her sales. She is then paid 3% on the next \$10,000 in sales, and 5% thereafter.

(i) Calculate her salary if her sales in January are \$50,000.

(ii) Calculate her salary if her sales in February are \$19,000.

(iii) Calculate her salary if her sales in March are \$9,000.

(iv) What single commission rate would represent her earnings in January?

Solution

Graduated commission:
- → 2% on the first \$10,000
- → 3% on the next \$10,000
- → 5% on the remaining

Solution *continued*

(i) If the sales in January are $50,000:

Amount eligible for 5% commission = 50,000 − (10,000 + 10,000) = $30,000

	Sales	Rate	Commission
First	$10,000	2%	$200
Second	$10,000	3%	$300
Remaining	$30,000	5%	$1500
Total	**$50,000**		**$2000**

Therefore, her salary will be $2000.00 if her sales in January are $50,000.00.

(ii) If her sales in February are $19,000:

Amount eligible for 3% commission = 19,000 − 10,000 = $9000

	Sales	Rate	Commission
First	$10,000	2%	$200
Second	$9000	3%	$270
Total	**$19,000**		**$470**

Therefore, her salary will be $470.00 if her sales in February are $19,000.00.

(iii) If her sales in March are $9000

Sales	Rate	Commission
$9000	2%	$180

Therefore, her salary will be $180.00 if her sales in March are $9000.00.

(iv) In January she earned $2000 from sales of $50,000.

$$\begin{aligned} \textit{Single commission rate} &= \frac{\textit{Total Commissions}}{\textit{Total Sales}} \\ &= \frac{2000}{50,000} = 0.04 \\ &= 4.00\% \end{aligned}$$

Therefore, a single commission rate of 4.00% would represent her earnings in January.

Base Salary + Commission

Base salary + commission is the most common form of commission that is paid to employees in sales environments. Organizations pay a fixed amount, called base salary, and they pay a commission on sales made by employees in addition.

Example 3.3(j)

Calculating Salary Based on Base Salary and Commission

Elan works for Future Store and gets paid a fixed amount of $1000 per month. In addition to this, he gets paid a commission of 4% on the sales he makes. What is his total salary if he made $50,000 in sales for the month?

Solution

Base salary per month = $1000.00

Solution continued

$$\text{Sales for the month} = \$50{,}000.00$$

$$\text{Commission of 4\% on sales} = 0.04 \times 50{,}000 = \$2000.00$$

$$\text{Total salary} = \text{Base Salary} + \text{Commission}$$

$$\text{Total salary} = 1000.00 + 2000.00 = \$3000.00$$

Therefore, his total salary is $3000.00 if he made $50,000.00 in sales for the month.

Quota then Commission

Quota then commission refers to a type of payment where the employee is required to sell a minimum sales amount (quota) before becoming eligible to earn income based on commissions.

Example 3.3(k)

Calculating Salary Based on Quota then Commission

Arkady works for a tourism company that requires him to sell vacation packages. He is paid a base salary of $500 per month in addition to a 10% commission on his sales exceeding $25,000. What would be his gross monthly salary if he sold $60,000 worth of vacation packages in a month?

Solution

$$\text{Base salary per month} = \$500.00$$

$$\text{Sales made for the month} = \$60{,}000.00$$

$$\text{Sales quota for the month} = \$25{,}000.00$$

$$\text{Sales amount exceeding the quota} = 60{,}000 - 25{,}000 = \$35{,}000.00$$

$$\text{Commission made on sales over quota} = 10\% \text{ of } \$35{,}000$$

$$= 0.1 \times 35{,}000 = \$3500.00$$

$$\text{Gross salary for the month} = 500.00 + 3500.00 = \$4000.00$$

Therefore, his gross monthly salary would be $4000.00.

Hourly Wages

If employees are paid hourly wages, then they are paid on an hour-by-hour basis. Pay for them is calculated as the number of hours worked multiplied by their hourly rate. The following are the minimum hourly rates (as of May 2011) set by the provinces and territories in Canada for experienced adult workers:

Table 3.3

Minimum Wage Rates by Province / Territory

Province / Territory	Minimum Wage	Province / Territory	Minimum Wage
Alberta	$8.80	Nunavut	$11.00
British Columbia	$8.75	Ontario	$10.25
Manitoba	$9.50	Prince Edward Island	$9.00
New Brunswick	$9.50	Quebec	$9.65
Newfoundland	$10.00	Saskatchewan	$9.25
Northwest Territories	$9.00	Yukon	$8.93
Nova Scotia & Labrador	$9.65		

Source: Human Resources and Skills Development Canada (Minimum Wage Database)

While most employees are eligible for minimum wage, some employees have jobs that are exempt from the minimum wage provisions. For example, in Ontario, the minimum hourly wage for students is $9.60, for liquor servers is $8.90, and for homeworkers is $11.28.

Hourly wage employees are also eligible for overtime pay and statutory or public holiday pay. For most employees, the maximum number of hours of work for a week is 44. After that time, they receive overtime pay. Normal working hours, unless specified, is 8 hours per day. At least one and one-half times the regular rate of pay (overtime factor of 1.5) is paid for hours worked during overtime.

Employees also receive their usual rate of pay on statutory or public holidays if they do not work on those days. Employees who have worked on holidays will receive their complete holiday pay plus additional pay at an overtime rate for the number of hours worked (based on the overtime rate for such holidays). However, the number of hours worked on holidays will not contribute towards the overtime for the work week.

If the nature of the work requires employees to work irregular hours or to work regularly scheduled hours which vary on certain days, then the employer may average the working hours over a selected period of two or more weeks. For example, employees may be scheduled to work 10 hours per day for 4 days a week, which exceeds the standard 8-hour workday.

Also, the maximum time an employee may work each week can be extended under exceptional circumstances such as during an emergency.

Unless specified in the contract of employment, an employee does not earn overtime pay on a daily basis by working more than the set number of hours for that day. Overtime is calculated only on a weekly basis or over a longer period under an averaging agreement.

Example 3.3(l) **Calculating Pay for Overtime work in a Normal Workweek with 1 Statutory Holiday**

Ryan's regular hourly rate of pay is $25.00 per hour and his employment allows overtime for any hours worked exceeding 40 hours. He receives holiday pay at the regular hourly rate for 8 hours. His overtime rate is at one-and-a-half times the regular rate and any work on statutory holidays is paid at the overtime rate. Last week Ryan worked 55 hours. Calculate Ryan's pay for last week.

Solution

$$\begin{aligned} \textit{Statutory holiday hours} &= 8 \text{ hours (standard working day)} \\ \textit{Regular working hours} &= 40 - 8 = 32 \text{ hours} \\ \textit{Overtime hours} &= 55 \text{ hours} - 32 \text{ hours} = 23 \text{ hours} \\ \textit{Overtime rate} &= (1.5 \times \$25.00) = \$37.50 \end{aligned}$$

Ryan's pay for the week is calculated as follows:

$$\begin{aligned} \textit{Regular pay} &= 32 \times \$25.00 = \$800.00 \\ \textit{Statutory holiday pay} &= 8 \times \$25.00 = \$200.00 \\ \textit{Overtime pay} &= 23 \times \$37.50 = \$862.50 \end{aligned}$$

Therefore Ryan's total pay ($800 + $200 + $862.50) = $1862.50

Piecework Rate

When employment is based on the number of units produced or task completed (output), an employee's gross pay is calculated based on an agreed flat rate for each item or task completed, called a piecework rate.

$$\textit{Gross Pay} = \textit{Number of units (or tasks) completed} \times \textit{Rate per unit (or task)}$$

Therefore, a piecework rate is performance-related rather than time-related, and encourages employees to produce more units rather than spend more time. Piecework encourages employees to complete tasks more efficiently to maximize their earnings, which in turn results in greater efficiency for the company.

Piecework rate could be straight piecework rate or graduated piecework rate. In straight piecework rate, a certain amount of pay per unit of output is given regardless of the output quantity. In graduated piecework rate, the rate per unit increases above a pre-determined output level (similar to that in commissions), which provides a greater incentive to the employee to increase output.

Example 3.3(m)

Calculating Piecework Wage

A company manufacturing tools pays its machine operators the greater of $5.50 for each item produced, or a graduated piece work rate of $5.25 per unit for the first 100 items and $6.25 per unit, thereafter. Robert, a machine operator, produced 190 items last week. What was his gross pay for last week?

Solution

Using, $\textit{Gross Pay} = \textit{Number of units produced} \times \textit{Rate per unit}$

$$\textit{Gross pay using straight piecework rate} = 190 \times \$5.50 = \$1045.00$$

$$\begin{aligned}\textit{Gross pay using graduated piecework rate} &= (100 \times \$5.25) + (90 \times \$6.25)\\ &= \$525.00 + \$562.50\\ &= 1087.50\text{, which is greater than } \$1045.00\end{aligned}$$

Therefore, Robert's gross pay for last week was $1087.50.

3.3 | Exercises

Answer the following problems assuming that there are 52 weeks per year. Round your final answer to two decimal places.

1. Roger received a job offer for a senior graphic designer position at a reputed e-learning company and is paid a gross salary of $60,000 per annum. Calculate his periodic payments if the pay period is (a) monthly, (b) semi-monthly, (c) bi-weekly, (d) weekly.

2. A Chief Executive Officer of a major bank receives a gross salary of $750,000 per annum. Calculate the payment for a pay period if paid (a) monthly, (b) semi-monthly, (c) bi-weekly, (d) weekly.

3. If a job pays $400 every week, calculate the annual salary and the equivalent monthly pay.

4. Nicole receives a gross pay of $1650 bi-weekly from her employer. If her employer changed her pay period to monthly instead of bi-weekly, calculate the monthly payment that she would receive.

5. A manufacturing company, that has 40-hour workweeks, pays its machine operators $18 per hour. Calculate the annual salary and the semi-monthly payment of their machine operators.

6. Al was being paid $2650 every other Wednesday at a web developing company. How much would he make per hour, assuming that he is required to work 40-hour workweeks?

7. Ruby earns a gross annual pay of $78,000, has a 40-hour workweek, and is paid bi-weekly. If her overtime factor is time and a half, calculate her gross pay for the pay period in which she worked a total of 95 hours.

8. Melanie receives a semi-monthly salary of $2600 and has 37.5-hour workweeks. If she worked 10 hours overtime during her last pay-period and her overtime factor is $1\frac{1}{2}$, calculate her gross payment for the last pay-period.

• 9. 10 technicians in a video production team were each being paid an annual salary of $35,000, with payments being made bi-weekly. Each member of the team is required to work 40 hours per week and their overtime factor is time and a half. Calculate each technician's payment for the last pay period if each of them worked for 43.5 hours and 42 hours for each of the weeks during that pay period.

- 10. A software development company that had 40-hour workweeks paid each of their developers an annual salary of $60,000 (payments made bi-weekly) with an overtime factor of time and a half. If each member of the team worked 46.5 hours and 48 hours for each of the weeks during the last pay period, calculate each person's payment for the last pay period.

11. A real-estate agent makes a commission of 2.5% on the sale of a condominium. If he sold a condominium for $450,000, calculate his commission from this sale.

12. A mutual fund broker receives a commission of 1.25% on all mutual funds he sells for the month. If he sells $560,000 worth of mutual funds to his clients, what is his commission for the month?

13. James, a sales representative at a computer retail outlet, receives a commission of 3% for every computer and 5% for every monitor he sells. The selling price of each computer is $800 and the selling price of each monitor is $250. If he sold 180 computers and 120 monitors in March, calculate his sales commission for March.

14. A sales representative at an electronics outlet mall receives sales commissions of 5% on Blu-ray players, 6% on laptops, and 8% on TVs. In April, if he sold 3 Blue-ray players that cost $450 each, 7 laptops that cost $700 each, and 5 TVs that cost $980 each, calculate his total sales commission earned for the month.

15. Abigail receives a graduated commission of 3% for her first $15,000 in sales, 4.5% on the next $15,000, and 5.75% thereafter on all sales she makes. Calculate her commission if she makes $60,450 in sales for the month. What single commission rate would her total earnings represent?

16. The sales commission of a pharmacy distribution company is structured such that their part-time sales representatives receive commissions of 5% for the first $10,000 they sell, 7% on the next $10,000, and 10% thereafter on all sales they make. Ivory, a new part-time sales representative of the company makes sales of $2000 in the first month, $11,000 in the second month, and $36,000 in the third month.
    a. What were her commissions for each of the first three months?
    b. What single commission rate would represent her earnings in the third month?

17. Sales people at a game developing company are paid a base salary of $40,000 per annum plus a commission of 7% on every sales order they make. If Jamie, one of the sales people, made sales orders worth $120,000 in his first year, calculate the total salary he earned during the year.

18. If Jasmine receives a base salary of $2200 bi-weekly and a commission of 8% on the sales she makes, calculate her last pay period payment if she made $8000 worth of sales during the period.

19. Ryan is paid a base salary of $1500 per month. In addition to this salary, he receives a commission of 4% on sales exceeding $18,000. Calculate his total salary if he made sales of $26,000 this month.

20. Banner House Inc. gives all its sales people a base salary of $30,000 per annum and a commission of 10% on all banners that they sell over $5000. Calculate Henry's salary last month if he sold $8000 worth of banners.

21. Stephen receives commissions of 3% for the first $5000 in sales he makes, 4% for the next $20,000, and 5% thereafter. If his pay last month was $2700, calculate the amount of sales he made.

22. Henry, a sales representative at a jewelers store, receives a 2.5% commission for the first $10,000 in sales he makes, 3% for the next $25,000, and 6% thereafter. If he was paid $1750 last month, calculate the amount of sales he made.

- 23. Rayne works for a clothing boutique store as a salesperson. He receives a monthly basic salary of $1000 and earns a commission on sales over $25,000. If he earned $4600 last month and he made $105,000 in sales, calculate his commission rate.

- 24. Kara's basic salary is $1250. However, she gets paid a commission on all sales she makes over $20,000. If she earned $3775 last month and she made sales of $83,125, calculate her commission rate.

- 25. Emma, who works for a software development company, has a 40-hour workweek and is paid a regular hourly rate of $20 per hour. She receives overtime pay for extra hours worked and holiday pay at regular hourly rate for 8 hours. Her overtime rate is $1\frac{1}{2}$ times the regular rate and any work on statutory holidays is paid at the overtime rate. In a week that has two statutory holidays, if she worked 36 hours including 4 hours on one of the statutory holidays, calculate her pay for the week.

- 26. Noah's employment at a coffee shop allows overtime pay for hours exceeding his regular 35-hour workweek. He is paid $14 per hour and receives holiday pay at regular hourly rate for hours. His overtime rate is $1\frac{1}{2}$ times the regular rate and any work on statutory holidays is paid at the overtime rate. If Noah worked for 35 hours in a week that has 2 statutory holidays including 2 hours on one statutory holiday, calculate his pay for the week.

27. Ruby had to quality test 1575 calculators in a production line of a factory. If she could test 75 calculators in 2 hours and her hourly rate is $30, calculate her earnings for that work.

28. Brian, an automobile production supervisor, can produce 5 doors in an 8-hour shift. If his hourly rate is $25 and he needs to produce 60 doors, calculate his earnings for the work.

3.4 | Taxes

Taxes are fees that federal or provincial governments charge organizations, properties, or individuals. This is a primary source of revenue for governments.

There are numerous types of taxes in Canada, some of which are income taxes, sales taxes, property taxes, payroll taxes, etc. In this chapter we will focus only on sales taxes and property taxes.

Sales Taxes

In Canada, three types of sales taxes are levied. These are as follows:

- **Goods and Services Tax (GST), levied by the federal government.**
  The federal GST rate for all provinces and territories is 5%.

- **Provincial Sales Tax (PST), levied by the provinces.**
  In Alberta, the Northwest territories, Nunavut, and Yukon, PST is not levied.
  In Prince Edward Island and Quebec, PST is applied to the combined cost of an item and the GST on the item.

- **Harmonized Sales Tax (HST), a single blended combination of the GST and PST.**
  In British Columbia, New Brunswick, Newfoundland, Nova Scotia, and Ontario, HST is collected by the Canada Revenue Agency and the appropriate amounts are remitted to the participating provinces.

Goods to which the tax is applied vary by province/territory, as does the rate. The table below provides the information on applicable sales tax rates for all provinces and territories.

Table 3.4

Summary of Sales Taxes Collected by Canadian Provinces as of April 01, 2011

Province	Type	PST(%)	GST* and PST Combined / HST (%)	Notes
Alberta	GST	0	5	No PST
British Columbia	HST	7	12	
Manitoba	GST + PST	7	12	
New Brunswick	HST	8	13	
Newfoundland	HST	8	13	
Nova Scotia & Labrador	HST	10	15	
Ontario	HST	8	13	
Prince Edward Island	GST + PST	10 (10.50 eff.)	15 (15.50 eff.)	PST is nominally 10%, but it is applied to the combined cost and federal 5% GST. Therefore, the effective PST is 10.5%.
Quebec	GST + PST	8.5** (8.925 eff.)	13.5 (13.925 eff.)	PST is nominally 8.5%, but it is applied to the combined cost and the federal 5% GST. Therefore, the effective PST is 8.925%.
Saskatchewan	GST + PST	5	10	
Nunavut, Yukon, Northwest territories	GST	0	5	No PST

Note:
*The federal GST rate for all provinces and territories is 5%.
** PST in Quebec is expected to increase to a nominal rate of 9.5% (9.975% effective) in January 2012.

Example 3.4(a)

Calculating the Cost After Taxes in Different Provinces in Canada

A brand new car costs $20,000 before taxes. Calculate the cost of the car after taxes in Ontario, Quebec, Alberta, and Nova Scotia using information provided in the table above.

Solution

Ontario: 13% HST

Cost before taxes = $20,000.00

13% HST = 0.13 × 20,000 = $2600.00

Total cost = 20,000 + 2600 = $22,600.00

Therefore, the cost of the car after taxes in Ontario is $22,600.00.

Cost before	100%	x	$20,000.00
HST	13%	$0.13x$	$2600.00
Total Cost	**113%**	$1.13x$	**$22,600.00**

Quebec: 5% GST, 8.5% PST on combined cost and GST (effective 8.925% PST)

Cost before taxes = $20,000.00

5% GST = 0.05 × 20,000.00 = $1000.00

Cost including GST = 20,000.00 + 1000.00
= $21,000.00

8.5% PST on Cost including GST
= 0.085 × 21,000
= $1785.00

Total cost = 21,000.00 + 1785.00 = $22,785.00

Cost before tax	100%	x	$20,000.00
GST	5%	$0.05x$	1000.00
PST	8.925% (eff.)	$0.08925x$	1785.00
Total Cost	**113.925%**	$0.13925x$	**$22,785.00**

In Quebec, the 8.5% PST is applied to the cost and 5% GST combined, resulting in an effective PST of 8.925% on cost.

Therefore, the cost of the car after taxes in Quebec is $22,785.00.

Solution *continued*

Alberta: 5% GST, 0% PST (Nil)

Cost before taxes = \$20,000.00

5% GST = 0.05 × 20,000 = \$1000.00

PST: Nil

Total cost = 20,000.00 + 1000.00

= \$21,000.00

Cost before tax	100%	x	\$20,000.00
GST	5%	$0.05x$	1000.00
PST	Nil	Nil	Nil
Total Cost	**105%**	**$1.05x$**	**\$21,000.00**

Therefore, the cost of the car after taxes in Alberta is \$21,000.00.

Nova Scotia: 15% HST

Cost before taxes = \$20,000.00

15% HST = 0.15 × 20,000 = \$3000.00

Total cost = 20,000.00 + 3000.00

= \$23,000.00

Cost before tax	100%	x	\$20,000.00
HST	15%	$0.015x$	\$3000.00
Total Cost	**115%**	**$1.15x$**	**\$23,000.00**

Therefore, the cost of the car after taxes in Nova Scotia is \$23,000.00.

Example 3.4(b)

Calculating the Total Cost After Taxes are Charged

Ron purchased a TV for \$500 (before taxes) in Ontario. What was the sales tax charged, and total cost of the TV including taxes?

Solution

Ontario 13% HST

Cost before taxes = \$500.00

HST = 13% × 500

= 0.13 × 500

= \$65.00

Total cost = 500 + 65

= \$565.00 Also equal to 1.13 × \$500

Cost before tax	100%	x	\$500.00
HST	13%	$0.13x$	\$65.00
Total cost	**113%**	**$1.13x$**	**\$565.00**

Therefore, the tax charged was \$65.00 and the total cost of the TV including taxes was \$565.00.

Example 3.4(c)

Calculating the Cost Before Taxes are Charged

Mark spent \$70 at a restaurant in Ontario for lunch with a client. This amount included the HST (13%). Calculate the cost of the meal before taxes and the HST on the meal.

Solution

Ontario 13% HST

Cost including taxes = \$70.00

$x + 0.13x = \$70.00$

$1.13x = \$70$

$x = \frac{70}{1.13} = 61.946902... = \$61.95$

13% HST = $0.13x$ = 0.13 × 61.95 = 8.053097... = \$8.05

Cost before tax	100%	x	**\$61.95**
HST	13%	$0.13x$	**\$8.05**
Total cost	**113%**	**$1.13x$**	**\$70.00**

Therefore, the cost of the meal before taxes was \$61.95 and HST was \$8.05.

Example 3.4(d)

Calculating the Total Cost After Taxes, Given the PST

Melody purchased a toaster in Manitoba and received a receipt for the purchase. When she reached home, she noticed that most of the numbers on the receipt were faded except the PST amount of \$5. Calculate the cost before taxes, GST, and total cost of her toaster.

Solution

Manitoba 5% GST, 7% PST

$$7\%\ PST = 0.07x = \$5.00$$
$$x = \$71.428571... = \$71.43$$
$$5\%\ GST = 0.05x = 0.05 \times 71.428571...$$
$$= \$3.571428$$
$$= \$3.57$$
$$\textit{Total Cost} = 1.12x$$
$$= 1.12 \times 71.428571...$$
$$= \$79.999999...$$
$$= \$80.00$$

Cost before taxes	100%	x	\$71.43
GST	5%	$0.05x$	\$3.57
PST	7%	$0.07x$	\$5.00
Total cost	**112%**	**$1.12x$**	**\$80.00**

Therefore, the cost before taxes, GST, and total cost of her toaster were \$71.43, \$3.57, and \$80.00, respectively.

Property Taxes

The owner of a property (land, houses, buildings, etc.) is required to pay the municipal government (county, city council, etc.) a property tax, calculated generally as a percentage of the value of the property that is being assessed. The local municipality collects this tax and this money is used to maintain the neighbourhood (parks, roads, street lights, garbage collection, etc.).

Tax authorities assess the value of the property based on the location and purpose of use of the property. For example, the value of land used for farming will be very different from that used to build apartments or houses. At the same time, the value of residences in the suburbs will be very different from that of residences in commercial locations within the city.

The assessed value of a property is generally a percentage of the market price (or fair market value) of that property. For example, the municipality may assess a condominium at \$120,000 in the year 2010 but the market price of the condominium may be \$150,000. Property taxes are charged only on the assessed value of the property and not on the purchase price or on the market value. Thus, the property tax is calculated with the following formula:

Formula 3.4(a)

Property Tax

$$\textit{Property Tax} = \textit{Assessed value of property} \times \textit{Tax Rate}$$

Example 3.4(e)

Calculating the Property Tax Using a Property Tax Rate

Andrew purchased a condominium for \$200,000 in the city of Toronto. The municipality assessed the value of the condominium at 70% of its purchase price. If the tax rate in this area is 1.1% per annum, how much will Andrew pay for property taxes the first year?

Solution

$$\textit{Assessed value of the condominium} = 0.70 \times 200{,}000 = \$140{,}000.00$$
$$\textit{Property Tax} = \text{Assessed Value of Property} \times \text{Tax Rate}$$
$$= 140{,}000 \times 0.011 = \$1540.00$$

Therefore, Andrew will have to pay \$1540.00 in property taxes for the first year.

Mill Rate: Porperty tax may also be expressed as a mill rate.

Mill Rate

Property taxes are generally a percentage of the assessed value of the property. It may also be expressed as a **mill rate** (or per mille, millage rate, millage, or mill levy), which is the amount of tax per thousand dollars of property value. For example, mill rate of 10 (10 mills) would mean your property tax rate is $10 for every $1000 worth of assessed value of property.

The property tax expressed as a mill rate is given by the following formula:

Formula 3.4(b)

Property Tax Expressed as a Mill Rate

$$Property\ tax = \frac{Assessed\ value\ of\ the\ property}{1000} \times Mill\ Rate$$

Example 3.4(f)

Calculating the Property Tax Using a Mill Rate

If a land is assessed for $100,000 and the property tax is 40 mills, what is the property tax amount the land owner would have to pay?

Solution

$$Property\ Tax = \frac{Assessed\ value\ of\ the\ property}{1000} \times Mill\ rate$$

$$Property\ Tax = \frac{100,000}{1000} \times 40 = \$4000.00$$

Therefore, the land owner would have to pay a property tax amount of $4000.00.

3.4 | Exercises

1. A business located in Toronto, Ontario purchased a photocopying machine that cost $9000 (before HST of 13%) from a local dealer. Calculate the amount of tax charged and the cost of the machine after taxes. How much would the business have paid for the same item in P.E.I. that cost $9000 (before PST of 10% and GST of 5%)?

2. Luke purchased 20 laptops from Edmonton, Alberta that cost $400 each (before GST of 5%). Calculate the amount he paid for the laptops after taxes and the total tax paid. How much would he have paid for the laptops (including PST of 8.5% and GST of 5%) if he had purchased them from Quebec?

3. Hansen took his family for a vacation to Halifax, Nova Scotia last summer. If his hotel room rental costs $232.50 per night (including HST of 15%), calculate the sales tax charged on the room rent per night.

4. If the cost of a diamond ring (including GST of 5%) in Alberta was $3230.58, calculate the cost of the same ring in New Brunswick. Assume that the cost before taxes in both provinces is the same.

5. Terrence, the purchase manager at a furniture outlet mall in London, Ontario, purchased 5 beds and 6 dining tables for his showroom. If the total HST he paid was $410.65, calculate the total cost of the furniture purchased (including taxes). Ontario has an HST of 13%.

6. Jessica, who lives in Halifax, Nova Scotia, bought a brand new bike for college. She lost the receipt for the bike but remembered that the total value of HST she paid was $100. Given this information, calculate the cost of her bike before and after the HST. Nova Scota has an HST of 15%.

7. Christina purchased a town-house for $280,000 in Toronto. If the municipality assessed the value of her house at 80% of its purchase price and the tax rate is 1.25% per annum on the assessed value, calculate how much she would have to pay in property tax this year.

8. Jason Forklifts, a successful heavy equipment manufacturer in Canada, decided to expand their production line and purchased land in Mississauga, Ontario for $3,890,000. If the municipality assessed the value of the industrial land at 65% of its purchase price and the tax rate is 0.85% per annum, calculate the amount of property tax they would have to pay in their first year.

9. If an industrial plot of land in British Columbia is assessed at $845,000 and the property tax is 30 mills, what is the property tax amount the land owner would have to pay?

10. A house in Manitoba is purchased at $375,000 and assessed at 80% of its purchase price. If the property tax on the house is 10 mills, calculate the property tax.

11. Magazines purchased by subscriptions in Ontario prior to July 01, 2010 were taxed only 5% GST (and no PST). However, since July 01, 2010, the HST of 13% has been charged for such purchases. How much more money will you pay now for a $75 (before taxes) magazine subscription in Ontario?

12. Home renovations in Ontario prior to July 01, 2010 were taxed only 5% GST. However, since July 01, 2010, the HST of 13% has been charged for such services. How much money would you have saved on a renovation costing $85,000 before taxes, if it was done in June rather than in July 2010?

13. Textbooks are always exempt from the PST in Ontario. If the total cost of a book including 5% GST is $147, how much GST is paid for the textbook?

14. Home insurance is always exempt from GST and only 8% PST is payable for such services in Ontario. If the insurance cost of a house in Ontario including taxes is $777.60 per year, calculate the amount of tax included in the total cost.

• 15. Property tax for a farmland is 75% of the municipal taxes levied for residential purposes. If the tax rate for residential buildings is 1.025%, calculate the property taxes for a farmland and residential property with assessed values of $300,000 and $180,000, respectively.

• 16. The mill rate of a residential property in a municipality is 8 Mills and the property tax for an industrial property is 1.25 times that of residential properties. Calculate the property taxes for a residential property and an industrial property that are assessed at $280,500 and $460,000, respectively.

3 | Review Exercises

Answers to odd-numbered problems are available at the end of the textbook

• 1. In 2008, 276,500 people immigrated to Canada. Of these, 3% were from the USA, 2% were from the UK, and the rest were from other countries.

a. How many more people immigrated to Canada from the USA than from the UK?

b. If the combined number of immigrants from the USA and the UK constituted 0.045% of the population of Canada, calculate the population of Canada in 2008.

• 2. Madison just received the first cheque from her salary and took her family out to dinner at a posh restaurant to celebrate. The waiter who was serving her was very hospitable so Madison left him a tip of 20% on the bill amount of $235.60.

a. Calculate the amount of tip that the waiter received from her.

b. If the tip was 1% of Madison's monthly salary, calculate her monthly salary.

- 3. Holistic Energy Ltd. spends $1200, $1400, $800, and $1700 on an average on replacing printer cartridges for their black & white inkjet printers, colour inkjet printers, black & white laser printers, and colour laser printers, respectively, every month.
  a. What percent of the total expenditure on printer cartridges do they spend on colour laser printers every month?
  b. If they decide to reduce the expense on both colour inkjet printers and colour laser printers by 50%, what percent of the total expenditure would they spend on black & white laser printers?

- 4. A manufacturing company has 280 production people, 21 quality inspectors, 15 sales people, 6 marketing people, and 15 other people in departments such as HR, Finance, etc.
  a. What percentage of the total employees are quality inspectors?
  b. If 15% of the production people quit their jobs, what percentage of the total remaining employees are quality inspectors?

5. The marketing department's expenses rose by 30% from last year. If this year's expenses were $234,260, calculate last year's expenses.

6. A manufacturing company paid $56,400 (after a discount) for a heavy-duty packing machine from Japan. If they received a discount of 21%, calculate the original price of the machine.

7. Katelyn's financial manager invested her savings in a portfolio of shares that comprised of investments of $2000, $1800, and $3100 in the infrastructure, hi-tech, and garment industries, respectively. Towards the end of 2010, if the value of her shares in the infrastructure industry rose by 20% while the rest remained the same, calculate the percent change in the value of her total investments.

8. Preston's website company invests their annual savings in different mutual funds. In 2010, they invested $12,500 in high-growth funds, $5000 in medium-growth funds, and $2000 in low-growth funds. If the value of their low-growth funds dropped by 10% this year, while the rest stayed the same, by what percent did the total value of their investments change?

- 9. Chelsea was excited that she secured the highest mark in her class on a mathematics quiz. If she scored 15% more than Zane who scored the 2nd highest, by what percent is Zane's score less than Chelsea's?

- 10. If Sabrina's annual salary is 10% more than Christina's, by what percent is Christina's annual earning less than Sabrina's?

11. A waitress is paid $18.60 per hour. If her workweek is 37.5 hours, calculate her monthly pay. Assume that there are 52 weeks per year.

12. A teller at a bank is paid a monthly salary of $3071.25. If he works 35 hours per week, calculate his hourly rate. Assume that there are 52 weeks per year.

- 13. Oliver is paid a base salary of $1000 per month. In addition to this salary, he receives commission on sales exceeding $20,000. His total salary for last month was $2225 and his sales were $30,000. Calculate his commission rate.

- 14. Heather's Leather Jacket Outlet pays all its sales representatives a base salary of $18,000 per annum and a commission on all jackets that they sell over $3000. If a sales representative's salary last month was $2500 and his sales were $11,000, calculate the commission rate.

15. Amy works at a pharmaceutical company as a sales representative and receives a graduated commission of 5% for the first $10,000 in sales, 6% on the next $12,000, and 7% thereafter. Calculate her commission if she makes $45,000 in sales for the month. What single commission rate would her total earnings represent?

16. A manufacturer of water purifiers offers sales people with the following commission structure: 2% for the first $5000 they sell, 3% on the next $3000, and 5% thereafter on all sales they make. Katherine, a new sales representative, makes sales of $6000 in the first month, $10,000 in the second month, and $15,000 in the third month.
  a. What were her commissions for the first three months?
  b. What single commission rate would represent her earnings in the third month?

17. Kristin was excited to furnish her new home. She purchased a couch, a dining set, and a bedroom set. When she returned home, she realized that she forgot to collect the invoice but remembered that she paid $580 in sales tax at the store. If the store is located in Toronto, Ontario, calculate the total amount she paid for the furniture (including 13% HST).

18. Scarlett was shocked to learn that a restaurant charged her a tax of $50 on a meal with her family. The manager explained to her that the restaurant charges 13% HST on the amount as per the rules of the province of Ontario. Calculate the cost of her meal including the HST.

19. Stephen and Hope purchased their first home in London, Ontario for $244,000. If the municipality assessed the value of their house at 85% of its purchase price and the tax rate is 1.15% per annum on the assessed value, calculate how much they would have to pay in property tax this year.

20. Marley purchased an industrial plot in Manitoba for $850,000 and it was assessed at 80% of its purchase price. If the property tax on the plot is 15 mills, calculate the property tax she would have to pay every year.

3 | Self-Test Exercises

Answers to all problems are available at the end of the textbook

1. Colton's store expenses for the month of July and August were $33,480 and $36,580, which were 110% and 90% of the budgeted expenditure for the months of July and August, respectively. Calculate the total budgeted expenses for the two months.

2. Sandra lives in a condominium in downtown Toronto and works for a leading telecommunications company as a multimedia specialist. She earns an annual take-home salary of $60,000, and every month she spends $1400 on rent, $600 on car expenses, $200 on a line-of-credit interest payment, $800 on miscellaneous expenses, and saves $2000.
   a. What percent of her annual take-home salary are her annual expenses?
   b. Her bank manager advised her to invest 10% of her annual take-home salary in a medium-risk mutual fund. What would this amount be every month and what percent of her current savings would this amount be?

3. Calculate the original price for a pair of shoes if Ruby paid $140 for it after receiving a discount of 7%.

4. Lindsey invested her savings in shares of her brother's engineering company. The value of the shares, which she owned, dropped by $1.25 at the end of the first year, and a further $2.50 at the end of the second year. If the price of the share at the end of the second year was $12.55,
   a. Calculate the percent change in the price of the share each year.
   b. What was the percent drop in the price over the two-year period?

5. The value of a currency appreciated by 20% of its value last month and then depreciated by 20% this month. By what percent did the currency appreciate or depreciate over the 2-month period?

6. Gracie received a job offer as a proofreader at a publishing company and is paid a gross salary of $38,000 per annum. Calculate her periodic gross payments if she is paid (a) monthly, (b) semi-monthly, (c) bi-weekly, (d) weekly.

7. Sandra works 'for a film production company and receives a bi-weekly pay of $1661.54. If she has 40-hour workweeks and worked a total of 97 hours during her last pay-period, calculate her gross payment for the last pay-period. Assume that her overtime factor is $1\frac{1}{2}$.

8. A sales representative at a furniture store receives sales commissions of 3% on the first $10,000 of sales made, 4% on the next $15,000, and 5% thereafter. If the sales representative earned $1912.50 last month from his commissions, calculate his total sales for last month.

9. If the cost (including the 5% GST) of a laptop in Alberta was $850.65, calculate the cost of the same laptop in New Brunswick (including the 13% HST in New Brunswick).

10. Wesley Steel Manufacturing Ltd. were expanding their production facilities and purchased large quantities of land in Oakville, Ontario for $8,560,000. If the municipality assessed the value of the industrial land at 65% of its purchase price and the tax rate is 0.85% per annum, calculate the amount of property tax they would have to pay in their first year.

CASE 3

Applying Percentages in Personal and Business Scenarios

Within two months of graduating from college, Heather got a job at a pharmaceutical company, where she earns a salary of $1750 bi-weekly. Her regular workweek is 35 hours and her overtime rate is twice the regular rate of pay.

To earn additional income, Heather took up a part-time job at a call center in the evenings and weekends, where she takes orders for a pizza company. Here, she receives a base salary of $750 per month plus commission. Her commission rate is 5% on the first $5000 in sales above her monthly quota of $10,000 and 7.5% on any additional sales thereafter.

After working for 6 months, Heather purchased a car for $13,560 (including the 13% HST) from a dealer in Toronto. Two years later, she purchased an apartment for $180,000 in Richmond Hill. Heather continued to do really well in her earnings and this year, she invested $5000 in shares of a software company that were selling at $2.50 per share.

a. What is Heather's hourly rate of pay and the equivalent monthly pay at the pharmaceutical company?

b. If Heather worked 77 hours during a pay period at the pharmaceutical company, what would her pay have been for that period?

c. Calculate her earnings for a month at the pizza company if her sales were worth $25,000. What straight commission would have resulted in the same earnings?

d. What were her sales last month if she received $1900 from the pizza company?

e. What was the cost of the car before the HST in Ontario and how much more would she have paid if she had purchased the car in Quebec, including the 5% GST and 8.5% PST?

f. The assessed value of her apartment is 80% of the purchase price and the property tax is 1.15% of the assessed value. Calculate her property tax amount for the year?

g. In the first six months of last year, the share price increased by 10% but decreased by 10% in the next six months. What was the percentage change in the share price over the one year period?

h. Calculate the total value of her shares at the end of the one year period.

3 | Summary of Notation and Formulas

NOTATION

P = Portion

B = Base

R = Rate

$\%C$ = Percent change

V_i = Initial value

V_f = Final value

FORMULAS

Portion | 3.1

$$P = R \times B$$

Percent Change | 3.2

$$\%C = \frac{(V_f - V_i)}{V_i} \times 100\%$$

Pay for pay period | 3.3 (a)

$$\text{Pay for pay period} = \frac{\text{Annual Salary}}{\text{Number of pay periods per year}}$$

Hourly rate of pay | 3.3 (b)

$$\text{Hourly rate of pay} = \frac{\text{Pay per week}}{\text{Number of working hours per week}}$$

Property tax | 3.4 (a)

$$\text{Property tax} = \text{Assessed value of property} \times \text{Tax rate}$$

Property tax expressed as mill rate | 3.4 (b)

$$\text{Property tax} = \frac{\text{Assessed value of the property}}{1000} \times \text{Mill Rate}$$

Ratios are widely used in our day-to-day lives to compare two or more quantities. Ratios are also used by businesses to compare their performance to the previous year's performance or to industry standards. This chapter will provide you with ample practice in using ratios and proportions. It will also provide you a thorough understanding of the numerous applications of ratios and proportions, such as converting currencies to foreign currencies, buying and selling currencies, importing goods into the country, and calculating the value of currencies when they fluctuate relative to foreign currencies.

4 Ratios, Proportions, and their Applications

LEARNING OBJECTIVES

- Set up ratios and use to solve allocation problems.
- Set up proportions and use to solve problems involving equivalent ratios.
- Solve problems involving pro-rating an amount using proportion method.
- Convert currencies between countries using exchange rates and proportion method.
- Understand buying and selling currencies by financial institutions.
- Understand currency appreciation and depreciation.
- Understand the role of exchange rates while importing goods from other countries.

CHAPTER OUTLINE

4.1 | Ratios

A **ratio** is a comparison or relationship between two or more quantities.

For example, Andy (A) invested \$5000 and Barry (B) invested \$4000 in a business. The comparison of A's investment to B's investment is called the ratio of their investments.

Expressing a Ratio of Two Quantities

Ratios **are comparisons or relationships between two or more quantities.**

When comparing two quantities, there are different ways to express the ratio. In the example above, the ratio of A's investment to B's may be expressed in any of the following forms:

5000 : 4000	(using a colon and read as '5000 is to 4000' or 'ratio of 5000 to 4000')
$\frac{5000}{4000}$	(as a fraction and read as '5000 over 4000')
1.25	(as a decimal equivalent of the fraction; i.e., A's investment is 1.25 times B's investment)
125%	(as a percentage equivalent of the decimal or fraction; i.e., A's investment is 125% of B's investment)

Expressing a Ratio of More than Two Quantities

When comparing more than two quantities, we use a colon to represent a ratio.

For example, if A's investment is \$5000, B's investment is \$4000, and C's investment is \$1000 in a business, then the ratio of their investments is given by,

$$A : B : C = 5000 : 4000 : 1000$$

Terms of a Ratio

When two ratios are equal, they give the same answer when reduced to their lowest terms.

The quantities in the ratio are called the terms of a ratio.

For example, the terms of the ratio 5 : 7 : 19 are 5, 7, and 19.

Equivalent Ratio

When all the terms of the ratio are multiplied by the same number or divided by the same number, the result will be an equivalent ratio.

For example, when the terms of a ratio 12 : 15 are multiplied by 2, we obtain an equivalent ratio of 24 : 30. When the terms of the ratio 12 : 15 are divided by the common factor 3, we obtain the equivalent ratio of 4 : 5.

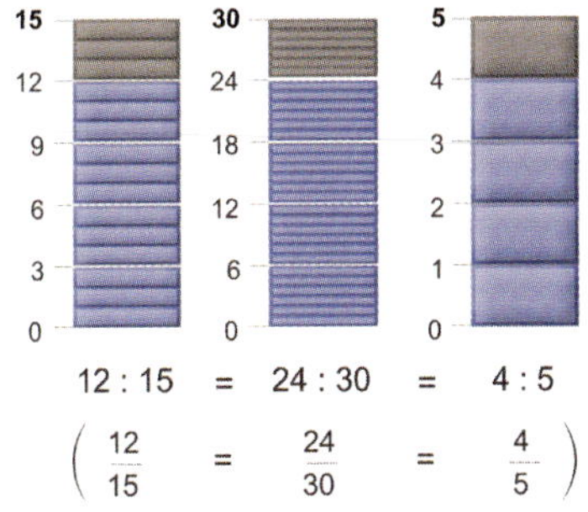

Therefore, ratios 12 : 15, 24 : 30, and 4 : 5 are called equivalent ratios.

Reducing a Ratio to its Lowest Terms

Comparisons are easier when ratios are reduced to their lowest terms. When all the terms of a ratio are integers, the ratio can be reduced to its lowest terms by dividing all the terms by their common factors.

For example, if *'A'* earns \$3000, *'B'* earns \$4500, and *'C'* earns \$6000, what is the ratio of their earnings (or compare their earnings)? Reduce the ratio to its lowest terms.

$A : B : C$	
3000 : 4500 : 6000	Dividing each term by the common factor 100, we obtain,
30 : 45 : 60	Dividing each term by the common factor 15, we obtain,
2 : 3 : 4	Now, the ratio is in its lowest terms.

By reducing this to lowest terms, we can say that the earnings of $A : B : C$ are in the ratio 2 : 3 : 4.

Reducing Ratios When One or More of the Terms of the Ratio Are Fractions

To reduce the ratio, first convert all the terms to integers by multiplying all terms by their lowest common denominator, and then reduce to its lowest terms.

For example,

$3 : \frac{9}{2} : 6$	Multiplying all terms by the common denominator 2, we obtain,
6 : 9 : 12	Dividing all terms by the common factor 3, we obtain,
2 : 3 : 4	

Reducing Ratios When One or More of the Terms of the Ratio Are Decimals

To reduce the ratio, first convert all the terms to integers by moving the decimal place of all terms to the right by the same number of places, and then reduce to its lowest terms.

For example,

2.25 : 3.5 : 5	Moving decimal by 2 places to the right, we obtain,
225 : 350 : 500	Dividing by the common factor 25, we obtain,
9 : 14 : 20	

Reducing Ratios When the Terms of the Ratio Are a Combination of Fractions and Decimals

To reduce the ratio, first convert all the fractional terms to decimals or decimal terms to fractions, then convert all terms to integers. Finally, reduce to its lowest terms.

For example,

$5.8 : \frac{9}{2} : 4$	Multiplying all terms by the common denominator 2, we obtain,
11.6 : 9 : 8	Moving decimal by 1 place to the right, we obtain,
116 : 90 : 80	Dividing by the common factor 2, we obtain,
58 : 45 : 40	

Reducing Ratios to an Equivalent Ratio Whose Smallest Term is 1

To make the comparison of quantities easier, we can also reduce a ratio to its equivalent ratio whose smallest term is equal to 1, by dividing all the terms by the smallest value.

For example, if the investment amount of 3 partners 'A', 'B', and 'C' are \$35,000, \$78,750, and \$59,500, respectively, what is the ratio of their earnings (or compare their earnings)? Reduce the ratio so the smallest value is 1.

A : B : C	
35,000 : 78,750 : 59,500	Dividing each term by the smallest term 35,000, we obtain,
1 : 2.25 : 1.7	Now the ratio is reduced to its equivalent ratio with the smallest term equal to 1.

By reducing it so that the smallest term is equal to 1, we can say: (i) B's investment is 2.25 times A's investment and (ii) C's investment is 1.75 times A's investment.

Order of a Ratio

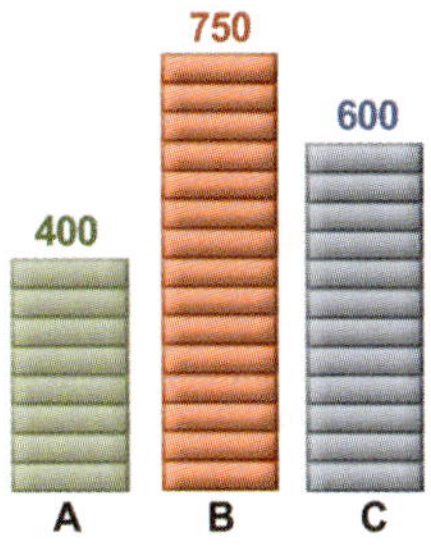

The order of presenting terms in a ratio is important.

For example, if A saves \$400, B saves \$750, and C saves \$600, then the ratio of the savings of $A : B : C$ is:

$A : B : C = 400 : 750 : 600$	Dividing each term by the common factor 50, we obtain,
$= 8 : 15 : 12$	

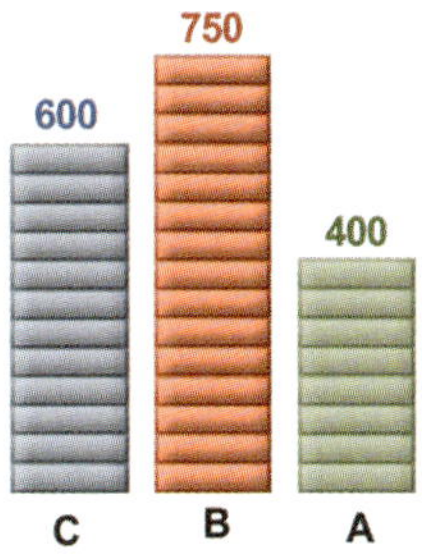

In the previous example, the ratio of the savings of $C : B : A$ is:

$C : B : A = 600 : 750 : 400$	Dividing each term by the common factor 50, we obtain,
$= 12 : 15 : 8$	

Notice that $C : B : A$ is not the same as $A : B : C$.

Comparing Quantities of Items that have the Same Kind of Measure

When comparing quantities of items that have the same kind of measure, the units have to be the same.

For example, in the ratio of 45 minutes to 2 hours, we are comparing 'time' in both these cases; therefore, the units used have to be the same. Converting hours to minutes (2 hours = 120 minutes), we obtain,

45 : 120	Dividing by the common factor 15, we obtain,
3 : 8	

Consider another example to find out the ratio of 2.5 kilometres to 3000 metres.

2.5 km : 3000 m	Converting km to m, (2.5 km = 2500 m), we obtain,
2500 : 3000	Dividing by the common factor 100, we obtain,
25 : 30	Dividing by the common factor 5, we obtain,
5 : 6	

Comparing Quantities of Items that have Different Kinds of Measure

When comparing quantities of items that have different kinds of measure, the units may be different.

For example, when baking a cake, Maggie uses 4 kilograms of flour, 2 litres of water, and 6 eggs. Therefore, the ratio of flour to water to eggs she uses while baking is given by,

The ratio of flour (kg) : water (l) : eggs (numbers) = 4 : 2 : 6   Dividing by the common factor 2, we obtain,

= 2 : 1 : 3

Rate is a ratio that is used to compare two quantities with different units of measure. It represents the number of units of the first type of quantity that corresponds to one unit of the second type of quantity. Rate is generally expressed by the word 'per'. For example, kilometres per hour, dollars per month, etc.

For example, a car travelled 300 kilometres in 5 hours.

The ratio of distance (km) to time (hr) = 300 : 5   Dividing by 5 to reduce the second unit to 1, we obtain,

= 60 : 1

Therefore, the rate (in this case speed) is 60 km per hour.

Sharing Quantities Using Ratios

This refers to the allocation or distribution of a quantity into two or more portions (or units) based on a given ratio.

For example, to share a $1000 profit among *A*, *B*, and *C* in the ratio of 2 : 3 : 5, first, add the terms in the ratio (i.e., 2, 3, and 5), which results in a total of 10 units. These 10 units represent the total profit of $1000, where *A*'s share constitutes 2 units, *B*'s 3 units, and *C*'s 5 units. Each person's share can then be calculated, as shown below:

The total of the amount shared individually will be equal to the original amount shared. Ratio of the amount shared individually, when reduced, will be equal to the original ratio.

$$A\text{'s share} = \frac{2}{10} \times 1000 = \$200.00$$

$$B\text{'s share} = \frac{3}{10} \times 1000 = \$300.00$$

$$C\text{'s share} = \frac{5}{10} \times 1000 = \$500.00$$

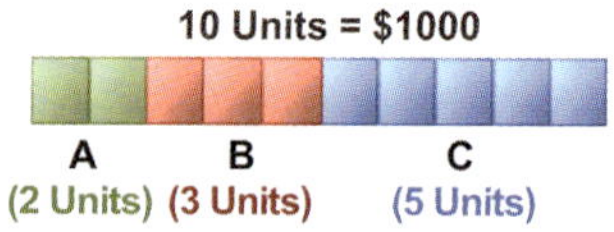

Note:

- The total of their shares will be equal to the amount shared (200 + 300 + 500 = 1000).
- If we reduce the ratio of the amounts shared to its lowest terms, the result is the original ratio (200 : 300 : 500 = 2 : 3 : 5).

Suppose the order of the ratio of *A*'s share : *B*'s share : *C*'s share is changed to 5 : 3 : 2 (instead of 2 : 3 : 5), their individual shares will change. Their shares are recalculated as shown below:

$$A\text{'s share} = \frac{5}{10} \times 1000 = \$500.00$$

$$B\text{'s share} = \frac{3}{10} \times 1000 = \$300.00$$

$$C\text{'s share} = \frac{2}{10} \times 1000 = \$200.00$$

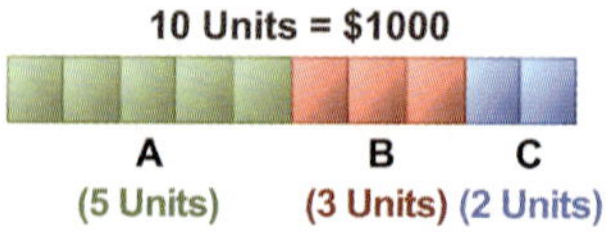

Note:

- The total of their shares will be equal to the amount shared (500 + 300 + 200 = 1000).
- If we reduce the ratio of the amounts shared to its lowest terms, the result is the original ratio (500 : 300 : 200 = 5 : 3 : 2).

Example 4.1(a)

Sharing Using Ratios

A, *B*, and *C* start a business and invest \$3500, \$2100, and \$2800, respectively. After a few months, if *C* decides to sell his shares to *A* and *B*, how much would *A* and *B* have to pay for *C*'s shares if they want to maintain their initial investment ratio?

Solution

Investments of *A*, *B*, and *C* are in the ratio of 3500 : 2100 : 2800, which can be reduced to 5 : 3 : 4. If *A* and *B* want to maintain their investment ratio at 5 : 3, then *C*'s share (of \$2800) has to be paid for by *A* and *B* in this ratio. By adding the ratio of *A* and *B*, we know that *C*'s share is to be divided into a total of 8 units as illustrated:

A would have to pay $C: \frac{5}{8} \times 2800 = \$1750.00$

B would have to pay $C: \frac{3}{8} \times 2800 = \$1050.00$

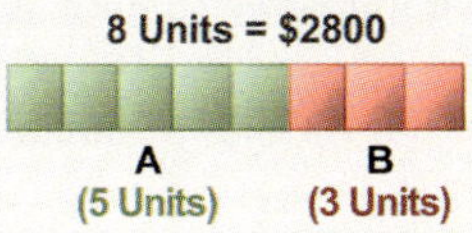

Therefore, A would have to pay \$1750.00 and B would have to pay \$1050.00 in order to maintain their initial investment ratio.

Example 4.1(b)

Application Using Equivalent Ratios

Andrew, Barry, and Cathy invested their savings in a bank. The ratio of the investment of Andrew's to Barry's is 2 : 3 and that of Barry's to Cathy's is 4 : 5. What is the investment ratio of Andrew: Barry: Cathy?

Solution

Find the equivalent ratio for $A : B$ and $B : C$ so that the number of units in B is the same in both cases.

This can be done by finding the equivalent ratio of $A : B$ by multiplying by 4 and that of $B : C$ by multiplying by 3.

$A : B = 2 : 3$ Multiplying both terms by 4, we obtain,

$= 8 : 12$

$B : C = 4 : 5$ Multiplying both terms by 3, we obtain,

$= 12 : 15$

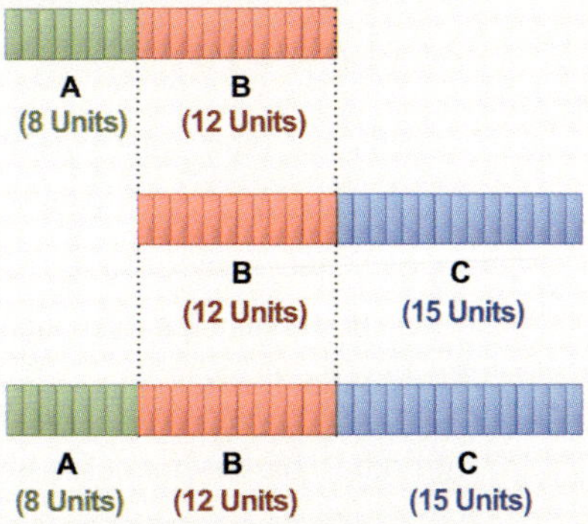

Therefore, the investment ratio of Andrew : Barry : Cathy is 8 : 12 : 15

4.1 | Exercises

1. Reduce the following ratios to their lowest terms and to an equivalent ratio having the smallest term 1.

   a. 500 : 400: 800 b. $12 : \frac{5}{3} : 3$ c. $1.7 : 8.5 : \frac{34}{3}$

2. Reduce the following ratios to their lowest terms and to an equivalent ratio having the smallest term 1.

   a. 420 : 280 : 140   b. $65 : 91 : \frac{13}{2}$ c. $12 : 1.5 : \frac{3}{2}$

3. Which of the following ratios are equal:

   a. 4 : 6 and 6 : 10   b. 8 : 10 and 28 : 35

   c. 6 : 8 and 27 : 32   d. 16 : 22 and 64 : 88

4. Which of the following ratios are equal:

   a. 16 : 20 and 24 : 30   b. 10 : 12 and 35 : 42

   c. 12 : 14 and 30 : 42   d. 12 : 26 and 30 : 65

5. Find the ratio of the following:

   a. 30 minutes to 3 hours and 15 minutes   b. 400 m to 3.5 km   c. 750 g to 12 kg

6. Find the ratio of the following:

   a. 55 minutes to 1 hours and 55 minutes   b. 990 m to 1.2 km   c. 120 g to 2 kg

7. What is the ratio of a Canadian dime (10¢) to a Canadian loonie ($1)?

8. What is the ratio of 12 minutes to 12 hours, reduced to its lowest terms?

9. An aircraft travels a distance of 3000 km in 6 hours. Calculate the ratio of the distance traveled to the time taken, reduced to a rate of kilometres per hour.

10. Speed is defined as the ratio of the distance travelled to the time taken. If Andrea, who lives in Toronto, took 6 hours to reach her parent's home in Montreal, which is 543 km away, calculate the speed at which she was travelling.

11. In a triathlon, participants are required to complete three successive events: swimming, bicycling and running without stopping. If they have to swim 3850 metres, bike 7 kilometres, and then run 3.5 kilometres, calculate the ratio of the distance covered by swimming to biking to running, in its lowest terms.

12. Rodney, a hardware engineer, wants to install a microchip that is 38.2 mm in length into his laptop. The length of the installation space provided in his laptop is 4.8 cm. Calculate the ratio of the length of the microchip to the installation space, provided in its lowest terms.

13. Martha was planning to make an authentic Indian dish for her guests. She planned to use 24 eggs, 4 litres of water, 2 tablespoons of chilli powder, and 8 tomatoes.
    a. What is the ratio of the ingredients in her recipe?
    b. If she decides to reduce the quantity of chilli powder to $1\frac{1}{2}$ tablespoons, calculate the new ratio of the ingredients in her recipe.

14. In Eddie's battery manufacturing company, they use 400 kg of lead, 30 kg of carbon, 20 litres of battery acid, and 80 kg of rubber per day to make batteries.
    a. What is the ratio of the raw materials used to make batteries per day?
    b. If he alters the quantity of carbon used in his battery and utilizes 20 kg of carbon per day, calculate the new ratio of raw materials used per day.

15. A TV cable bill of $120 is shared between two house-mates, Susan and Robert, in the ratio of $2 : 2\frac{1}{2}$. How much would each person pay?

16. Sherrie and Alexis invested a total of $10,000 in a web design business. If the ratio of their investments is 8 : 2, what are their investments?

17. Amanda and 2 of her friends received the first prize for a marketing case competition. They received an amount of $4500; however, they decided to share the prize in the ratio of the amount of time each of them spent on the marketing case. If Amanda spent 5 hours, Fredrick spent 8 hours, and Ronald spent 2 hours, what would be each person's share of the prize?

18. Three friends, Andrew, Baxter, and Cathy, *A*, *B*, and *C*, jointly insured a commercial property in the ratio of 12 : 8 : 5, respectively. How will an annual premium of $8000 be distributed to the three of them?

19. Three friends, Andrew, Brooks, and Charlie, have decided to invest $8,000, $12,000, and $4000, respectively, to start a software development business. If Charlie decided to leave the business, how much would Andrew and Brooks have to pay for Charlie's shares if they want to maintain their initial investment ratio?

20. Chuck decided to build a yacht with his two friends Rob and Bob and they invested $18,000, $22,000, and $13,000, respectively. After the yacht was built, Bob decided to sell his share of the investment to Chuck and Rob. How much would each of them have to pay if they want to maintain the same ratio of their investments in the yacht?

• 21. Abey and Bauxter invested equal amounts of money in a business. A year later, Abey withdrew $5000 making the ratio of their investments 5 : 9. How much money did each of them invest in the beginning?

• 22. Jocelyn and Haley invested equal amounts to start a business. Two months later, Jocelyn invested an additional $3000 in the business making the ratio of their investments 11 : 5. How much money did each of them invest in the beginning?

• 23. If $A : B = 3 : 4$ and $B : C = 5 : 6$, find $A : B : C$.

• 24. If $X : Y = 2 : 5$ and $Y : Z = 6 : 7$, find $X : Y : Z$.

25. If *A* earns $98 for working 8 hours and *B* earns $49 for working 5 hours, whose average hourly rate is higher?

26. If Amanda travelled 325 km in 4 hours and 15 minutes and Ashton travelled 290 km in 3 hours and 30 minutes, whose average speed was greater?

4.2 | Proportions and Pro-rations

Proportions

When two sets of ratios are equal, we say that they are proportionate to each other. In the proportion equation the ratios on the left side of the equation are equal to the ratios on the right side of the equation.

Consider an example where $A : B$ is 50 :100 and $C : D$ is 30 : 60. Reducing the ratio to its lowest terms, we obtain the ratio of $A : B$ as 1 : 2 and the ratio of $C : D$ as 1 : 2. Since these ratios are equal, they are equally proportionate to each other and their proportion equation is

$$A : B = C : D$$

The proportion equation can also be formed by representing the ratios as fractions.

The fraction obtained by dividing the 1st term by the 2nd term on the left side is equal to the fraction obtained by dividing the 1st term by the 2nd term on the right side.

$$\frac{A}{B} = \frac{C}{D}$$

If 3 terms of the proportion equation are known, the 4th term can be calculated using the method of cross-multiplication.

Cross-multiplication is accomplished by equating the product of the numerator of the 1st ratio and the denominator of the 2nd ratio with the product of the denominator of the 1st ratio and the numerator of the second ratio.

If two sets of fractions are equal, then the product obtained by cross-multiplying the fractions will be equal.

Cross-multiplying, $\frac{A}{B} \times \frac{C}{D}$ we obtain,

$$AD = BC$$

Notice that the cross-multiplication of $\frac{A}{B} = \frac{C}{D}$ also gives the same result.

Therefore, $A : B = C : D$ is equivalent to $\frac{A}{B} = \frac{C}{D}$ and is also equivalent to $\frac{A}{C} = \frac{B}{D}$.

Similarly, this principle can be extended to proportions with sets of ratios having more than 2 terms.

For example,

If $A : B : C = D : E : F$, then this ratio can be expressed as $\frac{A}{B} = \frac{D}{E}$, $\frac{B}{C} = \frac{E}{F}$, and $\frac{A}{C} = \frac{D}{F}$

This ratio can also be expressed as,

$$\frac{A}{D} = \frac{B}{E} = \frac{C}{F}$$

In both cases, cross-multiplying, gives the same result,

$$AE = BD,\ BF = CE, \text{ and } AF = CD$$

Example 4.2(a)

Solving for Unknowns in Proportions

Find the missing term in the following proportions:

(i) $5 : 8 = 10 : x$

(ii) $250 : x = 10 : 3$

(iii) $x : 3.8 = 5.2 : 19.76$

(iv) $2 : 2\frac{1}{2} = x : 3\frac{1}{2}$

Solution

(i) $5 : 8 = 10 : x$

In fraction form, $\frac{5}{8} = \frac{10}{x}$

Cross-multiplying, $5x = 80$

$x = \frac{80}{5}$

Therefore, $x = 16$

or, In fraction form, $\frac{5}{10} = \frac{8}{x}$

Cross-multiplying, $5x = 80$

$x = \frac{80}{5}$

Therefore, $x = 16$

(ii) $250 : x = 10 : 3$

In fraction form, $\frac{250}{x} = \frac{10}{3}$

Cross-multiplying, $750 = 10x$

$x = \frac{750}{10}$

Therefore, $x = 75$

or, In fraction form, $\frac{250}{10} = \frac{x}{3}$

Cross-multiplying, $10x = 750$

$x = \frac{750}{10}$

Therefore, $x = 75$

If $A : B = C : D$

then $\frac{A}{B} = \frac{C}{D}$

or, $\frac{A}{C} = \frac{B}{D}$

Solution *continued*

(iii) $x : 3.8 = 5.2 : 19.76$

In fraction form, $\frac{x}{3.8} = \frac{5.2}{19.76}$

Cross-multiplying, $19.76x = 3.8 \times 5.2$

$x = \frac{3.8 \times 5.2}{19.76}$

Therefore, $x = 1$

or, In fraction form, $\frac{x}{5.2} = \frac{3.8}{19.76}$

Cross-multiplying, $19.76x = 5.2 \times 3.8$

$x = \frac{5.2 \times 3.8}{19.76}$

Therefore, $x = 1$

(iv) $2 : 2\frac{1}{2} = x : 3\frac{1}{2}$

$4 : 5 = 2x : 7$

In fraction form, $\frac{4}{5} = \frac{2x}{7}$

Cross-multiplying, $10x = 28$

$x = \frac{28}{10}$

Therefore, $x = 2.8$

or, $4 : 5 = 2x : 7$

In fraction form, $\frac{4}{2x} = \frac{5}{7}$

Cross-multiplying, $28 = 10x$

$x = \frac{28}{10}$

Therefore, $x = 2.8$

Example 4.2(b)

Solving Word Problems Using Proportions

Ben can drive a distance of 18 km using 2 litres of gas. Calculate the distance (in km) Ben can drive using 30 litres of gas?

Solution

L : km = L : km

$2 : 18 = 30 : x$ — Using fractional notation, we obtain,

$\frac{2}{18} = \frac{30}{x}$ — Cross-multiplying, we obtain,

$2x = 18 \times 30$ — Dividing both sides by 2, the coefficient of x, we have,

$x = 270$ km

Therefore, Ben can drive a distance of 270 km using 30 litres of gas.

Example 4.2(c)

Sharing Using Proportions

Alex (A), Bebeto (B), and Carol (C) decide to start a lawn mowing business together and form a partnership. A invests \$105,000, B invests \$140,000, and C invests \$245,000. They agree to share the profits in the same ratio as their investments.

(i) What is the ratio of their investments?

(ii) In the first year of running the business, A's profit was \$30,000. What were B's and C's profits?

(iii) In the second year, their total profit was \$56,000. How much would each of them receive from this total profit?

Solution

(i) Ratio of their investments:

$A : B : C$

105,000 : 140,000 : 245,000 — Divide each term by the common factor of 1000

105 : 140 : 245 — Divide each term by the common factor of 5

Solution continued

$21 : 28 : 49$ Divide each term by the common factor of 7

$3 : 4 : 7$

Therefore, the ratio of their investments is 3 : 4 : 7.

> If $A : B : C = D : E : F$
>
> then $\frac{A}{B} = \frac{D}{E}, \frac{B}{C} = \frac{E}{F}, \frac{A}{C} = \frac{D}{F}$
>
> or, $\frac{A}{D} = \frac{B}{E} = \frac{C}{F}$

(ii) *A*'s profit was \$30,000. What were *B*'s and *C*'s profits?

Method 1:

$$\text{Ratio of investment} = \text{Ratio of profit}$$

$$A : B : C = A : B : C$$

Substituting terms, $3 : 4 : 7 = 30{,}000 : x : y$

So, $\frac{3}{4} = \frac{30{,}000}{x}$ and $\frac{3}{7} = \frac{30{,}000}{y}$

Cross-multiplying, we obtain,

$3x = 120{,}000$ $3y = 210{,}000$

$x = \$40{,}000.00$ $y = \$70{,}000.00$

Therefore, *B*'s profit is \$40,000.00. Therefore, *C*'s profit is \$70,000.00.

Method 2:

$$\text{Ratio of investment} = \text{Ratio of profit}$$

$$A : B : C = A : B : C$$

Substituting terms, $3 : 4 : 7 = 30{,}000 : x : y$

So, $\frac{3}{30{,}000} = \frac{4}{x} = \frac{7}{y}$

Hence, $\frac{3}{30{,}000} = \frac{4}{x}$ and $\frac{3}{30{,}000} = \frac{7}{y}$

Cross-multiplying, $3x = 120{,}000$ $3y = 210{,}000$

Solving, $x = \$40{,}000.00$ $y = \$70{,}000.00$

Therefore, *B*'s profit is \$40,000.00. Therefore, *C*'s profit is \$70,000.00.

(iii) In the second year, their total profit was \$56,000. How much would each of them receive from this total profit?

Method 1:

Since *A*, *B*, and *C* agreed to share profits in the same ratio as their investments, \$56,000 must be shared in the ratio, 3 : 4 : 7.

By adding the ratio of their investments (3 + 4 + 7), we know that the total profit of \$56,000 should be distributed over 14 units. Therefore,

$$A : B : C : \text{Total} = A : B : C : \text{Total}$$

Substituting terms, $3 : 4 : 7 : 14 = A : B : C : 56{,}000$

So, $\frac{3}{14} = \frac{A}{56{,}000}$, $\frac{4}{14} = \frac{B}{56{,}000}$, $\frac{7}{14} = \frac{C}{56{,}000}$

Solution *continued*

Cross-multiplying, we obtain,

$$14A = 168{,}000, \quad 14B = 224{,}000, \quad 14C = 392{,}000$$

$$A = \$12{,}000.00, \quad B = \$16{,}000.00, \quad C = \$28{,}000.00$$

Therefore, *A, B,* and *C* will receive profits of \$12,000.00, \$16,000.00, and \$28,000.00 respectively.

Method 2:

Ratio of investment = Ratio of profit

$$A : B : C : \text{Total} = A : B : C : 56{,}000$$

Substituting terms, $3 : 4 : 7 : 14 = A : B : C : 56{,}000$

So, $\frac{3}{A} = \frac{4}{B} = \frac{7}{C} = \frac{14}{56{,}000}$

$$\frac{3}{A} = \frac{14}{56{,}000}, \quad \frac{4}{B} = \frac{14}{56{,}000}, \quad \frac{7}{C} = \frac{14}{56{,}000}$$

Cross-multiplying, we obtain,

$$14A = 3 \times 56{,}000, \quad 14B = 4 \times 56{,}000, \quad 14C = 7 \times 56{,}000$$

$$A = \frac{3 \times 56{,}000}{14}, \quad B = \frac{4 \times 56{,}000}{14}, \quad C = \frac{7 \times 56{,}000}{14}$$

Simplifying,

$$A = \$12{,}000.00, \quad B = \$16{,}000.00, \quad C = \$28{,}000.00$$

Therefore, *A, B,* and *C* will receive profits of \$12,000.00, \$16,000.00, and \$28,000.00 respectively.

Pro-rations

Pro-ration is defined as sharing or allocating the quantities, usually the amounts, on a proportionate basis.

Consider an example where Kelly paid \$1200 for a computer course but decided to withdraw from the course after attending half the course. As she attended only half the course, the college decided to refund half her tuition fee, $\frac{\$1200}{2} = \$600$. As the college calculated the refund amount proportionate to the time she attended the course, we say that the college refunded her tuition fee on a **pro-rata basis.**

A few examples of pro-rated calculations are:

a. Cancellation of insurance premiums before the end of the premium period. On cancellation, the amount refunded is calculated on a pro-rata basis.

b. Employees' overtime pay, part-time pay, and vacation times are calculated on a pro-rata basis.

Example 4.2(d) **Calculating Pro-rated Amount of a Payment**

Find the pro-rated insurance premium for two months if the annual premium is \$4800.

Solution

Premium (\$) : time (months) = Premium (\$) : time (months)

$$4800 : 12 = x : 2$$

Solution continued

Expressed in fraction form, $\frac{4800}{12} = \frac{x}{2}$

$$x = \$800.00$$

Therefore, the pro-rated premium for two months is $800.00.

Example 4.2(e)

Calculating Pro-rated Amount of a Refund

Johnson paid $200 for a 1-year weekly subscription of a fashion journal. After receiving 15 issues of the journal, he decided to cancel his subscription. What should be his refund?

Assume 1 year = 52 weeks.

Solution

Paid for 52 issues, received 15 issues; therefore, refund for 37 issues (52 − 15).

$$\text{Issues (\#)} : \text{Cost (\$)} = \text{Issues (\#)} : \text{Cost (\$)}$$

Substituting values, $52 : 200 = 37 : x$

Solving for x, $\frac{52}{200} = \frac{37}{x}$

$$52x = 37 \times 200$$

$$x = 142.307692... = \$142.31$$

Therefore, his refund should be $142.31.

4.2 | Exercises

1. Calculate the missing terms:
   a. $1 : 2 = 5 : x$
   b. $x : 1.2 = 3.4 : 5.8$
   c. $1 : 4\frac{1}{2} = x : 2\frac{3}{4}$
   d. $2.25 : 1\frac{1}{2} = x : 1\frac{3}{4}$

2. Calculate the missing terms:
   a. $5 : 9 = x : 3$
   b. $12.34 : 1.8 = x : 2.2$
   c. $11\frac{3}{4} : 8 = 18\frac{1}{4} : x$
   d. $4.75 : x = 6\frac{3}{4} : 3.28$

3. A truck transporting material to a factory requires 180 litres of gas for every trip to cover 1500 km. How many litres of gas will it require to cover 1950 km?

4. Michael was the lead on a research project at a large pharmaceutical company. Based on his past experience, it would take his team 7 months to complete two projects. His director of research wants him to complete 6 similar projects. How long will his team take to complete all these projects?

5. Mike paid a property tax of $400 for his farm house that measures 110 square metres. What would his neighbour's property tax be if the size of her farm house is 70 square metres and she is taxed at the same rate?

6. The city of Ottawa charges $3760 in taxes per year for a 2000 square metre industrial shed. What taxes would Amazing Plastics Inc. have to pay if they have a 25,550 square metre shed in the same area?

7. On a map, 2.5 cm represents 2.0 km. If the distance between town *A* and town *B* on the map is 6.2 cm, how many kilometres apart are these towns?

8. On a house plan, 1.5 cm represents 1.25 metres. If the actual length of a room is 4.5 metres, how many centimetres will represent this length in the plan?

9. Harris invested his savings in telecommunications, real-estate, and technology stocks in the ratio of 4 : 5 : 3, respectively. If he invested $5450 in real-estate stocks, calculate his investments in the telecommunications and technology stocks.

10. The ratio of the distance from Alexandra's house to Mary's, Jane's, and Jill's house is 2 : 3.5 : 1, respectively. If the distance from Alexandra's house to Mary's is 4.75 km, calculate the distance from Alexandra's house to Jane's and to Jill's house.

11. Three friends, *A*, *B*, and *C*, start a business with investments in the ratio of 2 : 3 : 1, respectively. *A* invested $9130, and all three of them agree to share profits in the ratio of their investments.
    a. Calculate *C*'s investment.
    b. If *A*'s profit was $45,000 in the first year, calculate *B*'s and *C*'s profits.
    c. In the second year, their total profit was $180,000. How much would each of them receive from this total profit?

12. Adam, an entrepreneur, started an e-learning business with a personal investment of $110,000. He needed more funds and decided to raise money from two of his high-net-worth friends, Bill and Ted. In return for the money, he gave them ownership in his company. Based on their investments, Adam, Bill, and Ted own the company in the ratio of 11 : 5 : 2. All profits were also agreed to be shared in ratio of their investments.
    a. Calculate Bill's and Ted's investments in the business.
    b. If the business made a profit of $260,000 in the first year, calculate each partner's share of the profit.
    c. In the second year, if Adam made $60,000 in profit from the business, how much did Bill and Ted make?

13. If the annual salary of an employee is $45,000, calculate his weekly salary using pro-rations. Assume that there are 52 weeks in a year.

14. Addison got a job offer at a company that would pay her $2800 bi-weekly. How much is her annual salary, assuming that she will receive 26 payments in a year?

15. A student pays $1400 for a course that has 30 classes. Find the pro-rated refund she should receive if she only attended 2 classes before withdrawing from the course.

16. Angelina joined a driving school that charges $300 for 12 classes. After attending 5 classes, she did not like the training and wanted to cancel the remaining classes. Calculate the pro-rated refund she should receive.

17. Frank bought a brand new car on July 01, 2010 and obtained a pre-paid insurance of $1058 for the period of July 01, 2010 to June 30, 2011. After 2 months of using the car, he sold it and cancelled his insurance. Calculate the pro-rated refund he should receive from the insurance company.

18. The owner of a new gaming business decided to insure his servers and computers. His insurance company charged him a premium of $2000 per quarter starting January 01. If the insurance started on February 01, how much prorated insurance premium did he have to pay for the rest of the first quarter? Hint: Quarter of a year is 3 months.

19. Molly, Katie, and Timothy invested a total of $650,000 in the ratio of 2 : 4 : 7 to start a business. Two months later, each of them invested an additional $25,000 into the business. Calculate their new investment ratio after the additional investment.

20. Patrick and his two sisters purchased an office for $360,000. Their individual investments in the office were in the ratio of 2 : 4 : 3, respectively. After the purchase, they decided to renovate the building and purchase furniture, so each of them invested an additional $40,000. Calculate their new investment ratio after the additional investment.

21. Anthony set up a new charity fund to support needy children. For every $5 collected by the charity, the Government donated an additional grant of $1.50 to the charity. At the end of 3 months, if his charity fund had a total of $90,000, including the Government grant, calculate the amount the charity received from the Government.

22. The sales tax on many products sold in Ontario is such that for every $1.00 worth of a product sold, the buyer would have to pay an additional $0.13 in taxes. If a product was being sold at an exhibition for $18,500 before taxes, calculate the amount of sales tax to be paid by the buyer.

23. Bill, Blake, and Roy invested $45,000, $75,000, and $60,000, respectively, to start an e-learning business. They realized that they required an additional $60,000 for operating the business. How much did each of them have to individually invest to maintain their original investment ratio?

24. Three wealthy business partners decided to invest $120,000, $300,000, and $180,000, respectively, to purchase an industrial plot in the outskirts of the city. They required an additional $175,000 to build an industrial shed on the land. How much did each of them have to individually invest to maintain their original investment ratio?

• 25. Paul, Oliver, and Ellie decided to start a web design company and made investments in the ratio of 2 : 3 : 4, respectively. After one year, if Paul increased his initial investment by 50% and Oliver decreased his initial investment of $4500 by 25%, find the new ratio of their investments.

• 26. Jake, Kristen, and Destiny started a design studio and made investments in the ratio of 4 : 7 : 8, respectively, out of which Destiny's investment was $12,000. Calculate the new ratio of their investments if Jake and Destiny increased their investments by 25% and 50%, respectively.

27. A first semester class in a college has 9 more girls than boys and the ratio of the number of girls to boys in the class is 7 : 4.
    a. How many students are there in the class?
    b. If 4 girls and 3 boys joined the class, find the new ratio of girls to boys in the class.

28. The advisory board of a public sector company has 12 more men than women and the ratio of the number of men to women is 5 : 2.
    a. How many people are there on the board?
    b. If 4 men and 4 women joined the board, calculate the new ratio of men to women.

29. To estimate the number of tigers in a forest, a team of researchers tagged 91 tigers and released them into the forest. Six months later, 25 tigers were spotted, out of which 7 had tags. How many tigers are estimated to be there in the forest?

30. Researchers were conducting a study to estimate the number of frogs in a pond. They put a bright yellow band on the legs of 45 frogs and released them into the pond. A few days later, 12 frogs were spotted, out of which 5 had bands. How many frogs are estimated to be there in the pond?

4.3 | Exchange Rates and their Applications

Exchange Rates

Exchange rates: *used to convert currencies between countries.*

The exchange rate, also called the foreign exchange rate or forex rate, is used to convert currencies between countries. Therefore, knowing the exchange rate would allow you to calculate the amount of a currency required to purchase one unit of another currency.

For example, to convert Canadian currency to US currency, it is important to know how many Canadian dollars are equivalent to one US dollar, or vice versa.

The value of a currency may fluctuate constantly during the day and the exchange rate may vary accordingly. For example, on August 06, 2010, US$1 was equal to C$1.0273 and C$1 was equal to US$0.9734 at noon EST. Thus, the exchange rate on that date and time was US$1 = C$1.0273 and C$1 = US$0.9734.

Currency Cross-Rate Table

Currency exchange rates are generally displayed in a table called the currency cross-rate table for quick reference.

Exchange rates given in the currency cross-rate table below are as on August 06, 2010.

Table 4.3

Currency Cross-Rate Table

Currency	Symbol	C$	US$	€	£	¥	CHF	A$
Canadian dollar	**C$**	–	1.0273	1.3644	1.6414	0.012050	0.9909	0.9415
US dollar	**US$**	0.9734	–	1.3281	1.5978	0.011730	0.9646	0.9165
Euro	**€**	0.7329	0.7529	–	1.2030	0.008832	0.7263	0.6901
British pound	**£**	0.6092	0.6259	0.8312	–	0.007341	0.6037	0.5736
Japanese yen	**¥**	82.988	85.253	113.23	136.22	–	82.233	78.133
Swiss francs	**CHF**	1.0092	1.0367	1.3769	1.6565	0.012161	–	0.9501
Australian dollar	**A$**	1.0621	1.0911	1.4492	1.7434	0.012799	1.0525	–

The vertical column of the table represents one unit of the currency to be converted and the horizontal rows represent the equivalent value of it in another currency.

- For example, £1 = CHF1.6565, and US$1 = C$1.0273.

For calculations involving conversion from one currency to another, we will either use the cross-reference table or exchange rates provided in the question. We will be using the method of proportions to solve examples that follow.

Example 4.3(a)

Currency Conversion from Canadian Dollar (C$) to US$

Based on the exchange rates provided in Table 4.3 (Currency Cross-rate Table), how many US dollars would you receive when you convert C$400?

Solution

From the cross-rate table, US$1 = C$1.0273

$$\text{US\$} : \text{C\$} = \text{US\$} : \text{C\$}$$

$$1 : 1.0273 = x : 400$$

$$\frac{1}{1.0273} = \frac{x}{400}$$ Cross-multiplying and solving for x, we obtain,

$$x = \frac{400}{1.0273} = 389.370193... = \text{US\$}389.37$$

Therefore, you will receive US$389.37 when you convert C$400.00.

Example 4.3(b)

Currency Conversion from C$ to US$ and from US$ to C$

If US$1 = C$1.0273 then (i) how much will you receive if you convert US$1000 to Canadian dollars and (ii) how much will you receive if you convert C$1000 to US dollars?

Solution

(i)

$$\text{US\$} : \text{C\$} = \text{US\$} : \text{C\$}$$

$$1 : 1.0273 = 1000 : x$$

$$\frac{1}{1.0273} = \frac{1000}{x}$$ Cross-multiplying and solving for x, we obtain,

$$x = \text{C\$}1027.30$$

Therefore, you will receive C$1027.30 when you convert US$1000.00.

Solution continued

(ii)

$$US\$: C\$ = US\$: C\$$$

$$1 : 1.0273 = x : 1000$$

$$\frac{1}{1.0273} = \frac{x}{1000}$$ Cross-multiplying and solving for x, we obtain,

$$x = 973.425484... = US\$973.43$$

Therefore, you will receive US$973.43 when you convert C$1000.00.

Example 4.3(c)

Converting from One Currency to Another Currency, Given Exchange Rates

Samantha is travelling from Canada to London on vacation. If £1 = C$1.6414 then how much would she receive if she converted C$1000 to British pounds?

Solution

$$£ : C\$ = £ : C\$$$

$$1 : 1.6414 = x : 1000$$

$$\frac{1}{1.6414} = \frac{x}{1000}$$ Cross-multiplying and solving for x, we obtain,

$$x = 609.236018... = £609.24$$

Therefore, she will receive £609.24 when she converts C$1000.00.

Example 4.3(d)

Series of Currency Conversions

If US$1 = C$1.0273 and C$1 = A$1.0621, calculate the amount of US dollars you will receive with 100 Australian dollars.

Solution

First, find out how many Canadian dollars you can get with A$100.

$$C\$: A\$ = C\$: A\$$$

$$1 : 1.0621 = x : 100$$

$$\frac{1}{1.0621} = \frac{x}{100}$$ Cross-multiplying and solving for x, we obtain,

$$x = C\$94.153092...$$

Now, find out how many US dollars you can get with C$94.153092...

$$US\$: C\$ = US\$: C\$$$

$$1 : 1.0273 = x : 94.153092...$$

$$\frac{1}{1.0273} = \frac{x}{94.153092...}$$ Cross-multiplying and solving for x, we obtain,

$$x = 91.651020... = US\$91.65$$

Therefore, you will receive US$91.65 when you convert A$100.00.

Example 4.3(e)

Series of Currency Conversions and Converting Back to the Original Currency

Martha, a globe trotter, traveled from Canada to the US with C$3000 as backup cash. In the US, she converted this amount to US dollars. From there, she traveled to Japan. While in Japan, she converted her US dollars to Japanese yen. She finally returned to Canada and converted the Japanese yen to Canadian dollars.

(i) How many US dollars did she have as backup cash during her stay in the USA?

(ii) How many Japanese Yen did she have while she was in Japan?

(iii) Check to see if she received her original amount of C$3000 when she converted her Japanese Yen back to Canadian dollars.

Use these exchange rates: C$1 = US$0.9734, US$1 = ¥85.253, and C$1 = ¥82.988.

Solution

(i) How many US dollars did she have as backup cash during her stay in the USA?

$$\text{C\$} : \text{US\$} = \text{C\$} : \text{US\$}$$

$$1 : 0.9734 = 3000 : x$$

$$\frac{1}{0.9734} = \frac{3000}{x}$$ Cross-multiplying and solving for x, we obtain,

$$x = \text{US\$}2920.20$$

Therefore, she had US$2920.20 in the USA.

(ii) How many Japanese yen did she have while she was in Japan?

$$\text{US\$} : ¥ = \text{US\$} : ¥$$

$$1 : 85.253 = 2920.20 : x$$

$$\frac{1}{85.253} = \frac{2920.20}{x}$$ Cross-multiplying and solving for x, we obtain,

$$x = 248{,}955.8106 = ¥248{,}955.81$$

Therefore, she had ¥248,955.81 in Japan.

(iii) Check to see if she received her original amount of C$3000 when she converted her Japanese yen back to Canadian dollars.

$$\text{C\$} : ¥ = \text{C\$} : ¥$$

$$1 : 82.988 = x : 248{,}955.8106$$

$$\frac{1}{82.988} = \frac{x}{248{,}955.81}$$ Cross-multiplying and solving for x, we obtain,

$$x = 2999.901318... = \text{C\$}2999.90$$

Therefore, she would receive C$2999.90 in Canada.

Note: *The slight difference of C$0.10 is because of rounding every time she converts a currency.*

Buying and Selling Currencies

If you would like to convert currencies, you should go to a bank or other financial institution that is authorized to purchase and sell currencies. These financial institutions usually have different exchange rates for buying and selling currencies, which they call their buying rate and selling rate. They use the actual currency exchange rates and their rate of commission to create their own buying and selling rates for each currency. The commission is charged for their services on these transactions.

Example 4.3(f) **Currency Conversion Including Commission in Buying or Selling Currencies**

Sarah plans to travel to the US from Canada and approaches a local bank to purchase US$1000. Assume US$1 = C$1.0655 and the bank charges a commission of 0.75% to sell or buy US dollars.

(i) How much in Canadian dollars would Sarah have to pay for US$1000?

(ii) If Sarah changes her plan and wishes to convert US$1000 back to Canadian dollars, how much will she receive from the same bank, assuming the same exchange rate and the same commission rate?

Solution

(i) How much in Canadian dollars would she have to pay for US$1,000?

When you buy currencies, you will pay the converted amount and the financial institution's commission.

When calculating the buying or selling rate, it does not matter if you calculate the commission first and then convert the value, or vice-versa. You will always get the same answer.

$$\text{US\$} : \text{C\$} = \text{US\$} : \text{C\$}$$

$$1 : 1.0655 = 1000 : x$$

$$\frac{1}{1.0655} = \frac{1000}{x}$$ Cross-multiplying and solving for x, we obtain,

$x = \text{C\$}1065.50$ Amount in C$ before the bank's commission

$\text{US\$}1000 = \text{C\$}1065.50$

$0.0075 \times 1065.50 = + \text{C\$}7.99125$ Adding bank's 0.75% commission, we obtain,

$\text{Total} = \text{C\$}1073.49$ Amount that Sarah will pay the bank

Or

$$\text{C\$}1065.50\ (1 + 0.0075) = 1073.49125 = \text{C\$}1073.49$$

Therefore, Sarah would have to pay C$1073.49 for US$1000.00.

(ii) If Sarah changes her plan and wishes to convert US$1000 back to Canadian dollars, how much will she receive from the same bank, assuming the same exchange rate and the same commission rate?

$\text{US\$ } 1000 = \text{C\$}1065.50$ As calculated in (i)

$0.0075 \times 1065.50 = - \text{C\$}7.99125$ Subtracting 0.75% commission, we obtain,

$\text{Total} = \text{C\$}1057.51$ Amount the bank will pay Sarah

Or

$$\text{C\$}1065.50\ (1 - 0.0075) = 1057.50875 = \text{C\$}1057.51$$

Therefore, Sarah will receive C$1057.51 from the bank.

Example 4.3(g)

Calculating a Bank's Rate of Commission to Buy and Sell Currencies

A bank in Toronto has the following buying and selling rates against Canadian dollars:

Country	Currency name	Rate at which bank will buy from you	Rate at which bank will sell to you
Brazil	reals	0.54855	0.60629
South Africa	rand	0.13171	0.14557

(i) Calculate the rate of selling commission that the bank charges if you want to purchase 500 Brazilian reals. Exchange rate: R$1 = C$0.577426.

(ii) Calculate the rate of buying commission that the bank charges if you want to sell 2000 South African rands. Exchange rate: 1 rand = C$0.138647.

Solution

(i) **500 Brazilian reals**

Purchasing R$500 from the bank based on the bank's selling rate:

$$500 \times 0.60629 = \text{C\$}303.145$$

It would cost C$303.15 based on the bank's selling rate.

Although exchange rates may be the same, the buying and selling rates may be different at different financial institutions because of varying commissions.

Purchasing R$500 based on the exchange rate,

$$\text{R\$} : \text{C\$} = \text{R\$} : \text{C\$}$$

$$1 : 0.577426 = 500 : x$$

$$\frac{1}{0.577426} = \frac{500}{x}$$ Cross-multiplying and solving for x, we obtain,

Solution *continued*

$$x = \text{C\$}288.713$$

It would cost C$288.71 based on the exchange rate.

Therefore, the bank's commission is C$303.15 − C$288.71 = C$14.44

Using $R = \frac{P}{B}$, $\text{Rate of commission} = \frac{\text{Amount of Commission in C\$}}{\text{Amount based on exchange rate in C\$}}$

$$\text{Rate of commission} = \frac{14.44}{288.71} \times 100\% = 5.001558...\%$$

Therefore, the bank's selling commission rate is 5.00%.

(ii) 2000 South African rands

Selling 2000 rands based on the bank's rate:

$$2000 \times 0.13171 = \text{C\$}263.42$$

You would receive C$263.42 according to the bank's rate.

Selling 2000 rands based on the exchange rate:

$$\text{rand} : \text{C\$} = \text{rand} : \text{C\$}$$

$$1 : 0.138647 = 2000 : x$$

$$\frac{1}{0.138647} = \frac{2000}{x}$$ Cross-multiplying and solving for x, we obtain,

$$x = \text{C\$}277.294$$

You would receive C$277.29 according to the exchange rate.

Therefore, the bank's commission is C$277.29 − C$263.42 = C$13.87

Using $R = \frac{P}{B}$, $\text{Rate of commission} = \frac{\text{Amount of Commission in C\$}}{\text{Amount based on exchange rate in C\$}}$

$$\text{Rate of commission} = \frac{13.87}{277.29} \times 100\% = 5.001983...\%$$

Therefore, the bank's buying commission rate is 5.00%.

Currency Appreciation and Depreciation

The value of a currency can increase or decrease relative to the value of another currency.

For example, the exchange rate on March 1, 2009 was C$1 = US$0.78370. This means that on March 1, 2009 you could buy US$0.78 with C$1.

However, on March 1, 2010, the exchange rate changed to C$1 = US$0.9510. This means that on March 1, 2010 you could buy US$0.95 with C$1.

As you were able to purchase more US dollars with C$1 in 2010 than in 2009, the value of the Canadian currency strengthened or appreciated relative to the US currency in one year, or the value of the US currency weakened or depreciated relative to the Canadian currency in one year.

Understanding the Effect of Currency Appreciation and Depreciation

When the Canadian dollar appreciates in value compared to other currencies:

- It is cheaper for Canadian businesses to import from foreign countries and the consumer will benefit as the price on imported goods will drop.
- Export of goods to foreign countries and the demand for Canadian goods and services will decrease as foreign countries receive less money when exchanging their currencies.

When a currency appreciates, consumers will pay less for foreign goods and services. When a currency depreciates, consumers will pay more for foreign goods and services.

When the Canadian dollar depreciates in value compared to other countries:

- It is cheaper for foreign businesses to import more goods from Canadian businesses. It will cost more money for Canadian businesses to import goods from foreign countries and therefore, consumers will pay more for imported goods.
- When more Canadian goods are exported, the country must produce more goods and the employment rate will increase.

Example 4.3(h) **Application of Exchange Rate Fluctuation**

A large chocolate distributor in Canada purchased chocolates from a supplier in Switzerland last year for CHF100,000 when the exchange rate between the Canadian dollar and the Swiss franc was C$0.98940 = CHF1. This year they wanted to make a similar purchase as the price of the chocolates did not change in Swiss francs, however, the exchange rate changed to C$1.02570 = CHF1.

(i) Calculate the increase or decrease in the cost of the chocolates in Canadian dollars.

(ii) Which currency appreciated relative to the other?

Solution

(i) Cost of chocolates in Canadian dollars last year:

$$\text{C\\$} : \text{CHF} = \text{C\\$} : \text{CHF}$$

$$0.98940 : 1 = x : 100{,}000$$

$$\frac{0.98940}{1} = \frac{x}{100{,}000}$$

Cross-multiplying and solving for x, we obtain,

$$x = \text{C\\$}98{,}940.00$$

Cost of chocolates in Canadian dollars this year:

$$\text{C\\$} : \text{CHF} = \text{C\\$} : \text{CHF}$$

$$1.02570 : 1 = x : 100{,}000$$

$$\frac{1.02570}{1} = \frac{x}{100{,}000}$$

Cross-multiplying and solving for x, we obtain,

$$x = \text{C\\$}102{,}570.00$$

The cost of the chocolates have increased by 102,570 – 98,940 = C$3630.00

(ii) From the two exchange rates we see that this year you can purchase more Canadian dollars with 1 Swiss franc; therefore, the value of the Swiss franc has appreciated relative to the value of the Canadian dollar.

Importing Goods from Another Country

When you import an item, the authorities at the border will convert the value of the goods to the local currency based on current exchange rates and may impose an import duty or customs duty, which is the tax a government charges on imported goods. In addition to providing revenue for the government, import duties help to protect domestic trade from overseas products. Import duties vary depending on the product and/or the country of origin.

Importing goods to Canada are almost always subject to import duty and is normally charged on the converted rate in Canadian dollars. GST (Goods and Services Tax), PST (Provincial Sales Tax), or HST (Harmonized Sales Tax) will then be charged on the total value of the goods including duty.

Higher duties are applied on certain types of products as well as items of luxury or high-dollar value.

Example 4.3(i) **Calculating Cost of Importing Goods from Another Country**

Robert, who resides in Toronto, drove down to Buffalo, USA on Black Friday to purchase a leather jacket at a discounted price. He paid US$650 (including taxes) for the jacket that costs C$800 (including taxes) in Canada. While driving back into Canada, the customs authorities at the border charged a duty of 18% for the jacket. He also paid 13% HST on the amount after the duty was applied. Calculate the total amount he spent on the jacket and determine if it worked out to be cheaper for him to drive down to Buffalo to purchase this jacket. Assume US$1 = C$1.0655.

Solution

USD : CAD = USD : CAD

$1 : 1.0655 = 650 : x$

$$\frac{1}{1.0655} = \frac{650}{x}$$

$x =$ C$692.575 Value of the jacket in C$ based on the given exchange rate

Value of the jacket	= C$692.575	
Add 18% duty	= C$124.6635	(18% × 692.575) Amount of duty
Value including duty	= C$817.2385	
Add 13% HST	= C$106.241	(13% × 817.2385) Amount of HST
Total cost	= C$923.48	

Total cost including duty and HST:
650 (1.0655) (1.18) (1.13) = 923.48
$692.575
$817.23
$923.48

Therefore, the total amount he paid for the jacket was C$923.48.

It was more expensive for him to purchase the leather jacket from Buffalo. He would have saved C$123.48, plus the time and other costs related to driving down to Buffalo if he had bought the jacket in Canada.

4.3 | Exercises

1. How much would you receive if you convert the following:
   a. CHF200 to British pounds (£) b. C$3000 to US dollars (US$)
   c. US$5000 to Canadian dollars (C$) d. £10 to Canadian dollars (C$)
   Assume that the current exchange rates are:
   £1 = CHF1.6565, US$1 = C$1.0273, £1 = C$1.6414

2. How much would you receive if you convert the following:
   a. C$18,000 to Japanese yen (¥) b. US$2850 to Swiss francs (CHF)
   c. £18 to Swiss francs (CHF) d. CHF850,933 to Canadian dollars (C$)
   Assume that the current exchange rates are:
   ¥1 = C$0.012050, CHF1 = US$1.0367, £1 = CHF1.6565, CHF1 = C$0.9909

3. A Bank in Toronto charges 2.5% commission to buy and sell currencies.
   a. How many Canadian dollars would you have to pay to purchase US$1500?
   b. How much commission in Canadian dollars (C$) would you pay the bank for the above transaction?
   Assume that the current exchange rate is US$1 = C$1.0273.

4. A Bank in London, Ontario charges 2.25% commission to buy and sell currencies.
   a. How many Canadian dollars would you receive from the bank if you sell US$1375?
   b. How much commission would you pay the bank for this transaction?
   Assume that the current exchange rate is US$1 = C$1.0273.

5. Hailey found US$100 in her attic and sold it to a bank that charged her a commission of 0.25%. How much did she receive from the bank? Assume that the exchange rate was C$1 = US$0.9734.

6. Jo Ann's mother sent her ¥50,000 as a graduation gift and she wanted to convert the Japanese yen into Canadian dollars. If the commission the bank was charging was 0.90%, calculate how many Canadian dollars she received. Assume that the exchange rate was C$1 = ¥82.988.

7. Ronald planned to travel to Australia from Canada and purchased 5000 Australian dollars. A week later, he decided to cancel his trip and wanted to convert his Australian dollars back to Canadian dollars at the same bank. Did he lose any money by converting the money twice? If so, how much did he lose? Assume that the bank charged a commission of 0.5% to sell and 0.75% to buy currencies. Assume that the exchange rate was C$1 = A$1.0621.

8. Emma-Lee purchased US$10,000 from a bank in America, which charged her a commission of 0.80%, and sold the US dollars to a bank in Canada, which charged her a 0.25% commission. How much money did she lose or gain? Assume that the exchange rate was C$1 = US$0.9734.

9. If C$1 = ¥82.988 and ¥1 = US$0.011730, how many Canadian dollars would you receive with US$1000?

10. If C$1 = £0.6462 and £1 = US$1.5075, how many Canadian dollars would you receive with US$1000?

11. Bernie, a senior sales representative at a multinational company, travelled from Canada to Japan via the UK. He left Canada with C$8000. When he reached the UK he converted all his cash to British pounds. The conversion rate was £1 = C$1.5475. After spending £1000, he left for Japan where he converted the remaining British pounds to Japanese yen at an exchange rate of ¥1 = £0.007262. He spent ¥125,400 in Japan and finally returned to Canada. Based on the information in this question, calculate the number of Canadian dollars he received when he converted the remaining Japanese yen to Canadian dollars.

12. Kristin saved up C$3000 to use for her travels during her summer holidays. She first travelled from Toronto to Switzerland, where she converted all her Canadian dollars to Swiss francs at an exchange rate of C$1 = CHF1.0468. She spent CHF1652 and then travelled to London, where she converted the remaining Swiss francs to British pounds at an exchange rate of CHF1 = £0.6170. She spent £870.34 in London before returning to Toronto. How many Canadian dollars did she receive when she converted the remaining British pounds to Canadian dollars?

13. A bank in London, Ontario has a selling rate of £1 = C$1.6544. If the exchange rate is £1 = C$1.5756, calculate the rate of commission that the bank charges.

14. A bank in London, Ontario has a buying rate of CHF1 = C$1.0206. If the exchange rate is CHF1 = C$1.0468, calculate the rate of commission that the bank charges.

15. The following table provides you with exchange rates of different currencies on January 01, 2009 and January 01, 2010.

January 01, 2009	January 01, 2010
C$1 = US$0.82080	US$1 = C$1.0505
C$1 = US$0.82080	US$1 = C$1.0505
C$1 = €0.58460	€1 = C$1.8092
C$1 = £0.6075	£1 = C$1.6414

Did the Canadian dollar appreciate or depreciate relative to (a) US dollar (US$), (b) Euro (€), or (c) British pound (£) over the one year period? Explain your answer.

16. The following table provides you with exchange rates of different currencies on January 02, 2009 and January 04, 2010.

January 02, 2009	January 04, 2010
C$1 = A$1.17365	A$1 = C$0.94132
C$1 = ¥72.9880	¥1 = C$0.0127
C$1 = CHF0.9552	CHF1 = C$0.9909

Did the Canadian dollar appreciate or depreciate relative to (a) Australian dollar (A$), (b) Japanese yen (¥), or (c) Swiss franc (CHF) over the one year period? Explain your answer.

17. Helix, a motorbike manufacturer in Canada, has two paint suppliers – one is in the USA and the other is in Mexico. This month, the value of the Canadian currency appreciated relative to the US dollar but remained the same relative to the Mexican peso. If the paint suppliers did not change the price of the paint, in which country could he purchase more paint for the same amount of Canadian dollars and why?

18. Bob, a resident of Canada, was contemplating purchasing a motorbike from either the USA or Mexico. The cost of the bike, including shipment and taxes, after converting to Canadian dollars was the same whether purchased in the USA or Mexcio. A month later, the Canadian currency depreciated against the Mexican peso but remained the same relative to the US dollar. Where do you think he would get the bike cheaper and why?

19. If the Canadian dollar appreciated by US$0.0025 relative to the US dollar, what would be the new value of the Canadian dollar per US dollar? Assume that the current exchange rate is US$1 = C$1.0325.

20. If the US dollar depreciated by C$0.015 relative to the Canadian dollar, what would be the new value of the US dollar per Canadian dollar? Assume that the current exchange rate is C$1 = US$0.9875.

21. A Canadian businesswoman purchased an all-in-one printer for ¥80,000 while in Japan on business. On returning to Canada, she had to pay 15% customs duty, 5% GST, and 8% PST. What was the total cost of the printer in Canadian dollars if the exchange rate was ¥1 = C$0.008560?

22. What would it cost, in Canadian dollars, to import a set of Swiss skis priced at CHF850 and subject to an import duty of 10% and 13% HST if the exchange rate is CHF1 = C$0.7954?

23. A wholesaler in Ontario purchased a shipment of fruits from Australia for A$15,000. If his shipment was subject to customs duty of 5% and 13% HST, calculate the total cost of the shipment to the wholesaler in Ontario. Assume that the exchange rate was C$1 = A$1.0621.

24. Noah, who lives in Vancouver, British Columbia, purchased a yacht from Australia for A$535,280. He was charged 18% duty, and 12% HST to bring it home. Calculate the total amount he spent on the yacht. Assume that the exchange rate was C$1 = A$1.11401.

• 25. Harris drove down to the US and purchased an expensive set of golf clubs for US$900. While driving back into Canada, he had to pay 18% customs duty and 13% HST on the clubs. Calculate the total amount he paid for the clubs. If a similar set of clubs cost C$1000 plus 13% HST here in Canada, was it cheaper for him to buy it from the US? Assume that the exchange rate was US$1 = C$1.05214.

• 26. Joanne purchased a laptop from Los Angeles, California for US$1200 and brought it back with her to Toronto. At the US-Canada border, she was asked to pay customs duty of 14% on the laptop. In addition, she had to pay 13% HST. If the same model of laptop was available in Toronto for C$1500, was it cheaper for her to purchase the laptop from the US? Assume that the current exchange rate was US$1 = C$1.05214.

4 | Review Exercises

Answers to odd-numbered problems are available at the end of the textbook

1. Christopher, an investment banker, invests all his yearly earnings in stocks of high-tech, mining, and garment industries in the ratio of 2 : 5 : 7, respectively. Calculate his investment in mining stocks if his investment in high-tech stocks was $18,540.

2. The ratio of the driving distance from London to Hamilton, Mississauga, and Toronto is 3 : 4 : 5 ,respectively. If the distance from London to Hamilton is 125 km, calculate the distance from London to Mississauga and from London to Toronto.

3. Three college classmates, Sandra, Meghan, and Bob decided to start a small business and invest $1000, $2500, and $3500, respectively. If Bob decided to leave the business, how much did Sandra and Meghan have to pay for Bob's shares if they wanted to maintain their initial investment ratio?

4. Anthony decided to build a shopping complex with his two brothers Adrian and Andrew. They invested $200,000, $860,400, and $750,000, respectively. After the complex was built, Adrian decided to sell his share of the investment to Anthony and Andrew. How much did each of them have to pay if they wanted to maintain the same ratio of their investments in the complex?

5. If Lillian, a graphic designer, receives an annual salary of $55,000, calculate her weekly salary using pro-rations. Assume that there are 52 weeks in a year.

6. As the CFO of a technology company, every year, Tyler would receive 26 bi-weekly payments of $6000 each. Calculate his monthly salary.

• 7. If the ratio of sugar to flour in a pie is 2 : 3 and that of flour to salt is 2 : 1, calculate the ratio of sugar : flour : salt in the pie.

• 8. If the ratio of sales people to marketing people in an organization is 5 : 4 and the ratio of marketing people to finance people is 5 : 2, what is the ratio of sales people : marketing people : finance people in the organization?

9. Owen, Jamie, and Wayne invested a total of $800 in the ratio of 3 : 4 : 5 , respectively, to purchase a billiards table for their club house. After the table was delivered, each invested an additional $200 to purchase balls and cue sticks. Calculate their new investment ratio after their additional investment.

10. Gregory, his wife, and his mother jointly purchased an estate for $1,350,000. Their individual investments in the estate were in the ratio of 5 : 3 : 1 , respectively. Each of them decided to invest an additional $250,000 to develop the estate into a small family resort. Calculate their new investment ratio after the additional investment.

11. Dustin and Gina were classmates who graduated together from college. Dustin found a job as a banker that pays him $189 for 9 hours and Gina found a job as a freelance artist that pays her $174 for 8 hours of work. Who is being paid a higher hourly rate and by how much is it higher than the other person's hourly rate?

12. Jeffrey purchased a racing motorbike and Chris purchased a cruising motorbike. Jeffery travelled 765 km from Toronto to New York City and covered this journey in 8 hours and 20 minutes. Chris travelled for 165 km from Toronto to Buffalo in 2 hours and 10 minutes. Based on this information, whose average speed was greater and by how much is it greater (in km/hr) than the other person's average speed?

13. Lena, Maxwell, and Calvin invested $3750, $8000, and $6250, respectively, to start video production studio. The company did very well in the first year and they wanted to invest an additional $5250 to expand their business. How much did each of them have to individually invest to maintain their original investment ratio?

14. Dravid, an investment banker, invested $5000, $4300, and $3600 in stocks of three different companies. The market showed potential to grow so he decided to invest an additional $2000 in stocks of the same companies. How did he invest

this amount into stocks of the three companies to maintain the original investment ratio?

15. A bank in Vancouver, British Columbia has a selling rate of €1 = C$1.3949. If the exchange rate is €1 = C$1.3285, calculate the rate of commission that the bank charges.

16. A bank in Calgary, Alberta has a buying rate of ¥1 = C$0.0116171. If the exchange rate is ¥1 = C$0.0122286, calculate the rate of commission that the bank charges to buy currencies.

• 17. A software company in Canada outsourced 20 software development projects to Malaysia for 30,500 Malaysian ringgits (RM) last year. How many projects could they outsource this year for the same amount of Canadian dollars they spent last year if the cost to do the job remained the same but the exchange rate changed from C$1 = RM3.0425 last year to C$1 = RM2.8045 this year. Assume that each of the projects has the same value.

• 18. A telecommunication company in Vancouver hired an outsourced support team of 50 people from Italy. They paid them a total of €20,000 per person last year. If the exchange rate changed from C$1 = €0.7527 to C$1 = €0.6827 this year, calculate the number of people the telecommunication company could afford to hire for the support job. Assume that the cost to hire the people remained the same and the telecommunication company's yearly budget to hire people this year was the same as last year.

• 19. Ellen bought clothes from Los Angeles, California for US$1500 when the exchange rate was C$1 = U$0.9481. She then returned to Toronto and had to pay customs duty of 14% and HST of 13% on the clothes at the Canadian-US border based on that day's exchange rate of C$1 = US$0.9589. Calculate the total amount she spent on the clothes in Canadian dollars.

• 20. Alexandria went to Florida and purchased a laptop for US$650 when the exchange rate was C$1 = U$0.9485. After a month, she returned to Vancouver but the exchange rate fluctuated and was C$1 = US$0.9589 on the day of her return. At the border she paid customs duty of 14% and HST of 13% on the laptop based on that day's exchange rate. Calculate the total amount she spent on the laptop in Canadian dollars.

4 | Self-Test Exercises

Answers to all problems are available at the end of the textbook

1. If the Canadian dollar appreciated by C$0.0050 relative to the US dollar, what would be the new value of the Canadian dollar per US dollar? Assume the current exchange rate was US$1 = C$1.04354.

• 2. Zain and Cassie invested equal amounts of money in a business. A year later, Zain withdrew $10,000 making the ratio of their investments 3 : 5. How much money did each of them invest in the beginning?

3. If C$1 = ¥82.98755 and ¥1 = US$0.011729, how many Canadian dollars would you receive with US$1000?

4. For every $30 that a not-for-profit foundation transferred to a relief fund, the Government donated $10 towards the same cause. After 2 months of fund raising, the foundation had a total of $8500 including the Government's contribution. Calculate the amount donated by the Government.

5. Henry had a plan of a house he was building. If the scale ratio was 1 : 75 (i.e. the ratio of the measurements in the plan to the actual size was 1 : 75), calculate the width of the garage door, if it measured 5.75 cm on the plan.

• 6. Andrew's earnings to Bill's was in the ratio 5 : 6 and Bill's to Cathy's was in the ratio 5 : 7. What was the ratio of the earnings of Andrew : Bill : Cathy?

7. Antonio paid a yearly subscription amount of $250 to receive a business magazine monthly. After receiving two issues, he cancelled his subscription. Calculate the pro-rated refund he should receive from the magazine company.

8. After Georgia's grandfather died, she received his currency collection. She decided to sell the US$40 to a bank when the exchange rate was C$1 = US$0.9324. The bank charged her a commission of 0.35%. How much did she receive from the bank in Canadian dollars?

• 9. Russel who lives in Halifax, Nova Scotia purchased a dining table set from Brazil for 800 Brazilian reals (R$). At the Canadian border, he was charged 18% duty and 15% HST to bring the table back home. Calculate the total amount he spent on the dining table. The exchange rate was C$1 = R$1.70265.

10. Cheryl, a student at a college in Toronto, decided to travel to Switzerland and purchased CHF750 from her bank. However, two weeks later she canceled her trip and converted the Swiss Francs back to Canadian dollars at the same bank. Did she lose any money by converting the money twice? If so, how much did she lose? Assume C$1 = CHF0.9909 and that the bank charged a commission of 0.25% to sell and buy currencies.

CASE 4

Applying Ratios in Business

Lana, Ann, and Cecilia, three budding entrepreneurs formed a partnership to start a Belgian waffle restaurant in Toronto. They required funds to lease a place, hire staff, and purchase equipment and furniture. Their initial investments were in the ratio of 5 : 7 : 11, respectively and Ann's contribution was $14,700. Once the restaurant was ready for business, at the suggestion of Cecilia, the marketing specialist in the team, each of them contributed an additional $6300 for marketing and advertising expenses.

During the initial stage of operation of the restaurant, additional funds for miscellaneous expenses (repairs, maintenance, etc.) were required and the three partners decided to raise their total investment in their partnership to $87,400 while maintaining their original proportionate partnership. Also, the partners agreed that half of the annual profit shall be shared equally and the other half be shared in the ratio of their original investments. At the end of the first year, the total profit was $36,225.

Lana converted one-third of her profits to British pounds (£) and saved the balance in her bank in Toronto. Ann converted two-fifths of her profits to Swiss francs (CHF) and saved the balance in her bank in Toronto. Cecilia drove down to New York City and spent an amount equivalent to US$3000, including service charges, on clothes and designer accessories. On her return to Toronto, she converted the rest to Euros (€) at her bank and went on a vacation to France.

Assume the following exchange rates in answering the following:
C$1 = US$0.95756, C$1 = £0.6107, C$1 = CHF0.9939, C$1 = €0.7455

a. Calculate the amount initially invested by Lana and Cecilia.

b. Find the investment ratio of the three partners after their contributions for marketing and advertising expenses.

c. Calculate the amount contributed by each partner for miscellaneous expenses that was necessary to raise their total investment to $87,400 and to maintain the original proportionate partnership of 5 : 7 : 11?

d. What was the share of the profits of each partner?

e. How much did Lana save in British pounds and Ann save in Swiss francs, if the bank charged a commission of 0.75% for each transaction?

f. After 2 months, if the British pound appreciated by 10% relative to the Canadian dollar and Swiss Francs depreciated by 10% relative to the Canadian dollar, what was the equivalent value of money in Canadian dollars that Lana and Ann converted to British pounds and Swis francs, respectively.

g. On her return from New York, at the Canadian-US border, Cecilia paid 18% customs duty and 13% HST on the goods that she purchased. What was the total cost of her clothes and accessories in Canadian dollars? Note: HST is calculated on the amount that includes import duty.

h. How many Euros did Cecilia receive when she converted the balance of her profits if the bank's commission was 2%?

Have you ever wondered why prices of items sold at wholesalers like 'Costco' and 'Wal-Mart' are cheaper than prices of the same items sold at a convenience store, or why prices of items are cheaper online than at retail outlets, or how a 'Dollar Store' manages to sell items for a very cheap price? Large distributors buy directly from manufacturers to reduce the cost of the product offered to consumers. Online stores have less overhead expenses, employee time, storage costs, etc., which enable them to pass on the savings to customers. Although stores like the 'Dollar Store' make small profits on each item sold, they make high overall profits by selling large quantities of items. Pricing responsibilities such as these, and many more, lie in the hands of a seasoned merchandiser. This chapter will provide you with the basic analytical skills and terminology used in retail management that a merchandiser should possess to make intelligent business decisions.

5 Mathematics of Merchandising

LEARNING OBJECTIVES

- Solve problems involving a single trade discount rate, series of trade discount rates, and an equivalent discount rate for a series of trade discount rates.
- Solve problems involving cash discounts for full and partial payments.
- Calculate the amount of markup and rate of markup on the cost and selling price of items.
- Calculate the amount of markdown and rate of markdown on the selling price of items.
- Understand the application of markup and markdown in calculating profit or loss.

CHAPTER OUTLINE

5.1 | Introduction

Merchandising is a process that involves the buying and selling of goods (merchandise) from the manufacturer, to the final sale of those goods to the consumers. The process can include discounting, promoting, advertising, etc. Typically, manufactured goods are sold to consumers through a chain of distributors, wholesalers, and retailers. This is called a merchandising chain or distribution chain.

Merchandising is an essential part of commerce and involves the buying and selling of goods.

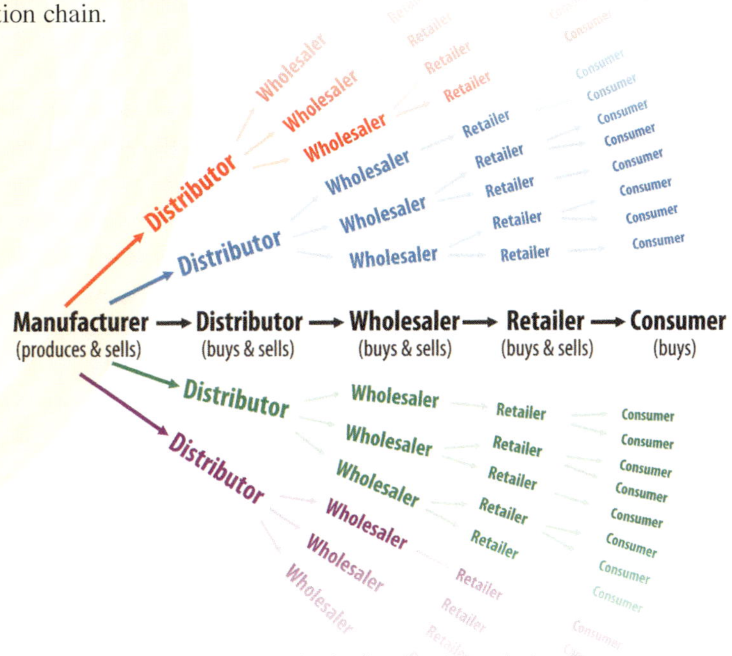

Note

- The illustration above is a typical distribution chain for most organizations. Some organizations may skip one or two members in this chain. For example, in some organizations, retailers may obtain goods directly from the manufacturer while in others, distributors may act as wholesalers and supply directly to retailers.
- Each manufacturer could have numerous distributors, wholesalers, retailers, or consumers located locally or in different countries depending on the type and nature of the organization, product, and consumer.
- Each member in this chain makes profits, except the consumer, as the consumer is only a buyer and not a seller.

Having fewer members in the distribution chain will usually result in a lower selling price of the product to the consumers.

- The selling price of a product at each stage of the distribution chain depends on many factors such as demand, competition, the cost of the product, operating costs, or the profit necessary to stay in business.

5.2 | Trade Discounts

The ***list price*** is the price quoted by a supplier for a product.

Manufacturers usually determine the price at which a product can be sold to the consumer. This is called the manufacturer's suggested retail price (MSRP), catalogue price, or **list price**.

A ***trade discount*** is a reduction on the list price of a product.

When a manufacturer sells the product to the distributor, the manufacturer deducts a certain amount from their list price, usually a percentage of the list price. This is known as a **trade discount**.

The ***net price*** is the price of a product after deducting trade discounts from the list price.

The distributor in turn gives a trade discount on their list price to the wholesaler and the wholesaler gives a trade discount to the retailer. The price each of them pays for the product after the trade discount is called their **net price** ***(N)***.

As the product goes through the distribution chain, the trade discount becomes smaller and smaller. Trade discounts are generally offered to increase sales, to reward valuable customers, to encourage large quantity purchases, to promote a new or seasonal product, etc.

Single Trade Discount

When one discount is offered by the seller to the buyer, it is called a single trade discount. The amount of trade discount is calculated by multiplying the single trade discount rate (d) and the list price (L).

$$\textit{Amount of trade discount} = \textit{Trade discount rate } (d) \times \textit{List price } (L)$$

This can be written as the following formula:

Formula 5.2(a)

Amount of Trade Discount

$$\textit{Amount of trade discount} = d \times L$$

Trade discount rate,

$$d = \frac{\textit{Amount of trade discount } (d \times L)}{\textit{List price } (L)}$$

The net price (N) is calculated by subtracting the amount of trade discount ($d \times L$) from the list price (L).

$$\textit{Net price } (N) = \textit{List Price } (L) - \textit{Amount of trade discount } (d \times L)$$

$$N = L - d \times L$$

Taking the common factor 'L', results in the follwoing formula for Net Price,

Formula 5.2(b)

Net Price

$$N = L(1 - d)$$

Note: $(1 - d)$ is the complement of the discount rate (d). It is known as the Net Cost Factor (NCF). The NCF is the percentage of the list price that has to be paid by the buyer.

$$NCF = 100\% - \textit{discount}\% = (1 - d)$$

Therefore, the Net Price can also be calculated by multiplying the list price by the complement of the discount rate (or NCF).

$$N = L(1 - d)$$

$$N = L(NCF)$$

Example 5.2(a)

Calculating the Amount of Trade Discount and Net Price

The list price of an item is \$640. The trade discount is 20%. Calculate the amount of trade discount and the net price of the item.

Solution

$L = \$640.00, \quad d = 20\% = 0.20$

$$\textit{Amount of trade discount} = d \times L$$

$$= 640.00 \times 0.20 = \$128.00$$

$$\textit{Net Price, } N = \textit{List price } (L) - \textit{Amount of trade discount } (d \times L)$$

$$= 640.00 - 128.00 = \$512.00$$

Solution continued

Or

$$\textit{Net Price}, N = L(1 - d) = 640.00(1 - 0.20)$$
$$= 640.00 \times 0.80 = \$512.00$$

$$\textit{Amount of trade discount} = \textit{List price}\ (L) - \textit{Net price}\ (N)$$
$$= 640.00 - 512.00 = \$128.00$$

Therefore, the amount of trade discount is $128.00 and the net price of the item is $512.00.

Example 5.2(b)

Calculating the List Price and Amount of Trade Discount

After a 40% trade discount, the net price of an item is $420. Calculate the list price of the item, and the amount of trade discount?

Solution

$d = 40\% = 0.40, \quad N = \$420.00, \quad L = ?$

Using Formula 5.2(b), $N = L(1 - d)$ Rearranging, we obtain,

Rearranging, $$L = \frac{N}{(1-d)} = \frac{420.00}{(1-0.40)} = \frac{420.00}{(0.60)} = \$700.00$$

Using Formula 5.2(a), $$\textit{Amount of trade discount} = d \times L$$
$$= 0.40 \times 700.00 = \$280.00$$

Or

$$\textit{Amount of trade discount} = L - N$$
$$= 700.00 - 420.00 = \$280.00$$

Therefore, the list price of the item is $700.00 and the amount of trade discount is $280.00.

Example 5.2(c)

Calculating the List Price and Net Price

An item is purchased after a trade discount of 25% and the amount of trade discount received is $150. Calculate the list price and net price of the item.

Solution

$d = 25\% = 0.25, \quad d \times L = \$150.00, \quad L = ?, \quad N = ?$

Using Formula 5.2(a), $$\textit{Amount of trade discount} = d \times L$$

Rearranging, $$L = \frac{\textit{Amount of trade discount}\ (d \times L)}{d}$$

Substituting the values, $$L = \frac{150.00}{d} = \frac{150.00}{0.25} = \$600.00$$

Using Formula 5.2(b), $$N = L(1 - d) = 600.00(1 - 0.25)$$
$$= 600.00(0.75) = \$450.00$$

Or

$$N = \textit{List price} - \textit{Amount of trade discount}$$
$$= 600.00 - 150.00 = \$450.00$$

Therefore, the list price is $600.00 and the net price is $450.00.

Example 5.2(d)

Calculating the Trade Discount Rate

The list price is \$500 and the net price is \$400 for an item. What is the trade discount rate?

Solution

$L = \$500.00, \quad N = \$400.00, \quad d = ?$

$$\textit{Amount of trade discount} = L - N$$

$$\textit{Amount of trade discount} = 500.00 - 400.00 = \$100.00$$

$$d \times L = \$100.00$$

Substituting the values, $d = \frac{100.00}{L} = \frac{100.00}{500.00} = 0.20 = 20.00\%$

Or

Using Formula 5.2(b), $N = L(1 - d)$

Substituting the values, $400.00 = 500.00(1 - d)$

Expanding, $400.00 = 500.00 - 500.00(d)$

Rearranging, $500.00(d) = 500.00 - 400.00$

$$d = \frac{100.00}{500.00} = 0.20 = 20.00\%$$

Therefore, the trade discount rate is 20.00%.

Series of Trade Discounts

As explained earlier, trade discounts are provided for various reasons. At times, a buyer may qualify to receive more than one trade discount rate on the list price of a product. In which case, the buyer may be offered a series of trade discount rates (also known as multiple discount rates or chain discount rates). These series of trade discounts are always applied in sequence, one after the other; i.e., the second discount is applied on the amount after the first discount and the third discount is applied on the amount after the first and second discounts.

Series of trade discount rates are never added to get a single trade discount rate.

Trade discounts of 10% followed by 5%, and followed by 2%, are not equal to 17%

For example, 3 trade discounts: a 10% seasonal discount, a 5% large purchase discount, and a 2% new product discount were offered on a product listed at \$1000. If a buyer is eligible for all 3 trade discounts, then the net price and amount of discount is calculated as follows:

The series of trade discount rates are usually written as 10%, 5%, and 2%.

$\textit{Net price after the } 1^{st} \textit{ discount} = 1000(1 - 0.10) = 1000 \times 0.90 = \$900.00$

Similarly, $\textit{Net price after the } 2^{nd} \textit{ discount} = 900(1 - 0.05) = 900 \times 0.95 = \$855.00$

and, $\textit{Net price after the } 3^{rd} \textit{ discount} = 855(1 - 0.02) = 855 \times 0.98 = \$837.90$

Therefore, $\textit{Net price after the series of 3 trade discounts} = \$837.90$

and, $\textit{Amount of trade discount} = 1000.00 - 837.90 = \$162.10$

Example 5.2(e)

Calculating the Net Price of an Item After 2 Trade Discount Rates

A department store gives a standard trade discount of 10% and an additional trade discount of 5%, if purchases are made during weekdays. How much would you pay for an item worth \$800 from this store on Monday and what is the amount of the trade discount offered?

Solution

$\textit{Net price after the } 1^{st} \textit{ trade discount} = 800(1 - 0.10) = 800 \times 0.90 = \$720.00$

Similarly, $\textit{Net price after the } 2^{nd} \textit{ trade discount} = 720(1 - 0.05) = 720 \times 0.95 = \$684.00$

Solution continued

Therefore, $\textit{Amount of the trade discount} = \textit{List price} - \textit{Net price after } 2^{nd} \textit{ discount}$

$$= 800.00 - 684.00 = \$116.00$$

Therefore, you would pay \$684.00 for the item and the amount of trade discount offered is \$116.00.

Calculating the Net Price of an Item Using the Formula for a Series of Trade Discounts

Let the list price of an item be 'L' and the series of trade discounts be d_1, d_2, d_3, ... d_n.

$$\textit{Net price after the } 1^{st} \textit{ trade discount} = L(1 - d_1)$$

Similarly, $\textit{Net price after the } 2^{nd} \textit{ trade discount} = L(1 - d_1)(1 - d_2)$

and, $\textit{Net price after the } 3^{rd} \textit{ trade discount} = L(1 - d_1)(1 - d_2)(1 - d_3)$

and, $\textit{Net price after the } n^{th} \textit{ trade discount} = L(1 - d_1)(1 - d_2)(1 - d_3) \ldots (1 - d_n)$

Therefore, the formula for the net price after a series of trade discounts si show below:

Formula 5.2(c)

Net Price After a Series of Trade Discounts

$$N = L(1 - d_1)(1 - d_2)(1 - d_3) \ldots (1 - d_n)$$

Example 5.2(f)

Calculating the Net Price of an Item After a Series of Trade Discounts

A manufacturer gives the following 3 discounts on the \$1250 list price of an item: 15% for the end-of-season sale, 10% for a large quantity purchase, and 5% if you collect the item on your own. Calculate the net price of the item if one qualifies for all 3 discounts.

Solution

Using Formula 5.2(c), $N = L(1 - d_1)(1 - d_2)(1 - d_3)$

Substituting values, $N = 1250(1 - 0.15)(1 - 0.10)(1 - 0.05)$

$$N = \underbrace{\underbrace{\underbrace{1250(0.85)}_{\$1062.50}(0.90)}_{\$956.25}(0.95)}_{\$908.4375} = \$908.44$$

Therefore, the net price of the item is \$908.44.

Example 5.2(g)

Comparing the Net Price of Similar Items that Have Different List Prices and Trade Discounts

Rudolph Electronics offers an HDTV for \$3500 with two trade discounts of 30% and 5%. Best Electronics offers the same model of HDTV for \$3430 with two trade discounts of 20% and 15%. Which offer is cheaper and by how much?

Solution

Using Formula 5.2(c), $N = L(1 - d_1)(1 - d_2)(1 - d_3)$

Substituting values for Rudolph Electronics, $N_{\textit{Rudolph Electronics}} = 3500.00(1 - 0.30)(1 - 0.05)$

$$= 3500.00(0.70)(0.95)$$

$$= \$2327.50$$

Solution *continued*

Substituting values for Best Electronics,

$$N_{Best\ Electronics} = 3430.00(1 - 0.20)(1 - 0.15)$$
$$= 3430.00(0.80)(0.85)$$
$$= \$2332.40$$

The difference in price = 2332.40 − 2327.50 = \$4.90

Therefore, Rudolph Electronic's offer is \$4.90 cheaper than that of Best Electronics.

Example 5.2(h) **Matching the Net Price of Similar Items**

Store A sells a camera that is listed at \$300 with two trade discounts of 20% and 5%. Store B sells the same item listed at \$375 with one trade discount of 10%. What further trade discount must Store B offer to match the price of the camera available at Store A?

Solution

Method 1:

Using Formula 5.2(c),

$$N = L(1 - d_1)(1 - d_2)(1 - d_3)$$

Substituting values for Store A,

$$N_{Store\ A} = 300.00(1 - 0.20)(1 - 0.05)$$
$$= 300.00(0.80)(0.95) = \$228.00$$

Substituting values for Store B,

$$N_{Store\ B} = 375.00(1 - 0.10)$$
$$= 375.00(0.90) = \$337.50$$

Store B has to provide an additional trade discount of 337.50 − 228.00 = \$109.50

$$\textit{Additional discount rate} = \frac{109.50}{337.50} \times 100\% = 0.324444... = 32.44\%$$

Therefore, Store B should provide an additional trade discount of 32.44% to match the price of the camera available at Store A.

Method 2:

Let the additional discount offered by Store B be d%.

$$N_{Store\ A} \text{ after trade discounts of 20\% and 5\%} = N_{Store\ B} \text{ after trade discounts of 10\% and } d\%$$

$$300.00(1 - 0.20)(1 - 0.05) = 375.00(1 - 0.10)(1 - d)$$

Rearranging and solving for d,

$$228.00 = 337.50(1 - d)$$
$$228.00 = 337.50 - 337.50d$$
$$d = \frac{337.50 - 228.00}{337.50}$$
$$= 0.324444... = 32.44\%$$

Therefore, Store B should provide an additional trade discount of 32.44% to match the price of the camera available at Store A.

Single Equivalent Trade Discount Rate for a Series of Trade Discount Rates

As explained in the previous section on series of trade discount rates, we cannot simply add trade discount rates to get the single equivalent trade discount rate. We can, however, find a formula to calculate the single equivalent trade discount rate for a series of trade discount rates.

Let d_e be the single equivalent trade discount rate for a series of trade discount rates $d_1, d_2, d_3, \ldots d_n$.

From Formula 5.2(c), $N = L(1 - d_e)$

From Formula 5.2(d), $N = L(1 - d_1)(1 - d_2)(1 - d_3) \dots (1 - d_n)$

Equating the above 2 formulas, $L(1 - d_e) = L(1 - d_1)(1 - d_2)(1 - d_3) \dots (1 - d_n)$

Dividing by L on both sides, $(1 - d_e) = (1 - d_1)(1 - d_2)(1 - d_3) \dots (1 - d_n)$

Rearranging the above will result in the formula for a single equivalent trade discount rate to a series of trade discount rates:

Formula 5.2(d)

Single Equivalent Trade Discount Rate

$$d_e = 1 - (1 - d_1)(1 - d_2)(1 - d_3) \dots (1 - d_n)$$

Example 5.2(i)

Calculating a Single Equivalent Trade Discount Rate for a Series of Trade Discount Rates

If an item with a list price of $1,000 is discounted under a series of trade discounts of 10%, 5%, and 2%, what is the single equivalent trade discount rate that represents all these three trade discount rates?

Solution

Method 1: Using the Single Equivalent Trade Discount Rate Formula

From Formula 5.2(d) $d_e = 1 - (1 - d_1)(1 - d_2)(1 - d_3)$

Substituting values, $= 1 - (1 - 0.10)(1 - 0.05)(1 - 0.02)$

$= 0.1621 = 16.21\%$

Therefore, the single equivalent trade discount rate that represents the series of three trade discount rates is 16.21%.

Method 2: Using the Amount of Trade Discount And List Price

$L = \$1000.00$

From Formula 5.2(c), $N = L(1 - d_1)(1 - d_2)(1 - d_3)$

Substituting values, $= 1000.00(1 - 0.10)(1 - 0.05)(1 - 0.02)$

$= \$837.90$

So, Amount of trade discount $= L - D$

$= 1000.00 - 837.90 = \$162.10$

Trade discount rate, $d = \dfrac{\textit{Amount of trade discount } (d \times L)}{\textit{List price } (L)}$

$de = \dfrac{162.10}{1000.00} = 0.1621 = 16.21\%$

Therefore, the single equivalent trade discount rate that represents the series of three trade discount rates is 16.21%.

Method 3: Using the Net Price Formula for a Series of Trade Discounts and the Equivalent Single Trade Discount Rate

$L = \$1000.00$

For a series of trade discounts:

From Formula 5.2(c), $N = L(1 - d_1)(1 - d_2)(1 - d_3)$

Substituting values, $= 1000.00(1 - 0.10)(1 - 0.05)(1 - 0.02)$

$= \$837.90$

Solution continued

or the equivalent trade discount d_e:

From Formula 5.2(b) $N = L(1 - d_e)$

$= 1000.00(1 - d_e)$

Equating both equations, we obtain,

$$837.90 = 1000.00(1 - d_e)$$

Solving for d_e, $837.90 = 1000.00 - 1000.00(d_e)$

$$1000.00\, d_e = 1000.00 - 837.90$$

$$d_e = \frac{1000.00 - 837.50}{1000.00} = \frac{162.10}{1000.00} \times 100\% = 16.21\%$$

Therefore, the single equivalent trade discount rate that represents the series of three trade discount rates is 16.21%.

Example 5.2(j) **Comparing a Series of Trade Discount Rates to an Equivalent Trade Discount Rate**

Is the series of trade discounts of 30%, 20%, and $2\frac{1}{2}$% equivalent to a discount rate of $52\frac{1}{2}$%?

Solution

$$d_e = 1 - (1 - d_1)(1 - d_2)(1 - d_3)$$
$$= 1 - (1 - 0.30)(1 - 0.20)(1 - 0.025)$$
$$= 0.454 = 45.4\%$$

Therefore, the given series of trade discount rates is not equivalent to a trade discount rate of $52\frac{1}{2}$%.

5.2 | Exercises

Calculate the missing values for problems 1 to 4:

1.

	List Price (L)	Single Trade Discount Rate (d)	Amount of Trade Discount ($d \times L$)	Net Price (N)
a.	?	20%	\$375.00	?
b.	?	?	\$27.60	\$202.40
c.	\$800.00	?	?	\$368.00
d.	\$500.00	?	\$10.00	?

2.

	List Price (L)	Single Trade Discount Rate (d)	Amount of Trade Discount ($d \times L$)	Net Price (N)
a.	?	5%	\$50.50	?
b.	?	?	\$217.50	\$652.50
c.	\$12,600.00	?	?	\$630.00
d.	\$30,750.00	?	\$3843.75	?

3.

	List Price (L)	Series of Trade Discount Rates	Equivalent Trade Discount Rate (d_e)	Net Price (N)	Amount of Trade Discount ($d \times L$)
a.	$540.00	20%, 10%	?	?	?
b.	?	22%, 12.5%, 10%	?	?	$760.00
c.	?	$5\frac{1}{2}$%, 3%, 1%	?	$2512.00	?
d.	$1200.00	10%, 6%, d%	?	$984.74	?

4.

	List Price (L)	Series of Trade Discount Rates	Equivalent Trade Discount Rate (d_e)	Net Price (N)	Amount of Trade Discount ($d \times L$)
a.	$850.00	10%, 5%	?	?	?
b.	?	5%, 4%, 3%	?	?	$80.50
c.	?	$5\frac{1}{2}$%, 2%, 1%	?	$1854.50	?
d.	$625	5%, 4%, d%	?	$558.60	?

5. A distributor of golf shoes lists a new model of shoes in his store at $110 per pair. If he offers a trade discount rate of 15% on the shoes, calculate the amount of trade discount and net price his retailer would have to pay for each pair of shoes.

6. Harold Electrical Fans Inc., a manufacturer of cutting edge table fans, lists Model A fans that they plan to sell through the summer at $165 each. They provide a trade discount rate of 8% on this model to all their distributors. Calculate the amount of trade discount each distributor would receive and the net price of each fan.

7. An accounting software developer sold software to their distributors at $780 per package. If the trade discount rate offered on the product was 10.5%, calculate the list price of the product and the amount of discount each distributor received.

8. A distributor of batteries received the complete payment of $8560.50 against an invoice for a shipment of 10 automobile batteries that they sold to their wholesaler. If the trade discount rate offered was 12%, calculate the list price and total amount of discount offered for each battery.

9. If a trade discount rate of 15% resulted in a trade discount amount of $18,200, calculate the list price and net price of the technology product that was subject to this discount.

10. A wholesaler was offered a discount of $20,400 on a shipment of designer clothes. If there was a trade discount rate of 5% on the shipment, calculate the list price and the net price of the clothes.

11. The list price of canned foods at a wholesaler's outlet is $50 and the net price is $46. What is the trade discount rate?

12. Dorris, the owner of a departmental retail chain of stores, was an excellent negotiator. She was known for getting the best trade discounts in the industry. Calculate the trade discount rate she received on a shipment of coffee whitener that cost her $787.20 but was listed for $960.00.

13. A clothing merchant listed a dress for $280 in his store and offered a standard trade discount rate of 10%. The dress did not sell for 2 months, so he offered an additional trade discount rate of 12% on the dress. If the dress finally sold at this rate, calculate the net price and the amount of discount offered.

14. A distributor of kitchen appliances could not sell a blender that was listed at $80.50 even after a trade discount of 25% on it. He decided to discount it further and offered an additional trade discount of 25%. If the distributor sold the blender at this new price, calculate the net price and amount of trade discount offered on the list price.

15. A list price is discounted under a series of three trade discount rates of 12% each. What is the single equivalent trade discount rate that represents all these three discount rates?

16. The owner of a manufacturing plant gives his distributors two consecutive trade discounts of 5% each and a final trade discount of 1%. He wanted to standardize these discounts and offer just one discount that was equivalent to all these three discounts. What equivalent trade discount rate should he offer?

17. If three successive trade discount rates of 5% each were offered on an air ticket that was listed at $1200, calculate the net price and amount of discount offered.

18. Towards the end of winter, a retail store was selling its winter clothes with the following discounts:
    - Regular trade discount: 15%
    - End of season trade discount: 10%
    - Weekend trade discount: 5%

    If you qualify for all three trade discounts, how much would you pay for a leather jacket that is listed at $2000 and what would be the total amount of trade discount?

• 19. A pet store in Toronto, Ontario sells a bag of dog food for $22 with two trade discount rates of 8% and 4%. At the same time, a store in Orillia, Ontario sells the same food for $21.50 with two trade discount rates of 7% and 5%. In which city is the dog food cheaper? What further trade discount rate should the store with the expensive dog food offer to match the price of dog food at the store where it is cheaper?

• 20. The Federal Government was accepting tenders for the creation of e-learning training courses for their staff. One of the tenders was received from a reputed Toronto based company that quoted $26,500 with two trade discount rates of 7% and 6%. Another tender was received from an American e-learning company that quoted $35,500 with two trade discount rates of 12% and 2%. Based on the quotes received, which tender should the Federal Government have accepted. What further trade discount rate would the highest bidder have had to provide to match the lower quote?

21. Martin, the purchase manager at an engineering company, was asked to source steel tubes. He received the following quotes from vendors:
    - Vendor A: $20,600 with three trade discount rates of 10%, 8% and 7.5%
    - Vendor B: $20,600 with two trade discount rates of 11% and 9.99%
    - Available online: $20,600 with one trade discount of 19.89%

    Who among the three has quoted the best price?

22. A distributor in Northern Canada sells a bag of raw material for $8700 with three trade discount rates of 10%, 8%, and 4%. Another distributor in Western Canada sells a bag of the same raw material for $8800 with two trade discount rates of 11% and 8%. The bag of raw materials is also available online for $8900 with a single trade discount rate of 22%. Where is this bag available the cheapest?

• 23. Is a series of trade discount rates of 15%, 10%, and 5% equal to an equivalent trade discount rate of 27.33%? Explain using calculations.

• 24. Is a series of trade discount rates of 50%, 40%, and 10% equal to an equivalent single trade discount rate of 85%? Explain using calculations.

5.3 | Cash Discounts

A cash discount is the amount of discount on the net price (invoice amount) that is offered by a seller to a buyer to encourage early payment of the invoice. Cash discounts are expressed as a percentage of the net price and have a time limit, after which, the full net price amount is due. A sample invoice with a description of its terms is illustrated in Exhibit 5.3(a).

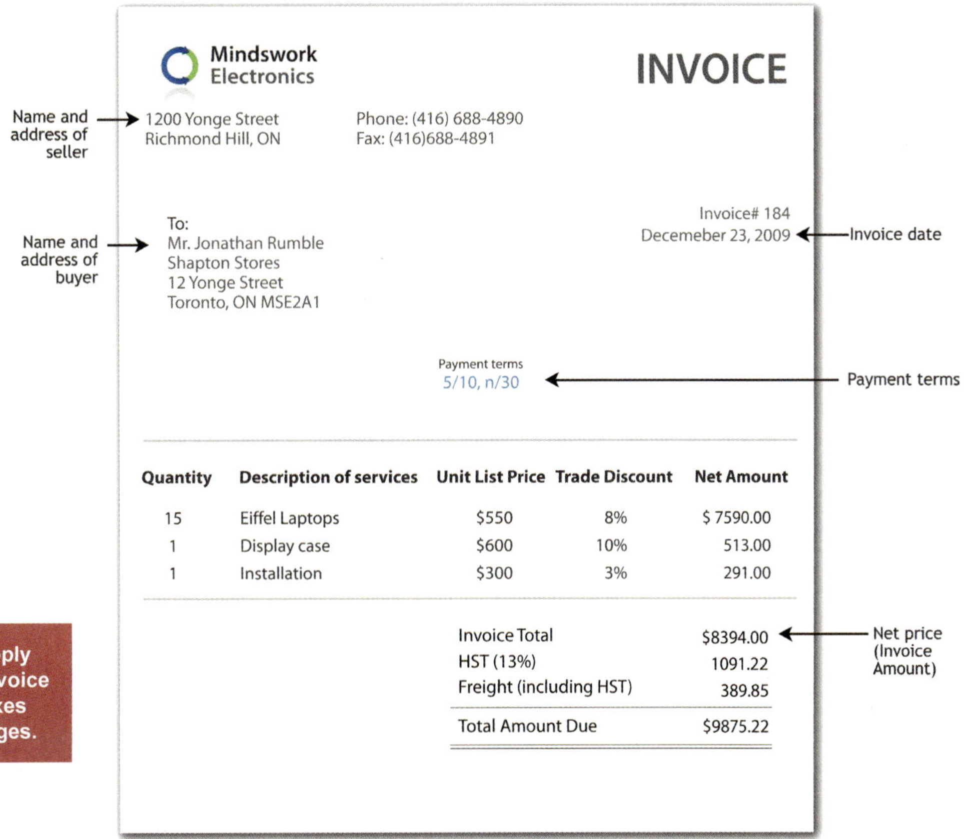

Quantity	Description of services	Unit List Price	Trade Discount	Net Amount
15	Eiffel Laptops	$550	8%	$ 7590.00
1	Display case	$600	10%	513.00
1	Installation	$300	3%	291.00

Invoice Total	$8394.00
HST (13%)	1091.22
Freight (including HST)	389.85
Total Amount Due	$9875.22

Exhibit 5.3: Sample Invoice with Description of Payment Terms

Cash discounts apply to the net price (invoice amount) before taxes and shipping charges.

In the invoice from 'Mindswork Electronics' in Exhibit 5.3(a), the 'payment terms' are 5/10, n/30. This provides information on cash discount terms, the discount period, and the credit period for the payment. Payment terms that end without any reference or code indicate that the payment follows *'ordinary dating'*, which will be explained later in this section.

The first term, 5/10 (read as five-ten), is the discount period, which implies that the buyer will receive a cash discount of 5% if the payment is made within 10 days of the invoice date. The buyer will not receive a discount after the discount period of 10 days.

The second term, n/30 (read as net thirty), is the credit period, which implies that the buyer is expected to settle the full payment within 30 days of invoice date (in other words, the full payment is expected within 20 days from the end of the discount period).

To count the days in the payment terms, the invoice date (December 23, 2009) is considered as day '0', December 24 is day '1', December 25 is day '2', and so on (or simply add 10 days to December 23, that is, 33 days. December has 31 days so the remaining two days are in January). Therefore, 10 days from the invoice date is January 02, 2010, and 30 days from the invoice date is January 22, 2010 as shown in the following time-line diagram:

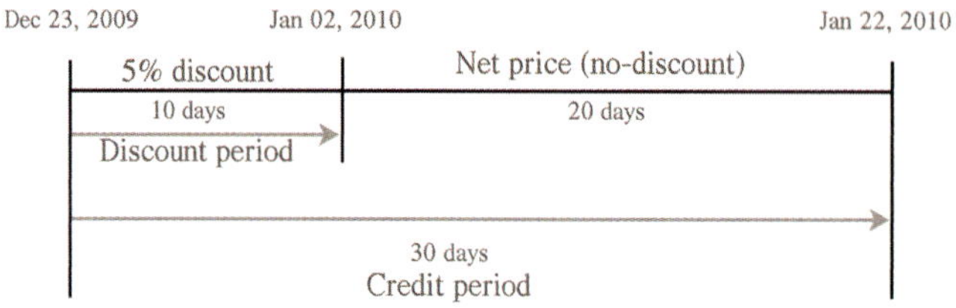

Description of payment terms 5/10, n/30 for the above invoice dated December 23, 2010 are:

- 5% discount for payment made on or before January 02, 2010 (discount period)
- Net price is due for payment made after January 02, 2010, but on or before January 22, 2010 (credit period)

Note: If the credit period is not stated, it is understood that the full payment is expected within 20 days from the end of the discount period: i.e., if only 5/10 is provided in the payment terms, it is understood that the payment terms are 5/10, n/30.

Example 5.3(a)

Calculating Payment Amounts, Given Ordinary Dating Payment Terms

Shawn purchased a computer and received an invoice for $2000 dated January 25, 2010 with terms 5/10, 2/25, n/45. What amount will settle the invoice if paid on: (i) February 03, (ii) February 04, (iii) February 19, (iv) February 20, or (v) March 11.

Solution

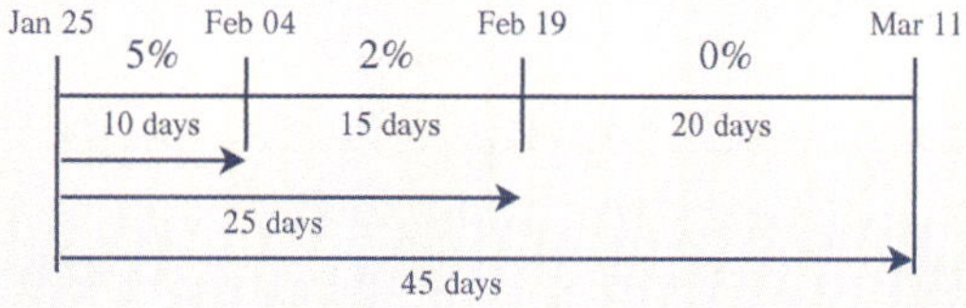

From the time-line diagram above,

- 5% discount for payment made on or before February 04 (1st discount period)
- 2% discount for payment made after February 04, but on or before February 19 (2nd discount period)
- Net price is due for payments made after February 19, but on or before March 11 (credit period)

(i) If paid on February 03:

He receives a 5% discount on his invoice as it falls within the first 10 days of the invoice date.

Therefore, he has to pay: $2000(1 - 0.05) = 2000 \times 0.95 = \$1900.00$.

(ii) If paid on February 04:

He receives a 5% discount on his invoice as it falls on the 10th day of the invoice date.

Therefore, he has to pay: $2000(1 - 0.05) = 2000 \times 0.95 = \$1900.00$.

(iii) If paid on February 19:

He receives a 2% discount on his invoice as it falls on the 25th day of the invoice date.

Therefore, he has to pay: $2000(1 - 0.02) = 2000 \times 0.98 = \$1960.00$.

(iv) If paid on February 20:

The net price has to be paid as it falls after the 25th day of the invoice date.

Therefore, he has to pay $2000.00.

Solution *continued*

(v) If paid on March 11:

The net price has to be paid as it falls on the 40th day (last day of credit period) of the invoice date.

Therefore, he has to pay $2000.00.

Cash Discount Terms

There are three ways by which cash discount terms are generally dated in an invoice under payment terms.

Ordinary Dating

In the previous examples in cash discounts, the payment terms are without any reference or code at the end of the terms and are called ordinary dating terms. For example, payment terms: 3/20, n/45 refers to ordinary dating where a 3% discount is offered when the payment is made within 20 days and the payment has to be settled within 25 days from the end of the discount period.

End-Of-Month Dating (E.O.M.)

When E.O.M. is included at the end of the payment terms, it refers to 'end-of-month dating' where the discount period and credit period start from the end of the month of the invoice date.

For example, if an invoice dated February 12, 2010 has payment terms 3/15, n/30, E.O.M., then the discount period and credit period start from the last day of the invoice month, which is February 28, 2010.

Therefore, a 3% cash discount is offered if a payment is made on or before 15 days following the end-of-month date (with the end-of-month date being day '0'), which is March 15, 2010, and the invoice is expected to be settled on or before March 30, 2010.

Receipt-Of-Goods Dating (R.O.G.)

When R.O.G. is included at the end of the payment terms, it refers to 'receipt-of-goods dating' where the discount period and credit period start from the date of receipt of goods.

When E.O.M. or R.O.G. are not specified in the payment terms of an invoice, it is ordinary dating.

For example, if an invoice dated March 12, 2010 has payment terms: 4/10, n/30, R.O.G. and goods are received on March 21, 2010, then the discount period and credit period start from March 21, 2010.

Therefore, a 4% cash discount is offered if the payment is made on or before 10 days from the date the goods were received (with date of the receipt of goods being day '0' or simply add 10 to March 21), which is March 31, 2010, and the invoice is expected to be settled on or before April 20, 2010.

Example 5.3(b)

Calculating Payment Amounts, Given E.O.M. Dating Payment Terms

An invoice dated March 25, 2010 for $650 has payment terms: 2/10, n/30, E.O.M. What payment will settle the invoice if it is paid on: (i) March 28, (ii) April 06, or (iii) April 11.

Solution

E.O.M. is specified at the end of the payment terms. Therefore, the discount period starts from the last day of the invoice month, which is March 30.

- 2% discount for payment made on or before April 10 (discount period)
- Net price is due for payments made after April 10, but on or before April 30 (credit period)

(i) If paid on March 28:

The date falls within the 2% discount period.

Therefore, payment amount = 650.00(1 – 0.02) = $637.00

Solution *continued*

(ii) If paid on April 06:

The date falls within the 2% discount period.

Therefore, payment amount = 650.00(1 − 0.02) = $637.00

(iii) If paid on April 11:

The date falls after the discount period, but within the credit period.

Therefore, the net payment is due and the payment amount is $650.00.

Example 5.3(c) **Calculating Payment Amounts, Given R.O.G. Dating Payment Terms**

A $5000 invoice dated March 20 has payment terms 5/10, R.O.G. However, the goods were received on March 25. Calculate the following:

(i) When does the discount period end?

(ii) When does the credit period end?

(iii) What is the amount of cash discount if the invoice is settled on April 02?

Solution

R.O.G. is specified at the end of the payment terms. Therefore, the discount period starts from the date of receipt of the goods, which is March 25.

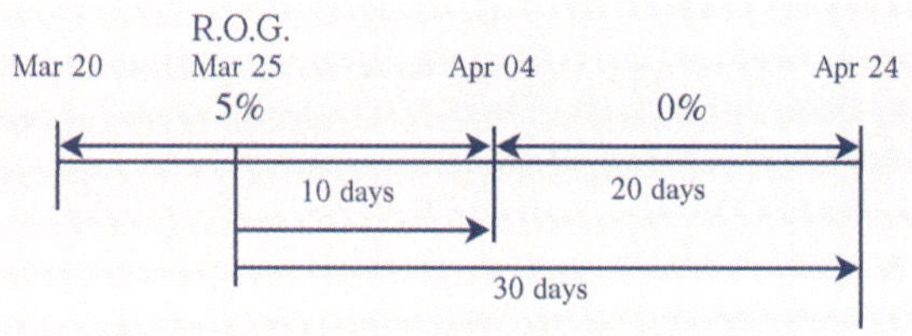

The net price period is not stated, therefore, it is understood to be 20 days after the end of the discount period, i.e., n/30.

Therefore, the net price is due after April 04, but on or before April 24 (credit period).

Therefore, the discount period ends on April 04, i.e., 10 days after R.O.G., and the credit period ends on April 24, i.e., 20 days after the end of the discount period.

If the invoice is settled on April 02, it is eligible for a 5% discount as it falls within the 5% discount period.

Therefore, the amount of cash discount = 5000(0.05) = $250.00

Partial Payments

Not all sellers allow buyers to make partial payments and receive cash discounts on the portion of invoice paid.

A partial payment is a portion of the invoice amount that a buyer pays within the discount period to take advantage of a cash discount.

The cash discount is applied to the amount paid. Therefore,

$$\textit{Amount Paid} = \textit{Amount Credited} - \textit{Amount of Discount}$$

$$= \textit{Amount Credited} - (d \times \textit{Amount Credited})$$

$$= \textit{Amount Credited}(1 - d) \qquad \text{[Compare with } N = L(1-d)\text{]}$$

$$\textit{Amount Credited} = \frac{\textit{Amount Paid}}{(1-d)}$$

The amount credited to the account is the partial payment plus the partial cash discount, as calculated using the following formula:

Formula 5.3

Amount Credited

$$Amount\ Credited = \frac{Amount\ Paid}{(1 - d)}$$

Note: The cash discount is only applied on the amount paid within the discount period and not on the invoice amount. If a payment of $1000 is made within the 10% discount period, the amount credited would be $\frac{1000}{(1 - 0.10)}$ = $1111.11 (i.e., $1000 payment in the 10% cash discount period has the equivalent value of $1111.11).

Example 5.3(d)

Calculating the Payment Amount When a Partial Payment is Made Within the Discount Period

Rolaxes Industries purchased a printing machine and received an invoice of $15,000 dated March 17, 2010 with terms 5/10, n/25. If they made a partial payment of $5000 on March 20 and settled the balance on April 08, calculate the total amount paid for the machine.

Solution

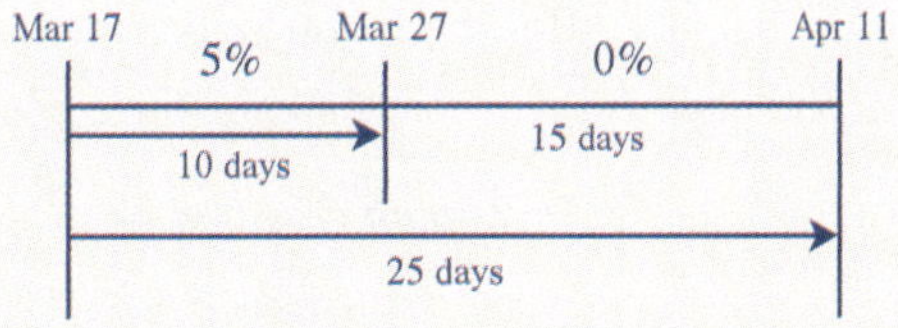

- 5% discount for the payment made on or before March 27 (discount period)
- Net price was due for payments made after March 27, but on or before April 11 (credit period)

The payment of $5000 on March 20 was within the 5% discount period. Therefore, the printing company would have received a credit equivalent to $\frac{5000}{(1 - 0.05)}$ = 5263.157895 = 5263.16.

Therefore, the balance that they would then have had to pay,

$$\$15,000.00 - \$5263.157895... = \$9736.842105... = \$9736.84$$

The balance payment on April 08 fell outside the discount period, but within the credit period. Since they would not have received any discount on this amount, they would have had to pay $9736.84.

Therefore, the total amount paid for the machine = $5000.00 + $9736.84 = $14,736.84.

Example 5.3(e)

Calculating the Payment Amount When Two Partial Payments are Made Within the Discount Periods

Alyssa purchased a desk from a wholesale furniture store and received an invoice dated January 15, 2010 for $2500 with the following terms: 4/10, 2/25, n/40.

(i) If she paid $1000 on January 20, what was the balance to be paid?

(ii) What was the amount of the second payment made on February 07 that reduced the balance to $700?

(iii) If she settled the balance on February 15, what was her total payment for the desk?

Solution

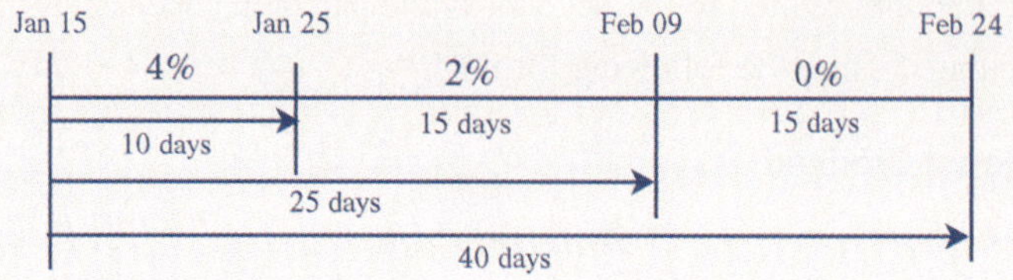

- 4% discount for payment made on or before January 25 (1st discount period)
- 2% discount for payment made after January 25, but on or before February 09 (2nd discount period)
- Net price was due for payment made after February 09, but on or before February 24 (credit period)

When amounts represent physical transactions, they are generally rounded to two decimal places before being used in further calculations.

(i) $1000 paid on January 20 was within the 4% discount period

$$\textit{Amount Credited} = \frac{\textit{Amount Paid}}{(1 - d)} = \frac{1000}{(1 - 0.04)} = \$1041.666666... = \$1041.67$$

Balance on that invoice after this payment on January 20:

$$\$2500.00 - 1041.67 = \$1458.33$$

(ii) Since the balance after the second payment was $700, the amount credited at the time the second payment was made should have been 1458.33 − 700.00 = $758.33

$$\textit{Amount Credited} = \frac{\textit{Amount Paid}}{(1 - d)}$$

$$758.33 = \frac{\textit{Amount Paid}}{(1 - 0.02)}$$

$$758.33 = \frac{\textit{Amount Paid}}{(0.98)}$$

$$\textit{Amount paid} = 0.98 \times 758.33 = \$743.1634 = \$743.16$$

Therefore, $743.16 was the amount of the second payment she made on February 07.

(iii) Her balance payment of $700.00 on February 15 was not eligible for any discounts and she should have paid the net price of $700.00.

Therefore, her total payment for the desk = 1000.00 + 743.16 + 700.00 = $2443.16

5.3 | Exercises

Identify the last date of the discount period and the credit period for the payment terms with ordinary, E.O.M., and R.O.G. dating in Problems 1 and 2.

1.

	Invoice date	Payment terms	Date goods were received (R.O.G.)	Last date of Discount Period	Last date of Credit Period
a.	January 01, 2008	3/10, n/30	January 03, 2008	?	?
b.	March 15, 2010	2/15, 1/20, n/45	March 19, 2010	?	?
c.	April 25, 2010	4/10, $3\frac{1}{2}$/15	April 27, 2010	?	?
d.	August 12, 2010	5/10, n/45, E.O.M.	August 15, 2010	?	?
e.	July 01, 2010	3/10, E.O.M.	July 05, 2010	?	?
f.	February 21, 2008	3/10, n/25, R.O.G.	February 28, 2008	?	?
g.	June 12, 2008	2/10, R.O.G.	July 16, 2008	?	?

2.

	Invoice date	Payment terms	Date goods were received (R.O.G.)	Last date of Discount Period	Last date of Credit Period
a.	February 18, 2008	2/15, n/30	February 21, 2008	?	?
b.	October 06, 2010	5/10, 4/15, n/30	October 08, 2010	?	?
c.	February 25, 2008	10/10, $8\frac{1}{2}$/15	February 26, 2008	?	?
d.	June 30, 2010	2/15, n/30, E.O.M.	July 05, 2010	?	?
e.	October 18, 2010	5/5, E.O.M.	October 25, 2010	?	?
f.	April 20, 2008	10/10, n/20, R.O.G.	May 10, 2008	?	?
g.	August 02, 2008	5/15, R.O.G.	August 23, 2008	?	?

3. Foresteel Inc., a manufacturer of steel tubes purchased raw materials for the month from Premier Controls Ltd. They received an invoice for \$20,500 dated February 28, 2010 with the following terms: 2/10, 1/20, n/30. What amount did they have to pay to settle the invoice if paid on the following days of 2010: (a) March 03, (b) March 10, (c) March 11, (d) March 22?

4. The purchase department of a leading information technology company received an invoice of \$260,800 for the purchase of new computers for their software development team. The invoice was dated February 14, 2010 and had the following payment terms: 6/15, 3/30, n/45. What amount did they have to pay to settle the invoice on the following days of 2010: (a) February 14, (b) February 28, (c) March 02, (d) March 31?

5. A retailer purchased winter clothes from a wholesaler and received an invoice for \$40,618 dated November 25, 2010 with payment terms 3/15, n/30. If the retailer made a partial payment of \$20,000 on December 10 and settled the balance on December 25, calculate the total amount paid for the clothes.

6. Nina received an invoice for $10,263 dated March 18, 2011 with payment terms 5/10, n/30 for the purchase of fertilizers for her vineyard. If she made a partial payment of $5000 on March 28 and settled the balance amount on April 17, what was the total amount paid for the fertilizers?

7. Whitney, the owner of a recording studio, received an invoice for $2500 that had payment terms $1\frac{1}{2}$/15, n/25. If he made a partial payment of $2000 during the discount period, calculate the balance on the invoice.

8. Suzanne received goods shipped to her from Halifax along with an invoice of $3000 that had payment terms 2.5/10, n/30. If she made a partial payment of $1000 during the discount period, calculate the balance on the invoice.

9. Nancy and Nikki run a very successful bakery in Oshawa, Ontario. On July 29, 2010 they received an invoice of $1750 with terms 3/10, 1.5/20, n/45 from their flour supplier. If they made a partial payment of $1250 on August 18, 2010, calculate the outstanding balance.

10. If a payment of $5000 was made on September 15, 2010 against an invoice for $30,000 dated September 05, 2010 with terms 5/15, 3/20, n/45, calculate the outstanding balance.

11. A company received an invoice dated October 20 with terms 1.5/15, 0.5/25, n/45 for an amount of $5050. They made a 1st payment of $2550 on November 04, a 2nd payment of $2000 on November 14, and the balance on December 04.
    a. What was the balance amount after the 1st payment?
    b. What was the amount paid on December 04?

12. Pamela, the purchase assistant of a small business, received an invoice for $2900 dated March 27, 2011 with payment terms 2/10, 1.5/20, n/30. She made a 1st payment of $1450 on April 06, a 2nd payment of $1000 on April 16, and the balance on April 26.
    a. What was the balance amount after the 1st payment?
    b. What was the amount paid on April 26?

13. What payment on October 23, 2010 will settle an invoice for $3150 dated September 28, 2010 and payment terms 4/10, 2.5/25, n/45?

14. Ella purchased some furniture for her office and received an invoice for $18,800 dated September 16, 2010 with payment terms 10/10, 5/15, n/45. What amount did she have to pay on October 01, 2010 to settle this invoice?

15. An invoice for $12,800 dated January 27, 2008 for a shipment of furniture has payment terms: 3/15, n/30, E.O.M. What payment will settle the invoice if it is paid on: (a) January 31, (b) February 15, (c) March 01?

16. Built-in Installers received an invoice dated February 24, 2008 for $8350 for electrical appliances that they purchased. If the payment terms on the invoice were 2/10, 1/20, n/30, E.O.M. what payment would have settled the invoice if it was paid on: (a) March 10, (b) March 20, (c) March 30?

17. Meghan, the owner of a brewery in Toronto, receives a shipment of barley on May 05, 2010 with an invoice dated May 01, 2010 valued at $30,600 and cash discount payment terms 3/10, n/30, R.O.G. What cash discount would she receive if the invoice is settled on the following dates: (a) May 10, (b) May 15, (c) June 04?

18. Seasoned Publishing, a Toronto based publishing firm, planned to ship a truck-load of textbooks to a college in Calgary. The invoice of $175,000 for the books was dated August 02, 2010. The textbooks were received by the college in Calgary on September 10, 2010. If the payment terms on the invoice were $3\frac{1}{2}$/10, 2/15, R.O.G., what cash discount would they have received if the invoice was settled on the following dates: (a) September 10, (b) September 25, (c) October 14?

• 19. An invoice for $5600 has terms 5/15, n/45. What payment should be made within the discount period to reduce the balance to $2500?

- 20. A purchase manager of a beverage bottling factory received a shipment of raw materials with an invoice for \$132,500 with terms 3/10, n/30. What payment should they make within the discount period to reduce the balance to \$50,000?

- 21. Markus, a furniture trader, purchased furniture from a wholesale furniture store and received an invoice dated April 25, 2010 for \$22,760 with the following terms: 3/10, 2/20.
    a. If he paid \$10,000 on May 05, what was the outstanding balance?
    b. After making the 1st payment on May 05, calculate the amount of the 2nd payment made on May 15 that reduced the balance to \$5000?
    c. What was his total payment for the desk (assuming that the balance after making the 2nd payment was paid during the non-discount period)?

- 22. Laura was in charge of sourcing chemicals for her pharmaceutical company. She received 300 bags of chemicals for \$280,400 from an overseas partner with an invoice dated October 12, 2010 and payment terms 10/3, 5/13.
    a. If she made a 1st payment of \$100,000 on October 15, what was the outstanding balance?
    b. What was the amount of the 2nd payment that she made on October 25 if it reduced the balance to \$69,288.89?
    c. What was her total payment for the chemicals (assuming the balance was paid during the non-discount period)?

5.4 | Markup

Markup ***(M)*** is the amount that a business adds to the **cost** ***(C)*** of the product to arrive at the **selling price** ***(S)*** of the product.

The relationship is expressed by the formula:

Formula 5.4(a)

Selling Price

$$S = C + M$$

The **cost** (*C*) of the product is the amount paid for the item after both trade discounts and cash discounts.

The **markup (M)** includes the business' **overhead expenses (*E*)** and the desired **operating profit (*P*)** of the business.

Amount of markup, also known as margin or gross profit, is the difference between the selling price and the cost of the product.

Overhead expenses (*E*), also known as operating expenses, include expenses such as salary, rent, utilities, insurance, advertising, etc., that are necessary to operate the business. Operating profit (*P*), also known as profit, is the amount of desired profit that is necessary to stay in the business.

This relationship is expressed by the formula:

Formula 5.4(b)

Amount of Markup

$$M = E + P$$

Combining the earlier two formulas, the formula for Selling Price (S) can be expressed as follows:

Formula 5.4(c)

Selling Price

$$S = C + E + P$$

Rate of Markup

The markup, expressed as a dollar amount (called amount of markup), can also be expressed as a percentage (called rate of markup) calculated as a ratio on the cost or on the selling price, as shown below:

Formula 5.4(d)

Rate of Markup on Cost

$$Rate\ of\ markup\ on\ cost = \frac{M}{C} \times 100\%$$

Formula 5.4(e)

Rate of Markup on Selling Price

$$Rate\ of\ markup\ on\ selling\ price = \frac{M}{S} \times 100\%$$

The relationship among S, C, E, P, and M as expressed by the above algebraic equations (formulas) can be represented by the illustration in Exhibit 5.4 below:

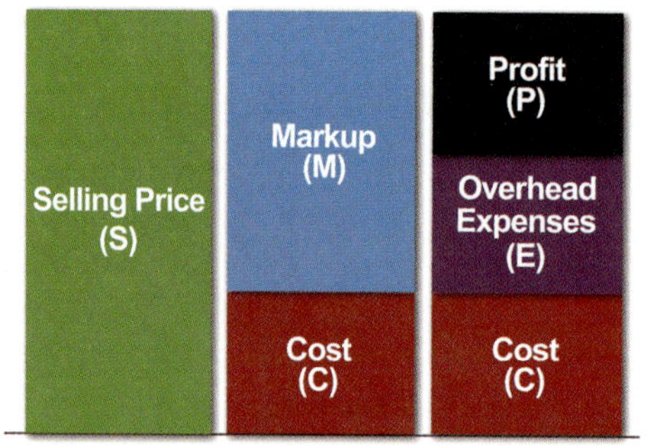

Exhibit 5.4: Relationship Among S, C, E, P, and M

The relationship established by the algebraic equations (formulas), which is illustrated in Exhibit 5.4, can also be represented by a table, as shown in Table 5.4. This is another representation of the formula, which allows the entry of values against those variables.

The first column represents the variables and their relationship in a vertical form, as expressed in the equations.

For example, Markup (M) is the sum of the operating profit (P) and the overhead expenses (E), as given in the formula: $M = E + P$.

Similarly, Selling Price (S) is the sum of Cost (C) and Markup (M), as given in the formula, $S = C + M$.

The second column ('Amount') represents the dollar amount of the variables.

Table 5.4: Merchandising Calculation Table

	Amount	Rate
P		
$+ E$		
M		
$+ C$		
S		

For example, if the cost of an item is \$2500, then \$2500 will be entered in the second column beside 'C'.

The third column ('Rate') represents the ratio between any two variables which is normally written in percentage form.

For example, if the rate of markup on cost is 25%, (i.e., $M =$ 25% of $C = 0.25C$), then $0.25C$ will be entered in the third column beside the variable 'M'.

This table is a useful tool for solving problems as it will allow you to organize the information provided and easily identify the values that need to be calculated, without repeatedly writing the same formulas.

	Amount	Rate
P		
$+ E$		
M		$0.25C$
$+ C$	\$2500.00	
S		

Example 5.4(a)

Markup Calculations, Given the Profit, Expenses, and Cost

A store purchases printers for \$800 each. The overhead expenses (E) on each printer are \$200. The store wants to sell each printer for an operating profit of \$400. Calculate:

(i) Amount of markup.

(ii) Selling price.

(iii) Rate of markup on cost.

(iv) Rate of markup on selling price.

Solution

Method 1: Using Formulas

Based on the information provided, C = \$800, E = \$200, P = \$400.

(i) Markup, $M = E + P = 200.00 + 400.00 = \$600.00$

Therefore, the amount of markup is \$600.00.

(ii) Selling Price, $S = C + M = 800.00 + 600.00 = \$1400.00$

Or, $S = C + E + P = 800.00 + 200.00 + 400.00 = \$1400.00$

Therefore, the selling price of each printer is \$1400.00.

(iii) $\textit{Rate of markup on cost} = \frac{M}{C} \times 100\% = \frac{600.00}{800.00} \times 100\% = 75.00\%$

Therefore, the rate of markup on cost is 75.00%.

(iv) $\textit{Rate of markup on selling price} = \frac{M}{S} \times 100\%$

$= \frac{600.00}{1400.00} \times 100\% = 0.428571... = 42.86\%$

Therefore, the rate of markup on selling price is 42.86%.

Method 2: Using Table 5.4

Enter the known quantities for the variables and identify the quantities that are to be calculated.

(i) $M = P + E = \$600.00$

(ii) $S = C + M = \$1400.00$

(iii) $\frac{M}{C} = \frac{600.00}{800.00} = 0.75 = 75.00\%$

(iv) $\frac{M}{S} = \frac{600.00}{1400.00} = 0.428571...t = 42.86\%$

	Amount	Rate
P	\$400.00	
$+ E$	\$200.00	
M	\$600.00	$M/C = 75.00\%$ $M/S = 42.86\%$
$+ C$	\$800.00	
S	\$1400.00	

Example 5.4(b) **Markup Calculations, Given the Cost, Rate of Markup on Cost, and Expenses on Cost**

A wholesaler purchases a product for \$2000 and has a rate of markup of 40% on the cost. His overhead expenses are 20% of the cost. Find his selling price, operating profit, amount of markup, and rate of markup on selling price.

Solution

Method 1: Using Formulas

Cost, $C = \$2000.00$

Markup, $M = 0.4C = 0.4(2000.00) = \$800.00$

Selling Price, $S = C + M = 2000.00 + \$800.00 = \$2800.00$

Expenses, $E = 0.2C = 0.2(2000.00) = \$400.00$

From Formula 5.4(b), $M = E + P$

Substituting the values, $800.00 = 400.00 + P$

Solving for P, $P = 800.00 - 400.00 = \$400.00$

$$\text{Rate of markup on selling price} = \frac{M}{S} \times 100\%$$

$$= \frac{800.00}{2800.00} \times 100\% = 0.285714... = 28.57\%$$

Therefore, the selling rice is \$2800.00, the operating profit is \$400.00, the amount of markup is \$800.00, and the rate of markup on selling price is 28.57%.

Method 2: Using Table 5.4

Enter the known quantities for the variable and identify the quantities that are to be calculated.

(i) $M = 0.40\ C = 0.40\ (2000.00) = \$800.00$

(ii) $E = 0.20\ C = 0.20\ (2000.00) = \$400.00$

(iii) $P = M - E = 800.00 - 400.00 = \$400.00$

(iv) $S = M = C = 800.00{=}2000.00 = \$2800.00$

(v) $\frac{M}{S} = \frac{800.00}{2800.00} = 0.285714... = 28.57\%$

	Amount	Rate
P	\$400.00	
+ E	\$400.00	0.20C
M	\$800.00	0.40C $M/S = 28.57\%$
+ C	\$2000.00	
S	\$2800.00	

Example 5.4(c) **Markup Calculations, Given the Selling Price and the Rate of Markup on Selling Price**

Madison, a retailer, sells a handbag for \$800. The rate of markup on her selling price for this bag is 40%. Calculate her cost for the bag and the markup amount.

Solution

$S = \$800.00$

$M = 0.40S = \$320.00$

From Formula 5.4(a), $S = C + M$

Substituting the values, $800.00 = C + 320.00$

Solving for C, $C = \$480.00$

Therefore, the bag cost her \$480.00 and her markup amount is \$320.00.

	Amount	Rate
P		
+ E		
M	\$320.00	$0.40S$
+ C	\$480.00	$0.60S$
S	\$800.00	S

Example 5.4(d)

Markup Calculations, Given the Selling Price and the Rate of Markup on Cost

Ashley, a wholesaler of handbags, sells each bag at \$600. If she has a rate of markup of 25% on the cost of the bag, calculate the cost of each bag.

Solution

From Formula 5.4(a), $S = C + M$

Substituting the values, $S = C + 0.25C$

$600.00 = 1.25C$

Solving for C, $C = \$480.00$

Therefore, the cost of each bag is \$480.00.

	Amount	Rate
P		
+ E		
M		$0.25C$
+ C	\$480.00	C
S	\$600.00	$1.25C$

Break-Even Price (BE)

The break-even (BE) price of a product refers to the selling price of an item which includes only the Cost (C) and the overhead expenses (E) of the product. Therefore, when a product is sold at a break-even price, there is no profit gained or loss incurred.

The relationship is expressed by the following formula:

Formula 5.4(f)

Break-Even Price

$$BE = C + E$$

Example 5.4(e)

Calculating the Break-Even Price

A furniture retail store received two successive trade discounts of 10% and 8% on the list price of \$1250 on a dining table and planned to sell it for \$1700 so that their operating profit would be 20% of their cost. If they were unable to sell it for this amount, what minimum selling price would allow them to break-even?

Solution

$Cost = Net\ Price = 1250.00(1 - 0.10)(1 - 0.08) = \$1035.00$

$P = 0.20C = 0.20 \times 1035.00 = \$207.00$

From Formula 5.4(a), $S = C + M$

Substituting values, $1700.00 = 1035.00 + M$

Solving for M, $M = \$665.00$

From Formula 5.4(b), $M = P + E$

Substituting values, $665.00 = 207.00 + E$

Solving for E, $E = \$458.00$

	Amount	Rate
P	\$207.00	$0.20C$
+ E	\$458.00	
M	\$665.00	
+ C	\$1035.00	
S	\$1700.00	

In order to break even, the minimum selling price would be the break-even price,
which is equal to $C + E$.

From Formula 5.4(f), $BE = C + E = 1035.00 + 458.00 = \$1493.00$

Therefore, the break-even price or selling price to break even would be \$1493.00.

5.4 | Exercises

Calculate the missing values in Problems 1 and 2:

1.

	Cost	Amount of Markup	Selling price	Profit	Expense	Rate of markup on cost	Rate of markup on selling price
a.	$1200.00	?	?	$350.00	$280.00	?	?
b.	$800.00	$85.75	?	$63.25	?	?	?
c.	?	?	$1545.75	$200.00	$120.50	?	?
d.	?	$2000.00	$12,455.00	$1551.25	?	?	?
e.	?	?	?	$400.00	$200.00	20.50%	?
f.	?	?	?	$380.75	$45.50	?	10.75%
g.	$7450.50	?	$10,500.00	?	$1375.40	?	?
h.	$6.50	?	$15.50	$4.50	?	?	?
i.	?	$100.00	?	$78.50	?	10.00%	?
j.	?	$20.50	?	?	$8.20	5.00%	?

2.

	Cost	Amount of Markup	Selling price	Profit	Expense	Rate of markup on cost	Rate of markup on selling price
a.	$400.00	?	?	$250.00	$150.00	?	?
b.	$75.30	$15.55	?	8.25	?	?	?
c.	?	?	$9480.45	$1800.50	$750.75	?	?
d.	?	$850.75	$6554.75	$240.25	?	?	?
e.	?	?	?	$125.50	$46.80	9.55%	?
f.	?	?	?	$21.50	$7.75	?	5.75%
g.	$1010.75	?	$1200.00	?	$110.35	?	?
h.	$40.50	?	$45.75	$1.50	?	?	?
i.	?	$20.00	?	$12.55	?	5.00%	?
j.	?	$284.50	?	?	$70.75	11.55%	?

3. If Mercer purchases a phone for $280.50 and sells it for $300.00, calculate the rate of markup on the cost and on the selling price.

4. Marlin buys printer cartridges for $1000 and has a rate of markup of 5% on the selling price. Calculate the selling price and rate of markup on the cost.

5. If the cost of a product is $480.75 and it has a 20% rate of markup on the selling price, calculate the selling price of the product.

6. A calendar reseller purchases calendars for \$5 each and has a 14.50% markup on the selling price. Calculate the selling price of each calendar.

7. A car dealership purchases a particular car model for \$16,500 each. If their overhead expenses on each car are \$1250 and they want to sell each car for a profit of \$3000, calculate the selling price of the car, amount of markup, and rate of markup on the cost.

8. A store that buys and sells laptops, purchases laptops for \$450 each. If the overhead expenses on each laptop are \$50 and they want to sell each laptop for a profit of \$200, calculate the selling price, amount of markup, and rate of markup on the cost of the laptop.

9. Rugged Hardware, a hardware store in London, Ontario, purchased industrial tool-kits for \$180 each. If their operating expenses are 15% on the cost and rate of markup is 35% on the cost, calculate the selling price and profit.

10. It costs a restaurant \$3.50 to make each waffle that they sell. If the restaurant's operating expenses are 105% of the cost and their profits are also 105% of the cost, calculate the selling price, amount of markup, rate of markup on cost, and rate of markup on selling price of each waffle.

11. Rafael, a clothing designer, creates designer jackets that he sells for \$1200 each. If the rate of markup is 90% on the selling price, what is his cost to produce the jackets and what is his amount of markup?

12. As Amber Cupcakes is the only cupcake shop in the city, the owner sells her cupcakes for a premium. The rate of markup on each cupcake is 95% on the selling price. If she sells each cupcake for \$4.25, what are the amount of markup and cost to make each cupcake?

13. Rudolf, a cloth merchant, buys special fabric and sells it for \$10 per metre. If he has a rate of markup of 30% on the cost, how much does he pay for the fabric and what is the amount of markup?

14. The bookstore of a college has a rate of markup of 10% on the cost for its textbooks. If they sell each book for \$140, what is their cost per textbook and amount of markup?

15. Kathy had a 20% rate of markup on the cost of the magazines she sold at her bookstore. Find the rate of markup on the selling price of the magazines.

16. If a car dealership sold its used cars at a 35.25% rate of markup on the cost, calculate the rate of markup on the selling price of the cars.

17. If a car dealership sold its brand new cars at a rate of markup of 40% on the selling price, calculate the rate of markup on the cost of the cars.

18. Amanda and Ruben had an 18% rate of markup on the selling price of the shoes that they sold at their store. Calculate the rate of markup on the cost of the shoes.

• 19. Henry purchased two computers for \$1000 each. If he had a rate of markup of 35% on the cost for the first computer and a markup of 25% of the selling price for the second computer, which computer did he sell for a cheaper price?

• 20. Lynn and Kim own two competing convenience stores. Both of them purchase a similar shipment of chocolate bars every month to sell at their store. If Lynn has a rate of markup of 45% on the cost of her chocolate bars and Kim has a markup of 30% of the selling price of her chocolate bars, which store sells them for a cheaper price?

21. Kayla started a computer retail store and negotiated a purchase price for computers from a distributor at \$1850. If her overhead expenses were 30% of the cost, calculate the minimum price she would have had to sell the computers in order to break-even.

22. A battery trader received two successive trade discounts of 8% and 6% on the list price of \$22,450 for a container shipment of batteries from an overseas country. If the trader has overhead expenses of 18% of the cost, calculate the minimum price at which he must sell the batteries to break-even.

5.5 | Markdown

Markdown (D) is the amount by which the selling price (S) of a product is reduced in determining the sale price or reduced selling price (S_{Red}). In business, the selling price of an item is often reduced for various reasons such as competition, clearance of seasonal items, out-of-fashion items, etc.

The relationship is given by the following formula:

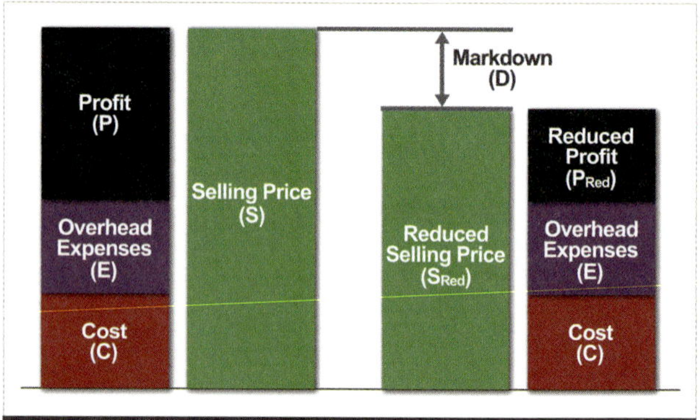

Exhibit 5.5(a): Relationship Between Markdown and Reduced Selling Price

Formula 5.5(a) **Reduced Selling Price**

$$S_{Red} = S - D$$

Amount of Markdown and Rate of Markdown

Markdown can be expressed as a dollar amount or as a percentage (called the rate of markdown) of the selling price as shown below:

Formula 5.5(b) **Amount of Markdown**

$$D = S - S_{Red}$$

Formula 5.5(c) **Rate of Markdown**

$$Rate\ of\ markdown = \frac{D}{S} \times 100\%$$

If the rate of markdown is 20%, then, $D = 0.20S$.

Unless otherwise stated, rate of markdown is calculated as a percentage of the selling price.

The relationship among S, D, and S_{Red} as given in Formula 5.5(a) and Formula 5.5(b) and the relationship among S, C, E, P, and M learned in section 5.4 (Exhibit 5.4), is incorporated into Exhibit 5.5(b).

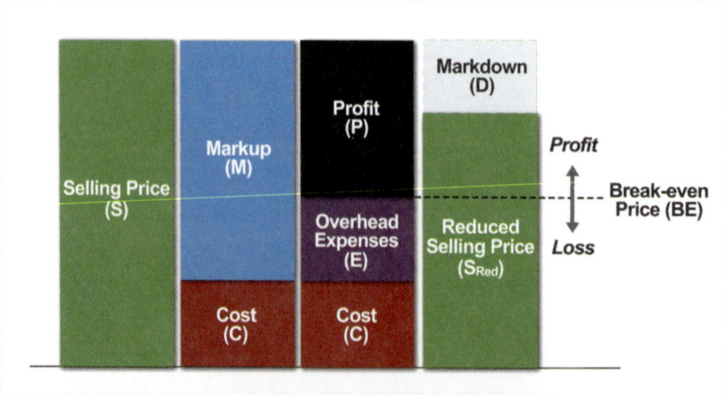

Exhibit 5.5(b): Relationship Among S, C, E, P, and M

The relationship established by the algebraic equations (formulas), which is illustrated in Exhibit 5.5(b), can also be represented using Table 5.5, an extension to Table 5.4.

Table 5.5: Merchandising Calculation Table

	Amount	Rate
P		
$+ E$		
M		
$+ C$		
S		
$- D$		
S_{Red}		

Example 5.5

Calculating the Rate of Markdown and Reduced Selling Price

A store purchases SLR cameras for $540 each. The store's overhead expenses are 20% of the cost and they want an operating profit of $200 on the sale of each camera. Since the store is unable to sell their cameras at the regular selling price, they mark down the price by $127.20. Calculate their rate of markdown and the reduced selling price.

Solution

Method 1: Using Formulas

$C = \$540, P = \$200, D = \$127.20$

$E = 0.20C = 0.20 \times 540 = \$108.00$

$S = C + E + P = 540 + 108 + 200 = \$848.00$

$$\text{Rate of markdown on selling price} = \frac{D}{S} \times 100\%$$

$$= \frac{127.20}{848.00} \times 100\%$$

$$= 15.00\%$$

Therefore, the rate of markdown is 15.00%

Reduced selling price (or sale price),

$S_{Red} = S - D = 848.00 - 127.20 = \$720.80$

Therefore, the reduced selling price is $720.80.

Method 2: Using Table 5.5

	Amount	Rate
P	$200.00	
+ E	$108.00	0.20C
M	$308.00	
+ C	$540.00	
S	$848.00	
- D	–$127.20	D/S = 15%
S_{Red}	$720.80	

5.5 | Exercises

Calculate the missing values in Problems 1 and 2 below:

1.

	Cost	Amount of Markup	Selling Price	Rate of Markup on Cost	Rate of Markup on Selling Price	Amount of Markdown	Rate of Markdown	Reduced Selling Price
a.	$50.75	?	$65.00	?	?	$5.50	?	?
b.	?	$26.50	$280.50	?	?	?	?	$240.75
c.	?	?	?	?	15.50%	$12.50	5.00%	?
d.	?	?	?	4.75%	?	$55.75	2.50%	?
e.	$456.50	?	$650.45	?	?	?	3.50%	?
f.	?	$100.25	?	?	?	$11.00	?	$580.75
g.	?	?	?	?	7.00%	$90.50	?	$940.25

2.

	Cost	Amount of Markup	Selling Price	Rate of Markup on Cost	Rate of Markup on Selling Price	Amount of Markdown	Reduced Selling Price	Rate of Markdown
a.	$250.50	?	$340.00	?	?	$42.75	?	?
b.	?	$120.00	$1200.00	?	?	?	$1145.50	?
c.	?	?	?	?	33.50%	$230.50	?	18.00%
d.	?	?	?	8.50%	?	$30.00	?	5.00%
e.	$5.50	?	$8.50	?	?	?	?	2.00%
f.	?	$20.75	?	?	?	$5.00	$65.75	
g.	?	?	?	?	5.00%	$450.50	$1840.25	?

3. What is the reduced selling price of a stereo that regularly sells for $200 at a store, but is now marked down by 20%?

4. Harris Steels was unable to sell steel rods when there was a slump in the construction industry so he offered a 60% markdown on the regular selling price of $80. Calculate the reduced selling price of his product.

5. Alessandria, a resident of Toronto, drives to Buffalo every year on Black Friday to purchase clothes from the retail outlets there. The markdown at the outlet this year was 70% on Black Friday and she spent $1000 on clothes. Calculate the regular selling price of the clothes she purchased and the amount of discount she received this year.

6. Tao was excited that he purchased a brand new car for $22,400 from a new dealership after it was marked down by 8%. Calculate the regular selling price of the car and the amount of markdown he received.

7. Winter Spree, a sporting store, regularly sells its snowboards at $800 each. However, as winter was coming to an end, they reduced the price to $680. Calculate the amount of markdown on the snowboards and the rate of markdown.

8. A sports jacket outlet in Kingston, Ontario sells its sports jackets for $1450 each. However, when they receive a big corporate order to supply sports jackets to a corporation, they sell them for $900 each. Calculate the amount of markdown on corporate orders and the rate of markdown.

9. Thomas owns a successful furniture distribution store. He purchases dining table sets at $200 each from a wholesaler and sells them after a rate of markup of 120% of the cost. Every summer he runs a seasonal sale and offers a markdown of 30%. Calculate the regular selling price and the discounted selling price of the set.

10. A retailer buys portable hard-disks for $500 each and has a rate of markup of 60% of the selling price. During a sale, he offers a markdown of 75%. Calculate the reduced selling price of the hard-disk.

11. During a sale, a kitchen utensils store marks down its utensils by 40%. If the amount of markdown on an expensive dinner set is $435.00, calculate the regular selling price and sale price of the dinner set.

12. Skis were being marked down by 25% towards the end of the season. If the amount of markdown is $180.50, calculate the regular selling price and sale price of a set of skis.

13. Lisabet, a shoe store owner, purchases snow boots for $600 each and has a rate of markup of 25% on the cost. If she marks them down to a reduced selling price of $525 every January, calculate the rate of markdown on the price of the boots.

14. Kaycie buys chocolates for $7 and marks them up by 10% of the cost. During a sale, he marks them down to $6. Calculate the rate of markdown on the price of the chocolates.

- 15. The cost of an item is $450 and it is marked up by 40% of the cost. During a sale, it is marked down to sell at the break-even price. If the overhead expenses are 15% of the selling price, calculate the rate of markdown.
- 16. Karina owns a boutique where she sells designer dresses. She purchases the dresses for $280 each and has a rate of markup of 35% of the cost. At the end of every season, she has a sale and marks down the dresses to sell them at the break-even price. If the overhead expenses are 10% of the selling price, calculate the rate of markdown on these dresses.

5.6 | Applications of Markup and Markdown

Calculating the Reduced Profit or Loss at the Sale Price

When a product is sold at its break-even price, there is neither profit gained nor loss incurred. As described earlier, the break-even price of a product is the selling price of an item, which includes the cost (C) and overhead expenses (E) of the product.

At the reduced selling price (S_{Red}), the desired or operating profit (P) will be reduced by the amount equal to the amount of markdown (D), as shown in the diagram below:

$P_{Red} = P - D$
$P_{Red} = S_{Red} - BE$

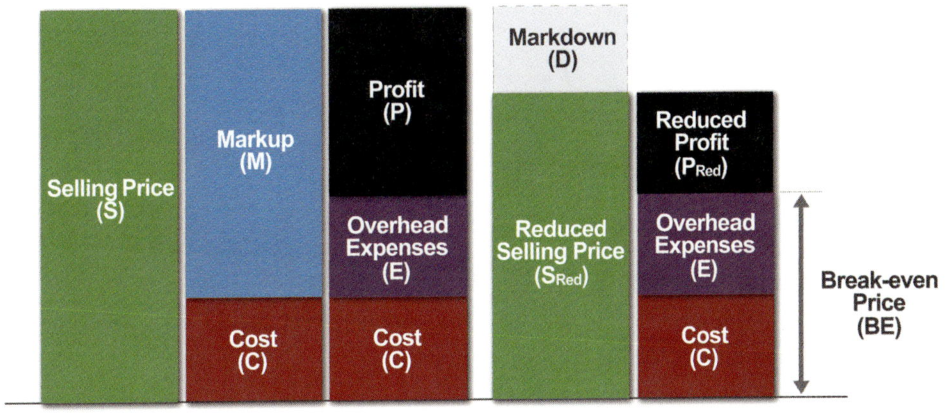

Exhibit 5.6: Reduced Profit or Loss After Markdown

From the above diagram you will also note the following:

- If $D < P$, then the reduced profit (P_{Red}) will be positive. Also, S_{Red} will be greater than BE. Therefore, there will be reduced profit at the sale price.
- If $D = P$, then P_{Red} will be 0. Also, S_{Red} will be equal to BE. Therefore, there will be neither profit nor loss at the sale price.
- If $D > P$, then P_{Red} will be negative. Also, S_{Red} will be less than BE. Therefore, there will be loss at the sale price.

Therefore, we can conclude that

$$P_{Red} = S_{Red} - BE$$
$$= S_{Red} - (C + E)$$

If P_{Red} is negative, then there is a loss at sale price.

Removing the brackets, results in the following formula:

Formula 5.6(a)

Reduced Profit

$$P_{Red} = S_{Red} - C - E$$

The relationship established by the algebraic equations (formulas) which is illustrated by the diagram on the previous page can also be represented using Table 5.6, an extension of Table 5.5.

Table 5.6: Merchandising Calculation Table

		Amount	Rate
	P		
	$+E$		
	M		
	$+C$		
	S		
	$-D$		
	S_{Red}		
$-BE$	$-C$		
	$-E$		
	P_{Red}		

From 5.6(a), $P_{Red} = S_{Red} - C - E$

Substituting $S_{Red} = S - D$ from Formula 5.5(a), we obtain,

$$P_{Red} = S - D - C - E$$

Regrouping , we obtain,

$$P_{Red} = (S - C - E) - D$$

Substituting $P = (S - C - E)$ from 5.4 (c), we obtain the following formula:

Formula 5.6(b)

Reduced Profit

$$P_{Red} = P - D$$

Example 5.6(a)

Calculating Profit or Loss

A store that purchases printers for \$800 each has overhead expenses (E) of \$200 on each printer. The store wants to sell each printer for an operating profit of \$400. During a sale, they offer a markdown rate of 25%. At the sale price, calculate the store's profit or loss.

Solution

Method 1: Using Formulas

$M = P + E = 400.00 + 200.00 = \$600.00$

Also, $S = C + M = 800.00 + 600.00 = \$1400.00$

and, $D = 0.25S = 0.25 \times 1400.00 = \$350.00$

Therefore, $S_{Red} = 1400.00 - 350.00 = \$1050.00$

Thus, $P_{Red} = S_{Red} - C - E$

$= 1050.00 - 800.00 - 200.00$

$= \$50.00$ Profit

Or,

$P = \$400.00, D = \$350.00$

Using Formula 5.6(b),

$P_{Red} = P - D$

$= 400.00 - 350.00$

$= \$50.00$

Therefore, at the sale price, the store's profit is \$50.00.

Method 2: Using Table 5.6

		Amount	Rate
	P	\$400.00	
	$+E$	\$200.00	
	M	\$600.00	
	$+C$	\$800.00	
	S	\$1400.00	
	$-D$	–\$350.00	$0.25S$
	S_{Red}	\$1050.00	
$-BE$	$-C$	–\$800.00	
	$-E$	–\$200.00	
	P_{Red}	\$50.00	

Example 5.6(b)

Calculating Profit or Loss

An item costs \$500, the overhead expenses are 20% of the cost, and the operating profit is 30% of the cost. If the item is marked down by 15% during a sale, calculate the profit or loss on the sale of this item.

Solution

Method 1: Using Formulas

$C = \$500.00$

$E = 0.20C = \$100.00$

$P = 0.30C = \$150.00$

$D = 0.15S$

P_{Red} or Loss = ?

$$S = C + M = C + E + P$$
$$= 500.00 + 100.00 + 150.00$$
$$= \$750.00$$

Also, $D = 0.15 \times 750.00$
$$= \$112.50$$

and, $S_{Red} = S - D$
$$= 750.00 - 112.50$$
$$= \$637.50$$

$$P_{Red} \text{ or } Loss = S_{Red} - C - E$$
$$= 637.50 - 500.00 - 100.00$$
$$= \$37.50 \text{ profit}$$

Therefore, at the sale price, the store's profit is \$37.50.

Method 2: Using Table 5.6

	Amount	Rate
P	\$150.00	$0.30C$
+ E	\$100.00	$0.20C$
M	\$250.00	
+ C	\$500.00	
S	\$750.00	
- D	-\$112.50	$0.15S$
S_{Red}	\$637.50	
$-BE$: - C	-\$500.00	
$-BE$: - E	-\$100.00	$0.20C$
P_{Red}	\$37.50	

Example 5.6(c)

Calculating Profit or Loss on Sales Involving the Regular Selling Price, Sale Price, and Break-Even Price

A retailer of electronic goods purchases 1000 HDTVs from a distributor after trade discounts of 10% and 8% on the list price of \$600 per unit. The retailer marks up the HDTVs by \$603.20 per unit and sells 660 units at this price. During a sale, he offers a markdown of 30% and sells another 300 units at the sale price. He then sells the remaining units at the break-even price. If the retailer's overhead expenses are 20% of the cos t, calculate the following:

(i) Price at which 660 units were sold.

(ii) Sale price at which 300 units were sold.

(iii) Break-even price at which the remaining units were sold.

(iv) Total profit or loss from the sale of 1000 units.

Solution

Using, $N = L(1-d_1)(1-d_2)$

$C = 600.00(1 - 0.10)(1 - 0.08) = \$496.80$

(i) Regular selling price is $1100.00 per unit.

(ii) Sale price is $770.00 per unit.

(iii) Number of units sold at *BE* price

= 1000 – (660 + 300)

= 40 units

There is no profit or loss for the remaining 40 units sold at break-even price.

BE price = *C* + *E*

= 496.80 + 99.36= $596.16

(iv) Total profit from the sale of all 1000 units

= (660 × 503.84) + (300 × 173.84) + (40 × 0)

= $384,686.40

	Amount	Rate
P	$503.84	
+ E	$99.36	0.20C
M	$603.20	
+ C	$496.80	
S	$1100.00	
- D	–$330.00	0.30S
S_{Red}	$770.00	
–BE: - C	–$496.80	
–BE: - E	–$99.36	
P_{Red}	$173.84	

This is the profit per unit for 660 units sold at the regular selling price. (P)

This is the profit per unit for 300 units sold at the sale price. (P_{Red})

5.6 | Exercises

Calculate the missing values for Problems 1 and 2:

1.

	Cost	Amount of Markup	Selling Price	Profit	Expenses	Rate of Markup on Cost	Rate of Markup on Selling Price	Rate of Markdown	Reduced Selling Price	Reduced Profit
a.	?	?	$2150.00	$850.00	$300.00	?	?	25.00%	?	?
b.	$900.25	?	?	$600.00	$200.50	?	?	35.00%	?	?
c.	$15.75	?	?	$2.18	?	15.50%	?	5.50%	?	?
d.	?	?	$678.75	?	$76.50	?	25.00%	12.50%	?	?
e.	?	$656.50	$4555.50	?	$140.75	?	?	?	$4180.00	?
f.	$38.00	?	$59.50	$10.00	?	?	?	?	?	–$2.50

2.

	Cost	Amount of Markup	Selling Price	Profit	Expenses	Rate of Markup on Cost	Rate of Markup on Selling Price	Rate of Markdown	Reduced Selling Price	Reduced Profit
a.	?	?	$12.00	$2.50	$3.00	?	?	17.00%	?	?
b.	$450.75	?	?	$40.50	$80.50	?	?	5.00%	?	?
c.	$1.50	?	?	$0.25	?	30.00%	?	5.50%	?	?
d.	?	?	$12,400.00	?	$1280.50	?	23.00%	9.00%	?	?
e.	?	$180.50	$750.50	?	$45.75	?	?	?	$710.50	?
f.	$12.50	?	$18.50	$4.00	?	?	?	?	?	–$1.30

3. A diamond merchant purchased Canadian solitaire diamonds for $2800. If the markup on these diamonds is 15% of the cost and his operating expenses are 10% of the cost, calculate his profit on each diamond. During a sale, if he offers a markdown of 15%, calculate the reduced selling price and profit or loss he makes at the sale price.

4. A jean retail outlet purchases pairs of jeans for $30 each and expects to make a profit of 20% of the cost. If the amount of markup on each pair of jeans is $9, calculate the selling price per pair of jeans. During a boxing week sale, they marked down the price by 10%. Calculate the sale price and profit or loss made per pair of jeans at the sale price.

5. Henry, the owner of a music store, purchased acoustic guitars for $80 each and has marked them up by 20% of the cost. His overhead expenses were 10% of the cost.
   a. What is the regular selling price of the guitar?
   b. If he decides to offer a markdown of 5%, what would be the reduced selling price and profit or loss he would make on the sale of each guitar?

6. Amanda purchases flowers for $2 each and her regular selling price is $4.25.
   a. If she makes a profit of $1.85 on each flower, calculate her overhead expenses.
   b. During Valentine's Day, if she offers a rate of markdown of 30%, calculate the reduced selling price and the profit or loss that she makes on the sale of each flower.

• 7. The profit of an item from the regular selling price of $500 is $150. If a 20% markdown is offered during a sale, calculate the profit or loss at the sale price.

• 8. Hollis Sound Equipments Ltd. makes a profit of $100 on an acoustic guitar that they sell at the regular selling price of $600. During a boxing week sale, if they marked down the guitar by 20%, calculate the profit or loss at the sale price.

9. Jacy, a reseller of ink jet printers, purchases printers for $300 each and marks them up by 40% of the cost to make a profit of $70 on each printer. If he marks them down by 10% during a sale, calculate his profit or loss on each printer at the sale price.

10. Frank is in the business of buying and selling expensive yachts to wealthy immigrants in Canada. He recently bought a yacht for $420,500 and marked it up by 20% of the cost hoping to make a profit of $70,000. Since, it did not sell for many months, he marked down the price by 30% and was then able to sell it. Calculate his profit or loss on the yacht at the sale price.

11. Miranda purchases a computer desk from a wholesaler listed at $800 less 20% and 10%. She has overhead expenses of 20% of the cost and wants to have an operating profit of 30% of the cost. After listing the item for one month, she marked it down by 10%.
    a. Calculate the reduced selling price and the profit or loss she will make at the reduced selling price.
    b. What is the maximum rate of markdown she can offer so that she breaks even on the sale?

12. Gabriella was in the business of purchasing sculptures from Brazil and selling them in Toronto in her boutique. On one consignment listed at $2400, she received trade discounts of 10%, 8%, and 6%. If her overhead expenses were 15% of her costs and she wanted to make a profit of 20% on costs:
    a. Calculate the regular selling price of the sculptures.
    b. The profit of loss she will make if she decides to markdown the selling price by 15%.
    c. The maximum markdown she can offer so that she breaks even on the sale.

• 13. A torch supplier purchased 1000 torches for $5 per torch. She sold 500 torches at their regular selling price of $12 per torch, 300 torches at a discount of 20%, and the remaining at a price to break-even. If her overhead expenses were 20% of costs, calculate her total profit or loss made from the sale of all torches. What is the discount offered on the remaining torches that were sold at break-even?

• 14. Rodney runs a cell phone store in Mississauga, Ontario. He purchases 400 phones from a distributor with trade discounts of 12% and 5% on the list price of $50 per phone. He sold 300 phones at the regular selling price of $75 each and offered a markdown of 25% on the next 75 phones. To ensure that he completes the stock, he sold the rest at break-even. If his store's overhead expenses are 10% on the cost, calculate his total profit or loss made from the sale of the phones. What is the discount offered on the remaining phones that are being sold at break-even?

15. The cost of an electric toy train was $300 and the store owner marked it up by 40% of the cost as he wanted to make a profit of $75. During the Christmas sale, he marked it down by 10% and sold it. Calculate the profit or loss at the sale price.

16. Jesse had a rate of markup of 25% on the cost of leather belts that he was selling in his store. He purchased them for $15 each and wanted to make a profit of $1.50 per belt. During a sale, he marked them down by 10%. Calculate the profit or loss at sale price.

5 | Review Exercises

Answers to odd-numbered problems are available at the end of the textbook

1. A ream of paper was sold by a wholesaler for $15.75 after a trade discount of 7%. Calculate the list price and the amount of discount offered.

2. A wholesaler paid a net price of $180,446.50 for the shipment of a container load of raw materials. If the trade discount offered was 18%, calculate the list price and the amount of discount received on the container load of raw materials.

3. A used car dealer listed a four-door sedan for $12,400 in his showroom and offered a standard trade discount of 10%. Since the car did not sell for 4 months, he offered an additional trade discount of 15% and the car was sold. Calculate the net price and amount of trade discount offered.

4. A wholesaler listed firewood at $2 per kg. Last winter, he offered 10% and 5% trade discounts to a retailer. Calculate the net price and the amount of trade discount per kg to the retailer.

5. A bag of basmati rice in a wholesale grocery store in Toronto was listed for $11 less 5% and 3%. Another wholesaler in Oakville listed the same brand of rice for $11.25 less 8%. What additional trade discount rate must the wholesaler in Oakville offer to match the price of the bag sold in Toronto?

6. The government wanted bids for a highway construction project. Company A's bid was $850,000 less 15% and 8%. Company B's bid was $1,140,000 less 20% and 20%. Which company won the bid? What additional trade discount rate should the highest bidder provide to match the other bidder?

7. An expensive wine rack in a furniture store listed for $900 was sold after trade discounts of 50%, 25%, and 15%. Calculate the net price and single equivalent trade discount rate that represents all these three trade discounts?

8. A grocery chain purchased its meat wholesale from a supplier for $750 less 10%, 5%, and 3%. Calculate the net price and the equivalent trade discount rate that represents these three discounts?

9. A publishing company delivered textbooks worth $45,000 to a college bookstore. The invoice is dated August 18 and has the following payment terms: 5/10, 2/20, n/35. What amount paid by the bookstore to the publisher will settle the invoice on: (a) August 28, (b) September 06, (c) September 22?

10. A video production house sent Harry an invoice of $18,500 for the creation of an advertising video for his designer clothes store. The invoice was dated April 05 and had the following payment terms 3/5, 2/10, n/30. Calculate the amount paid by Harry and the cash discount if the invoice was settled on (a) April 09, 2010, (b) April 11, 2010, (c) May 04, 2010.

• 11. A computer assembly company received a shipment of monitors from its supplier with an invoice of $185,650 dated November 23 and payment terms 5/10, 4/15, n/30.

   a. If the company paid $75,000 on December 02 what was the balance to be paid?

   b. What further payment on December 06 will reduce the balance to $50,000?

   c. If the invoice is settled with a balance payment on December 15, what was the total payment for the shipment?

• 12. Maya, the general manager at a gym, received a shipment of new equipment for her gym. The invoice dated March 04 was for $30,000 with payment terms of 5/5, 2/15, n/30.

   a. If she made a payment of $10,000 on March 09, calculate the balance amount on the invoice.

   b. What further payment on March 18 will reduce the balance to $2000?

   c. If the invoice was settled with a balance payment on April 02, what was the total payment for the shipment?

13. A shoe store purchases a new model of walking shoes at $60 per pair. The store's operating expenses are 10% of the cost and the rate of markup on cost is 40%. Calculate the selling price, rate of markup on selling price, and the profit on each pair of shoes sold.

14. Vanessa, a florist, buys and sells flowers at her store. If she purchases roses at $1.50 each, has operating expenses of 22% of cost, and profits of 60% of cost, calculate the selling price, amount of markup, rate of markup on the selling price, and the profit on each rose that she sells.

15. Emma runs a successful department store in Toronto. The demand for coffee powder in her neighbourhood is really high so she buys large quantities of it and sells it for $4 per kg. If she has a rate of markup of 80% on cost, calculate the cost of the coffee powder per kg and the amount of markup?

16. A watch store in a mall has a markup rate of 35% on the cost of their watches. If they sell each watch for $440, calculate their cost on each watch and the amount of markup.

17. Rodney, the owner of a clothing retail outlet, purchases jeans at $25 per pair from a distributor and sells them after a markup of 80% of the cost. During the summer, he offers a markdown of 20% for college students. Calculate the regular selling price and discounted selling price of each pair of jeans.

18. A kitchen utensil store purchased a new model of cutlery for $125 and has a markup rate of 60% on the selling price. During a sale, the store offered a markdown of 50%. Calculate the regular selling price and the reduced selling price of the cutlery.

• 19. A wholesaler listed a printer for $150 with two trade discounts of 15% and 10%. Tyler purchased this printer and showcased it for sale in his computer store. His overhead expenses are 30% of the cost and his desired profit is 25% of the cost. To clear the item, he offered a markdown of 20%.

   a. Calculate the regular selling price of the printer.

   b. Calculate Tyler's profit or loss at the clearance price.

   c. What is the maximum markdown rate he can offer to sell at the break-even price?

• 20. Ella buys paintings from Paris and sells them in her studio in London. She purchases her paintings from a gallery in Paris for $8500, less 20% and 15%. Her overhead expenses are 8% on the cost and her desire is to make a profit of 60% on the cost. Calculate the following:

   a. Regular selling price of the paintings.

   b. Her profit or loss if she offers a markdown of 22%.

   c. Maximum markdown rate she can offer to sell at the break-even price

5 | Self-Test Exercises

Answers to all problems are available at the end of the textbook

1. The net price of an item after trade discounts of 40%, 10%, and 5% is $1077.30.
   a. What is the list price of the item?
   b. Calculate the equivalent trade discount rate of the series of discount rates.

2. A clothing store in Ajax, Ontario sells a designer suit for $1500 less 30%. Another store in Oshawa, Ontario sells a similar designer suit for $1440 less 25%.
   a. In which store will you get the suit for the best price?
   b. What further trade discount rate should the other store give to match the price of the suit at this store?

• 3. Timothy, an entrepreneur, received a shipment of clothes on March 25 and an invoice for $5000 dated March 30 with terms 3/10, 2/15, n/30, R.O.G. What payment on April 09 would reduce the balance (a) by $2000, (b) to $2000?

4. An item is listed at $750 less 15%, 8%, and 5%.
   a. What is the net price of the item?
   b. What is the equivalent single trade discount rate of the given series of discounts?
   c. What is the amount of discount offered?

5. A newspaper company received an invoice for $180,540 dated August 28 with payment terms 10/10, 5/20, n/30 for the supply of a truck load of paper. Calculate the cash discount the newspaper company would receive if the invoice was paid on: (a) September 07, (b) September 17, (c) September 25.

6. Amanda received an item on June 17 with an invoice dated June 10 with payment terms 3/10, 1.5/20, n/30, E.O.M. She made a payment of $425 on July 19 which settled the entire invoice amount. Calculate the invoice amount.

• 7. Lily, had to settle an invoice of $70,000 dated July 09 with terms of 2.5/10, 1.5/25, n/45. If she made a payment of $4000 on July 19 and another payment of $2000 on August 03, calculate:
   a. The balance after the 1st payment.
   b. The balance after the 2nd payment.
   c. The payment which will settle the invoice on August 23.

• 8. A stationery store in Mississauga has operating expenses of 20% of the selling price and the operating profit is 25% of the selling price. During a sale, the laser printers were marked down by 30%. What is the profit or loss at sale price if they purchased the laser printers at $600 each?

9. A tractor dealer purchases high-end tractors for $55,000 each. His operating expenses are 20% of the cost and he desires a profit of 15% of the cost. During a sale, he offers a markdown of 25%. Calculate the profit or loss made at the sale price.

10. Molly imported a dresser and marked it up by 35% of the cost. If the amount of markup was $157.50, calculate the cost of the dresser and the markup as a percentage of the selling price.

11. If the markup on a phone is 40% of its selling price, calculate the markup as a percentage of the cost of the phone?

• 12. William purchased dress shirts to sell in his clothing store that has overhead expenses equal to 18% of costs. To make a profit of 12% of the cost, he sells them at a regular price of $75 each.
   a. What rate of markdown is required to sell the shirts at break-even?
   b. What rate of markdown is required to sell the shirts at cost?

CASE 5

Merchandising Cycle of a Product: Manufacturer to Consumer

Isabelle, a college student, enjoyed this chapter on the mathematics of merchandising and wanted to see for herself how a product moves through the merchandising cycle from a manufacturer to the consumer. During her 2010 summer holidays, she decided to study the merchandising cycle at her father's clothing store.

The store is located in Toronto and purchases dress shirts from a garment manufacturer in Vancouver. During her study period, the store ordered 100 dress shirts after negotiating a series of trade discounts of 10%, 8%, and 6% with the garment manufacturer. The invoice for the shipment for $2500 was dated April 28 with payment terms 4/10, 3/20, n/45. Her father settled this invoice by making payments of $500 on May 08, $600 on May 18, and the balance on May 25. The store's operating expenses were 10% of the cost and rate of markup was 30% on the selling price.

The store sold 45 shirts at the regular selling price. During a sale, they offered a markdown of 10% and sold another 25 shirts. They then sold the remaining shirts at the break-even price.

Isabelle created her report and wanted to cross-check her answers. Calculate the following for her:

a. The garment manufacturer's list price of each shirt and the amount of trade discount received by the store from the manufacturer.

b. The single equivalent discount rate for the given three trade discounts.

c. The cost of each shirt to the store after both trade discounts and cash discounts.

d. The regular selling price at which 45 shirts were sold.

e. The sale price at which 25 shirts were sold.

f. The break-even price at which the remaining shirts were sold.

g. The total profit or loss from the sale of 100 shirts.

h. If the payment terms were 4/10, 3/20, n/45, R.O.G. instead of the given ordinary dating terms and the shipment arrived on May 02, calculate the answers for questions (c) to (g) above.

5 | Summary of Notation and Formulas

NOTATION

L = List price

d = Single discount rate

$d \times L$ = Amount of trade discount

d_e = Single equivalent discount rate to a series of discount rates

N = Net price

C = Cost

M = Markup

S = Selling price (or regular selling price)

D = Markdown

BE = Break-even price

S_{Red} = Reduced selling price (or sale price)

P_{Red} = Reduced profit

FORMULAS

Amount of Trade Discount | 5.2 (a)

$$\text{Amount of trade discount} = d \times L$$

Net Price | 5.2 (b)

$$N = L(1 - d)$$

Net Price After a Series of Trade Discounts | 5.2 (c)

$$N = L(1 - d_1)(1 - d_2)(1 - d_3) \ldots (1 - d_n)$$

Single Equivalent Trade Discount Rate | 5.2 (d)

$$d_e = 1 - (1 - d_1)(1 - d_2)(1 - d_3) \ldots (1 - d_n)$$

Amount Credited | 5.3

$$\text{Amount Credited} = \frac{\text{Amount Paid}}{(1 - d)}$$

Selling Price | 5.4 (a)

$$S = C + M$$

Amount of Markup | 5.4 (b)

$$M = E + P$$

Selling Price | 5.4 (c)

$$S = C + E + P$$

Rate of Markup on Cost | 5.4 (d)

$$\text{Rate of markup on cost} = \frac{M}{C} \times 100\%$$

Rate of Markup on Selling Price | 5.4 (e)

$$\text{Rate of markup on selling price} = \frac{M}{S} \times 100\%$$

Break-Even Price | 5.4 (f)

$$BE = C + E$$

Reduced Selling Price | 5.5 (a)

$$S_{Red} = S - D$$

Amount of Markdown | 5.5 (b)

$$D = S - S_{Red}$$

Rate of Markdown | 5.5 (c)

$$\text{Rate of markdown} = \frac{D}{S} \times 100\%$$

Reduced Profit | 5.6 (a)

$$P_{Red} = S_{Red} - C - E$$

Reduced Profit | 5.6 (b)

$$P_{Red} = P - D$$

If P_{Red} is negative, then there is a loss at sale price.

Table 5.6: Merchandising Calculation Table

		Amount	Rate
	P		
	$+ E$		
	M		
	$+ C$		
	S		
	$- D$		
	S_{Red}		
$-BE$	$- C$		
	$- E$		
	P_{Red}		

Many word problems can be solved easily by translating them to systems of equations with two or more variables. A 'system' of equations is a set of equations considered together. 'Linear' equations produce straight lines when we graph them. The simplest linear system is one with two equations and two variables. A system of linear equations can be solved by several methods. In this chapter, you will learn to solve them by plotting the equations on the same graph or by using algebraic approaches such as the substitution and elimination methods.

6 Linear Systems

LEARNING OBJECTIVES

- Understand the coordinate system in graphs.
- Graph linear equations.
- Understand systems of linear equations.
- Solve systems of linear equations with two variables.

CHAPTER OUTLINE

6.1 | Introduction

A linear equation is an algebraic equation with one or more variables, where the variables are all raised to the power of one.Linear equations produce a straight line when plotted on a graph.

A linear equation is an algebraic equation with one or two variables (each to the power of one) which produces a straight line when plotted on a graph.

- Examples of linear equations with one variable are:
  - $3x - 5 = 0$
  - $5y + 7 = 0$
- Examples of linear equations with two variables are:
  - $2x + 3y - 6 = 0$
  - $y = 4x + 9$

Linear equations commonly have two variables, generally represented by the variables x and y and expressed in the form $y = mx + b$ (m and b are constants). The process of finding the value of the variables for which the equation(s) are true is called solving the equations. In this chapter we will learn how to solve systems of linear equations with two variables using both graphical and algebraic methods.

Terminology Used in the Rectangular Coordinate System in Graphs

Graphs are used to provide information in a visual form to illustrate the relationship between variables easily and clearly. Graphs of equations refer to a drawing that represents the solutions to that equation.

Graphs are drawn on a **rectangular coordinate system** known as the **Cartesian coordinate system** (invented by René Descartes). This system uses two perpendicular number lines: one horizontal and the other vertical, each called an **axis**, which cross each other at zero (0), known as the **origin**.

The horizontal number line (moving to the left or the right) is called the **X-axis** and the vertical number line (moving up or down) is called the **Y-axis**, as illustrated in Exhibit 6.1(a).

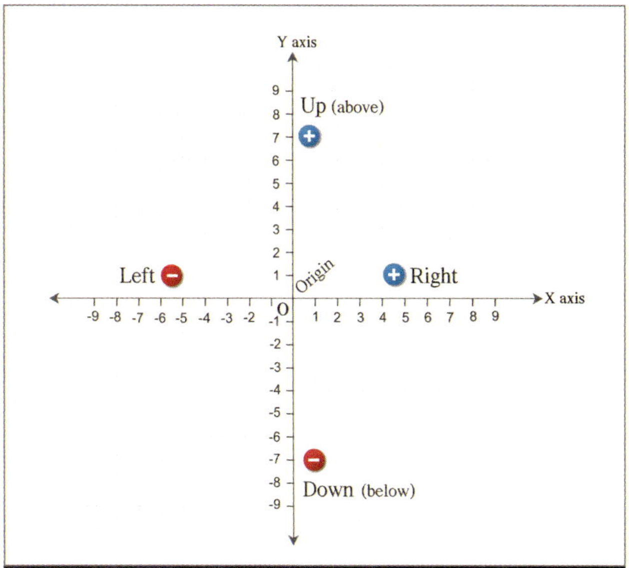

Exhibit 6.1(a): Rectangular Coordinate System

Sign Convention

The numbers to the **right** of the origin along the X-axis are **positive** and that to the left are negative. The numbers **above** the origin along the Y-axis are **positive** and those that are below are negative.

The purpose of the rectangular coordinate system and the sign convention is to locate a point relative to the X and Y axes and in reference to the origin 'O'.

Ordered pairs are used to locate a point in the coordinate system. The ordered pair (x, y) describes a point in the plane by its x- and y-coordinates.

For example, the coordinate of a point P written as an ordered pair (2, 3) refers to the point P which is 2 units to the right and 3 units above in reference to the origin, as illustrated in Exhibit 6.1(b).

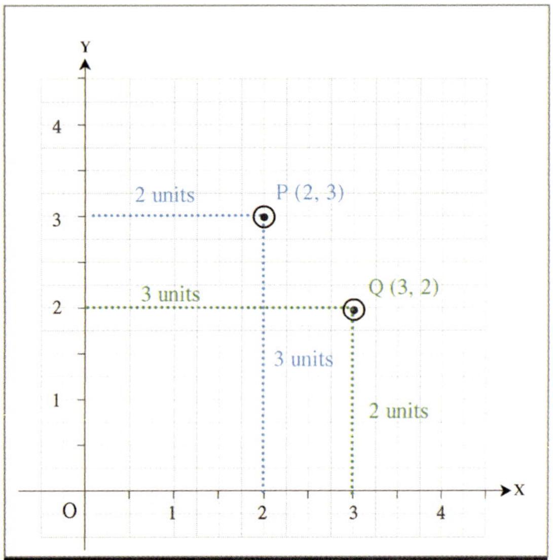

Exhibit 6.1(b): Ordered Pairs

Note:

- The first value in the bracket gives the x-coordinate (horizontal distance from the Y-axis) and the second value in the bracket gives the y-coordinate (vertical distance from the X-axis) of the point; i.e., x-coordinate of point P is 2 units and y-coordinate of point P is 3 units, as illustrated in Exhibit 6.1(b).
- It is called a rectangular coordinate system because the x and y-coordinates form a rectangle with the X- and Y- axes.
- It is important to identify the coordinate numbers in their order. They are called ordered pairs because the order in which they appear determines where they lie on the graph. Changing their order will result in a different point.

Pay close attention to the order in which coordinate pairs are written.

- (2, 3) and (3, 2) are different points.
- (2, 3) refers to a point 'P', which is 2 units to the right of the origin and 3 units above the origin.
- (3, 2) refers to a point 'Q', which is 3 units to the right of the origin and 2 units above the origin.

Quadrants

The X and Y axes divide the coordinate plane into 4 parts, called quadrants. Quadrants are numbered counter-clockwise from one (I) to four (IV), as illustrated in Exhibit 6.1(c).

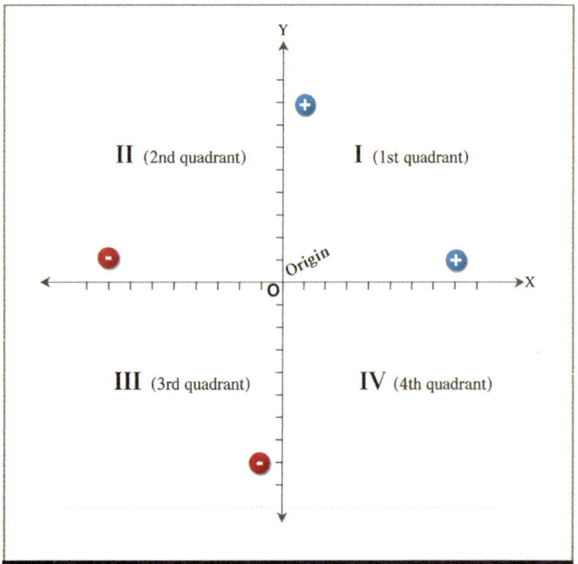

Exhibit 6.1(c): Quadrants

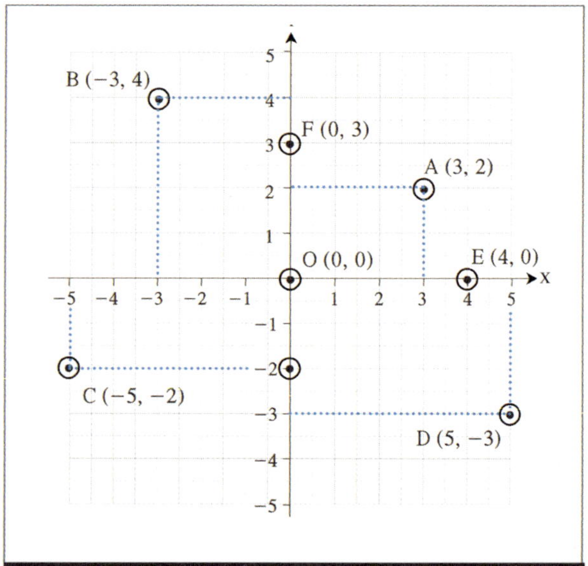

Exhibit 6.1(d): Coordinates in Different Quadrants

The table below shows the sign convention of coordinates in each of the quadrants with examples that are plotted on the graph in Exhibit 6.1(d).

Table 6.1 **Sign Convention of Coordinates in Different Quadrants**

Quadrant	Sign of x-coordinate	Sign of y-coordinate	Example as plotted in Exhibit 6.1(d)
I	Positive (+)	Positive (+)	A (3, 2)
II	Negative (−)	Positive (+)	B (−3, 4)
III	Negative (−)	Negative (−)	C (−5, −2)
IV	Positive (+)	Negative (−)	D (5, −3)

Note:

- Points on the X-axis will have y-coordinates of zero.
    - For example, E (4, 0).
- Points on the Y-axis will have x-coordinates of zero.
    - For example, F (0, 3).
- Origin has coordinates O (0, 0).

6.1 | Exercises

1. Plot the following points on a graph:
   a. A (−3, 5) b. B (5, −3) c. C (0, −4)
   d. D (6, 0) e. E (−2, −4) f. F (5, 2)

2. Plot the following points on a graph:
   a. A (−6, 0) b. B (4, −2) c. C (0, −7)
   d. D (8, 0) e. E (−3, −5) f. F (5, 5)

3. In which quadrant or axis do the following points lie?
   a. A (−1, 2) b. B (5, −1) c. C (3, 5)
   d. D (−4, 0) e. E (−2, −7) f. F (0, 5)

4. In which quadrant or axis do the following points lie?
   a. A (1, 6) b. B (4, −3) c. C (−7, 3)
   d. D (6, 0) e. E (−1, −13) f. F (0, −7)

5. Plot the following pairs of points on a graph and calculate the length of each horizontal line joining the pair of points:
   a. (3, 4) and (5, 4) b. (−7, 1) and (2, 1) c. (−5, 3) and (0, 3) d. (−2, −2) and (6, −2)

6. Plot the following pairs of points on a graph and calculate the length of each vertical line joining the following pairs of points:
   a. (5, 6) and (5, 2) b. (7, 2) and (7, −4) c. (−3, 5) and (−3, 0) d. (−3, 5) and (−3, −4)

- 7. Three vertices of a square, ABCD, have points A (−3, 3), B (1, 3), and C (1, −1). Find the coordinates of the 4th vertex, D.
- 8. Three vertices of a rectangle, PQRS, have points P (−3, 4), Q (6, 4), and R (6, −1). Find the coordinates of the 4th vertex, S.
- 9. A vertical line has a length of 7 units and the coordinates of one end of the line is (1, 5). Find the possible coordinates of the other end of the line.
- 10. A horizontal line has a length of 6 units and the coordinates of one end of the line is (−1, 3). Find the possible coordinates of the other end of the line.

6.2 | Graphing Linear Equations

Consider a simple linear equation with two variables.

$2x - y + 3 = 0$ This equation is in the form of $Ax + By + C = 0$ and is called the equation in 'standard' form, where $A = 2$, $B = -1$, and $C = 3$.

This equation in standard form, could be rearranged to:

$y = 2x + 3$ This equation is in the form of $y = mx + b$ and is called the equation in 'slope-intercept' form, where the slope, $m = 2$, and the y-intercept, $b = 3$.

It is not possible to solve the equation because it has two variables, x and y. However, it is possible to solve for a set of values by replacing one variable (either x or y) with any number and then solving for the value of the other variable. Therefore, if an equation has two variables, then the solutions are pairs of values.

Consider the same equation

$y = 2x + 3$ Substituting for $x = 1$ in the equation, we obtain,

$y = 2(1) + 3 = 5.$

Therefore, $x = 1$ and $y = 5$ is one of the solutions to the equation; i.e., (1, 5) is a point on the line that represents the equation.

Similarly, we can obtain any number of points on the line by using different values for x.

$y = 2x + 3$ Substituting for $x = 2$ in the equation, we obtain,

$y = 2(2) + 3 = 7$

Therefore, $x = 2$ and $y = 7$ is another solution to the equation; i.e., (2, 7) is another point on the line.

Graphing a linear equation means representing the solution of the equation on a graph.

Conversely, any point on the line is a solution to the linear equation.

Graphing Linear Equations Using a Table of Values

Steps in drawing the graph of a linear equation using a table of values:

Drawing a linear graph requires only two points. However, at least 3 points will ensure that the formed line truly represents the given linear equation.

1. Create a table of values by choosing a few different values for the variable x.
2. Compute the corresponding value for the variable y.
3. Form the ordered pairs (x, y).
4. Repeat 2 more times to create 3 ordered pairs.
   Plot the ordered pairs (points) on the coordinate system, choosing a scale.
5. Join the points in a straight line.
6. Label the graph with the equation of the line.

$y = 2x + 3$		
x	y	(x, y)
3	9	(3, 9)
2	7	(2, 7)
1	5	(1, 5)
0	3	(0, 3)

For example, let $x = 3$,

$$y = 2x + 3$$
$$= 2(3) + 3$$
$$= 6 + 3 = 9$$

(3, 9) is a point on the line.

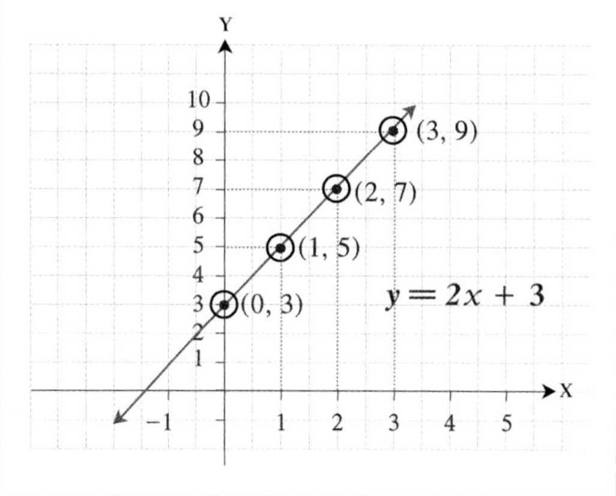

Exhibit 6.2(a): Graphing a Linear Equation Using a Table of Values

Graphing Linear Equations Using the x-intercept and the y-intercept

We may use the x-intercept and y-intercept as two points to draw a linear graph and use a 3rd point to test the drawn line.

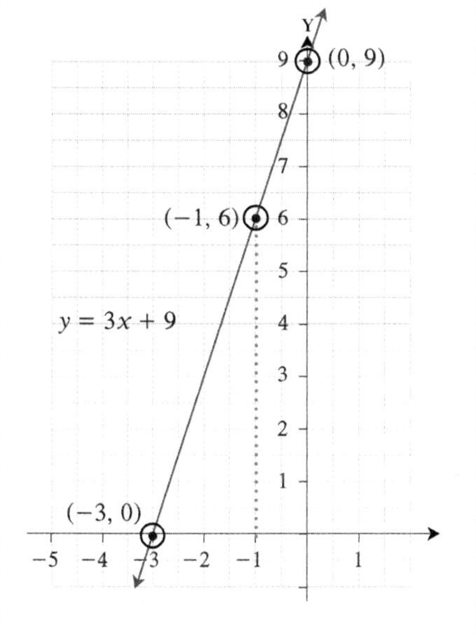

Exhibit 6.2(b): Graphing a Linear Equation Using the x-intercept and the y-intercept.

Let us consider another equation $y = 3x + 9$, as shown in Exhibit 6.2(b).

x-intercept: it is the point at which the line crosses the X-axis and where the y-coordinate is zero.

Substituting $y = 0$ in the above equation and solving for x, we obtain,

$$0 = 3x + 9, \text{ thus, } x = -3.$$

Therefore, $(-3, 0)$ is the x-intercept.

y-intercept: it is the point at which the line crosses the Y-axis and where the x-coordinate is zero. Substituting $x = 0$ in the above equation and solving for y, we obtain,

$$y = 3(0) + 9, \text{ thus, } y = 9.$$

Therefore, $(0, 9)$ is the y-intercept.

To test the line, let us find another point on this line.

Let $x = -1$.

Substituting this in the equation, we obtain,

$$y = 3(-1) + 9 = 6$$

Since the point $(-1, 6)$, when plotted on the graph, falls on the line, it verifies that the plotted line represents the equation.

Graphing Linear Equations Using the Slope and the y-intercept

As noted earlier, a linear equation in the form of $y = mx + b$ is known as the equation in slope-intercept form, where 'm' is the slope and 'b' is the y-intercept.

If the equation is in the standard form $Ax + By + C = 0$, it can be rearranged to represent the slope-intercept form as follows:

$$Ax + By + C = 0$$
$$By = -Ax - C$$
$$y = -\frac{A}{B}x - \frac{C}{B}$$

This is of the form $y = mx + b$

Where, $m = -\frac{A}{B}$ and $b = -\frac{C}{B}$

The Slope and y-intercept of a Line

The Slope (m) is the steepness of the line relative to the X-axis. It is the ratio of the change in value of y (called 'rise') to the corresponding change in value of x (called 'run').

If $P(x_1, y_1)$ and $Q(x_2, y_2)$ are two different points on a line, then the slope of the line between the points PQ is given by,

$$m = \frac{\text{Change in } y \text{ value}}{\text{Change in } x \text{ value}} = \frac{\Delta y}{\Delta x} = \frac{\text{Rise}}{\text{Run}} = \frac{y_2 - y_1}{x_2 - x_1}$$

as illustrated below, in Exhibit 6.2(c) and Exhibit 6.2(d):

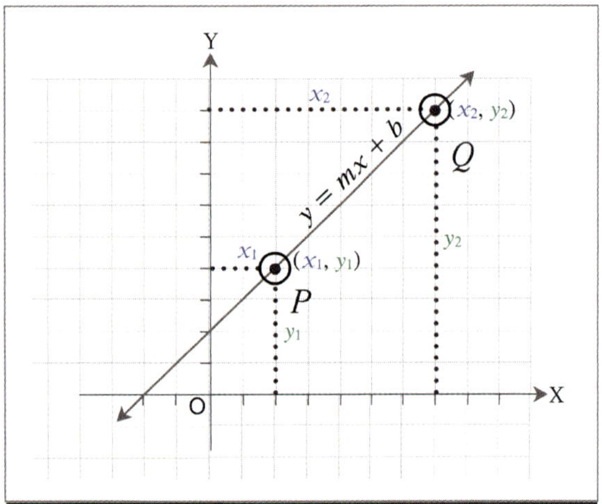

Exhibit 6.2(c): Coordinates of Points P and Q

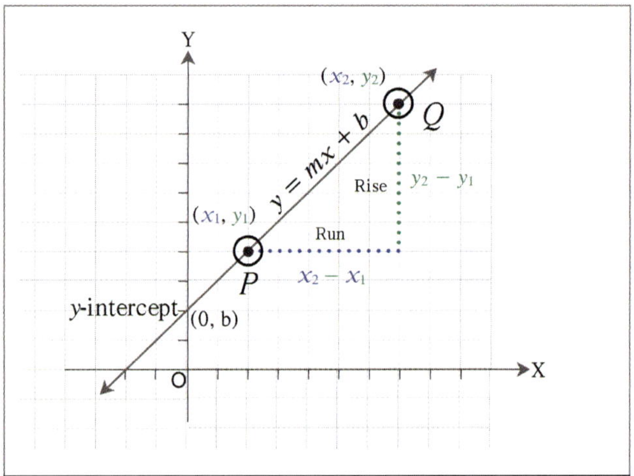

Exhibit 6.2(d): Rise and Run Between Points P and Q

As defined earlier, the y-intercept (b) is the point where the line crosses the Y-axis and is calculated by substituting zero for the x-coordinate of the equation.

Example 6.2(a)

Finding the Slope and y-intercept of an Equation and Graphing the Equation

Find the slope and y-intercept of the linear equation $-2x + 3y - 12 = 0$ and graph the equation.

Solution

Rearranging, $-2x + 3y - 12 = 0$

$$3y = 2x + 12$$

Therefore, $y = \frac{2}{3}x + 4$

This is in the form $y = mx + b$,

where, the y-intercept, $b = 4$, and the slope $m = \frac{2}{3}$.

Therefore, (0, 4) is a point on the line and slope,

$$m = \frac{\text{Change in } y \text{ value}}{\text{Change in } x \text{ value}} = \frac{\text{Rise}}{\text{Run}} = \frac{2}{3}$$

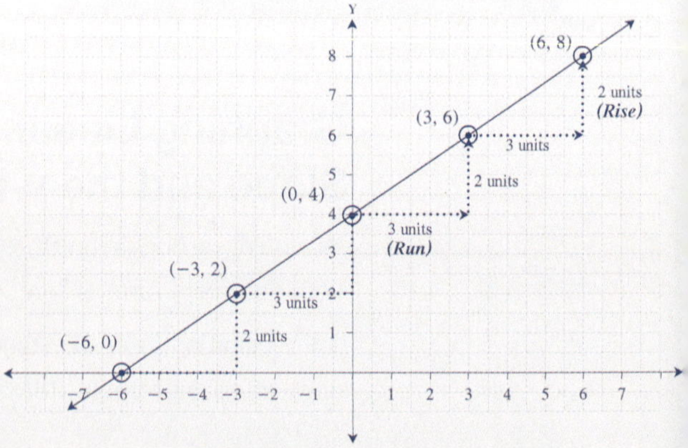

Representing this on a graph:

(i) First plot the y-intercept (0, 4).

Solution continued

(ii) From this point, move 3 units to the right and then move 2 units up to locate the new point (3, 6). This is the same as moving 2 units up, then 3 units to the right to locate the new point (3, 6).

(iii) Similarly, from the point (3, 6) move 3 units to the right and 2 units up to locate another point (6, 8).

(iv) Draw the line through these points to graph the equation.

Or,

(i) From the y-intercept (0,4), move 3 units to the left and then move 2 units down to locate a point (−3, 2).

(ii) Similarly, by using the same order for both the rise and the run find another point (−6,0).

(iii) Draw the line through these points to graph the equation.

Note: *All the points will lie on the same line.*

Example 6.2(b)

Graphing a Linear Equation in the Slope-intercept Form

Graph the equation $y = -\frac{3}{4}x - 2$.

Solution

The equation is in the form $y = mx + b$.

Therefore, the slope, $m = \dfrac{\text{Change in } y \text{ value}}{\text{Change in } x \text{ value}}$

$$= \frac{\text{Rise}}{\text{Run}} = -\frac{3}{4}.$$

$$m = \frac{-3}{4} \; or = \frac{3}{-4}$$

The y-intercept $= -2$, which gives the point $(0, -2)$.

First plot the point $(0, -2)$. Then, using the slope, $m = \frac{-3}{4}$, from the point $(0, -2)$, move 4 units to the right and 3 units down to locate the new point, $(4, -5)$.

Alternatively, first plot the point $(0, -2)$. Then, using the slope, $m = \frac{3}{-4}$, from the point$(0, -2)$, move 4 units to the left and 3 units up to get another point on the line,$(-4, 1)$.

Draw a line through these points to graph the equation.

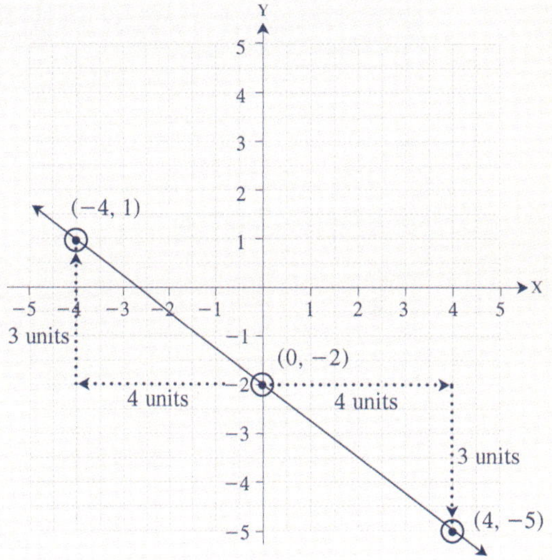

Note:

- The sign of the coefficient *'m'* of the equation $y = mx + b$ indicates the direction of the line.

If the sign of the coefficient *'m'* is positive, then the line slopes upwards to the right, as illustrated in Exhibit 6.2(e).

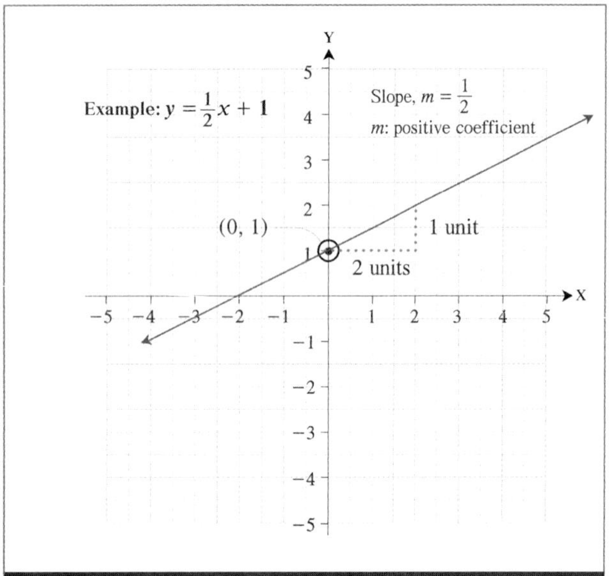

Exhibit 6.2(e): Slope of a Line When *'m'* is Positive

If the sign of the coefficient of *'m'* is negative, then the line slopes downwards to the right, as illustrated in Exhibit 6.2(f).

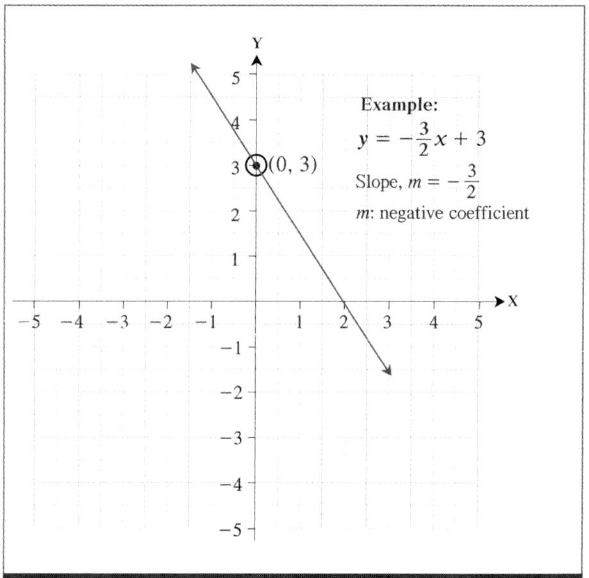

Exhibit 6.2(f): Slope of a Line When *'m'* is Negative

- The slope of a line parallel to the X-axis is zero; i.e., if the slope of a line is zero, then the line is horizontal, as shown in Exhibit 6.2(g).

For example, in the equation, $y = 3$, ($y = 0x + 3$) the slope is zero and the value of the y-coordinate is 3 for all values of x. Therefore, the line is horizontal and passes through (0, 3), as illustrated in Exhibit 6.2(g).

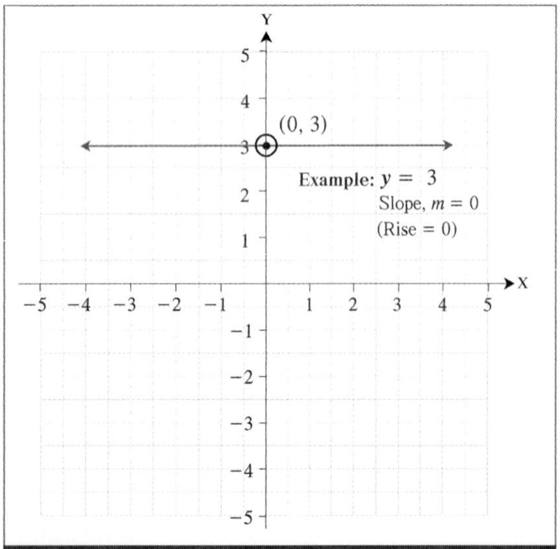

Exhibit 6.2(g): Slope of a Line Parallel to the X-axis

- The slope of a line parallel to the Y-axis is undefined; i.e., if the slope of a line is undefined, then the line is vertical, as shown in Exhibit 6.2(h).

For example, in the equation, $x = 2$, the value of the x-coordinate is 2 for all values of y. Therefore, the line is vertical and passes through (2, 0), as illustrated in Exhibit 6.2(h).

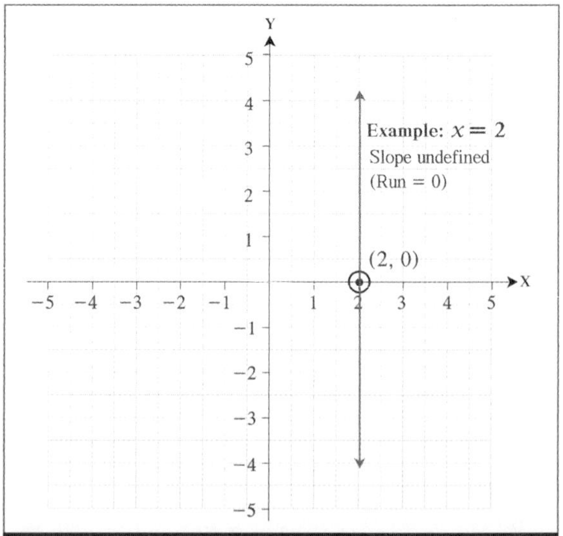

Exhibit 6.2(h): Slope of a Line Parallel to the Y-axis

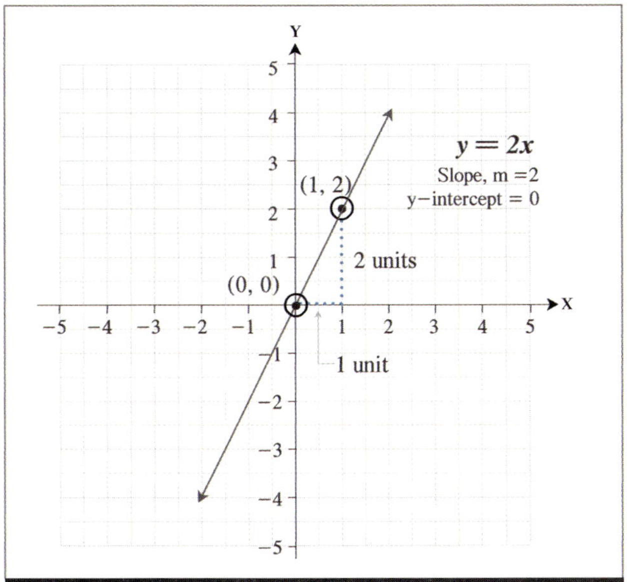

Exhibit 6.2(i): Slope of a Line When the y-intercept is 0

An equation with a y-intercept equal to 0 will have the graph passing through the origin.

For example, in the equation, $y = 2x$,

the slope $(m) = 2 = \frac{2}{1}$, and the y-intercept $= 0$.

Therefore, the line passes through (0, 0), as illustrated in Exhibit 6.2(i).

Example 6.2(c)

Finding the Slope and the Equation of a Line Given 2 Points

Find the equation of a line that passes through points (3, 2) and (4, 5).

Solution

Step 1: Calculate the slope

$$m = \frac{\text{Change in } y \text{ value}}{\text{Change in } x \text{ value}} = \frac{y_2 - y_1}{x_2 - x_1} = \frac{5-2}{4-3} = \frac{3}{1}$$

Step 2: Replace m with the calculated slope

Substituting for m in the slope-intercept equation $y = mx + b$, we obtain, $y = 3x + b$.

Step 3: Substitute one ordered pair into the equation to solve for b

Substituting the coordinate (3,2) into the above equation to solve for b,

$$2 = 3(3) + b, \qquad b = -7.$$

Step 4: Write the equation $y = mx + b$ with the value of m and b calculated

Therefore, the equation of the line is $y = 3x - 7$.

Example 6.2(d)

Finding the Equation of a Line Given the Slope and One Point

Find the equation of a line having a slope of −2 and passing through (3, 5).

Solution

$m = -2$, point = (3, 5)

Substituting for m in the slope-intercept equation $y = mx + b$, we obtain, $y = -2x + b$.

Substituting the coordinates of the given point (3, 5) in the above equation to solve for b,

$$5 = -2(3) + b, \qquad b = 5 + 6 = 11.$$

Therefore, the equation of the line is $y = -2x + 11$.

Example 6.2(e)

Finding the Equation of a Line in the Standard Form Given a Graph

Find the equation of the line that is plotted in the graph shown:

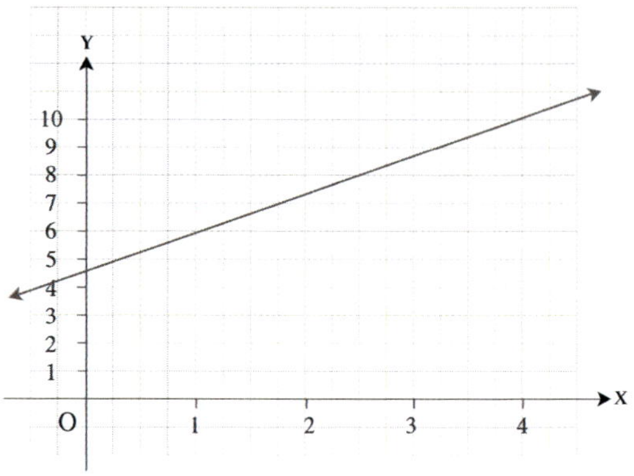

Solution

Start by choosing any 2 points (with integer coordinates) on the line: e.g., (1, 6) and (4, 10).

The slope of the line is, $m = \dfrac{y_2 - y_1}{x_2 - x_1} = \dfrac{10 - 6}{4 - 1} = \dfrac{4}{3}$.

Let the equation be $y = mx + b$.

Therefore, $y = \dfrac{4}{3}x + b$.

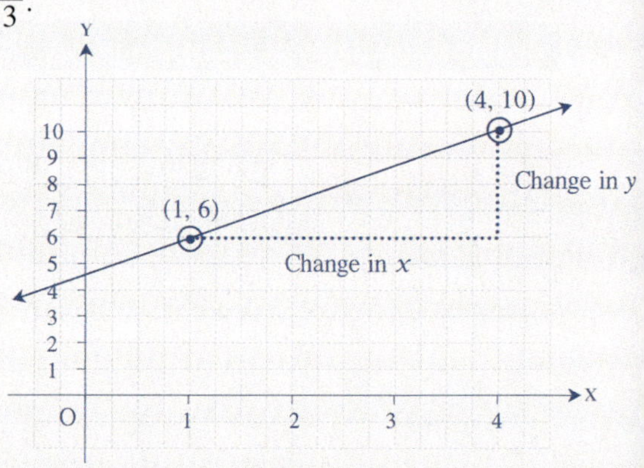

Substituting the coordinates of one of the points (1, 6) into the above equation, we obtain,

$$6 = \frac{4}{3}(1) + b$$

Solving for b, $b = 6 - \dfrac{4}{3}(1) = \dfrac{14}{3}$

Therefore, the equation of the line is

$$y = \frac{4}{3}x + \frac{14}{3}$$ This is in the slope-intercept form.

Multiplying both sides by 3, we obtain,

$$3y = 4x + 14.$$

Rearranging, $4x - 3y + 14 = 0$

Therefore, the equation of the line in standard form is $4x - 3y + 14 = 0$.

A higher value for a slope indicates a steeper incline.

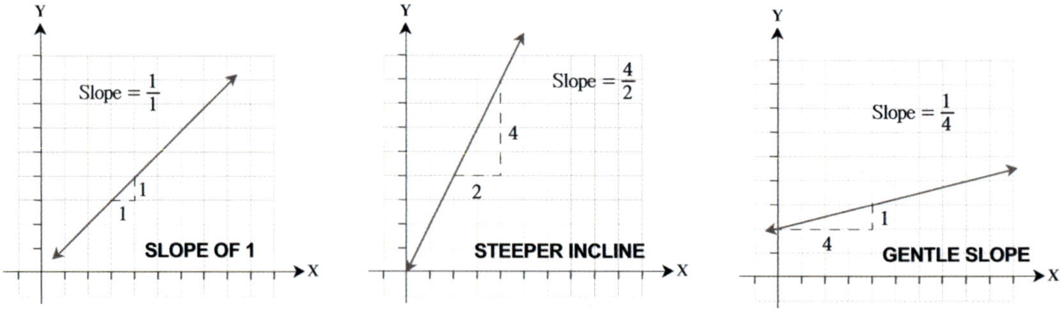

6.2 | Exercises

1. For the equation $2x + 3y = 18$, find the missing value of the following ordered pairs:
   a. (3, ?) b. (−6, ?) c. (0, ?)
   d. (?, 0) e. (?, −4) f. (?, 2)

2. For the equation $x + 5y = 20$, find the missing value of the following ordered pairs:
   a. (0, ?) b (−15, ?) c. (5, ?)
   d. (?, 6) e. (?,−3) f. (?, 0)

3. Graph the following equations using a table of values:
   a. $y = x + 3$ b. $y = -5x + 1$ c. $2x + y + 1 = 0$ d. $2x - y - 3 = 0$

4. Graph the following equations using a table of values:
   a. $y = 3x + 2$ b. $y = -2x + 3$ c. $4x + y + 2 = 0$ d. $x - y - 1 = 0$

5. Find the x-intercepts and y-intercepts for the following equations:
   a. $3x + y = -2$ b. $x + y - 3 = 4$ c. $y = 2x + 4$

6. Find the x-intercepts and y-intercepts for the following equations:
   a. $5x + y = -3$ b. $x + y - 4 = 7$ c. $y = 4x + 1$

7. Point 'A' is in the 3rd quadrant and Point 'B' is in the 1st quadrant.
   Find the sign of the slope of the line AB.

8. Point 'C' is in the 4th quadrant and Point 'D' is in the 2nd quadrant.
   Find the sign of the slope of the line CD.

9. Find the slope and y-intercept of the following equations and graph the equations:
   a. $2x - 3y - 18 = 0$ b. $-4x + 7y - 21 = 0$

10. Find the slope and y-intercept of the following equations and graph the equations:
    a. $5x - 2y + 10 = 0$ b. $-7x + 8y - 32 = 0$

11. Find the equation of the line that passes through the following points:
    a. (1, 2) and (5, 2) b. (−3, −5) and (3, 1)

12. Find the equation of the line that passes through the following points:
    a. (5, 0) and (4, 5) b. (−4, −7) and (5, 2)

13. Find the equation of the following lines that have:
    a. Slope 1 and passing through (2, 6). b. Slope 2 and passing through the origin.
    c. x-intercept 4 and y-intercept −5.

14. Find the equation of the following lines that have:
    a. Slope = −5 and passing through (3, −2). b. Slope = 4 and passing through the origin.
    c. x-intercept = −3 and y-intercept 3.

15. Find the slope of the line passing through:
    a. (2, 1) and (6, 1) b. (−5, 4) and (3, −1)

16. Find the slope of the line passing through:
    a. (−6, 4) and (2, 4) b. (5, 6) and (5, −4)

17. The slope of a line is 3. The line passes through A (4, y) and B (6, 8). Find y.

18. The slope of a line is 2. The line passes through A (x, 8) and B (2, 4). Find x.

19. Points A (2, 3), B (6, 5), and C (10, y) are on a line. Find y.

20. Points D (3, 2), E (6, 5), and F (x, 1) are on a line. Find x.

21. Find the equation of the line (in standard form) for the graph shown below:

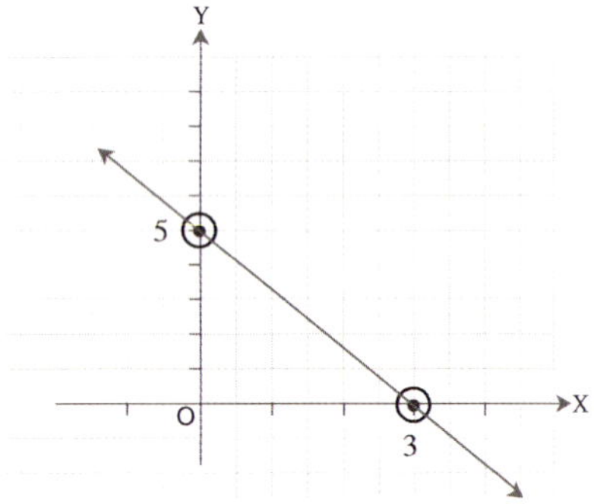

22. Find the equation of the line (in standard form) for the graph shown below:

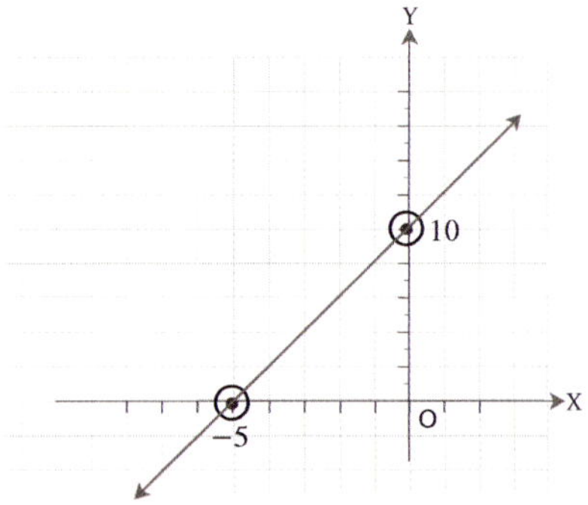

6.3 | Solving Systems of Linear Equations with Two Variables Graphically

Two or more equations analyzed together are called systems of equations. In this section, we will be analyzing two linear equations with two variables.

The solution to a system of two equations with two variables is an ordered pair of numbers (coordinates) that satisfy both equations.

If the graph of an equation is linear, then every point on the line is a solution to that equation. If we graph a system of two linear equations, then the point at which the two lines intersect will be a solution to both lines.

- **Graphs of linear equations may not be parallel and intersect, be parallel and distinct, or be parallel and coincident.**
  - If they intersect once (lines are not parallel), it indicates that there is one solution, as in Exhibit 6.3(a).

- If they do not interesct (lines parallel and distinct), it indicates that there is no solution, as in Exhibit 6.3(b).
- If they intersect at every point (lines are parallel and coincident), it indicates that there are infinitely many solutions, as in Exhibit 6.3(c).

Consistent and Inconsistent Systems

A system of equations that has **one or many solutions** is called a **consistent linear system**.

A system of equations that has **no solution** is called an **inconsistent linear system**.

Dependent and Independent Equations

If the system of equations has **many solutions** then the **equations are dependent**.

If the system of equations has **one or no solution** then the **equations are independent**.

Non-Parallel and Intersecting Lines

Slope of lines:	Different
***y*-intercept:**	May or may not be same (will be different, unless the lines intersect on the Y-axis or at the origin)
Number of solutions:	One
System:	Consistent
Equations:	Independent

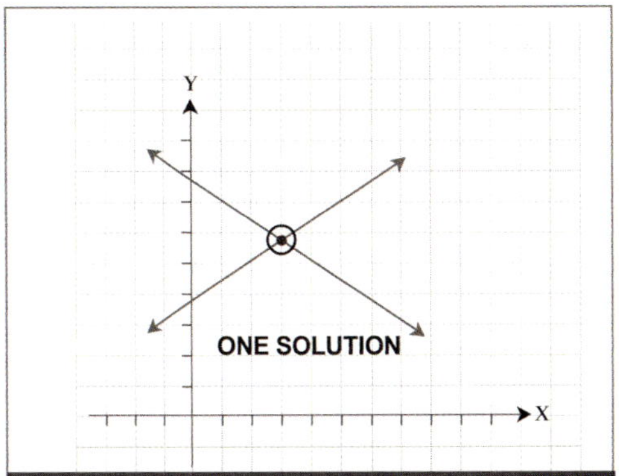

Exhibit 6.3(a): Solution of Non-Parallel and Intersecting Lines

Parallel and Distinct Lines

Slope of lines:	Same
***y*-intercept:**	Different
Number of solutions:	None
System:	Inconsistent
Equations:	Independent

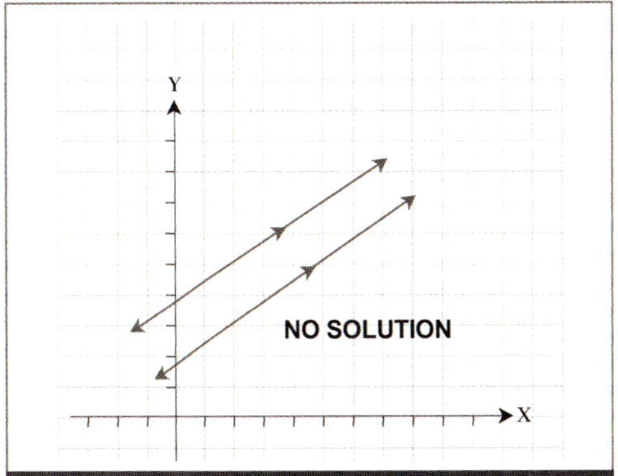

Exhibit 6.3(b): Solution of Parallel and Distinct Lines

Parallel and Coincident Lines

Slope of lines:	Same
***y*-intercept:**	Same
Number of solutions:	Infinitely many
System:	Consistent
Equations:	Dependent

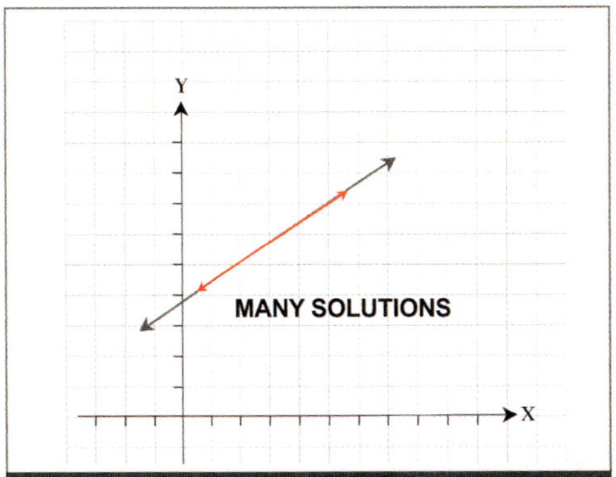

Exhibit 6.3(c): Solution of Parallel and Coincident Lines

Example 6.3(a)

Classifying the Systems of Linear Equations

Solve this system of equations by graphing and classifying the system as consistent or inconsistent and the equations as dependent or independent.

$y = x + 1$ Equation (1)

$y = -x + 3$ Equation (2)

Solution

Equation (1): $y = x + 1$

Slope, $m = 1 = \frac{1}{1}$

$b = 1$, therefore, y-intercept is (0, 1).

Equation (2): $y = -x + 3$

Slope, $m = -1 = \frac{-1}{1}$

$b = 3$, therefore, y-intercept (0, 3).

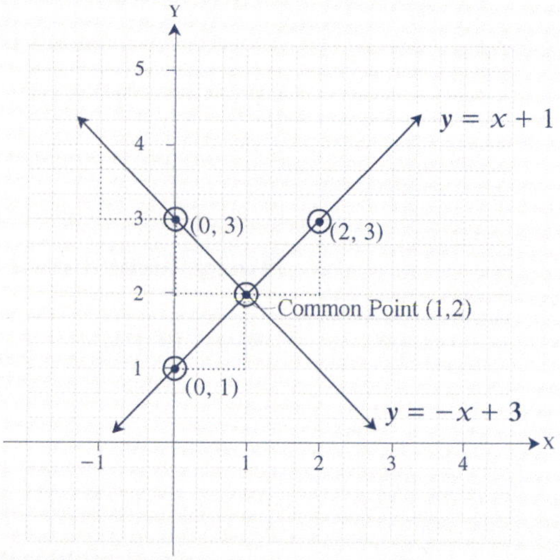

Plot the graph using the slope-intercept method. The two lines intersect at a common point (1, 2), i.e., the solution (1, 2) satisfies both equations.

Therefore, the system is consistent with independent equations.

Example 6.3(b)

Classifying the Systems of Linear Equations

Solve this system of equations by graphing and classifying the system as consistent or inconsistent and the equations as dependent or independent.

$y = -3x + 3$ Equation (1)

$y = -3x - 2$ Equation (2)

Solution

Equation (1): $y = -3x + 3$

Slope, $m = -3 = \frac{-3}{1}$

$b = 3$, therefore, y-intercept is (0, 3).

Equation (2): $y = -3x - 2$,

Slope, $m = -3 = \frac{-3}{1}$

$b = -2$, therefore, y-intercept is (0, −2).

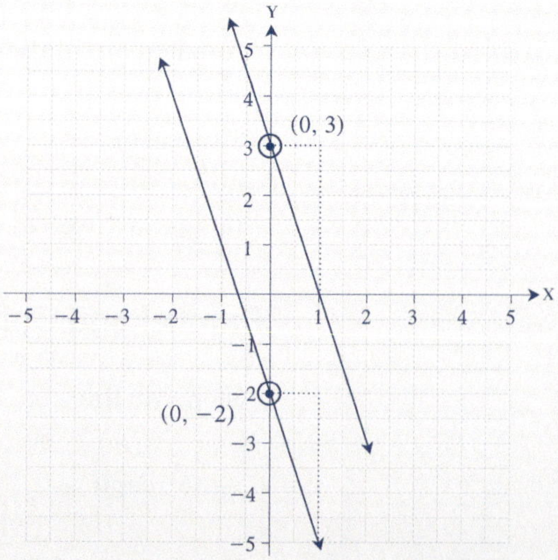

The lines have the same slope but different y-intercepts. Therefore, the lines are parallel and distinct; i.e., they have no solutions.

The system is inconsistent and the equations are independent.

6.3 | Exercises

1. Solve the system of equations by graphing.
   a. $y = 3x - 2$ and $y = -7x + 8$ b. $y = -x + 2$ and $2y = -2x + 6$ c. $y = -4x + 7$ and $2y + 8x = 14$
2. Solve the system of equations by graphing.
   a. $y = 3x + 9$ and $y = x - 4$ b. $y = 2x + 6$ and $2y = -3x + 6$ c. $y = -2x + 3$ and $2y + 4x = 6$
3. By determining the slope and y-intercept of each pair of equations in Problem 1, classify the system of equations as dependent or independent.
4. By determining the slope and y-intercept of each pair of equations in Problem 2, classify the system of equations as dependent or independent.
5. By determining the slope and y-intercept of each pair of equations in Problem 1, classify the system of equations as consistent or inconsistent.
6. By determining the slope and y-intercept of each pair of equations in Problem 2, classify the system of equations as consistent or inconsistent.
7. Find the value of 'A' for which the lines $Ax - 2y - 5 = 0$ and $8x - 4y + 3 = 0$ are parallel.
8. Find the value of 'B' for which the lines $3x - 2y + 8 = 0$ and $6x - By - 3 = 0$ are parallel.
9. Solve the following system of equations by graphing
   a. $5x + y + 9 = 0$ and $x - 3y + 5 = 0$ b. $3x + 2y = -4$ and $y + \frac{3}{2}x + 2 = 0$
   c. $4x - 2y = 6$ and $-2y + 4x - 8 = 0$
10. Solve the following system of equations by graphing
    a. $3x - 2y + 1 = 0$ and $y + 4x - 6 = 0$ b. $2x - y = 6$ and $6x - 3y = 15$
    c. $2y - x - 6 = 0$ and $y = \frac{1}{2}x + 3$

6.4 | Solving Systems of Linear Equations with Two Variables Algebraically

Solving systems of linear equations using algebraic methods is the most accurate for the following reasons: It eliminates graphing errors.

(i) It gives the exact answer with systems of equations that have fractions or that have fractional answers.

There are basically two methods involved in solving systems of linear equations. They are the **substitution method** and the **elimination method**.

The Substitution Method

The substitution method is preferable when the coefficient of any one of the variables is either 1 or -1 in either one of the equations in the system.

In this method, the following steps are used to solve systems of two linear equations with two variables:

1. Solve one of the equations for either x or y.
2. Substitute that result into the second equation to obtain an equation with one variable.
3. Solve the equation obtained from the step above for that variable.
4. Substitute that value into any one of the equations to find the value of the other variable.

Example 6.4(a) **Solving a System of Equations by Substituting for the Variable 'y'**

Solve this system:

$y - 3x + 2 = 0$ Equation (1)

$2y + x - 10 = 0$ Equation (2)

Solution

From Equation (1), $y - 3x + 2 = 0$

$$y = 3x - 2$$

Substitute this into Equation (2)

$$2y + x - 10 = 0$$

Solving for 'x', $2(3x - 2) + x - 10 = 0$

$$6x - 4 + x - 10 = 0$$

$$7x = 14$$

$$x = 2$$

Substituting $x = 2$ in Equation (1),

$$y = 3x - 2 = 3(2) - 2 = 4$$

Therefore, the solution is (2, 4).

Example 6.4(b) **Solving System of Equations by Substituting for the Variable 'x'**

Solve this system:

$x + 2y = 6$ Equation (1)

$4x + 3y = 4$ Equation (2)

Solution

From Equation (1), $x = 6 - 2y$

Substituting in Equation (2), $4(6 - 2y) + 3y = 4$

Solving for 'y', $24 - 8y + 3y = 4$

$$20 = 5y$$

$$y = 4$$

Substituting $y = 4$ in equation (1),

$$x = 6 - 2y = 6 - 2(4) = -2$$

Therefore, the solution is (−2, 4).

The Elimination Method

The elimination method is preferable when none of the the variables' coefficient is either 1 or −1, in either one of the equations in the system.

In this method, the following steps are used to solve systems of two linear equations with two variables:

1. Write both equations in the form $Ax + By = C$.
2. Simplify the equations to eleminate decimals and fraction.
3. Choose a variable to eliminate.
4. Multiply one or both equations by a constant to obtain the least common multiple for the coefficient of the variable to be eliminated.
5. Add or subtract the two equations so that the variable is eliminated.
6. Solve the equation for the remaining variable.
7. Substitute that value into any one of the equations to find the value of the other variable.

Example 6.4(c) **Solving System of Equations by Eliminating the Variable 'x'**

Solve the system:

$$2x + 3y = 13 \quad \text{Equation (1)}$$

$$-3x + 6y = 12 \quad \text{Equation (2)}$$

Solution Choose the variable 'x' to eliminate.

It has coefficients of 2 and -3.

Multiplying Equation (1) by 3, and multiplying Equation (2) by 2,

$$3(2x + 3y) = 3(13) \qquad 2(-3x + 6y) = 2(12)$$

$$6x + 9y = 39 \qquad -6x + 12y = 24$$

$$(6x + 9y) + (-6x + 12y) = 39 + 24 \quad \text{Adding Equations (3) and (4)}$$

$$6x - 6x + 9y + 12y = 63$$

$$21y = 63,$$

$$y = \frac{63}{21} = 3$$

Substituting $y = 3$ into Equation (1), we obtain,

$$2x + 3y = 13$$

Solving for 'x', $2x + 3(3) = 13$

$$2x = 13 - 9 = 4$$

$$x = 2$$

Therefore, the solution is (2, 3)

Example 6.4(d) **Solving Systems of Equation by Eliminating the Variable 'y'**

Solve the system:

$$3x + 2y = 8 \quad \text{Equation (1)}$$

$$8x + 5y = 18 \quad \text{Equation (2)}$$

Solution Choose the variable 'y' to eliminate.

It has coefficients of 2 and 5.

Multiplying Equation (1) by 5, we obtain,

$$15x + 10y = 40 \quad \text{Equation (3)}$$

Multiplying Equation (2) by 2, we obtain,

Solution *continued*

$$16x + 10y = 36 \qquad \text{Equation (4)}$$

Subtract Equation (3) from (4), we obtain,

$$x = -4$$

Substituting $x = -4$ into Equation (1), we obtain,

$$3(-4) + 2y = 8$$

Rearranging, $$2y = 20$$

$$y = 10$$

6.4 | Exercises

1. Solve the following by the substitution method:
   a. $y - 3x + 8 = 0$ and $y - x + 4 = 0$
   b. $3x - 2y = 8$ and $x + 3y = 15$
   c. $x - 3y = 12$ and $5x + 2y = 9$

2. Solve the following by the substitution method:
   a. $4x - 7y + 6 = 0$ and $x - 3y + 2 = 0$
   b. $6x - 9y + 2 = 0$ and $x - 2y - 5 = 0$
   c. $3x + y = -8$ and $3x - 4y = -23$

3. Solve the following by the substitution method:
   a. $5x + 4y = 14$ and $x - 3y = -1$
   b. $3x - 2y = 20$ and $y + 4x = 23$
   c. $7x - 5y + 3 = 0$ and $-3x + y + 1 = 0$

4. Solve the following by the substitution method:
   a. $x - 9y = 6$ and $3x - 7y = 16$
   b. $9x - 2y = 12$ and $5y + 3x = 21$
   c. $6x - 5y + 13 = 0$ and $-3x + y - 8 = 0$

5. Solve the following by the elimination method:
   a. $3y + 2x = 24$ and $2x - 2y = 14$
   b. $5x + 3y = 19$ and $3x - 5y = -9$
   c. $5x - 2y + 1 = 0$ and $2x - 3y - 4 = 0$

6. Solve the following by the elimination method:
   a. $7x - 3y = -5$ and $5x - 9y = 7$
   b. $5x - 3y = 2$ and $3x - 5y = 7$
   c. $4x + 5y = 11$ and $2x + 3y = 5$

7. Solve the following by the elimination method:
   a. $5x - 7y = 19$ and $2x + 3y = -4$
   b. $2y + 3x = 14$ and $9x - 4y = 2$
   c. $3y + 7x = 15$ and $3x + 5y + 1 = 0$

8. Solve the following by the elimination method:
   a. $9x + 8y = 10$ and $3x + 2y = 4$
   b. $3x - 5y = 4$ and $5x + 3y = -16$
   c. $9y + 4x - 1 = 0$ and $4x + 5y + 3 = 0$

9. Solve the following equations:
   a. $0.5x - 0.3y = -1.2$ and $0.2x - 0.7y = 0.1$
   b. $0.4x - 0.5y = -0.8$ and $0.3x - 0.2y = 0.1$
   c. $0.7x - 0.4y = 2.9$ and $0.6x - 0.3y = 2.4$

10. Solve the following equations:

    a. $1.2x + 0.6y = 0$ and $3.5x + 1.7y = 0.01$

    b. $0.2x - 0.3y = -0.6$ and $0.5x + 0.2y = 2.3$

    c. $1.5x + y = 1$ and $0.8x + 0.7y = 1.2$

11. Solve the following equations:

    a. $\frac{x}{5} + \frac{y}{6} = 3$ and $\frac{x}{2} - \frac{y}{3} = 3$

    b. $\frac{5x}{3} - \frac{5y}{2} = -5$ and $\frac{x}{3} - \frac{y}{4} = 2$

    c. $\frac{x}{4} + \frac{y}{2} = 2\frac{1}{4}$ and $\frac{2x}{3} + \frac{y}{6} = \frac{3}{2}$

12. Solve the following equations:

    a. $\frac{x}{6} - \frac{y}{3} = \frac{2}{3}$ and $\frac{x}{4} - \frac{y}{12} = -\frac{3}{2}$

    b. $\frac{x}{4} + \frac{y}{2} = 2$ and $\frac{x}{6} + \frac{2y}{3} = \frac{4}{3}$

    c. $\frac{3x}{10} + \frac{y}{5} = \frac{1}{2}$ and $\frac{x}{3} + \frac{y}{3} = \frac{1}{2}$

13. Solve the following equations:

    a. $4(x - 3) + 5(y + 1) = 12$ and $(y + 7) - 3(x + 2) = 1$

    b. $2(x - 2) - 3(y - 1) = 11$ and $5(x + 1) + 2(y - 4) = 8$

    c. $3(2x + 1) - 2(y + 7) = -1$ and $4(x + 5) + 3(y - 1) = 28$

14. Solve the following equations:

    a. $4(x + 3) - 3(y + 4) = 21$ and $2(x + 4) + 5(y - 3) = 10$

    b. $3(x + 1) - 6(y + 2) = 6$ and $5(2x - 4) + 7(y + 1) = -17$

    c. $2(3x + 2) + 5(2y + 7) = 13$ and $3(x + 1) - 4(y - 1) = -15$

15. 2 adult meals and 3 children meals cost \$48, whereas, 3 adult meals and 2 children meals cost \$52. How much is 1 adult meal?

16. 3 DVDs and 4 movie tickets cost \$94.00, whereas, 4 DVDs and 3 movie tickets cost \$81. How much is 1 DVD?

17. The sum of a son's age and of his father's age in years is 92. The difference in their ages is 28. How old are the son and father?

18. The sum of 2 numbers is 56 and their difference is 22. What are the numbers?

• 19. Hanna charges \$20 for the first shirt that you purchase at her store. However, for every additional shirt, she charges \$15. Write an equation that shows the relationship between her total revenue (y) and number of shirts sold (x). If you plot a graph of y vs. x, what is the y-intercept and slope of the line that represents the equation?

• 20. An online music store charges \$2 for the first song that you download. For every additional song you download, you will be charged only \$1.50. Write an equation that shows the relationship between the total revenue (y) and the number of songs sold (x). If you plot a graph of y vs. x, what is the y-intercept and slope of the line that represents the equation?

• 21. Henry works in a computer store and earns \$500 a month plus a commission of 10% on the sales he makes. The relationship between his earnings (y) in a month and the number of computers he sells (x) is given by the equation $y = 500 + 0.10x$.

    a. What would his commission be if his earnings are \$14,000 in a month?

    b. What would his earnings be if his sales are \$250,000 in a month?

- 22. The fixed costs (FC) of a factory for the month are \$5000 and the variable costs (VC) to manufacture each product are \$5. The total costs (TC) for the month are the sum of the fixed costs and the variable costs per unit, times the number of products produced and sold. The relationship between *TC*, *FC*, *VC*, and x is given by the equation $TC = (VC)x + FC$.
    a. What would be the total cost if 90 products were sold this month?
    b. How many products were sold this month if the total cost is \$11,375?

6 | Review Exercises

Answers to odd-numbered problems are available at the end of the textbook

1. In which quadrant or axis do the following points lie?
   a. A (5, –1) b. B (–2, 3) c. C (3, 0)
   d. D (4, –2) e. E (2, 0) f. F (0, 4)

2. In which quadrant or axis do the following points lie?
   a. A (–4, 5) b. B (–5, 0) c. C (–2, –7)
   d. D (0, –3) e. E (6, 6) f. F (5, 4)

3. Plot the following points and join them in the order A, B, C, D. Identify the type of quadrilateral and find its area and perimeter.
   a. A (6, –3) b. B (6, –6)
   c. C (–2, –6) d. D (–2, –3)

4. Plot the following points and join them in the order P, Q, R, S. Identify the type of quadrilateral and find its area and perimeter.
   a. P (–2, 4) b. Q (–8, 4)
   c. R (–8, –2) d. S (–2, –2)

5. Graph the following equations using a table of values with four points:
   a. $4x - y = 2$ b. $x + y - 4 = 0$
   c. $y = \frac{1}{2}x + 2$

6. Graph the following equations using a table of values with four points:
   a. $2x + 3y = 12$ b. $x + 2y - 4 = 0$
   c. $y = -\frac{1}{3}x - 2$

7. Graph the following equations using the x-intercept, y-intercept, and another point.
   a. $3x - 4y = 12$ b. $x - 2y - 6 = 0$
   c. $y = 4x$

8. Graph the following equations using the x-intercept, y-intercept, and another point.
   a. $x - 2y = -1$ b. $3x + y - 4 = 0$
   c. $x = 2y$

9. Graph the following equations using the slope and y-intercept method.
   a. $y = 4x + 6$ b. $y = -\frac{3}{4}x - 1$
   c. $3x + 2y - 12 = 0$

10. Graph the following equations using the slope and y-intercept method.
    a. $y = 5x + 4$ b. $y = -\frac{1}{3}x - 1$
    c. $2x + 3y + 6 = 0$

11. Find the equation of the line that passes through the following points:
    a. (3, 2) and (7, 5) b. (5, –4) and (–1, 4)
    c. (1, –2) and (4, 7)

12. Find the equation of the line that passes through the following points:
    a. (4, 6) and (2, 4) b. (0, –7) and (–6, –1)
    c. (3, –4) and (–1, 4)

13. Solve the following pairs of equations by using the graphing method:
    a. $y = -2x - 1$ and $y = 3x - 11$
    b. $2x - 3y - 6 = 0$ and $x + 2y - 10 = 0$
    c. $2y = x$ and $y = -x + 3$

14. Solve the following pairs of equations by using the graphing method:
    a. $y = 2x + 3$ and $y = -2x - 1$
    b. $3x + 4y - 5 = 0$ and $2x - y + 4 = 0$
    c. $3y = 2x$ and $y = -3x + 11$

15. Solve the following pairs of equations by using the substitution method:
    a. $x + 4y = 8$ and $2x + 5y = 13$
    b. $x + 4y + 12 = 0$ and $9x - 2y - 32 = 0$
    c. $3x + 2y = 5$ and $y = 2x - 1$

16. Solve the following pairs of equations by using the substitution method:
    a. $x + y = 3$ and $2x - y = 12$
    b. $x - y - 1 = 0$ and $2x + 3y - 12 = 0$
    c. $4x + 3y = 12$ and $9 - 3x = y$

17. Solve the following pairs of equations by using the elimination method:
    a. $8x + 7y = 23$ and $7x + 8y = 22$
    b. $9x - 2y = -32$ and $x + 4y = -12$
    c. $4x + 3y = 12$ and $18 - 6x = 2y$

18. Solve the following pairs of equations by using the elimination method:
    a. $2x + y = 8$ and $3x + 2y = 7$
    b. $5x - 2y + 3 = 0$ and $3x - 2y - 1 = 0$
    c. $2x + y + 2 = 0$ and $6x = 2y + 9$

19. The slope of a line is 2 and it passes through A (2, 3) and B (–1, y). Find 'y' and the equation of the line.

20. The slope of a line is –3 and it passes through P (2, –2) and Q (x, 7). Find 'x' and the equation of the line.

6 | Self-Test Exercises

Answers to all problems are available at the end of the textbook

1. Three vertices of a rectangle ABCD have points. A (–3, 4), B (5, 4), and C (5, –1). Find the coordinate of the 4th vertex and the area of the rectangle.

2. Find the slope and y-intercept of the line $2x - 3y + 6 = 0$.

3. Find the equation of the line in standard form that passes through the points P (–4, 5) and Q (1, 1).

4. Given the following slopes (m) and y-intercepts (b), write the equations in standard form:
   a. $m = -\frac{1}{2}$, $b = -4$
   b. $m = \frac{2}{3}$, $b = -2$

5. Find the x-intercept, y-intercept, and another point on the line and graph the following lines.

6. Write the equation of a line in standard form that is parallel to $3x - 2y + 9 = 0$ and passing through the point (–6, –3).
   (Hint: Parallel lines will have the same slope.)

7. Solve the system of equations by using the graphical method:
   a. $y = 3x + 6$ and $6x - 2y + 12 = 0$
   b. $2x + 3y + 4 = 0$ and $3x - y + 7 = 0$

8. Solve the system of equations by using the substitution method:
   a. $2x + 4y + 6 = 0$ and $y - 3x + 9 = 0$
   b. $3x + y = -8$ and $2x + 3y = 4$

9. Solve the system of equations by using the elimination method:
   a. $6x - 4y + 3 = 0$ and $4x - 6y - 3 = 0$
   b. $3x + 5y - 19 = 0$ and $5x - 2y + 11 = 0$

10. The equation of a line is $8x - By - 6 = 0$. If the line passes through (1, –2), find the value of 'B' and write the equation in slope-intercept form.

In any business evaluation, a good understanding of how revenue and costs change with the quantity produced and sold is important. It is also necessary to understand the relationships among fixed costs, variable costs, selling price, etc. To be competitive in the market, businesses should look into ways of lowering their costs by reducing fixed costs and unit variable costs, while optimizing the quantities of items produced and sold, as well as by analyzing the resulting effects on their revenue. In this chapter, you will learn to answer some of the important questions in making such business decisions.

7 Break-Even and Cost-Volume-Profit Analysis

LEARNING OBJECTIVES

- Understand terms used in break-even analysis and their relation to each other.
- Understand assumptions and limitations in break-even analysis.
- Calculate the break-even point in terms of number of units produced and total revenue.
- Use formulas in cost-volume-profit (CVP) analysis.
- Use the contribution margin approach in CVP analysis.
- Use break-even charts in CVP analysis.
- Use the Texas Instruments BA II Plus calculator in break-even analysis.

CHAPTER OUTLINE

7.1 | Introduction

In any business, the goal is to make a profit. To achieve this goal, the **total revenue** from the business should exceed the **total costs** associated with it. Revenue is earned from the sales of the product manufactured or produced, but there are numerous costs incurred in manufacturing or producing a product before selling it. Therefore, it is important to determine the number of units of the product that needs to be manufactured and sold in order to cover all of the costs related to manufacturing it.

Break-even point is the point at which the total revenue equals the total costs.

The point at which the total sales or total revenue equals the total costs is known as the **break-even point**. At the break-even point, the profit (net income) or loss is zero; i.e., there is no profit made nor loss incurred. The break-even point is generally expressed in terms of volume (or quantity produced and sold). It may also be expressed in terms of total revenue. Any quantity that is produced and sold over this break-even point would result in a profit, while any quantity that is produced and sold below this break-even point would result in a loss.

Businesses analyze the break-even point and their profit or loss in relation to the costs incurred, volume of sales, and selling price using (i) cost-volume-profit analysis, (ii) the contribution margin approach, or (iii) break-even charts (graphical analysis).

Terms used in Break-Even Analysis

To understand break-even analysis, it is necessary to define the following terms and understand how they relate to each other.

Total Costs (TC)

There are several types of costs to consider in a business and these are classified into the two most relevant categories: fixed costs (FC) or total variable costs (TVC). The sum of the fixed costs and total variable costs is the total cost of the business and is expressed by the following formula:

Formula 7.1(a)

Total Costs

$$TC = FC + TVC$$

Fixed Costs (FC)

Fixed Costs (FC) are always for a period of time.

These are costs that remain the same irrespective of how many items are produced to sell. Fixed costs are calculated for a specific period (per annum, per month, etc.) to produce a predetermined quantity of products, known as the maximum capacity of the facility for that period.

Examples of fixed costs are generally administrative salaries, rent or lease of the facility, insurance cost, property tax, equipment rental or depreciation, and marketing and advertising costs.

Total Variable Costs (TVC)

These are costs that vary directly with the number of units of items produced. Examples of total variable costs are generally cost of all materials, cost of labour, and revenue-related costs, such as commission, etc., that are necessary to produce the number of items for the specific period. If no quantity is produced, then the total variable cost is zero.

Variable Costs per Unit (VC)

These are costs from producing one unit of the item. This is the ratio of the total variable costs to the total number of units produced:

$$VC = \frac{TVC}{x}$$

where x is the number of units produced and sold.

Variable Costs (VC) and Selling price (S) are always per unit.

Rearranging results in the following formula for TVC:

Formula 7.1(b)

Total Variable Costs

$$TVC = VC \times x$$

Selling Price per Unit (S)

This is the amount a business charges its customers to buy a single unit of item produced. This is critical in calculating the revenue for the business.

Total Revenue (TR)

This is the amount of money received or brought into the business from the sales of the items produced and is expressed by the following formula:

Formula 7.1(c)

Total Revenue

$$TR = S \times x$$

where 'x' is the number of units produced and sold.

Profit or Net Income (NI)

This defines the success of the business by determining the difference between the total revenue (TR) collected and the total costs (TC) incurred in the business. If the total revenue exceeds the total costs, then there is a net profit. If the total revenue is less than the total costs, then there is a net loss. If the total revenue is equal to the total costs, then the business breaks even.

Formula 7.1(d)

Net Income

$$NI = TR - TC$$

If $TR > TC$, then $NI > 0$	Profit
If $TR = TC$, then $NI = 0$	Break-even
If $TR < TC$, then $NI < 0$	Loss

Formula 7.1(e)

At the break-even point

$$\text{At the break-even point, } TR = TC$$

Contribution Margin per Unit (CM)

This is the amount remaining from sales per unit after deducting the variable costs per unit, as shown below:

Formula 7.1(f)

Contribution Margin

$$CM = S - VC$$

The contribution amount from the sale of all units during a period is first used to cover the fixed costs (*FC*); amount that remains is the net income (*NI*). If the contribution amount from the sale of all units exceeds the fixed costs for a period, then there is a profit; similarly, if the contribution amount from the sale of all units is less than the fixed costs, then there is a loss.

Contribution Ratio (*CR*)

This is the ratio of the contribution margin (*CM*) to the selling price (*S*) and is expressed as a percentage, as shown in the formula below:

Formula 7.1(g)

Contribution Ratio

$$CR = \frac{CM}{S} \times 100\%$$

Assumptions and Limitations

There are a number of assumptions made and limitations present in break-even analysis and cost-volume-profit analysis in this chapter. These assumptions are made to focus on the main concepts in this topic and to simplify theoretical calculations. However, in practical situations, variations to these assumptions must be taken into account before making business decisions, and this is accomplished using more advanced mathematical models.

The following outlines are the assumptions and limitations in this chapter::

a. Selling price per unit (*S*) is constant and is not affected by a change in the number of units sold.

b. Quantity of items (x) produced is equal to the quantity of items sold.

c. Variable Costs per unit (*VC*) is constant and is not affected by a change in the number of units sold.

d. Fixed Costs (*FC*) remain the same over the specified period.

e. When multiple products are produced in a company, the ratio of various products produced remains constant.

Break-even point: The point at which the total revenue (*TR*) equals the total costs (*TC*).

Break-Even Point

As explained earlier, the break-even point in a business is when the total revenue from the sale is equal to the total costs. The break-even point may be expressed in terms of the number of units produced or in terms of the total revenue.

Note:

The break-even point can be lowered by any or all of the following measures:

a. Reducing the variable costs (*VC*) per unit by more cost-effective scheduling or by using technology.

b. Reducing the fixed costs (*FC*) by cost control measures in marketing, rentals, etc.

c. Increasing the selling price (*S*). However, businesses may be reluctant to increase the price of the product due to a competitor's selling price of similar items.

Example 7.1(a)

Calculating the Break-Even Point in Terms of the Number of Units Produced

A company produces calculators and sells them at $50 each. Their total fixed costs are $4000 per month and the variable cost per unit is $30. Calculate the number of units needed to be produced per month to break even.

Solution

$S = \$50.00, \quad FC = \$4000.00, \quad VC = \$30.00$

Let x be the number of units needed per month to break even.

Using Formula 7.1(c), $TR = S \times x = 50x$

Total Cost at the break-even point $TC = FC + VC \times x = 4000 + 30x$

At the break-even point, $TR = TC$

Therefore, $50x = 4000 + 30x$

Solving for x, $20x = 4000$

$x = 200$ units

Therefore, 200 units should be produced per month to break even.

Example 7.1(b)

Calculating the Break-Even Point in Terms of the Total Revenue

A tire manufacturing company must produce 3200 tires per annum to break even and has total fixed costs of $80,000 per annum. The variable costs are $40 per tire. Calculate the total revenue per annum required to break even. Also, find the selling price per tire.

Solution

$x = 3200$ units, $\quad FC = \$80{,}000, \quad VC = \$40, \quad TR = ?$

Using Formula 7.1(a), $TC = FC + TVC$

Substituting TVC with Formula 7.1(b), $= FC + (VC \times x)$

$= 80{,}000 + (40 \times 3200)$

Total Cost at the break-even point $= \$208{,}000.00$

At the break-even point, $TR = TC$

Therefore, the total revenue required to break even is $208,000.00 per annum.

Let 'S' be the selling price per unit.

Using Formula 7.1(c), $TR = S \times x$

Substituting values, $208{,}000 = S\,(3200)$

$S = \$65.00$

Therefore, the selling price per tire is $65.00.

7.1 | Exercises

Calculate the missing values in Problems 1 and 2:

1.

	Fixed Cost (FC) per month	Variable Cost (VC) per unit	Selling Price (S) per unit	Break-even Volume (x) per month	Total Variable Cost (TVC) per month	Total Revenue (TR) per month ($TR = TC$ at Break-even)
a.	$1000	$3	$13	?	?	?
b.	$8000	?	$110	200	?	?
c.	$5890	?	$156	62	?	?
d.	?	$45	$91	50	?	?
e.	$4250	?	$75	?	?	$18,750
f.	?	$300	?	?	$150,000	$158,500

2.

	Fixed Cost (FC) per month	Variable Cost (VC) per unit	Selling Price (S) per unit	Break-even Volume (x) per month	Total Variable Cost at Break-even (TVC) per month	At Break-even Total Cost = Total Revenue $TR = TC$ per month
a.	\$8400	\$25	\$36	?	?	?
b.	\$125,000	?	\$475	1000	?	?
c.	\$720	?	\$74	20	?	?
d.	?	\$30	\$50	400	?	?
e.	\$7800	?	\$150	?	?	\$30,000
f.	?	\$120	?	?	\$84,000	\$108,500

3. The selling price per unit of a product is \$30, the fixed costs per month are \$12,560, and the total variable costs per month are \$11,440 at the break-even point. Calculate the number of units required to be sold per month to break even.

4. Harris owns a DVD manufacturing factory that produces DVDs and sells them for \$0.30 each. Their total fixed costs are \$8640 per month and the total variable costs at the break-even point are \$1800 per month. Calculate the number of DVDs he needs to produce per month to break even.

5. Calculate the selling price per unit of a product and the total revenue per month to break even if the fixed costs per month are \$390,500, the number of units required to be sold per month to break even is 3550, and the variable costs per unit are \$70.

6. A factory that manufactures and sells computer hard-drives has fixed costs of \$183,000 and variable costs of \$106 per hard-drive sold. If they need to sell 2440 hard-drives per month to break even, calculate the selling price of each hard-drive and the total revenue per month required to break even.

7. A firm selling snowboots has variable costs of \$65 per pair of boots. The fixed costs for the firm are \$2100 per month, and they have to sell 84 pairs of boots to break even. Calculate their total revenue at the break-even point and the selling price per pair of boots.

8. A phone manufacturing company has to produce and sell 225 phones every month to break even. If the company's fixed costs are \$2227.50 per month and their variable costs are \$10 per phone, calculate their total revenue and selling price per phone at the break-even point.

9. A ski company manufactured and sold skis for \$400 per set. If the variable costs to manufacture each set were \$290 and the break-even volume was 740 units per month, calculate their fixed costs and total revenue at the break-even point.

10. Chu-hua sold calendars at her store for \$15.40 each. If her variable costs to create each calendar are \$12 and she needs to sell 625 calendars per month to break even, calculate her fixed costs and total revenue at the break-even point.

11. A large music store must sell 292 headphones every week to break even. If the total revenue per week at the break-even point is \$27,000 and the fixed costs are \$10,220 per week, calculate the variable costs per headphone.

12. Alora and Jacey run a travel agency that makes commissions on selling air tickets. They need to sell 520 tickets per month to break even and their total revenue at the break-even point is \$45,000. Calculate their variable costs per ticket if their fixed costs are \$26,000 per month.

7.2 | Cost-Volume-Profit (CVP) Analysis

Cost-Volume-Profit analysis commences with the following profit equation:

Profit or Net Income (NI) = Total Revenue (TR) − Total Costs (TC)

From Formula 7.1(d) $NI = TR - TC$

Rearranging, $TR = TC + NI$

Substituting $TR = S \times x$ from Formula 7.1(c), and $TC = FC + TVC$ from Formula 7.1(a), we obtain,

$$S \times x = FC + TVC + NI$$

Substituting $TVC = VC \times x$ from Formula 7.1(b) results in the cost-volume-profit analysis formula,

Formula 7.2(a) **Cost-Volume-Profit Analysis**

$$S \times x = FC + (VC \times x) + NI$$

When $TR > TC$, NI is positive (i.e. profit), as illustrated in Exhibit 7.2(a).

$$S \times x = FC + (VC \times x) + NI$$

Rearranging, we obtain,

$$(S \times x) - (VC \times x) = FC + NI$$

By factoring, we obtain,

$$x\,(S - VC) = FC + NI$$

Rearranging and isolating x results in the following formula:

Formula 7.2(b) **Number of Units**

$$x = \frac{FC + NI}{(S - VC)}$$

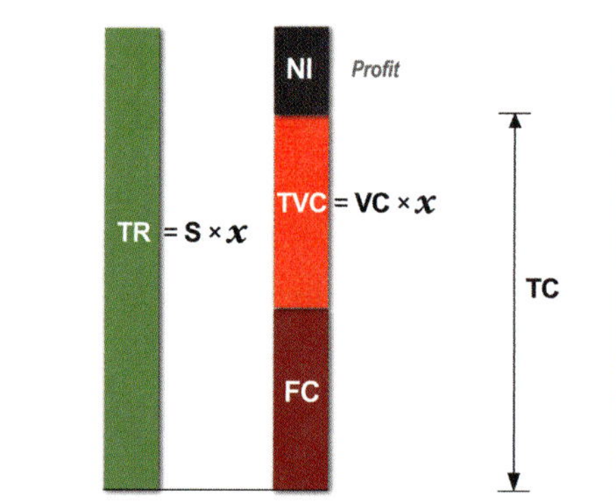

Exhibit 7.2(a): When $TR > TC$, NI is Positive (Profit)

When $TR = TC$, $NI = 0$ (i.e., break-even), as illustrated in Exhibit 7.2(b).

$$S \times x = FC + (VC \times x) + NI$$

When $NI = 0$, we obtain,

$$S \times x = FC + (VC \times x) + 0$$

Rearranging, we obtain,

$$S \times x - (VC \times x) = FC$$

Factoring the x, we have,

$$x\,(S - VC) = FC$$

Rearranging and isolating x, we have,

$$x = \frac{FC}{(S - VC)}$$

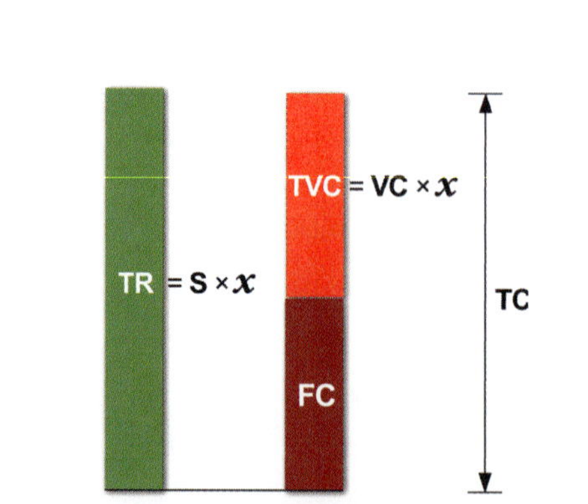

Exhibit 7.2(b): When $TR = TC$, NI is Zero (Break-even)

When $TR < TC$, NI is negative (i.e., loss), as illustrated in Exhibit 7.2(c).

From Formula 7.2(b), $x = \dfrac{FC + NI}{(S - VC)}$

In this case, NI is entered as a negative number as it is a loss.

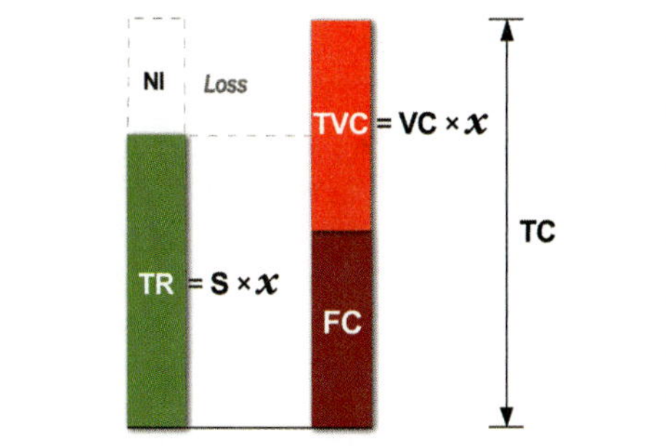

Exhibit 7.2(c): When $TR < TC$, NI is Negative (Loss)

Example 7.2(a) **Use of Formulas in Cost-Volume-Profit (CVP) Analysis**

Sam has a printing company that prints textbooks, which are then sold to customers. His printing facility can produce a maximum of 3000 textbooks per annum (maximum capacity of the facility). The fixed costs per annum are \$100,000, the variable costs per unit are \$75, and the selling price per unit is \$125.

a. Calculate the number of books he should produce and sell per year to break even.

b. In 2007, Sam produced and sold 1200 textbooks. Did he make a profit or incur a loss and by what amount?

c. In 2008, Sam produced and sold 2250 textbooks. Did he make a profit or incur a loss and by what amount?

d. In 2009, Sam utilized 80% of his facility to produce and sell textbooks. Calculate the profit made or loss incurred.

e. In 2010, Sam wanted a profit of \$40,000. How many books did he have to produce and sell and what percentage of his facility would he have utlitized?

f. What is the maximum profit per annum that he can expect from his facility?

Solution

a. **Calculate the number of books he should produce and sell per year to break even.**

Assume that he has to produce and sell x books to break even.

Maximum capacity = 3000 books, $FC = \$100{,}000$, $S = \$125$, $VC = \$75$

Total revenue, $TR = S \times x = 125x$

Total costs, $TC = FC + (VC \times x) = 100{,}000 + 75x$

At the break-even point, $TR = TC$

So, $125x = 100{,}000 + 75x$

Solving for x, $125x - 75x = 100{,}000$

$$50x = 100{,}000$$

$$x = \frac{100{,}000}{50} = 2000 \text{ units per year}$$

Therefore, Sam should produce and sell 2000 textbooks per year to break even.

Solution *continued*

b. In 2007, Sam produced and sold 1200 textbooks. Did he make a profit or incur a loss and by what amount?

Sam would have incurred a loss since the 1200 textbooks produced in 2007 is less than the break-even volume of 2000 textbooks per year.

$$TR = S \times x = 125 \times 1200 = \$150{,}000.00$$

And, $TC = FC + (VC \times x) = 100{,}000 + (75 \times 1200) = \$190{,}000.00$

Also, $NI = TR - TC = 150{,}000 - 190{,}000 = -\$40{,}000.00$ (loss)

Therefore, Sam incurred a loss of $40,000.00 in 2007.

c. In 2008, Sam produced and sold 2250 textbooks. Did he make a profit or incur a loss and by what amount?

Sam would have made a profit since the 2250 textbooks produced in 2008 is greater than the break-even volume of 2000 textbooks per year.

Using Formula 7.1(c), $TR = S \times x = 125 \times 2250 = \$281{,}250.00$

Using Formula 7.1(a), $TC = FC + (VC \times x) = 100{,}000 + (75 \times 2250) = \$268{,}750.00$

Using Formula 7.1(d), $NI = TR - TC = 281{,}250 - 268{,}750 = \$12{,}500.00$ (profit)

Therefore, Sam made a profit of $12,500.00 in 2008.

d. In 2009, Sam utilized 80% of his facility to produce and sell textbooks. Calculate the profit made or loss incurred.

$$\text{Maximum capacity} = 3000 \text{ textbooks}$$

$$80\% \text{ of } 3000 = 2400 \text{ textbooks}$$

This is greater than the break-even volume of 2000 textbooks and therefore, he would have made a profit.

Using Formula 7.1(c), $TR = S \times x = 125 \times 2400 = \$300{,}000.00$

Using Formula 7.1(a), $TC = FC + (VC \times x)$

$$= 100{,}000 + (75 \times 2400) = \$280{,}000.00$$

Using Formula 7.1(d), $NI = TR - TC = 300{,}000 - 280{,}000 = \$20{,}000.00$ (profit)

Therefore, Sam made a profit of $20,000.00 in 2009.

e. **In 2010, Sam wanted a profit of $40,000. How many books did he have to produce and sell and what percentage of his facility would he have utilized?**

Using Formula 7.1(d), $NI = TR - TC$

$$NI = S \times x - (FC + VC \times x)$$

Expanding, $40{,}000 = 125x - (100{,}000 + 75x)$

Solving for x, $40{,}000 = 125x - 100{,}000 - 75x$

$$140{,}000 = 50x$$

Therefore, $x = \dfrac{140{,}000}{50} = 2800$ textbooks in 2010

To make a profit of $40,000.00, Sam would have had to produce and sell 2800 textbooks in 2010, out of a maximum of 3000 textbooks.

Therefore, percentage of the facility utilized $= \dfrac{\text{Quantity produced}}{\text{Maximum capacity of the facility}} \times 100\%$

$$= \frac{2800}{3000} \times 100\% = 0.933333... = 93.33\%$$

Therefore, Sam would have had to produce and sell 2800 textbooks in 2010 and he would have utilized 93.33% of his facility.

Solution ***continued***

f. What is the maximum profit per annum that he can expect from his facility?

He should utilize 100% of the facility to maximize profit. Therefore, he should produce and sell 3000 textbooks (maximum capacity of the facility).

$$TR = S \times x = 125 \times 3000 = \$375{,}000.00$$

And, $$TC = FC + (VC \times x) = 100{,}000 + (75 \times 3000) = \$325{,}000.00$$

Also, $$NI = TR - TC = 375{,}000 - 325{,}000 = \$50{,}000.00$$

Therefore, he can expect a maximum profit of $50,000.00 per annum from his facility.

Example 7.2(b) **CVP Analysis Where there are Several Fixed Costs and Variable Costs**

A furniture manufacturer who sells chairs for $210 each has the following monthly fixed costs: $2500 in rent, $350 in utilities, and $150 in insurance. The variable costs to produce each chair are $60 for the material and 3 hours of labour at $30.00 per hour.

a. Calculate the break-even volume per month.

b. If the profit last month was $1800, how many chairs were produced and sold?

Solution

a. **Calculate his break-even volume per month.**

Assume that he needs to produce and sell x chairs per month to break even.

$$FC = Rent + Utilities + Insurance$$
$$= 2500 + 350 + 150 = \$3000.00 \text{ per month}$$

$$VC \text{ per chair} = \text{Material cost} + \text{Labour costs}$$
$$= 60 + (30 \times 3) = \$150.00 \text{ per chair}$$

At the break-even point, $NI = 0$,

Using Formula 7.1(a), $S \times x = FC + (VC \times x) + NI$

Substituting values, $210x = 3000 + 150x + 0$

Solving for x, $60x = 3000$

$x = 50$ units per month

Therefore, the manufacturer's break-even volume is 50 chairs per month.

b. If the profit last month was $1800, how many chairs were produced and sold?

Using Formula 7.1(a), $S \times x = FC + (VC \times x) + NI$

Substituting values, $210x = 3000 + 150x + 1800$

Solving for x, $60x = 4800$

$x = 80$ units per month

Therefore, if the profit last month was $1800, 80 chairs were produced and sold.

Example 7.2(c) **CVP Analysis When the Selling Price and/or Fixed Costs Change**

Pierre runs a small garment manufacturing company. He has fixed costs of $2500 per month and variable costs of $25 per unit. He sells each garment for $35 per unit.

a. Calculate his break-even volume and revenue per month.

b. If he increases his selling price by 10%, calculate his new break-even volume per month.

c. If he reduces his fixed costs by $250 per month with no changes to the variable costs and selling price, calculate his new break-even volume per month.

d. If his fixed costs increase by 5% and he decreases his selling price by 10%, calculate his new break-even volume per month if there were no changes to the variable costs.

Solution

a. **Calculate his break-even volume and revenue per month.**

Assume that he sells x garments per month.

$$S = \$35, FC = \$2500$$

Using Formula 7.1(b), $TVC = VC \times x = 25x$

Using Formula 7.1(c), $TR = S \times x = 35x$

Using Formula 7.1(a), $TC = FC + TVC = 2500 + 25x$

At the break-even point, $TR = TC$

$$35x = 2500 + 25x$$

Solving for x, $10x = 2500$

$$x = 250 \text{ units per month}$$

Therefore, his break-even volume is 250 garments per month.

$$TR = S \times x = 35 \times 250 = \$8750.00$$

Therefore, his break-even revenue is \$8750.00 per month.

b. **If he increases his selling price by 10%, calculate his new break-even volume per month.**

New selling price, $S = 1.10 \times 35 = \$38.50$

Fixed Costs, $FC = \$2500.00$

Using Formula 7.1(b), $TVC = VC \times x = 25x$

Using Formula 7.1(c), $TR = S \times x = 38.50x$

Using Formula 7.1(a), $TC = FC + TVC = 2500 + 25x$

At the break-even point, $TR = TC$

$$38.50x = 2500 + 25x$$

Solving for x, $13.50x = 2500$

$$x = 185.185185... \text{ units per month}$$

The number of units produced must be rounded up to the next whole number.

Therefore, his new break-even volume is 186 garments per month.

c. **If he reduces his fixed costs by \$250 per month with no changes to the variable costs and selling price, calculate his new break-even volume per month.**

$$FC = 2500 - 250 = \$2250.00$$

$$S = \$35.00$$

Using Formula 7.1(b), $TVC = VC \times x = 25x$

Using Formula 7.1(c), $TR = S \times x = 35x$

Using Formula 7.1(a), $TC = FC + TVC = 2250 + 25x$

At the break-even point, $TR = TC$

Solving for x, $35x = 2250 + 25x$

$$10x = 2250$$

$$x = 225 \text{ units per month}$$

Therefore, his new break-even volume is 225 garments per month.

Solution *continued*

d. **If his fixed costs increase by 5% and he decreases his selling price by 10%, calculate his new break-even volume per month if there were no changes to the variable costs.**

$$FC = 2500 \times 1.05 = \$2625.00$$

$$S = 35 \times 0.90 = \$31.50$$

Using Formula 7.1(b), $TVC = VC \times x = 25x$

Using Formula 7.1(c), $TR = S \times x = 31.50x$

Using Formula 7.1(a), $TC = FC + TVC = 2625 + 25x$

At the break-even point, $TR = TC$

$$31.50x = 2625 + 25x$$

Solving for x, $6.50x = 2625$

$$x = 403.846153... \text{ units per month}$$

Therefore, his new break-even volume is 404 garments per month.

7.2 | Exercises

1. Hayden runs a hot dog stand at Toronto's Harbourfront Center and only sells vegetarian hot dogs for \$3 each. If her fixed costs are \$1900 per month and variable costs are \$0.50 per hot dog, calculate the number of hot dogs she would have to sell to break even.

2. Precision engineers have been making hi-tech watches for over three decades. Their new CEO would like to diversify the business and start making precision grandfather clocks. To conduct a cost-volume-profit analysis, he gathers the following costs for this new division: \$280,455 in fixed costs per annum and \$1800 in variable costs per clock. Calculate the number of grandfather clocks they would have to make and sell to break even if they plan to sell each clock for \$8000.

3. Rodney's toy manufacturing company can produce a maximum of 6000 dolls per annum and sells each doll for \$80. His company has fixed costs of \$385,500 per annum and variable costs of \$5 per doll.
   a. How many dolls must he produce and sell to break even?
   b. If he used 85% of his facility to produce and sell dolls, calculate the profit made or loss incurred.
   c. If he wants to make a profit of \$50,000, how many dolls must he produce and sell and what percentage of his facility will he utilize?

4. Sandra started a Belgian waffle restaurant and purchased equipment that can produce a maximum of 50,000 waffles per annum. She sells each waffle for \$3.50. She has fixed costs of \$36,000 per annum and variable costs of \$0.35 per waffle.
   a. How many waffles must she produce and sell to break even?
   b. If she produced and sold 13,500 waffles, did she make a profit or incur a loss and by what amount?
   c. What is the maximum profit she can expect from her restaurant?

5. An e-learning company manager identified a new course that he could create and sell in the market for \$90 per student. The costs for adding this new course to their product offering would be:
   - Lease for additional space = \$1800 per month
   - Insurance costs = \$300 per month

- Support staff cost = $5000 per month
- Sales staff cost = $4000 per month
- Variable costs to host each course = $2 per month

a. Calculate his break-even volume per month.

b. If his profit last month was $32,460, how many courses did he sell?

6. Olga was planning to set up a business where she would purchase paintings for $1000 per unit and sell them for $1600 per unit. She wanted to conduct a break-even analysis and identified the following costs for running her business: $4450 per month for store leasing, $50 per month for website hosting fee, $5000 per month for staff salary, $2000 per month for advertising costs, and $25 per unit for labour charges to pack the paintings.

   a. How many paintings would she have to sell per month to break even?

   b. If she wants to make a profit of $23,000 in a month, how many paintings would she have to sell?

• 7. Sylvester, the CEO of a manufacturing company, decided to expand the product offering of his business to include the manufacture of automobile wheels. To include this product, his business would incur fixed costs of $120,000 per year and variable costs of $750 per wheel. He plans to sell each wheel in the market for $1250.

   a. Calculate the number of wheels he would have to manufacture to break even.

   b. While manufacturing the product, he realized that he required an additional expense of $3000 per year, and also realized that to be more competitive in the market he had to drop the selling price of the wheels by 20%. Calculate the new break-even quantity.

• 8. Samantha and Baxter started an animal spa and charged $80 per dog grooming session. Their monthly fixed costs included $3800 for the building lease and $2800 for salaries. The cost of supplies for each grooming session was $12.

   a. To break even, how many animals did they serve every month?

   b. If the cost of supplies for each grooming session was reduced to $10 and they hired one more person for $2000 per month, calculate the minimum number of animals they had to serve to ensure that they did not have any losses.

7.3 | Contribution Margin (CM) Approach to CVP Analysis

As defined earlier in Formula 7.1(f), the unit contribution margin (CM) is the amount remaining from the sales per unit after deducting the variable costs per unit.

$$CM = S - VC \qquad \text{from Formula 7.1(f)}$$

We know that the number of units produced (x) is given by:

$$x = \frac{FC + NI}{(S - VC)} \qquad \text{from Formula 7.2(b)}$$

At the break-even point, $NI = 0$

Therefore, $$x = \frac{FC}{(S - VC)}$$

Substituting $CM = (S - VC)$ in the above formula, we obtain,

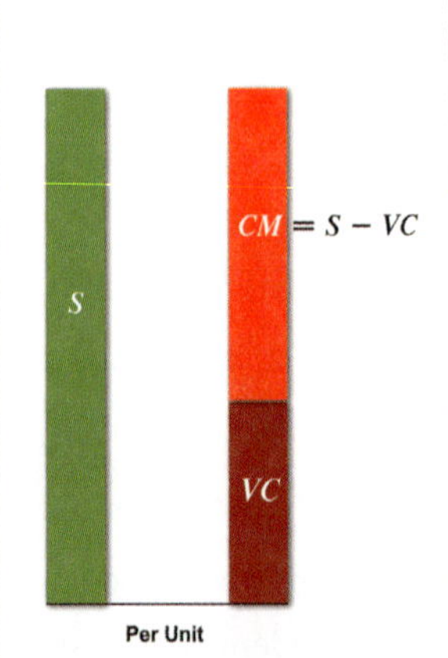

Exhibit 7.3: $CM = S - VC$

Formula 7.3 | **Number of Units at the Break-Even Point**

$$x = \frac{FC}{CM}$$

The contribution margin from each unit produced and sold is used to cover fixed costs (FC) until the break-even point is reached.

Once the break-even volume is reached, every unit produced above the break-even volume will result in a profit equal to the contribution margin amount.

If the contribution margin from the number of units produced and sold is not sufficient to cover the fixed costs, then a loss occurs; i.e., every unit produced below the break-even volume will result in a loss equal to the contribution margin amount.

For example, if FC = \$100,000, S = \$125 per unit, and VC = \$75 per unit,

$$\begin{aligned} CM &= S - VC \\ &= 125 - 75 \\ &= \$50.00 \text{ per unit} \end{aligned}$$

$$\begin{aligned} \text{Break-even volume, } x &= \frac{FC}{CM} \\ &= \frac{100{,}000}{50} \\ &= 2000 \text{ units} \end{aligned}$$

Therefore, every unit produced above the break-even volume of 2000 units gives a profit of \$50.00 and every unit produced below the break-even volume of 2000 units will result in a loss of \$50.00.

Example 7.3(a)

Use the Contribution Margin (CM) Approach in Cost-Volume-Profit Analysis to Solve Example 7.2(a)

Sam has a printing company that prints textbooks, which are then sold to customers. His printing facility can produce a maximum of 3000 textbooks per annum (maximum capacity of the facility). The fixed costs per annum are \$100,000, the variable costs per unit are \$75, and the selling price per unit is \$125.

a. Calculate the number of books he should produce and sell per year to break even.

b. In 2007, Sam produced and sold 1200 textbooks. Did he make a profit or incur a loss and by what amount?

c. In 2008, Sam produced and sold 2250 textbooks. Did he make a profit or incur a loss and by what amount?

d. In 2009, Sam utilized 80% of his facility to produce and sell textbooks. Calculate the profit made or loss incurred.

e. In 2010, Sam wanted a profit of \$40,000. How many books did he have to produce and sell and what percentage of his facility would he have utlitized?

f. What is the maximum profit per annum that he can expect from his facility?

Solution

Let's first calculate his contribution margin per textbook.

S = \$125 per unit, VC = \$75 per unit

$CM = S - VC = 125 - 75 = \$50.00$ per unit

a. Calculate the number of books he should produce and sell per year to break even.

$$FC = \$100{,}000$$

Using Formula 7.3,

$$\begin{aligned} x &= \frac{FC}{CM} \\ &= \frac{100{,}000}{50} = 2000 \text{ units} \end{aligned}$$

Therefore, Sam should produce and sell 2000 textbooks per year to break even.

Solution
continued

b. In 2007, Sam produced and sold 1200 textbooks. Did he make a profit or incur a loss and by what amount?

If Sam sold 1200 textbooks in 2007, then this was 800 textbooks below the break-even volume of 2000 textbooks per year; therefore, he incurred a loss.

Since, CM = \$50 per textbook, the amount of loss = 800 × 50 = \$40,000.00.
Therefore, he incurred a loss of \$40,000.00 in 2007.

c. In 2008, Sam produced and sold 2250 textbooks. Did he make a profit or incur a loss and by what amount?

If Sam sold 2250 textbooks in 2008, then this was 250 textbooks above the break-even volume of 2000 textbooks; therefore, he made a profit.

Since, CM = \$50 per textbook, the amount of profit is 250 × 50 = \$12,500.00.

Therefore, he made a profit of \$12,500.00 in 2008.

d. In 2009, Sam utilized 80% of his facility to produce and sell textbooks. Calculate the profit made or loss incurred.

$$\textit{Maximum Capacity} = 3000 \text{ textbooks},$$

$$80\% \text{ of } 3000 = 2400 \text{ textbooks}$$

This was 400 textbooks above the break-even volume of 2000 textbooks; therefore, he made a profit.

Since, CM = \$50 per textbook, the amount of profit is 400 × 50 = \$20,000.00 per year.
Therefore, he made a profit of \$20,000.00 in 2009.

e. In 2010, Sam wanted a profit of \$40,000. How many books did he have to produce and sell and what percentage of his facility would he have utilized?

Since he wanted a profit of \$40,000 he should have produced books above the break-even volume of 2000 textbooks per year.

The number of units above the break-even volume that he had to produce and sell to give him \$40,000:

$$\textit{Textbooks to Produce} = \frac{40{,}000}{50} = 800 \text{ units}$$

Therefore, he had to produce and sell (2000 + 800) = 2800 textbooks per year.

$$\textit{Percentage Utilized} = \frac{2800}{3000} \times 100\% = 0.933333... = 93.33\%$$

In order to produce and sell 2800 textbooks in 2010, 93.33% of his facility would have been utilized.

f. What would be the maximum profit per annum that he can expect from his facility?

This would be 1000 textbooks above the break-even volume of 2000 textbooks per year. Therefore, the profit would be 1000 × 50 = \$50,000.00 per year.

Example 7.3(b)

Use the Contribution Margin (CM) Approach in Cost-Volume-Profit Analysis

An audio equipment manufacturer produced and sold 725 sound systems and made a net income of \$50,000 last year, with total revenues of \$1,015,000. The manufacturer's break-even volume is 600 units.

a. Calculate the selling price of each sound system.

b. Calculate the variable costs for each sound system.

c. Calculate the fixed costs per year.

Solution $NI = \$50{,}000, \quad TR = \$1{,}015{,}000, \quad x = 725$

a. Calculate the selling price of each sound system.

Using Formula 7.1(c), $TR = S \times x$

$$1{,}015{,}000 = S \times 725$$

$$S = \frac{1{,}015{,}000}{725} = \$1400.00$$

Therefore, the selling price of each sound system was $1400.00 per unit.

b. Calculate the variable costs for each sound system.

The manufacturer produced 725 sound systems last year.

This is 125 units above the break-even volume, contributing to a profit of $50,000.

$$125 \times CM = 50{,}000$$

Therefore, $CM = \frac{50{,}000}{125} = 400.00$

Using Formula 7.1(f), $CM = S - VC$

$$400.00 = 1400.00 - VC$$

$$VC = \$1000.00 \text{ per unit}$$

Therefore, the variable cost for each sound system was $1000.00 per unit.

Every unit produced above the break-even volume results in a profit equal to the contribution margin amount. Similarly every unit produced below the break-even volume results in a loss equal to the contribution margin amount.

c. Calculate the fixed costs per year.

Using Formula 7.3, $x = \frac{FC}{CM}$

$$600 = \frac{FC}{400.00}$$

Rearranging, $FC = \$600 \times 400 = \$240{,}000$ per year

Therefore, the fixed costs per year are $240,000.00.

7.3 | Exercises

Calculate the missing values for Problems 1 and 2:

1.

	Fixed Costs (*FC*) per period	Variable Costs (*VC*) per unit	Selling Price (*S*) per unit	Total Variable Costs (*TVC*) per period	Total Revenue (*TR*) per period	Total Costs (*TC*) per period	Net Income (*NI*) per period	Number of units produced and sold (*x*)
a.	$9000	?	$65	?	?	$31,500	$33,500	?
b.	?	$75	$145	?	?	$168,500	?	1200
c.	$1440	?	?	$22,500	$33,750	?	?	750
d.	?	?	$135	$62,500	?	?	$62,200	1500

2.

	Fixed Costs (*FC*) per period	Variable Cost (*VC*) per unit	Selling Price (*S*) per unit	Total Variable Costs (*TVC*) per period	Total Revenue (*TR*) per period	Total Costs (*TC*) per period	Net Income (*NI*) per period	Number of units produced and sold (*x*)
a.	$22,500	?	$910	?	?	$364,500	$418,100	?
b.	?	$280	$420	?	?	$55,480	?	170
c.	$120,800	?	?	$342,000	$570,000	?	?	1900
d.	?	?	$1480	$37,800	?	?	$4,300	30

3. The variable costs to manufacture digital e-books are $280 per e-books and the selling price is $800 per e-book. If the manufacturer has fixed costs of $44,460 per month, calculate the contribution margin per e-book and the number of books that need to be sold to break even.

4. A plumber offers his plumbing services of fixing tubs and jacuzzis at $350 per job. If his fixed costs are $1400 per month and variable costs are $30 per job, calculate the contribution margin on each job and the number of orders he needs to have per month to break even.

5. A roof insulation company charges a flat rate of $1400 for insulating roofs of town houses. Monthly administrative costs of the company are $3540, cost of supplies is $130 per job, and wages are $300 per job. Calculate the company's profit or loss if they insulated 15 roofs in a particular month.

6. A solar water heating distributor buys water heaters for $5850 and sells them for $7600 each. If he pays $2000 per month as lease for his store, $5950 per month for staff salary, and $800 per month for marketing, calculate the amount of profit made or loss incurred if he sold 4 heaters in a particular month.

7. Ching Lan sells designer caps in her store at $28 each. If her fixed costs are $2700 per month and she needs to sell 310 caps to break even, calculate:

   a. Contribution margin per cap.

   b. Variable costs per cap.

   c. Net income at 50% above break-even volume.

8. Dmytro runs a sports shop in Markham, Ontario. He sells pairs of skates for $450 each and has fixed costs of $28,500 per annum. If he needs to sell 190 pairs of skates to break even, calculate:

   a. Contribution margin per pair of skates.

   b. Variable costs per pair of skates.

   c. Net income if he sells 100 units above the break-even point.

9. Belle sells popular designer watches for $36 each. If her total revenue at the break-even point is $81,000 per month and the contribution margin per watch is $27, calculate the fixed costs, break-even volume, and total revenue should she sell 2500 watches.

10. Elise and her friend Eloi developed an online car-repair course and sell it for $62.50 per course. If the contribution margin per course is $20 and to break even they need to have a total revenue of $175,000 per annum, calculate the fixed costs per annum, break-even volume, and total revenue should they sell 3000 courses this year.

• 11. Zenith Lighting Inc. introduced a new line of chandeliers in their retail store that they were selling for $650 each. To secure additional space to store and sell these chandeliers they had to pay an additional rent of $2800 per month. They also recruited a full time sales person for a base salary of $2000 to sell this line of chandeliers. The sales person's commission on the sale of each chandelier was 5% on the selling price and it cost them $75 to purchase these chandeliers from an overseas vendor. If they could only purchase a maximum of 38 chandeliers of this type every month from their current vendor, calculate the maximum profit they could make on this product in any month.

• 12. Mark, a first semester student at a college, decided to start a trading business buying formal dress shirts for $10 from an overseas country and selling them to his college peers for $35 each. As he is not good at selling, he hired his friend Ruby to sell these shirts and paid her 10% of the selling price as commission on every shirt she sold. If he spent a flat rate of $20 on storage charges every month and could only purchase a maximum of 500 shirts every month from his overseas vendor, calculate the maximum monthly profit he could make in his business.

7.4 | Graphical Approach to CVP Analysis (Break-Even Chart)

A break-even chart is a graphical representation of the following two graphs on the same axis:

1. Total costs at various levels of quantity produced (Total Costs vs. Quantity Produced)
2. Total revenue at various levels of quantity sold (Total Revenue vs. Quantity Sold)

The vertical axis (Y-axis) of the graph represents total cost or total revenue (in dollars).

The horizontal axis (X-axis) of the graph represents quantity of items produced or sold (in number of units).

These graphs are useful tools in break-even analysis and make it easy to observe how total costs and total revenue change with the quantity produced and sold. It also makes it easy to see at which point neither profit is made nor loss is incurred in the business (i.e., break-even point) and the amount of profit or loss if the quantity produced and sold is known.

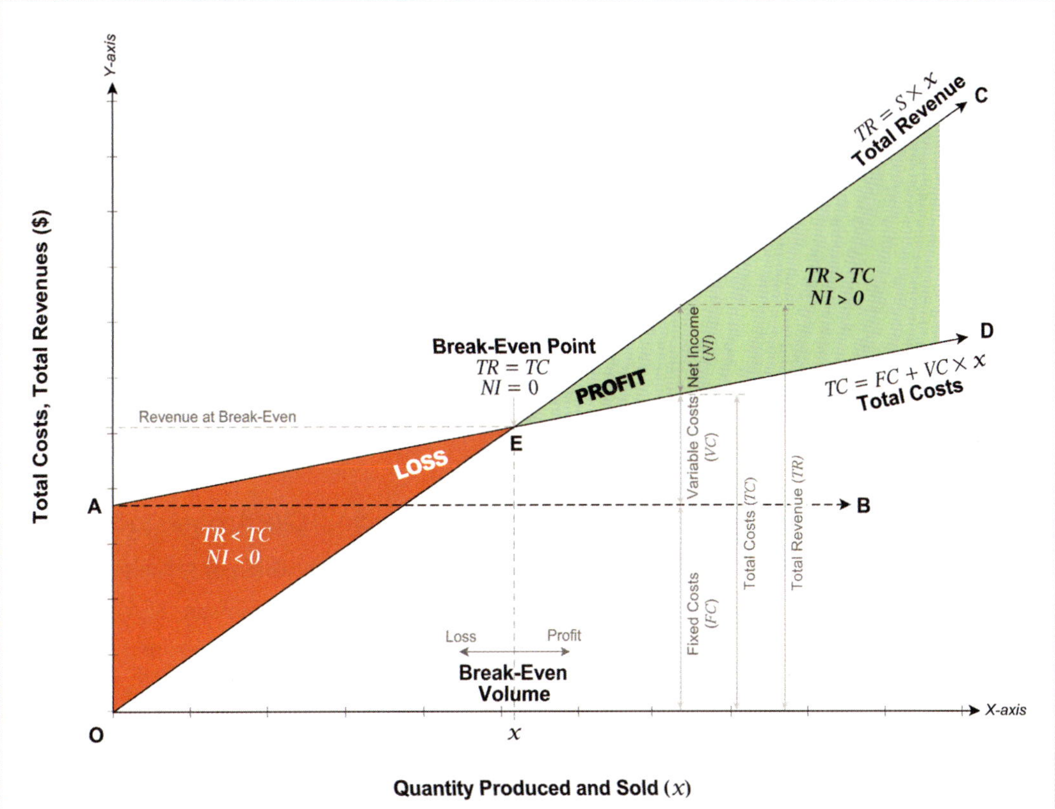

Exhibit 7.4: Graph of Total Costs vs. Quantity Produced and Total Revenue vs. Quantity Sold

As sales increase, net income becomes less negative until it equals Zero ($NI = 0$). At this point it reaches the break-even point. The intersection point of the two graphs represents the break-even point, where the total revenue and the total costs from the business are equal.

Therefore, sales before the break-even point would result in a negative net income ($NI < 0$) indicating a **loss**, while sales beyond the break-even point will result in a positive net income ($NI > 0$), indicating a **profit**.

The quantity produced and sold above the break-even volume will result in a profit for a business while that below the break-even volume will result in a loss.

Steps in Drawing the Break-Even Chart

1. Draw the horizontal axis (X-axis) to represent the quantity produced and sold. Use a ruler to draw a straight line and mark this X-axis to represent volume in number of units (x).
2. Draw the vertical axis (Y-axis) to represent both the total costs or the total revenue. Use a ruler to draw a straight line and mark this Y-axis to represent the amount in dollars ($).
3. Mark 'O', the origin.
4. Draw a horizontal line (AB), using a broken line, to represent the amount of the Fixed Costs (FC). This line is parallel to the X-axis.
5. Draw a line AD to represent the Total Cost (TC) where $TC = FC + (VC \times x)$

   $$TC = (VC \times x) + FC$$

   $$(y = mx + b)$$

   Use coordinates (x, y) to represent the above equation and use a table of values to draw the line.
6. Draw the line OC to represent the Total Revenue (TR)

   where, $TR = S \times x$

   $$(y = mx)$$

   Use coordinates (x, y) to represent the above equation and use a table of values to draw the line.
7. Find the intersecting point E of the lines OC and AD. This is the break-even point.
8. The x coordinate of point E is the break-even volume.coordinate.
9. The y coordinate of point E is the total revenue at the break-even volume.
10. A quantity produced and sold greater than the break-even volume will generate a profit, while a quantity produced and sold less than the break-even volume will result in a loss.

Example 7.4

Use Break-Even Charts (Graphical Approach) in CVP Analysis to Solve Example 7.2(a)

Sam has a printing company that prints textbooks, which are then sold to customers. His printing facility can produce a maximum of 3000 textbooks per annum (maximum capacity of the facility). The fixed costs per annum are $100,000, the variable costs per unit are $75, and the selling price per unit is $125.

a. Calculate the number of books he should produce and sell per year to break even.

b. In 2007, Sam produced and sold 1200 textbooks. Did he make a profit or incur a loss and by what amount?

c. In 2008, Sam produced and sold 2250 textbooks. Did he make a profit or incur a loss and by what amount?

d. In 2009, Sam utilized 80% of his facility to produce and sell textbooks. Calculate the profit made or loss incurred.

e. In 2010, Sam wanted a profit of $40,000. How many books did he have to produce and sell and what percentage of his facility would he have utlitized?

f. What is the maximum profit per annum that he can expect from his facility?

Solution $FC = \$100{,}000$, $VC = \$75$, $S = \$125$, Maximum capacity = 3000 units

Use the following steps in drawing the break-even chart:

Step I: Draw the X-axis and Y-axis as explained earlier.

Step II: Draw the horizontal line (AB) using a broken line from A (0, 100,000) to represent the amount of fixed costs.

Step III: Draw the line AD to represent the Total Cost (TC) with coordinates as calculated below:

$$TC = FC + (VC \times x)$$

$$TC = 100{,}000 + 75x$$

$$TC = 75x + 100{,}000 \text{ (This is in the form } y = mx + b\text{)}$$

Calculate the value of TC, when $x = 0$, 1000, and 3000

x	0	1000	3000
y	100,000	175,000	325,000

These are the coordinates for the graph of Total Costs vs. Quantity Produced.
Using these coordinates, construct AD.

Step IV: Draw the line OC to represent the Total Revenue (TR) with coordinates as calculated below:

$$TR = S \times x$$

$$TR = 125 \times x \text{ (This is in the form } y = mx\text{)}$$

Calculate the value of TR, when $x = 0$, 1000, and 3000

x	0	1000	3000
y	0	125,000	375,000

These are the coordinates for the graph of Total Revenue vs. Quantity Sold. Using these coordinates, construct OC.

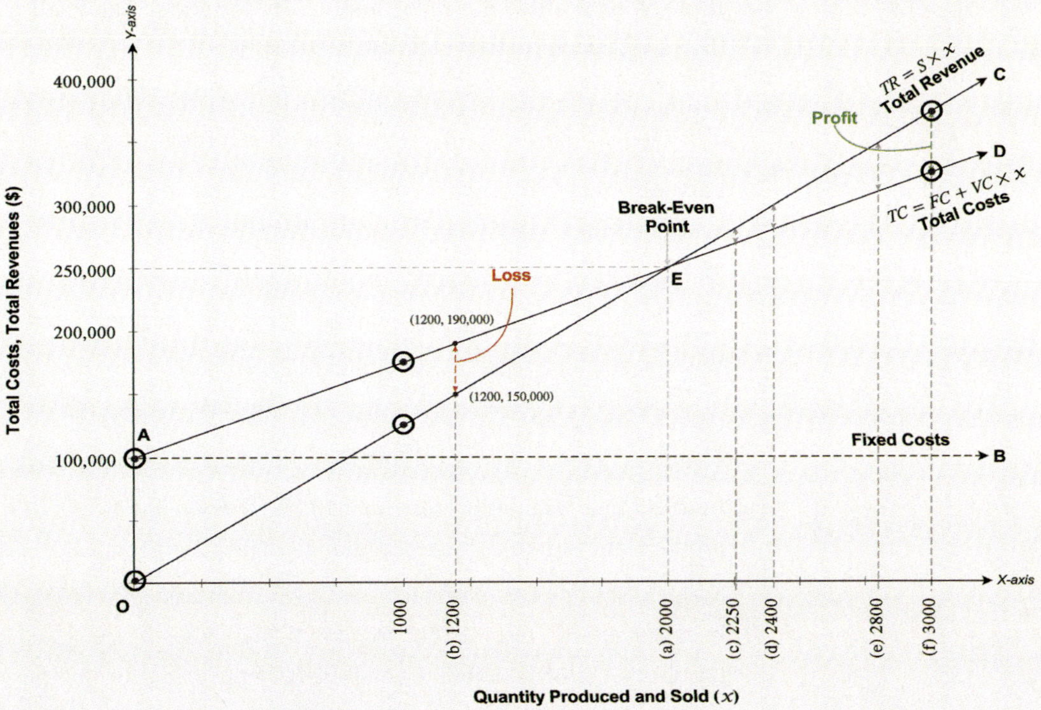

Solution *continued*

Now, let us answer the questions:

a. Calculate the number of books he should produce and sell per year to break even.

The x coordinate of the break-even point (intersection point E of the lines OC and AD) will provide us with this value. As seen from the graph, this is equal to 2000. Therefore, he must produce and sell 2000 books to break even.

b. In 2007, Sam produced and sold 1200 textbooks. Did he make a profit or incur a loss and by what amount?

If Sam sold 1200 textbooks in 2007, then this was 800 textbooks below the break-even volume of 2000 textbooks per year; therefore, he incurred a loss.

The amount of loss is calculated by subtracting the value for the y coordinate in line AD (i.e., Total Cost), from the y coordinate in line OC (i.e., Total Revenue) , when $x = 1200$.

When $x = 1200$, $TR = \$150{,}000$, and $TC = \$190{,}000$

$$TR - TC = 150{,}000 - 190{,}000 = -\ \$40{,}000.00$$

Therefore, he incurred a loss of $40,000.00 by producing 1200 textbooks in 2007.

c. In 2008, Sam produced and sold 2250 textbooks. Did he make a profit or incur a loss and by what amount?

If Sam sold 2250 textbooks in 2008, then this was 250 textbooks above the break-even value of 2000 textbooks; therefore, he made a profit.

The amount of loss is calculated by subtracting the value for the y-coordinate in line AD (i.e., Total Cost), from the y-coordinate in line OC (i.e., Total Revenue), when $x = 2250$.

When $x = 2250$, $TR = 281{,}250$, and $TC = 268{,}750$

$$TR - TC = 281{,}250 - 268{,}750 = \$12{,}500.00$$

Therefore, he incurred a profit of $12,500.00 by producing 2250 textbooks in 2008.

d. In 2009, Sam utilized 80% of his facility to produce and sell textbooks. Calculate the profit made or loss incurred.

$$\textit{Maximum Capacity} = 3000 \text{ textbooks}$$

$$80\% \text{ of } 3000 = 2400 \text{ textbooks}$$

This was 400 textbooks above the break-even volume of 2000 textbooks; therefore, he made a profit.

The amount of loss is calculated by subtracting the value for the y-coordinate in line AD (i.e., Total Cost), from the y-coordinate in line OC (i.e., Total Revenue), when $x = 2400$.

When $x = 2400$, $TR = 300{,}000$, and $TC = 280{,}000$

$$TR - TC = 300{,}000 - 280{,}000 = \$20{,}000.00$$

Therefore, he incurred a profit of $20,000.00 by producing 2400 textbooks in 2009.

e. In 2010, Sam wanted a profit of $40,000. How many books did he have to produce and sell and what percentage of his facility would he have utilized?

$40,000 should be the difference when TC is subtracted from TR, the y coordinates in lines AD and OC, respectively, for a particular value of x. By examining the graph for this difference of $40,000, you will identify the corresponding x coordinate = 2800.

Therefore, he had to produce and sell 2800 textbooks to make a profit of $40,000 in 2010.

Solution continued

$$Percentage\ of\ Facility\ Utilised = \frac{2800}{3000} = 0.093333... = 93.33\%$$

In order to produce and sell 2800 textbooks in 2010, 93.33% of his facility would have been utilized.

f. **What would be the maximum profit per annum that he can expect from his facility?**

He will make the maximum profit when he completely utilizes his facility, i.e., when $x = 3000$. This is 1000 textbooks above the break-even volume of 2000 textbooks per year.

The amount of loss is calculated by subtracting the value for the y-coordinate in line AD (i.e., Total Cost), from the y-coordinate in line OC (i.e., Total Revenue), when $x = 3000$.

When $x = 3000$, $TR = 375{,}000$ and $TC = 325{,}000$

$$TR - TC = 375{,}000 - 325{,}000 = \$50{,}000.00$$

Therefore, $50,000.00 would be the maximum profit per annum that he could expect.

7.4 | Exercises

Use the graphical approach (break-even charts) to solve the following problems.

Problems 1 and 2 are the same as Problems 3 and 4 from Section 7.1.

1. The selling price per unit of a product is $30, the fixed costs per month are $12,560, and the total variable costs per month are $11,440 at the break-even point. Calculate the number of units required to be sold per month to break even.

2. Harris owns a DVD manufacturing factory that produces DVDs and sells them for $0.30 each. Their total fixed costs are $8640 per month and the total variable costs at the break-even point are $1800 per month. Calculate the number of DVDs he needs to produce per month to break even.

Problems 3 to 8 are the same as Problems 1 to 6 from Section 7.2

3. Hayden runs a hot dog stand at Toronto's Harbourfront Center and only sells veggie hot dogs for $3 each. If her fixed costs are $1900 per month and variable costs are $0.50 per hot dog, calculate the number of hot dogs she would have to sell to break even.

4. Precision engineers have been making hi-tech watches for over three decades. Their new CEO would like to diversify the business and start making precision grandfather clocks. To conduct a cost-volume-profit analysis, he gathers the following costs for this new division: $280,455 in fixed costs per annum and $1800 in variable costs per clock. Calculate the number of grandfather clocks they would have to make and sell to break even if they plan to sell each clock for $8000.

5. Rodney's toy manufacturing company can produce a maximum of 6000 dolls per annum and sells each doll for $80. His company has fixed costs of $385,500 per annum and variable costs of $5 per doll.
   a. How many dolls must he produce and sell to break even?
   b. If he used 85% of his facility to produce and sell dolls, calculate the profit made or loss incurred.
   c. If he wants to make a profit of $50,000, how many dolls must he produce and sell and what percentage of his facility will he utilize?

6. Sandra started a Belgian waffle restaurant and purchased equipment that can produce a maximum of 50,000 waffles per annum. She sells each waffle for $3.50. She has fixed costs of $36,000 per annum and variable costs of $0.35 per waffle.

a. How many waffles must she produce and sell to break even?

b. If she produced and sold 13,500 waffles, did she make a profit or incur a loss and by what amount?

c. What is the maximum profit she can expect from her restaurant?

7. An e-learning company manager identified a new course that he could create and sell in the market for $90 per student. The costs for adding this new course to their product offering would be:
   - Lease for additional space = $1800 per month
   - Insurance costs = $300 per month
   - Support staff cost = $5000 per month
   - Sales staff cost = $4000 per month
   - Variable costs to host each course = $2 per month

   a. Calculate his break-even volume per month.

   b. If his profit last month was $32,460, how many courses did he sell?

8. Ramona was planning to set up a business where she would purchase paintings for $1000 per unit and sell them for $1600 per unit. She wanted to conduct a break-even analysis and identified the following costs for running her business: $4450 per month for store leasing, $50 per month for website hosting fee, $5000 per month for staff salary, $2000 per month for advertising costs, and $25 per unit for labour charges to pack the paintings.

   a. How many paintings would she have to sell per month to break even?

   b. If she wants to make a profit of $23,000 in a month, how many paintings would she have to sell?

Problems 9 to 12 are the same as Problems 3 to 6 from Section 7.3.

9. The variable costs to manufacture digital e-books are $280 per e-book and the selling price is $800 per e-book. If the manufacturer has fixed costs of $44,460 per month, calculate the contribution margin per e-book and the number of books that need to be sold to break even.

10. A plumber offers his plumbing services of fixing tubs and jacuzzis at $350 per job. If his fixed costs are $1400 per month and variable costs are $30 per job, calculate the contribution margin on each job and the number of orders he needs to have per month to break even.

11. A roof insulation company charges a flat rate of $1400 for insulating roofs of town houses. Monthly administrative costs of the company are $3540, cost of supplies is $130 per job, and wages are $300 per job. Calculate the company's profit or loss if they insulated 15 roofs in a particular month.

12. A solar water heating distributor buys water heaters for $5850 and sells them for $7600 each. If he pays $2000 per month as lease for his store, $5950 per month for staff salary, and $800 per month for marketing, calculate the amount of profit made or loss incurred if he sold 4 heaters in a particular month.

7.5 | Break-Even Analysis Using a Financial Calculator

If you are routinely solving break-even problems, the Texas Instruments BA II Plus calculator would help you solve them quickly, without the need for you to remember any formulas.

The exhibit below shows methods to access your worksheet and the five break-even variables (fixed costs, variable costs per unit, selling price per unit, profit, and quantity) as seen in your calculator. It also shows the corresponding algebraic reference variables. You will get a better idea on how to use your calculator by working through Example 7.5.

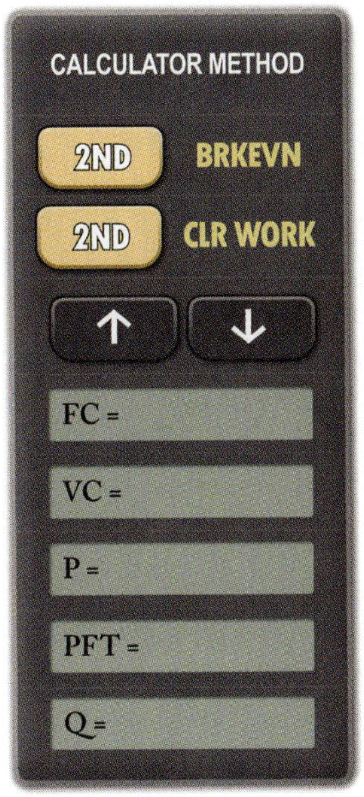

Press the **2ND** key then the **BRKEVN** key (secondary function of the number 6 key) to open the break-even worksheet.

Press the **2ND** key then the **CLR WORK** key (secondary function to the **CE|C key**) to clear all values from memory.

Press the **up** and **down arrow** keys to access the different break-even variables.

Fixed Cost — Represented by *'FC'* in algebraic calculations.

Variable Cost per unit — Represented by *'VC'* in algebraic calculations.

Selling Price per unit — Represented by *'S'* in algebraic calculations.

Profit — Represented by *'NI'* in algebraic calculations.

Quantity — Represented by *'x'* in algebraic calculations.

Note: *At the break-even point, PFT = 0*

Example 7.5

Break-Even Analysis Using a Financial Calculator

A shoe manufacturer has fixed costs of $3000 per week, variable costs of $15 per pair of shoes, and sells each pair of shoes for $20.

a. How many pairs of shoes must he sell per week to break even?

b. How many pairs of shoes must he sell to have a net income of $1000 per week?

c. Find the profit or loss if (i) 700 pairs of shoes are produced and sold per week and (ii) 500 pairs of shoes are produced and sold per week.

Solution

a.

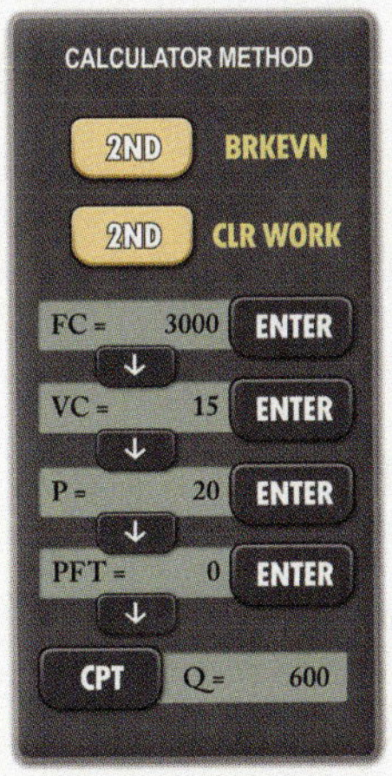

Therefore, he must sell 600 pairs of shoes per week to break even.

b.

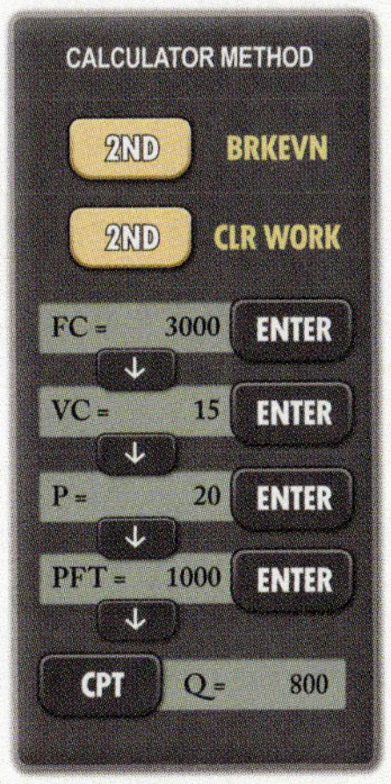

Therefore, he must sell 800 pairs of shoes per week to have a net income of $1000 per week.

Solution
continued

c. (i)

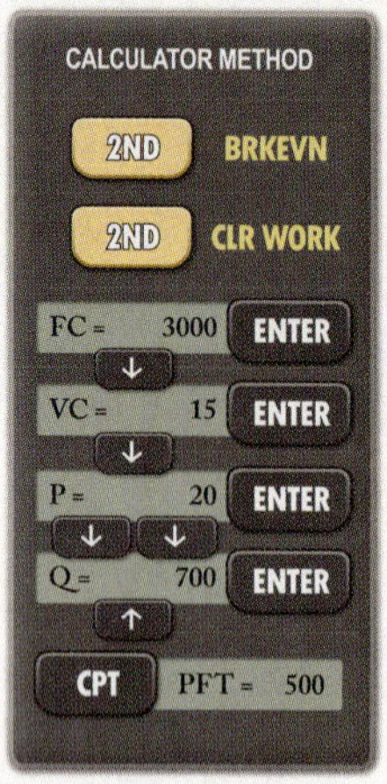

Therefore, he will make a profit of $500 per week if 700 pairs of shoes are produced and sold per week.

c. (ii)

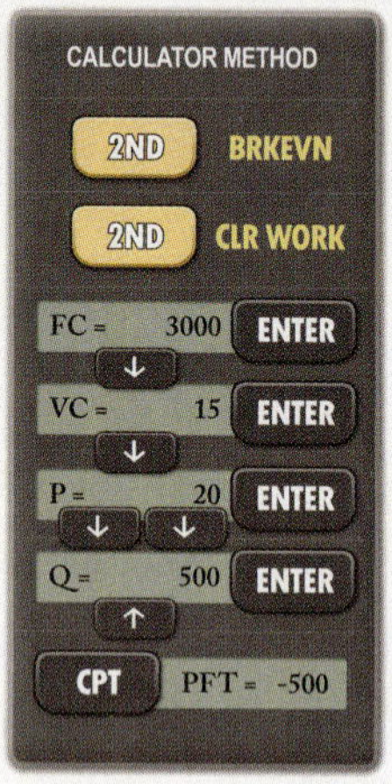

Therefore, he will incur a loss of $500 per week if 500 pairs of shoes are produced and sold per week.

7.5 | *Exercises*

Use tha financial calculator to solve the following problems.

Problems 1 and 2 are the same as Problems 3 and 4 from Section 7.1.

1. The selling price per unit of a product is $30, the fixed costs per month are $12,560, and the total variable costs per month are $11,440 at the break-even point. Calculate the number of units required to be sold per month to break even.

2. Harris owns a DVD manufacturing factory that produces DVDs and sells them for $0.30 each. Their total fixed costs are $8640 per month and the total variable costs at the break-even point are $1800 per month. Calculate the number of DVDs he needs to produce per month to break even.

Problems 3 to 8 are the same as Problems 1 to 6 from Section 7.2.

3. Hayden runs a hot dog stand at Toronto's Harbourfront Center and only sells veggie hot dogs for $3 each. If her fixed costs are $1900 per month and variable costs are $0.50 per hot dog, calculate the number of hot dogs she would have to sell to break even.

4. Precision engineers have been making hi-tech watches for over three decades. Their new CEO would like to diversify the business and start making precision grandfather clocks. To conduct a cost-volume-profit analysis, he gathers the following costs for this new division: $280,455 in fixed costs per annum and $1800 in variable costs per clock. Calculate the number of grandfather clocks they would have to make and sell to break even if they plan to sell each clock for $8000.

5. Rodney's toy manufacturing company can produce a maximum of 6000 dolls per annum and sells each doll for $80. His company has fixed costs of $385,500 per annum and variable costs of $5 per doll.

   a. How many dolls must he produce and sell to break even?

   b. If he used 85% of his facility to produce and sell dolls, calculate the profit made or loss incurred.

   c. If he wants to make a profit of $50,000, how many dolls must he produce and sell and what percentage of his facility will he utilize?

6. Sandra started a Belgian waffle restaurant and purchased equipment that can produce a maximum of 50,000 waffles per annum. She sells each waffle for $3.50. She has fixed costs of $36,000 per annum and variable costs of $0.35 per waffle.

    a. How many waffles must she produce and sell to break even?

    b. If she produced and sold 13,500 waffles, did she make a profit or incur a loss and by what amount?

    c. What is the maximum profit she can expect from her restaurant?

7. An e-learning company manager identified a new course that he could create and sell in the market for $90 per student. The costs for adding this new course to their product offering would be:

    - Lease for additional space = $1800 per month
    - Insurance costs = $300 per month
    - Support staff cost = $5000 per month
    - Sales staff cost = $4000 per month
    - Variable costs to host each course = $2 per month

    a. Calculate his break-even volume per month.

    b. If his profit last month was $32,460, how many courses did he sell?

8. Ramona was planning to set up a business where she would purchase paintings for $1000 per unit and sell them for $1600 per unit. She wanted to conduct a break-even analysis and identified the following costs for running her business: $4450 per month for store leasing, $50 per month for website hosting fee, $5000 per month for staff salary, $2000 per month for advertising costs, and $25 per unit for labour charges to pack the paintings.

    a. How many paintings would she have to sell per month to break even?

    b. If she wants to make a profit of $23,000 in a month, how many paintings would she have to sell?

Problems 9 to 12 are the same as Problems 3 to 6 from Section 7.3.

9. The variable costs to manufacture digital e-books are $280 and the selling price is $800 per e-book. If the manufacturer has fixed costs of $44,460 per month, calculate the contribution margin per e-book and the number of books that need to be sold to break even.

10. A plumber offers his plumbing services of fixing tubs and jacuzzis at $350 per job. If his fixed costs are $1400 per month and variable costs are $30 per job, calculate the contribution margin on each job and the number of orders he needs to have per month to break even.

11. A roof insulation company charges a flat rate of $1400 for insulating roofs of town houses. Monthly administrative costs of the company are $3540, cost of supplies is $130 per job, and wages are $300 per job. Calculate the company's profit or loss if they insulated 15 roofs in a particular month.

12. A solar water heating distributor buys water heaters for $5850 and sells them for $7600 each. If he pays $2000 per month as lease for his store, $5950 per month for staff salary, and $800 per month for marketing, calculate the amount of profit made or loss incurred if he sold 4 heaters in a particular month.

7 | Review Exercises

Answers to odd-numbered problems are available at the end of the textbook

1. A nursery sells a bouquet of roses for $14 each. The variable costs are $8.50 per bouqet and the fixed costs per week are $2700.
   a. Calculate the break-even number of bouquets to be sold per week.
   b. What is the net income in a week in which 900 bouquets are sold?
   c. Calculate the number of bouquets to be sold to earn a profit of $1000 per week.
2. Don owns a specialized store that sells portable hard drives for $81 each. The variable costs per drive are $33 and the fixed costs per week are $1200.
   a. Calculate the number of drives he needs to sell per week to break even.
   b. What net income will he make in a week in which he sells 35 drives?
   c. If he wants to make a profit of $960 in a week, how many drives must he sell?
3. A publishing company sells its Biology textbooks for $125 each. Their office overhead costs are $48,000 per year, equipment maintenance costs are $18,000 per year, printing costs are $40 per textbook, and advertisement and promotional costs are $2875 per year. In addition, the author receives a royalty that is 10% of the selling price.
   a. How many books must be sold to break even?
   b. Calculate the net income with the sale of 3500 books per year.
   c. How many books must be sold to earn a net income of $435,000 per year?
4. AWM Inc., a plastic chair manufacturing company, produces and sells chairs for $28 each. Their administrative costs are $54,000 per year, machinery maintenance costs are $85,500 per year, packing costs are $7.72 per chair, marketing and advertising costs are $10,500 per year, and shipment costs 1% of the selling price.
   a. How many chairs must be sold to break even?
   b. Calculate the net income with the sale of 8,000 chairs per year.
   c. How many chairs must be sold to earn a net income of $40,000 per year?
- 5. A store that sells video games at $65 each has fixed costs of $8400 per month and variable costs of $23 per game. The store can sell a maximum of 350 games per month. Calculate the following:
   a. The break-even revenue and volume per month.
   b. The number of games they would have to sell to have a net income of $5600 per month.
   c. The net income at maximum capacity if the variable costs decreased by $3 per game.
- 6. A saloon charges $25 per haircut. They have fixed costs of $2025 per month and variable costs of $2.50 per haircut. If they have the capacity to provide 3000 haircuts per month, calculate:
   a. The break-even revenue and volume per month.
   b. The number of haircuts they would have to provide to have a net income of $6750 per month.
   c. The net income at maximum capacity if the variable costs decreased by $0.50 per haircut.

7. A store sells toys at $12.50 each. The variable costs per toy are $7.50 and fixed costs are $20,000 per year.
   a. What are the contribution margin and contribution ratios?
   b. How many toys must be sold per year for a net income of $48,000 per year?
   c. What will be the net income in a year in which 10,000 toys were sold?
8. A music store sells violins for $286 each. The variable costs per violin are $111 and fixed costs are $31,500 per year.
   a. What are the contribution margin and contribution ratios?

b. How many violins must be sold per year for a net income of $63,000 per year?

c. What will be the net income in a year in which 450 violins were sold?

9. To achieve a total revenue target of $86,400 per month, Henry has to sell 320 cameras. If his store can sell a maximum of 600 cameras and the variable costs per camera are $150 and the fixed costs are $54,000 per month, calculate the following:

a. The selling price of each camera.

b. The new break-even volume if the fixed costs decreased by $6000 per month.

c. The new break-even volume as a percentage of the maximum capacity.

10. Jerry purchased a new printing machine and started a small printing shop. As per his calculations, to earn a revenue of $5000 per month, he needs to sell printouts of 25,000 pages per month. If the printing machine has a capacity of printing 40,000 sheets per month and the variable costs are $0.02 per sheet and the fixed costs are $1800 per month, calculate:

a. The selling price of each printout.

b. The new break-even point if the fixed costs decreased by $360 per month.

c. The new break-even point as a percentage of the maximum capacity.

11. Xing-fu and his business partner sell car tires in their showroom at $105 per tire. Their fixed costs are $180,000 per year and variable costs are $75 per tire.

a. Calculate their net income assuming that their annual sales are $840,000.

b. How many units would they be required to sell to make a net income of $75,000 per year?

c. Find the break-even point if the variable costs increase by $5 per tire.

12. A management consulting company charges $275 per hour for their consulting services. Their fixed costs are $780,000 per annum and variable costs are $25 per hour.

a. Calculate their net income assuming that their annual sales are $2,579,500.

b. How many hours of consultation service would they be required to provide to make a net income of $3,000,000 per year?

c. Find the break-even point if the variable costs increase by $10 per hour.

13. Vibol sells love seats in her furniture store for $925 each. The store has a maximum capacity of selling 320 love seats and has variable costs of $785 per item and fixed costs of $15,680 per year.

a. Calculate the break-even point as a percentage of the capacity.

b. If the fixed costs are reduced to $13,440, find the new break-even point.

c. After the decrease in the fixed costs in (b), what quantity should be produced to have a profit of $35,000 per year?

14. An electronic store sells car navigation systems for $225 each. The store has a maximum capacity of selling 1600 systems and has variable costs of $75 per system and fixed costs of $122,400 per year.

a. Calculate the break-even point as a percentage of the capacity.

b. If the fixed costs are reduced to $112,500, find the new break-even point.

c. After the decrease in the fixed costs in (b), what quantity should be produced to have a profit of $18,600 per year?

• 15. A store has the capacity to sell 600 electronic readers per annum for $500 each. The variable costs are $250 per unit and the fixed costs are $100,000 per year.

a. What quantity should they sell to have a net income of $60,000 per year?

b. What is their net income at maximum capacity?

c. Calculate the quantity they need to sell to have a net income of $60,000 per year if the selling price of the reader is reduced by 10% and variable costs increase by 10%.

• 16. Marge, a painter, has the capacity to paint and sell 56 paintings every year at $12,500 each. If the variable costs are $800 per painting and fixed costs are $58,500 per year,

a. how many paintings should she paint and

sell to have a net income of $479,700 per year?

b. what is her net income at maximum capacity?

c. calculate the number of paintings she needs to sell to have a net income of $407,420 per year if the selling price of the painting is reduced by 20% and variable costs increased by 30%.

17. Tom has a garment manufacturing factory that has the capacity to make and sell 700 dress shirts per week. They sell each shirt for $16 to wholesalers, have fixed costs of $2880 per week, and variable costs of $9.60 per shirt.

    a. Calculate the contribution margin and contribution ratio.

    b. What sales amount will result in a net income of $960 for the week.

    c. What will be their net income at maximum capacity?

18. A magazine company has the capacity to print and sell 200,000 magazines per month. They sell each magazine for $4.50 each, have fixed costs of $520,000 per month, and variable costs of $0.50 per magazine.

    a. Calculate the contribution margin and contribution ratio.

    b. What sales amount will result in a net income of $21,000 for the month?

    c. What will be their net income at maximum capacity.

• 19. An automobile plant produced 9000 cars and lost $6,000,000 last year. The total revenue for the year was $135,000,000. The break-even volume of the plant is 10,000 cars.

    a. Calculate the selling price of each car.

    b. Calculate the variable costs for each car.

    c. Calculate the fixed cost per year.

• 20. A garment manufacturing company produced and sold 2800 dress shirts and made a net income of $1750 last year. The total revenue for the year was $35,000. The break-even volume of the company is 2200 shirts.

    a. Calculate the selling price of each shirt.

    b. Calculate the variable costs for each shirt.

    c. Calculate the fixed costs per year?

7 | Self-Test Exercises

Answers to all problems are available at the end of the textbook

1. Vibol Manufacturing is evaluating the introduction of a new product that would have a unit selling price of $100. The total annual fixed costs are estimated to be $200,000 and the unit variable costs are projected at $60.

    a. What sales volume (in units) is required to break even?

    b. What volume is required to generate an income of $100,000?

2. A manufacturer of major appliances provided the following information. The maximum capacity of the facility is 900 units per month. The fixed costs are $175,000 per month and the variable costs are $360 per unit. The product currently sells for $640.

    a. What is the break-even volume as a percent of capacity?

    b. If the variable costs decreased by $20 per unit, what would be the net income per month at maximum capacity?

• 3. A company manufactures a product that currently sells for $30. The fixed costs are $100,000 per year and the variable costs are $20. The maximum capacity of the production facility is 50,000 units per year.

    a. How many units must be produced to attain a net income of $80,000 per year?

    b. If sales dropped to 50% of the maximum capacity and the selling price reduced by $3 per unit, what would be the net income?

4. A manufacturer of ovens sells them for $2050 each. The variable costs are $1400 per unit. The manufacturer's factory has annual fixed costs of $2,100,000.

   a. Given the expected sales volume of 3000 units for this year, what will be this year's net income?

   b. How many units must the manufacturer produce to break even if the fixed costs increased by 10%?

• 5. Abban manufactures a product that sells very well. The maximum capacity of his facility is 50,000 units per month. The fixed costs are $150,000 per month and the variable costs are $12 per unit. The product currently sells for $20.

   a. What total revenue of the sales is required for a net income of $100,000 per year?

   b. If sales dropped to 75% of the maximum capacity and the variable costs decreased by 25%, what would be the net income?

• 6. Last year, a battery manufacturing company in Winnipeg incurred a loss of $835,000 by producing and selling 45,000 batteries. If their total revenue for the year was $12,600,000 and the break-even volume of the plant is 49,900 batteries, calculate:

   a. The selling price of each battery.

   b. The fixed costs and variable costs for each battery.

7. A publishing company decided to create a new textbook in Chemistry to be sold to bookstores for $120 each. Their costs for adding this new textbook to their products are:

   - Rent for additional space to hold their editorial and research team = $2000 per month
   - Insurance costs for the building = $330 per month
   - Cost for support staff = $4250 per month
   - Sales and marketing costs = $2500 per month
   - Variable costs associated with each textbook = $18 per month

   a. Calculate their break-even volume.

   b. If their profit last month was $55,460, how many textbooks did they sell?

8. Grace runs a boutique designer clothing store where she sells tank-tops for $45 each. If her fixed costs are $3000 per month and she needs to sell 480 tops to break even, calculate:

   a. The variable costs per top.

   b. The contribution margin per top.

   c. The net income at 60% above break-even volume.

• 9. A retail store has fixed costs of $180,000 per year and a maximum capacity to store and sell 850 dishwashers every year. They sell each unit for $500 and their variable costs are $140 per unit.

   a. How many units should they sell to have a net income of $45,000 per year?

   b. What is their net income at maximum capacity?

   c. Calculate the number of units they need to sell to have a net income of $45,000 per year if they decide to reduce the selling price of each unit by 15% and variable costs increase by 15%.

10. Robert, the owner of a large stationery store in a mall, sells a particular brand of pen for $40 each. If his total revenue from these pens at the break-even point is $70,520 per month and the contribution margin per pen is $12, calculate the fixed costs, break-even volume, and total revenue if he sells 1500 pens.

CASE 7

Cost-Volume-Profit Analysis at a Manufacturing Company

Madison is the newly appointed manager of Spark Communications, a small computer monitor manufacturing company based out of Halifax, Nova Scotia. During her first few days on the job, she collected the following data about the company:

The company has a maximum capacity of producing 750 monitors per month and is currently producing 525 monitors every month and selling it to a wholesaler. The company's expenses are: rent of $4000 per month, salaries of $12,500 per month, insurance of $1500 per month, materials at $6 per monitor, labour of $35 per monitor, and sales commissions of $19 per monitor. Each monitor is sold for $105.

a. What are the contribution margin and the contribution ratio?

b. What are the break-even volume and break-even revenue?

c. How much net income would be earned at the current level of production?

d. At the current level of production, what percentage of the facility is utilized?

e. Madison decided to increase the quantity produced to the facility's maximum capacity and reduce the selling price from $105 to $95. What would be the impact of this decision on the company's net income?

f. At the new selling price of $95, another store wanted to purchase an additional 750 units per month on a regular basis. Madison expanded the facility by renting additional space, which increased the fixed costs by 25% and doubled the capacity of the facility. What would be the company's net income per month if they were operating at 100% of the new facility's capacity?

7 | Summary of Notation and Formulas

NOTATION

TR = Total Revenue

TR = Total Costs

VC = Variable Costs per unit

TVC = Total Variable Costs

FC = Fixed Costs for a specific period

x = Number of units produced and sold

S = Selling Price per unit

NI = Net Income

CM = Contribution Margin per unit

CR = Contribution Ratio

BEP = Break-Even Point

FORMULAS

Total Cost | 7.1 (a)

$$TC = FC + TVC$$

Total Variable Cost | 7.1 (b)

$$TVC = VC \times x$$

Total Revenue | 7.1 (c)

$$TR = S \times x$$

Net Income | 7.1 (d)

$$NI = TR - TC$$

At the break-even point | 7.1 (e)

At the break-even point, $TR = TC$

Contribution Margin | 7.1 (f)

$$CM = S - VC$$

Contribution Ratio | 7.1 (g)

$$CR = \frac{CM}{S} \times 100\%$$

Cost-Volume-Profit Analysis | 7.2 (a)

$$S \times x = FC + (VC \times x) + NI$$

Number of Units | 7.2 (b)

$$x = \frac{FC + NI}{(S - VC)}$$

Number of Units at the Break-Even Point | 7.3

$$x = \frac{FC}{CM}$$

Given a choice, would you prefer to receive $1000 today or $1000 in 1 year? Even though these amounts are the same, you would certainly prefer to have the money now because you could invest this amount in a bank and earn interest on the investment over time. The value of money changes over a period of time and is called the time value of money. Many business transactions either involve lending or borrowing money, with money-lenders (typically financial institutions like banks, credit unions, etc.) charging an amount for lending money. Therefore, it costs to borrow money and different financial institutions charge different amounts while lending. The amount charged to 'use' money is a percentage of the amount loaned and is known as interest. In this chapter, you will learn the fundamental relationship that is necessary to calculate the time value of money and the simple interest charged or earned.

8 Simple Interest and its Applications

LEARNING OBJECTIVES

- Understand the concept of simple interest and calculate the amount of interest, principal, time, interest rate, and maturity value of investments and loans.
- Determine the number of days between two calendar dates using different methods, including the use of the Texas Instruments BA II Plus Calculator.
- Calculate equivalent payments that replace another payment or a series of payments.
- Understand the use of simple interest in business applications such as demand loans, promissory notes, treasury bills, commercial papers, and discounting.

CHAPTER OUTLINE

8.1 | Introduction

Interest is a fee paid by borrowers to lenders for using money temporarily. Interest is an expense when we borrow money and an income when we invest money.

For example, when we invest money, the financial institution uses our money and therefore, pays us interest for the use of the money for the time period it has been invested. Similarly, when we borrow money from a financial institution, we pay interest to them for the use of the money for the time period borrowed. In both cases, when money is returned after a period of time, interest is added to the original amount borrowed. Therefore, as time goes by, the value of money increases by the amount of interest earned for that period. This is called **time value of money**: money grows with time when it is invested or borrowed at a particular interest rate.

Interest is a fee paid by borrowers to lenders for using money temporarily.

In simple interest calculations, interest is calculated only on the initial amount invested or borrowed (not on any interest earned during the past periods). For this reason, simple interest is usually used for short term investments or loans.

For long term investments or loans, compound interest is used, where interest is calculated on the amount borrowed or invested in addition to the interest earned during the previous period. You will learn about compound interest in Chapter 9.

8.2 | Calculating the Amount of Simple Interest

In simple interest calculations, the amount of interest, for a period of time, is calculated as a percentage of the amount invested or borrowed. This percentage is referred to as the rate of interest (or interest rate), which is always stated for a unit period of time; i.e., r% per annum (r% p.a.) or r% per year.

In simple interest calculations, interest is calculated only on the principal and not on the interest earned.

For example,

Interest for \$1000 at 10% p.a. for 1 year $= 1000 \times 0.10 \times 1 = \$100.00$

Interest for \$1000 at 10% p.a. for 3 years $= 1000 \times 0.10 \times 3 = \$300.00$

Similarly,

Interest for $\$P$ at $r\%$ p.a. for t years $= P \times r \times t$

Therefore, $\textit{Amount of Interest} = \textit{Principal} \times \textit{Rate} \times \textit{Time Period}$

In calculations, '*r*' is used in decimal or fractional equivalent of the percentage rate.

Therefore, the amount of interest is expressed by the following formula:

Formula 8.2

Amount of Interest

$$I = Prt$$

Notation

***I* = Amount of interest.** It is the amount (in dollars) paid for using the principal amount for a period of time.

P = **Principal.** It is the amount of money borrowed or invested at the beginning of a period.

r = **Simple interest rate.** It is the rate at which the principal is borrowed or invested. It is expressed as a percentage for a given period of time, usually per year, unless otherwise specified. If the interest rate is $r\%$, it is understood that $r\%$ is an annual interest rate ($r\%$ p.a.).

t = **Time period.** It is the period of time for which the principal amount is borrowed or invested during which interest is charged or earned.

Note:

Since $r \times t$ refers to the interest percentage of the principal $\left(r \times t = \frac{I}{P}\right)$, the units for '$r$' and '$t$' should match.

For example,

- If 'r' is per annum ($r\%$ p.a.) then 't' should be in years.
- If 'r' is per month ($r\%$ p.m.) then 't' should be in months.

Usually, the unit of 't' is converted to match the unit of 'r' using 1 year = 12 months or 1 year = 365 days.

Example 8.2(a)

Calculating 'I' When 't' is Expressed in Years

Mercy borrowed $4250 from her friend for 2 years. If she was charged a simple interest rate of 6% per annum, how much interest would she have to pay on the loan?

Solution

P = \$4250, r = 6% p.a. = 0.06 p.a., t = 2 years (unit of 't' and unit of 'r' are in matching units)

Using Formula 8.2, $I = Prt$

Substituting values, $I = (4250)(0.06)(2)$

$= \$510.00$

Therefore, she would have to pay interest of $510.00.

Example 8.2(b)

Calculating 'I' When 't' is Expressed in Months

Calculate the amount of interest earned from an investment of \$1750 for 9 months at $4\frac{1}{2}\%$p.a.

Solution

P = \$1750, $r = 4\frac{1}{2}\%$ p.a., t = 9 months

Method 1

Match the unit of 't' to that of 'r'

$r = 4\frac{1}{2}\%$ p.a. = 0.045 p.a.

$t = 9$ months $= \frac{9}{12}$ years = 0.75 years

Using Formula 8.2, $I = Prt$

Substituting values, $I = (1750)(0.045)(0.75)$

$= \$59.06$

Method 2

Match the unit of 'r' to that or 't'

$t = 9$ months

$r = 4\frac{1}{2}\%$ p.a. $= \frac{0.045}{12}$ p.m.

Using Formula 8.2, $I = Prt$

Substituting values, $I = (1750)\left(\frac{0.045}{12}\right)(9)$

$= \$59.06$

Therefore, interest of $59.06 will be earned.

Example 8.2(c)

Calculating 'I' When 't' is Expressed in Days

Calculate the amount of interest charged on a loan of $3200 at 6% p.a. for 125 days.

Solution

$P = \$3200$, $r = 6\%$ p.a. $= 0.06$ p.a., $t = 125$ days (unit of 't' is converted to match the unit of 'r') $= \frac{125}{365}$ years

Using Formula 8.2, $I = Prt$

Substituting values, $I = (3200)(0.06)\left(\frac{125}{365}\right)$

$= \$65.75$

Therefore, interest of $65.75 will be charged.

Example 8.2(d)

Calculating 'I' When 't' is Expressed in Days and 'r' is Expressed per Month

Calculate the amount of interest earned on an investment of $2275 earning interest at 0.75% per month for 90 days.

Solution

$P = \$2275$, $r = 0.75\%$ p.m. $= 0.0075$ p.m., $t = 90$ days (unit of 't' is converted to months to match units of 'r') $= \frac{90}{365} \times 12$ months

Using Formula 8.2, $I = Prt$

Substituting values, $I = (2275)(0.0075)\left(\frac{90}{365} \times 12\right)$

$= \$50.49$

Therefore, interest of $50.49 is earned.

Example 8.2(e)

Calculating 'I' When 't' is Expressed in Years and 'r' is Expressed per Month

Calculate the amount of interest earned on an investment of $5680 at 0.25% per month for $1\frac{1}{2}$ years.

Solution

$P = \$5680$, $r = 0.25\%$ p.m. $= 0.0025$ p.m., $t = 1\frac{1}{2}$ years (unit of 't' is converted to months to match unit of 'r') $= 1\frac{1}{2} \times 12$ months $= 18$ months

Using Formula 8.2, $I = Prt$

Substituting values, $I = (5680)(0.0025)(18)$

$= \$255.60$

Therefore, interest of $255.60 will be charged.

Determining the Time Period in Days Between Dates

Since simple interest is mostly used for loans or investments with short time periods, it is necessary to calculate the time period in days, unless it is given in months or years. The time period in days is then converted to its equivalent in years to use as 't' in the simple interest formula.

The following months have 31 days: *January, March, May, July, August, October,* and *December*

The following months have 30 days: *April, June, September*, and *November*

There are 28 days in *February*, *except on leap years* when there are 29 days.

Leap years occur every 4 years. For example, 1996, 2000, 2004, 2008, 2012, 2016, etc. are leap years.

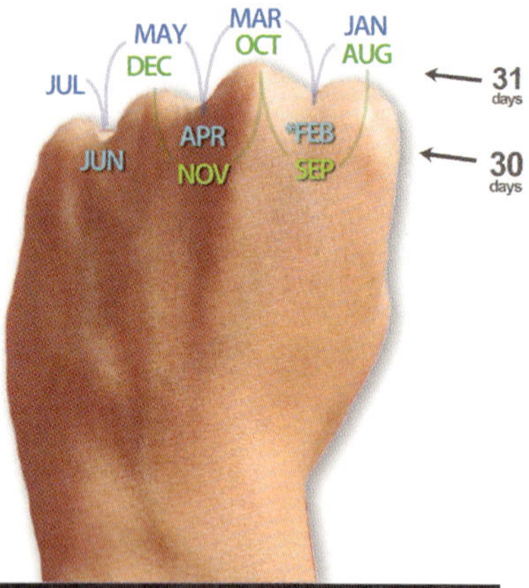

Exhibit 8.2: Days in Each Month

An Easy Way to Remember the Number of Days in Each Month

Make a fist with one hand, hiding your thumb.

Using your other hand, start counting **January, February, March, April, May, June, July,** on the knuckle and the space in between the knuckles, as shown in blue on the left.

When you reach the end, go back to the first knuckle and continue counting **August, September, October, November, and December,** as shown in green.

All months that fall on a knuckle have 31 days and the others have 30 days, except for February.

*February usually has 28 days, except in leap years where it has 29 days.

Described below are 3 methods to determine the number of days for a time period between two dates:

Method 1: Determining the Number of Days Using Calendar Days in Each Month

In calculating the number of days in a time period, you must either exclude the first day or the last day in the day count.

While counting the number of days in a time period, we include either the first day or the last day of the investment or loan, but not both days.

Financial institutions generally include the first day of the period and exclude the last day. This is done because they base their financial calculations on the end of the day's closing balance. On the first day, as you would either borrow or invest money, the closing balance would not be zero. However, on the last day of the period, since you would either pay-back the loan or withdraw the investment making the closing balance zero, financial institutions would not include the last day in calculations.

For example, the number of days between January 25 and February 05 are:

January 25 to January 31:	7 days (First day included)
February 01 to February 05:	4 days (Last day excluded)

Therefore, there are 11 days between January 25 and February 05.

In the following two examples, we have illustrated calculations that :

- include the first day and exclude the last day, as done by financial institutions
- exclude the first day and include the last day, which can also be done to determine the number of days.

Example 8.2(f)

Calculating the Number of Days in a Time Period During a Non-Leap Year

Calculate the number of days in the time period from October 18, 2009 to April 05, 2010.

Solution

Calculating by ***including*** first day and ***excluding*** last day

October: 14 days
(First day included, counting from October 18 to October 31 = 14 days)

November: 30 days

December: 31 days

January: 31 days

February: 28 days
(Year 2010 is not a leap year)

March: 31 days

April: 4 days
(Last day excluded, counting from April 01 to April 04 = 4 days)

Total number of days = 169 days

$$t = \frac{169}{365} \text{ years}$$

Calculating by ***excluding*** first day and ***including*** last day

October: 13 days
(First day excluded, counting from October 19 to October 31 = 13 days or 31 − 18 = 13 days)

November: 30 days

December: 31 days

January: 31 days

February: 28 days
(Year 2010 is not a leap year)

March: 31 days

April: 5 days
(Last day included, counting from April 01 to April 05 = 5 days)

Total number of days = 169 days

$$t = \frac{169}{365} \text{ years}$$

Example 8.2(g)

Calculating the Number of Days in a Time Period During a Leap Year

Calculate the number of days in the time period from January 15, 2008 to March 20, 2008.

Solution

Calculating by ***including*** first day and ***excluding*** last day

January: 17 days
(First day included, counting from January 15 to January 31 = 17 days)

February: 29 days
(Year 2008 is a leap year)

March: 19 days
(Last day excluded, counting from March 01 to March 19 = 19 days)

Total number of days = 65 days

$$t = \frac{65}{365} \text{ years}$$

Calculating by ***excluding*** first day and ***including*** last day

January: 16 days
(First day excluded, counting from January16 to January 31 = 16 days or 31 − 15 = 16)

February: 29 days
(Year 2008 is a leap year)

March: 20 days
(Last day included, counting from March 01 to March 20 = 20 days)

Total number of days = 65 days

$$t = \frac{65}{365} \text{ years}$$

Method 2: Determining the Number of Days Using a Days-Table

In this method, we use a table that has the days of the year serially numbered from 1 to 365 as shown in Table 8.2. The number of days between two dates that are in the same calendar year is determined by calculating the difference between the serial numbers of those dates in the table.

Table 8.2

Table to Determine the Number of Days in a Time Period

DAY OF MONTH	JAN	FEB	MAR	APR	MAY	JUN	JUL	AUG	SEP	OCT	NOV	DEC	DAY OF MONTH
1	1	32	60	91	121	152	182	213	244	274	305	335	**1**
2	2	33	61	92	122	153	183	214	245	275	306	336	**2**
3	3	34	62	93	123	154	184	215	246	276	307	337	**3**
4	4	35	63	94	124	155	185	216	247	277	308	338	**4**
5	5	36	64	95	125	156	186	217	248	278	309	339	**5**
6	6	37	65	96	126	157	187	218	249	279	310	340	**6**
7	7	38	66	97	127	158	188	219	250	280	311	341	**7**
8	8	39	67	98	128	159	189	220	251	281	312	342	**8**
9	9	40	68	99	129	160	190	221	252	282	313	343	**9**
10	10	41	69	100	130	161	191	222	253	283	314	344	**10**
11	11	42	70	101	131	162	192	223	254	284	315	345	**11**
12	12	43	71	102	132	163	193	224	255	285	316	346	**12**
13	13	44	72	103	133	164	194	225	256	286	317	347	**13**
14	14	45	73	104	134	165	195	226	257	287	318	348	**14**
15	15	46	74	105	135	166	196	227	258	288	319	349	**15**
16	16	47	75	106	136	167	197	228	259	289	320	350	**16**
17	17	48	76	107	137	168	198	229	260	290	321	351	**17**
18	18	49	77	108	138	169	199	230	261	291	322	352	**18**
19	19	50	78	109	139	170	200	231	262	292	323	353	**19**
20	20	51	79	110	140	171	201	232	263	293	324	354	**20**
21	21	52	80	111	141	172	202	233	264	294	325	355	**21**
22	22	53	81	112	142	173	203	234	265	295	326	356	**22**
23	23	54	82	113	143	174	204	235	266	296	327	357	**23**
24	24	55	83	114	144	175	205	236	267	297	328	358	**24**
25	25	56	84	115	145	176	206	237	268	298	329	359	**25**
26	26	57	85	116	146	177	207	238	269	299	330	360	**26**
27	27	58	86	117	147	178	208	239	270	300	331	361	**27**
28	28	59	87	118	148	179	209	240	271	301	332	362	**28**
29	29		88	119	149	180	210	241	272	302	333	363	**29**
30	30		89	120	150	181	211	242	273	303	334	364	**30**
31	31		90		151		212	243		304		365	**31**

Note: *For leap years, February 29 becomes day number 60. Therefore, you will need to add one day to any date that includes February 29 in a leap year.*

Example 8.2(h)

Calculating the Number of Days Within a Single Calendar Year

Calculate the number of days in the time period from February 18, 2010 to May 17, 2010.

Solution

February 18, 2010: 49th day of the year (using the table)

May 17, 2010: 137th day of the year (using the table)

Difference = 137 – 49 = 88 days

Therefore, the number of days in the time period = 88 days ($t = \frac{88}{365}$ years)

Example 8.2(i)

Calculating the Number of Days in a Time Period During a Non-Leap Year When the Time Period is Over Two Calendar Years

Calculate the number of days in the time period from October 18, 2009 to April 05, 2010.

Solution

October 18, 2009 to December 31, 2009: 74 days in 2009
(365 − 291 = 74)

Up to April 05: 95 days in 2010
(Note: As it is a continuation from the previous year, January 01 is included)

Therefore, the number of days in the time period = 74 + 95 = 169 days ($t = \frac{169}{365}$ years)

Example 8.2(j)

Calculating the Number of Days in a Time Period During a Leap Year

Calculate the number of days in the time period from January 15, 2008 to March 20, 2009.

Solution

January 15, 2008:	15th day of the year
December 31, 2008:	366th day of the year (leap year)
Difference:	351 days (366 − 15)
March 20, 2009:	79th day of the year
Total:	430 days

Therefore, the number of days in the time period = 430 days ($t = \frac{430}{365}$ years)

Method 3: Determining the Number of Days Using a Financial Calculator

You can use a financial calculator, such as the Texas Instruments BA II Plus, to determine the number of days in a time period as illustrated below:

The following example will illustrate the use of the calculator to determine the number of days.

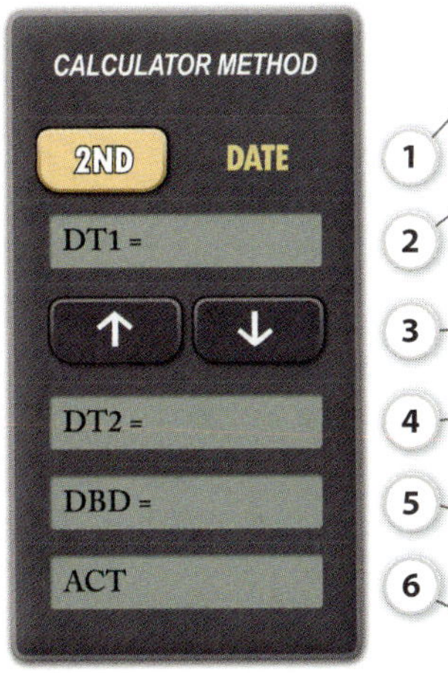

1. ***Pressing the 2ND button then DATE (press 1 to access DATE)*** will take you to the date worksheet to determine the number of days between two dates.
2. ***Date 1*** is the earlier date or the first date you will enter. Dates are shown in mm-dd-yyyy format and entered as mm-dd-yy (you will understand this better while working through an example).
3. This is to toggle between different items in the date worksheet.
4. ***Date 2*** is the later date or the second date you will enter, If you enter the dates in a reverse order you will get a negative value for the number of days.
5. Days between dates will give you the number of days between the first date entered and the second date entered. It includes the first day and excludes the last day in the calculation.
6. It shows you that the setting for your date worksheet takes the actual number of days into consideration: i.e., it includes adjustments for leap years. If it is set to '360', change it by pressing 2ND then SET to get ACT.

Example 8.2(k) **Calculating the Number of Days in a Time Period Using a Financial Calculator**

Calculate the number of days in the time period from October 18, 2009 to April 05, 2010.

Solution

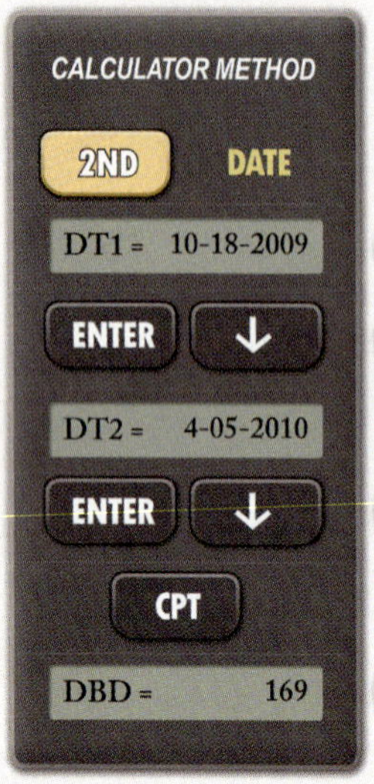

1. ***Enter Oct 18, 2009 as 10.1809*** then press **ENTER**
2. ***Use the down arrow to go to DT2*** and enter Apr 05, 2010 as 4.0510 then press **ENTER**.
3. ***Use the down arrow to go to DBD*** and press CPT to compute the number of days.
4. Therefore, the number of days in the time period is 169.

8.2 | *Exercises*

1. Calculate the number of days in the following periods and express it in terms of years:
   a. January 01, 2011 to February 19, 2011
   b. February 26, 2010 to December 02, 2010
   c. November 23, 2010 to April 04, 2011
   d. August 25, 2011 to September 06, 2012
2. Calculate the number of days in the following periods and express it in terms of years:
   a. August 18, 2011 to September 19, 2011
   b. January 23, 2010 to October 06, 2010
   c. July 18, 2010 to July 18, 2011
   d. October 19, 2011 to November 06, 2012
3. Calculate the amount of interest earned on the following investments:

	Principal	Rate	Time period
a.	$200	10% p.a.	200 days
b.	$2200	4% p.a	April 15, 2010 to November 01, 2010
c.	$5605	1.2% p.m	January 24, 2010 to February 15, 2011
d.	$150	0.8% p.m	1 year and 9 months

4. Calculate the amount of interest earned on the following investments:

	Principal	Rate	Time period
a.	$20,000	5% p.a.	250 days
b.	$200	12% p.a.	November 06, 2010 to February 28, 2011
c.	$800	1.10% p.m	March 15, 2010 to August 25, 2011
d.	$500	0.75% p.m	2 years and 3 months

5. Hua borrowed $5000 from her friend Owen, with a promise to return it to him in 1 year and 3 months. If Owen charged Hua a simple interest at 5% per annum for this loan, calculate the amount of interest he will receive at the end of the time period.

6. Madison won a prize amount of $1500 and she deposited the entire amount in a savings account of a local bank. How much interest would she have earned after 18 months if interest on the savings account was 3% p.a.?

7. Nathan obtained a loan of $750 to purchase a bike. How much interest would Nathan have to pay at the end of 11 months if the loan was at an interest rate of 5.5% p.a.?

8. Logan wanted to purchase a motorbike but was short $4350. He approached his friend who agreed to give him the amount as long as he paid back the money in 4 months at an interest rate of 6% p.a. How much interest would Logan have to pay his friend at the end of 4 months?

9. Abbey withdrew $8000 from her business and deposited this amount in a savings account on January 02, 2011. If the account provided her with an interest rate of 4% p.a., calculate the amount of interest she would earn by March 02, 2012.

10. Rajesh's website development business was doing well and he wanted to lend the surplus earnings he made to his friend who was in need of money. He lent $5000 at 6% p.a. to his friend on February 7, 2011. Calculate how much interest his friend had to pay Rajesh on July 11, 2012.

11. Benjamin borrowed $2500 from a money lender. If the money lender charges interest at 24% p.a., calculate the amount of interest Benjamin had to pay the lender at the end of 20 days.

12. Zack wanted to propose to his girlfriend and decided to give her a diamond ring. The ring he liked was selling for $3200 but he only had $1500 with him. His friend, Ethan, agreed to loan him the remaining amount at an interest rate of 12% p.a. If Zack returned the money in 40 days, calculate the amount of interest he had to pay Ethan for the loan.

13. A money lender was known to lend money at an exuberant rate of 6% per month. Aidan was in desperate need of $5000 and borrowed the money from this lender. If Aidan repaid the amount in 45 days, calculate the amount of interest he had to pay at the end of the time period.

14. Maya had a savings account with a multinational bank in Canada that was providing her with a very low interest rate of 0.05% per month. If she deposited $10,000 in her savings account, calculate how much interest she earned after 60 days.

15. Which rate is more attractive for a lender of a loan: 9.8% per annum or 0.85% per month? Explain your answer.

16. Lian's friend offered to lend her $1000 at an interest rate of 6.5% per annum. However, her sister offered her the same amount at 0.52% per month. Who was charging her lesser interest for the loan? Explain your answer.

17. Angelo took a loan of $2500 from a bank at 4.6% p.a. for 18 months and gave it to his friend Alisa as a loan at a rate of 0.5% per month. At the end of 18 months, how much interest should Alisa have paid Angelo? Of this amount, how much interest should Angelo have paid the bank?

18. Aba invested \$5200 for 210 days at 0.4% per month. Tabita invested the same amount for the same period but at 4.3% p.a. Who earned more and by how much?

19. Jada invested a total of \$7500. Out of this, \$3500 was invested at 4.6% p.a. and the remainder at 0.4% per month. Calculate the total interest earned from both investments after 8 months.

20. Babiya borrowed a total of \$3250 to pay for college fees. \$2000 of this was from a bank at 6.25% p.a and the remainder from a credit union at 0.9% per month. Calculate the total interest she should have paid after 9 months for both the loans.

21. Yara took a loan of \$2600 for 180 days at 11% per annum. How much more or less money would be required to pay off the loan if the interest rate is 1.2% per month instead of 11% per annum?

22. Afsoon invested \$9500 for 320 days at 8% per annum. How much more or less interest would he have earned on the investment if his money was growing at an interest rate of 0.75% p.a. instead of 8% p.a.?

8.3 | Calculating Principal, Interest Rate, Time, and Maturity Value

In simple interest calculations, depending on the information provided, the simple interest Formula 8.2 can be rearranged to solve for the unknown variable, as shown below:

Using Formula 8.2, $I = Prt$

Therefore, $Prt = I$

Dividing both sides by,

(i) rt, we have, $P = \frac{I}{rt}$

(ii) Pt, we have, $r = \frac{I}{Pt}$

(iii) Pr, we have, $t = \frac{I}{Pr}$

P, r, t Triangle

Here is a triangle that can be used to help in rearranging the formula $I = Prt$ to find the variable P, r, or t.

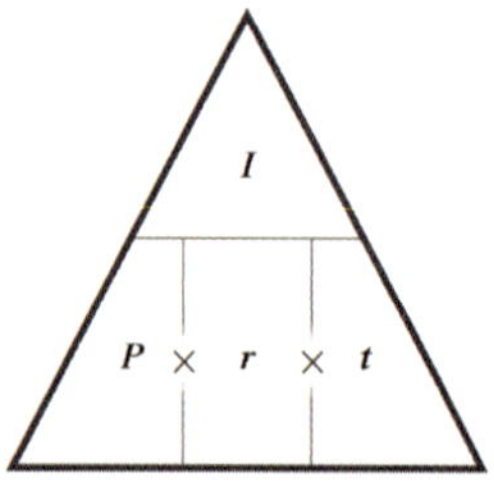

Variables beside each other at the bottom are multiplied ($P \times r \times t$, as shown).

Variables at the bottom are divided by the variable on top: I.

Cover the variable that you want to solve to see the new formula.

For example, if you want to solve for 'P', the formula can be found by covering 'P' and reading the remaining variables in the above triangle, to get $P = \frac{I}{rt}$.

Example 8.3(a) **Calculating the Principal**

A 5-month term deposit at Andrew's bank offers a simple interest rate of 3.5% p.a. If Andrew earned an interest amount of \$75 over the 5-month period, how much did he deposit in this term deposit?

Solution

$I = \$75, \quad r = 3.5\%$ p.a., $\quad t = 5$ months

$= 0.035$ p.a. $\quad = \frac{5}{12}$ years ('t' is converted into years as 'r' is per annum)

Rearranging Formula 8.2, $P = \frac{I}{rt}$

$$= \frac{75}{0.035 \times \frac{5}{12}}$$

$$= \$5142.857143...$$

Therefore, Andrew had to deposit \$5142.86 in his term deposit to earn interest of \$75.

Example 8.3(b)

Calculating the Time Period

A short-term loan of \$30,000 was issued to an employee at 9.5% p.a. What was the time period of the loan (rounded up to the next day) if the interest charged was \$1750?

Solution

$P = 30{,}000, \quad r = 9.5\%$ p.a., $\quad I = \$1750,$

$= 0.095$ p.a.

Rearranging Formula 8.2,

$$t = \frac{I}{Pr}$$

$$t = \frac{1750}{30{,}000 \times 0.095} \text{ years}$$ Since the unit of 'r' is p.a., units of 't' will be in years

$= 0.614035...$ years

$= 0.614035... \times 365$ days — Multiplying by 365 to convert years to days

$= 224.122807...$ days — Rounding up to the next day

$= 225$ days

Therefore, the time period of the loan was 225 days.

Example 8.3(c)

Calculating the Rate of Interest

Calculate the rate of simple interest per annum offered on savings of \$2900 if interest earned is \$170 over a period of 8 months.

Solution

Method 1: Using unit of 't' in months

$P = \$2900, I = \$170, t = 8$ months, $r = ?$ p.a.

Rearranging Formula 8.2,

$$r = \frac{I}{Pt}$$

$$= \frac{170}{2900 \times 8}$$

$= 0.007327...$

$= 0.73\%$ per month — Multiplying by 12 to convert per month to per annum.

$= 0.007327... \times 12 = 0.087931... = 8.79\%$ per annum

Therefore, the rate of interest is 8.79% p.a.

Solution *continued*

Method 2: Using unit of 't' in years

$P = \$2900, \quad I = \$170, \quad t = 8 \text{ months}, \quad r = ? \text{ p.a.}$

$= \frac{8}{12} \text{ years}$

Rearranging Formula 8.2,

$$r = \frac{I}{Pt}$$

Substituting values, we obtain,

$$= \frac{170}{\left(2900 \times \frac{8}{12}\right)}$$

$$= 0.087931... = 8.79\% \text{ p.a.}$$

Therefore, the rate of interest is 8.79% p.a.

Calculating Maturity Value

Maturity value (*S*) is the accumulated value of money over a period of time. It is the sum of the principal amount and the amount of interest.

Therefore, *Maturity Value = Principal + Amount of Interest*

This is given by the formula,

Formula 8.3 (a)

Maturity Value

$$S = P + I$$

This can be rearranged to obtain, $I = S - P$

And, $P = S - I$

Formulas 8.2 and 8.3(a) can be combined by substituting for 'I' as follows:

$I = Prt$ From Formula 8.2

$S = P + I$ From Formula 8.3(a)

Substituting 'I' from Formula 8.2 into Formula 8.3(a), we obtain,

$$S = P + Prt$$

Isolating the common factor 'P', results in the following formula:

Formula 8.3 (b)

Maturity Value

$$S = P(1 + rt)$$

This can be rearranged to obtain,

Formula 8.3 (c)

Principal

$$P = \frac{S}{(1 + rt)} \quad \text{or} \quad P = S(1 + rt)^{-1}$$

Example 8.3(d)

Calculating the Maturity Value and Amount of Interest

Ruth received an amount of \$700 from a pawnbroker at an interest rate of 3% per month. Calculate the maturity value of her loan and amount of interest she would have to repay at the end of 4 months.

Solution

$P = \$700 \qquad r = 3\%$ p.m. $= 0.03$ p.m. $\qquad t = 4$ months

Using Formula 8.3(b),

$$S = P(1 + rt)$$
$$S = 700(1 + 0.03 \times 4) = \$784.00$$

Therefore, the maturity value of her loan is \$784.00.

Using Formula 8.3(a), $S = P + I$ Rearranging, we obtain,

$$I = S - P = 784 - 700 = \$84.00$$

Therefore, the interest she would have to repay is \$84.00.

Example 8.3(e)

Calculating the Principal and Amount of Interest

If Margaret had an amount of \$2264.50 in an investment fund at the end of 10 months if the fund was growing at a simple interest rate of 8% p.a., calculate:

(i) The amount she invested.

(ii) The interest earned

Solution

$S = \$2264.50 \qquad r = 8\%$ p.a. $= 0.08$ p.a. $\qquad t = 10$ months $= \frac{10}{12}$ years

(i) Using Formula 8.2(c),

$$P = \frac{S}{(1 + rt)} = \frac{2264.50}{\left(1 + 0.08 \times \frac{10}{12}\right)} = \$2122.97$$

Or, $P = S(1 + rt)^{-1} = 2264.50\left(1 + 0.08 \times \frac{10}{12}\right)^{-1} = \$2122.97$

Therefore, she invested \$2122.97.

(ii) Using Formula 8.2(a), $S = P + I$

$$I = S - P = 2264.50 - 2122.97 = \$141.53$$

Therefore, she earned \$141.53 in interest.

8.3 | Exercises

Calculate the missing values for Problems 1 and 2.

Round your answer to the nearest day wherever applicable:

1.

	Principal Amount	Date of Receiving Loan	Date of Repayment	Interest Rate	Amount of Interest Earned
a.	?	January 18, 2008	April 24, 2008	1.20% p.m.	$480.00
b.	$12,400	July 16, 2010	August 05, 2011	?% p.m.	1862.50
c.	?	April 19, 2010	September 09, 2010	18% p.a.	$280.40
d.	$6740	May 12, 2010	October 16, 2011	?% p.m.	$640.75
e.	$19,865	August 08, 2010	?	5% p.a.	$375.50
f.	$1675	?	January 18, 2010	0.60% p.m.	$163.00

2.

	Principal Amount	Date of Investment	Date of Maturity	Interest Rate	Amount of interest Earned
a.	?	February 08, 2008	March 08, 2008	0.80% p.m.	$1435.00
b.	$26,850	December 12, 2009	April 19, 2010	?% p.m.	$724.75
c.	?	May 01, 2010	October 06, 2010	12% p.a.	$180.75
d.	$13,480	June 19, 2010	July 07, 2011	?% p.m.	$1208.50
e.	$180	September 17, 2010	?	5% p.a.	$12.00
f.	$7890	?	February 12, 2010	0.90% p.m.	$295.00

3. Calculate the amount of money that was loaned at 8% p.a. to Amanda on March 3, 2010 if she repaid the loan on December 16, 2010 with interest of $420.

4. On November 23, 2010, Maya paid her uncle $868.75 in interest for a loan that he had given her on June 12, 2010. Calculate the amount she borrowed from him if he charged her interest of 12% p.a.

5. Danielle borrowed $7400 at 7.35% p.a. simple interest. Calculate the term of the loan (rounded to the nearest day) if she was charged interest of $300.

6. Ruben invested $9180 in an account that was earning simple interest at a rate of 3.23% p.a. How long did it take (rounded to the nearest day) for his investment to earn $160?

7. What annual rate of simple interest was charged on a loan of $4600 that was issued to Mary on August 03, 2007 if she settled the loan on September 03, 2008 with $380.50 in interest?

8. Sarah received an academic achievement prize of $4000 from her college. She deposited this money on August 08, 2011 in a savings account. If the interest she earned when she withdrew the money on October 09, 2012 was $75.75, calculate the annual rate of simple interest that the savings account was providing her.

9. An investment of $8000 for 18 months in an account earning simple interest resulted in a maturity value of $8600. If the interest rate had been 3% more, what would have been the maturity value?

10. A loan of $3700 charging simple interest for 1 year and 3 months requires a repayment of $3954.38. If the interest rate had been 1% lower, what would have been the repayment amount?

11. Emily invested \$400 in her savings account for a period of 6 months. If the savings account was offering her a simple interest rate of 2.5% p.m., calculate the maturity amount of her investment and the interest she earned at the end of the time period.

12. Hannah received a loan of \$700 from her aunt to purchase a new bike. She had to repay the loan in 45 days at a simple interest rate of 7% p.a. Calculate the total amount she would have had to repay her aunt and the interest charged at the end of the time period.

13. What is the term (rounded to the nearest month) for an investment of \$2000 earning 5.6% p.a. simple interest to grow to \$2133.67.

14. What was the term of a \$6500 loan (rounded to the nearest month) that was settled with an amount of \$7280.50, if it had a simple interest rate of 4.5% p.a.

15. Ryan invested \$20,000 in a short term investment that was offering a simple interest rate of 4% p.a. Calculate the interest earned and maturity amount of his investment if the investment time period was 320 days.

16. Isabella learned that she could invest her money in a short-term investment that was offering a simple interest rate of 3.5% p.a. If she invested \$10,000 for a period of 91 days, calculate the amount of interest she earned and the maturity value of her investment at the end of the time period.

17. At the end of the first quarter (March 31, 2010) Rachel deposited the net earnings of \$6790.25 from her business into a short-term investment that was offering a simple interest rate of 5.75% p.a. Calculate the interest earned and the maturity amount if she wanted to withdraw the entire amount at the end of the second quarter (June 30, 2010).

18. Katelyn's clothing retail startup business urgently required an operational investment of \$12,500. She approached a local money lender who agreed to give her the amount at an interest rate of 3% p.m. If Katelyn borrowed the amount on April 03, 2010 and returned the loan on August 03, 2010, calculate the total amount she had to repay and the interest charged on the loan.

19. The maturity value of an investment is twice the amount invested. If the rate on the investment earns 0.98% p.m., what is the term of the investment rounded to the nearest month?

20. The interest paid on a loan is equal to the amount of the loan. If the rate charged on the loan is 1.5% p.m., calculate the time period of the loan to the nearest month.

21. Calculate the amount of money Nicholas lent his friend and the interest he earned if his friend repaid him \$3684.50 (including interest) at the end of 80 days. Assume that Nicholas charged his friend a simple interest rate of 5% p.a.

22. Sophia decided to deposit all the profits of her game developing business into a savings account at the beginning of this year. The bank was offering a simple interest rate of 5% p.a. on the investment in her savings account. At the end of the first 6 months, her deposited amount matured to \$18,546.75. Calculate her business profit this year and the interest she earned over the second half of the year.

23. If the interest earned on an investment that is growing at 0.42% p.m. simple interest for 180 days is \$250, calculate the principal and maturity amount of this investment.

24. If Rachel earned \$20 as interest by lending a certain amount at 2% p.m. to her friend for 3 months, calculate the amount she lent to her friend and the amount she received from her friend at the end of the loan period.

• 25. Ben invested a certain amount of money at 6% p.a. and another \$6000 at 7% p.a. After 15 months, the total interest from both investments was \$716.50. Calculate the amount that was invested at 6% p.a.

• 26. Alice obtained a loan of \$1750 at 6.5% p.a. and another loan at 7.5% p.a. She settled both loans 9 months later with a payment of \$1868.49. Calculate the amount of the loan taken at 7.5% p.a.

8.4 | Calculating Equivalent Payments that Replace Another Payment or a Series of Payments

Time value of money: A dollar is worth more today than a dollar in the future since it can be invested today to earn interest over time.

We have learned that the value of money changes over a period of time when invested or borrowed at an interest rate (time value of money).

For example, \$100 invested or borrowed today is neither equivalent to \$100 a year ago nor equivalent to \$100 a year from now. It is equivalent to:

- \$90.91 a year ago or
- \$110 a year from now,

assuming money earns 10% p.a. simple interest.

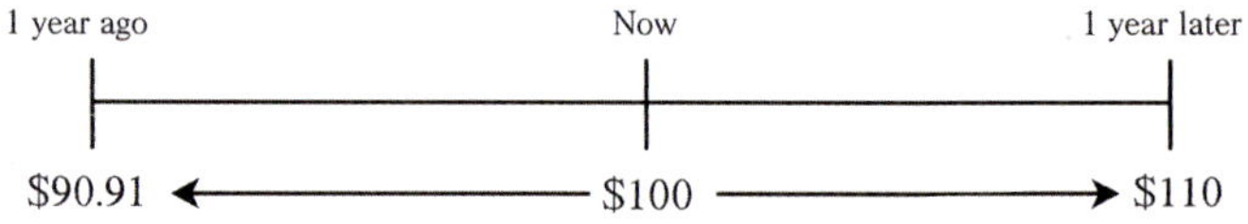

Similarly, \$100 invested a year ago is equivalent to:

- \$110 now or
- \$120 a year from now,

assuming money earns 10% p.a. simple interest.

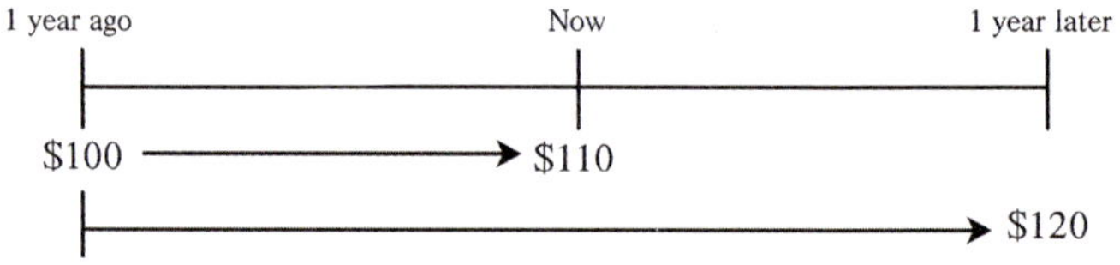

There may be times when it may be necessary to change or reschedule the due date of a payment for various reasons. When the due date is changed, the value of money on the new date is called the equivalent value; i.e., a new value equivalent to the value of money on the old date.

Equivalent Payment of a Single Payment

If the rescheduled date of a payment is after the due date, it is similar to moving money in the forward direction. Therefore, the equivalent value of the payment on the rescheduled date is calculated using Formula 8.3(b) $S = P(1 + rt)$.

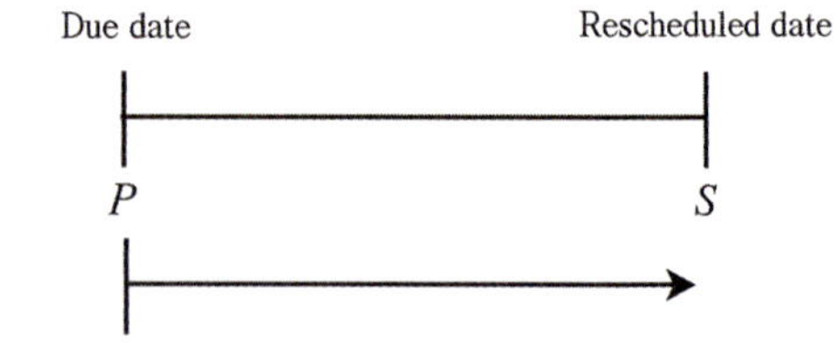

If the rescheduled date of a payment is before the due date, it is similar to moving money in the reverse direction. Therefore, the equivalent value of the payment on the rescheduled date is calculated using Formula 8.3(c):

$$P = \frac{S}{(1 + rt)} \text{ or } P = S(1 + rt)^{-1}$$

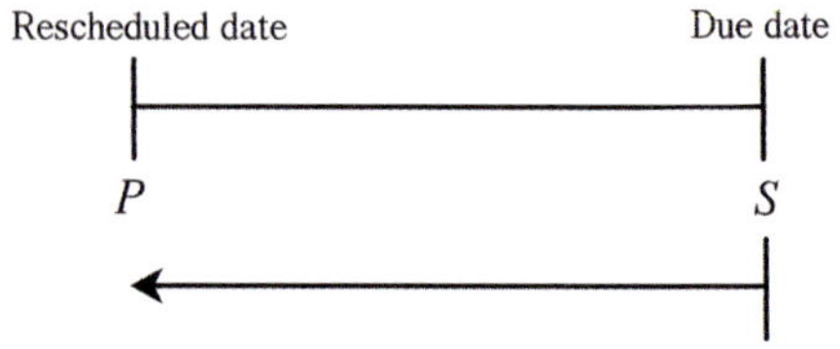

Example 8.4(a) **Equivalent Payment of a Single Payment to be Received in the Future**

Harry realizes that he is unable to repay a matured loan amount of \$2500 that is due today. If he is charged 5% p.a. (simple interest) for this loan, what equivalent payment is required to repay this amount in 6 months?

Solution

$P = \$2500, \quad r = 5\%$ p.a., $\quad t = 6$ months

$= 0.05$ p.a. $\quad = \frac{6}{12}$ years

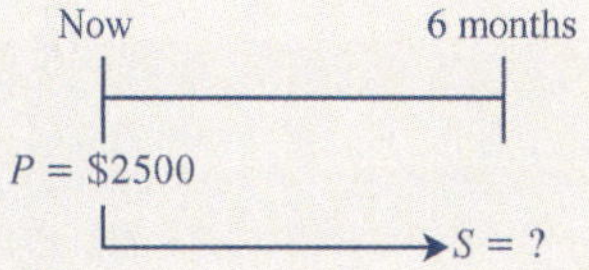

Using Formula 8.3(b), $\quad S = P(1 + rt)$

Substituting values, $\quad S = 2500\left(1 + 0.05 \times \frac{6}{12}\right)$

$= \$2562.50$

Therefore, Harry has to make an equivalent payment of $2562.50 in 6 months.

Example 8.4(b)

Equivalent Payment of a Single Payment to be Received on an Earlier Date

Grace is required to repay a matured loan amount of $1500 in 9 months. However, she realized that she can clear the loan amount in 6 months instead. How much would she have to pay to clear the loan in 6 months if the interest charged is 4.5% p.a. (simple interest)?

Solution

$S = \$1500 \quad r = 4.5\%$ p.a. $\quad t = 3$ months

$= 0.045$ p.a. $\quad = \frac{3}{12}$ years

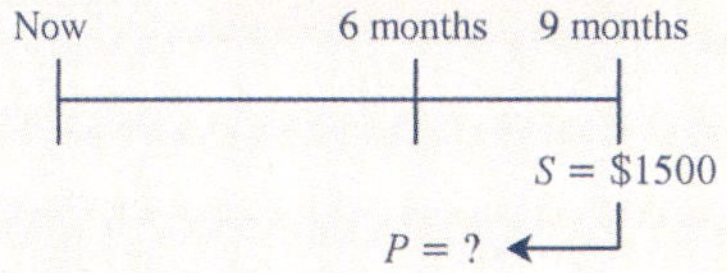

Using Formula 8.3(c), $\quad P = S(1 + rt)^{-1}$

Substituting values, $\quad P = 1500\left(1 + 0.045 \times \frac{3}{12}\right)^{-1}$

$= \$1483.31$

Therefore, she would have to pay $1483.31 to clear the loan in 6 months.

Equivalent Payment of a Series of Payments

Since the value of money will be different at different points of time, equivalent payment calculations involving more than one payment will require a defined comparison point, known as the focal date. It is a reference date for calculating and equating the equivalent values of all payments. A timeline diagram will assist in calculating the equivalent value of a series of payments.

Example 8.4(c)

Single Equivalent Payment that Replaces Two Payments

A payment of $5000 is due in 3 months and another payment of $8000 is due in 9 months. Calculate the value of a single payment to be made in 5 months that is equivalent to these two payments if money earns 6% p.a. simple interest. Use 5 months from now as the focal date.

Solution

Let the single unknown payment in 5 months that is equivalent to the two payments be 'x'.

Single unknown payment at the focal date = Equivalent value of $5000 at the focal date
+ Equivalent value of $8000 at the focal date.

- Equivalent value of $5000 at the focal date is the maturity value of $5000 at the focal date ($S_1$).
- Equivalent value of $8000 at the focal date is the principal amount of $8000 at the focal date ($P_2$).

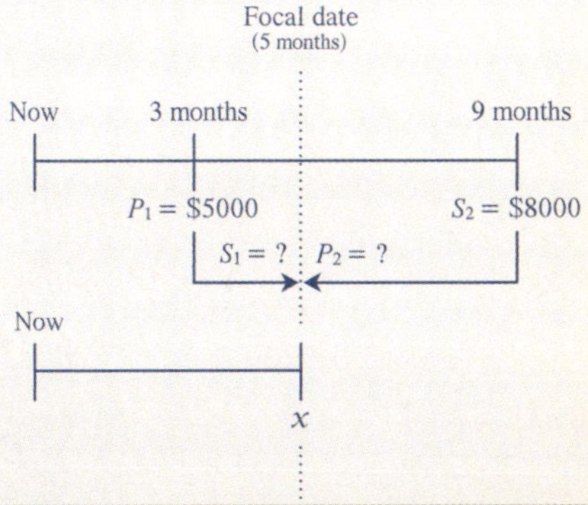

$$x = S_1 + P_2$$

$$S_1 = P_1(1 + rt_1)$$

Solution continued

$$= 5000\left(1 + 0.06 \times \frac{2}{12}\right) \qquad [t_1 = 2 \text{ months} = \tfrac{2}{12} \text{ years}]$$

$$= \$5050.00$$

In simple interest calculations, different focal dates will give slightly different values for the equivalent payment. Therefore, the focal date is to be determined before calculating the equivalent payment.

$$P_2 = S_2\,(1+rt_2)^{-1}$$

$$= 8000\left(1 + 0.06 \times \frac{4}{12}\right)^{-1} \qquad [t_2 = 4 \text{ months} = \tfrac{4}{12} \text{ years}]$$

$$= \$7843.14$$

$$x = S_1 + P_2$$

$$x = 5050.00 + 7843.14$$

$$= \$12{,}893.14$$

Therefore, when the focal date is 5 months from now, the single payment to be made in 5 months that is equivalent to the two payments is $12,893.14.

Example 8.4(d) **Single Equivalent Payment that Replaces Two Payments at a Different Focal Date**

Repeat Example 8.4(c) using 'now' as the focal date.

Solution

Let the single unknown payment in 5 months that is equivalent to the two payments be 'x'.

Equivalent value of 'x' at the focal date = Equivalent value of $5000 at the focal date + Equivalent value of $8000 at the focal date.

- Equivalent value of 'x' at the focal date is the principal amount of 'x' at the focal date.
- Equivalent value of $5000 at the focal date is the principal amount of $5000 at the focal date ($P_1$).
- Equivalent value of $8000 at the focal date is the principal amount of $8000 at the focal date ($P_2$).

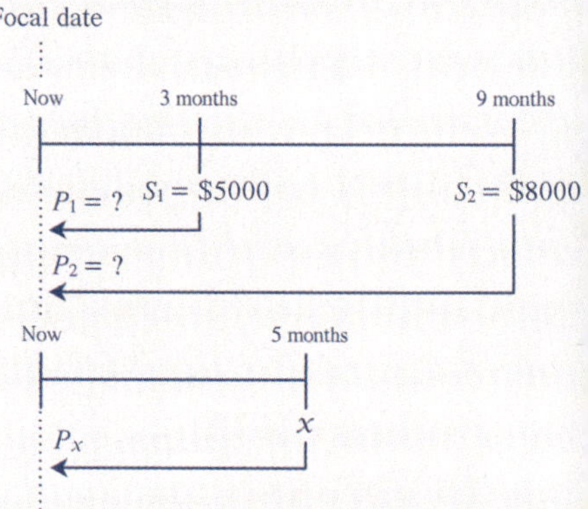

$$P_x = P_1 + P_2$$

And,
$$P_x = S_x\,(1 + rt_x)^{-1}$$

$$= x\left(1 + 0.06 \times \frac{5}{12}\right)^{-1} \qquad [t_x = 5 \text{ months} = \tfrac{5}{12} \text{ years}]$$

$$= x(0.975609...)$$

Also,
$$P_1 = S_1\,(1 + rt_1)^{-1}$$

$$= 5000\left(1 + 0.06 \times \frac{3}{12}\right)^{-1} \qquad [t_x = 3 \text{ months} = \tfrac{3}{12} \text{ years}]$$

Simplifying,
$$= \$4926.108374...$$

Also,
$$P_2 = S_2\,(1 + rt_2)^{-1}$$

$$= 8000\left(1 + 0.06 \times \frac{9}{12}\right)^{-1} \qquad [t_x = 9 \text{ months} = \tfrac{9}{12} \text{ years}]$$

Simplifying,
$$= \$7655.502392...$$

Recalling,
$$P_x = P_1 + P_2$$

Solving for x,
$$x(0.975609...) = 4926.108374... + 7655.502392...$$

$$x = \$12{,}896.15$$

Solution continued

Therefore, when the focal date is 'now', the single payment in 5 months that is equivalent to the two payments is $12,896.15.

Note: *Notice that when the focal date changes, the value of the equivalent payment is slightly different from the value of the equivalent payment in Example 8.6(c).*

Example 8.4(e)

Single Equivalent Payment that Replaces Two Payments When No Focal Date is Provided

Abdul was supposed to pay $500 six ago months and $900 in 10 months. He did not make these payments as scheduled. However, he wanted to clear the loan in 18 months from now. What would be the value of this single payment if interest on the loan is 9% p.a.?

Solution

As no focal point is provided, we use the single payment date as the focal date. Therefore, the focal date is 18 months.

When no focal date is provided, the last payment date is usually used as the focal date.

Let the single unknown payment in 18 months that is equivalent to the two payments be 'x'.

Value of 'x' at the focal date = Equivalent value of $500 at the focal date + Equivalent value of $900 at the focal date.

- Equivalent value of $500 at the focal date is the maturity value of $500 at the focal date ($S_1$)
- Equivalent value of $900 at the focal date is the maturity value of $900 at the focal date ($S_2$)

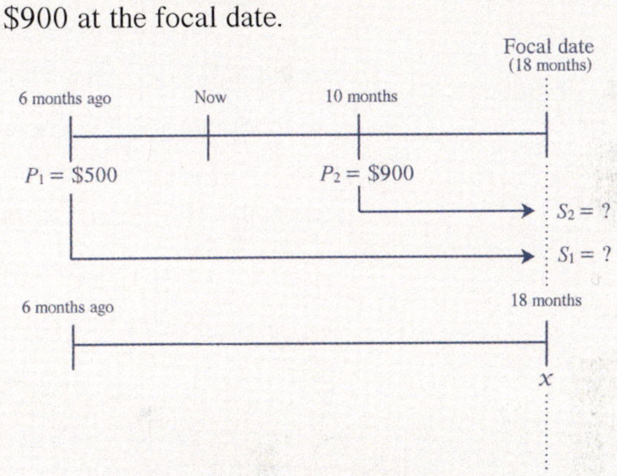

$$x = S_1 + S_2$$

And, $S_1 = P_1(1 + rt_1)$

$= 500(1 + 0.09 \times 2)$ $\quad [t_1 = 24 \text{ months} = \frac{24}{12} = 2 \text{ years}]$

Simplifying, $= \$590.00$

Also, $S_2 = P_2(1 + rt_2)$

$= 900\left(1 + 0.09 \times \frac{8}{12}\right)$ $\quad [t_2 = 8 \text{ months} = \frac{8}{12} \text{ years}]$

Simplifying, $= \$954.00$

Therefore, $x = 590.00 + 954.00$

$= \$1544.00$

Therefore, the single equivalent payment in 18 months that would replace the two payments is $1544.00.

Example 8.4(f)

Comparison of Two Different Payment Streams

A furniture supplier sold some furniture to a clothing store and provided them with two options to make a payment for the purchase:

Option (i): $4000 in 2 months and $1800 in 6 months.

Option (ii): $2150 in 4 months and $3732 in 8 months.

If money earns 6% p.a. simple interest, calculate which option is economically better for the store.

Solution

We use the last payment date of 8 months as the focal date and compare the equivalent values of the payments in Option (i) and Option (ii) at the focal date.

Equivalent value of payments using Option (i) at the focal date = $S_1 + S_2$

$$S_1 = P_1(1 + rt_1)$$
$$= 4000\left(1 + 0.06 \times \frac{6}{12}\right)$$
$$= \$4120.00$$

$$S_2 = P_2(1 + rt_2)$$
$$= 1800\left(1 + 0.06 \times \frac{2}{12}\right)$$
$$= \$1818.00$$

$$S_1 + S_2 = \$4120.00 + \$1818.00$$
$$= \$5938.00$$

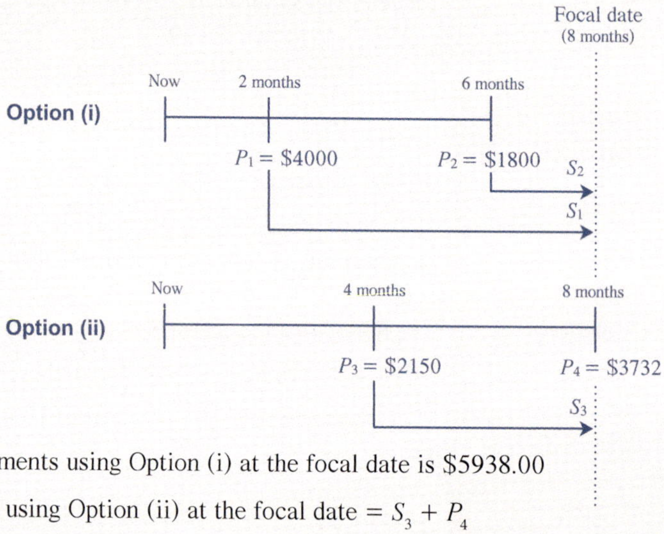

Therefore, the equivalent value of payments using Option (i) at the focal date is $5938.00

Equivalent value of payments using Option (ii) at the focal date = $S_3 + P_4$

(As the fourth payment is on the focal date, the equivalent value of the payment on the focal date will be its principal amount, P_4.)

$$S_3 = P_3(1 + rt_3)$$
$$= 2150\left(1 + 0.06 \times \frac{4}{12}\right) \qquad [t_1 = 4 \text{ months} = \frac{4}{12} \text{ year}]$$
$$= \$2193.00$$

$$S_3 + P_4 = \$2193.00 + \$3732.00$$
$$= \$5925.00$$

Therefore, the equivalent value of payments using Option (ii) at the focal date is $5925.00.

The equivalent value of the payments in Option (ii) is economically better than that of Option (i). Therefore, the store should choose Option (ii).

Example 8.4(g)

Two Equal Payments Replacing a Stream of Payments

Karen has to repay a personal loan in two installments of $1280 in 5 months and $2193 in 15 months. If she wants to reschedule these payments by two equal payments, one in 8 months and the other in 12 months, what will be the amount of her new payments? Assume money is earning 8% p.a. simple interest.

Solution

Let the two equal payment amounts be $\$x$ each.

Choose the last payment date of 15 months as the focal date.

Option (i)		Option (ii)
Equivalent value of scheduled payments at the focal date	=	Equivalent value of rescheduled payments at the focal date

Solution *continued*

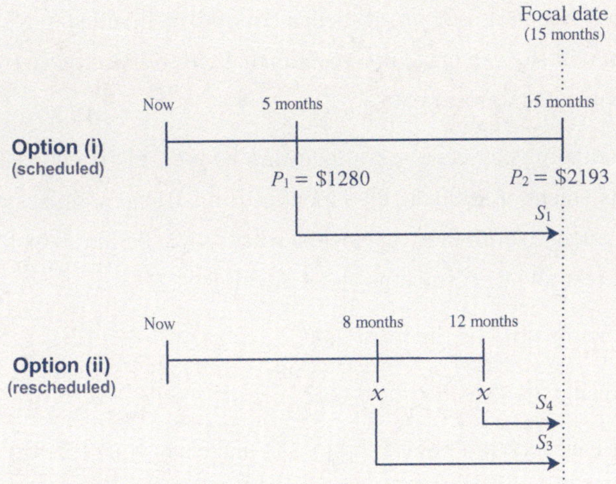

$$S_1 + P_2 = S_3 + S_4$$

Substituting values, $1280\,(1 + rt_1) + 2193 = x(1 + rt_3) + x(1 + rt_4)$

And, $1280\left(1 + 0.08 \times \frac{10}{12}\right) + 2193 = x\left(1 + 0.08 \times \frac{7}{12}\right) + x\left(1 + 0.08 \times \frac{3}{12}\right)$

Solving for x, $3558.333333... = x(1.046666...) + 1.02x$

$$3558.333333... = x(2.066666...)$$

$$x = \$1721.77$$

Therefore, the two equal payments that will replace her original payments will be $1721.77 each.

8.4 | Exercises

1. A company has two outstanding loans. The first one is for $20,000 at an interest rate of 1.25% p.m. due 6 months ago and the second one is for $15,000 at an interest rate of 9.5% p.a. due today. The company re-negotiated to pay both loans in a single payment in 4 months. Calculate the repayment amount. (Use 4 months from now as the focal date.)

2. Sabir planned to make the following two investments: $7500 in 5 months at 0.9% p.m. and $5000 in 7 months at 6.5% p.a. Find the maturity value of both investments in 15 months. (Use 15 months from now as the focal date.)

3. Debt payments of $1250 and $1450 are due in 4 months and 7 months, respectively. What single payment is required to settle both debts in 1 month? Assume an interest rate of 7.25% p.a. and use 1 month from now as the focal date.

4. A payment of $4500 was due 3 years ago and another payment of $2750 is due in 4 years. Find the single payment that will settle both payments in 2 years. Assume an interest rate of 1.1% p.m. and use 2 years from now as the focal date.

5. A loan payment of $2900 was due 60 days ago and $3200 is due in 90 days. What single payment in 45 days is required to settle the two payments? Assume an interest rate of 4.2% p.a. and use 45 days from now as the focal date.

6. Saburi had to pay her landlord a payment of $750 that was due 2 months ago and $1250 in 8 months. What single payment must she give her landlord that will settle these amounts in 3 months if interest is 0.75% p.m. Use 3 months from now as the focal date.

7. Victoria has to repay a loan in two installments: $1000 in 6 months and $1200 in 10 months. Calculate the single equivalent payment that she can make in 8 months that will replace these two payments if interest is 4% p.a. simple interest. Use 8 months as the focal date.

8. Jacob has two outstanding payments for a loan that he gave his friend: $3650, due 2 months ago, which was not paid, and another payment of $900,due in 8 months. If his friend promises to make one single payment in 5 months that would be equivalent to both these payments, what should be the size of the payment? Assume that money earns 3% p.a. simple interest and use 5 months as the focal date.

9. Repeat Problem 7 using 'now' as the focal date.

10. Repeat Problem 8 using 'now' as the focal date.

11. A supplier of doors gave a contractor two options to make a payment for the supply of doors for a new condominium development project:
    - Option (a): $120,500 immediately and another payment of $75,600 in 6 months.
    - Option (b): $30,000 immediately and another payment of $165,500 in 5 months.

    If money earns 4% p.a. simple interest, calculate which option is economically better for the contractor. You may use any date as the focal date for this question.

12. Samantha won a lottery; however, the lottery company gave her the following two options to receive her prize money:
    - Option (a): $10,000 in 2 months and $16,000 in 8 months.
    - Option (b): $5000 immediately and $22,000 in 10 months.

    Which option would be economically better for Samantha if money earns 7% p.a.? You may use any date as the focal date for this question.

• 13. The Director of Sales of a management consulting company was preparing a quotation for a potential client. He wanted to provide two payment options in the quote:
    - Payment Option (a): $4500 in 4 months and another payment of $7630 in 13 months.
    - Payment Option (b): Two equal payments, one in 6 months and the other in 12 months.

    If money earns 4% p.a., what must be the value of payments in Option (b) such that they are equivalent to the payments in Option (a)? You may use any date as the focal date for this question.

• 14. What two equal payments, one on March 05, 2010 and the other on June 15, 2010 will be equivalent to the following two payments: $2400 on April 01, 2010 and $3500 on August 15, 2010. Assume that money earns 5% p.a. You may use any date as the focal date for this question.

15. $1800 due 2 months ago and $700 due in 3 months are to be repaid by a payment of $1500 today and the balance payment in 4 months. Find the balance if interest is 6% p.a. and the agreed focal date is 4 months from now.

16. Yan was supposed to receive $1350 that was due 150 days ago and $450 due in 30 days from her friend Mee. If Mee promised to repay $1000 today and the balance in 60 days, calculate how much she would have to repay in 60 days if the interest is 0.75% p.m. and the agreed focal date is 60 days from now.

8.5 | Applications of Simple Interest

Some common applications of simple interest are:

- Savings accounts, Term deposits, and Guaranteed Investment Certificates
- Demand loans and partial payments of demand loans
- Promissory notes

- Treasury bills and Commercial paper
- Discounting and proceeds

Savings Accounts, Term Deposits, and Guaranteed Investment Certificates

Financial institutions offer different types of investment options to investors. Some of the secure investment options are savings accounts, term deposits, and Guaranteed Investment Certificates. Investors are not charged any special fee to invest in these options. When they invest money in these options, the financial institution makes use of the money for a period of time and therefore, pays an interest to the investors. At the same time, the financial institution charges a higher interest rate to those borrowing money from them. Even though there is no fee when money is invested in these accounts, financial institutions make money on the difference between the interest it pays investors and the interest it charges borrowers.

Savings Accounts

A savings account provides people with a safe place to deposit their money. It is an option where funds are usually easily accessible; i.e., people can deposit and withdraw money from a savings account at any convenient time.

In a savings account, the interest is often calculated on the daily balance and posted monthly.

For example, if you have invested \$1000 in a savings account for the month of March at a bank that is offering you an interest of 1% p.a.,

Interest rate per day $= \frac{1}{365}\%$

Interest amount per day $= \frac{0.01}{365} \times \$1000 = \$0.03$

Interest paid at the end of March = \$0.03 x 31 days = \$0.93

Term Deposits

Term deposits, also known as fixed deposits or time deposits, are investment options where money is invested for a fixed period of time. If an investor wants to withdraw their money from a term deposit prior to the end of the term, they may have to pay a penalty as determined by the financial institution. As this investment is fixed for a period of time, the interest rate is higher than that of a savings account.

Guaranteed Investment Certificate (GIC)

The interest earned from savings accounts, term deposits, and GICs are taxable income.

Purchasing a GIC refers to investing a sum of money for a specific period of time. It is similar to a term deposit or fixed deposit. The investor is guaranteed to receive the full principal investment plus interest at the end of the specified time period. The time period for a GIC can range from a few days to five years or even ten years. The interest rate for a longer investment period or a larger amount of investment will be higher than that of a shorter period or smaller amount of investment.

GICs can also be redeemable or non-redeemable. In a redeemable GIC, the deposit may be withdrawn in whole or in part before the maturity date. In a non-redeemable GIC, the deposit usually cannot be redeemed or withdrawn before the maturity date. As redeemable GICs offer the option to withdraw before maturity, their interest rate is less than that offered on non-redeemable GICs.

Example 8.5(a)

Comparing GICs

A bank offers 1.75% p.a. on investments of \$5000 to \$99,999 and 1.95% on investments of \$100,000 to \$249,000 for 2-year to 4-year GICs. What additional amount will Harold earn from a \$160,000, 3-year GIC than from two \$80,000, 3-year GICs?

Solution

Earnings from the $160,000, 3-year GIC:

$I = Prt = 160{,}000 \times 0.0195 \times 3 = \$9360.00$

Earnings from two $80,000, 3-year GICs:

$I = Prt = 80{,}000 \times 0.0175 \times 3 = \$4200.00$

Total earnings from two $80,000, 3-year GICs $= 4200 \times 2 = \$8400.00$

Additional earnings $= 9360 - 8400 = \$960.00$

Therefore, he will earn $960.00 more from the $160,000, 3-year GIC.

Demand loan

A demand loan is a loan that is payable when it is demanded by the lender who issues the loan. The borrower signs a demand note agreeing to pay the interest and the principal on demand. Once the borrower signs the demand note, the lender has the right to ask for full payment at any time for any reason.

A demand loan requires no regular repayments of the principal amount, but the lender may request for regular payments to cover the interest on the loan. The borrower has an option to make a payment to settle the loan either in part (partial payment) or in full anytime without paying a penalty.

The interest rate on a demand loan is generally a few percentage points above the prime rate. Prime rate is the lowest lending interest rate that is set by the Bank of Canada. The Bank of Canada changes the prime rate periodically. The rate on a demand loan will change when the prime rate changes. A demand loan is usually not a secured loan; i.e., no protection (collateral) is required with assets to obtain the loan. Therefore, it is a high risk loan and the borrower will pay a high interest rate for the loan.

Example 8.5(b)

Calculating the Interest Paid on a Loan with a Varying Interest Rate

Peter obtained a demand loan on April 13, 2010 for $4200 at 4.1% p.a. simple interest. On June 01, 2010, the prime rate increased and the rate on the demand loan changed to 4.35% p.a. If the loan was repaid on July 15, 2010, what was the interest paid on the loan?

Solution

Let P be the principal amount of the loan

April 13 to June 01 = 49 days, $t_1 = \dfrac{49}{365}$ years, $r_1 = 9.1\%$ p.a.

I_1 = Interest charged for the above period at 4.1% p.a.

$= Prt = 4200 \times 0.041 \times \dfrac{49}{365} = \$23.117260...$

June 01 to July 15 = 44 days, $t_2 = \dfrac{44}{365}$ years, $r_2 = 4.35\%$ p.a.

I_2 = Interest charged for the above period at 4.35% p.a.

$= Prt = 4200 \times 0.0435 \times \dfrac{44}{365} = \$22.024109...$

Therefore, the interest paid on the loan was $23.117260... + 22.024109... = 45.141369... = \$45.14$

Partial Payments of Demand Loans

When partial payments (more than one payment) are made to reduce a loan, each payment amount is first used to reduce the interest on the loan and the remainder is used to reduce the amount of principal. This method of dealing with repayments is called the declining balance method.

Example 8.5(c)

Partial Payments Using the Declining Balance Method

A demand loan of $18,500 on March 10, 2010 at 18% p.a. simple interest was settled by a payment of $800 on May 15, another payment of $200 on June 18, and the outstanding balance on August 20, 2010 . Using the declining balance method, calculate the amount of the last payment.

Solution

Balance after 1st payment of $800 on May 15, 2010

March 10, 2010 to May 15, 2010 = 66 days = $\frac{66}{365}$ years

Using the formula, $I = Prt$,

The interest accumulated on the principal of $18,500 for the above period at 18% p.a.:

$$I = 18{,}500 \times 0.18 \times \frac{66}{365} = \$602.14$$

The partial payment of $800 is first used to clear the interest.

$$\textit{Amount left after clearing interest} = 800 - 602.14 = \$197.86$$

This balance amount from the partial payment is used to reduce the principal.

Therefore, $\textit{Principal Balance} = \$18{,}500.00 - \$197.86 = \$18{,}302.14$

Balance after 2nd payment of $200 on June 18, 2010

May 15, 2010 to June 18, 2010 = 34 days = $\frac{34}{365}$ years

Using the formula, $I = Prt$,

The interest accumulated on the principal of $18,302.14 for the above period at 18% p.a.:

$$I = 18{,}302.14 \times 0.18 \times \frac{34}{365} = \$306.87$$

The partial payment of $200 is first used to clear the interest. Now, as the partial payment is less than the accumulated interest, there will be an interest balance.

$$\textit{Interest Balance} = 306.87 - 200.00 = \$106.87$$

Principal Balance will remain the same = $18,302.14

Last payment on August 20, 2010

June 18, 2010 to August 20, 2010 = 63 days = $\frac{63}{365}$ years

Using the formula, $I = Prt$,

The interest accumulated on the principal of $18,302.14 for the above period at 18% p.a.:

$$I = 18{,}302.14 \times 0.18 \times \frac{63}{365} = \$568.62$$

The balance to be paid:

Interest balance as on June 18, 2010 = $106.87

Interest accumulated from June 18, 2010 to August 20, 2010 = $568.62

Principal amount remaining on August 10, 2010 = $18,302.14

Total = 106.87 + 568.62 + 18,302.14 = $18,977.63

Therefore, the amount of the last payment is $18,977.63.

Promissory Notes

A promissory note is a written promise to repay a borrowed amount of money to the lender on an agreed date. The borrower of the amount is called the 'maker' of the note (as they are making a promise to pay the amount) and the lender is called the 'payee' (as the borrower promises to pay them the amount).

The amount shown on the promissory note is called the 'face value' of the note. The time period negotiated is known as the 'term or the maturity date', which may be in days, months, or years.

The legal due date of a promissory note is 3 days after the term of the note.

For a promissory note, the legal due date is 3 days after the maturity date, known as the 'grace period'. If a promissory note is issued with 'no grace period' marked on the note, then the maturity date and the legal due date will be the same. The interest period is the time period from the date of issue to the legal due date.

There are two types of promissory notes: interest-bearing notes and non-interest-bearing notes.

The face value of an interest-bearing promissory note is the principal amount.

Interest-Bearing Promissory Note

The face value of the note is the amount of loan that must be repaid with the interest calculated based on the interest rate specified on the note. Therefore, the maturity value (S) is the amount to be repaid and is calculated using Formula 8.3(b): $S = P(1 + rt)$.

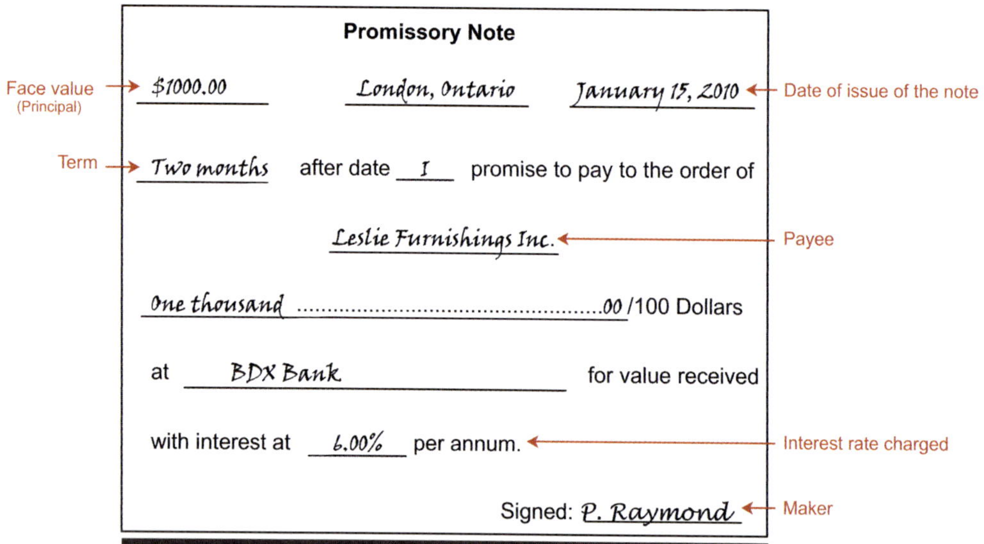
Promissory Note
$1000.00 London, Ontario January 15, 2010
Two months after date I promise to pay to the order of
Leslie Furnishings Inc.
One thousand ....00 /100 Dollars
at BDX Bank for value received
with interest at 6.00% per annum.
Signed: P. Raymond

Exhibit 8.5(a): Sample Interest-Bearing Promissory Note

Example 8.5(d)

Calculating the Maturity Date, Legal Due Date, and Maturity Value of an Interest-Bearing Promissory Note

Tony signs an interest-bearing promissory note for $3500 at an interest rate of 6% p.a. The date of the note is April 15, 2010 and the term is 60 days. Find the maturity date, legal due date, and the maturity value.

Solution

Maturity date:

Using the days table,

April 15, 2010: 105th day of the year
+ 60 days

165th day of the year,

which is June 14, 2010

Solution continued

Legal due date = 3 days after the maturity date

= June 17, 2010

Calculating the Maturity Value:

$$P = \$3500$$

Using Formula 8.3(b), $S = P(1 + rt)$

Substituting values, $S = 3500\left(1 + 0.06 \times \frac{63}{365}\right)$

$$= 3536.25$$

Therefore, the maturity value is $3536.25.

Example 8.5(e)

Calculating the Face Value of an Interest-Bearing Promissory Note

Compute the face value of a 90-day promissory note dated October 25, 2010 that has a maturity value of $3566.88 and an interest rate of 7.5% p.a.

Solution

The face value is the principal amount of the maturity value. The legal due date is 93 days from October 25, 2010 (including 3-day grace period).

Using Formula 8.3(c), $P = S(1 + \text{rt})^{-1}$

Substituting values, $P = 3566.88\left(1 + 0.075 \times \frac{93}{365}\right)^{-1}$

$$= \$3500.00$$

Therefore, the face value of the promissory note is $3500.00.

Non-Interest-Bearing Promissory Note

The face value of a non-interest-bearing promissory note is the maturity value of the note; i.e., interest is calculated and included in the face value. The interest rate may not be specified on the note and the lender usually agrees on the interest rate on the loan. The loan amount is calculated using the formula: $P = S(1 + rt)^{-1}$.

The face value of a non-interest-bearing promissory note is the maturity value. Also. note that there is no interest rate given on the note.

Non-Interest-Bearing Promissory Note

Face value (Maturity amount) → $1080.00   Toronto, Ontario   July 18, 2010 ← Date of issue of the note

Term → Two months after date I promise to pay to the order of

Speedy Web Hosting Ltd. ← Payee

One thousand and eighty ....00 /100 Dollars

at Toronto Bank for value received.

Signed: M. Chang ← Maker

Exhibit 8.5(b): Sample Non-Interest-Bearing Promissory Note

Example 8.5(f)

Calculating the Loan Amount of a Non-Interest-Bearing Promissory Note

A 90-day non-interest-bearing promissory note dated March 25, 2010 has a face value of $4000. If the note is discounted at 5.5% p.a. on the date of issue, calculate the amount of the loan. Assume no grace period on the note.

Solution

The legal due date is 93 days from March 25,2010 (including 3-day grace period).

Using Formula 8.3(c), $P = S(1 + rt)^{-1}$

Substituting values, $P = 4000\left(1 + 0.055 \times \frac{93}{365}\right)^{-1}$

$= \$3944.719884...$

Therefore, the amount of the loan is $3944.72.

Treasury Bills and Commercial Paper

A treasury bill, also known as a T-bill, is a written agreement or contract issued to investors for a short term (less than a year) and is issued by the federal government on every other Tuesday through major financial institutions as their agents. The maturity period of a T-bill is usually 13, 26, or 52 weeks (91, 182, or 364 days). Some provincial governments also issue T-bills, but on irregular dates or intervals. T-bills are generally available in denominations of $1000, $5000, $25,000, $100,000, and $1,000,000.

A T-bill is similar to a non-interest-bearing promissory note. The face value of a T-bill is the amount shown on it and it is the maturity value that the government guarantees to pay on the maturity date. Therefore, the purchase price of a T-bill is calculated as a principal amount of the face value shown (maturity value) using the interest rate (called discount rate) offered at the time of purchase, which is based on market conditions.

T-bills are transferable and its value at the time of selling or buying is determined by the market rate for the time remaining until maturity.

Commercial paper is similar to T-bills, except that it is issued by large corporations. The maturity period of commercial paper is generally 1, 3, or 6 months (30, 90, or 180 days).

Example 8.5(g)

Calculating the Purchase Price of a T-bill

Benjamin, an investor, purchased a 182-day T-bill that had an interest rate of 3.5% p.a. and face value of $25,000. Calculate the price he paid for the T-bill.

Solution

$S = \$25{,}000,\ r = 0.035,\ t = \frac{182}{365}$ years

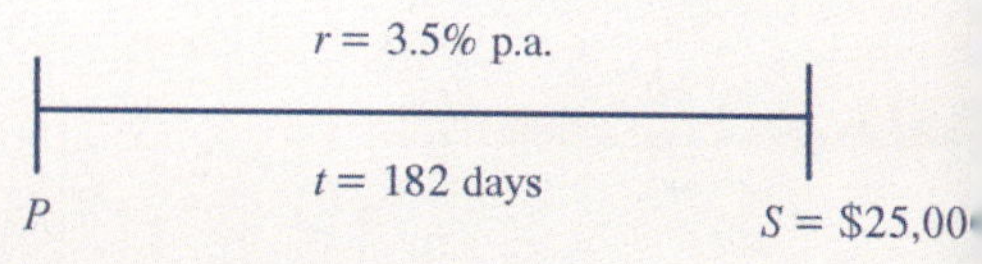

Using Formula 8.3(c), $P = S(1 + rt)^{-1}$

Substituting values, $P = 25{,}000\left(1 + 0.035 \times \frac{182}{365}\right)^{-1}$

$= \$24{,}571.18$

Therefore, he paid $24,571.18 for the T–bill.

Example 8.5(h)

Calculating the Purchase Price of a T-bill

An investor purchased a 91-day T-bill with a face value of $5000 discounted at 3% p.a.

(i) Calculate the purchase price of the T-bill.

(ii) In 30 days, he needed the money and therefore, sold the T-bill to another investor. The rate for this investment in the market was 2.8% at the time of the sale. Calculate his selling price and profit or loss on the transaction.

(iii) What rate of return did he realize while holding the T-bill?

Solution

(i) $S = \$5000$, $r = 3\%$ p.a. $= 0.03$, $t = \frac{91}{365}$ years

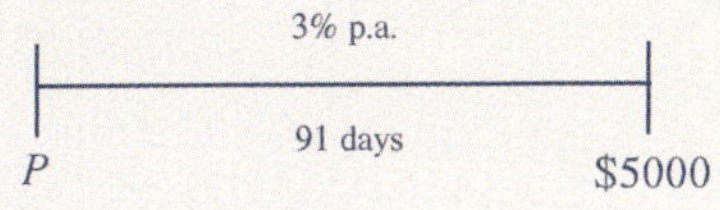

Using Formula 8.3(c), $P = S(1 + rt)^{-1}$

Substituting values, $P = 5000\left(1 + 0.03 \times \frac{91}{365}\right)^{-1}$

$= \$4962.88$

Therefore, the purchase price was $4962.88.

(ii) Days remaining on T-bill = 91 days − 30 days passed = 61 days

Using Formula 8.3(c), $P = S(1 + rt)^{-1}$

Substituting values for P_1, $P_1 = 5000\left(1 + 0.028 \times \frac{61}{365}\right)^{-1}$

$= \$4976.71$

Therefore, he sold it for $4976.71.

He sold it for more; hence, he made a profit.

His profit on the sale of the T-Bill was $P_1 - P = 4976.71 - 4962.88 = \$13.83$

Since he held it for 30 days,

Rearranging Formula 8.2, $r = \frac{I}{Pt}$

Substituting values, $r = \frac{13.83}{4962.88\left(\frac{30}{365}\right)}$

$= 0.033904...$

$= 3.39\%$ p.a.

Therefore, he realized a rate of return of 3.39% p.a. while holding the T-bill.

Discounting and Proceeds

Discounting a promissory note refers to the process of finding the value of a note on a specific date before its specific legal due date. Sometimes notes and bills are resold before their maturity dates for various reasons. For example, the owner of the note may want to repay the loan earlier than the maturity date or the owner may require cash on the bill before its maturity date.

Proceeds: the amount of money for which a promissory note is bought or sold at the discounting date

The amount received by the owner of the note at the time of the discount is called "proceeds" and the interest rate used or agreed to calculate the proceeds is called "discount rate". The discount rate may not be the same as the rate of interest on the note at the time of purchase.

The notes and bills are legal contracts. Therefore, it is necessary to find its maturity value first before calculating the proceeds.

For non-interest-bearing notes (T-bills and commercial papers), the maturity value is the face value. The maturity value is discounted using the discount rate to calculate the proceeds.

For interest-bearing notes, the face value is the amount of loan and the maturity value is to be calculated using $S = P(1 + rt)$. The maturity value is discounted using the discount rate to calculate the proceeds.

Example 8.5(i)

Calculating the Proceeds and Discount of a Non-Interest-Bearing Note

A non-interest-bearing note with a face value of $3000 is due in 120 days. If the note is discounted 30 days from the date of issue at a rate of 9% p.a., calculate the amount of proceeds and the amount of discount.

Solution

Since it is a non-interest-bearing note, the legal due-date is 123 days (including the 3-day grace period) from the date of issue and the maturity value is equal to the face value of the note.

The time remaining is 123 − 30 = 93 days.

Using Formula 8.3(c), $P = S(1 + rt)^{-1}$

Substituting values, $P = 3000\left(1 + 0.09 \times \frac{93}{365}\right)^{-1}$

$= \$2932.75$

The amount of proceeds is $2932.75.

The amount of discount = 3000 − 2932.75 = $67.25.

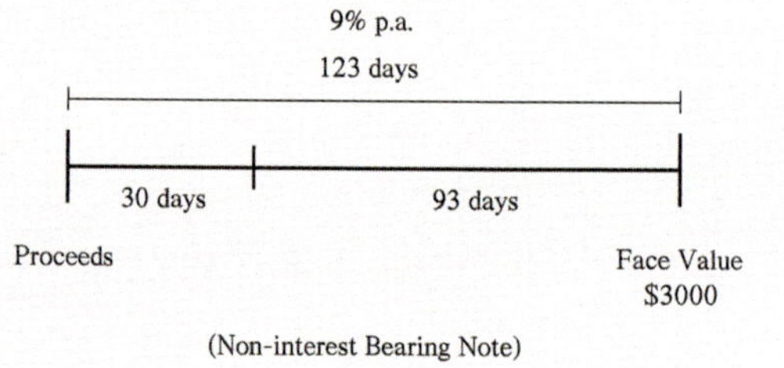

Example 8.5(j)

Calculating the Proceeds and Discount of an Interest-Bearing Note

An interest-bearing note for 93 days at 8% p.a. simple interest has a face value of $4000. If the note is settled in 20 days at a discounted rate of 10% p.a., calculate the proceeds.

Solution

Since it is an interest-bearing note, the principal is the face value.

First calculate the maturity value of the note.

$S = 4000\left(1 + 0.08 \times \frac{93}{365}\right) = 4081.534247...$

$= \$4081.53$

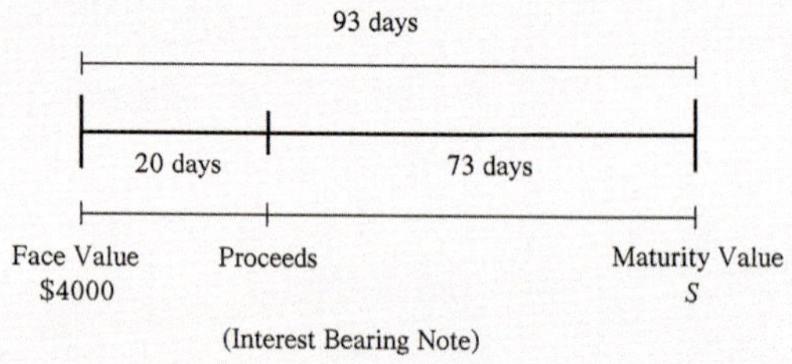

Now, since it is discounted in 20 days,

$t = 93 - 20 = 73 \text{ days} = \frac{73}{365} \text{ years}$

$P = S(1 + \text{rt})^{-1}$

$= 4081.53\left(1 + 0.10 \times \frac{73}{365}\right)^{-1}$

$= \$4001.50$

Therefore, the proceeds will be $4001.50.

8.5 | Exercises

1. Lea's bank offers interest rates of 1.50% p.a. for 1-year GICs and 1.85% p.a. for 2-year GICs for investments of $5000 to $99,000. Lea was considering the following two investment options:
   a. Invest $50,000 in a 2-year GIC.
   b. Invest $50,000 in a 1-year GIC then invest the maturity amount in a second 1-year GIC, assuming that the interest rate remains constant over the second 1-year period.

   In which of the above two options will she earn more and by how much?

15. An interest-bearing promissory note for $7500 is due in 180 days with simple interest at 6.25% p.a. If this note is sold after 70 days by discounting at a rate of 9% p.a., calculate the proceeds of the note.

16. Lisa purchased an interest-beatring promissory note for $5000 at 5% p.a., due in 90 days. If she sold the note in 30 days by discounting it at 6% p.a., calculate the proceeds of the note.

17. A six month non-interest-bearing note was issued on August 08, 2010 for $1750. The note was discounted at 6.75% p.a. on October 30, 2010. Calculate the proceeds of the note.

18. David, a wealthy businessman, purchased a 120-day, $100,000 non-interest-bearing note on January 01, 2011. If he discounted the note at 8% p.a. on April 01, 2011, calculate the proceeds of the note.

• 19. Roanna borrowed $2500 at 7% p.a. She wanted to settle this loan with 2 equal payments, one in 5 months and another in 16 months. Determine the size of the payments using 'now' as the focal date.

• 20. Phoenix loaned $10,000 to a friend at 1.2% p.m. He wanted the amount to be paid in 2 equal payments, one immediately and the other in 4 months. Calculate the size of the payments using 4 months from now as the focal date.

8 | Self-Test Exercises

Answers to all problems are available at the end of the textbook

1. Tim invested his savings of $2000 in a savings account that was earning simple interest at 3% p.a. He also invested $1500 in his friend's business at 0.95% p.m. How much interest did he earn from both these investments at the end of 10 months?

2. On September 11, 2010, Ali received $5000 from his father. If he settled this amount on May 01, 2011 with an interest of $180, calculate the monthly rate of simple interest he was charged for this loan.

3. Angelia invested $200 for 16 months in a bank and received a maturity amount of $270.50. If she had invested the amount in a fund earning 2.5% p.a. more, how much would she have had received at maturity?

4. Calculate the amount of money Victoria invested in the savings account of her bank if it matured to $6740.75 at the end of 100 days. Assume that the simple interest rate was 3% p.a. How much of this amount was interest?

5. Ryan had to make payments of $2000 and $3000 in 10 months and 18 months, respectively, to a raw material supplier. What single payment in 5 months would settle both these payments? Assume an interest rate of 6% p.a. and use 5 months as the focal date.

• 6. Brenda's lawyer gave her the following two options to settle his invoice:

   a. $1800 in 1 month and the balance $2100 in 3 months.

   b. Two equal payments, one in 20 days and the other in 4 months.

   If money earned 3.5% p.a., what was the value of the equal payments in Option (b) such that it is equivalent to the payments in Option (a)? Use any date as the focal date for this question.

7. Thomas was supposed to pay Logan $3800 six months ago and $1240 in five months. If he wants to repay this amount with two equivalent payments of $3000 today and the balance amount in 2 months, calculate the balance amount. Assume interest is 4% p.a. and the agreed focal date is 2 months from now.

8. Hanna received a demand loan for $8000 from her bank on February 16, 2011 at 6% p.a. simple interest. On May 23, 2011, the interest rate on the loan decreased to 5.75% p.a. and Hanna settled the loan on July 14, 2011. Calculate the total interest paid on the loan.

• 9. A bank offers interest rates of 1.50% p.a. for 60-day GICs and 1.75% p.a. for 120-day GICs. Roberto was considering the following two investment options at this bank:

   a. Invest an amount in a 120-day GIC.

   b. Invest an amount in a 60-day GIC then invest the maturity amount in a second 60-day GIC.

   What interest rate should be offered on the 60-day GIC after 60 days from now for Roberto to earn the same amount of money from either option?

10. Abbey bought a 182-day T-bill that has an interest rate of 4% p.a. and a face value of $25,000.

    a. How much did she pay for the T-bill?

    b. After 90 days, she sold the T-bill to her friend when the interest rate for this T-bill in the market increased to 4.25% p.a. What was her selling price and profit or loss on the transaction?

    c. What rate of return did she realize while holding the T-bill?

11. James purchased a 90-day interest-bearing note at 5% p.a. and that has a face value of $25,000. If he settles the note in 60 days at a discounted rate of 6% p.a., calculate his proceeds.

CASE 8

Borrowing and Investing Using Simple Interest

Shing and Benjamin, two classmates at a college, decided to use their free time after classes to create video games. On October 07, 2010, they received a loan of $3000 from a bank at 8.5% p.a. to start their small business. Two months later, they launched their first game in the community and it was highly successful. On March 02, 2011, a larger gaming company paid them $50,000 to purchase copyrights to their game. Shing and Benjamin used $5000 from this amount to settle the bank loan and to cover other miscellaneous expenses.

They then2 shared the balance of $45,000 equally between themselves.

Shing invested a portion of it in a 182-day T-bill that has an interest rate of 4% p.a. and face value of $7500 and used the balance in a 270-day interest-bearing promissory note at 6% p.a.

Benjamin, on the other hand, invested a portion of it in a 270-day non-interest-bearing note that has an interest rate of 5% p.a. and face value of $9000, and loaned the balance to his friend who was running a successful website design business for 182 days.

a. Calculate the total amount they paid to settle the bank loan.

b. i) Calculate the amount invested by Shing in the T-bill and in the interest-bearing note.

   ii) Calculate the amount invested by Benjamin in the non-interest-bearing promissory note and the amount he loaned to his friend.

c. Shing decided to discount his interest-bearing promissory notes at the time of maturity of his T-bill (182 days) and used the money to purchase a car for himself. Calculate the total proceeds from his investments if he discounted his interest-bearing promissory note at 6.50% p.a.

d. Benjamin wants to have the same amount as Shing in 182 days. If he discounts his non-interest-bearing promissory note at 7% p.a., what interest rate should he charge his friend for the loan?

e. If Benjamin invested the total amount from (d) at the rate that he lend to his friend calculated in (d), how long would it take for his investment to double?

8 | Summary of Notation and Formulas

NOTATION

I = *Amount of Interest*

P = *Principal*

r = *Simple Interest Rate*

t = *Time Period*

S = *Maturity Value*

FORMULAS

Amount of Interest | 8.2

$I = Prt$

Maturity Value | 8.3 (a)

$S = P + I$

Maturity Value | 8.3 (b)

$S = P(1 + rt)$

Principal | 8.3 (c)

$$P = \frac{S}{(1 + rt)} \quad \text{or} \quad P = S(1 + rt)^{-1}$$

In the previous chapter, you learned that money grows linearly when invested over a period of time at simple interest. Have you ever wondered if money could grow exponentially? This chapter will teach you a method to have your money grow in leaps and bounds! It uses a concept called compound interest, where interest is earned upon interest. Compound interest is often remarked as being an extremely powerful force; it can either work for you when you invest, or against you when you borrow!

9 Compound Interest

LEARNING OBJECTIVES

- Understand the concept of compound interest and how it differs from simple interest.
- Calculate the future value and present value of investments and loans in compound interest applications using both algebraic and financial calculator methods.
- Calculate equivalent payments that replace another payment or a set of payments.
- Calculate the time period of an investment or loan and the number of compoundings.
- Calculate the effective and equivalent interest rates for nominal interest rates.

CHAPTER OUTLINE

9.1 | Introduction

Compound interest is a procedure where interest is added to the principal at the end of each compounding period to earn interest in the subsequent compounding period.

Compound interest is a procedure where interest is calculated periodically (at regular intervals, known as compounding periods) and reinvested to earn interest at the end of each compounding period during the term; i.e., interest is added to the principal to earn interest. This is different from simple interest where interest is calculated only on the original amount (principal) for the entire term.

In compound interest, the interest earned in the previous compounding period also earns interest in subsequent compounding periods. For any given interest rate, the shorter the compounding period, the greater the interest earned because the number of compoundings during the term will be more. Generally, the compounding period can be one year (annually), 6 months (semi-annually), 3 months (quarterly), one month (monthly), or one day (daily).

Consider an example of $1000 invested or borrowed at 10% compounded annually for 4 years. Interest earned in the 1st year is added to the principal at the end of the 1st year. In the 2nd year, interest is calculated on the sum of the principal and interest earned. This is continued similarly at the end of each year.

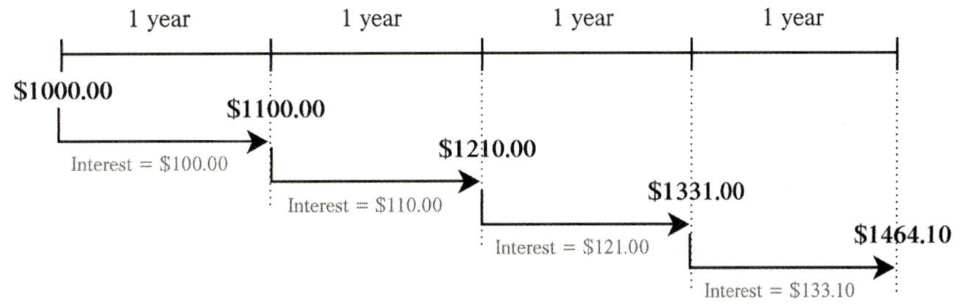

Exhibit 9.1: Interest Calculated Upon Interest

The value at the:

Beginning (initial value)	= $1000.00	
End of the 1st year	= $1000(1.10)	= $1100.00
End of the 2nd year	= $1000(1.10)^2	= $1210.00
End of the 3rd year	= $1000(1.10)^3	= $1331.00
End of the 4th year	= $1000(1.10)^4	= $1464.10

Now consider an investment of '*PV*' compounded '*n*' times at the rate of '*i*'

The value of the initial investment = *PV*

The value at the end of the 1st compounding period $= PV(1 + i)^1$

The value at the end of the 2nd compounding period $= PV(1 + i)^2$

The value at the end of the 3rd compounding period $= PV(1 + i)^3$

⋮

The value at the end of the nth compounding period $= PV(1 + i)^n$

If 'FV' is the value at the end of the nth compounding period, we obtain the following formula for Future Value:

Formula 9.1(a)

Future Value

$$FV = PV(1 + i)^n$$

Future Value **(FV):** the accumulated value or maturity value of an investment or loan.

Formula 9.1 (a) is the basic compound interest formula where:

- 'FV' is the future value (accumulated value or maturity value)
- 'PV' is the present value (discounted value or principal amount)
- 'i' is the interest rate per compounding period
- 'n' is the total number of compounding periods during the term

Present Value **(PV):** the principal amount or discounted value of an investment or loan.

Rearranging the terms of Formula 9.1(a), $FV = PV(1 + i)^n$, results in the following formula for Present Value:

Formula 9.1(b)

Present Value

$$PV = \frac{FV}{(1+i)^n} \quad \text{or} \quad PV = FV(1 + i)^{-n}$$

The amount of compound interest during the period, 'I', is the difference between the Future Value and the Present Value, which gives us the formula:

Formula 9.1(c)

Amount of Compound Interest During the Period

$$I = FV - PV$$

Notation

m = **compounding frequency:** it is the number of times interest is compounded every year. It usually appears after the word 'compounding' or 'compounded'.

Compounding frequency **(m):** the number of times interest is compounded every year.

For example, 6% compounded **monthly**: $m = 12$

Compounding period or interest period: it is the time interval between two successive interest calculation dates.

Table 9.1

Compounding Frequencies for Different Compounding Periods

Compounding period: the time interval between two successive interest calculation dates.

Compounding Period	Compounding Frequency (m)
Annually (every year)	1
Semi-annually (every 6 months)	2
Quarterly (every 3 months)	4
Monthly (every month)	12
Daily (every day)	365

If the compounding period is quarterly (every 3 months), then m = 4 because there are four 3-month periods in a year.

Nominal interest rate (j): the quoted interest rate per annum.

j = nominal interest rate: it is the quoted or stated interest rate per annum on which the compound interest calculation is based for a given compounding period. It is the rate (expressed as a percentage) that usually precedes the word *'compounding'* or *'compounded'*.

For example, **6%** compounded monthly: $j = 6\% = 0.06$

The nominal interest rate (j) is always provided with a compounding frequency (m) and can easily be remembered as: *'j'* compounding *'m'* times.

i = periodic interest rate: it is the interest rate for a given compounding period and is calculated as follows:

$$\textit{Periodic Interest Rate} = \frac{\textit{Nominal Interest Rate}}{\textit{Compounding Frequency}}$$

This is given by the formula,

Formula 9.1(d)

Periodic interest rate

$$i = \frac{j}{m}$$

Periodic interest rate (i): the interest rate for a given compounding period.

For example, **6%** compounded **monthly**: $i = \frac{j}{m} = \frac{0.06}{12} = 0.005$

n = total number of compounding periods during the term: it is calculated as follows:

$$\textit{Total Number of Compounding Periods} = \textit{Compounding Frequency} \times \textit{Time in Years}$$

This is given by the formula,

Formula 9.1(e)

Number of compounding periods

$$n = m \times t$$

Where 't' is the time period in years.

For example,

- 6% compounded semi-annually for 2 years, the number of compounding periods,
  $$n = m \times t = 2 \times 2 = 4$$
- 5% compounded quarterly for 18 months, the number of compounding periods,
  $$n = m \times t = 4 \times \frac{18}{12} = 6$$

Time period (t): the period of time, in year, during which interest is calculated.

t = time period: it is the period of time (in years) during which interest is calculated.

The time period in the previous example, $t = 18 \text{ months} = \frac{18}{12} = 1.5 \text{ years}$

Example 9.1(a)

Identifying and Calculating the Compound Interest Terms

An investment is growing at 6% compounded monthly for 10 years.

(i) Identify the nominal interest rate, compounding frequency, and time period.

(ii) Calculate the periodic interest rate and number of compounding periods.

Solution

(i) **6%** compounded **monthly** for **10 years**

$j = 0.06$ $\quad m = 12$ $\quad t = 10$

Therefore, the nominal interest rate is 6%, compounding frequency is 12, and time period is 10 years.

Solution continued

(ii) Periodic interest rate: $i = \frac{j}{m} = \frac{0.06}{12} = 0.005 = 0.5\%$

Number of compounding periods: $n = m \times t = 12 \times 10 = 120$ compounding periods

Therefore, the periodic interest rate is 0.5% per month, and the number of compounding periods is 120.

Example 9.1(b)

Identifying and Calculating the Compound Interest Terms When the Time Period is in Years and Months

An investment is earning 8.2% compounded quarterly for 5 years and 3 months.

(i) Identify the nominal interest rate, compounding frequency, and time period.

(ii) Calculate the periodic interest rate and number of compounding periods.

Solution

(i) **8.2%** compounded **quarterly** for **5 years and 3 months**

$j = 0.082$ $\quad m = 4$ $\quad t = \left(5 + \frac{3}{12}\right)$ years $= 5.25$ years

Therefore, the nominal interest rate is 8.2%, compounding frequency is 4, and time period is 5.25 years.

(ii) Periodic interest rate: $i = \frac{j}{m} = \frac{0.082}{4} = 0.0205 = 2.05\%$

Number of compounding periods: $n = m \times t = 4 \times 5.25 = 21$ compounding periods

Therefore, the periodic interest rate is 2.05% per month and the number of compounding periods is 21.

Example 9.1(c)

Identifying and Calculating the Compound Interest Terms When the time Period is in Days

A loan is issued at 4.33% compounded semi-annually for 225 days.

(i) Identify the nominal interest rate, compounding frequency, and time period.

(ii) Calculate the periodic interest rate and number of compounding periods.

Solution

(i) **4.33%** compounded **semi-annually** for **225 days**

$j = 0.0433$ $\quad m = 2$ $\quad t = \frac{225}{365}$ years

Therefore, the nominal interest rate is 4.33%, compounding frequency is 2, and time period is $\frac{225}{365}$ years.

(ii) Periodic interest rate: $i = \frac{j}{m} = \frac{0.0433}{2} = 0.02165 = 2.165\%$

Number of compounding periods: $n = m \times t = 2 \times \frac{225}{365} = 1.232876...$

Therefore, the periodic rate is 2.17% per half-year and the number of compounding periods is 1.23.

9.1 | Exercises

Calculate the missing values for Problems 1 and 2:

1.

	Nominal Interest Rate, Compounding Frequency, and Time Period	Number of Compounding Periods per Year (m)	Periodic Interest Rate (i)	Term in Years (t)	Number of Compounding Periods for the Term (n)
a.	5% compounded semi-annually for 2 years	?	?	?	?
b.	11.4% compounded quarterly for 1 year and 6 months	?	?	?	?
c.	?% compounded monthly for 1 year and 7 months	?	0.70%	?	?
d.	?% compounded daily for 120 days	?	0.02%	?	?

2.

	Nominal Interest Rate, Compounding Frequency, and Time Period	Number of Compounding Periods per Year (m)	Periodic Interest Rate (i)	Term in Years (t)	Number of Compounding Periods for the Term (n)
a.	11.40% compounded monthly for 15 months	?	?	?	?
b.	8.76% compounded daily for 310 days	?	?	?	?
c.	?% compounded semi-annually for $4\frac{1}{2}$ years	?	2.775%	?	?
d.	?% compounded quarterly for 1 year and 9 months	?	0.98%	?	?

3. Calculate the nominal interest rate compounded monthly for a credit card that has a periodic interest rate of 2.2% per month.

4. A bank released a new credit card that charges interest at a rate of 1.84% per month. Calculate the nominal interest rate compounded monthly for the credit card.

5. Martha invested some money in a savings account that was giving her a nominal interest rate of 4.28% and periodic interest rate of 2.14%. Calculate the compounding frequency at which the money was growing.

6. If the nominal interest rate of an investment is 12% and the periodic interest rate is 3%, calculate the compounding frequency.

7. Calculate the number of compounding periods during the term of a loan that Harry received if the time period is 6 years and the compounding frequency is semi-annual.

8. If an investment has a time period of 5 years and 9 months and the compounding frequency is monthly, calculate the number of compounding periods during the term.

9. Lila receives a personal loan that has 66 compoundings for a period of 16 years and 6 months. Calculate the compounding frequency of the loan.

10. If Carrey invested money for 1 year and 3 months in a low-risk investment vehicle that had 15 compounding periods over the term, calculate the compounding frequency of the investment.

11. The periodic interest rate and nominal interest rate of a loan are 2.25% and 4.5%, respectively. Calculate the number of compounding periods if the loan is for a period of 8 years?

12. Ramona deposits her savings in an investment that has nominal and periodic interest rates of 4.48% and 2.24%, respectively. If she invests this money for a period of 2 years, calculate the number of compounding periods during the term.

• 13. Calculate the nominal interest rate of a loan that has 16 compounding periods over 4 years and a periodic interest rate of 0.5%.

• 14. Roger deposits his money for 9 years in a savings account that has a periodic interest rate of 1.1%. Calculate the nominal interest rate of the account if there are 18 compoundings during the period of investment.

9.2 | Calculating the Future Value (*FV*)

The following examples will illustrate future value calculations using the future value Formula 9.1(a) :

$$FV = PV(1 + i)^n$$

Example 9.2(a)

Calculating Future Value and Interest Earned

Hassan Furnishings Inc. invested $400 for 2 years at 5% compounded annually.

(i) Calculate the accumulated value of their investment at the end of 2 years.

(ii) Calculate the compound interest earned on this amount.

Solution

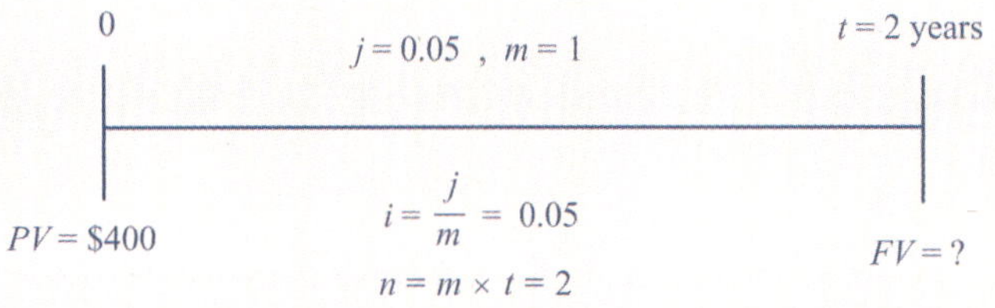

Although $441 is numerically different from $400, they are economically equal in value, considering the time value of money; i.e., money grows with interest over time.

(i) $FV = PV(1 + i)^n = 400(1 + 0.05)^2 = 400(1.1025) = \$441.00$

Therefore, the accumulated value of their investment at the end of 2 years would be $441.00.

(ii) Compound interest, $I = FV - PV = 441.00 - 400.00 = \$41.00$

Therefore, the compound interest earned was $41.00.

Using the Financial Calculator to Solve Problems

Solving problems algebraically will significantly improve your understanding of the subject; however, if you have to routinely solve financial problems and would like an easy and fast method of solving problems, without having to remember formulas, financial calculators (that are pre-programmed) can be used. There are many calculators in the market, but we will use the Texas Instruments BA II Plus calculator to solve problems in this course.

We will be using the following function keys that are present in the 3rd row of your calculator (also known as the TVM row, or time value of money row) as shown:

1. ***Number of compounding periods;*** represented by 'n' in algebraic calculations.
2. ***Interest rate per year (nominal interest rate);*** represented by 'j' in algebraic calculations. This is entered in percentage form (without the % sign) directly and is not converted to a decimal. E.g. 5% is entered as 5.
3. Pressing the **2ND** key then **I/Y** (to access the secondary key above the I/Y key) will open the P/Y-C/Y worksheet. P/Y stands for 'periodic payments per year' and is a concept that will be covered in the next chapter on annuities. Pressing the '**down arrow**' key will take you to C/Y which stands for '***compoundings per year'***: represented by 'm' in algebraic calculations. Pressing **2ND** then **Quit** will close the P/Y-C/Y worksheet.
4. ***Present value;*** represented by 'PV' in algebraic calculations.
5. ***Periodic annuity payment;*** represented by 'PMT'. This is a concept that will be covered in the next chapter on annuities.
6. ***Future value;*** represented by 'FV' in algebraic calculations.

Cash-Flow Sign Convention

When money is received, cash is flowing in and is called a cash-inflow. This amount has to be entered in your calculator as a positive amount. Similarly, when money is paid out, it is called a cash-outflow. This amount has to be entered as a negative amount. This cash-flow sign convention has to be followed in all calculators.

For example, if you make an investment in a bank, this is considered as a cash-outflow for you (money paid-out) and the value of the amount invested (PV) should be entered in your calculator as a negative amount. However, at the end of the time-period, when you receive your matured investment back from the bank, this is considered as a cash-inflow for you (money received) and the value of the amount received (FV) should be entered in your calculator as a positive amount.

Let's look at another example: if you take a loan, then the loan amount (PV) is considered as a cash-inflow, and therefore, has to be entered as a positive amount. When the loan amount is repaid, it is considered as a cash-outflow, and therefore, the amount paid (FV) has to be entered as a negative amount.

Before you start solving problems, you need to set the number of decimal places on your calculator to 9. Follow these instructions on your calculator:

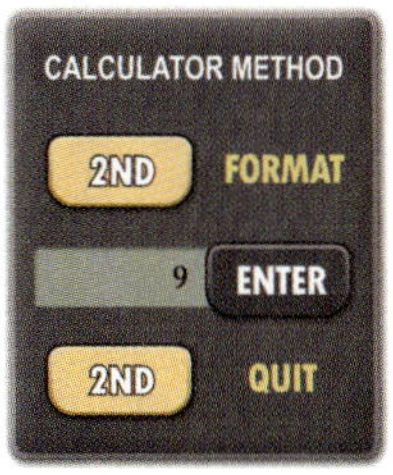

1. Press **2ND** then press **FORMAT** *(this is the secondary key above the decimal key)*.
2. Enter **9** then press **ENTER** to set the number of decimals to 9.
3. Press **2ND** and press **QUIT** (*this is the secondary key above CPT*).

Let us solve Example 9.2(a) using the *Texas Instruments BA II Plus* calculator as shown below:

Example 9.2(b)

Using the Financial Calculator to Solve Example 9.2(a)

Hassan Furnishings Inc. invested $400 for 2 years at 5% compounded annually.

(i) Calculate the accumulated value of their investment at the end of 2 years.

(ii) Calculate the compound interest earned on this amount.

Solution

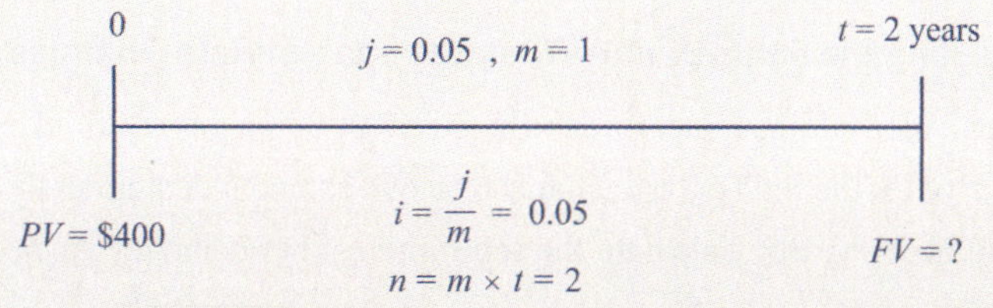

Solution continued

(i) In the example we have identified $PV = 400$, $j = 5\%$, $m = 1$ and $n = 2$.

We need to enter these values into the calculator and compute 'FV'.

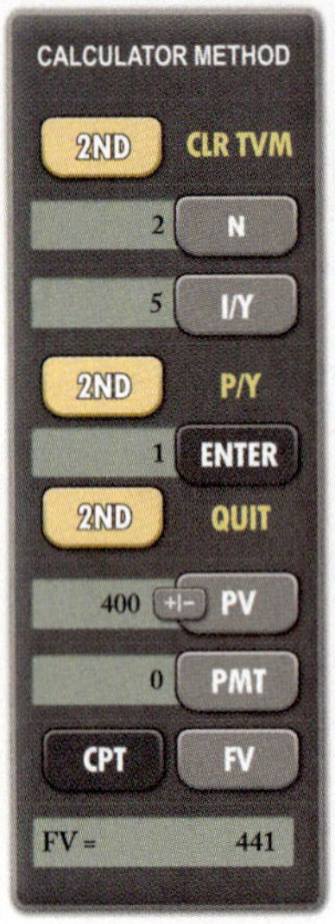

1. Press **2ND** then **CLR TVM** *(secondary function of the FV key)* to clear the memory of the TVM function keys.
2. Enter the number of ***compounding periods***, 'n', as **2** then press **N**.
3. Enter the ***interest per year***, 'j' *(nominal rate)*, directly as **5** (*not as 5% or 0.05*) then press **I/Y**.
4. As the calculation does not involve an annuity, we need to set ***payments per year*** *(P/Y)* to the same value as *the* ***number of compounding periods per year*** *(C/Y)*. To do this, press **2ND** then **P/Y** *(secondary function of the I/Y key)*, which opens the P/Y-C/Y worksheet. To set P/Y to 1 (as $m = 1$) enter **1** then press **Enter**. When you scroll down (using the **down arrow key**), you will notice that C/Y will automatically be set to 1. Press **2ND** then press **Quit** *(secondary function of the CPT key)* to close the P/Y-C/Y worksheet.
5. Enter the ***investment amount*** as a negative value, as it is a cash-outflow (cash paid/invested), by entering **400** and pressing the **+/− key**. Then press **PV**.
6. As the calculation does not involve annuity payments, enter '**0**' then press **PMT**.
7. To compute FV, press **CPT** then **FV**.
8. The calculator will display *441***.** The value is positive as it is a cash-inflow (cash received).

Therefore, the accumulated value of their investment at the end of 2 years is $441.00.

(ii) The compound interest, $I = FV - PV = 441.00 - 400.00 = \$41.00$

Therefore, the compound interest earned is $41.00.

Example 9.2(c) Calculating the Future Value and Interest Earned When 'n' is a Fraction

Executive International Inc. invested $80,000 in an investment fund at 8% compounded quarterly for 3 years and 5 months.

(i) Calculate the accumulated value of this amount for this period.

(ii) Calculate the compound interest earned on this amount.

Solution

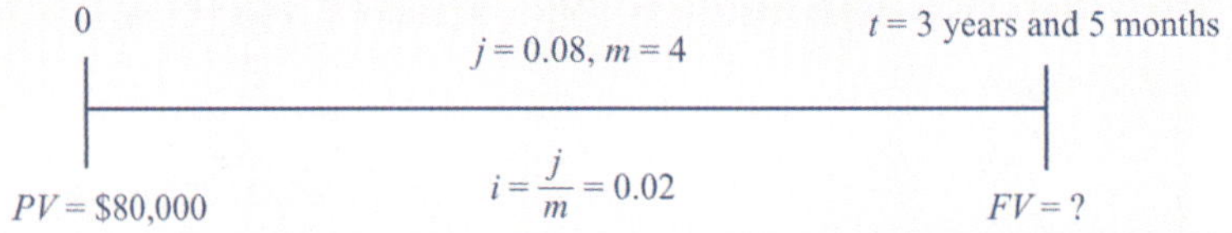

> Do not round numbers in intermediate steps, such as 'n' in this case. However, round your final answer to 2 decimal places.

(i) $t = 3$ years and 5 months $= \left(3 + \frac{5}{12}\right)$ years $= 3\frac{5}{12}$ years

$n = m \times t = 4 \times 3\frac{5}{12} = 4 \times 3.416666... = 13.666666...$ compounding periods

$FV = PV(1 + i)^n = 80{,}000(1 + 0.02)^{13.666666...} = \$104{,}863.8184...$

Therefore, the accumulated amount at the end of the period is $104,863.82.

(ii) Interest earned, $I = FV - PV$

$= 104{,}863.82 - 80{,}000.00 = \$24{,}863.82$

Therefore, the compound interest earned on this amount is $24,863.82.

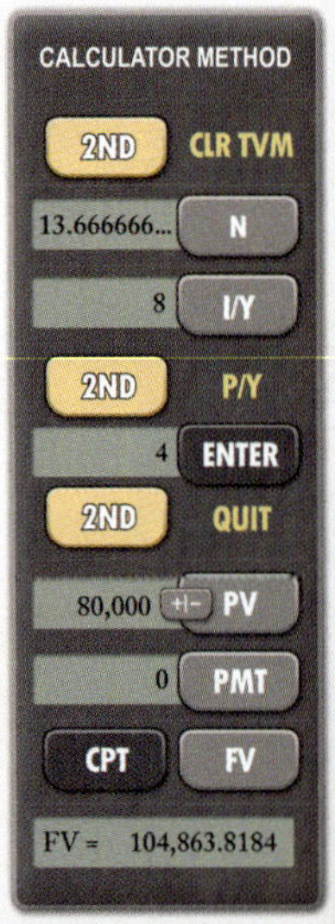

Example 9.2(d) Calculating the Future Value When the Interest Rate Changes

Amanda's consulting company deposited $50,000 in a growth fund at 8% compounded semi-annually. After 2 years the interest rate changed to 6% compounded annually. What is the value of the fund at the end of $5\frac{1}{2}$ years? Calculate the total interest her company earned over the entire period.

Solution

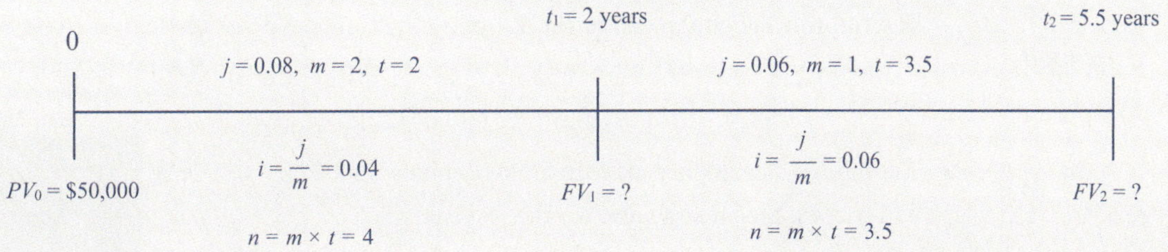

First we need to find the future value of the fund at the end of 2 years. The future value at the end of 2 years will become the present value in calculating the future value for the next $3\frac{1}{2}$ years.

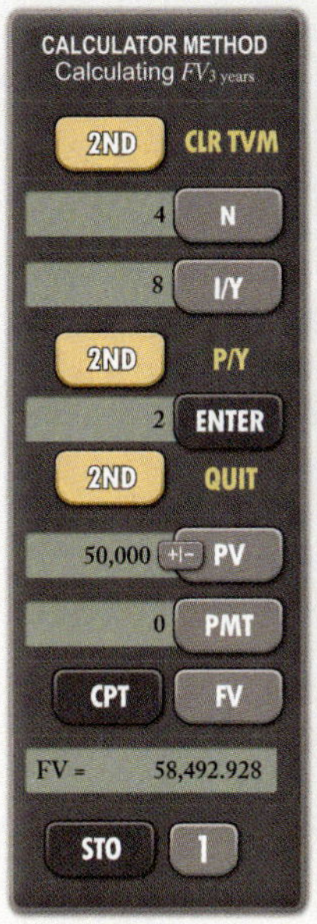

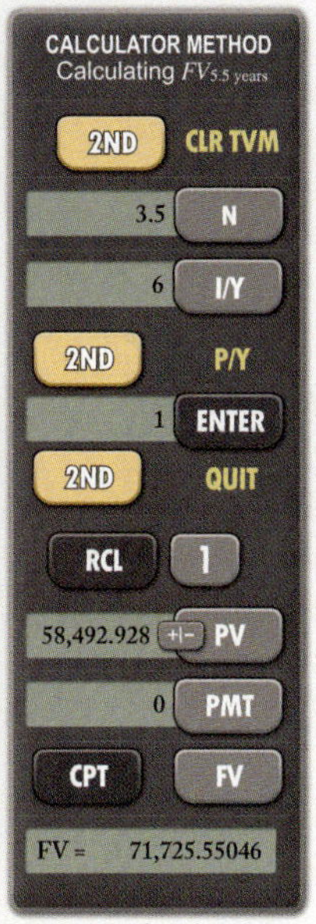

The future value at the end of 2 years :

$$FV_1 = PV_0(1 + i)^n$$
$$= 50,000\ (1 + 0.04)^4$$
$$= \$58,492.928 = PV_1$$

The future value at the end of $5\frac{1}{2}$ years:

$$FV_2 = PV_1\ (1 + i)^n$$
$$= 58,492.928...(1 + 0.06)^{3.5}$$
$$= \$71,725.55046...$$

Therefore, the value of the fund at the end of $5\frac{1}{2}$ years is \$ 71,725.55.

$$\text{The total interest earned} = FV_2 - PV_0$$
$$= 71,725.55 - 50,000.00$$
$$= \$21,725.55$$

Therefore, the total interest earned over the entire period is \$21,725.55.

Example 9.2(e)

Calculating the Future Value When the Principal Changes

Huan borrowed \$10,000 from the bank at 8% compounded quarterly. He repaid \$5000 at the end of the 1st year and another \$2000 at the end of the 2nd year. What amount at the end of the 3rd year will settle this loan?

Solution

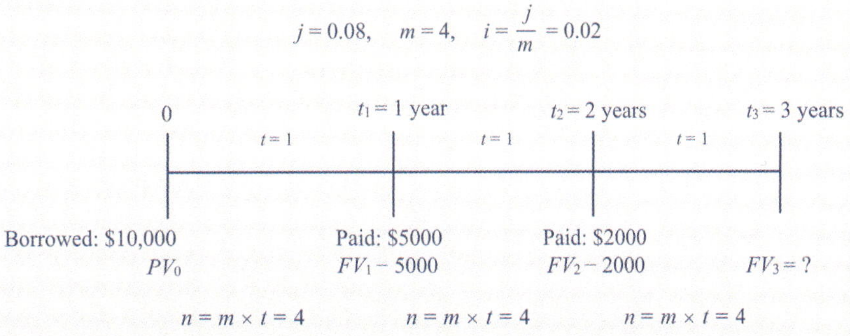

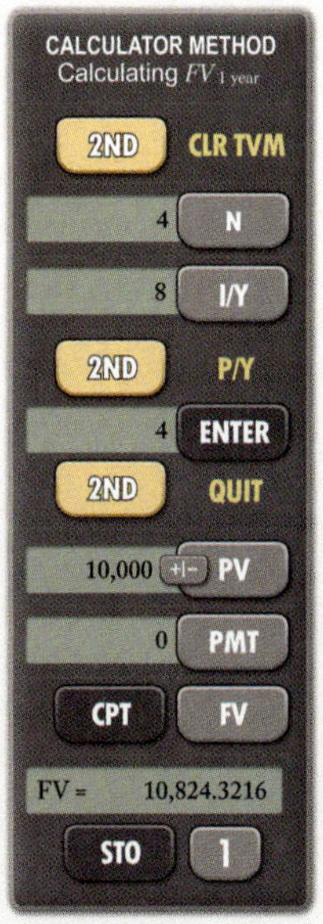

The future value at the end of the 1st year

$$FV_1 = PV_0(1 + i)^n = 10,000(1 + 0.02)^4 = \$10,824.3216$$

The future value at the end of 1st year minus \$5000.00 will become the present value for the 2nd year.

$$FV_1 - 5000 = 10,824.3216 - 5000.00$$
$$= \$5824.3216 = PV_1$$

Solution *continued*

The future value at the end of the 2nd year

$$FV_2 = PV_1(1 + i)^n$$

$$= 5824.3216(1 + 0.02)^4 = \$6304.43301...$$

The future value at the end of the 2nd year minus $2000.00 will become the present value for the 3rd year.

$$FV_2 - 2000.00 = 6304.43301... - 2000.00$$

$$= \$4304.43301... = PV_2$$

The future value at the end of the 3rd year

$$FV_3 = PV_2(1 + i)^n$$

$$= 4304.43301...(1 + 0.02)^4 = \$4659.256721...$$

Therefore, $4659.26 at the end of the 3rd year will settle this loan.

Note:
If you do not clear the data stored in the TVM keys (2ND, CLR TVM), you need to enter only the values that are different.

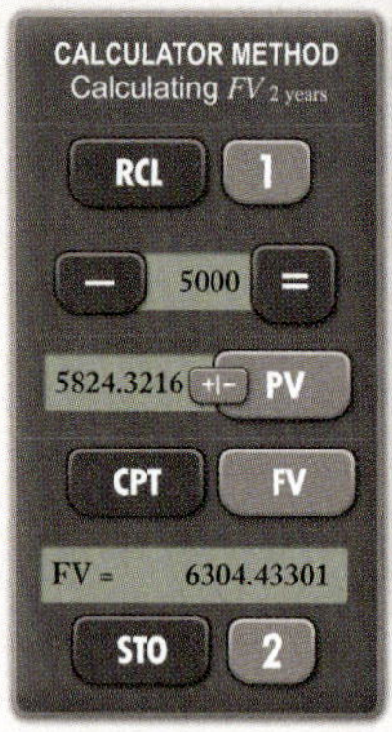

9.2 | Exercises

Calculate the missing values for Problems 1 and 2:

1.

	Present Value (*PV*)	Nominal Interest Rate (*j*)	Compounding Frequency (*m*)	Time Period (*t*)	Periodic Interest Rate (*i*)	Number of Compounding Periods (*n*)	Future Value (*FV*)
a.	$1000.00	5.11%	2	5 years and 6 months	?	?	?
b.	$3550.50	?	4	2 years and 3 months	1.1625%	?	?
c.	$16,500.00	6.30%	?	219 days	0.525%	?	?
d.	$9650.75	6.57%	1	?	?	11.25	?

2.

	Present Value (*PV*)	Nominal Interest Rate (*j*)	Compounding Frequency (*m*)	Time Period (*t*)	Periodic Interest Rate (*i*)	Number of Compounding Periods (*n*)	Future Value (*FV*)
a.	$12,450.50	4.95%	?	10 years	1.2375%	?	?
b.	$540.75	7.30%	365	292 days	?	?	?
c.	$16,400.00	5.84%	2	?	?	19.5	?
d.	$4500.00	?	12	3 years and 9 months	0.6050%	?	?

3. Ben invested $8450 for 5 years in his savings account that was earning 3.2% compounded annually. Calculate the future value of his investment at the end of the term and the amount of interest earned during the period.

4. Shirley borrowed $3000 at 9.45% compounded annually. She repaid the loan in 4 years. Calculate the accumulated value of the laon at the end of the term and the interest charged during the period.

5. Power Printers received a loan of $25,000 from a bank at 8% compounded quarterly for 1 year and 5 months. Calculate the accumulated amount and the interest charged on this loan.

6. Robbie invested $250,000 in a small business at 15% compounded semi-annually for 1 year and 2 months.
    a. How much would the business have to repay Robbie at the end of the period?
    b. How much interest did Robbie earn from this investment over the period?

7. Lee's real estate agency borrowed $10,000 from a credit union at 8% compounded quarterly for 6 years and 9 months.
    a. How much should Lee's agency repay the credit union at the end of the time period?
    b. If the agency decides to keep the money for another 3 months, calculate the total repayment amount and the amount of interest for the extended period.

8. Carleen Corporation borrowed a $2000 entrepreneurship loan for office renovations from The Business Development Bank for 3 months at 6% compounded semi-annually.
    a. Calculate the value of the corporation's debt at the end of the time period.
    b. If the corporation decides to keep the money for another 2 months, calculate the repayment amount, total interest, and interest for the extended period.

9. Rebecca Smith, a successful recruitment agency in Montreal, loaned $1000 to one of its partners for 5 years. The interest rate for the first 2 years was 2% compounded quarterly and for the next 3 years it was 2.3% compounded semi-annually. How much should the partner have repaid Rebecca Smith at the end of the period?

10. Brandon, an investment banker, took a risk and invested $350,000 in a high-growth fund that had a yield of 16.45% compounded quarterly. After 2 years, the fund did poorly and its yield dropped to 7.02% compounded semi-annually. Brandon waited for 8 months and withdrew all of his money. Calculate the accumulated money in his fund at the time of withdrawal.

11. Maxwell Servers Inc. wants to invest its net profits to gain highest returns. Which of the following two options will yield the highest returns? (Hint: Assume $1000 for present value and 1 year for time period.)
    a. A credit union that provides an interest of 6.09% compounded semi-annually.
    b. A local business development bank that provides an interest rate of 6.07% compounded quarterly.

    Show your calculations.

12. Roy was offered a choice between two interest rates for a loan: 5.13% compounded monthly or 5.14% compounded quarterly. Which one should he choose and why? (Hint: Assume $1000 for present value and 1 year for time period.)

13. How much more interest (in dollars) would you earn by investing $10,000 for 6 years at 10% compounded annually rather than at 10% per annum (simple interest)?

14. How much more interest (in dollars) would you earn by investing $5850 for 3 months at 8% compounded semi-annually rather than at 8% per annum (simple interest)?

15. Interest rates for Guaranteed Investment Certificates (GIC) depend on the time period of the investment. The following are the advertised rates for GICs at a local bank:
    - 1-year GIC: 1.50% compounded semi-annually
    - 2-year GIC: 2.70% compounded semi-annually
    - 3-year GIC: 4.28% compounded semi-annually
    - 4-year GIC: 4.80% compounded semi-annually

    In which of the following investments would you earn more and by how much:
    a. $1000 in a 4-year GIC.
    b. $1000 in a 2-year GIC, then at the end of the 2 years, re-invest the maturity amount in another 2-year GIC.

16. Based on the information provided in Problem 15, which of the following investments would yield higher returns and how much more interest would you be receiving compared to the lesser option:
    a. \$1000 in a 3-year GIC.
    b. \$1000 in a 1-year GIC, then at the end of the 1 year, re-invest the maturity amount in a 2-year GIC.

17. Martha deposited \$1000 in her bank savings account that earns 2% compounded quarterly. At the end of 2 years, she deposited an additional \$1500 into this account. What was the balance in her account at the end of 5 years?

18. Ace Publishing Company invested \$50,000 in an investment fund that was growing at a rate of 4% compounded monthly. After one year, the company deposited an additional \$30,000 in the same fund. Calculate the balance in the fund at the end of 3 years (2 years later).

19. Ferne has an option to either receive \$4000 today or \$5000 in 3 years. Which option is economically better for her if money earns 7.64% compounded monthly and why?

20. Eva won a lottery of \$18,000. However, the lottery company gave her the option of either receiving \$18,000 today or \$30,000 in 10 years. Assuming that money was earning 4% compounded quarterly throughout the time period, which option was economically better for her and why?

• 21. Harris learned that a demand loan is a loan that is payable when the lender (a financial institution) makes a demand for it (without prior notice). He decided to take a demand loan of \$25,000 to start his software company. He repaid \$5000 at the end of the first year, \$10,000 at the end of the second year, and the balance at the end of the third year. If the interest rate charged was 4% compounded semi-annually for the first year, 6% compounded quarterly for the second year, and 7.25% compounded monthly for the third year, calculate his final payment.

• 22. Sparco Medicals took a loan of \$285,000 from a Canadian financial institution. They repaid \$50,000 in 1 year, \$110,000 in 2 years, and the balance in 3 years. If the financial institution charged them an interest rate of 11% compounded quarterly for the first year, 10.5% compounded semi-annually for the second year, and 10% compounded monthly for the third year, calculate their final payment.

• 23. Matthew received a personal loan from his local bank at an interest rate of 11% compounded semi-annually for 1 year. If the amount of interest charged at the end of the period was \$280.50, calculate the accumulated value of the loan. (Hint: use the formula $FV = PV(1 + i)^n$ and substitute $PV = FV - I$ in the formula to solve the problem.)

• 24. The interest amount charged on a student loan that Hannah took from a bank for 4 years was \$1855. If the bank charged an interest rate of 4.35% compounded monthly, calculate the accumulated value of the loan at the end of the period. (Hint: use the formula $FV = PV(1 + i)^n$ and substitute $PV = FV - I$ in the formula to solve the problem.)

9.3 | Calculating the Present Value (PV)

As described in Section 9.1, present value (or discounted value or principal) can be calculated by rearranging the future value Formula 9.1(a), $FV = PV(1 + i)^n$:

$$PV = \frac{FV}{(1+i)^n} \quad \text{or} \quad PV = FV(1+i)^{-n}$$

The following examples will illustrate present value calculations.

Example 9.3(a)

Calculating the Present Value

Calculate the present value of \$5000 due in 2 years. The interest rate is 4% compounded semi-annually.

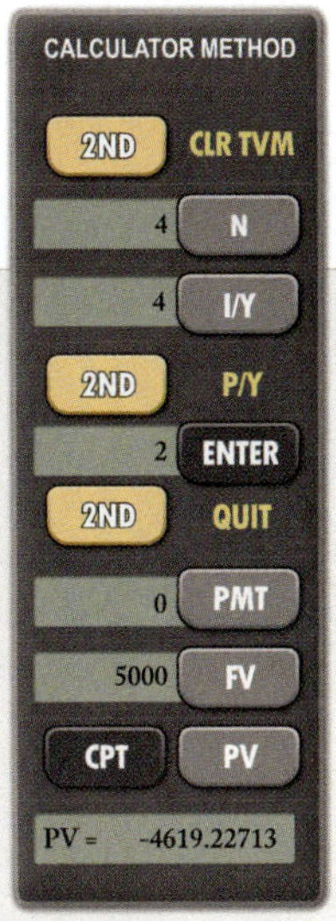

Solution

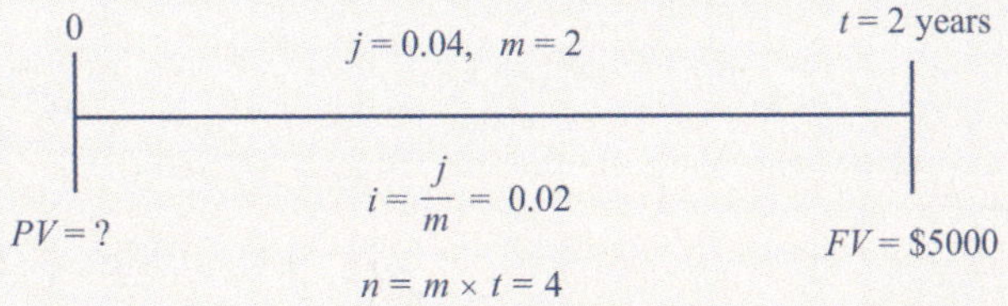

Present value is always numerically smaller than the future value. For this reason, it is also known as the discounted value. The interest rate is known as the discount rate.

$$PV = FV(1 + i)^{-n} = 5000.00(1 + 0.02)^{-4} = 5000(0.923845...) = \$4619.22713...$$

Therefore, the present value of \$5000 due in 2 years is \$4619.23.

Example 9.3(b)

Calculating the Present Value When 'n' is a Fraction

Rodney Lawn Mowers wants \$1000 in 3 years and 7 months. How much must they invest now to meet their goal, if the interest rate is 8% compounded quarterly?

Solution

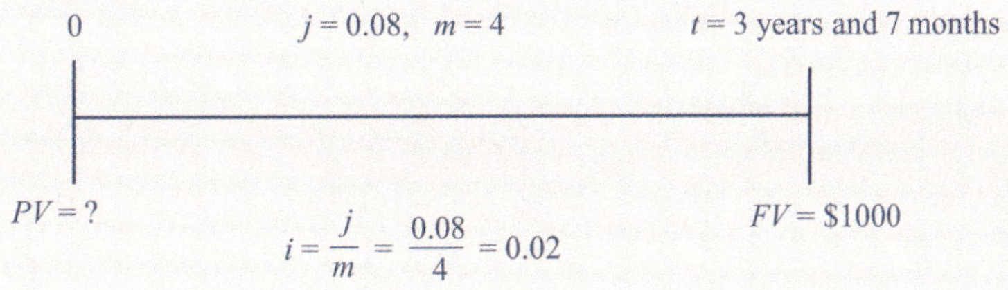

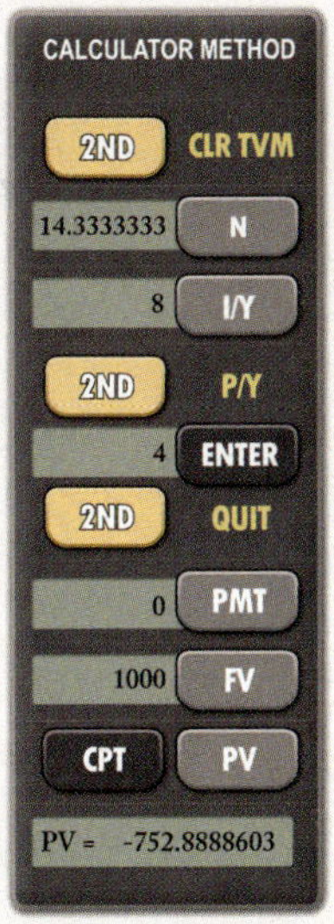

$$t = 3 \text{ years and } 7 \text{ months} = \left(3 + \frac{7}{12}\right)\text{years} = 3\tfrac{7}{12} \text{ years}$$

$$n = m \times t = 4 \times 3\tfrac{7}{12} = 4 \times 3.583333... = 14.333333... \text{ compounding periods}$$

$$\begin{aligned} PV &= FV(1 + i)^{-n} \\ &= 1000(1 + 0.02)^{-14.333333...} \\ &= 1000(0.752888...) \\ &= \$752.888860... \end{aligned}$$

Therefore, they must invest \$752.89 now to meet their goal.

Example 9.3(c)

Comparing Two Payment Options

RC Printers had the following two options to pay for printing supplies:

(i) A single payment of \$650 at the beginning of the year.

(ii) \$200 at the beginning of the year and \$480 at the end of the year.

Which option should they choose if money can earn 8% compounded quarterly?

Solution

This can be solved using the following two methods:

Method 1: Comparing the Present Values of Both Options

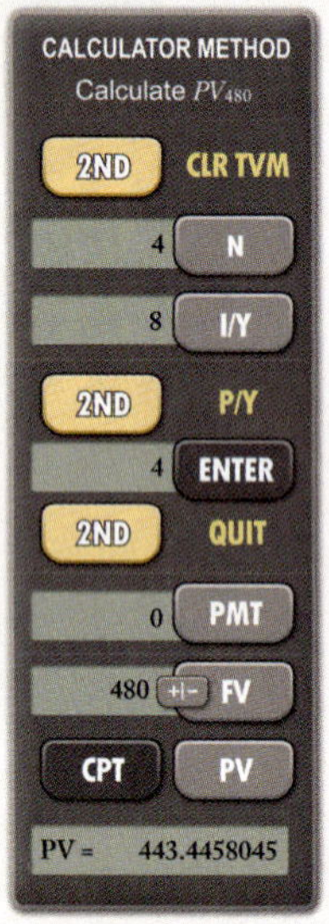

First, calculate the present value of Option (i).

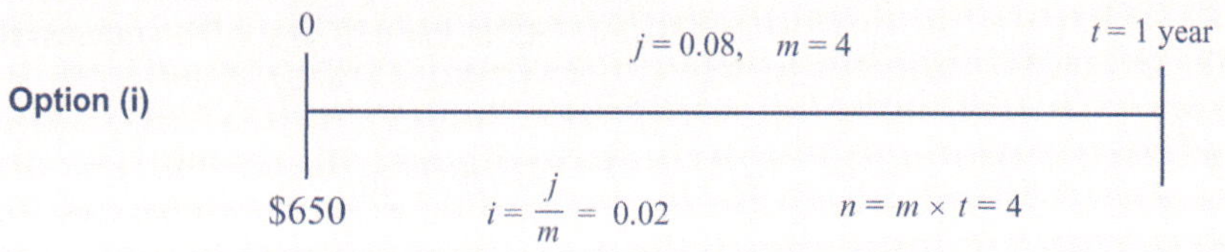

$$PV_{\text{Option (i)}} = \$650.00$$

Now, calculate the present value of Option (ii)

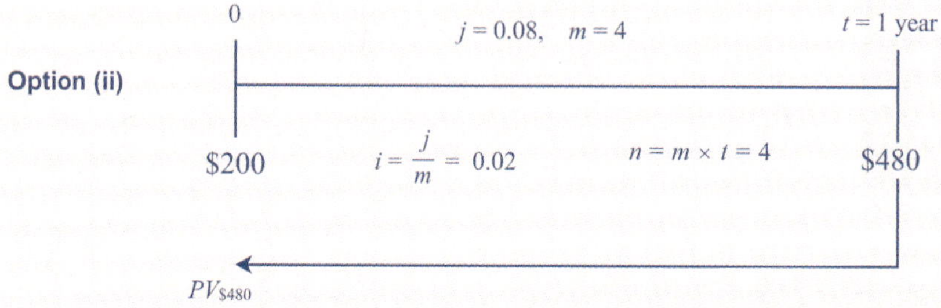

$$PV_{\$480} = 480(1 + 0.02)^{-4} = 480(0.923845...) = \$443.445804...$$

$$PV_{\text{Option (ii)}} = 200 + 443.445804... = 643.4458045... = \$643.45$$

They should choose Option (ii) as they will be paying a lesser amount than in Option (i).

Method 2: Comparing Future Values of Both Options

First, calculate future value of Option (i).

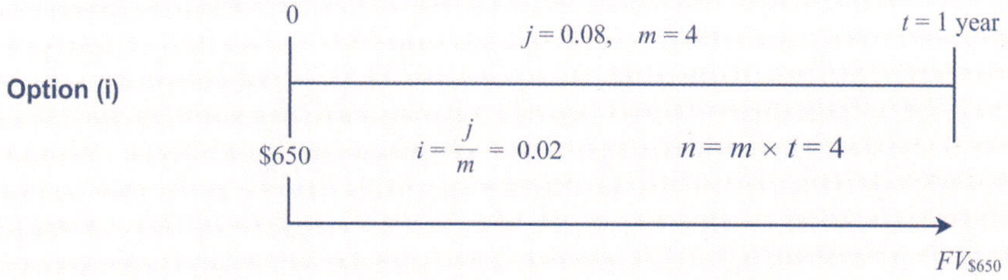

$$FV_{\text{Option (i)}} = FV_{\$650} = 650(1 + 0.02)^4 = \$703.580904...$$

Now, calculate the future value of Option (ii).

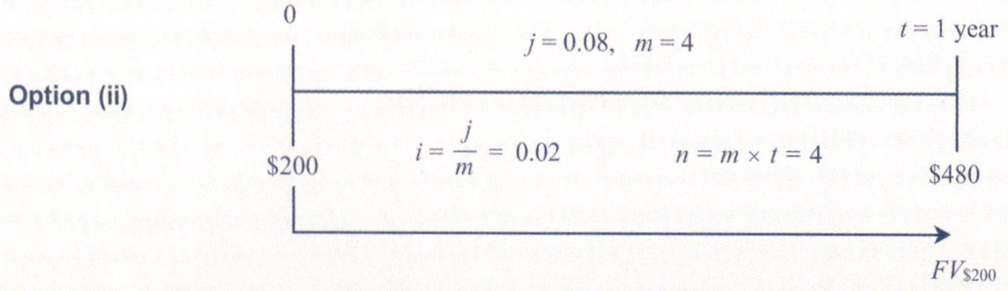

$$FV_{\$200} = 200(1 + 0.02)^4 = \$216.486432...$$

$$FV_{\text{Option (ii)}} = 480 + 216.486432... = 696.486432... = \$696.49$$

Therefore, they should choose payment Option (ii).

Note: *The calculator method of solving the preceding problem has been omitted in Method 2 and may be worked out as practice.*

9.3 | Exercises

Calculate the missing values for Problems 1 and 2:

1.

	Present Value (PV)	Nominal Interest Rate (j)	Compounding Frequency (m)	Time Period (t)	Periodic Interest Rate (i)	Number of Compounding Periods (n)	Future Value (FV)
a.	?	5.38%	2	5 years	?	?	$6500.00
b.	?	?	4	10 years and 9 months	1.4550%	?	$16,000.00
c.	?	4.89%	?	7 years	0.4075%	?	$16,886.44
d.	?	7.42%	1	?	?	2.25	$8810.55

2.

	Present Value (PV)	Nominal Interest Rate (j)	Compounding Frequency (m)	Time Period (t)	Periodic Interest Rate (i)	Number of Compounding Periods (n)	Future Value (FV)
a.	?	6.90%	?	4 years	1.725%	?	$17,500.00
b.	?	10.95%	365	219 days	?	?	$12,450.00
c.	?	7.45%	2	?	?	13.5	$49,152.74
d.	?	?	12	30 months	0.670%	?	$19,856.11

3. What amount invested today would yield $50,000 in 10 years and 5 months if it were invested at 8.20% compounded semi-annually?

4. The interest rate on a Guaranteed Investment Certificate (GIC) is 6.5% compounded semi-annually. What was the purchase price if it has a maturity value of $38,430 in 15 years and 1 month?

5. If you wish to have a million dollars 30 years from today, how much should you invest in your savings account that earns you 5% compounded monthly?

6. Cheryl would like to accumulate $35,000 for her retirement in 30 years. If she is promised 8.4% compounded monthly by her local bank, how much should she invest?

7. Samantha purchased a Guaranteed Investment Certificate (GIC) that has a maturity value of $25,865 in 6 years and 4 months. What was the purchase price of the GIC if it earns 6% compounded quarterly?

8. What is the discounted value of $5000 that is due in $5\frac{1}{2}$ years if the interest rate is 4% compounded quarterly?

9. How much money should Geoffrey invest today at 6.35% compounded semi-annually if he wants to have $20,800 in 5 years and 5 months to use as a deposit for the purchase of his home?

10. How much interest did Speedy Movers pay for a debt that accumulated to $58,556 in 4 years? The interest rate is 4.5% compounded quarterly.

11. A law firm invested its net profit into an investment that provided interest of 6% compounded monthly. After 6 months, there was a boom in the market and the interest rate rose to 13.07% compounded monthly. If the accumulated fund value 1 year after the boom was $480,000, calculate the amount that was originally invested.

12. Kyle invested his savings in a Registered Retirement Savings Plan (RRSP) at an interest rate of 9.6% compounded semi-annually. After one year, his investment grew to $24,600; however, the interest rate on the RRSP dropped to 8% compounded quarterly and remained constant for the next two years. Calculate the original amount he invested into his RRSP and the accumulated amount at the end of 3 years (2 years after the rate drop).

13. It was time for Bolder Cans Ltd. to repay its accumulated debt of $83,232. The original amount was received from a high net-worth individual at 8% compounded quarterly for 5 years. How much would have been saved if the loan had been received at 8% compounded semi-annually?

14. A loan accumulated to $25,050 in 10 years at 5.5% compounded monthly. If this loan had been issued at 5.48% compounded quarterly instead of 5.5% compounded monthly, would there have been any savings? Show calculations to support your answer.

15. Which option should Ramona Bookkeepers Inc. choose to invest its savings and why?
    a. 5.02% compounded quarterly.
    b. 5.05% compounded semi-annually.

    (Hint: Assume either a future value or present value and a time period.)

16. Tao learned that he could save his money in a term deposit (savings account that is fixed for a period of time). Which ten-year term deposit should he choose if one is providing him with an interest rate of 6% compounded quarterly and the other 6.5% compounded monthly? Show calculations to support your answer.

17. What single payment today would be economically equivalent to a payment of $25,485 in 3 years if money earns 8% compounded monthly?

18. Excite Party Rentals Ltd. received some money and decided to clear an outstanding loan of $30,500 that has to be paid in 1 year. How much would the company have to pay today to clear this debt if the interest on the loan is 12% compounded monthly?

19. A manufacturing firm purchased a heavy duty drilling machine and had to make a payment of $19,000 immediately to settle the invoice for the machine. However, the firm received another option of making payments of $10,000 immediately and the balance of $9500 in 6 months to settle the invoice. If money earns 4% compounded quarterly, which option is economically better for the manufacturing firm?

20. Karen was to receive a payment of $5000 today. However, the borrower agreed to pay Karen this amount in two parts: $3000 immediately and $2000 in 1 month. By agreeing to this new payment option, how much would Karen lose or gain if money earns 5.35% compounded semi-annually?

• 21. A bank offered a personal loan to George at an interest rate of 6.5% compounded semi-annually for 2 years. At the end of the period if the amount of interest charged was $880.50, calculate the present value of the loan. (Hint: use the formula $FV = PV(1 + i)^n$ and substitute $FV = PV + I$ in the formula to solve the problem.)

• 22. The interest amount charged on a personal loan for 10 years was $2450.75. If the interest rate charged on the loan was 9.5% compounded quarterly, calculate the present value of the loan. (Hint: use the formula $FV = PV(1 + i)^n$ and substitute $FV = PV + I$ in the formula to solve the problem.)

9.4 | Calculating Equivalent Payments

A single payment or a set of payments, at a given interest rate, can be replaced by a single equivalent payment or an equivalent set of payments on any common date, known as the focal date, as illustrated in the following examples:

Example 9.4(a)

Calculating a Single Payment Equivalent to Two Payments

What single payment in 3 years would be equivalent to $1000 1 year ago and $2000 in 6 years? Assume a rate of 5% compounded semi-annually during this period.

Solution

First, create the line-diagram showing the given payments and select a focal date. We will find the value of all the payments on this date and equate them to find the value of the unknown payment.

Let the focal date be the date of the unknown payment, i.e., 3 years. We are asked to find the payment on this focal date that is equivalent to the other two payments. To do so, we find the future value of the first payment (FV_1) on this focal date and the present value of the second payment (PV_2) on this focal date.

You can choose any date as the focal date. However, it is easier to choose the focal date on the date of one of the unknown payments.

$$\text{Equivalent payment} = FV_1 + PV_2$$

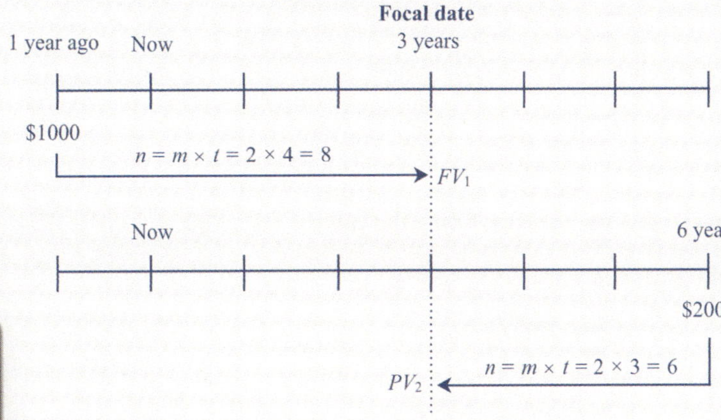

$$j = 0.05, \quad m = 2$$

$$i = \frac{j}{m} = \frac{0.05}{2} = 0.025$$

$$FV_1 = 1000(1 + 0.025)^8 = \$1218.402897...$$

$$PV_2 = 2000(1 + 0.025)^{-6} = \$1724.593732...$$

$$\text{Equivalent single payment in 3 years} = 1218.402897... + 1724.593732... = \$2942.996629...$$

Therefore, a single payment of $2943.00 in 3 years would be equivalent to $1000.00 1 year ago and $2000.00 in 6 years.

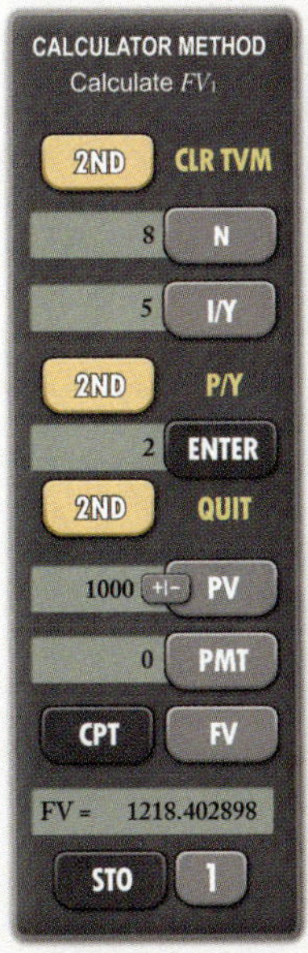

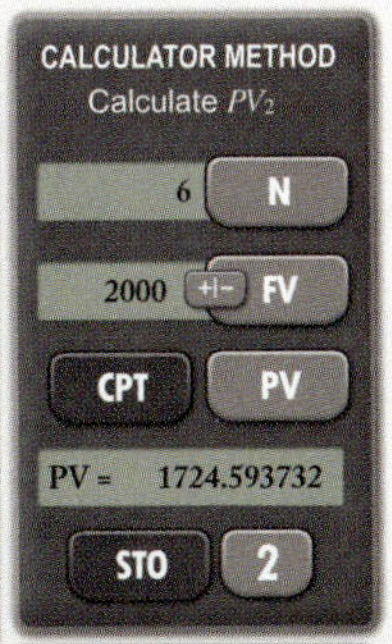

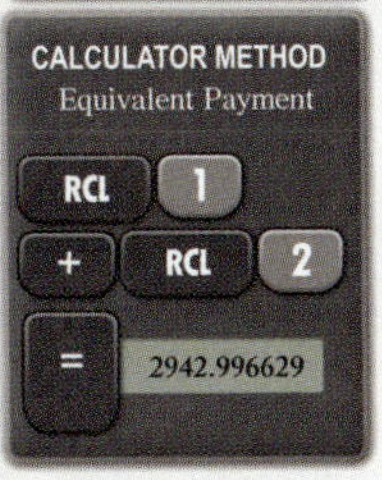

Example 9.4(b) Calculating Two Equal Payments Equivalent to a Single Payment

A scheduled payment of $5000 due in 3 months is to be replaced by 2 equal payments. The 1st payment is due in 1 month and the 2nd payment in 6 months. Calculate the size of the equal payments if money can earn 6% compounded monthly.

Solution

This question can be solved by choosing different focal dates, as explained by Methods 1, 2, and 3 below:

Method 1: Let the focal date be in 3 months.

Let '$x' be the value of each equal payment.

Note that in this example there will only be one unknown variable 'x', since the two unknown payments are equal.

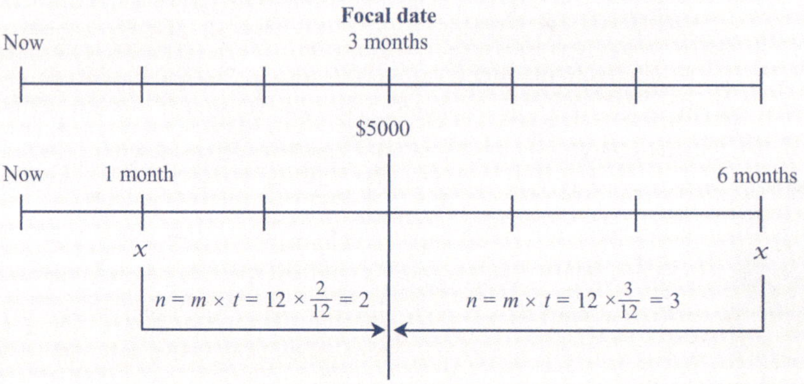

$$j = 0.06, \quad m = 12$$

$$i = \frac{j}{m} = \frac{0.06}{12} = 0.005$$

$$\$5000 = FV_{\text{1st payment in 3 months}} + PV_{\text{2nd payment in 3 months}}$$

Substituting the values, $5000 = x(1+0.005)^2 + x(1+0.005)^{-3}$

$5000 = x(1.010025) + x(0.985148...)$

Solving for x, $5000 = x(1.995173...)$

$x = \$2506.047394...$

Therefore, the size of each of the two equal payments is $2506.05.

In the calculator method, assume that the equal payments are $1 each.

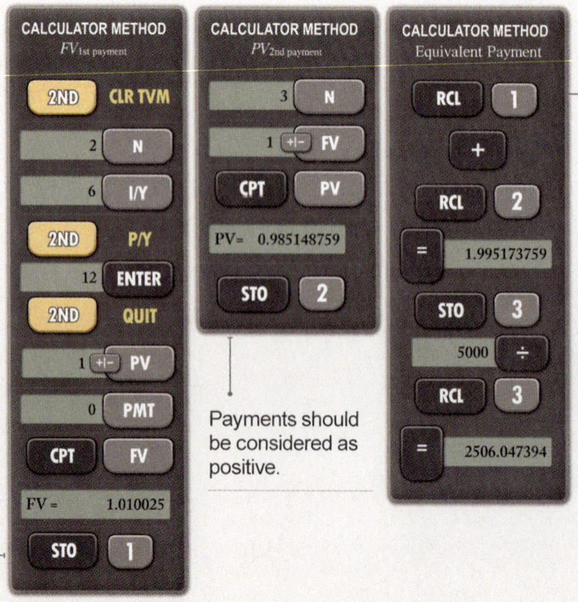

Stores value under '1'

Payments should be considered as positive.

Recalls stored value under '1'

Solution *continued*

Method 2: Let the focal date be in 6 months.

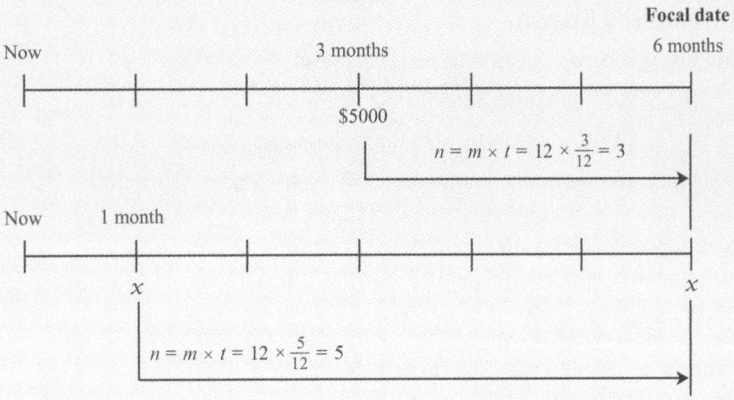

$$j = 0.06, \quad m = 12, \quad i = \frac{j}{m} = \frac{0.06}{12} = 0.005$$

$$FV_{\$5000 \text{ in 3 months}} = FV_{1^{st} \text{ payment in 6 months}} + \text{Value of } 2^{nd} \text{ payment } x$$

Substituting the values, $5000(1 + 0.005)^3 = x(1 + 0.005)^5 + x$

Simplifying, $5075.375625... = x(1.025251...) + x$

Solving for x, $5075.375625... = x(2.025251...)$

$$x = \$2506.047394...$$

Therefore, the size of each of the two equal payments is $2506.05.

Method 3: Let the focal date be in 1 month.

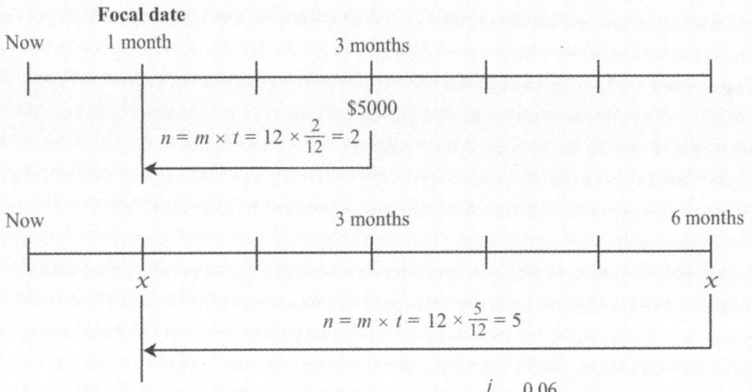

$$j = 0.06, \quad m = 12, \quad i = \frac{j}{m} = \frac{0.06}{12} = 0.005$$

$$PV_{\$5000 \text{ in 1 month}} = PV_{2^{nd} \text{ payment in 1 month}} + \text{Value of } 1^{st} \text{ payment } x$$

$$5000(1 + 0.005)^{-2} = x(1 + 0.005)^{-5} + x$$

Solving for x, $4950.372516... = x(0.975370...) + x$

$$4950.372516... = x(1.975370...)$$

$$x = \$2506.047394...$$

Therefore, the size of each of the two equal payments is $2506.05.

***Note:** The calculator method of solving the preceding problem has been omitted in Methods 2 and 3 and may be worked out as practice.*

Example 9.4(c)

Calculating Two Payments Equivalent to Two Other Payments When One of the Two Payments is Known

You are given two options to settle a loan:

(i) \$2000 now and \$3000 in 2 years.

(ii) \$2500 in 6 months and the balance in 3 years.

Calculate the payment required in 3 years under Option (ii) if money earns 8% compounded quarterly.

Solution

This question can be solved by choosing different focal dates, as demonstrated in Methods 1, 2, and 3 below:

Method 1: Let the focal date be in 3 years.

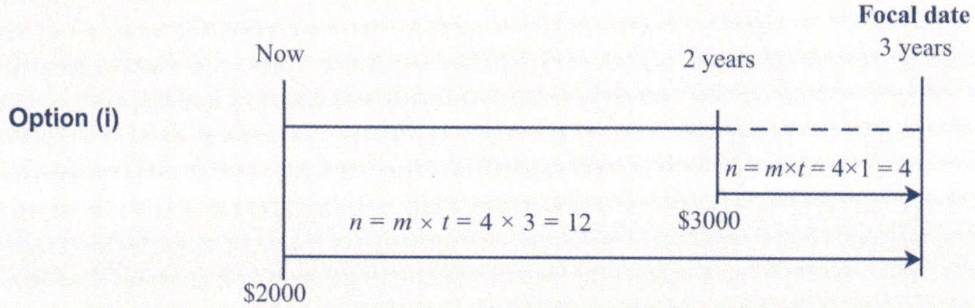

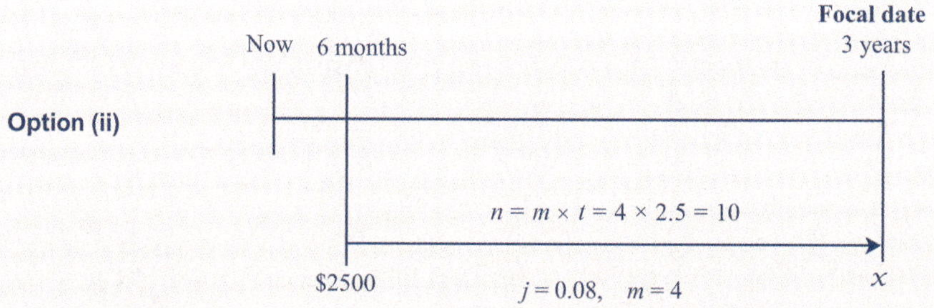

$j = 0.08, \quad m = 4$

$i = \frac{j}{m} = \frac{0.08}{4} = 0.02$

$$FV_{1^{st}\text{ Option(i) payment}} + FV_{2^{nd}\text{ Option(i) payment}} = FV_{1^{st}\text{ Option(ii) payment}} + 2^{nd}\text{ Option(ii) payment}$$

$$2000(1 + 0.02)^{12} + 3000(1 + 0.02)^{4} = 2500(1 + 0.02)^{10} + x$$

$$2536.483589... + 3247.29648 = 3047.48605 + x$$

$$2536.483589... + 3247.29648 - 3047.48605 = + x$$

$$x = \$2736.294019...$$

Therefore, the payment required in 3 years under Option (ii) is \$2736.29.

Solution continued

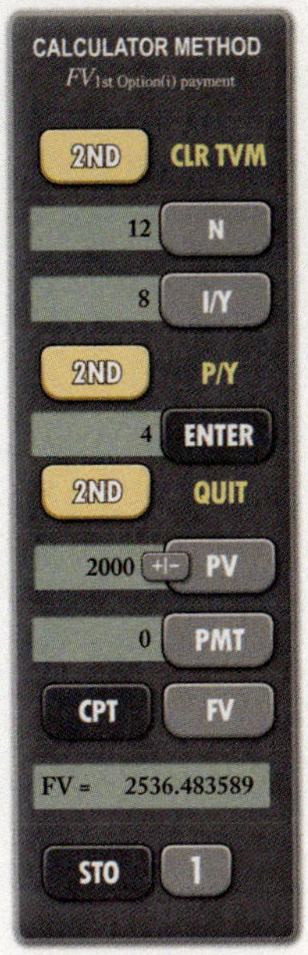

Note:
It is not necessary to re-enter I/Y, P/Y, and PMT as they have not changed and have not been cleared (*by CLR TVM*).

Method 2: Let the focal date be in 6 months.

Option (i)

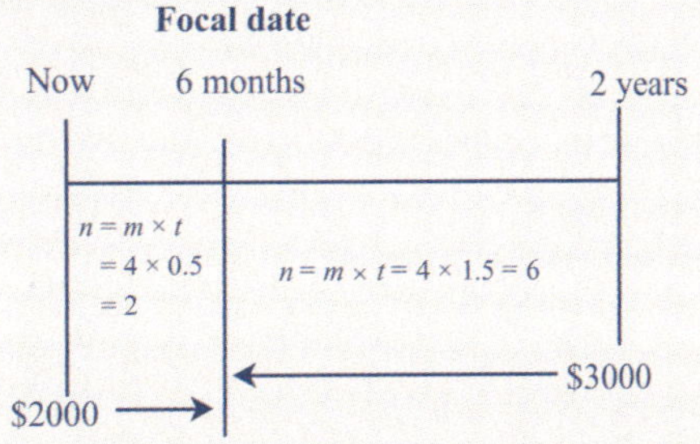

Option (ii)

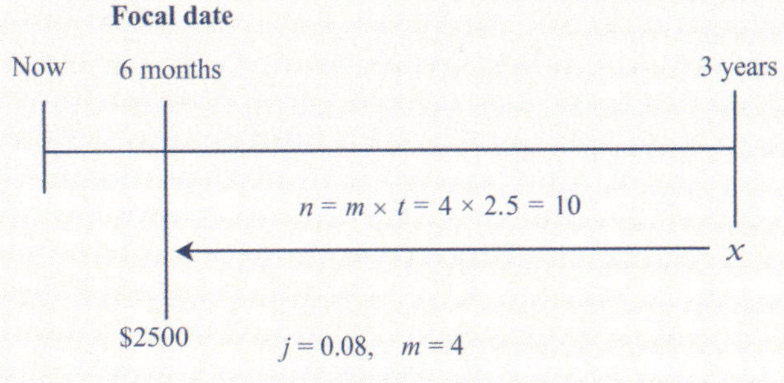

$$j = 0.08, \quad m = 4$$

$$i = \frac{j}{m} = \frac{0.08}{4} = 0.02$$

$$FV_{1^{st}\text{ Option(i) payment}} + PV_{2^{nd}\text{ Option(i) payment}} = 1^{st}\text{ Option(ii) payment} + PV_{2^{nd}\text{ Option(ii) payment}}$$

$$2000(1+0.02)^2 + 3000(1+0.02)^{-6} = 2500 + x(1+0.02)^{-10}$$

$$2080.80 + 2663.914147... = 2500 + x(0.820348...)$$

$$\frac{2080.80 + 2663.914147... - 2500}{0.820348} = x$$

$$x = \$2736.294019...$$

Therefore, the payment required in 3 years under Option (ii) is $2736.29.

Solution *continued*

Method 3: Let the focal date be now.

Option (i)

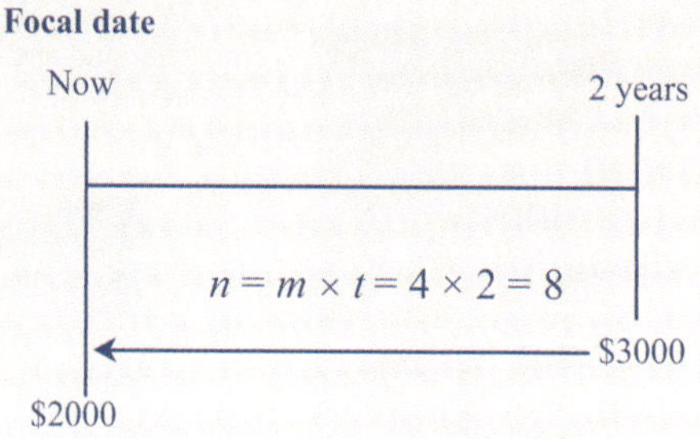

Option (ii)

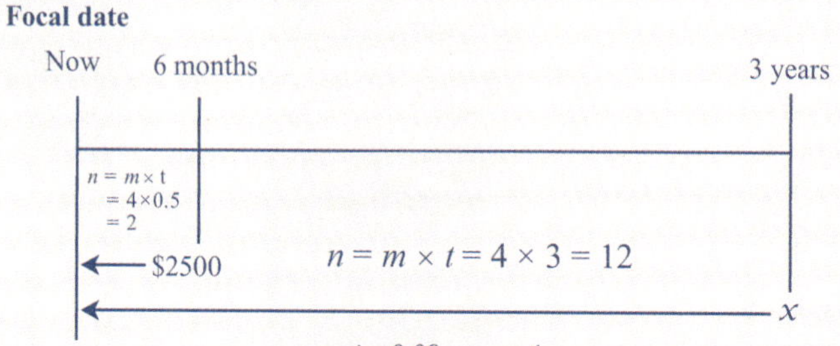

$$j = 0.08, \quad m = 4$$

$$i = \frac{j}{m} = \frac{0.08}{4} = 0.02$$

$$1^{st} \text{ Option (i) payment} + PV_{2^{nd}\text{ Option(i) payment}} = PV_{1^{st}\text{ Option(ii) payment}} + PV_{2^{nd}\text{ Option(ii) payment}}$$

Substituting values, $2000 + 3000(1+0.02)^{-8} = 2500(1+0.02)^{-2} + x(1+0.02)^{-12}$

Solving for x, $2000 + 2560.471114... = 2402.921953... + x(0.788493...)$

$$\frac{2000 + 2560.471114... - 2402.921953...}{0.788493...} = x$$

$$x = \$2736.294019...$$

Therefore, the payment required in 3 years under the Option(ii) is $2736.29.

Note:

- *The calculator method of solving this problem has been omitted from Methods 2 and 3 and may be worked out as practice.*
- *Choosing 2 years as the focal date has been omitted and may be done as practice.*

9.4 | Exercises

1. If money earns 8.5% compounded monthly, what single payment in one year would be equivalent to a payment of:
   a. $2340 two years ago, but not paid, and $500 today?
   b. $880 two years ago, but not paid, and $850 in five years?

   Show your calculation with a time-line diagram, choosing 1 year from now as the focal date.

2. If money earns 6.25% compounded quarterly, what single payment today would be equivalent to an amount of:
   a. $300 in two years and $780 in four years?
   b. $8020 six months ago, but not paid, and $9050 in one year?

   Show your calculation with a time-line diagram, choosing 1 year from now as the focal date.

3. If money earns 4% compounded semi-annually, what two equal payments in one year and in three years would be equivalent to:
   a. $8000 today?
   b. $5650 one year ago, but not paid, and $6800 two years ago, but not paid?

4. If money earns 6.26% compounded quarterly, what two equal payments today and in 2 years would be equivalent to:
   a. $550 today and $680 in nine months?
   b. Two equal payments of $5000 two years ago, but not paid, and a payment today?

5. Markson Industries was supposed to have received a payment of $10,000 two years ago and $20,000 one year ago from a customer who could not make either payment as scheduled. If the customer would like to settle both the payments today, what total amount would he have to pay Markson Industries if interest of 8% compounded quarterly is charged?

6. What single payment in two years would replace a payment of $18,650 one year ago and a payment of $21,400 two years and two months ago? Assume both payments were not paid and that the interest rate is 4% compounded quarterly.

7. What single payment today would replace a payment of $5000 in one year and $8000 in two years if the interest rate is 4% compounded monthly?

8. Calculate the single equivalent payment today that would replace three payments of $18,400, $21,065, and $12,560, in 2 years, 4 years, and 5 years, respectively, if money is earning interest at a rate of 3% compounded monthly.

9. You had an agreement to pay $6070 and $10,500 in 3 years and 5 years, respectively. What single payment would pay off this debt two years earlier than the first scheduled payment? Assume money earns 3% compounded quarterly.

10. You are expected to settle a loan by making payments of $1200, $1560, and $3200 in one, two and three years, respectively. What single payment in two years would be equivalent to these scheduled payments if money is worth 6% compounded semi-annually?

11. What three equal payments in 1 year, 2 years, and 3 years would replace one single payment of $4000 today at an interest rate of 6% compounding monthly?

12. A year ago, Aaisha, a money lender, loaned $12,000 to her client Chang at the rate of 4% compounded quarterly. Chang was required to repay this amount in three equal installments every year, with payments starting from the end of the 1st year. How much interest did Aaisha earn from this transaction?

13. What single payment in one year would be equivalent to $60,500 three years ago, but not paid, and $12,025 in four years? Assume an interest rate of 12% compounded monthly.

14. John had an agreement to repay Harry payments of $6500 and $11,225 in 4 years and 7 years, respectively. How much should John pay 5 years from now in order to clear the debt? Assume an interest rate of 5% compounded quarterly.

• 15. When Rutherford Steels bid for an infrastructure project with the government, the company was offered the following two payment options:
   a. A payment of $750,000 at the end of one year, which is the scheduled completion time for the project.
   b. $100,000 paid upfront on commencement of the project and the balance payment in 2 years.

   If the two payments are economically equivalent and the interest rate is 3% compounded semi-annually, calculate the balance payment offered in Option (b).

• 16. Thomas, an architect, is expected to make a first payment of $4000 in 1 year and a second payment in 4 years to a designer. Calculate his second payment if both these payments are economically equivalent to a single payment of $8000 today. Assume money can earn 6% compounded monthly.

• 17. What equal payments in one year and five years would replace payments of $8000 and $10,000 in four and six years, respectively? Assume money can earn 8% compounded annually.

- 18. Calculate the two equal installments, at the end of 1 year and 2 years from now, that would replace two payments of \$2000 today and \$8500 in 5 years, respectively. Assume money is worth 4% compounded semi-annually.

9.5 | Calculating the Periodic Interest Rate (i), and the Nominal Interest Rate (j)

We can calculate the periodic interest rate 'i' by rearranging Formula 9.1(a),

$FV = PV(1+i)^n$ — Dividing by 'PV' on both sides, we obtain,

$(1+i)^n = \frac{FV}{PV}$ — Taking the nth root on both sides, we obtain,

$$(1+i) = \left(\frac{FV}{PV}\right)^{\frac{1}{n}}$$

Rearranging to isolate 'i' results in the following formula for periodic interest rate:

Formula 9.5(a)

Periodic Interest Rate

$$i = \left(\frac{FV}{PV}\right)^{\frac{1}{n}} - 1$$

We can calculate the nominal interest rate 'j' by rearranging Formula 9.1(d): $i = \frac{j}{m}$

Rearranging to isolate 'j' results in the following formula for nominal interest rate:

Formula 9.5(b)

Nominal Interest Rate

$$j = m \times i$$

Example 9.5(a)

Calculating the Nominal Interest Rate When 'FV' and 'PV' are Known

At what rate compounded monthly will an investment of \$4500 grow to \$10,000 in 4 years?

Solution

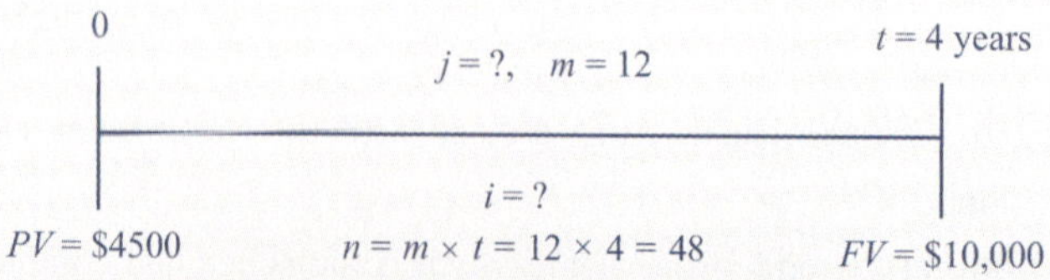

$$i = \left(\frac{FV}{PV}\right)^{\frac{1}{n}} - 1 = \left(\frac{10{,}000}{4500}\right)^{\frac{1}{48}} - 1 = 0.016774...$$

$$j = m \times i = 12 \times 0.016774... = 0.201296... = 20.13\%$$

Therefore, the investment will grow to \$10,000 in 4 years at an interest rate of 20.13% compounded monthly.

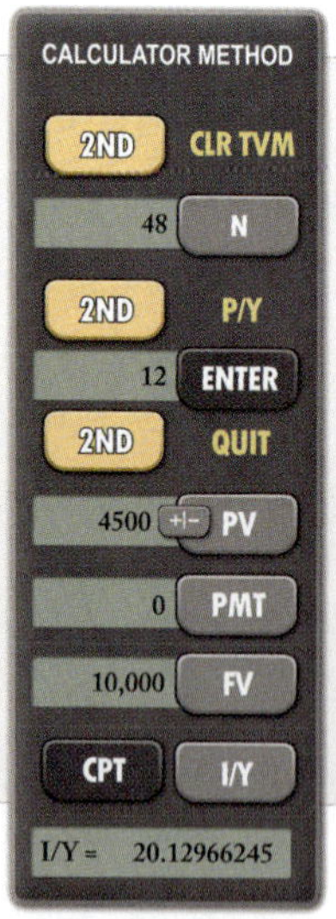

Example 9.5(b)

Calculating the Nominal Interest Rate When '*PV*' and '*I*' are Known

The interest on a 3-year investment bond is $1072.97. If the bond was purchased for $4000, what is the nominal interest rate of the bond if interest is compounded quarterly?

Solution

Note that *FV* is not directly provided, but the amount of interest is provided.

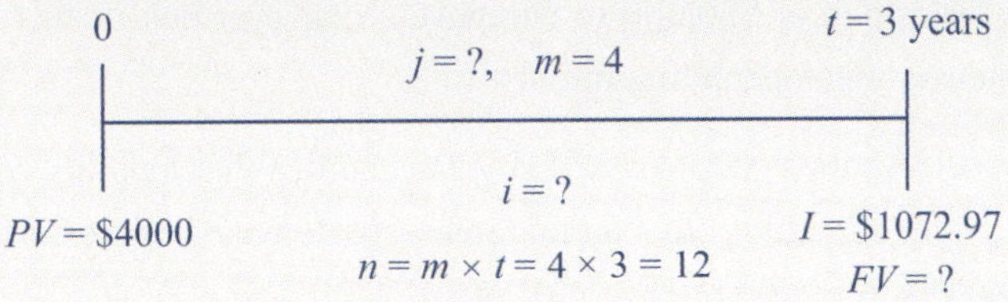

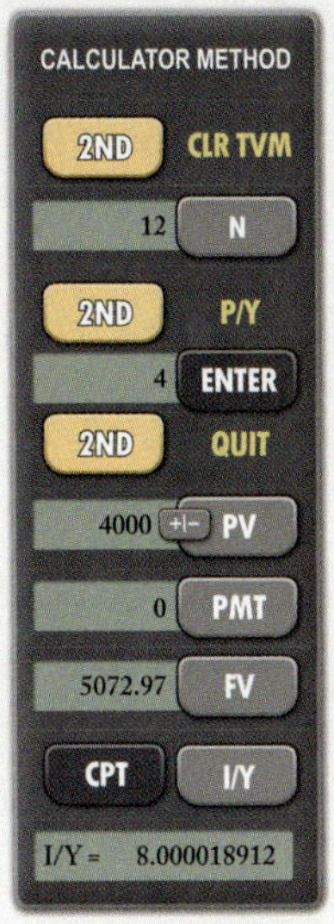

We know that $FV = PV + I$

$$FV = 4000 + 1072.97$$

$$= \$5072.97$$

$$i = \left(\frac{FV}{PV}\right)^{\frac{1}{n}} - 1$$

$$= \left(\frac{5072.97}{4000}\right)^{\frac{1}{12}} - 1$$

$$i = 0.020000...$$

$$j = m \times i = 4 \times 0.020000... = 0.080000... = 8.00\%$$

Therefore, the nominal interest rate of the bond is 8.00%.

Example 9.5(c)

Calculating Nominal Interest Rate When an Investment Triples

At what nominal interest rate compounded semi-annually will an investment triple in 12 years?

Solution

Assume $PV = \$1000$. If the investment triples, $FV = \$3000$.

Note that when an investment triples, the ratio $\frac{FV}{PV} = \frac{3}{1}$

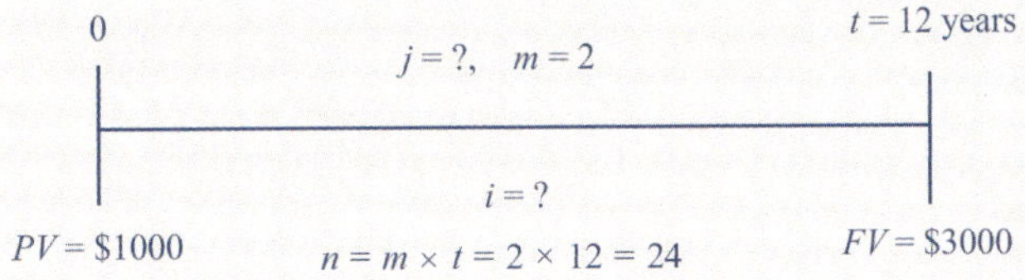

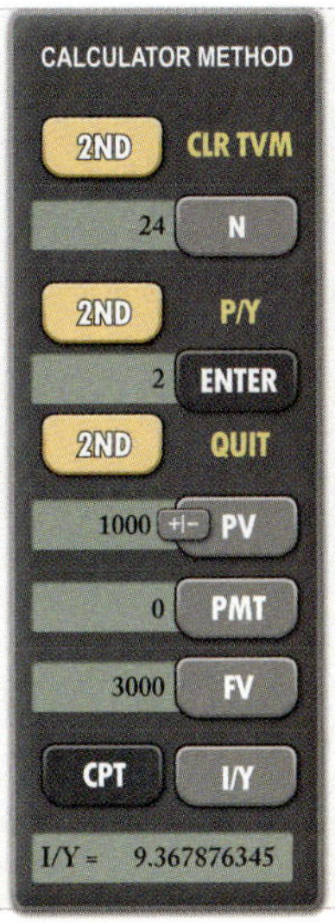

$$i = \left(\frac{FV}{PV}\right)^{\frac{1}{n}} - 1 = \left(\frac{3000}{1000}\right)^{\frac{1}{24}} - 1 = 0.046839...$$

$$j = m \times i = 2 \times 0.046839... = 0.093678... = 9.37\%$$

Therefore, the investment will triple at 9.37% compounded semi-annually.

9.5 | Exercises

1. Calculate the nominal interest rate and periodic interest rate for an investment of $100,000 that matures to $200,000 in 10 years if interest is compounded quarterly.

2. Canary Calendars Inc. invested this year's profits of $64,000 in a bond that matured to $84,500 in 2 years. Calculate the fund's quarterly compounding nominal interest rate and periodic interest rate.

3. Rose received an excellent interest rate for her car loan of $11,000. Calculate the nominal interest rate and periodic interest rate of her loan if it accumulated to $11,170 in 5 months and interest is compounded quarterly.

4. A calculator distributor invested its net income of $35,000 in a mutual fund. Calculate the nominal interest rate compounded semi-annually if the accumulated value in 2 years and 7 months is $44,650.

5. If you have $20,000 in your savings account and wish to grow it to a million dollars in 40 years, calculate the semi-annually compounding interest rate.

6. A computer assembling company took a loan of $30,000 to purchase a conveyer belt. If the debt accumulated to $45,850 in 2 years, calculate the quarterly compounding interest rate.

7. D'Anah wants to double his money in 15 years in a low-risk savings account. What monthly compounding interest rate do you suggest that he look for? What monthly compounding interest rate would allow him to double his money within 10 years? (Hint: If money doubles, the ratio of FV to PV is 2.)

8. Mark heard that he could triple his money in 15 years if he invested it in his friend's telecommunications business. What monthly compounding interest rate should the business offer?

9. An investment of $5000 in a TFSA (Tax Free Savings Account) accumulated to $5280 at the end of one year at a monthly compounding interest rate. However, the monthly compounding interest rate for the second year changed and the balance in the account at the end of the second year was $5875. Calculate the nominal interest rate for the first year and the nominal interest rate for the second year.

10. The nominal interest rate on a car loan that was compounded semi-annually changed at the end of one year. If the initial loan amount was $8000 and the accumulated balance at the end of the first year and second year were $8656 and $9100.50, respectively, calculate the nominal interest rates for each year.

11. Amex Industries Ltd. invested $30,000 in a low-growth mutual fund that earned them an interest amount of $12,000 in 14 years. Calculate the nominal interest rate compounded quarterly for the fund.

12. If an investment grew to $12,000 in 2 years and the interest amount earned was $800, calculate the monthly compounding interest rate.

9.6 | Calculating the Number of Compounding Periods (n), and the Time Period (t)

We can calculate the number of compounding periods 'n' from Formula 9.1(a) as follows:

$$FV = PV(1 + i)^n$$

Dividing by 'PV' on both sides, we obtain,

$$\frac{FV}{PV} = (1 + i)^n$$

Taking the natural logarithm on both sides, we obtain,

$$\ln\left(\frac{FV}{PV}\right) = \ln(1 + i)^n$$

Using the laws of logarithms, we obtain,

$$\ln\left(\frac{FV}{PV}\right) = n \times \ln(1+i)$$

Rearranging to isolate 'n' results in the following formula for calculating the number of compounding periods:

Formula 9.6(a) **Number of Compounding Periods**

$$n = \frac{\ln\left(\frac{FV}{PV}\right)}{\ln(1 + i)}$$

We can calculate term 't' in years by rearranging Formula 9.1(e), $n = m \times t$

Rearranging to isolate 't' results in the following formula for calculating the time period in years:

Formula 9.6(b)

Time Period in Years

$$t = \frac{n}{m}$$

Note: *In determining the time period, 't', in years and months, the value of 'n' is not to be rounded to the nearest (or rounded up the next) compounding period.*

Example 9.6(a)

Calculating the Time Period When 'PV' and 'FV' are Known

How long will it take for an investment of $30,000 to mature to $100,000 if it is growing at the rate of 12% compounded semi-annually? Provide your answer rounded up to the next month.

Solution

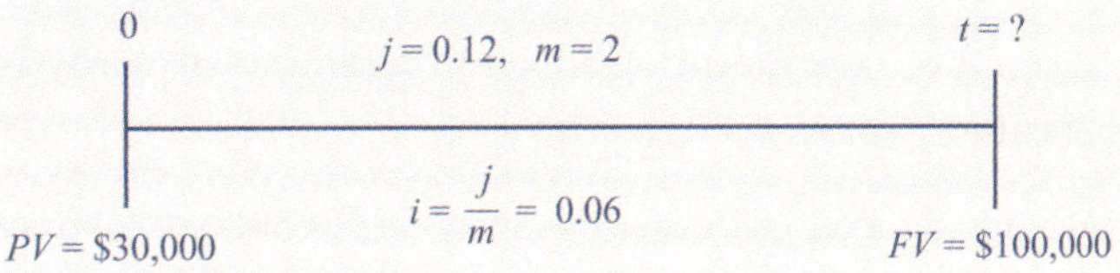

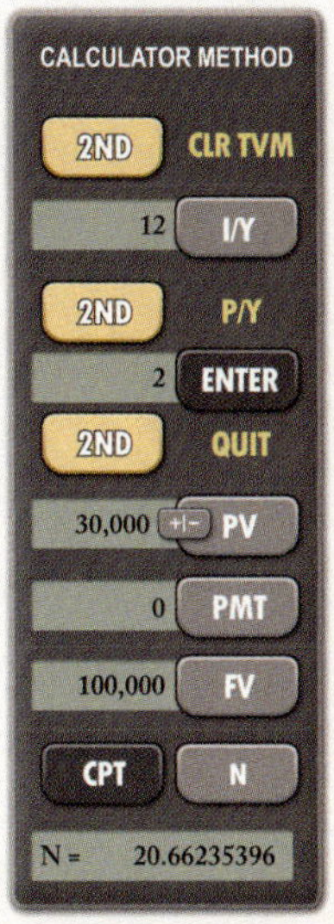

$$n = \frac{\ln\left(\frac{FV}{PV}\right)}{\ln(1+i)} = \frac{\ln\left(\frac{100{,}000}{30{,}000}\right)}{\ln(1+0.06)} = 20.662353\text{... compounding periods}$$

$$t = \frac{n}{m} = \frac{20.662353...}{2} = 10.331176\text{... years}$$

$= 10$ years $+ (0.331176... \times 12$ months$)$

$= 10$ years $+ 3.974123...$ months

Rounding 't' up to the next month, $= 10$ years and 4 months

Therefore, it will take 10 years and 4 months for the investment to mature.

Note: *In the above example, if the value of 'n', 20.662353..., is rounded up to the next compounding period (n = 21), then the time period, t, will be* $\frac{21}{2}$ *= 10 years and 6 months. However, the investment of $30,000 will mature to $100,000 in 10 years and 4 months as calculated above. For this reason, we do not round the value of 'n' in compound interest calculations.*

Example 9.6(b)

Calculating the Time Period When 'PV' and 'I' are Known

What is the term for an investment of $8000 that earns interest of $3000 at the rate of 8% compounded annually? Provide your answer rounded up to the next month.

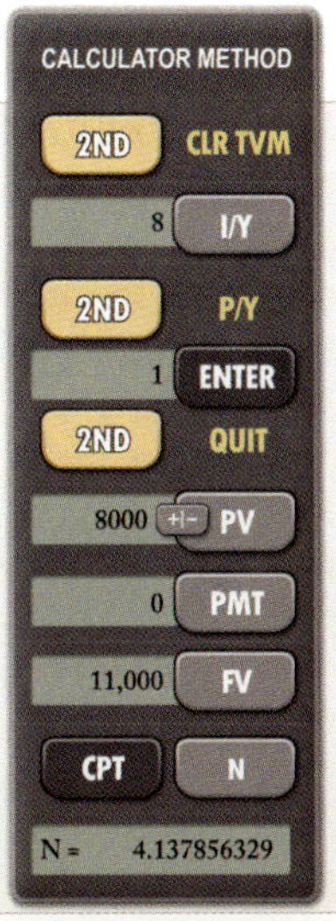

Solution

Note that FV is not directly provided but interest has been provided.

We know that $FV = PV + I$.

$$FV = 8000.00 + 3000.00 = \$11{,}000.00$$

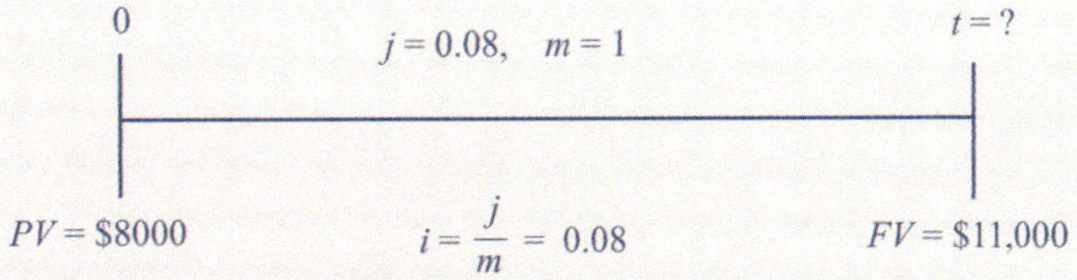

$$n = \frac{\ln\left(\frac{11{,}000}{8000}\right)}{\ln(1+0.08)}$$

Solution
continued

$= 4.137856...$ compounding periods

$t = \frac{n}{m} = \frac{4.137856...}{1} = 4.137856...$ years

$= 4$ years $+ (0.137856... \times 12$ months$)$

$= 4$ years $+ 1.654275...$ months

Rounding 't' up to the next month, $= 4$ years and 2 months

Therefore, the term for the investment is 4 years and 2 months.

9.6 | Exercises

In the following problems, provide your answer rounded up to the next month when calculating the term.

1. How long would it take for an investment of $2500 to result in a maturity value of $3000 at the rate of 10% compounded semi-annually?
2. How long would it take a loan of $15,625 to accumulate to $18,500 at the rate of 8% compounded quarterly?
3. A sugar processing unit invested its profits of $27,000 in a GIC at 8% compounded quarterly. How long would it take for this amount to grow to $60,000?
4. Rudolph invested $5000 in his RRSP that was earning 9.55% compounded semi-annually. How long would it take for his investment to grow to $100,000?
5. How long would it take an investment to double in value if it earns:
   a. 6% compounded monthly.
   b. 5% compounded semi-annually.
6. How long would it take for an investment to triple in value if it earns:
   a. 6% compounded monthly?
   b. 5% compounded semi-annually?
7. Apiscon Farms decided to invest its net profit in a low-risk fund that promised to double the investment at 2.3% compounded monthly. How long would it take for the investment to double?
8. Texas Equipments wanted to invest in a bond that promises to triple its investment at 12.5% compounded quarterly. How long would it take for the bond to mature?
9. Your bank offers you a personal loan of $5000 at an interest rate of 6% compounded monthly. At the end of the term, the debt accumulated an interest of $2100. Calculate the term of this loan?
10. Hewlett Plastics Inc. received a loan of $860,000 at 11% compounded quarterly to purchase a heavy-duty machinery for its factory. Calculate the time period of the loan if the interest accumulated on the loan was $80,000.
11. If the accumulated value of a balanced-fund is $25,000, the interest earned on this fund is $7000, and it is growing at 8% compounded semi-annually, calculate the time period of this investment.
12. The maturity value of a bond is $10,850 and it has grown at an interest rate of 6% compounded quarterly. Calculate the time period of the bond if the interest earned is $2300.

9.7 | Calculating the Effective Interest Rate (f) of a Given Nominal Interest Rate

Effective interest rate **(f):** the annually compounding interest rate.

The effective interest rate 'f' is the annually compounding interest rate. We have learned that the nominal interest rate 'j' (nominal meaning 'in name only') is the quoted or stated interest rate per annum on which the compound interest calculation is based for the given compounding period. The nominal interest rate is commonly used to express compounding periods that are annual, semi-annual, quarterly, monthly, or daily and is used to calculate the periodic interest rate 'i'.

Effective interest rate 'f' is the actual annually compounding interest rate of a given nominal interest rate 'j' at a different compounding frequency.

When the nominal interest rate is compounded annually it is called the **effective interest rate.** The effective interest rates is used to compare the annual interest rate between loans and investments that have different compounding periods. By definition, the effective interest rate 'f' results in the same future value as a nominal rate with a given compounding frequency.

Therefore, the formula for calculating the effective interest rate can be derived by equating the following two equations:

a) The future value of an investment for one year at an effective rate 'f' (annually compounding rate with 1 compounding period per year).

Using, $FV = PV(1 + i)^n$ In this case, $n = m \times t = 1 \times 1 = 1$ and $i = \frac{j}{m} = \frac{f}{1} = f$

$FV = PV(1 + f)^1$ Equation (a)

b) The future value of the same investment for one year at a different compounding rate 'j' ($= m \times i$) with 'm' compoundings per year and a periodic interest rate of 'i'.

Using, $FV = PV(1 + i)^n$ In this case, $n = m \times t = m \times 1 = m$

$FV = PV(1 + i)^m$ Equation (b)

Equating equations (a) and (b), we obtain,

$PV(1 + f)^1 = PV(1 + i)^m$ Dividing by 'PV' on both sides, we obtain,

$(1 + f)^1 = (1 + i)^m$

Rearranging to solve for 'f' results in the following formula for calculating the effective interest rate:

Formula 9.7

Effective Interest Rate

$$f = (1 + i)^m - 1$$

Example 9.7(a)

Calculating the Effective Interest Rate When the Nominal Rate is Given

What is the effective interest rate that corresponds to:

(i) 9% compounded semi-annually?

(ii) 9% compounded quarterly?

Solution

(i) 9% compounded semi-annually: $j = 9\%$, $m = 2$, $i = \frac{j}{m} = \frac{0.09}{2} = 0.045$

$$f = (1 + i)^m - 1 = (1 + 0.045)^2 - 1 = 0.092025 = 9.20\%$$

Therefore, 9.20% compounded annually is the effective interest rate that corresponds to 9% compounded semi-annually.

Solution *continued*

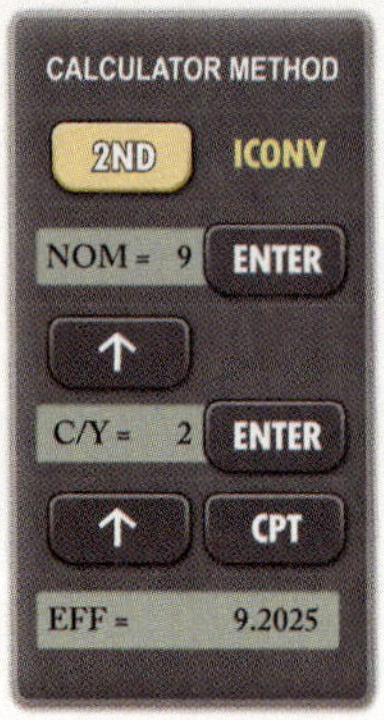

1. Press **2ND** then **ICONV** *(Secondary function over the 2 key).*
2. Enter the ***nominal interest rate.***
3. Scroll to see *C/Y.*
4. Enter the ***compoundings per year.***
5. Compute the ***effective interest rate.***

As the compounding frequency for the given nominal interest rate increases, so does the corresponding effective interest rate.

(ii) 9% compounded quarterly: $j = 9\%,\ m = 4,\ i = \frac{j}{m} = \frac{0.09}{4} = 0.0225$

$$f = (1 + i)^m - 1 = (1 + 0.0225)^4 - 1 = 0.093083... = 9.31\%$$

Therefore, 9.31% compounded annually is the effective interest rate that corresponds to 9% compounded quarterly.

Example 9.7(b) Calculating the Effective Interest Rate When 'i' is Given

If an interest rate of 1.2% per month is charged by a credit card company, what effective interest rate should be disclosed to the borrower?

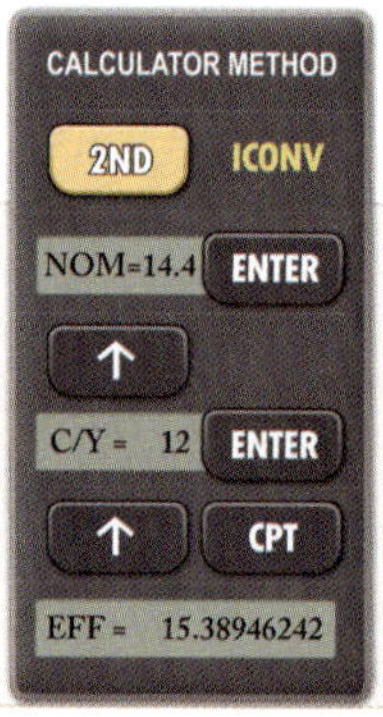

Solution

$m = 12,\ i = 1.2\%$

$j = i \times m = 1.2 \times 12 = 14.4$

$$f = (1 + i)^m - 1 = (1 + 0.012)^{12} - 1 = 0.153894... = 15.39\%$$

1.2% per month is effectively 15.39% compounded annually.

Therefore, 15.39% compounded annually should be disclosed to the borrower.

"An interest rate of 1.2% per month" refers to the periodic interest rate 'i' that is compounding monthly.

Example 9.7(c) Calculating the Effective Interest Rate When 'PV', 'FV', and 't' are Given

At what effective interest rate would \$8000 grow to \$13,663.19 in 6 years?

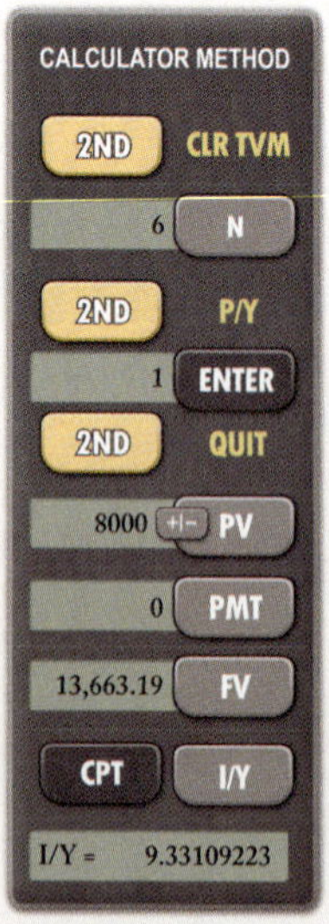

Solution

The effective interest rate is the annually compounding rate, so in this case, to find the effective interest rate, we can set $m = 1$ and calculate 'i'.

$$m = 1, \quad t = 6$$

$$n = m \times t = 1 \times 6 = 6$$

$$i = \left(\frac{FV}{PV}\right)^{\frac{1}{n}} - 1 = \left(\frac{13{,}663.19}{8000}\right)^{\frac{1}{6}} - 1 = 0.093310... = 9.33\%$$

Since the amount is compounded once a year the periodic interest rate 'i' will be equal to the effective interest rate 'f'.

We can check this by using the formula:

$$f = (1 + i)^m - 1 = (1 + 0.093310...)^1 - 1 = 0.093310... = 9.33\%$$

Therefore, \$8000.00 will grow to \$13,663.19 at an effective interest rate of 9.33%.

9.7 | Exercises

1. Calculate the effective interest rate for each of the following nominal interest rates:
   a. 4% compounded semi-annually.
   b. 4% compounded quarterly.
   c. 4% compounded monthly.

2. Calculate the effective interest rates for the following nominal interest rates:
   a. 6% compounded semi-annually.
   b. 6.03% compounded quarterly.
   c. 6.75% compounded monthly.

3. If an $8,000 investment grew to $13,000 in 6 years, what effective interest rate would have provided the same benefit?

4. Matthew invested $230,000 to purchase a home. After 10 years, he sold the home for $340,000. Calculate the effective interest rate of growth of the value of the home.

5. A software development company lent $20,000 to an employee for 2 years. If interest of $880 was charged on this loan amount for the entire time period, calculate the effective interest rate of the loan.

6. Pierre invested $15,500 in shares of a blue-chip company. After 5 years, he sold the shares at market price and made a profit of $10,000. Calculate the effective interest rate of growth of the value of his shares.

7. Which of the following rates offers a higher rate of return?
   a. 6% compounded monthly.
   b. 6.12% compounded quarterly.

8. Which of the following rates offers a higher rate of return?
   a. 10% compounded annually.
   b. 9.7% compounded daily.

9. If an interest rate of 1.75% per month is charged by a credit card company, what effective interest rate should be disclosed to the borrower?

10. Amanda's utility bill stated that interest would be charged at a rate of 2.5% per month on any outstanding payments on the invoice. What effective interest rate would be charged on outstanding payments?

11. Ace Machinery wants to save an amount in an account that gives the company the highest return over a two-year period. The Bank of Halifax is offering the company interest on its savings at a rate of 2% compounded monthly and Bank of Sarnia is offering the company an interest rate of 2.1% compounded semi-annually. Which bank should the company choose? Show calculations to support your answer.

12. Where do you suggest that Best Electronics invest its savings of $200,000 for 2 years and why?
    a. The Bank of Kingston provides an interest rate of 4.5% compounded annually.
    b. The Bank of London provides an interest rate of 4.45% compounded monthly.

• 13. If the effective rate of the nominal interest rate of 4.8% compounded monthly is increased by 1.2%, calculate the new monthly compounding nominal interest rate.

• 14. If the effective rate of the nominal interest rate of 4% compounded quarterly decreases by 1%, calculate the new quarterly compounding nominal interest rate.

15. Alyssa was in need of a personal loan urgently so she approached a trust company that offered her the loan at an effective interest rate of 24%. However, she could also have taken the loan from her credit card company that charged her 1.8% p.m. Where would it have been cheaper for her to take this loan?

16. If a credit card company is offering a loan at an interest rate of 1.55% p.m, what effective interest rate should a bank offer to match this rate?

9.8 | Calculating the Equivalent Interest Rate of a Given Nominal Interest Rate at a Different Compounding Frequency

Equivalent interest rates are nominal interest rates with different compounding periods that result in the same future value of a given principal for any fixed period of time. Equivalent interest rates are used to compare the interest rates between loans and investments that have different compounding periods.

Finding the equivalent interest rate is a 2-step approach, as shown below:

Step I: Find the Equivalent Periodic Interest Rate

As the future values of two investments with equivalent interest rates are the same for a fixed period, for example, one year ($t = 1$), they can be equated:

$$FV = PV(1 + i_2)^{m_2} \quad , \quad FV = PV(1 + i_1)^{m_1}$$

Equating FV from the above two equations, we obtain,

$$PV(1 + i_2)^{m_2} = PV(1 + i_1)^{m_1}$$

Dividing both sides by PV, we obtain,

$$(1 + i_2)^{m_2} = (1 + i_1)^{m_1}$$

Dividing the exponents on both sides by m_2, we obtain

$$(1 + i_2)^{m_2/m_2} = (1 + i_1)^{m_1/m_2}$$

Rearranging to isolate 'i_2' results in the following formula for calculating the equivalent periodic interest rate:

Formula 9.8(a)

Equivalent Periodic Interest Rate

$$i_2 = (1 + i_1)^{m_1/m_2} - 1$$

Equivalent interest rates **(*j_2*)**: nominal interest rates with different compounding periods that result in the same future value of a given principal at any fixed period of time.

Step II: Find the Equivalent Nominal Interest Rate

We can multiply the equivalent periodic interest rate by the compounding frequency to find the equivalent nominal interest rate, using Formula 9.5 (b),

$$j = m \times i$$

Using our values for 'j_2', 'i_2', and 'm_2' results in the following formula for calculating the equivalent nominal interest rate:

Formula 9.8(b)

Equivalent Nominal Interest Rate

$$j_2 = m_2 \times i_2$$

Example 9.8

Calculating the Equivalent Nominal Interest Rate

16% compounded monthly is equivalent to what rate compounded quarterly?

Solution

16% compounded monthly = ?% compounded quarterly

$j_1 = 0.16$, $m_1 = 12$, $j_2 = ?$, $m_2 = 4$

> **'m_1' is the compounding frequency of the known nominal interest rate 'j_1', and 'm_2' is the compounding frequency of the unknown nominal interest rate 'j_2'.**

$$i_1 = \frac{0.16}{12}$$

$$i_2 = (1 + i_1)^{m_1/m_2} - 1$$

Substituting the values, $$i_2 = \left(1 + \frac{0.16}{12}\right)^{12/4} - 1$$

$$= 0.040535...$$

$$j_2 = m_2 \times i_2 = 4 \times 0.040535... = 0.162142... = 16.21\%$$

Therefore, 16.21% compounded quarterly is equivalent to 16% compounded monthly.

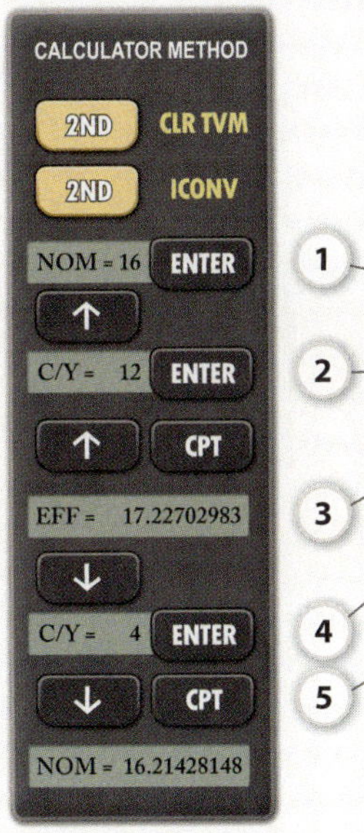

1. Enter the *given* ***nominal interest rate.***
2. Enter the ***compoundings per year*** related to the nominal interest rate.
3. Compute the ***effective rate of interest.***
4. Enter the required ***compounding periods per year*** for the **equivalent nominal rate.**
5. Compute the ***equivalent nominal interest rate.***

9.8 | *Exercises*

1. What rate compounded quarterly is equivalent to:
   a. 7% compounded semi-annually
   b. 6.05% compounded monthly
   c. 8% compounded semi-annually
2. Find the equivalent interest rate compounded monthly for the given effective interest rates:
   a. 8%
   b. 12%
   c. 5.34%
3. What nominal rate compounded semi-annually would place investors in exactly the same financial position as 8.25% compounded annually?

4. A credit union pays 8.00% compounded annually on its 5-year investments. What semi-annually compounded rate would place investors in exactly the same financial position?

5. What semi-annually compounded rate would place you in the same financial position as 6.16% compounded quarterly?

6. What quarterly compounded rate would result in the same amount of interest earned as 12.13% compounded monthly?

7. The ABC Bank offers 5-year loans at 3.25% compounded semi-annually. What quarterly compounded rate would a local bank have to offer you so that you would not be disadvantaged by going with them?

8. The ABC Bank has decided to set its interest rates to compound daily on all deposits in order to give customers the same benefits as its current offering of 10% compounded quarterly. At what value should the daily compounded interest rate be set?

9. Tom is offered a loan from Bank A at 8.00% compounded semi-annually. Bank B offers similar terms, but at a rate of 8.16% compounded annually. Which loan should he accept?

10. Harold and Jeena were shopping around for a good interest rate and they received the following rates from three different banks: 5.84% compounded monthly, 5.92% compounded quarterly, and 6% compounded annually. Which rate should they pick and what would be that chosen rate compounded semi-annually?

11. Henry wanted a loan and was offered these two rates: 16% compounded quarterly or 1.5% per month. Which rate would be most advantageous to him?

12. Francesca was offered rates of 1.2% per month or 14% compounded monthly for an upcoming investment. Which rate would earn the most interest?.

9 | Review Examples

Example 1

Compute the maturity value of $27,449.80 invested for 10 years at 8% compounded semi-annually.

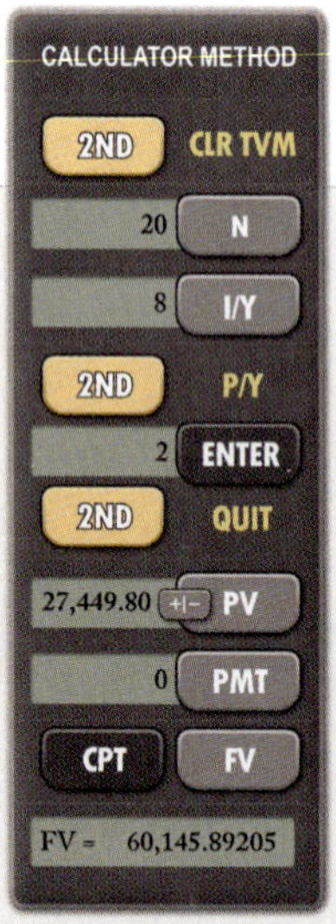

Solution

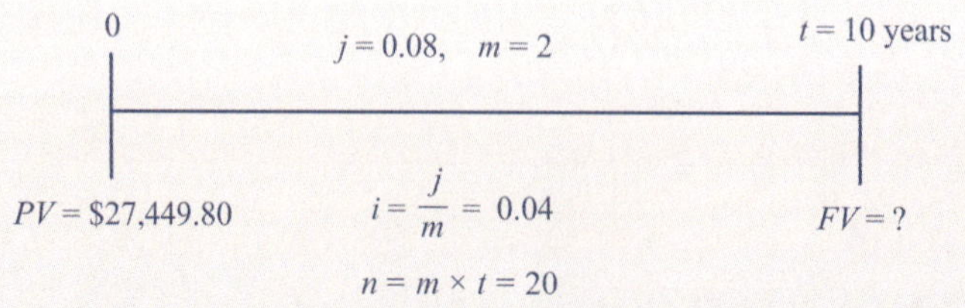

$$FV = PV\,(1 + i)^n = 27{,}449.80(1+0.04)^{20} = \$60{,}145.89205...$$

Therefore, the maturity value is $60,145.89.

Example 2

What amount invested today would accumulate to \$60,145.89 in 10 years if it is invested at 8% compounded semi-annually?

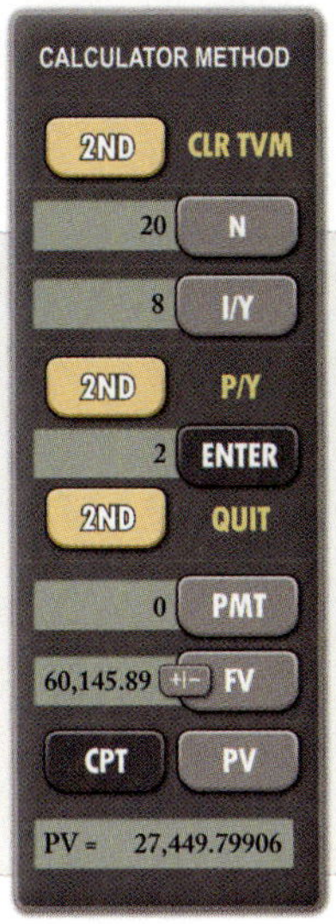

Solution

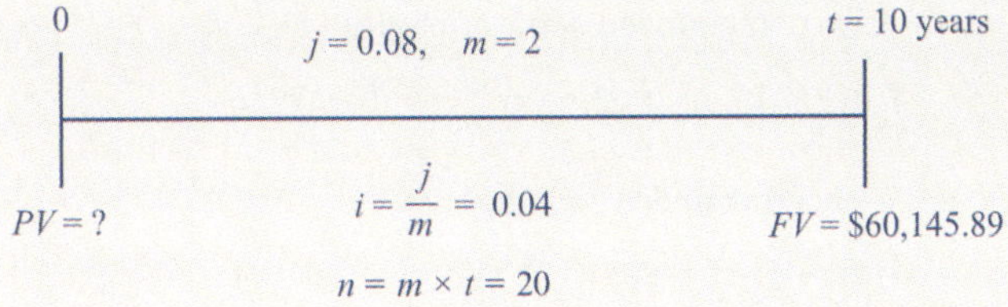

$$PV = FV(1 + i)^{-n} = 60{,}145.89(1 + 0.04)^{-20} = \$27{,}449.79906...$$

Therefore, \$27,449.80 invested today would accumulate to \$60,145.89.

Example 3

At what rate compounded semi-annually will an investment of \$27,449.80 grow to \$60,145.89 in 10 years?

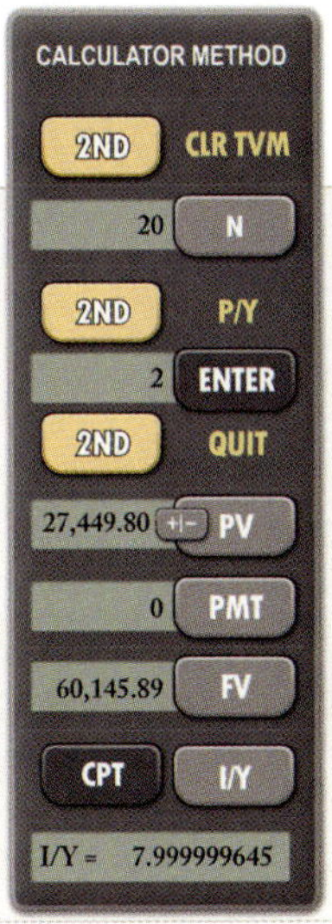

Solution

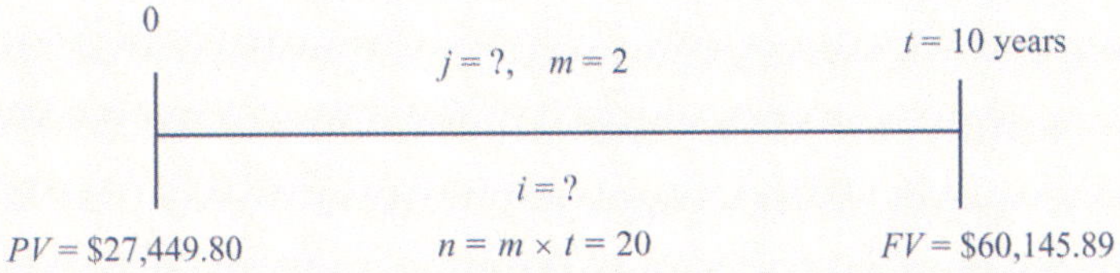

$$i = \left(\frac{FV}{PV}\right)^{\frac{1}{n}} - 1 = \left(\frac{60{,}145.89}{27{,}449.80}\right)^{\frac{1}{20}} - 1 = 0.039999...$$

$$j = m \times i = 2 \times 0.0399999... = 0.079999... = 7.999999...\%$$

Therefore, \$27,449.80 will grow to \$60,145.89 at 8% compounded semi-annually.

Example 4

How long will it take for an investment of \$27,449.80 to grow to \$60,145.89 if it earns 8% compounded semi-annually?

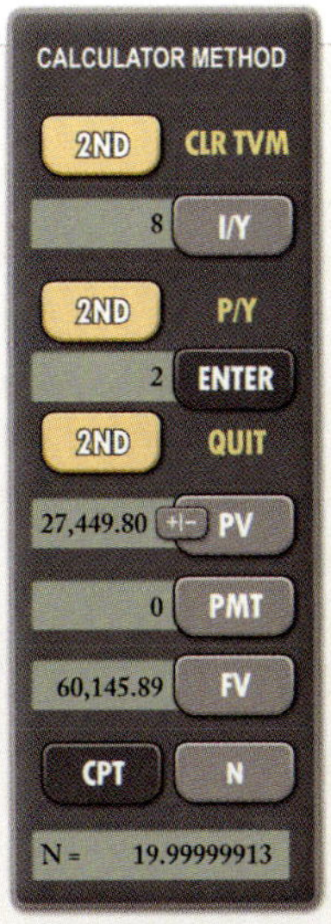

Solution

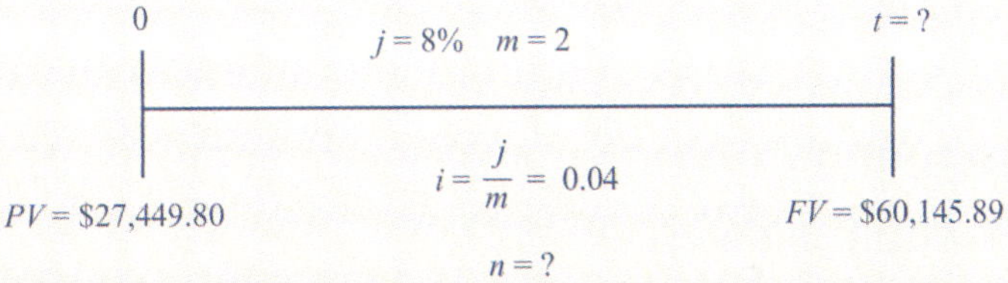

$$n = \frac{\ln\left(\frac{FV}{PV}\right)}{\ln(1+i)} = \frac{\ln\left(\frac{60{,}145.89}{27{,}449.80}\right)}{\ln(1 + 0.04)} = 19.999999... \text{ compounding periods}$$

$$t = \frac{n}{m} = \frac{19.999999...}{2} = 9.999999... \text{ years}$$

Therefore, \$27,449.80 will grow to \$60,145.89 in 10 years with an interest rate of 8% compounded semi-annually.

Example 5

What monthly interest rate is equivalent to 7.5% compounded semi-annually?

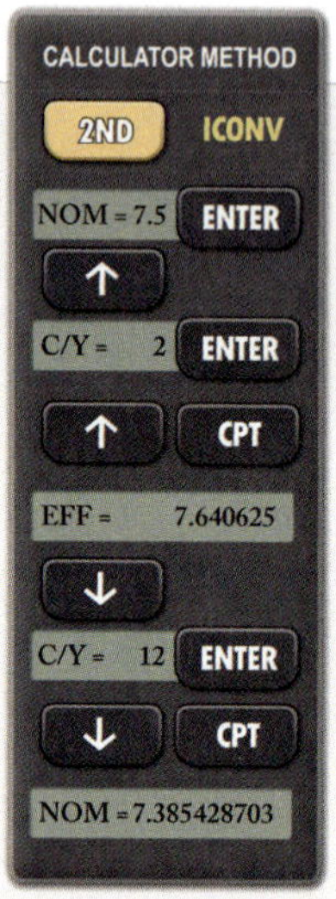

Solution

We can solve this using two different methods:

Method 1: Using an equivalent interest rate

7.5% compounded semi-annually

$j_1 = 0.075, m_1 = 2, i_1 = \frac{j_1}{m_1} = 0.0375$

? % compounded monthly

$j_2 = ?, m_2 = 12, i_2 = ?$

Use the formula: $i_2 = (1 + i_1)^{m_1/m_2} - 1$

$$i_2 = (1 + 0.0375)^{2/12} - 1 = 0.006154...$$

$$j_2 = m_2 \times i_2 = 12 \times 0.006154... = 0.073854... = 7.39\%$$

Therefore, 7.5% compounded semi-annually is equivalent to 7.39% compounded monthly.

Method 2: Assuming values for '*PV*' and '*t*'

In this method, we assume $PV = \$1000$ and $t = 1$ year. We calculate 'FV' using the provided interest rate and then use this calculated 'FV' value to find the interest for the second case.

$$PV = \$1000,\ t = 1,\ j = 7.5\%, \text{ and } m = 2,$$

$$i = \frac{j}{m} = \frac{0.075}{2} = 0.0375 \text{ and } n = m \times t = 2 \times 1 = 2$$

$$FV = PV(1 + i)^n = 1000(1 + 0.0375)^2 = \$1076.40625$$

Using the value of 'FV', we can now find the value for 'i' by using the second value of 'm'.

In this case $n = m \times t = 12 \times 1 = 12$

$$i = \left(\frac{FV}{PV}\right)^{\frac{1}{n}} - 1$$

$$i = \left(\frac{1076.40625}{1000}\right)^{\frac{1}{12}} - 1 = 0.615452...\%$$

$$j_2 = m \times i = 12 \times 0.615452...\% = 7.385428...\%$$

Therefore, 7.5% compounded semi-annually is equivalent to 7.39% compounded monthly.

Note: *The calculator method of solving this problem has been omitted in Method 2 and may be worked out as practice.*

Example 6

A bank in Toronto offers John a loan at 8% compounded semi-annually. A bank in Montreal offers a similar loan for 4 years, but at a rate of 8.20% compounded annually. Which loan will be economically better for him.

Solution

Method 1: Using effective interest rates

Find the effective interest rate that is equivalent to the Toronto bank's offer of 8% compounded semi-annually.

Toronto bank:

$j = 0.08, m = 2, i = \frac{j}{m} = 0.04$

$f = (1 + i)^m - 1 = (1.04)^2 - 1 = 0.0816 = 8.16\%$

8.00% compounded semi-annually is equivalent to 8.16% compounded annually.

Solution ***continued***

The Montreal bank offers 8.20% compounded annually. This is the effective rate. As John is taking a loan, he should be looking for the lowest interest rate. The Toronto bank is offering a lower interest rate of 8.16% compounded annually. Therefore, John should accept the loan offered by the Toronto bank.

Method 2: Using a financial calculator

Follow these steps in your calculator to find the effective interest rate compounded semi-annually that is equivalent to the Toronto bank's offer of 8% compounded semi-annually.

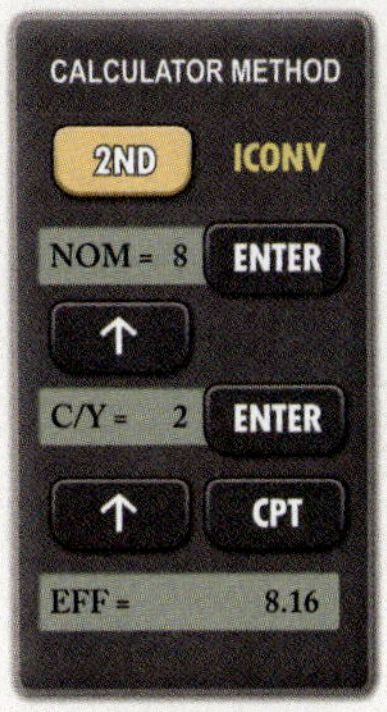

As John is taking a loan, he should be looking for the lowest interest rate. The Montreal bank is offering a rate of 8.2% compounded annually, whereas the Toronto bank is offering a lower interest rate of 8.16% compounded annually. Therefore, John should accept the loan offered by the Toronto bank.

Method 3: Using equivalent interest rates

Find the nominal interest rate compounded semi-annually that is equivalent to the Montreal bank's offer of 8.20% compounded annually.

Montreal bank:

$$j_1 = 8.20\%,\ m_1 = 1,\ i_1 = \frac{j}{m} = \frac{8.20\%}{1} = 8.20\%$$

? % compounded semi-annually

$$i_2 = (1 + i_1)^{m_1/m_2} - 1 = (1.082)^{1/2} - 1 = 0.040192...$$

$$j_2 = i_2 \times 2 = 0.080384... = 8.04\%$$

Therefore, 8.20% compounded annually is equivalent to 8.04% compounded semi-annually.

As John is taking a loan, he should be looking for the lowest interest rate. The Toronto bank is offering a lower interest rate of 8% compounded semi-annually. Therefore, John should accept the loan offered by the Toronto bank.

Method 4: Using the Future Value

Assume: $PV = \$1000$, $t = 1$ year

Toronto bank: 8.00% compounded semi-annually

$$j = 8.00\%,\ m = 2,\ i = \frac{j}{m} = 4\% = 0.04,\ n = m \times t = 2$$

$$FV = PV(1 + i)^n = 1000(1.04)^2 = \$1081.60$$

Montreal bank: 8.20% compounded annually

$$j = 8.20\%,\ m = 1,\ i = \frac{j}{m} = 8.20\% = 0.082,\ n = m \times t = 1$$

$$FV = PV(1 + i)^n = 1000(1.082)^1 = \$1082.00$$

As John is taking a loan, he should be looking for the rate which results in the lowest accumulated value (i.e., 'FV') at the end of the time period. The Toronto bank's rate results in a lower accumulated value. Therefore, John should accept the loan offered by the Toronto bank.

Note: The calculator method of solving this problem has been omitted in Methods 1 and 4 and may be worked out as practice.

9 | Review Exercises

Answers to odd-numbered problems are available at the end of the textbook

1. $200,000 was deposited in a Swiss savings bank account by a large software company for 10 years and 6 months at 8% compounded quarterly. Calculate the accumulated value of the investment at the end of the period and the interest earned during the period.

2. Micropore LLP, a small law firm, borrowed $280,000 for 3 years and 2 months at 12% compounded semi-annually from a credit union. Calculate the amount the law firm would have to repay at the end of the period. What is the amount of interest charged on the loan?

3. Romba, a smart money lender, offers personal loans at an interest rate of 8.16% compounded annually for the first year and 8% compounded semi-annually thereafter. How much money did she lend Martha 3 years ago, if Martha owes her $45,450 today?

4. Westin Lord Braking Company invested $150,650 in a fund at an interest rate of 11% compounded monthly. At the end of 5 months, the company's investment advisor transferred these funds to another investment that was yielding 13% compounded monthly. Calculate the amount by which the fund grew at the end of 15 months from the initial investment.

5. How much more would an investment of $5000 be worth after 5 years if it was earning 10% compounded semi-annually instead of 10% compounded annually?

6. How much more would a loan of $11,860.50 accumulate to in 2 years if the interest rate charged was 4% compounded monthly instead of 4% compounded annually?

7. Determine the discounted value of an investment with a maturity value of $12,000, if it is discounted 5 years before maturity at 8% compounded quarterly. Also calculate the compound discount (amount by which the money is discounted).

8. Calculate the amount by which the money is discounted (compound discount) and the discounted value (present value) of an investment that has a maturity value of $22,450 and is discounted 2 years before maturity at 4% compounded monthly.

9. What single payment today would replace a payment stream of $50,000 due today, $60,000 due in 1 year, and $80,000 due in 2 years if money earns 8% compounded semi-annually?

10. Amanda won a lottery that would pay her $5000 in a year and $10,000 in two years. If the lottery company had another option where she could get an upfront amount now and another $7000 in one year, calculate the upfront amount that she would receive now from the second option, assuming that money is worth 2% compounded semi-annually.

11. What monthly compounding nominal interest rate is earned on an investment that doubles in 8 years? What semi-annual compounding nominal interest rate will give the same benefit?

12. What monthly compounding nominal interest rate is earned on an investment that triples in 2 years? What quarterly compounding nominal interest rate will result in the same benefit?

13. After 10 years of semi-annual compounding, an $8000 investment in a GIC earns $3000 in interest. What are the periodic and nominal interest rates?

14. If Jane wants to earn interest of $5000 on her $20,000 savings in 2 years, at what nominal interest rate compounded semi-annually do you suggest she invest her money?

15. The maturity value of the GIC you bought for $10,000 at 7.2% compounded quarterly is $21,000. Calculate the term of the GIC.

16. Calculate the time period of an investment in a mutual fund that matured to $43,676.25 yielding an interest of $13,676.25 at 8% compounded monthly.

17. Zack shopped around for a good interest rate to invest the prize amount that he received from an inter-college tennis competition. He narrowed down his search to two banks: one was offering him 6% compounded semi-annually and the other 6.09% compounded annually. Which bank should he choose to save his prize money and why?

18. Which of the following interest rates would have a higher effective interest rate: 6.00% compounded quarterly or 6.09% compounded semi-annually?

• 19. A mortgage has a nominal interest rate of 2.65% compounded semi-annually. If the bank that issued the mortgage increases the effective interest rate by 1.5%, calculate the new mortgage rate compounded semi-annually.

• 20. Henrietta went to a bank and obtained a personal loan with an interest rate of 3.18% compounded monthly. If the effective interest rate on the loan were to decrease by 1%, calculate the new nominal rate compounded monthly.

21. What nominal interest rate compounded quarterly would place investors in exactly the same financial position as 6.55% compounded annually?

22. What nominal interest rate compounded monthly would place investors in exactly the same financial position as 8% compounded annually?

9 | Self-Test Exercises

Answers to all problems are available at the end of the textbook

1. A small telecommunications company invested its 2010 net income of $580,900 in a savings account for 2 years and 4 months. Calculate the amount it would have in this account at the end of the period and the interest earned if money was earning interest at a rate of 6.25% compounded quarterly.

2. Peter borrowed $28,000 from a local bank at 5% compounded semi-annually to start an organic cafeteria on a university campus. After 2 years, the interest rate on the debt changed to 5% compounded quarterly. What would be the accumulated amount of the debt in 4 years?

3. Rodney opened an RRSP account and deposited $1500 into it. He then deposited $500 and $600 at the end of the 1st and 2nd years,respectively, into the account.. If the RRSP was earning 4% compounded quarterly, calculate the accumulated value of his investments at the end of 4 years from the initial deposit.

4. The maturity value of a savings account that belonged to Paulo Window Manufacturing Ltd. was $30,223.50. If the money it deposited earned 6% compounded semi-annually for the first 3 years and 4% compounded quarterly for the next 2 years, calculate the amount it deposited in this savings account.

5. What would the total savings be if a loan that accumulates to $12,000 in 4 years was issued at 4% compounding semi-annually instead of 4.04% compounded annually?

6. You wish to accumulate $12,000 in four years. How much should you deposit if your investment accumulates interest at a rate of 4% compounded semi-annually?

• 7. Two payments of $10,000 and $5000 are due in 1 year and 2 years, respectively. Calculate the two equal payments that would replace these payments in 6 months and 3 years if money is worth 8% compounded quarterly.

8. If $18,850 is the interest earned on lending $82,400 for 3 years, calculate the nominal interest rate if the compounding frequency is monthly.

9. If Gaya invested $18,000 in an RRSP on her 21st birthday, how long would it take for the RRSP to earn interest of $10,000 if it is growing at 8% compounded quarterly?

10. If the Government invested $1,455,680 for 10 years in international bonds, what was the effective rate of interest earned on the investment if the amount matured to $2,120,235.50?

11. Roxy took a loan of $100,000 $4\frac{1}{2}$ years ago. The interest rate on the loan was 4% compounded semi-annually for the first 6 months, 6% compounded semi-annually for the next $1\frac{1}{2}$ years, and 8% compounded semi-annually thereafter. Calculate the accumulated value of the loan today.

CASE 9a

Investing for the Future

Martin, a 45-year-old shoe sales man, decided that it was time he started saving for retirement. He had money in his checking account that was earning 1% compounded annually, and he decided to transfer this amount into an RRSP that invested in the bond market. The manager at his local bank assured him that the RRSP he chose would generate returns of 8% compounded quarterly. Martin learned mathematics of finance during his college days to be a well-informed investor and knew the right questions to ask the bank manager. What answers would the bank manager provide Martin for the following questions?

a. How long will it take for an investment to double while earning interest at the offered rate of 8%?

b. If the offered rate was compounded daily instead of quarterly, how long would it take for an investment to double?

c. Martin wanted to triple his original investment in the RRSP before his retirement in 15 years. Is this achievable at the offered rate? Support your answer with an example.

d. At what rate compounded monthly would his investment triple in 15 years?

e. What is the effective rate of the monthly compounded rate calculated in part (d)?

f. He wanted to know if investing his money at 8% compounded monthly or at 8% compounded semi-annually would give him a higher accumulated value than the offered rate at the end of the same time period. Provide a suitable example with calculations to demonstrate the manager's approach to answering his question.

g. If he wants to withdraw an amount equal to 50% of the original amount invested at the end of 5 years and another amount equal to 50% of the original amount invested at the end of 10 years, what percentage of his original investment would be available for withdrawal at the end of 15 years?

h. If he would like to make a deposit equal to 25% of the original investment in 5 years and another deposit equal to 75% of the original investment in 10 years, what percentage of his original investment would be available for withdrawal at the end of 15 years?

CASE 9b

Borrowing to Start a Business

Susan, a budding entrepreneur, was excited that her presentation at her college annual entrepreneurial competition was voted the best by every judge. An angel investor in the audience was very impressed by her business plan and offered to help her start her designer clothing store by offering her a loan at 6% compounded semi-annually.

After 2 years, her business had savings of $80,654 and she used the entire amount to completely pay off her outstanding debt with the investor.

a. What was the loan amount given to her by the angel investor and what was the accumulated interest over the two-year period?

b. What rate, compounded monthly, would have resulted in the same accumulated debt?

c. How long would it take for her debt to reach $100,000 if she does not repay any amount throughout the term? Assume the same interest rate of 6% compounded semi-annually throughout this extended period.

d. If she had taken the same loan amount from a local bank, it would have accumulated to $80,654 in 18 months instead of 2 years. What is the interest rate compounded semi-annually charged by the local bank?

e. What would her savings be if the loan had been issued to her at an annually compounding frequency?

f. If her contract with the investor required that she settle all dues in 2 years, how much could she have borrowed initially if she was sure that she could repay $25,000 in 1 year and $40,000 at the end of 2 years?

g. What was the loan amount given to her by the investor if she was charged 6% compounded semi-annually for the first year, and 8% compounded quarterly for the second year and it accumulated to $80,654 in two years?

9 | Summary of Notation and Formulas

NOTATION

FV = Future value (maturity value or accumulated value) of a loan or investment

PV = Present value (discounted value or principal amount) of a loan or investment

I = Amount of compound interest of a loan or investment

j = Nominal (stated or quoted) annual interest rate

i = Periodic rate of interest (interest rate per compounding period)

m = Number of compounding periods per year (compounding frequency)

n = Number of compounding periods during the term

t = Time period or term in years

f = Effective interest rate (annually compounding rate)

FORMULAS

Future Value | 9.1 (a)

$$FV = PV(1 + i)^n$$

Present Value | 9.1 (b)

$$PV = \frac{FV}{(1+i)^n} \quad \text{or} \quad PV = FV(1 + i)^{-n}$$

Amount of compound interest | 9.1 (c)

$$I = FV - PV$$

Periodic interest rate | 9.1 (d)

$$i = \frac{j}{m}$$

Number of compounding periods | 9.1 (e)

$$n = m \times t$$

Periodic interest rate | 9.5 (a)

$$i = \left(\frac{FV}{PV}\right)^{\frac{1}{n}} - 1$$

Nominal interest rate | 9.5 (b)

$$j = m \times i$$

Number of compounding periods | 9.6 (a)

$$n = \frac{\ln\left(\frac{FV}{PV}\right)}{\ln(1+i)}$$

Time period in years | 9.6 (b)

$$t = \frac{n}{m}$$

Effective interest rate | 9.7

$$f = (1 + i)^m - 1$$

Equivalent periodic interest rate | 9.8 (a)

$$i_2 = (1 + i_1)^{m_1/m_2} - 1$$

Equivalent nominal interest rate | 9.8 (b)

$$j_2 = m_2 \times i_2$$

Many financial transactions involve investing or borrowing fixed amounts of money at regular intervals for a fixed period of time. Some examples from our day-to-day lives include regular contributions to an RRSP, RESP, or an investment fund, or making mortgage payments, insurance payments, or repayments to student loans. Businesses and governments also save for future expansion projects by making regular deposits into investment funds. These regular payments and investments are called annuities and in this chapter, you will learn about different types of annuities and their related calculations.

10 Annuities

LEARNING OBJECTIVES

- Identify annuities based on a payment date and compounding period.
- Calculate the future value and present value of ordinary simple annuities.
- Calculate the future value and present value of ordinary general annuities.
- Calculate the future value and present value of simple annuities due and general annuities due.
- Calculate the amount of the periodic payments (PMT), the number of payments (n), term (t), periodic interest rate (i), and nominal interest rate (j) of an annuity.

CHAPTER OUTLINE

10.1 | Introduction

An annuity is a **series of payments** (usually in equal amounts) made at **regular intervals** for a **fixed period of time**.

Consider an example where Melanie made regular deposits of $100 at the end of every month for the past 2 years at an interest rate of 6% compounded monthly. This series of equal deposits that she made at regular intervals for a fixed period of time is called an annuity.

Annuities are series of payments made at regular intervals for a period of time.

The timeline diagram below illustrates this annuity:

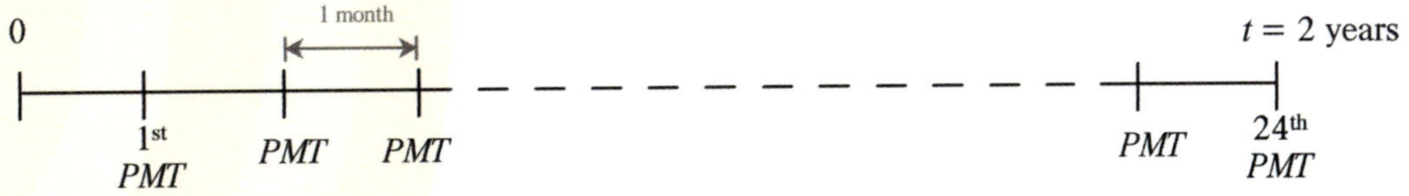

Periodic Payment (PMT) = $100

Notation

t = **term of an annuity**: time from the first payment interval to the end of the last payment interval.

PMT = amount of the periodic payment of an annuity

n = **total** number of payments during the term of an annuity
= number of payments per year × time period in years

j = nominal interest rate

m = compounding frequency (number of compounding periods per year)

i = periodic interest rate (interest rate per compounding period)

Payment interval (or payment period) = time between two successive payments

FV = accumulated value or future value of an annuity. It is the equivalent value of the series of payments at the **end of the term.**

PV = discounted value or present value of an annuity. It is the equivalent value of the series of payments **at the beginning of the term.**

Table 10.1: Number of Payments per Year for Different Payment Intervals

Payment Interval	Number of payments per year
Daily (every day)	365
Monthly (every month)	12
Quarterly (every 3 months)	4
Semi-annually (every 6 months)	2
Annually (every year)	1

In the above example,

Term = 2 years, Payment interval = 1 month

$PMT = \$100.00$

$n = 12$ payments per year × 2 years
= 24 monthly payments

$j = 0.06$

$m = 12$ compoundings per year

$$i = \frac{0.06}{12} = 0.005 \text{ per month}$$

Example 10.1(a) **Calculating the Number of Payments During the Term of an Annuity**

Calculate the number of payments during the term for the following annuities:

(i) The deposit of $500 at the end of every 3 months for 7 years.

(ii) The deposit of $700 at the end of every 6 months for 3 years and 6 months.

(iii) You receive $100 at the end of every month for the first 5 years and thereafter, $150 at the end of every month for the next 2 years.

Solution

(i) The payment interval is 3 months. In one year, you would have to make $\frac{12}{3} = 4$ payments.

Therefore, n, the number of payments in 7 years = $4 \times 7 = 28$ payments.

(ii) The payment interval is 6 months. In one year, you would have to make $\frac{12}{6} = 2$ payments.

Therefore, n, the number of payments in 3 years and 6 months = $2 \times 3.5 = 7$ payments.

(iii) The entire set of payments for the 7-year period is not one annuity. The periodic payment amount of \$100 for the first 5 years forms one annuity with 60 payments and the periodic payment amount of \$150 for the next 2 years forms another annuity with 24 payments, as shown in the timeline below:

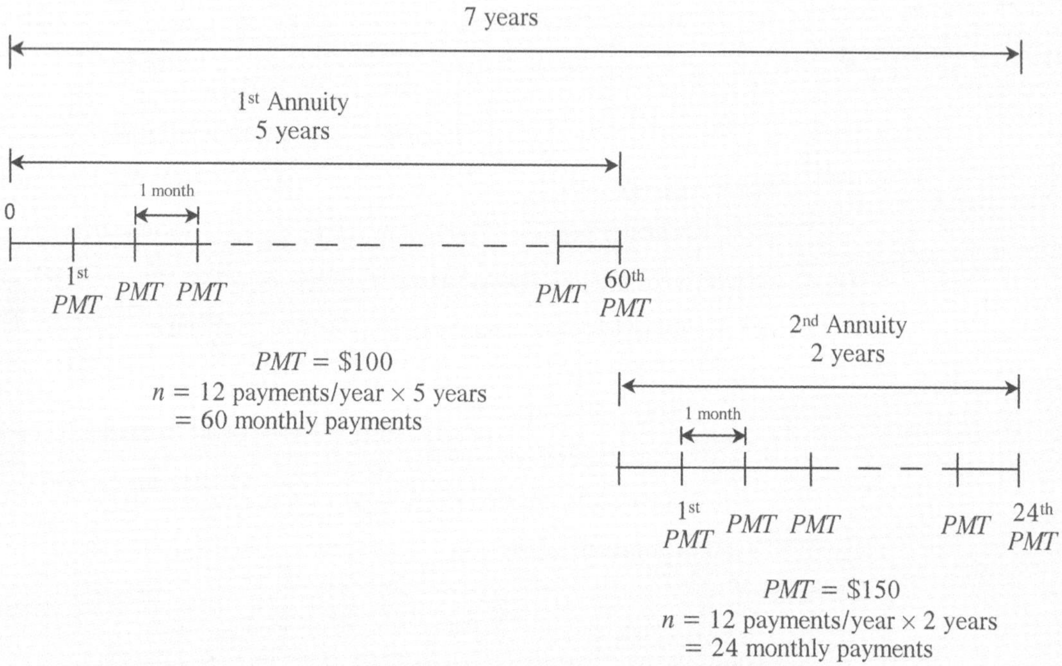

Types of Annuities Based on Payment Dates

When the payments are made at the **end of each payment period**, the annuity is referred to as an **ordinary annuity**.

When the payments are made at the **beginning of each payment period**, the annuity is referred to as an **annuity due**.

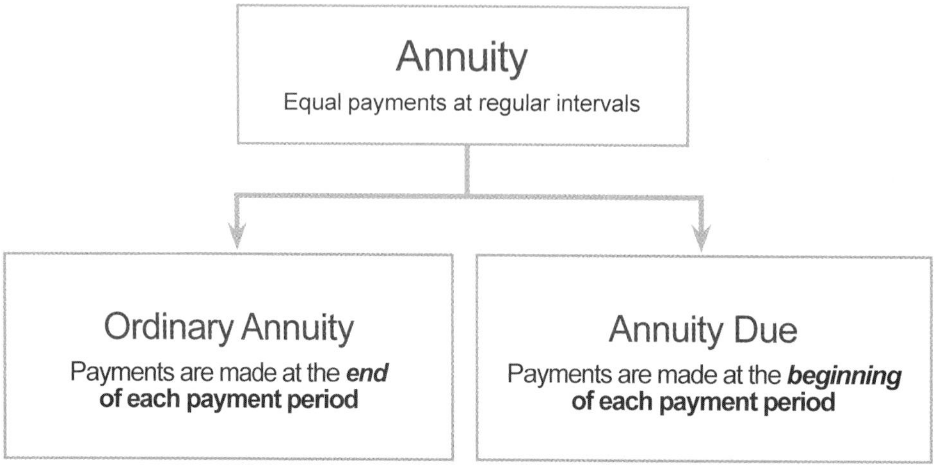

Exhibit 10.1(a): Types of Annuities Based on Payment Dates

Example 10.1(b)

Identifying the Types of Annuities Based on Payment Dates

Maggie is required to pay auto insurance of $150 at the end of every month for one year. She is also required to pay rent of $500 at the beginning of every month for one year for her property. Identify the type of each of the annuity payments.

Solution

Both these payments are annuities of different types.

The insurance payments of $150 are payable at the **end** of every month. Therefore, these payments form an **ordinary annuity**.

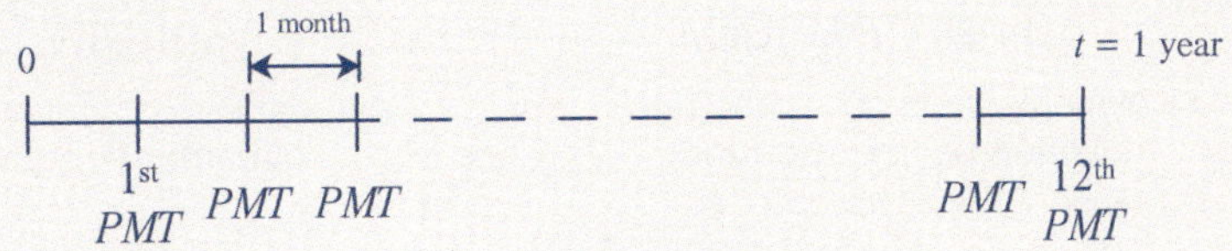

$$PMT = \$150$$
$$n = 12 \text{ payments/year} \times 1 \text{ year}$$
$$= 12 \text{ monthly payments}$$

The rent payments of $500 are payable at the **beginning** of every month. Therefore, these payments form an **annuity due**.

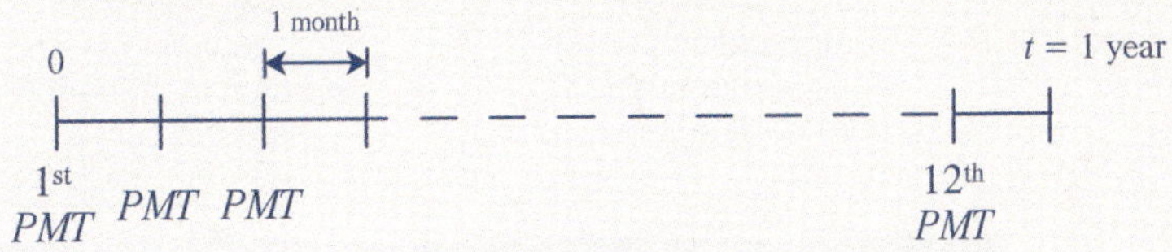

$$PMT = \$500$$
$$n = 12 \text{ payments/year} \times 1 \text{ year}$$
$$= 12 \text{ monthly payments}$$

Types of Annuities Based on Compounding Periods

When the **payment period** (or payment interval) and the interest **compounding period** (or compounding frequency) are the **same** (or equal), then the annuity is referred to as a **simple annuity**.

> In an annuity, if the compounding period is equal to the payment period then it is a simple annuity, otherwise, it is a general annuity.

When the **payment period** (or payment interval) and the interest **compounding period** (or compounding frequency) are **not the same** (or not equal), then the annuity is referred to as a **general annuity**.

This applies to both ordinary annuities and annuities due:

In an **ordinary annuity** (when the payments are made at the end of each payment period):

- If the compounding period and the payment period are the same, then it is called an **ordinary simple annuity**.
- If the compounding period and the payment period are **not** the same, then it is called an **ordinary general annuity**.

In an **annuity due** (when the payments are made at the beginning of each payment period):

- If the compounding period and the payment period are the same, then it is called a **simple annuity due**.
- If the compounding period and the payment period are **not** the same, then it is called a **general annuity due**.

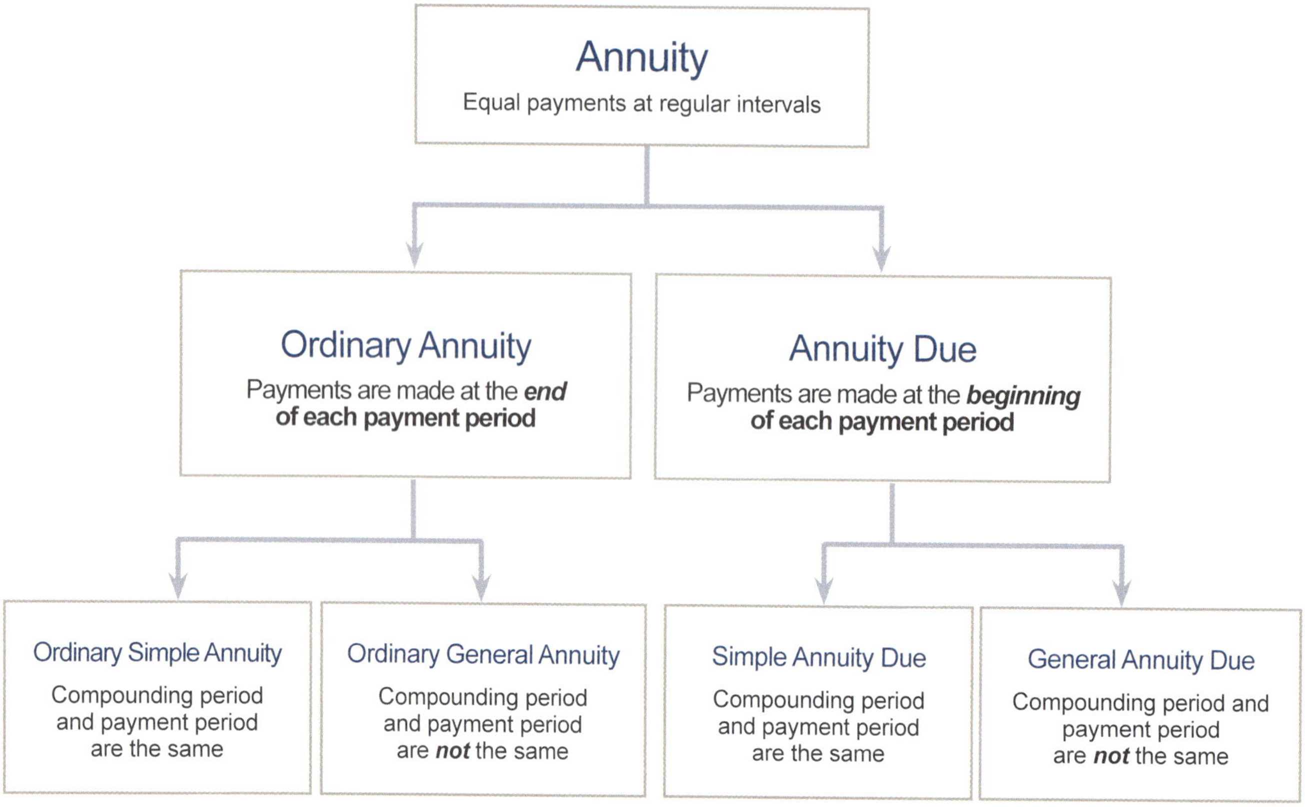

Exhibit 10.1(b): Types of Annuities Based on Compounding Periods

Example 10.1(c)

Identifying Types of Annuities Based on Payment Dates and Compounding Periods

Identify the following types of annuities:

(i) Payments of \$500 at the end of every month for 10 years at 9% compounded monthly.

(ii) Payments of \$500 at the end of every month for 10 years at 9% compounded quarterly.

(iii) Payments of \$500 at the beginning of every month for 10 years at 9% compounded monthly.

(iv) Payments of \$500 at the beginning of every month for 10 years at 9% compounded quarterly.

Solution

(i) Payments of \$500 at the end of every month for 10 years at 9% compounded monthly.

- Payments are made at the **end** of every month
- Compounding period (monthly) = payment period (monthly)

Therefore, this is an ordinary simple annuity.

(ii) Payments of \$500 at the end of every month for 10 years at 9% compounded quarterly.

- Payments are made at the **end** of every month
- Compounding period (quarterly) ≠ payment period (monthly)

Therefore, this is an ordinary general annuity.

(iii) Payments of \$500 at the beginning of every month for 10 years at 9% compounded monthly.

- Payments are made at the **beginning** of every month
- Compounding period (monthly) = payment period (monthly)

Therefore, this is a simple annuity due.

Solution continued

(iv) Payments of $500 at the beginning of every month for 10 years at 9% compounded quarterly.

- Payments are made at the **beginning** of every month
- Compounding period (quarterly) ≠ Payment period (monthly)

Therefore, this is a general annuity due.

Example 10.1(d)

Identifying Types of Annuities with Change in Compounding Periods of Interest

An investor deposited $400 into an investment at the end of every month for 6 years. The interest rate for the first 4 years was at 6% compounded monthly and thereafter was at 6% compounded quarterly. Identify the type of annuity in this scenario.

Solution

This forms two different annuities.

- 1st annuity for 4 years with month-end payments (PMT = $400)
  - Payment period (monthly) = compounding period (monthly)

  Therefore, it is an ordinary simple annuity
- 2nd annuity for 4 years with month-end payments (PMT = $400)
  - Payment period (monthly) ≠ compounding period (quarterly)

  Therefore, it is an ordinary general annuity

When the payment amount, interest rate, payment period, or compounding period changes, a new annuity is formed.

10.1 | Exercises

Identify the type of annuity and calculate the number of payments during the term in the following problems:

1. Ronda pays $1000 at the end of every three months for 5 years and 9 months towards her student loan at 4% compounded quarterly.
2. Isabella receives $5000 at the end of every six months for 10 years and 6 months for money that she loaned to a friend at 7.50% compounded semi-annually.
3. Mike receives $1500 at the end of every month for 15 years from a retirement fund at 4% compounded every 6 months.
4. Afsoon pays $800 at the end of every month for 20 years towards a retirement fund at 2.5% compounded every 6 months.
5. Mary pays $1800 for a loan at the beginning of every 3 months for 2 years at 7% compounded quarterly.
6. Michael pays $246.50 for a car lease at the beginning of every month for 4 years at 0.90% compounded monthly.
7. Merlin pays $280 for a lease at the beginning of every month for 3 years and 5 months at 7% compounded annually.
8. Anming receives $2400 from an investment at the beginning of every month for 5 years and 11 months at 5% compounded semi-annually.
9. Armas receives $280 at the beginning of every month for 6 years at 7% compounded annually and thereafter receives $580 at the end of every month for another 2 years at 7.25% compounded semi-annually.
10. Eva pays $1200 at the end of every quarter for 2 years at 2% compounded annually and thereafter receives $1120 at the beginning of every month for another 1 year at 1.25% compounded semi-annually.

10.2 | Future Value and Present Value of an Ordinary Simple Annuity

In an ordinary simple annuity, payments are made at the end of each payment period and the compounding period is equal to the payment period. In this section, you will learn how to calculate the future value and present value of an ordinary simple annuity.

Future Value of an Ordinary Simple Annuity

Consider an example where Abriella decides to invest $1000 at the end of every year for 5 years in a savings account that earns an interest rate of 10% compounded annually. She wants to find out how much she would have at the end of the 5-year period. In other words, she wants to find out the future value of her investments at the end of 5 years.

To calculate the future value of her investments at the end of 5 years, we could calculate the future value of each of her investments using the compound interest formula and then add all the future values.

From the compound interest Formula 9.1(a), we know that the future value of each payment is

$$FV = PV(1 + i)^n$$

where, FV = future value,

PV = present value,

i = interest rate for the compounding period (periodic interest rate), and

n = total number of compounding periods for each payment.

In this example:

In compound interest, '*n*' is the number of compounding periods during the term.

- '*PV*' for each payment is $1000
- '*i*' for each payment is $i = \frac{j}{m} = \frac{0.10}{1} = 0.10$ per annum
- '*n*' for each payment is not the same. '*n*' for each payment starting from the 1st payment is 4, 3, 2, 1, and 0.

The future value of an annuity is the sum of the accumulated value of each periodic payment.

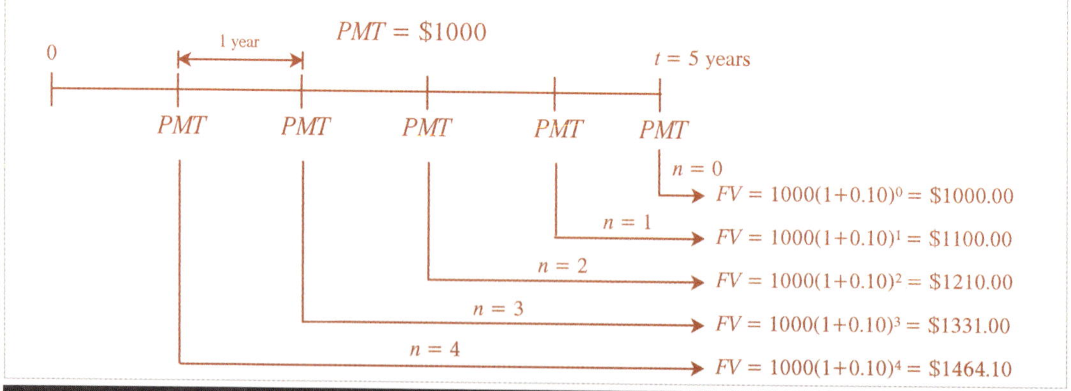

Exhibit 10.2(a): Future Value of Ordinary Simple Annuity Payments

Individual future values calculated are in geometric series with '*n*' terms, where the 1st term is *PMT* and the common ratio is (1+*i*). By applying the formula for the sum of a geometric series you will get the simplified '*FV*' Formula 10.2 (a).

Sum of the future values of her investment = 1464.10 + 1331.00 + 1210.00 +1100.00 + 1000.00

= $6105.10

Therefore, if she invests $1000 every year for five years at 10% compounded annually in a savings account, she would have a total of $6105.10 at the end of five years.

Now, if there were many payments for an annuity (e.g., she invested the same amount for 15 years, compounded annually), the above method would become too time-consuming.

A simplified formula to calculate the future value of an ordinary simple annuity is given by:

Formula 10.2(a)

Future Value of an Ordinary Simple Annuity

$$FV = PMT\left[\frac{(1+i)^n - 1}{i}\right]$$

where 'n' is the number of payments during the term, 'PMT' is the amount of the periodic payment, and 'i' is the periodic interest rate.

Calculating the future value of her investment at the end of five years using this simplified formula,

In an annuity, '*n*' is the number of payments during the term.

$$n = 1 \text{ payments/year} \times 5 \text{ years} = 5 \text{ annual payments}$$

$$i = \frac{j}{m} = \frac{0.10}{1} = 0.10$$

$$PMT = \$1000$$

$$FV = PMT\left[\frac{(1+i)^n - 1}{i}\right]$$

$$= 1000\left[\frac{(1+0.10)^5 - 1}{0.10}\right]$$

$$= 1000\,[6.1051]$$

$$= \$6105.10$$

Therefore, the future value of the investment is $6105.10.

In the calculation of the future value of annuities, the amount of interest is calculated as follows:

Amount of Interest Earned = Future Value of the Investments − Amount Invested Over the Term

$$I = FV - n(PMT)$$

In this example,

$$I = 6105.10 - 5(1000.00)$$

$$= 6105.10 - 5000.00$$

$$= \$1105.10$$

Therefore, she would earn $1105.10 from this investment.

Example 10.2(a)

Calculating the Future Value, Total Investment, and Interest Earned in an Ordinary Simple Annuity

Ruth would like to invest $200 at the end of every month for 20 years in an RRSP. Assuming that the interest rate is constant at 6% compounded monthly over the 20-year period, calculate the following:

(i) The accumulated value of her investment.

(ii) Her total investment over the term.

(iii) The interest she would earn from this investment.

Solution

(i) This is an ordinary simple annuity as:

- Payments are made at the end of each payment period (monthly)
- Compounding period (monthly) = payment period (monthly)

Solution continued

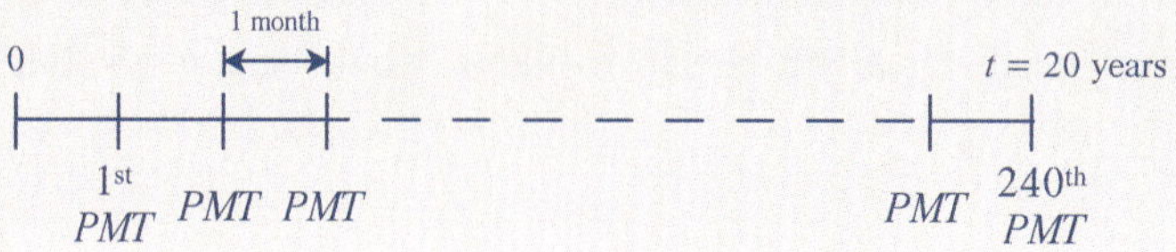

$$PMT = \$200$$

$$n = 12 \text{ payments/year} \times 20 \text{ years}$$
$$= 240 \text{ monthly payments}$$

$$j = 0.06, \quad m = 12, \quad i = \frac{j}{m} = 0.005 \text{ per month}$$

Using Formula 10.2(a),

$$FV = PMT\left[\frac{(1+i)^n - 1}{i}\right]$$

$$= 200\left[\frac{(1+0.005)^{240} - 1}{0.005}\right]$$

$$= 200\,[462.040895...] = \$92{,}408.17903...$$

Therefore, the accumulated value of her investment at the end of 20 years would be \$92,408.18.

(ii) *Total Investment* = 200 per month × 240 payments = \$48,000.00.

Therefore, her total investment over the term would be \$48,000.00.

(iii) *Interest Earned* = \$92,408.18 − \$48,000.00 = \$44,408.18

Therefore, the interest she would earn is \$44,408.18.

Using the Financial Calculator to Solve Problems

Before you start solving problems, check and set the following in the Texas Instruments BA II Plus financial calculator:

1. Set the number of decimals to 9. (You need to set this only when you start using the calculator.)

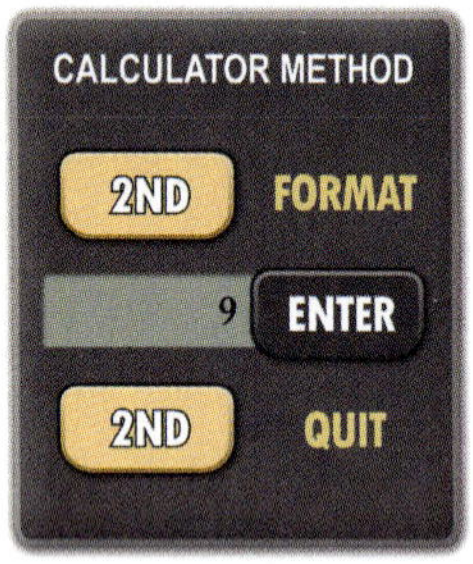

1. Press **2ND** then press **FORMAT** (this is the secondary function of the decimal key).
2. Enter **9** then press **ENTER** to set the number of decimals to 9
3. Press **2ND** then **QUIT** (this is the secondary key above CPT)

2. Check the settings for end-of-period (ordinary annuity) or beginning-of-period (annuity due) calculations. (You need to check this before you work out problems.)

1. Pressing **2ND** then **BGN** (secondary function above **PMT**) will display the current setting - either **END** or **BGN**. (Select END for ordinary annuity problems and BGN for annuity due problems.)
2. **END** would mean end-of-period setting (for an ordinary annuity). To change this setting to beginning-of-period setting (for annuity-due), press **2ND** then **SET** (secondary function above **ENTER**). You can switch between **END** and **BGN** by pressing **2ND** then **SET** again.
3. If **BGN** setting is selected, a small **BGN** appears at the top-right corner of your screen and will remain there throughout your calculations. However, if **END** is selected, nothing will appear.
4. Once you select your setting, press **2ND** then **QUIT** (secondary function above **CPT**) and return to your calculation.

Solving Example 10.2(a)(i) using the Texas Instruments BA II Plus calculator, to find 'FV'

Where, $n = 240$, I/Y = 6, P/Y = 12, C/Y = 12, $PMT = \$200$

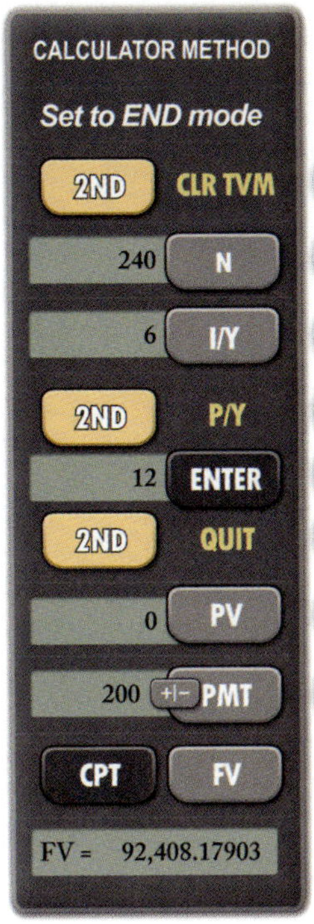

1. **Clear past values in the memory** of the function keys.
2. ***Number of payments*** (n).
3. ***Nominal interest rate per year*** (j).
4. This **opens** the **P/Y, C/Y worksheet** to set values.
5. Set ***payments per year*** (P/Y) equal to compounding periods per year (**C/Y**) as 12. You can scroll down using the down arrow key to view **C/Y**, which will be automatically set to 12.
6. This **closes** the **P/Y, C/Y worksheet**.
7. In annuity problems, we will usually find either ***FV*** or **PV**. To avoid errors when you are finding ***FV*** set **PV** to '0' and vice versa.
8. ***Periodic payments*** can be cash inflows or outflows, so set the sign accordingly. In this problem, it is a cash outflow (money paid out for the investment), therefore, the periodic payment is negative.

Example 10.2(b)

Calculating the Future Value, Total Investment, and Interest Earned in an Ordinary Simple Annuity Combined with a Compound Interest Period

When the payment date of the investment is not stated, it is assumed to be at the end of the payment period.

Brad deposited \$1500 at the end of every 3 months into a savings account. His savings earned 6% compounded quarterly for a 4-year period. He then decided to let his savings grow for another 6 years without investing any more money into the account. At that time, the interest rate on the account increased to 9% compounded quarterly for 6 years. Calculate the accumulated amount of money in his account and the total interest he earned over the 10-year period.

Solution

This is an ordinary simple annuity as:

- Payments are assumed to be at the end of each payment period (quarterly)
- Compounding period (quarterly) = payment period (quarterly)

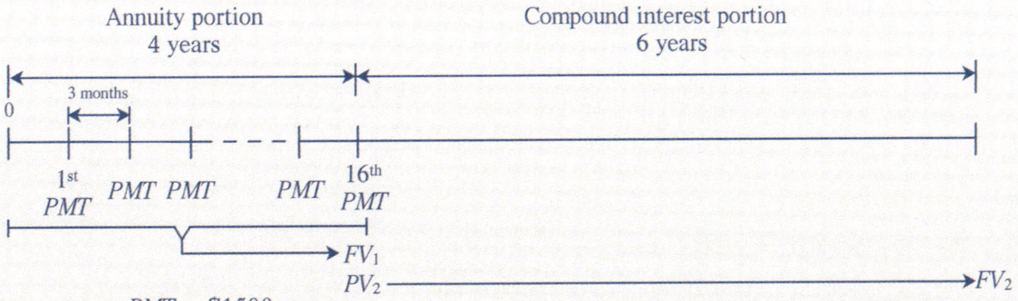

$PMT = \$1500$

$n = 4$ payments/year $\times$ 4 years $= 16$ quarterly payments

$j = 0.06, \quad m = 4, \quad i = \frac{j}{m} = 0.015$ per quarter

$n = m \times t = 4 \times 6 = 24$ compounding periods

$j = 0.09, \quad m = 4, \quad i = \frac{j}{m} = 0.0225$ per quarter

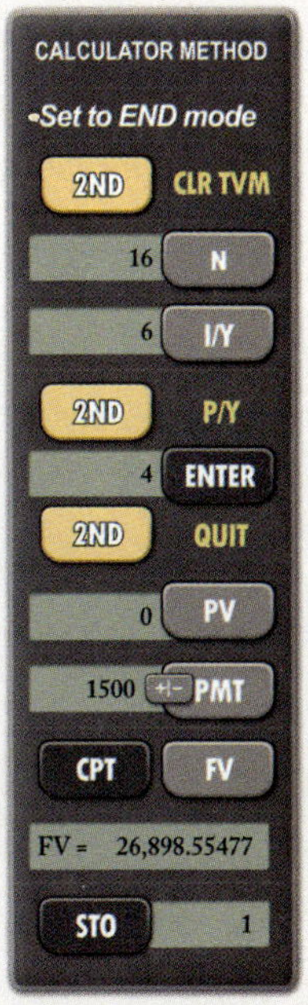

Solution continued

Using Formula 10.2(a),

$$FV = PMT\left[\frac{(1+i)^n - 1}{i}\right]$$

$$FV_1 = 1500\left[\frac{(1+0.015)^{16} - 1}{0.015}\right] = 1500[17.932369...]$$

$$= \$26,898.55477...$$

This 'FV_1' amount now becomes the present value for the compounding period. We now need to find the future value of this amount using the compound interest formula.

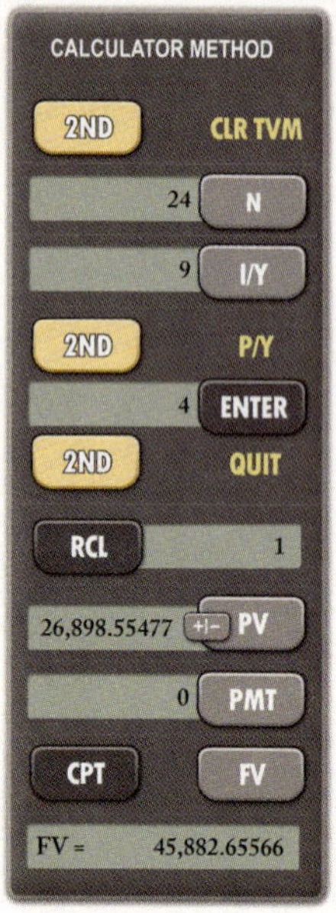

$$FV_2 = PV_2(1+i)^n$$

In an annuity, '*n*', is the number of payments during the term, but in compound interest, '*n*' is the number of compounding periods during the term.

Here, 'n', the number of compounding periods = $m \times t = 24$

$$FV_2 = 26,898.55477...(1 + 0.0225)^{24} = \$45,882.65566...$$

$$Total\ Investment = n(PMT)$$

$$= 16 \times 1500.00 = \$24,000.00$$

$$Interest\ earned\ over\ the\ entire\ period = FV - n(PMT)$$

$$= 45,882.65566... - 24,000.00$$

$$= \$21,882.65566...$$

Therefore, he has accumulated \$45,882.66 in his account and has earned \$21,882.66 in interest over the 10-year period.

Present Value of an Ordinary Simple Annuity

Consider an example where Margaret wishes to withdraw \$1000 at the end of every year for the next 5 years from an account that pays interest at 5% compounded annually. How much money should she deposit into this account now?

The present value of an annuity is the sum of the discounted values of each periodic payment.

To calculate the present value of all the payments at the beginning of the 5-year period, we can calculate the present value of each payment and then add all the present values using the compound interest formula as shown below:

As payments that she would be receiving in the future have to be discounted, the present value of each payment is given by the compound interest formula: $PV = \frac{FV}{(1+i)^n} = FV(1+i)^{-n}$

where 'n' is the number of compounding periods for each payment. 'n' for each payment starting from the 1st payment is 1,2,3,4, and 5.

Individual present values calculated are in geometric series with '*n*' terms, where the 1st term is '*PMT*' and the common ratio is $(1+i)^{-1}$. By applying the formula for the sum of a geometric series you will get the simplified '*PV*' Formula 10.2 (b).

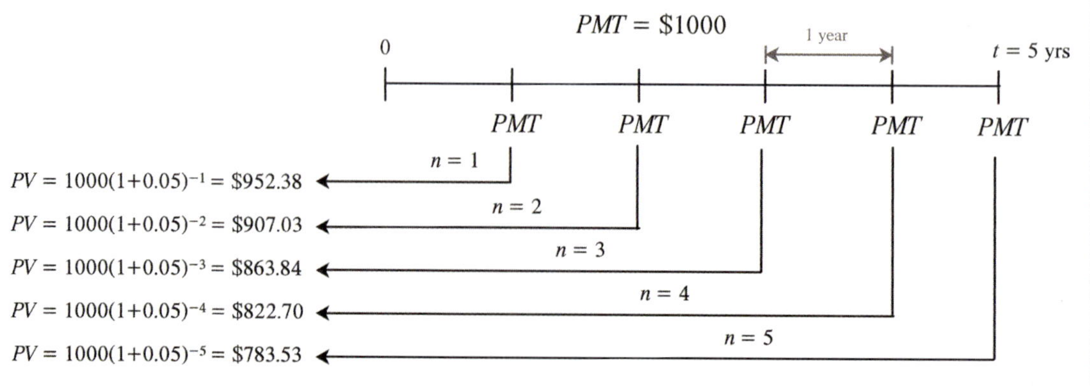

Exhibit 10.2(b): Present Value of Ordinary Simple Annuity Payments

$$\text{Sum of Present Values of her Investment} = 952.38 + 907.03 + 863.84 + 822.70 + 783.53$$
$$= \$4329.48.$$

Now, similar to the simplified formula used in *FV* calculations, the simplified *PV* formula is given by:

Formula 10.2(b)

Present Value of an Ordinary Simple Annuity

$$PV = PMT\left[\frac{1-(1+i)^{-n}}{i}\right]$$

where '*n*' is the number of payments during the term and '*PMT*' is the periodic payment.

Calculating the present value of her payments using this simplified formula:

$$PV = 1000\left[\frac{1-(1+0.05)^{-5}}{0.05}\right] = 1000[4.329476...]$$
$$= \$4329.476671$$

Therefore, she would have to deposit $4329.48 at the beginning of the 5-year period to be able to withdraw $1000 at the end of each year for 5 years.

In the calculation of the present value of an annuity, the amount of interest is calculated as follows:

$$\text{Amount of Interest Earned} = \text{Amount Received over the Term} - \text{Present Value}$$
$$I = n(PMT) - PV$$

In this example,

$$I = 5(1000.00) - 4329.48$$
$$= 5000.00 - 4329.48$$
$$= \$670.52$$

Therefore, she would earn interest of $670.52.

Example 10.2(c)

Calculating the Present Value and Interest Earned in an Ordinary Simple Annuity

Zack purchased an annuity that provided him with payments of $1000 every month for 25 years at 5.4% compounded monthly. How much did he pay for the annuity? Over the 25-year time period, what was the total amount he received from this annuity and how much of this amount was interest earned?

Solution

This is an ordinary simple annuity as:

- Payments are assumed to be made at the end of each payment period (monthly)
- Compounding period (monthly) = payment period (monthly)

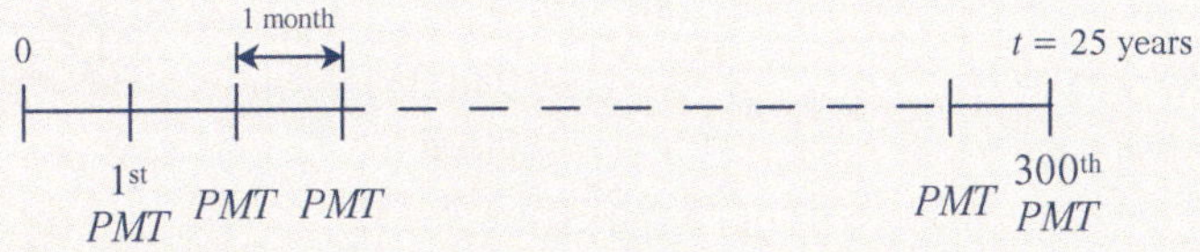

$$PMT = \$1000$$
$$n = 12 \text{ payments/year} \times 25 \text{ years}$$
$$= 300 \text{ monthly payments}$$
$$j = 0.054, \quad m = 12, \quad i = \frac{j}{m} = 0.0045 \text{ per month}$$

Solution continued

Using Formula 10.2(b),

$$PV = PMT\left[\frac{1-(1+i)^{-n}}{i}\right]$$

$$= 1000\left[\frac{1-(1+0.0045)^{-300}}{0.0045}\right]$$

$$= 1000\,[164.438546...]$$

$$= \$164{,}438.546990...$$

Therefore, he paid $164,438.55 for the annuity.

$$\textit{Amount Paid over the Term} = n(PMT)$$

$$= 300 \times \$1000.00 = \$300{,}000.00$$

$$\textit{Interest Earned Over the Entire Period} = n(PMT) - PV$$

$$= 300{,}000.00 - 164{,}438.55$$

$$= \$135{,}561.45$$

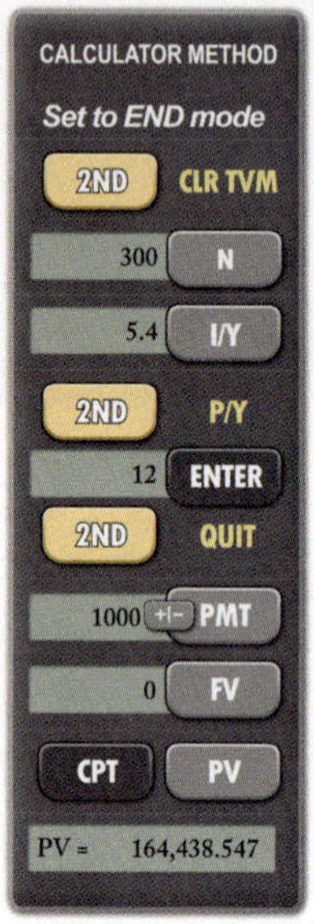

Example 10.2(d)

Calculating the Present Value, Amount Invested, and Total Interest Charged in an Ordinary Simple Annuity

Andrew paid $20,000 as a down payment towards the purchase of a house and received a mortgage from a bank to complete the purchase of his house. He was required to pay the bank an amount of $1500 at the end of every month for 30 years at an interest rate of 3% compounded monthly.

(i) What was the purchase price of his house?

(ii) What was the total amount he would have paid over the 30-year period to settle the mortgage and how much of this would have been his interest payment towards the mortgage?

Solution

(i) This is an ordinary simple annuity as:

- Payments are made at the end of each payment period (monthly)
- Compounding period (monthly) = payment period (monthly)

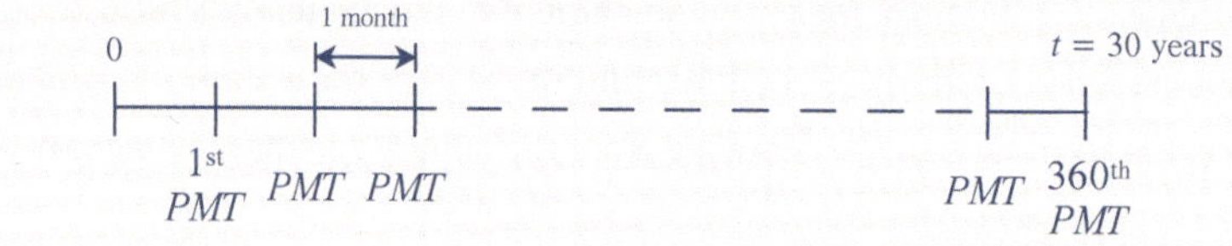

$PV = ?$

$PMT = \$1500$

$n = 12$ payments/year × 30 years = 360 monthly payments

$j = 0.03, \quad m = 12, \quad i = \frac{j}{m} = 0.0025$ per month

Using Formula 10.2(b),

$$PV = PMT\left[\frac{1-(1+i)^{-n}}{i}\right]$$

$$= 1500\left[\frac{1-(1+0.0025)^{-360}}{0.0025}\right]$$

$$= 1500[237.189381...]$$

$$= \$355{,}784.0723...$$

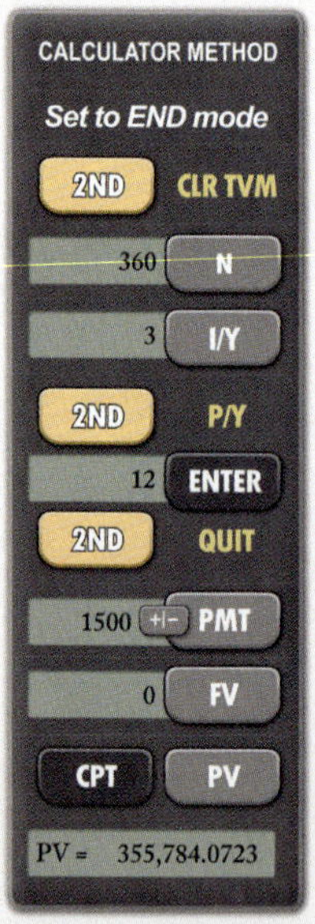

As he paid $20,000.00 as down payment for the house, the purchase price of the house was:

$$\textit{PV of All Payments} + \textit{Down Payment} = 355{,}784.07 + 20{,}000.00 = \$375{,}784.07$$

(ii) We are now required to find out how much he would have paid for the house at the end of 30 years.

Solution continued

$$\textit{Amount Paid over the Term} = n(PMT) = 360 \times 1500.00 = \$540,000.00$$

$$\begin{aligned}\textit{Total Interest on this Mortgage} &= n(PMT) - PV \\ &= 540,000.00 - 355,784.07 \\ &= \$184,215.93\end{aligned}$$

At the end of 30 years, Andrew would have paid a total of $540,000.00 to settle the mortgage, of which, $184,215.93 would have been his interest payment.

10.2 | Exercises

1. Aliana saved $50 at the end of every month in her savings account at 6% compounded monthly for 5 years. Calculate:
   a. The accumulated value of money at the end of the period in her savings account.
   b. The interest earned over the period.

2. Sharleen contributed $330.50 towards an RRSP at the end of every month for 4 years at 0.9% compounded monthly. Calculate:
   a. The accumulated value of money at the end of the period in the RRSP.
   b. The interest earned over the period.

3. Lue made deposits of $25 at the end of every month for 10 years in a savings account paying 3.5% compounded monthly. He plans on leaving his savings in the account for another 5 years. Assuming that the interest rate in his savings account is fixed during the entire time period, what would be the total interest earned on this investment?

4. Shanelle saves $75 at the end of every month in a savings account at 6% compounded monthly for 15 years for her child's education. How much would she have at the end of 15 years? If she leaves the accumulated money in the savings account for another 2 years earning the same interest rate, how much would she have at the end of the period?

5. Robert invests $500 at the end of every 3 months in a savings account with the Bank of Toronto at 6% compounded quarterly for 7 years and 9 months. How much more would he have earned if he had saved it in the Bank of London that was providing an interest rate of 6.5% compounded quarterly?

6. Carrie saved $750 of her salary every month in an RRSP earning 4% compounded monthly for 20 years. How much more would she have earned if she had saved this amount in an RRSP that was earning an interest rate of 4.25% compounded monthly?

7. What is the discounted value of payments of $10,000 made at the end of every year for 10 years at 5% compounded annually?

8. If the discount rate is 3% compounded quarterly, what is the present value of $3000 paid at the end of each quarter for 10 years and 6 months?

9. Calculate the amount of money Chin Ho would have to deposit in a savings account at 6% compounded monthly to provide his daughter with $700 every month for 4 years through her undergraduate studies.

10. Cortland wants to receive $1500 at the end of every month from a retirement investment plan for 10 years. If the investment plan is earning a rate of 4% compounded monthly, how much would he have to invest in this plan to ensure that he receives his monthly payments for 10 years?

11. What would be the purchase price of an annuity that provides $500 at the end of every month for 5 years and earns an interest rate of 4% compounded monthly?

12. Adler took a loan from a bank at 9% compounded monthly to purchase a car. He was required to pay the bank $300 at the end of every month for the next 4 years and 2 months. What was the cost of the car?

13. Sharla wants to buy a house but can afford to pay only $5000 at the end of every 6 months for a mortgage with an interest rate of 2% compounded semi-annually for 20 years. If she has $7500 for the down payment, calculate the value of a house she can afford, her total investment, and interest paid over the mortgage period.

14. Falco paid $25,000 as a down payment for a condominium he purchased in Toronto. He received a mortgage from a bank at the rate of 3.25% compounded semi-annually, which required a payment of $9000 at the end of every 6 months for 25 years for the balance payment of the condominium. Calculate the purchase price of the condominium and the total amount of interest charged on the mortgage over the 25-year period.

15. Alexander received a loan from his bank at 6% compounded monthly to purchase a home theatre system. He was required to pay monthly installments of $100 for the next 18 months to clear the loan. By how much would the loan amount change if the interest rate was 5% compounded monthly while his monthly payments and repayment term remained the same?

16. Leesha was required to make month-end payments of $35.75 for 1 year for a loan with an interest rate of 2% compounded monthly. By how much would the loan amount change if it were offered to her at 2.5% compounded monthly, with the same month-end payment terms and time period?

17. How much would you have to pay now for a retirement annuity that would provide $3000 at the end of every 3 months at 5% compounded quarterly for the first 10 years and $2500 at the end of each month at 6% compounded monthly for the following 5 years?

18. Mark purchased an annuity that pays him $1000 every month for the first 2 years, while money was worth 2% compounded monthly. It then paid him $1100 every 6 months for the next 3 years, while money was worth 2.5% compounded semi-annually. How much should he have paid for this annuity?

• 19. Reeta purchased furniture from Rafique's store that did not require her to make an immediate payment. However, she could settle the invoice over the next 24 months by paying $150 at the end of every month. They charged her an interest rate of 0.75% compounded monthly. How much would she have saved if she had paid them the invoice amount of $3000 immediately instead of taking the loan?

• 20. Ronald and Jill were wondering if they should pay an amount of $30,000 for a parking space that was for sale in their condominium building or take a loan from the bank at 4% compounded monthly for 5 years, paying month-end repayment amounts of $550. Which option should they choose and why?

• 21. Calculate the value of a loan that requires a payment of $400 at the end of every 3 months for 5 years at 5% compounded quarterly. If the first 4 payments are missed, what amount should be paid with the 5th payment to bring the original loan agreement back into effect?

• 22. Claretta received a loan and is required to make payments of $300 at the end of every month for the next 8 years, at 6% compounded monthly. Calculate the amount of the loan received if all the payments for the first year are missed, what amount must be paid at the end of the first month of the second year to bring the payments up to date?

10.3 | Future Value and Present Value of an Ordinary General Annuity

In an ordinary general annuity, payments are made at the end of each payment period and the compounding period is not equal to the payment period.

In this case, if we find the equivalent periodic rate that matches the payment period, then using this equivalent periodic rate we can use the ordinary simple annuity formula to calculate the future value and present value.

To calculate this, we first find the number of compounding periods per payment period (c) and then the equivalent periodic interest rate per payment period (i_2) using the following two formulas:

Formula 10.3(a)

Number of Compounding Periods per Payment Period

$$c = \frac{\textit{Number of compounding periods per year}}{\textit{Number of payments per year}}$$

Formula 10.3(b)

Equivalent Periodic Interest Rate per Payment Period

$$i_2 = (1 + i)^c - 1$$

Note: The value of 'c' as calculated from Formula 10.3(a) is used in calculating 'i_2' in Formula 10.3(b).

Substitute the value of 'i_2' for 'i' in the ordinary simple annuity Formula 10.2(a) and Formula 10.2(b) to solve for 'FV' and 'PV' of an ordinary general annuity:

$$FV = PMT\left[\frac{(1 + i_2)^n - 1}{i_2}\right] \text{ and } PV = PMT\left[\frac{1 - (1 + i_2)^{-n}}{i_2}\right]$$

Example 10.3(a)

Calculating the Compounding Periods per Payment Period (c) and the Equivalent Periodic Interest Rate (i_2) that Matches the Payment Period

Complete the table by calculating the number of compounding periods per payment period (c) and the equivalent periodic interest rate (i_2) that matches the payment period for the related interest rates:

Solution

Interest Rate	Payment Period	c	i_2
8% compounded quarterly	Monthly	$\frac{4}{12}$	$\left(1 + \frac{0.08}{4}\right)^{\frac{4}{12}} - 1 = 0.006622...$ per month
9% compounded semi-annually	Quarterly	$\frac{2}{4}$	$\left(1 + \frac{0.09}{2}\right)^{\frac{2}{4}} - 1 = 0.022252...$ per quarter
6% compounded monthly	Semi-annually	$\frac{12}{2}$	$\left(1 + \frac{0.06}{12}\right)^{\frac{12}{2}} - 1 = 0.030377...$ per half year
5% compounded annually	Monthly	$\frac{1}{12}$	$\left(1 + \frac{0.05}{1}\right)^{\frac{1}{12}} - 1 = 0.004074...$ per month

The following two examples will demonstrate future value and present value calculations of an ordinary general annuity:

Example 10.3(b) **Calculating the Future Value of an Ordinary General Annuity**

Sarah would like to save $100 every month for the next 4 years. If the interest rate is 2% compounded quarterly, what would the accumulated value of her investments be at the end of 4 years?

Solution

This is an ordinary general annuity as:

- Payments are made at the end of each payment period (monthly)
- Compounding period (quarterly) ≠ payment period (monthly)

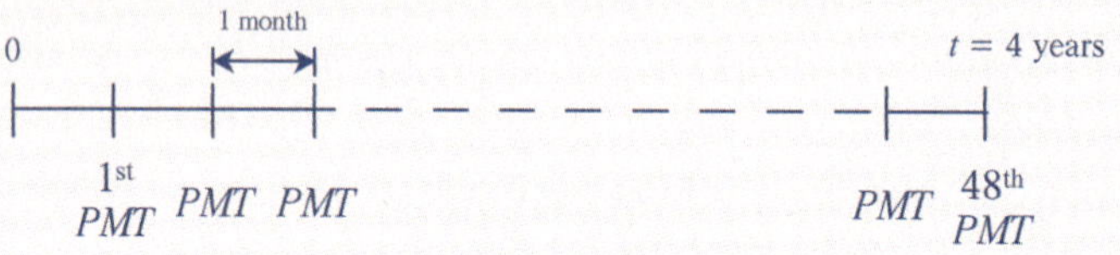

$$PMT = \$100 \qquad FV = ?$$

$$n = 12 \text{ payments/year} \times 4 \text{ years}$$
$$= 48 \text{ monthly payments}$$

$$j = 0.02, \quad m = 4, \quad i = \frac{j}{m} = 0.005 \text{ per quarter}$$

Using Formula 10.3(a),

$$c = \frac{\textit{Number of compounding periods per year}}{\textit{Number of payments per year}} = \frac{4}{12}$$

Using Formula 10.3(b),

$$i_2 = (1 + i)^c - 1 = (1 + 0.005)^{(4/12)} - 1$$
$$= 0.001663\ldots \text{ per month}$$

Using Formula 10.2(a) and substituting i_2 for i,

$$FV = PMT\left[\frac{(1 + i_2)^n - 1}{i_2}\right]$$

$$= 100\left[\frac{(1 + 0.001663...)^{48} - 1}{0.001663...}\right]$$

$$= 100\,[49.925669...] = \$4992.566985...$$

The accumulated value of Sarah's investments at the end of four years would be $4992.57.

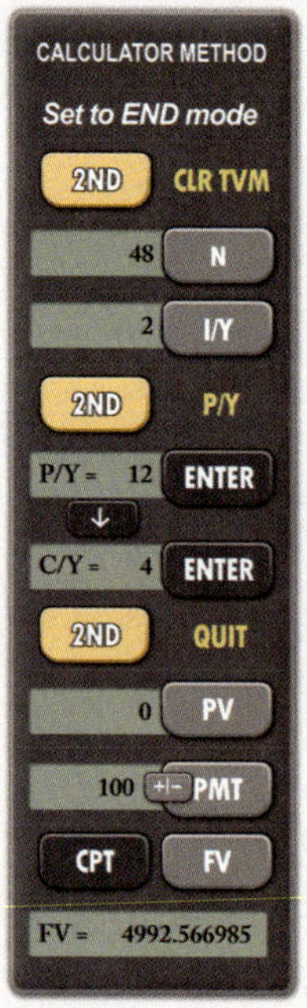

Enter ***payment periods per year*** first

Next, Enter ***compoundings per year***

Example 10.3(c) **Calculating the Present Value of an Ordinary General Annuity**

Joseph requires a student loan but can afford to pay only $500 towards repayment of the loan at the end of every month for 6 years. How much would the bank give him at an interest rate of 6% compounded annually?

Solution

This is an ordinary general annuity as:

- Payments are made at the end of each payment period (monthly)
- Compounding period (annually) ≠ payment period (monthly)

Solution continued

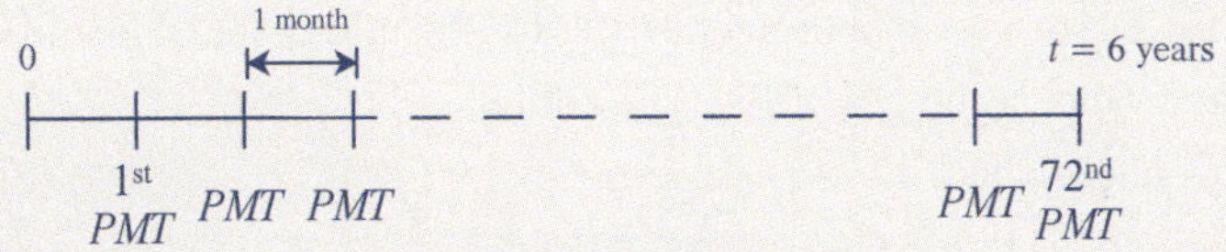

$PV = ?$

$PMT = \$500$

$n = 12$ payments/year × 6 years
$= 72$ monthly payments

$j = 0.06, \quad m = 1, \quad i = \frac{j}{m} = 0.06$ per annum

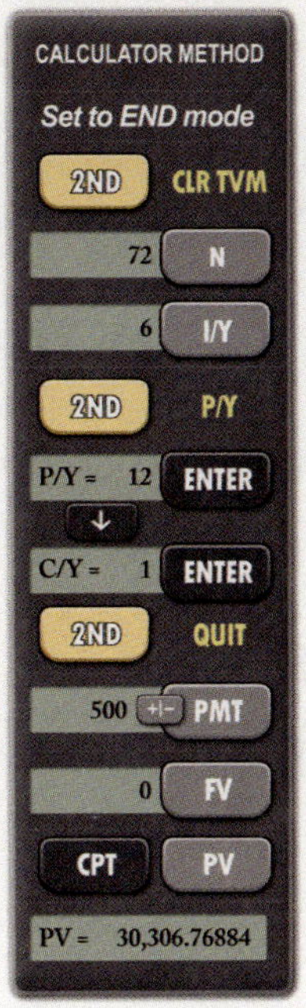

Using Formula 10.3(a),

$$c = \frac{\textit{Number of compounding periods per year}}{\textit{Number of payments per year}} = \frac{1}{12}$$

Using Formula 10.3(b),

$$i_2 = (1 + i)^c - 1 = (1 + 0.06)^{1/12} - 1 = 0.004867... \text{ per month}$$

Using Formula 10.2(b) and substituting i_2 for i,

$$PV = PMT\left[\frac{1 - (1 + i_2)^{-n}}{i_2}\right]$$

$$= 500\left[\frac{1 - (1 + 0.004867...)^{-72}}{0.004867...}\right]$$

$$= 500[60.61537...] = \$30{,}306.768845...$$

Therefore, the bank would give him $30,306.77.

10.3 | Exercises

1. Adrian, an employee at a coffee shop, instructed his employer to deduct $100 at the end of every month from his salary and to contribute it to an RRSP for 5 years. If the RRSP was providing an interest rate of 5% compounded quarterly, how much did he have in the RRSP at the end of the 5-year period?

2. If Bina saved $250 at the end of every month for 2 years in a savings account that earns 5% compounded quarterly, how much money would she have had at the end of 2 years and how much interest would she have earned over the period?

3. Calculate the future value of month-end payments of $180 for 10 years at the following interest rates:
   a. 7.8% compounded monthly.
   b. 8% compounded quarterly.

4. Calculate the accumulated value of end-of-quarter payments of $800 made at the following interest rates for 5 years:
   a. 6.23% compounded quarterly.
   b. 6.24% compounded semi-annually.

5. Tom has been contributing $1000 quarterly into a retirement fund for the past 10 years. He decided to stop making payments and to allow his investment to grow for another 5 years. If money could earn 8% compounded semi-annually, how much interest would he have earned over the 15-year period?

6. Femi deposited $300 in a savings account every 3 months for 5 years. If the amount earned 5% compounded monthly, and if he left the accumulated money in the account to grow for another 3 years, calculate the balance in his savings account at the end of the period. What was his total deposit and total earnings?

7. If an annuity payment for 5 years is $200 at the end of every month, compare the future values if the investment earns 4% compounded monthly, 4% compounded quarterly, and 4% compounded semi-annually.

8. Becca can afford to invest $400 every month in an RRSP for the next 5 years. Identify the RRSP that provides her with a larger accumulated value at the end of the time period:
   a. RRSP 1: 7% compounded annually.
   b. RRSP 2: 5% compounded semi-annually.

9. Calculate the accumulated value of the following investment options if the bank offers an interest rate of 5% compounded semi-annually:
   a. A single amount of $5000 saved for 5 years.
   b. A series of payments of $100 at the end of every month for 5 years.

10. A credit union offers an interest rate of 4.50% compounded monthly for all investments. Which of the following would result in a higher future value when invested at the credit union?
    a. $18,250 invested for 10 years.
    b. Annuity payments of $475 at the end of every quarter for 10 years.

11. What will the future value of a series of $1000 payments made at the end of each quarter for 10 years be, if the interest rate is 5% compounded monthly for the first half of the term and 4% compounded annually for the second half of the term?

12. Amanda invested $500 at the end of every month into an RRSP that had an interest rate of 3% compounded quarterly. Two years later, the interest rate on her RRSP increased to 3.25% compounded quarterly and remained the same thereafter. How much did she accumulate in her RRSP after a period of 6 years?

13. What is the discounted value of annuity payments of $2000 made at the end of every year for $5\frac{1}{2}$ years at 6% compounded semi-annually?

14. How much should Rod pay for a 10-year annuity that provides month-end payments of $1800 at 4.5% compounded quarterly?

15. Calculate the cost of Troy's car if he has to make a down payment of $1000 at the time of purchase and payments of $330 per month for 3 years and 3 months at an interest rate of 6% compounded semi-annually. What is the total interest he would pay for the car?

16. David has $30,000 to use as a down payment to purchase a house. What would be the size of the loan that he would receive from a bank if he could only afford to pay $1400 at the end of each month for a mortgage with an interest rate of 4.5% compounded semi-annually, assuming that the rate is constant for 25 years? What would be the amount of interest he would be paying for the mortgage over the period?

17. Ellen decided to retire in Canada and wants to receive a retirement income of $3000 every month for 20 years from her savings. If the Bank of London could give her an interest rate of 6% compounded semi-annually, how much would she have to invest to get her planned retirement income? By how much would it be cheaper for her to invest her money with the Bank of Toronto if they are offering her an interest rate of 5.98% compounded quarterly?

18. Two annuities that provide end-of-quarter payments of $850 for a period of 5 years have the following interest rates:
    a. Annuity A: 9.45% compounded monthly.
    b. Annuity B: 9.50% compounded semi-annually.

    Which one would have a cheaper purchase price?

19. How much should Emma pay for an annuity that would give her $5000 at the end of every year for the first 7 years and $8000 at the end of every year for the next 4 years, if the interest rate is 6% compounded semi-annually throughout the time period?

20. What is the purchase price of an annuity that provides month-end payments of $500 for the first 2 years and $1000 for the next 3 years? Assume that the interest rate is 3% compounded quarterly throughout the time period.

10.4 | Future Value and Present Value of a Simple Annuity Due

In a simple annuity due, payments are made at the beginning of each payment period, and the compounding period is equal to the payment period. In this section, you will learn how to calculate the future value and present value of a simple annuity due.

Future Value of a Simple Annuity Due

In an annuity due, as each payment is made at the beginning of the payment period, you will notice that the future value (accumulated value) of each payment is a multiple of the future value (accumulated value) of each payment in an ordinary annuity by a factor of $(1+i)$. Let us compare two examples of an annuity with 5 annual payments, where in the first example, payments are made at the beginning of each year (annuity due) and in the second example, payments are made at the end of each year (ordinary annuity):

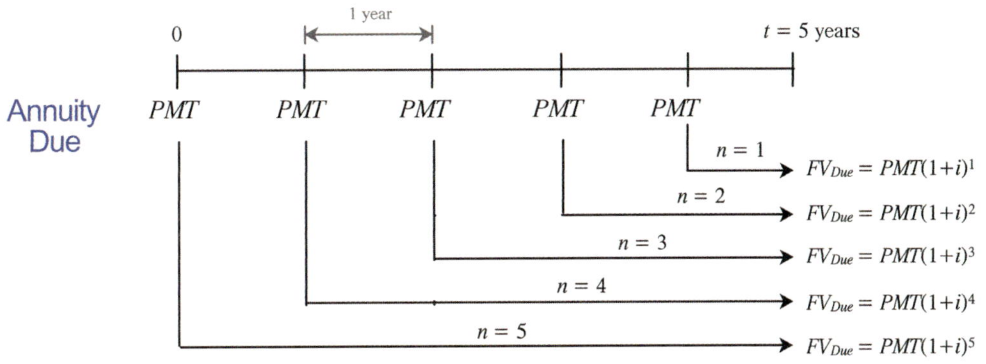

$$FV_{Due} = PMT(1+i)^5 + PMT(1+i)^4 + PMT(1+i)^3 + PMT(1+i)^2 + PMT(1+i)^1$$

Exhibit 10.4 (a): Future Value of Simple Annuity Due Payments (FV_{Due})

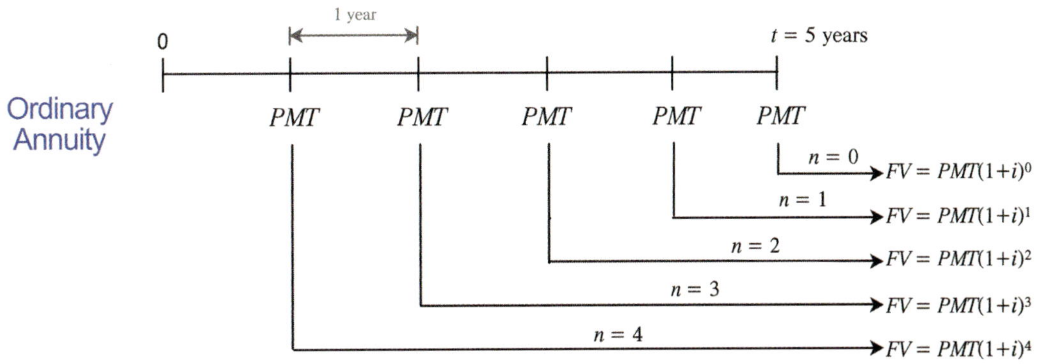

$$FV = PMT(1+i)^4 + PMT(1+i)^3 + PMT(1+i)^2 + PMT(1+i)^1 + PMT(1+i)^0$$

Exhibit 10.4 (b): Future Value of Ordinary Simple Annuity Payments (FV)

Comparing the two equations in the preceding two diagrams:

$$FV_{Due} = PMT(1+i)^5 + PMT(1+i)^4 + PMT(1+i)^3 + PMT(1+i)^2 + PMT(1+i)^1$$

$$FV = PMT(1+i)^4 + PMT(1+i)^3 + PMT(1+i)^2 + PMT(1+i)^1 + PMT(1+i)^0$$

You will notice that each term in FV_{Due} is a multiple of the corresponding term in FV by a factor of $(1 + i)$.

Therefore, $FV_{Due} = FV(1 + i)$ and can be expressed by the following formula:

Formula 10.4(a)

Future Value of a Simple Annuity Due

$$FV_{Due} = PMT\left[\frac{(1+i)^n - 1}{i}\right](1+i)$$

Present Value of a Simple Annuity Due

In an annuity due, as the payment is made at the beginning of the payment period, you will notice that the present value (discounted value) of each payment is a multiple of the present value (discounted value) of each payment in an ordinary annuity by a factor of $(1+i)$. Let us compare two examples of an annuity with 5 annual payments, where in the first example, payments are made at the beginning of each year (annuity due) and in the second example, payments are made at the end of each year (ordinary annuity):

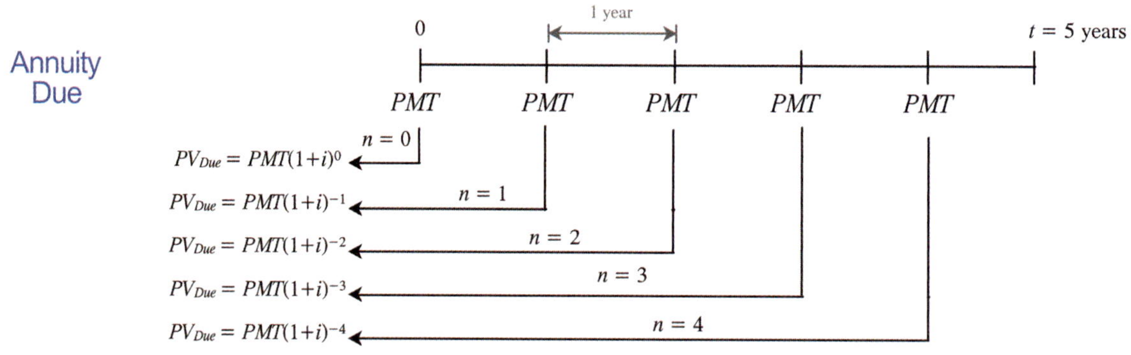

$$PV_{Due} = PMT(1+i)^0 + PMT(1+i)^{-1} + PMT(1+i)^{-2} + PMT(1+i)^{-3} + PMT(1+i)^{-4}$$

Exhibit 10.4 (c): Present Value of Simple Annuity Due Payments(PV_{Due})

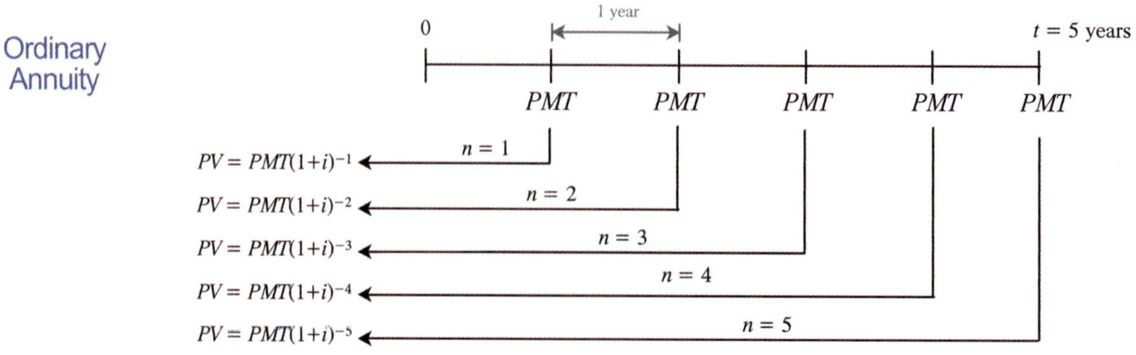

$$PV = PMT(1+i)^{-1} + PMT(1+i)^{-2} + PMT(1+i)^{-3} + PMT(1+i)^{-4} + PMT(1+i)^{-5}$$

Exhibit 10.4 (d): Present Value of Ordinary Simple Annuity Payments (PV)

Comparing the above two equations:

$$PV_{Due} = PMT(1+i)^0 + PMT(1+i)^{-1} + PMT(1+i)^{-2} + PMT(1+i)^{-3} + PMT(1+i)^{-4}$$

$$PV = PMT(1+i)^{-1} + PMT(1+i)^{-2} + PMT(1+i)^{-3} + PMT(1+i)^{-4} + PMT(1+i)^{-5}$$

You will notice that each term in PV_{Due} is a multiple of the corresponding term in PV by a factor of $(1 + i)$.

Therefore, $PV_{Due} = PV\,(1+i)$ and can be expressed by the following formula:

Formula 10.4(b)

Present Value of a Simple Annuity Due

$$PV_{Due} = PMT\left[\frac{1-(1+i)^{-n}}{i}\right](1+i)$$

Example 10.4(a)

Calculating the Future Value of a Simple Annuity Due

Madison makes contributions of \$500 at the beginning of every 6 months for 10 years towards an RRSP. If the RRSP earns interest at 5% compounded semi-annually, what be would the value of her RRSP at the end of the time period?

Solution

This is a simple annuity due as:

- Payments are made at the beginning of each payment period (semi-annually)
- Compounding period (semi-annually) = payment period (semi-annually)

In using the financial calculator for annuity due calculations, set the calculator to beginning of period ('BGN' mode). This is described in Section 10.2

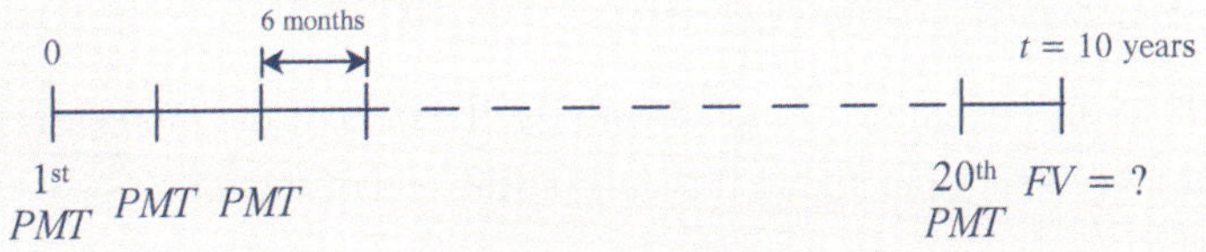

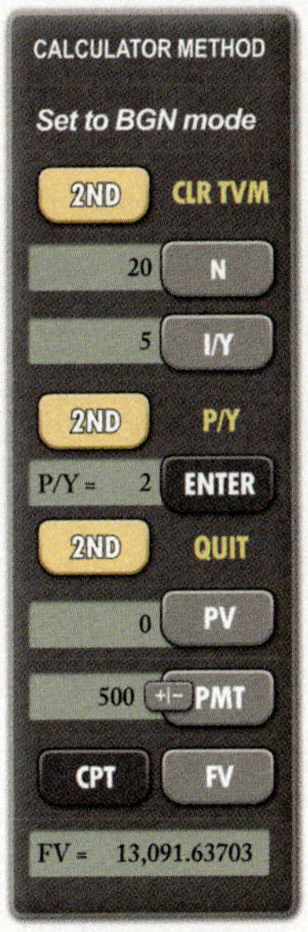

$$PMT = \$500$$

$$n = 2 \text{ payments/year} \times 10 \text{ years} = 20 \text{ semi-annual payments}$$

$$j = 0.05, \quad m = 2, \quad i = \frac{j}{m} = 0.025 \text{ per half-year}$$

Using Formula 10.4(a),

$$FV_{Due} = PMT\left[\frac{(1+i)^n - 1}{i}\right](1+i)$$

$$= 500\left[\frac{(1+0.025)^{20} - 1}{0.025}\right](1+0.025)$$

$$= 500\,[25.544357...]\,(1.025) = \$13{,}091.63703$$

Therefore, the value of her RRSP would be \$13,091.64 at the end of the time period.

Example 10.4(b)

Calculating the Present Value of a Simple Annuity Due

What is the present value of an annuity that pays \$3000 at the beginning of every 3 months for 8 years? Assume the interest rate is 4% compounded quarterly.

Solution

This is a simple annuity due as:

- Payments are made at the beginning of each payment period (quarterly)
- Compounding period (quarterly) = payment period (quarterly)

Solution continued

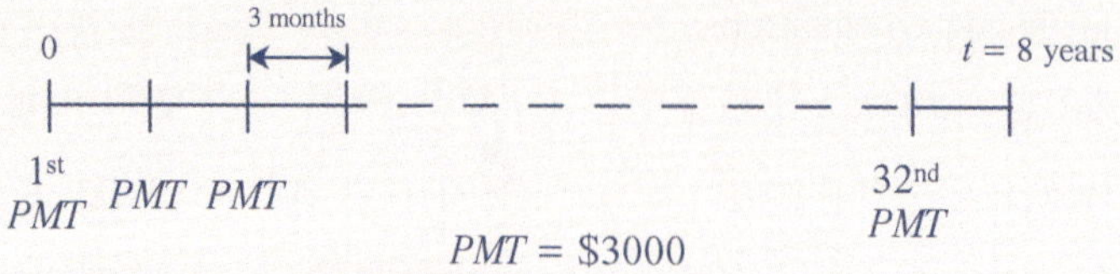

$$PMT = \$3000$$

$PV = ?$ $\quad n = 4 \text{ payments/year} \times 8 \text{ years} = 32 \text{ quarterly payments}$

$$j = 0.04, \quad m = 4, \quad i = \frac{j}{m} = 0.01 \text{ per quarter}$$

Using Formula 10.4(b),

$$PV_{Due} = PMT\left[\frac{1-(1+i)^{-n}}{i}\right](1+i)$$

$$= 3000\left[\frac{1-(1+0.01)^{-32}}{0.01}\right](1+0.01)$$

$$= 3000\,[27.269589...](1.01) = \$82{,}626.8561$$

Therefore, the present value of the annuity is \$82,626.86.

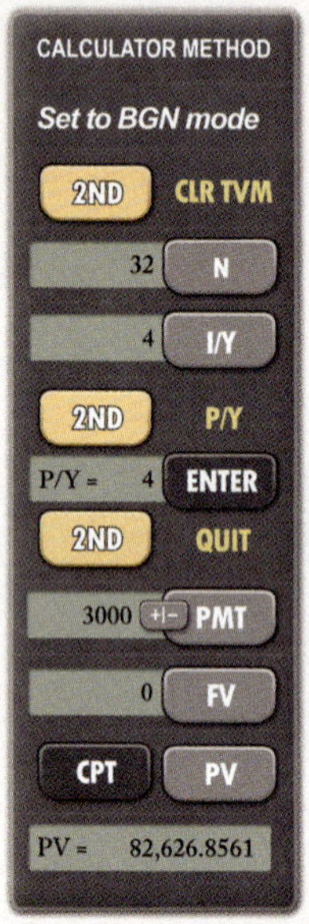

10.4 | Exercises

1. What is the accumulated value of periodic deposits of \$3000 at the beginning of every quarter for 4 years if the interest rate is 6% compounded quarterly?

2. Zach deposited \$200 at the beginning of each month for 10 years. If the fund earned 7.25% compounded monthly, how much would have been accumulated in this fund at the end of the term?

3. From the day Donald was born, his mother has invested \$50 every month for 15 years in a savings account at 2% compounded monthly. How much did Donald have in this account on his 15th birthday? Assume that there was no deposit on that day. What was his mother's total investment and the interest earned?

4. Rodney plans to retire on his 45th birthday and has saved \$10,000 every year since his 25th birthday in a fund that earns 8.5% compounded annually. What would the balance be in the fund on his 45th birthday, assuming that he did not make an investment on his 45th birthday? What would have been his contribution and interest earned through the years?

5. Trista invested \$1850 at the beginning of every 3 months in an RRSP for 20 years. For the first 9 years it earned interest at a rate of 6% compounded quarterly and for the next 11 years it earned interest at a rate of 6.75% compounded quarterly. Calculate the accumulated value of her investment and earnings.

6. Amanda made contributions of \$200 at the beginning of each month to an RRSP for 10 years. If it was earning 5% compounded monthly for the first 5 years and 6% compounded monthly for the next 5 years, calculate the accumulated value of her investment and earnings.

7. Loan payments of \$600 at the beginning of each month were being made towards a brand new luxury car for a term of 8 years at 4% compounded monthly. Calculate the cost of the car if a down payment of \$1000 was also required at the time of purchase.

8. Eric purchased a diamond ring for his girlfriend with a loan at 10% compounded quarterly. If he had to pay a down payment of \$500 and then \$250 at the beginning of every 3 months for 3 years, what was the cost of the ring and how much interest did he have to pay over the period of the loan?

9. What single payment now is equivalent to 12 payments of \$750 payable at the beginning of each month, assuming that money can earn interest at 3% compounded monthly?

10. How much should Kyle's dad invest in a savings account today to pay for Kyle's rent for the next 4 years, if the rent is \$500 per month payable at the beginning of each month? The account earns 4% compounded monthly.

11. Harry has invested \$3000 at the beginning of every 3 months in a savings account with the Brampton Bank at 6% compounded quarterly for 9 years and 9 months. How much more would he have earned if he had saved it in the Bank of Sudbury that was providing an interest rate of 6.5% compounded quarterly?

12. Ruba saved \$1200 of her salary at the beginning of every month in an RRSP earning 3.5% compounded monthly for 30 years. How much more would she have saved if she had put this amount in an RRSP that was earning an interest rate of 4.5% compounded monthly?

CFA Prep.

13. What's the maximum an investor should be willing to pay for an annuity that will pay out \$10,000 at the beginning of each year for the next 10 years, given that the investor wants to earn 12.5% compounded annually?

14. Lilia took a loan from a bank at 11% compounded monthly to purchase a lawnmower. To settle the loan, she was required to pay the bank \$100 at the beginning of every month for the next 3 years and 6 months. What was the cost of the lawnmower?

15. Mandy made deposits of \$350 at the beginning of every month for 7 years in an investment fund that was earning 7.25% compounded monthly. She then left the money in the fund for another 3 years to accumulate interest. Assuming that the fund earns the same interest rate during the entire time period, what is the total interest earned on her investment during the term?

16. Hilda saved \$150 at the beginning of every month in a savings account for 10 years. After this period, she stopped making periodic deposits and left the accumulated amount to grow for another 4 years. How much interest did she earn if the interest rate on the account was 3.55% compounded monthly for the entire term?

10.5 | Future Value and Present Value of a General Annuity Due

In a general annuity due, payments are made at the beginning of each payment period, and the compounding period is not equal to the payment period. In this section, you will learn how to calculate the future value and present value of a general annuity due.

Similar to the ordinary general annuities, we first need to calculate the equivalent periodic interest rate per payment period (i_2) using Formulas 10.3(a) and 10.3(b):

$$c = \frac{\text{Number of compounding periods per year}}{\text{Number of payments per year}}$$

$$i_2 = (1 + i)^c - 1$$

Then, substituting the value of 'i_2' for 'i' in the simple annuity due Formula 10.4(a) and Formula 10.4(b), solve for 'FV_{Due}' and 'PV_{Due}', as follows:

$$FV_{Due} = PMT\left[\frac{(1 + i_2)^n - 1}{i_2}\right](1 + i_2) \quad \text{and} \quad PV_{Due} = PMT\left[\frac{1 - (1 + i_2)^{-n}}{i_2}\right](1 + i_2)$$

***Note:** In using the Texas Instruments BA II Plus calculator for annuity due calculations, set the calculator to beginning of period calculations ('BGN' mode) as described in Section 10.2.*

Example 10.5(a) Calculating the Future Value, Amount Invested, and Total Interest of a General Annuity Due

Tao invested $5000 at the beginning of every year for 5 years in a web design company that assured him an interest rate of 5% compounded quarterly on his investment. Calculate the following:

(i) The total amount he invested in the business.

(ii) The accumulated value of his investments.

(iii) The interest earned over the period.

Solution

(i) This is a general annuity due as:

- Payments are made at the beginning of each payment period (annually)
- Compounding period (quarterly) ≠ payment period (annually)

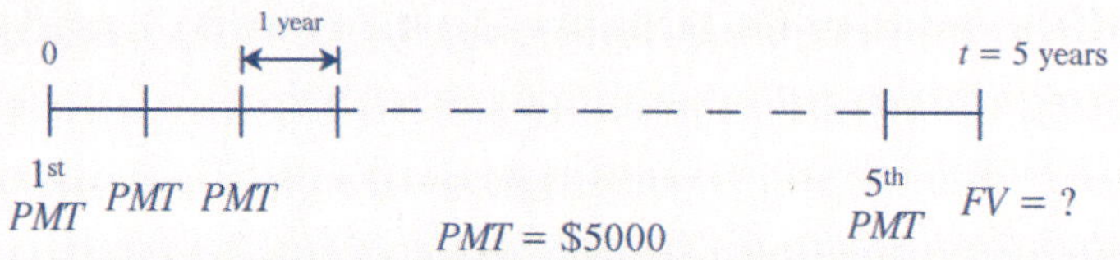

$$PMT = \$5000$$
$$n = 1 \text{ payments/year} \times 5 \text{ years} = 5 \text{ annual payments}$$

$$j = 0.05, \quad m = 4, \quad i = \frac{j}{m} = 0.0125 \text{ per quarter}$$

The total amount he invested in the business $= n(PMT) = 5 \times 5000.00 = \$25{,}000.00$

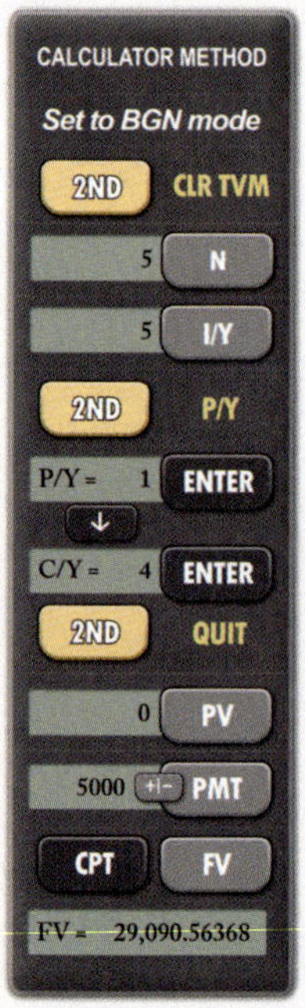

(ii) The accumulated value of his investments:

$$c = \frac{\text{Number of compounding periods per year}}{\text{Number of payments per year}} = \frac{4}{1}$$

$$i_2 = (1 + i)^c - 1 = (1 + 0.0125)^4 - 1 = 0.050945\ldots \text{ per year}$$

Using Formula 10.4(a) and substituting i_2 for i,

$$FV_{Due} = PMT\left[\frac{(1 + i_2)^n - 1}{i_2}\right](1 + i_2)$$

$$= 5000\left[\frac{(1 + 0.050945\ldots)^5 - 1}{0.050945\ldots}\right](1 + 0.050945\ldots)$$

$$= 5000\,[5.536075\ldots]\,(1.050945\ldots) = \$29{,}090.563686\ldots$$

Therefore, the accumulated value of his investments would be $29,090.56.

(iii) The interest earned over the period $= FV_{Due} - n(PMT)$

$$= 29{,}090.56 - 25{,}000.00 = \$4090.56$$

Example 10.5(b) Calculating the Present Value of a General Annuity Due

Alexandria inherited money that was invested in an account which provided her $4500 at the beginning of every month for 30 years. If the interest rate on the savings account was 4% compounded semi-annually, what was the total amount of money she inherited? Round your answer to the nearest hundred dollars.

Solution

This is a general annuity due as:

- Payments are made at the beginning of each payment period (monthly)
- Compounding period (semi-annually) ≠ payment period (monthly)

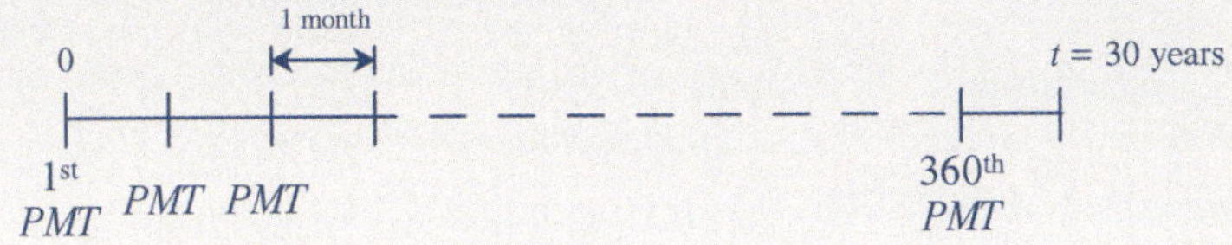

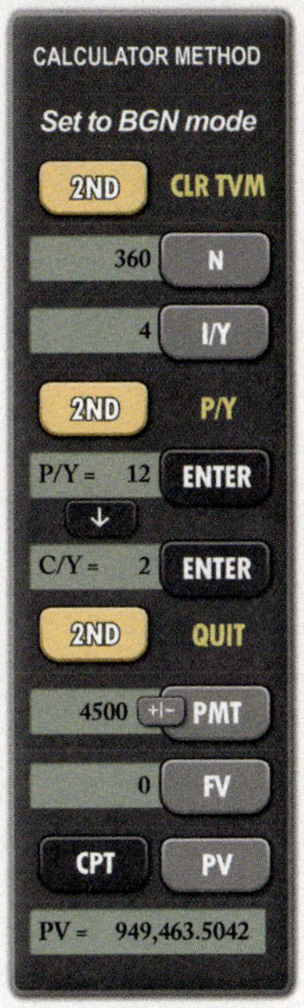

$PV = ?$

$$PMT = \$4500$$

$$n = 12 \text{ payments/year} \times 30 \text{ years} = 360 \text{ monthly payments}$$

$$j = 0.04, \quad m = 2, \quad i = \frac{j}{m} = 0.02 \text{ per half-year}$$

$$c = \frac{\textit{Number of compounding periods per year}}{\textit{Number of payments per year}} = \frac{2}{12}$$

$$i_2 = (1+i)^c - 1 = (1+0.02)^{(2/12)} - 1 = 0.003305... \text{ per month}$$

Using Formula 10.4(b) and substituting i_2 for i,

$$PV_{Due} = PMT\left[\frac{1-(1+i_2)^{-n}}{i_2}\right](1+i_2)$$

$$= 4500\left[\frac{1-(1+0.003305...)^{-360}}{0.003305...}\right](1+0.003305...)$$

$$= 4500\,[210.296672...](1.003305...) = \$949{,}463.504172...$$

Therefore, she inherited \$949,500.00 (rounded to the nearest \$100).

Example 10.5(c)

Lease or Buy Option

Erica was not sure whether she should lease or buy the car that she liked. The salesman at the car showroom informed her that she could either purchase the car by paying \$17,500 immediately or she could lease it by making payments of \$180 at the beginning of every month for 4 years. At the end of 4 years, she would have to pay a residual value of \$10,000 to purchase the car. Which option would be less expensive if money earns:

(i) 3% compounded annually?

(ii) 2% compounded annually?

Solution

The lease payments form a general annuity due as:

- Payments are made at the beginning of each payment period (monthly)
- Compounding period (annually) ≠ payment period (monthly)

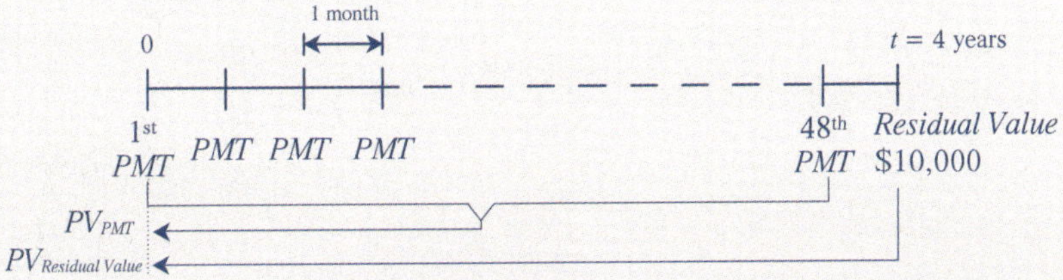

$$PMT = \$180$$

$$n = 12 \text{ payments/year} \times 4 \text{ years} = 48 \text{ monthly payments}$$

$$j = 0.03, \quad m = 1, \quad i = \frac{j}{m} = 0.03 \text{ per year}$$

$$PV_{\text{Lease option}} = PV_{PMT} + PV_{\text{Residual Value}}$$

Solution *continued*

(i) If money is worth 3% compounded annually

$$c = \frac{\textit{Number of compounding periods per year}}{\textit{Number of payments per year}} = \frac{1}{12}$$

$$i_2 = (1 + 0.03)^{(1/12)} - 1 = 0.002466\ldots \text{ per month}$$

Substituting 'i_2' in Formula 10.2(b)

$$PV_{Due} = PMT\left[\frac{1-(1+i_2)^{-n}}{i_2}\right](1+ i_2)$$

$$PV_{PMT} = 180\left[\frac{1 - (1+0.002466\ldots)^{-48}}{0.002466\ldots}\right](1+0.002466\ldots)$$

$$= 180[45.215228\ldots](1.002466\ldots)$$

$$= \$8158.813519\ldots$$

Using Formula 9.1(b), $PV = FV(1 + i)^{-n}$

$$PV_{Residual\ Value} = 10{,}000(1 + 0.03)^{-(1\times 4)}$$

$$= 10{,}000(0.888487\ldots)$$

$$= \$8884.870479\ldots$$

$$PV_{Lease\ Option} = PV_{PMT} + PV_{Residual\ Value}$$

$$= 8158.813519\ldots + 8884{,}870479\ldots$$

$$= \$17{,}043.684\ldots$$

The present value of the lease option is less than the purchase price of $17,500.

Therefore, if money is worth 3% compounded annually, leasing the car is less expensive.

Using the financial calculator, you can either compute 'PV' separately and add the answers together, or you can do the entire calculation in one step as shown here.

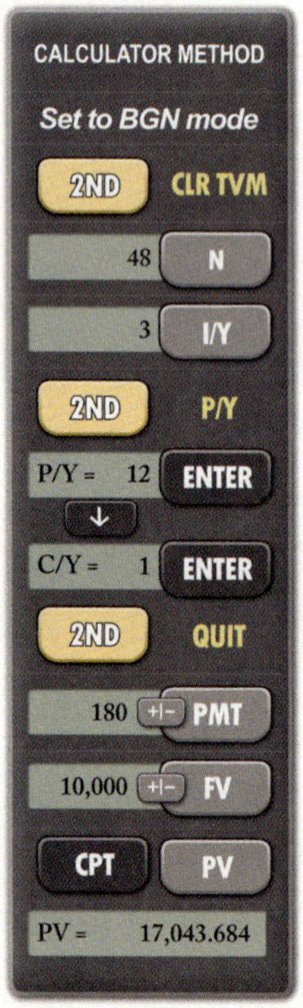

In an annuity, '*n*', is the number of payments during the term, but in compound interest, '*n*' is the number of compounding periods during the term.

(ii) If money is worth 2% compounded annually

$$c = \frac{\textit{Number of compounding periods per year}}{\textit{Number of payments per year}} = \frac{1}{12}$$

$$i_2 = (1 + 0.02)^{(1/12)} - 1 = 0.001651\ldots \text{ per month}$$

Substituting 'i_2' in Formula 10.2(b)

$$PV_{Due} = PMT\left[\frac{1-(1+i_2)^{-n}}{i_2}\right](1+ i_2)$$

$$PV_{PMT} = 180\left[\frac{1 - (1+0.001651\ldots)^{-48}}{0.001651\ldots}\right](1+0.001651\ldots)$$

$$= 180[46.110096\ldots](1.001651\ldots)$$

$$= \$8313.525277\ldots$$

Using Formula 9.1(b), $PV = FV(1 + i)^{-n}$

$$PV_{Residual\ Value} = 10{,}000(1 + 0.02)^{-(1\times 4)}$$

$$= 10{,}000(0.923845\ldots)$$

$$= \$9238.45426\ldots$$

$$PV_{Lease\ Option} = PV_{PMT} + PV_{Residual\ Value}$$

$$= 8313.525277\ldots + 9238.45426\ldots$$

$$= \$17{,}551.97954\ldots$$

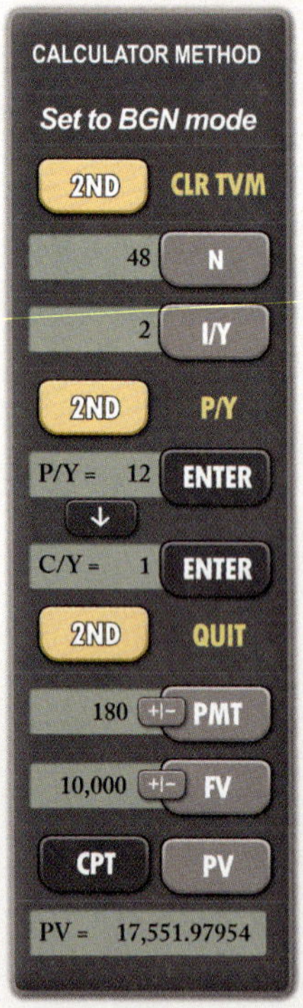

The present value of the lease option is more than the purchase price of $17,500.

Therefore, if money is worth 2% compounded annually, purchasing the car is less expensive.

10.5 | Exercises

1. What would the accumulated value of a fund be if \$2500 was deposited at the beginning of each quarter for 2 years and 9 months and the fund was earning 2.85% compounded monthly?

CFA Prep.

2. As part of his New Year's resolution, Clive committed to save \$500 per month in a mutual fund account. He deposited the money at the beginning of every month and projected that he would earn 8.5% compounded annually on the funds. At the end of 12 months, how much did Clive accumulate?

3. How much would you have to invest today in an investment fund that is earning 4% compounded annually, if you want to withdraw \$200 at the beginning of each month for the next 10 years?

4. What amount of loan would you receive from a bank if you can make payments of \$450 at the beginning of each month for 5 years? Assume an interest rate of 6% compounded semi-annually.

5. Nina purchased a car using a 6-year car lease at 3% compounded quarterly that required her to make payments of \$500 at the beginning of each month. Calculate the cost of the car if she made a down payment of \$1500.

6. Marlin purchased a large truck for his business using a 5-year lease that had an interest rate of 5.55% compounded quarterly. Calculate the cost of the truck and the cost of financing it, assuming that Marlin made a down payment of \$4500 and regular payments of \$1250 at the beginning of each month for the term of the lease.

7. Roger has been contributing \$1500 into a retirement fund at the beginning of each quarter for the past 15 years. He decided to stop making payments and to allow his investment to grow for another 5 years. If money can earn 8% compounded monthly, how much interest would he have earned over the 20-year period?

8. Andrew deposited \$1000 in a savings account at the beginning of every year for 10 years. If the amount earned 3% compounded monthly, and if she left the accumulated money in the account to grow for another year, calculate the balance in her savings account at the end of the period. What was her total deposit and total earnings?

9. What will be the amount of the 10-year loan at 4.5% compounded annually that Joyce would receive from a bank if she can only afford to make payments of \$400 at the beginning of every month? By how much would the loan amount change if the bank's interest rate was 4.5% compounded daily?

10. Soong decided to retire in Canada and wants to receive a retirement income of \$4000 at the beginning of every month for 15 years from her savings. If the Bank of Vancouver is offering her an interest rate of 5% compounded annually, how much would she have to invest to get her planned retirement income? By how much would it be cheaper for her to invest in the Bank of Niagara if they are offering her an interest rate of 4.99% compounded quarterly?

11. How much should Main Corp. pay for an annuity that would give it \$20,000 at the beginning of every year for the first 5 years and \$30,000 at the beginning of every year for the next 3 years, if the interest rate is 7% compounded monthly throughout the term?

12. What is the purchase price of an annuity that provides beginning-of-month payments of \$400 for the first 3 years and \$600 for the next 2 years? Assume that the interest rate is 4% compounded quarterly throughout the time period.

13. Amy, an office administrator, was evaluating the following quotation that she received for the purchase of a printing machine for her office:
    - Lease Option: Make payments of \$750 at the beginning of every month for 2 years. At the end of 2 years purchase the printer for \$3000.
    - Purchase Option: Make a payment of \$19,500 immediately.

Which option is economically better if money is worth:

a. 6% compounded semi-annually.

b. 8% compounded semi-annually.

14. If money is worth 7% compounded quarterly, how much would Madison save if she purchased a machine for \$59,000 instead of leasing it by making month-beginning payment of \$1200 for 4 years and then purchasing it for \$15,000 at the end of the 4th year?

10.6 | Calculating the Periodic Payment (*PMT*)

If the future value of an annuity, the periodic interest rate, '*i*', and the number of payment periods, '*n*', are known, we can use the future value formula to solve for the unknown '*PMT*'.

Similarly, if the present value of an annuity, the periodic interest rate, '*i*', and the number of payment periods, '*n*', are known, we can use the present value formula to solve for the unknown '*PMT*'.

Example 10.6(a) **Calculating the Periodic Payment of an Ordinary Simple Annuity, Given the Present Value**

Rodney received a \$35,000 home improvement loan from his bank at an interest rate of 6% compounded monthly. How much would he need to pay every month to settle the loan in 10 years?

Solution

This is an ordinary simple annuity as:

- Payments are made at the end of each payment period (monthly)
- Compounding period (monthly) = payment period (monthly)

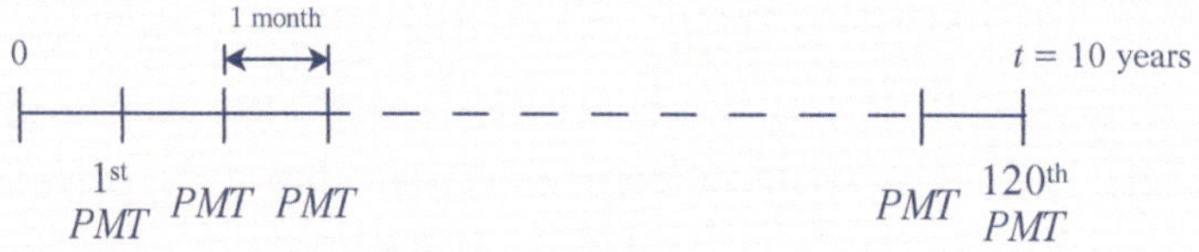

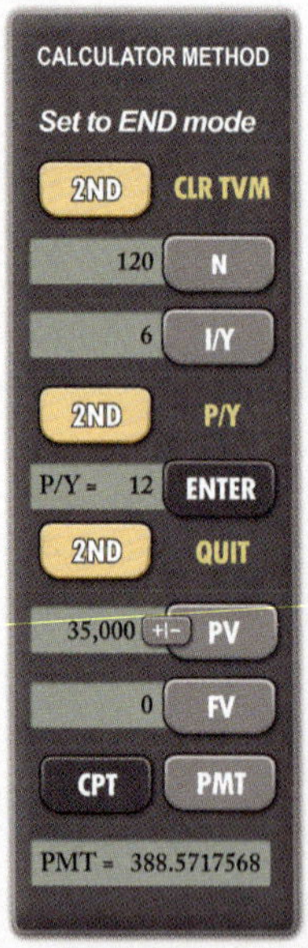

$PV = \$35{,}000$ $\qquad PMT = ?$

$n = 12 \text{ payments/year} \times 10 \text{ years}$

$= 120 \text{ monthly payments}$

$j = 0.06, \quad m = 12, \quad i = \frac{j}{m} = 0.005 \text{ per month}$

Using Formula 10.2(b),

$$PV = PMT\left[\frac{1-(1+i)^{-n}}{i}\right]$$

$$35{,}000 = PMT\left[\frac{1-(1+0.005)^{-120}}{0.005}\right]$$ Solving for '*PMT*', we obtain,

$$PMT = \frac{35{,}000}{\left[\frac{1-(1+0.005)^{-120}}{0.005}\right]}$$

$$= \frac{35{,}000}{[90.073453...]} = \$388.571756...$$

Therefore, he paid \$388.57 every month to settle the loan in 10 years.

Example 10.6(b) **Calculating the Periodic Payment of an Ordinary General Annuity, Given the Future Value**

What quarterly payments should Ben pay in order to save \$60,000 in 10 years if money can earn 8% compounded semi-annually?

Solution

This is an ordinary general annuity as:

- Payments are made at the end of each payment period (quarterly)
- Compounding period (semi-annually) ≠ payment period (quarterly)

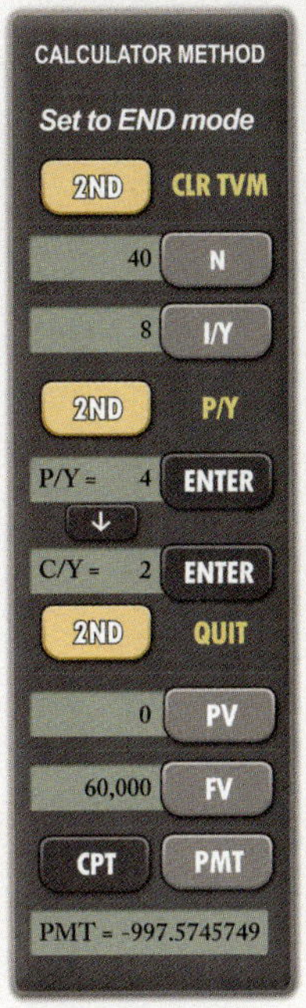

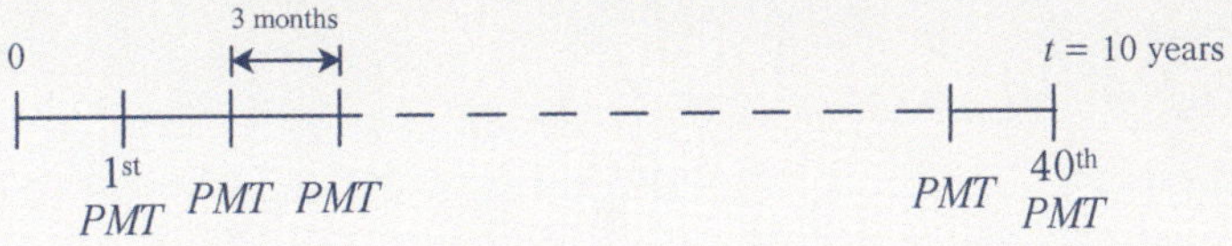

$PMT = ?$ $\qquad FV = \$60{,}000$

$n = 4$ payments/year × 10 years
$= 40$ quarterly payments

$j = 0.08, \quad m = 2, \quad i = \frac{j}{m} = 0.04$ per half-year

$$c = \frac{\text{Number of compounding periods per year}}{\text{Number of payments per year}} = \frac{2}{4}$$

$i_2 = (1 + i)^c - 1 = (1.04)^{2/4} - 1 = 0.019803\ldots$ per quarter

Using Formula 10.2(a), and substituting i_2 for i,

$$FV = PMT\left[\frac{(1+i_2)^n - 1}{i_2}\right]$$

$$60{,}000 = PMT\left[\frac{(1 + 0.019803\ldots)^{40} - 1}{0.019803\ldots}\right]$$ Solving for PMT, we obtain,

$$PMT = \frac{60{,}000}{\left[\frac{(1 + 0.019803\ldots)^{40} - 1}{0.019803\ldots}\right]} = \$997.574574\ldots$$

Therefore, Ben should pay quarterly payments of \$997.57.

Example 10.6(c) **Calculating the Periodic Payment of a General Annuity Due, Given the Present Value**

After winning a lottery, \$10,000 is deposited into an account earning interest at 4% compounded annually. What is the largest withdrawal which could be made at the beginning of each month from this account for the next 5 years?

Solution

This is a general annuity due as:

- Withdrawals are made at the beginning of each payment period (monthly)
- Compounding period (annually) ≠ payment period (monthly)

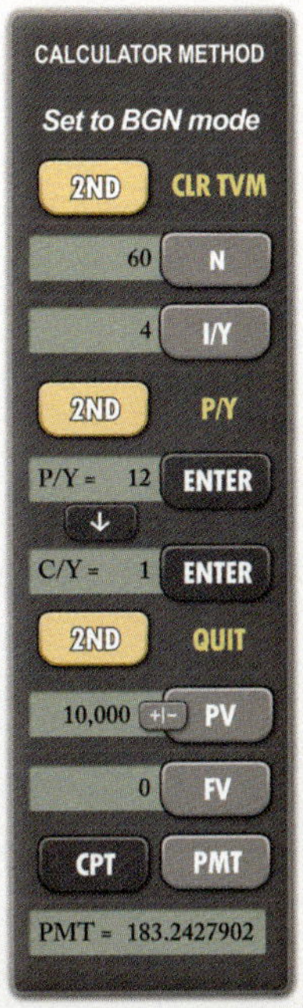

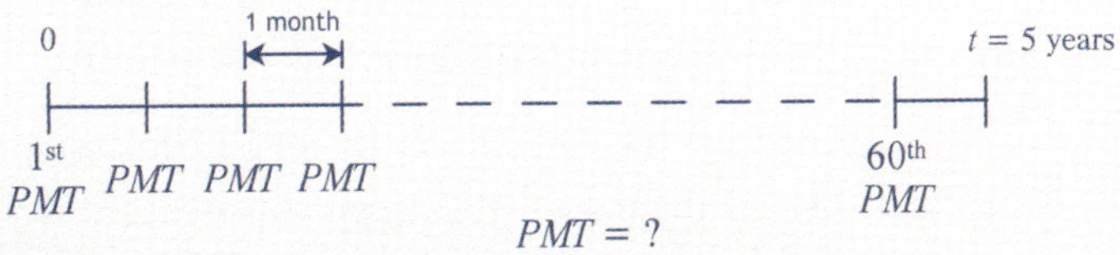

$PMT = ?$

$PV = \$10{,}000$ $\qquad n = 12$ withdrawals/year × 5 years
$= 60$ monthly withdrawals

$j = 0.04, \quad m = 1, \quad i = \frac{j}{m} = 0.04$ per month

$$c = \frac{\text{Number of compounding periods per year}}{\text{Number of payments per year}} = \frac{1}{12}$$

$i_2 = (1 + i)^c - 1 = (1.04)^{1/12} - 1 = 0.003273\ldots$ per month

While using the financial calculator for annuity due calculations, set the calculator to the beginning of period calculations ('BGN' mode) as described in Section 10.2.

Solution continued

Using Formula 10.4(b) and substituting i_2 for i,

$$PV_{Due} = PMT\left[\frac{1-(1+i_2)^{-n}}{i_2}\right](1+i_2)$$

$$10{,}000 = PMT\left[\frac{1-(1+0.003273...)^{-60}}{0.003273...}\right](1+0.003273...)$$

Solving for PMT, we obtain,

$$PMT = \frac{10{,}000}{\left[\frac{1-(1+0.003273...)^{-60}}{0.003273...}\right](1+0.003273...)}$$

$$= \frac{10{,}000}{[54.394333...](1.003273...)} = \$183.242790...$$

Therefore, the largest withdrawal which could be made is \$183.24.

10.6 | Exercises

1. An investment fund growing at 9% compounded monthly has an accumulated value of \$50,000. The fund has been receiving equal payments at the end of each month for the past 2 years. Calculate the size of the payments.

2. CFA Prep. At an expected rate of return of 7% compounded annually, how much must be deposited at the end of each year for the next 15 years to accumulate \$3000?

3. John, an automobile salesman, just sold a car to Rosemary. The car costs \$25,000 and is financed by a loan, to be repaid in 5 years. If she makes a down payment of \$3000, what should be the size of her loan payments at the end of each month if an interest rate of 7% compounded monthly is charged?

4. CFA Prep. Suppose you are considering applying for a \$2000 loan that will be repaid with equal end-of-year payments over the next 13 years, what will be the size of your payments? Assume that the interest rate for the loan is 6% compounded annually.

5. An investment fund was earning an interest rate of 5% compounded semi-annually for 10 years. If the accumulated value of the fund at the end of the time period was \$30,000, calculate the size of the month-end contributions to the fund.

6. An independent bush-pilot is saving up to purchase a new plane which will cost \$420,000, in 5 years. He plans on putting money away at the end of every month into an investment earning 8% compounded quarterly. How much will he have to put away every month so that he can afford the plane in 5 years?

7. Cyrus purchased an expensive networking system for his office for \$20,000 using a 5-year loan at 6.5% compounded quarterly. If the first payment was made a month from when he purchased the computer, what is the size of the monthly payments?

8. Gertrude sold her \$2 million business and has invested the money in a fund that will allow her to withdraw a regular payment every month for the next 20 years, while the fund grows at 4% compounded annually. How much will she be able to withdraw at the end of every month?

9. Martha's retirement fund has an accumulated amount of \$45,000. If it has been earning interest at 5% compounded semi-annually for the past 20 years, calculate the size of the equal payments that she deposited at the beginning of each month in this fund for the past 20 years.

10. Metal Equipment Co. has an investment fund that has accumulated \$180,500 in 3 years. If the fund has been earning 9% compounded quarterly for the past 3 years, calculate the size of the equal payments that was deposited into this fund at the beginning of each month for the past 3 years?

11. Christopher received a loan of \$230,000 for a term of 20 years. If the interest rate was fixed at 2.65% compounded annually for the entire term, calculate the size of his monthly payments that had to be made at the beginning of each month.

12. A municipality had a \$650,000 surplus in property tax collections for 2009 and decided to use the money for a parks renewal project. The city can earn 4% compounded quarterly by investing the money in a fund. How much money could be taken out of the fund at the beginning of each month so as to sustain the renewal project from the beginning of 2010 until the end of 2014?

13. What deposits should Tyler make at the beginning of each month in order to have a million dollars in 30 years if money can earn 8.5% compounded monthly?

14. What amount saved at the beginning of every 3 months will accumulate \$100,000 in 10 years, if money can earn 4.2% compounded quarterly?

15. Ivan made equal deposits at the end of every month for 5 years into an investment fund. He then left the money in the fund to grow for another 4 years. If the fund was earning 4% compounded monthly for the entire period and the accumulated amount at the end of the term was \$100,000, calculate the size of his periodic deposits.

16. Quincy made equal deposits at the end of every 3 months into a savings account for 12 years. After this period, he stopped making deposits and left the accumulated amount to grow for another 5 years. What was the size of his periodic deposits if the accumulated amount at the end of the term was \$37,450? Assume that the interest rate on

10.7 | Calculating the Number of Payments (n), and Time Period (t)

If the periodic payment (PMT), periodic interest rate (i), and either Present Value (PV) or Future Value (FV) of an annuity are known, then we can calculate the number of payments, 'n', and the time period, 't', as follows.

In a Simple Annuity

If 'FV' is known, we can calculate the number of payments, 'n', using Formula 10.2(a),

$$FV = PMT\left[\frac{(1+i)^n - 1}{i}\right]$$

Rearranging and isolating 'n' using natural logarithms (ln) results in the following formula:

Formula 10.7(a) **Number of Payments, Given 'FV'**

$$n = \frac{\ln\left(1 + \frac{i \times FV}{PMT}\right)}{\ln(1+i)}$$

If 'PV' is known, using Formula 10.2(b),

$$PV = PMT\left[\frac{1-(1+i)^{-n}}{i}\right]$$

Rearranging and isolating 'n' using natural logarithms (ln) results in the following formula:

Formula 10.7(b)

Number of Payments, Given 'PV'

$$n = -\frac{\ln\left(1 - \frac{i \times PV}{PMT}\right)}{\ln(1+i)}$$

We know that the number of payments during the term of annuity, 'n', is given by

$$n = \text{number of payments per year} \times \text{number of years } (t)$$

Rearranging to isolate 't' results in the following formula for the time period:

Formula 10.7(c)

Time Period

$$t = \frac{n}{Number\ of\ payments\ per\ year}$$

To round the time period up to the next payment period, the value of 'n' can be rounded up to the next whole number of payments. In such situations, the last payment will be of a smaller value than the other payments (PMT).

In an Annuity Due

If 'FV_{Due}' is known, using Formula 10.4(a),

$$FV_{Due} = PMT\left[\frac{(1+i)^n - 1}{i}\right](1+i)$$

Rearranging and isolating 'n' using natural logarithms (ln) results in the following formula:

Formula 10.7(d)

Number of Payments, Given 'FV_{Due}'

$$n = \frac{\ln\left[1 + \frac{i \times FV_{Due}}{PMT(1+i)}\right]}{\ln(1+i)}$$

If 'PV_{Due}' is known, using Formula 10.4(b),

$$PV_{Due} = PMT\left[\frac{1-(1+i)^{-n}}{i}\right](1+i)$$

Isolating 'n' using natural logarithms (ln) results in the following formula:

Formula 10.7(e)

Number of Payments, Given 'PV_{Due}'

$$n = -\frac{\ln\left[1 - \frac{i \times PV_{Due}}{PMT(1+i)}\right]}{\ln(1+i)}$$

Knowing the number of payments, 'n', from above, we can calculate the time period using Formula 10.7(c).

Example 10.7(a)

Calculating the Time Period of an Ordinary General Annuity Given the Future Value

Steve was planning for retirement and invested \$5000 at the end of every year into an RRSP that was earning 12% compounded monthly. How long will it take fo his RRSP fund to grow to \$500,000. Round your answer up to the next payment period.

Solution

This is an ordinary general annuity as:

- Payments are made at the end of each payment period (annually)
- Compounding period (monthly) ≠ payment period (annually)

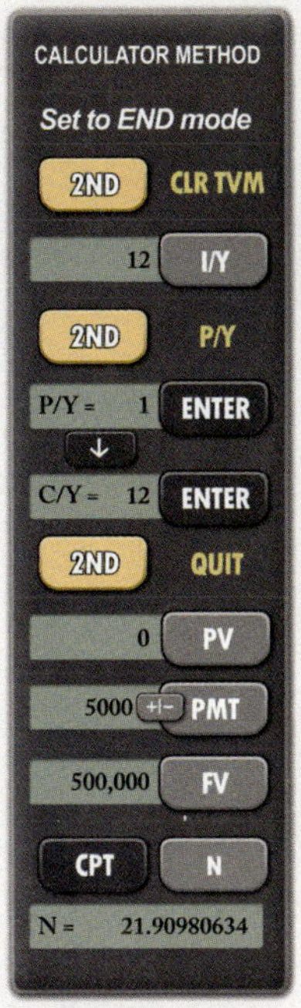

For an ordinary general annuity or a general annuity due, use 'i_2' in place of 'i'.

$PMT = \$5000$ $\quad FV = \$500,000$

$n = ?$

$$j = 0.12, \quad m = 12, \quad i = \frac{j}{m} = 0.01 \text{ per month}$$

$$c = \frac{\textit{Number of compounding periods per year}}{\textit{Number of payments per year}} = \frac{12}{1} = 12$$

$$i_2 = (1 + i)^c - 1 = (1 + 0.01)^{12} - 1 = 0.126825\ldots \text{ per year}$$

Using Formula 10.7(a) and substituting 'i_2' for 'i',

$$n = \frac{\ln\left(1 + \frac{i_2 \times FV}{PMT}\right)}{\ln(1 + i_2)}$$

$$n = \frac{\ln\left(1 + \frac{0.126825\ldots \times 500,000}{5000}\right)}{\ln(1 + 0.126825\ldots)} = 21.909806\ldots$$

By rounding up the number of contributions, the 22nd contribution will be of a smaller amount than the other contributions.

$n = 22$ contributions (rounded up to the next payment)

Time period, $$t = \frac{n}{\textit{Number of payments per year}}$$

$$= \frac{22}{1} = 22 \text{ years}$$

Therefore, it will take 22 years for the funds in the RRSP to grow to \$500,000.

Example 10.7(b) Calculating the Time Period of an Ordinary General Annuity Given the Present Value

James won a lottery of \$50,000 and he deposited the money in an investment fund earning 6% compounded semi-annually. If he were to withdraw \$5000 at the end of every 3 months, how long (rounded up to the next payment period) would the money last in the fund?

Solution

This is an ordinary general annuity as:

- Payments are made at the end of each payment period (quarterly)
- Compounding period (semi-annually) ≠ payment period (quarterly)

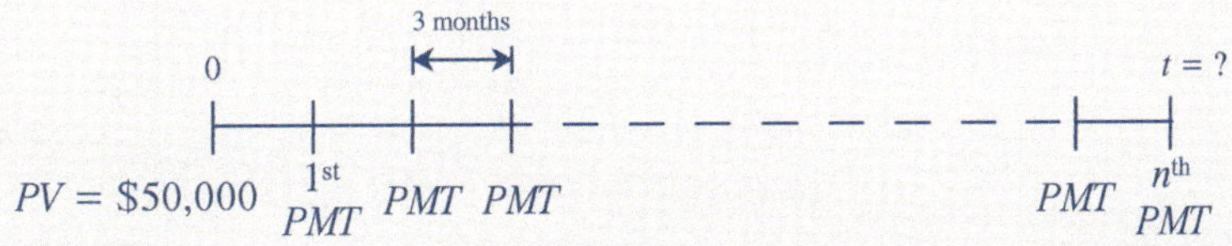

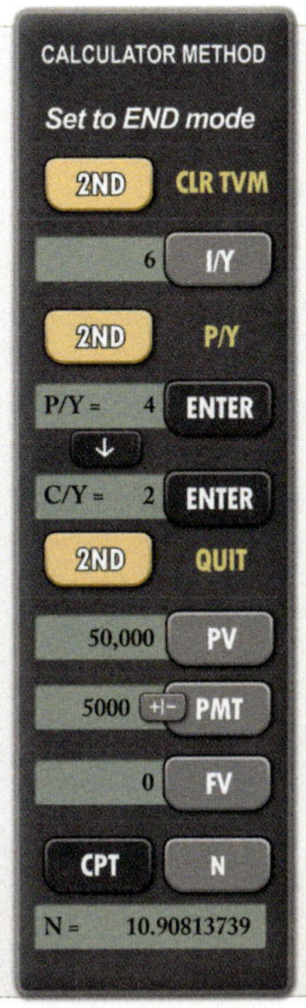

$PMT = \$5000$

$n = ?$

$$j = 0.06, \quad m = 2, \quad i = \frac{j}{m} = 0.03 \text{ per half-year}$$

$$c = \frac{\textit{Number of compounding periods per year}}{\textit{Number of payments per year}} = \frac{2}{4}$$

$$i_2 = (1 + i)^c - 1 = (1 + 0.03)^{2/4} - 1 = 0.014889\ldots \text{ per quarter}$$

Solution continued

Using Formula 10.7(b) and substituting 'i_2' for 'i',

$$n = -\frac{\ln\left(1 - \frac{i_2 \times PV}{PMT}\right)}{\ln(1 + i_2)}$$

$$= -\frac{\ln\left(1 - \frac{0.014889... \times 50,000}{5000}\right)}{\ln(1 + 0.014889...)} = 10.908137...$$

= 11 withdrawals (rounded up to the next withdrawal)

Note that by rounding up the number of withdrawals, the 11th withdrawal will be of a smaller amount than the other withdrawals.

$$t = \frac{n}{Number\ of\ payments\ per\ year} = \frac{11}{4}$$

= 2.75 years = 2 years and (0.75 × 12 months) = 2 years and 9 months

Therefore, it would take him 2 years and 9 months to receive the entire payment.

Example 10.7(c)

Calculating the Time Period of a General Annuity Due Given the Present Value

Campwood Inc. invested $20,000 in an investment fund that is growing at 10% compounded semi-annually. If Campwood were to withdraw $1600 from this fund at the beginning of every month, how long (rounded up to the next payment period) will the money last?

Solution

This is a general annuity due as:

- Payments are made at the beginning of each payment period (monthly)
- Compounding period (semi-annually) ≠ payment period (monthly)

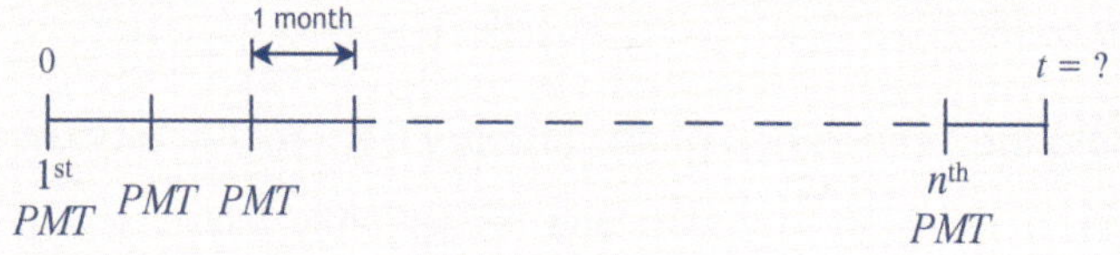

PV = $20,000

PMT = $1600

n = ?

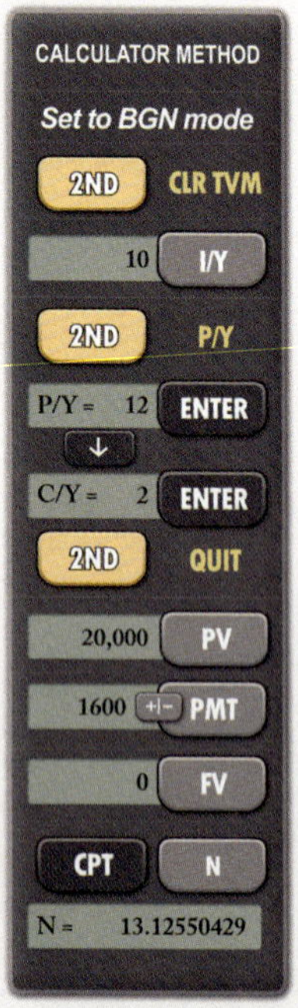

$$j = 0.10, \quad m = 2, \quad i = \frac{j}{m} = 0.05 \text{ per half-year}$$

$$c = \frac{Number\ of\ compounding\ periods\ per\ year}{Number\ of\ payments\ per\ year} = \frac{2}{12}$$

$$i_2 = (1 + i)^c - 1 = (1 + 0.05)^{2/12} - 1 = 0.008164... \text{ per month}$$

Using Formula 10.7(e) and substituting 'i_2' for 'i',

$$n = -\frac{\ln\left[1 - \frac{i_2 \times PV_{Due}}{PMT(1 + i_2)}\right]}{\ln(1 + i_2)}$$

$$= -\frac{\ln\left[1 - \frac{0.008164... \times 20,000}{1600(1 + 0.008164...)}\right]}{\ln(1 + 0.008164...)} = 13.125504...$$

= 14 withdrawals (rounded up to the next withdrawal)

Note that by rounding up the number of withdrawals, the 14th withdrawal will be a smaller amount than the other withdrawals.

Solution continued

$$t = \frac{n}{\textit{Number of payments per year}} = \frac{14}{12}$$
$$= 1.166666...\text{ years}$$
$$= 1\text{ year and }(0.166666... \times 12\text{ months})$$
$$= 1\text{ year and }2\text{ months}$$

Therefore, the money will last for 1 year and 2 months in the fund.

10.7 | Exercises

In the following problems, round the time period up to the next payment period wherever applicable.

CFA Prep.
1. How many $100 end-of-year payments are required to accumulate at least $920 if the discount rate is 9% compounded annually?

2. Bridgette has been depositing $400 at the end of every month in a savings account with a goal of accumulating $25,000. If her account earns 4% compounded monthly, many deposits will she have to make to reach her goal?

CFA Prep.
3. If you purchased a $1000 annuity that is earning 8% compounded annually, then how many annual end-of-year $150 withdrawals would this annuity provide you?

4. Longcore Technologies has to settle a personal loan of $80,000, which has an interest rate of 12% compounded semi-annually, by making semi-annual payments of $20,000 (with the first payment being made 6 months from now). How many payments will it take to settle the loan?

5. Ashton deposits $1000 at the end of every month in an RRSP for 20 years. If the RRSP is earning 5% compounded quarterly, how long will it take for his investment to accumulate to $40,000?

6. Lilly has been depositing $2000 into a fund at the end of every 3 months to save for her daughter's education. If the fund earns 6% compounded monthly, how long will it take for the investment to grow to $20,000?

7. Dao-ming will make payments of $50 at the end of each month to settle a loan of $1200 that he used to purchase a television. How long will it take for him to settle the loan if the interest rate charged was 4% compounded quarterly?

8. Lush Gardens Co. bought a new truck for $40,000, financed by a loan with interest rate of 8.5% compounded semi-annually. If the company makes payments of $1500 at the end of every month, how long will it take to pay off the loan?

• 9. Samantha made regular equal deposits into a savings account at the end of every month for 3 years. Her investments were earning 5% compounded quarterly and grew to $12,800 at the end of 3 years. Calculate the size of her month-end deposits. How long will it take for the $12,800 to accumulate to $45,000 if the interest rate remains the same and she continues making the same month–end deposits?

• 10. Wang's RRSP investment, which has month-end contributions, accumulated $18,435 in 2 years at 2.5% compounded quarterly. What was the size of his month-end contributions to the RRSP? How long did it take for $18,435 to accumulate to $35,000 if the interest rate changed to 2.75% compounded monthly? Assume that the size of his contributions were the same throughout the period.

10.8 | Calculating the Periodic Interest Rate (i), and Nominal Interest Rate (j)

Calculating the periodic interest rate 'i' using algebraic methods is difficult as 'i' cannot be isolated easily from the present value and future value formulas. Thus, there is no formula to calculate 'i', although the value for 'i' can be calculated using a trial-and-error method – a time-consuming procedure with some 'guessing'. However, the financial calculator can be used to calculate the value of 'j'. Therefore, in this section you will learn only the financial calculator method to calculate 'j'. Once 'j' is calculated, the periodic interest rate (i) can be calculated using the formula $i = \frac{j}{m}$.

Example 10.8(a)

Calculating the Nominal and Periodic Interest Rates of an Ordinary Simple Annuity,Given the Present Value

What are the nominal interest rate compounded monthly and the periodic interest rate per month of a $25,000 loan that can be settled by making payments of $240 at the end of every month for 10 years?

Solution

From the calculator computations shown, the interest rate is 2.88% compounded monthly.

Therefore, the nominal interest rate is 2.88% compounded monthly and the periodic interest rate can be calculated as follows:

$$i = \frac{j}{m}$$

Substituting values, $$i = \frac{0.028783...}{12} = 0.002398...$$

$$= 0.24\% \text{ per month.}$$

CALCULATOR METHOD

Set to END mode

2ND CLR TVM

120 N

2ND P/Y

P/Y = 12 ENTER

2ND QUIT

25,000 PV

240 +/- PMT

0 FV

CPT I/Y

I/Y = 2.87830165

Example 10.8(b)

Calculating the Nominal and Periodic Interest Rates of a General Annuity Due, Given the Future Value

At what nominal interest rate compounded quarterly would payments of $1500 to an RRSP at the beginning of every six months give a maturity value of $50,000 in 12 years? Also, find the corresponding periodic interest rate per quarter.

Solution

From the calculator computations shown, the interest rate is 5.05% compounded quarterly.

Therefore, the nominal interest rate would be 5.05% compounded quarterly and the periodic interest rate can be calculated as follows:

$$i = \frac{j}{m}$$

Substituting values, $$i = \frac{0.050472...}{4} = 0.012618...$$

$$= 1.26\% \text{ per quarter.}$$

For all annuity due calculations, remember to set your calculator to 'BGN' mode.

CALCULATOR METHOD

Set to BGN mode

2ND CLR TVM

24 N

2ND P/Y

P/Y = 2 ENTER

↓

C/Y = 4 ENTER

2ND QUIT

0 PV

1500 +/- PMT

50,000 FV

CPT I/Y

I/Y = 5.047278144

10.8 | Exercises

CFA Prep.

1. You invested $100 at the end of each year for 5 years in an investment fund. At the end of the 5th year, if the balance in the fund was $600, what was the annual compounding rate of return on your investment?

2. Oliver deposits $300 in his savings account at the end of every month for 3 years and 6 months. What nominal interest rate compounded monthly is his savings account earning if it accumulates to $14,575?

CFA Prep.

3. What is the annual compounding rate of return that you will earn on an ordinary annuity that requires a $700 deposit today and promises to pay $100 at the end of every year for the next 10 years?

4. Rebecca can afford to pay $750 at the end of every month as repayment for a 5-year loan from a bank. If she wants to purchase a parking space in her apartment that costs $40,745 with the loan, calculate the nominal interest rate compounded annually that she should secure for the loan.

5. Robert and Martha wanted to ensure that they had $100,000 for their child's university education. As soon as their child was born, they started saving $500 every quarter in an investment fund. If they achieved their investment target on their child's 21st birthday, calculate the nominal interest rate compounded quarterly and the effective rate for the investment. Assume no deposit was made on the child's 21st birthday.

6. If the accumulated value of an investment was $10,000 after deposits of $200 were made to the investment at the beginning of each quarter for a period of 10 years, calculate the nominal interest rate of the fund if the investment was compounded quarterly. Also, find the effective interest rate of the fund.

7. Raga Steel Corporation took a loan of $1,780,000 to build a new office complex for the staff. Calculate the semi-annually compounding interest rate charged on the loan if $10,000 was repaid at the beginning of every month and the loan was paid off in 25 years.

8. Paul received a car loan of $18,000 and had to make regular payments of $300 at the beginning of every month. What was the quarterly compounding interest rate charged on the loan if he settled the loan in 5 years and 9 months?

9. Nailah made payments of $200 at the end of every 3 months into a retirement fund, which had accumulated $40,000 over 20 years.
   a. At what interest rate compounded quarterly was she earning interest in the fund (assuming the rate remained constant throughout the 20-year term)?
   b. At what interest rate compounded quarterly would she have been able to accumulate the same $40,000 in only 15 years?

10. Standard Co. makes deposits of $5000 at the end of every month into an investment fund which will accumulate to $1.5 million in 15 years.
    a. At what interest rate compounded monthly is Standard Co. earning interest in the fund (assuming the rate remains constant throughout the 15-year term)?
    b. At what interest rate compounded monthly would the fund accumulate to $1.5 million in 10 years, rather than 15 years (without changing the size of the monthly payments).

10 | Review Examples

Example 1

Find the maturity value of $1000 invested at the end of every 3 months for 10 years at 8% compounded semi-annually.

Solution

This is an ordinary general annuity as:

- Payments are made at the end of each payment period (quarterly)
- Compounding period (semi-annually) ≠ payment period (quarterly)

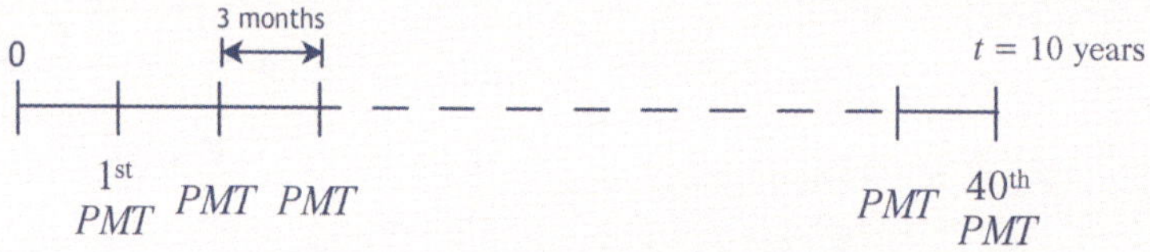

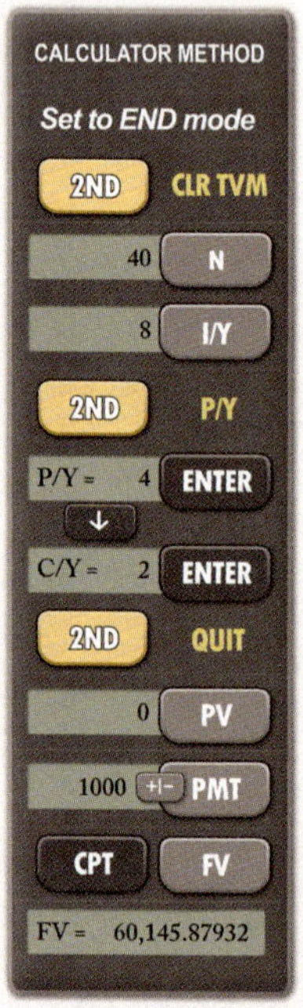

$PMT = \$1000$ $\qquad FV = ?$

$n = 4$ payments/year × 10 years = 40 quarterly payments

$j = 0.08, \quad m = 2, \quad i = \frac{j}{m} = 0.04$ per half-year

$$c = \frac{\text{Number of compounding periods per year}}{\text{Number of payments per year}} = \frac{2}{4}$$

$i_2 = (1 + i)^c - 1 = (1+0.04)^{(2/4)} - 1 = 0.019803...$ per quarter

Using Formula 10.2(a) and substituting 'i_2' for 'i',

$$FV = PMT\left[\frac{(1 + i_2)^n - 1}{i_2}\right] = 1000\left[\frac{(1 + 0.019803...)^{40} - 1}{0.019803...}\right]$$

$$= 1000[60.145879...] = \$60,145.879322...$$

Therefore, the maturity value is $60,145.88.

Example 2

What amount of loan at 8% compounded semi-annually can be repaid in 10 years with payments of $1000 at the end of every quarter?

Solution

This is an ordinary general annuity as:

- Payments are made at the end of each payment period (quarterly)
- Compounding period (semi-annually) ≠ payment period (quarterly)

$PV = ?$ $\qquad PMT = \$1000$

$n = 4$ payments/year × 10 years = 40 quarterly payments

$j = 0.08, \quad m = 2, \quad i = \frac{j}{m} = 0.04$ per half-year

$$c = \frac{\text{Number of compounding periods per year}}{\text{Number of payments per year}} = \frac{2}{4}$$

Solution continued

$i_2 = (1 + i)^c - 1 = (1+0.04)^{(2/4)} - 1 = 0.019803...$ per quarter

Using Formula 10.2(b) and substituting 'i_2' for 'i',

$$PV = PMT\left[\frac{1-(1+i_2)^{-n}}{i_2}\right]$$

$$= 1000\left[\frac{1-(1+0.019803...)^{-40}}{0.019803...}\right]$$

$$= 1000\,[27.449794...] = \$27,449.79419...$$

Therefore, a loan of \$27,449.79 can be repaid in 10 years.

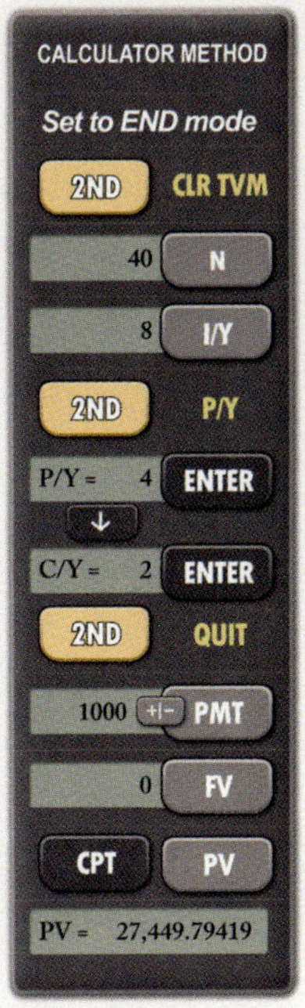

Example 3

What payments at the end of every 3 months at 8% compounded semi-annually will accumulate \$60,145.88 in 10 years?

Solution

This is an ordinary general annuity as:

- Payments are made at the end of each payment period (quarterly)
- Compounding period (semi-annually) ≠ payment period (quarterly)

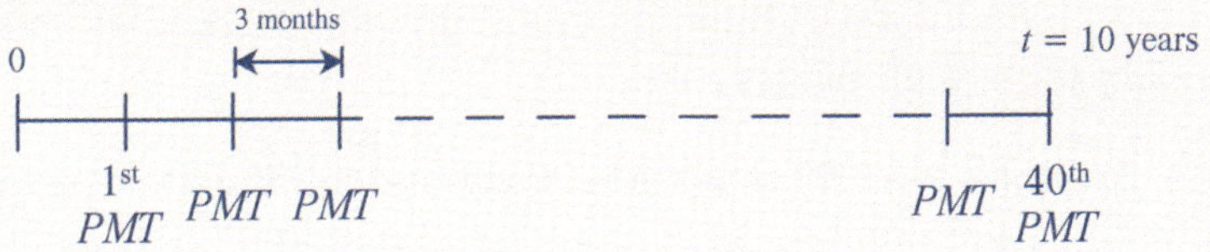

$PMT = ?$ $FV = \$60,145.88$

$n = 4$ payments/year × 10 years $= 40$ quarterly payments

$j = 0.08, \quad m = 2, \quad i = \frac{j}{m} = 0.04$ per half-year

$$c = \frac{\textit{Number of compounding periods per year}}{\textit{Number of payments per year}} = \frac{2}{4}$$

$i_2 = (1 + i)^c - 1 = (1+0.04)^{(2/4)} - 1 = 0.019803...$ per quarter

Using Formula 10.2(a) and substituting 'i_2' for 'i',

$$FV = PMT\left[\frac{(1+i_2)^n - 1}{i_2}\right]$$

$$60,145.88 = PMT\left[\frac{(1+0.019803...)^{40} - 1}{0.019803...}\right]$$

$$60,145.88 = PMT\,[60.145879...]$$

$$PMT = \$1000.000011...$$

Therefore, payments of \$1000 at the end of every 3 months will accumulate \$60,145.88 in 10 years.

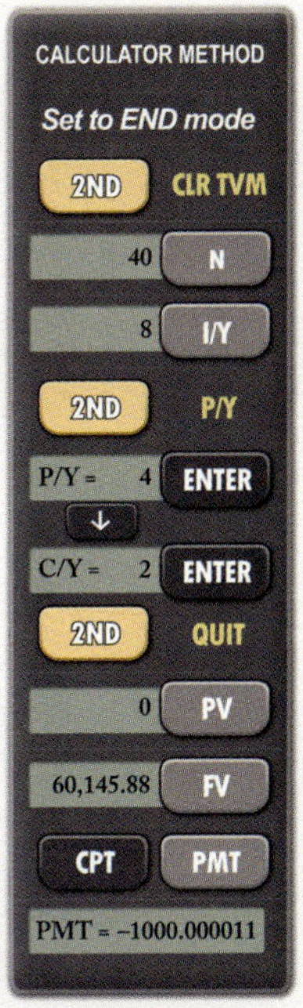

Example 4

What payments at the end of every quarter will pay off a loan of $27,449.79 in 10 years at 8% compounded semi-annually?

Solution

This is an ordinary general annuity as:

- Payments are made at the end of each payment period (quarterly)
- Compounding period (semi-annually) ≠ payment period (quarterly)

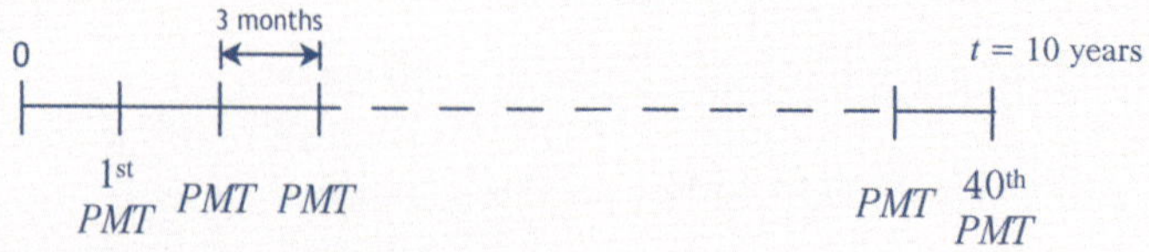

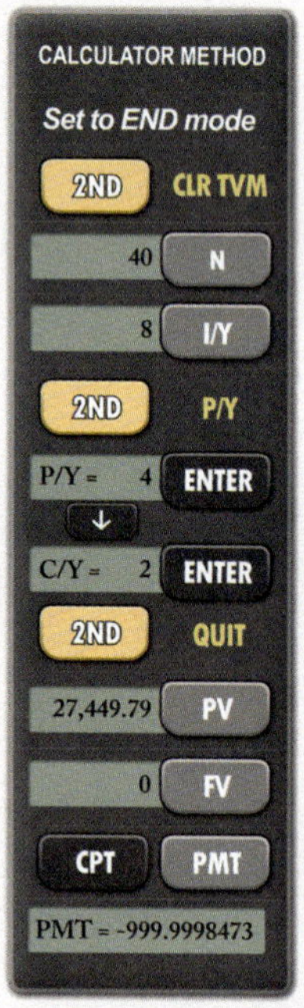

PV = $27,449.79 PMT = ?

n = 4 payments/year × 10 years = 40 quarterly payments

$j = 0.08, \quad m = 2, \quad i = \frac{j}{m} = 0.04$ per half-year

$$c = \frac{\textit{Number of compounding periods per year}}{\textit{Number of payments per year}} = \frac{2}{4}$$

$i_2 = (1 + i)^c - 1 = (1+0.04)^{(2/4)} - 1 = 0.019803...$ per quarter

Using Formula 10.2(b) and substituting 'i_2' for 'i',

$$PV = PMT\left[\frac{1-(1+i_2)^{-n}}{i_2}\right]$$

$$27{,}449.79 = PMT\left[\frac{1-(1+0.019803...)^{-40}}{0.019803...}\right]$$

$$27{,}449.79 = PMT\,[27.449794...]$$

$$PMT = \$999.999847...$$

Therefore, payments of $1000 at the end of every quarter will settle a loan of $27,449.79 in 10 years.

Example 5

How long would it take to accumulate $60,145.88 with $1000 payments at the end of every 3 months if invested at 8% compounded semi-annually?

Solution

This is an ordinary general annuity as:

- Payments are made at the end of each payment period (quarterly)
- Compounding period (semi-annually) ≠ payment period (quarterly)

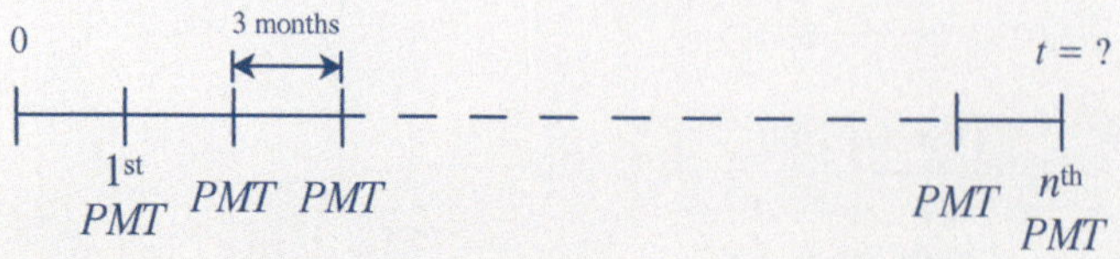

PMT = $1000 FV = $60,145.88

n = ?

$j = 0.08, \quad m = 2, \quad i = \frac{j}{m} = 0.04$ per half-year

10 | Review Exercises

Answers to odd-numbered problems are available at the end of the textbook

1. How much interest would be earned if \$800 is invested at the end of every 3 months at 6% compounded quarterly for 5 years.

2. Paul contributed \$1250 at the end of every 6 months to an RRSP fund earning 5% compounded semi-annually for 15 years. Calculate the amount of interest earned over this period.

3. What single payment now is equivalent to month-end payments of \$1000 for 10 years. Assume money earns 9% compounded monthly.

4. Calculate the amount of a loan that can be settled by payments of \$750 at the end of every 3 months for 3 years if money earns 6% compounded quarterly.

5. Evelyn saved \$1000 at the end of every 6 months for 5 years in a savings account that earned 4% compounded semi-annually. At the end of the 5 years, she let her money compound at 6% compounded quarterly for the next 5 years. Calculate the balance in her savings account at the end of 10 years and the total interest earned over this term.

6. Schmidt invested \$5540 at the end of every 3 months in an investment that was earning interest at a rate of 9% compounded quarterly. He stopped making regular deposits at the end of 5 years when the interest rate changed to 8.75% compounded monthly. However, he let the money grow in this investment account for the next 2 years. Calculate the accumulated balance in his investment account at the end of the 7-year period and the total interest earned over this period.

7. Deposits of \$1500 are made to an investment fund at the end of each month for 8 years. What will be the accumulated value of the fund if the interest earned is 6% compounded annually for the first half of the term and 3% compounded quarterly for the second half of the term?

8. Zoe started investing \$700 at the end of every month into an RRSP that has an interest rate of 4% compounded semi-annually. Three years later, the interest rate on her RRSP increased to 5% compounded monthly and remained the same thereafter. How much would she have accumulated in her RRSP after a period of 7 years?

9. Albert purchased a property by making a down payment of \$50,000 and month-end payments of \$1500 for 15 years. What was the value of the property if money is worth 6% compounded semi-annually.

10. Lina wants to receive \$5000 at the end of every 6 months for the next 7 years. How much money should she invest now at 3.75% compounded monthly?

11. For the past 10 years, Anton has been depositing \$1000 into an RRSP at the beginning of each year. If the interest rate for the first 4 years was 6.0% compounded annually and for the next 6 years was 6.5% compounded annually, calculate the accumulated value of his investment at the end of the 10 years. How much of this was earned from interest?

12. Since the birth of her daughter, 16 years ago, Solange has deposited \$50 at the beginning of every month into an RESP. The interest rate on the plan was 4.8% compounded monthly for the first 8 years and 4.2% compounded monthly for the next 8 years. Calculate the value of the fund today (the end of a 16-year term). How much of this is interest?

13. Henry wanted to accumulate \$25,000 in 8 years, by making equal deposits into an investment fund at the end of every 3 months. What must be the size of each deposit if the fund earns 5% compounded quarterly.

14. How much did Alexis deposit every month in her savings account if she had $15,000 after 24 month-end deposits. The money in her account was growing at 4.8% compounded monthly.

15. melia received a loan of $30,000 at an interest rate of 9.5% compounded monthly to renovate her basement. What is the size of her month-end payments that is required to clear the loan in 6 years?

16. Marblestone, a retail appliance store, sold a refrigerator that costs $1,599.97 with 3-year financing to a customer who made a down payment of $599.97. What should be the size of the loan payments at the end of each month if an interest rate of 12% compounded monthly is charged?

• 17. Rosy wanted to have savings of $100,000 in 10 years so she made equal deposits at the end of every 6 months into a savings account at 5% compounded semi-annually. If the interest rate offered was 5% compounded monthly instead of 5% compounded semi-annually, by how much would the size of her deposits reduce to ensure that she would have the same accumulated amount at the end of 10 years?

• 18. Amanda's bank offers her an interest rate of 7% compounded monthly on her investments. How much more money would she have to deposit at the end of every month for her fund to accumulate to $30,000 in 8 years if the interest rate was 7% compounded semi-annually?

19. Harris took a loan to purchase a large offset printing machine. He had to make payments of $500 at the beginning of each month for 3 years at an interest rate of 5.5% compounded monthly. What was the cost of the printer if he had to make a down payment of $1000 when purchasing it?

20. Irene purchased a scooter for her grandmother and financed it with a loan at 8% compounded quarterly. If she had to pay a down payment of $200 and then $70 at the beginning of every 3 months for 4 years, what was the cost of the scooter at the time of purchase and how much interest did she have to pay over the period of the loan?

21. A car was purchased with a down payment of $4000 and monthly loan payments of $360 payable at the beginning of each month for 5 years. If the interest charged on the loan was 5% compounded annually, calculate the purchase price of the car.

22. Edwin wants to set up a fund for his son's education so that he would be able to withdraw $2000 at the beginning of every 3 months for the next 5 years. If the fund can earn 3.6% compounded semi-annually, what amount must he deposit today to provide the payment?

23. How long will it take (rounded up to the next payment period) for Carol to settle her student loan of $25,000 that has an interest rate of 6% compounded monthly if she makes end-of-month payments of $500 each?

24. Bilal has a loan of $55,000 that has an interest rate of 12% compounded quarterly. How long (rounded up to the next payment period) will it take him to clear the loan if he makes end-of-quarter payments of $10,000 each?

25. How long (rounded up to the next payment period) will it take to repay a student loan of $30,000 if payments of $500 are made at the end of every month and the interest rate on the loan is 5.4% compounded semi-annually?

26. A $325,000 mortgage loan is to be repaid by monthly payments of $1750.00. If the interest rate on the loan is 4.5% compounded semi-annually, what is the term of the loan (rounded up to the next payment period)?

27. Jerry and Jill were saving up for a $25,000 European tour. Together, they've been putting away $2000 at the end of every month into an investment providing them with an interest rate that was compounding monthly. If they achieved their investment target in one year, calculate the nominal and periodic interest rates of the investment.

28. Shortboard Inc. is investing in a new manufacturing process which will cost them $220,000. To accumulate this amount, they save $8,000 at the end of every quarter for 6 years in an investment fund that provides interest compounding quarterly. Calculate the required nominal and periodic interest rates of the investment.

29. A car loan of $20,000 was settled in 4 years with quarterly payments of $2000. Calculate the monthly compounding interest rate on this loan.

30. Month-end contributions of $150 were made to an RESP fund for 10 years. If the accumulated value of the fund at the end of the last contribution was $25,000, calculate the annually compounding interest rate at which the fund was growing.

10 | Self-Test Exercises

Answers to all problems are available at the end of the textbook

1. Ronny had a balance of $2000 in his RRSP. In addition to this, he invested $500 at the end of every 3 months for 5 years and 6 months. If his RRSP earned 4% compounded quarterly for the first 2 years and 4.25% compounded quarterly for the rest of the period, how much did he have in the RRSP at the end of the time period? What were his total earnings?

2. Andrew won a lottery and must decide among the following options:
   a. $50,000 cash today.
   b. $1250 at the end of every 3 months for 20 years.
   c. $400 at the end of every month for 20 years.

   If money is worth 9% compounded annually, which option is best, based on the present value of the offer?

3. Hurd Corporation wants to save $10,000 at the end of every year for 5 years. Bank A offers an interest rate of 6% compounded quarterly and Bank B offers an interest rate of 6% compounded monthly. Hurd Corporation is considering the following two options:
   a. Save $4000 annually in Bank A and $6000 annually in Bank B.
   b. Save $6000 annually in Bank A and $4000 annually in Bank B.

   Which option is economically better?

4. A 20-year loan is amortized by payments of $1200 made at the end of each month. If the interest rate is 4% compounded semi-annually, what is the loan principal?

5. How long would it take to save at least $50,000 by making month-end deposits of $500 in a savings account that earns 3.5% compounded semi-annually?

6. How many more payments would be required to be able to accumulate at least $200,000 by saving $1500 at the end of every 3 months instead of $1500 at the beginning of every month? Assume an interest rate of 6% compounded quarterly.

7. How much more money should be invested now in order to receive $900 at the beginning of each month for 10 months instead of $300 at the beginning of each month for 30 months? Assume an interest rate of 6% compounded semi-annually.

8. Nuben obtained a business loan of $300,000 at 4.5% compounded semi-annually.
   a. What is the size of the semi-annual payments to be made over 20 years in order to pay off the loan?
   b. Calculate the interest paid on the loan.

9. Ann obtained a loan of $50,000 at 3.6% compounded monthly. How long (rounded up to the next payment period) will it take to settle the loan with month-end payments of $500?

10. Stephanie paid off her student loan in 5 years by making payments of $750 at the beginning of every month. If the interest rate on her loan was 6.0% compounded monthly, calculate the size of the original loan and the amount of interest paid on the loan.

11. Atif plans to retire on his 40th birthday. He has been saving $1200 every month since his 22nd birthday in a fund that earns 7.5% compounded annually. What would the balance be in the fund on his 40th birthday, assuming that he did not make any investment on his 40th birthday? What was his contribution and interest earned through the years?

12. The interest rate on a 15-year, $100,000 mortgage is 4% compounded semi-annually. Calculate the amount of interest saved if the mortgage was settled with month-end payments in 10 years instead of month-end payments in 15 years.

• 13. How much more money should be deposited at the end of every month to accumulate $50,000 in 10 years at 6.2% compounded quarterly instead of 6.2% compounded monthly?

14. For how long can $750 be withdrawn at the beginning of each month from a fund of $35,000 if the interest rate is 3.6% compounded monthly?

• 15. A mortgage of $190,000 was settled in 25 years with payments of $2750 at the end of every 3 months. Calculate the monthly compounded interest paid on this loan. At this rate, what month-end payments would have settled the loan in 15 years?

CASE 10
Saving for Retirement

At the age of 30, Logan decided to create a financial plan to retire in 25 years. He had the following retirement objectives:

- Home purchase objective: Own a home worth at least $800,000 with no mortgage.
- Vacation objective: Have an amount of $45,000 for a European tour.
- Monthly allowance objective: Receive a month-beginning allowance of $2000 for 20 years after retirement.

He created the following financial plans to achieve the above retirement objectives. Answer the questions related to each plan.

Plan to achieve his home purchase objective

Assuming that the value of a property in a Toronto suburb would double over 25 years, Logan would purchase a house worth $400,000 by paying a down-payment of $20,000 and taking a mortgage for the balance amount from a local bank at 4% compounded semi-annually for 25 years.

a. If the interest rate is constant over the 25 year period, calculate his month-beginning payments for the mortgage. What would be his total investment in the house over the term?

Plan to achieve his vacation objective

Deposit $150 at the end of every month for 10 years into a savings account that earns 3% compounded monthly. At the end of 10 years, transfer the accumulated money into an investment fund that earns 6% compounded quarterly. Let the money grow in this fund until retirement.

b. Rounding to the nearest month, how long would it take to accumulate the required amount of $45,000 to pay for his vacation?

c. To ensure that the amount accumulates to only $45,000 at the time of retirement, by how much should he change his monthly deposit?

Plan to achieve his monthly allowance objective

He will save $500 at the beginning of every month until retirement in an RRSP that has a constant interest rate of 5.4% compounded monthly.

d. What would be the accumulated value in the RRSP at the time of retirement?

e. What should the monthly compounding interest rate on the RRSP change to through the period of retirement for him to be able to withdraw the required amount of $2000 for 20 years? Assume the same interest rate of 5.4% compounded monthly during this period.

Summary of the Types of Annuities and their Formulas

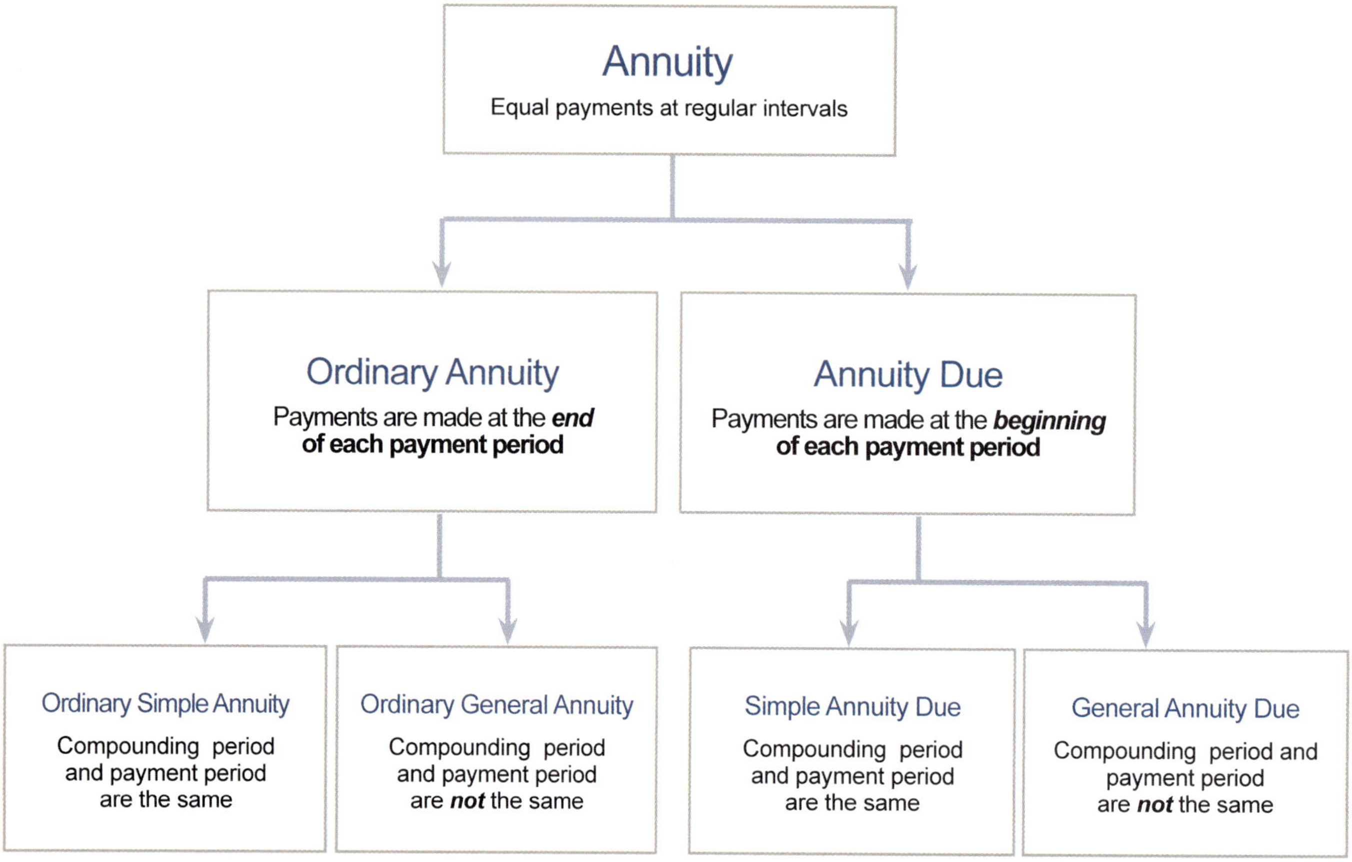

$$FV = PMT\left[\frac{(1+i)^n - 1}{i}\right]$$

$$PV = PMT\left[\frac{1-(1+i)^{-n}}{i}\right]$$

$$FV_{Due} = PMT\left[\frac{(1+i)^n - 1}{i}\right](1+i)$$

$$PV_{Due} = PMT\left[\frac{1-(1+i)^{-n}}{i}\right](1+i)$$

In the case of ordinary general annuity and general annuity due, substitute 'i_2' for 'i' in the annuity formulas.

$$c = \frac{\text{Number of compounding periods per year}}{\text{Number of payments per year}}$$

$$i_2 = (1+i)^c - 1$$

10 | Summary of Notation and Formulas

NOTATION

PMT = Amount of periodic payment in an annuity

n = Number of payments during the term of an annuity

= Number of compounding periods during the term of a single payment in compound interest

i = Interest rate per conversion period (periodic interest rate)

c = Number of compounding periods per payment period

i_2 = Equivalent interest rate per payment period

j = Nominal interest rate

t = Time period or Term

FV = Accumulated value or future value of an ordinary annuity

FV_{Due} = Accumulated value or future value of an annuity due

PV = Discounted value or present value of an ordinary annuity

PV_{Due} = Discounted value or present value of an annuity due

FORMULAS

Future Value of an Ordinary Simple Annuity | 10.2 (a)

$$FV = PMT\left[\frac{(1+i)^n - 1}{i}\right]$$

Present Value of an Ordinary Simple Annuity | 10.2 (b)

$$PV = PMT\left[\frac{1-(1+i)^{-n}}{i}\right]$$

Number of Compounding Periods per Payment Period | 10.3 (a)

$$c = \frac{\textit{Number of compounding periods per year}}{\textit{Number of payments per year}}$$

Equivalent Periodic Interest Rate per Payment Period | 10.3 (b)

$$i_2 = (1+i)^c - 1$$

In the case of ordinary general annuity and general annuity due, substitute 'i_2' for 'i' in the formulas.

Future Value of a Simple Annuity Due | 10.4 (a)

$$FV_{Due} = PMT\left[\frac{(1+i)^n - 1}{i}\right](1+i)$$

Present Value of a Simple Annuity Due | 10.4 (b)

$$PV_{Due} = PMT\left[\frac{1-(1+i)^{-n}}{i}\right](1+i)$$

Number of Payments, Given 'FV' | 10.7 (a)

$$n = \frac{\ln\left(1 + \frac{i \times FV}{PMT}\right)}{\ln(1+i)}$$

Number of Payments, Given 'PV' | 10.7 (b)

$$n = -\frac{\ln\left(1 - \frac{i \times PV}{PMT}\right)}{\ln(1+i)}$$

Time Period | 10.7 (c)

$$t = \frac{n}{\textit{Number of payments per year}}$$

Number of Payments, Given 'FV_{Due}' | 10.7 (d)

$$n = \frac{\ln\left[1 + \frac{i \times FV_{Due}}{PMT(1+i)}\right]}{\ln(1+i)}$$

Number of Payments, Given 'PV_{Due}' | 10.7 (e)

$$n = -\frac{\ln\left[1 - \frac{i \times PV_{Due}}{PMT(1+i)}\right]}{\ln(1+i)}$$

Expert Advice

Understanding Your Investment Options

Armed with the knowledge of annuities, it is important to know the different investment options that are available in Canada.

The Canadian investment landscape is structured to cater to the needs of individuals with low-, medium-, and high-risk tolerance. Low-risk investments yield low returns, whereas, high-risk investments yield high returns. The appropriate investment for individuals is determined by three things: investment objective, risk profile, and time period of investment. Investments can be made directly into investment vehicles such as bonds, shares, T-bills, etc., or through investment plans such as RRSPs, RESPs, etc., which have particular tax benefits, as you will see later in this section.

Investment vehicles are differentiated based on their risk and return. If you are a low-risk person, you can invest in debt instruments, which are low-risk and provide low returns. However, if you are a high-risk person, you can invest in the equity market, which has higher risk and higher returns.

HIGH RISK, HIGH RETURN

Equity Investments

5

Shares (*or stocks*):
In order to raise money, companies offer ownership of their business either to the public or a select, private group of people in the form of shares or stock.

4

Mutual Funds:
Investment vehicles that contain a portfolio of investments that are managed to provide the required rate of return.

3

Bonds:
Investment where you lend money to a bond-issuer (who may be the government, or a corporation) who gives you a bond that promises to pay you a specified interest during the bond's life and the face value (principal) on maturity.

2

Treasury Bills (*T-Bills*):
Investment offered and guaranteed by the Government of Canada.

1

Guaranteed Investment Certificate (*GIC*):
Investment where the principal and return are guaranteed. These investments are offered by banks, credit unions, and trust companies.

Debt Investments

LOW RISK, LOW RETURN

> *"Buy when everyone else is selling and hold until everyone else is buying. That's not just a catchy slogan. It's the very essence of successful investing."*
>
> *J. Paul Getty, Industrialist*

Investment Plans are methods of investing in investment vehicles. Investment plans are non-registered when you directly invest in an investment vehicle, or registered when they are approved by the Federal Government and may have special tax advantages to the investor. Registered plans contain a mix of one or many investment vehicles in different proportions. The rate of return of the plan is the average of the individual rates of returns of each investment vehicle in the plan. The four most popular investment plans are described below.

Registered Retirement Savings Plan:
Initiated by the Federal Government to encourage people to invest towards their retirement with a tax deduction as incentive.

RRSP

Registered Education Savings Plan:
Initiated by the Federal Government to encourage parents to save for the education of their children. The investment will grow tax-free and will be given to the child on enrolment in a post-secondary educational program at low or no tax.

RESP

Tax Free Savings Account :
Recent initiative of the Federal Government offering tax-free investment with a maximum of $5000 per individual per year.

TFSA

Registered Retirement Income Fund:
A plan to convert RRSPs to a tax-efficient annuity where the RRSP investment will be distributed in regular instalments with low tax.

RRIF

Source: World Financial Group

In the previous chapter, we learned how to analyze situations when series of equal payments are invested or borrowed at regular intervals for a fixed period of time. However, there are many practical situations when an annuity begins after a certain time interval, known as deferred annuities, or there may be no fixed period of time for the annuity payments (i.e., payments are continued indefinitely, known as a perpetuity), or the size of the payment may be increasing at a constant growth rate. This chapter deals with these three different types of annuities called deferred annuities, perpetuities, and constant-growth annuities.

11 Other Types of Annuities

LEARNING OBJECTIVES

- Calculate the present value, number of payments, term, and periodic payment of a deferred annuity.
- Calculate the present value and periodic payment of a perpetuity.
- Calculate the future value and present value of a constant-growth annuity.

CHAPTER OUTLINE

11.1 | Deferred Annuities

A deferred annuity is an annuity in which the first periodic payment is made after a certain interval of time, known as the **deferral period**. The deferral period is the time interval from 'now' to the beginning of the annuity period.

A deferred annuity is an annuity in which the first periodic payment is made after a certain interval of time.

Ordinary Deferred Annuity

In a deferred annuity, if the periodic payments are made at the end of each payment period, then it is an ordinary deferred annuity. Here, the deferral period ends one payment interval before the first periodic payment, as shown in the line diagram below:

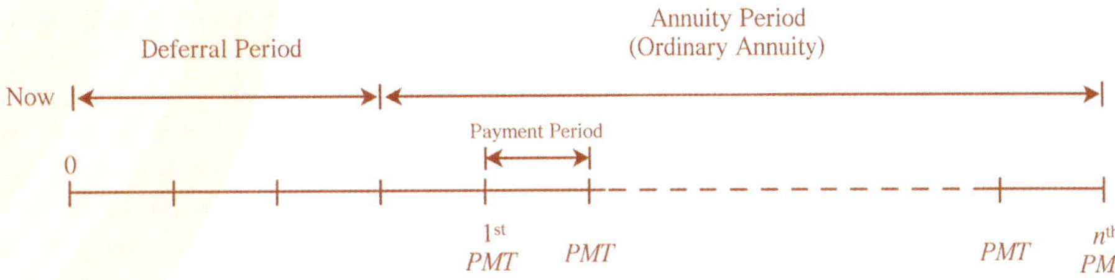

Ordinary deferred annuity

The ordinary deferred annuity can be simple or general based on the payment period and the compounding period.

Deferred Annuity Due

In a deferred annuity, if the periodic payments are made at the beginning of each payment period, then it is a deferred annuity due. Here, the deferral period ends at the beginning of the first periodic payment, as shown in the line diagram below:

The deferred annuity due can be simple or general based on the payment period and the compounding period.

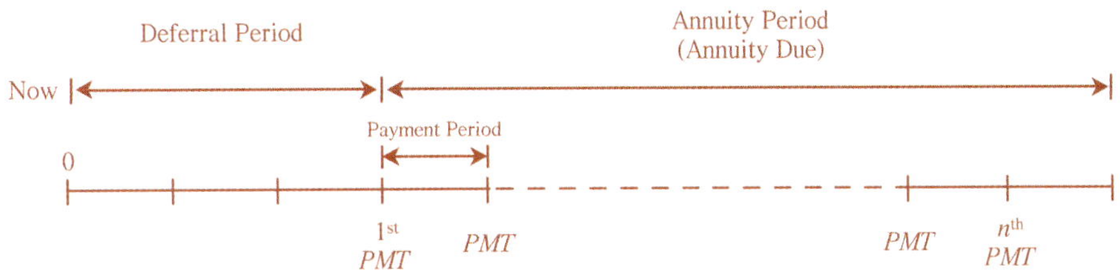

Deferred annuity due

A deferred annuity due can be modified to become an **ordinary deferred annuity** by shortening the deferral period by one payment period. By doing this, the payments made at the beginning of each payment period could be accommodated by making them into payments made at the end of each payment period, as shown below:

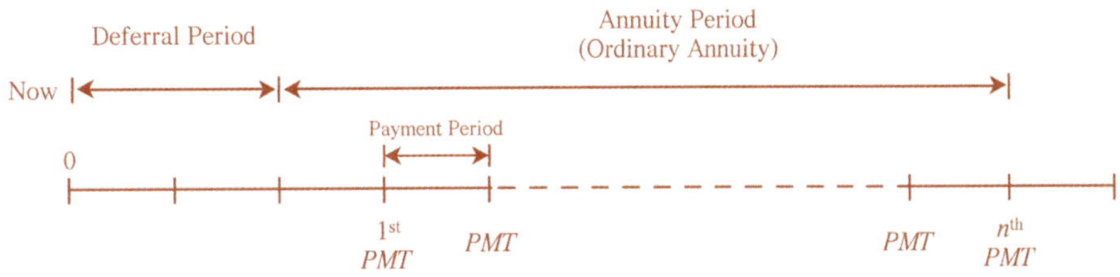

Ordinary deferred annuity

Example 11.1(a) **Identifying the Type of Annuity, Deferral Period, Annuity Period, and the Number of Payments (n) in an Annuity**

Identify the type of annuity (based on the periodic payment date), deferral period, annuity period, and total number of payments in the following:

(i) $1000 is deposited in a savings account at the end of each year for 10 years and the first deposit is made 3 years from now.

(ii) $1000 is deposited in a savings account at the beginning of each year for 10 years and the first payment is made 2 years from now.

(iii) $200,000 is invested in a savings account today and $5000 is withdrawn at the end of every six months for 15 years. The first amount is withdrawn 5 years from now.

(iv) $100,000 is invested in a retirement fund today providing payments of $1000 at the beginning of every month for 8 years. The first payment will be received 2 years from now.

Solution

(i) $1000 is deposited in a savings account at the end of each year for 10 years and the first deposit is made 3 years from now.

Type of Annuity (based on the periodic payment date): The payments are made at the end of each payment period and the annuity is deferred. Therefore, it is an ordinary deferred annuity.

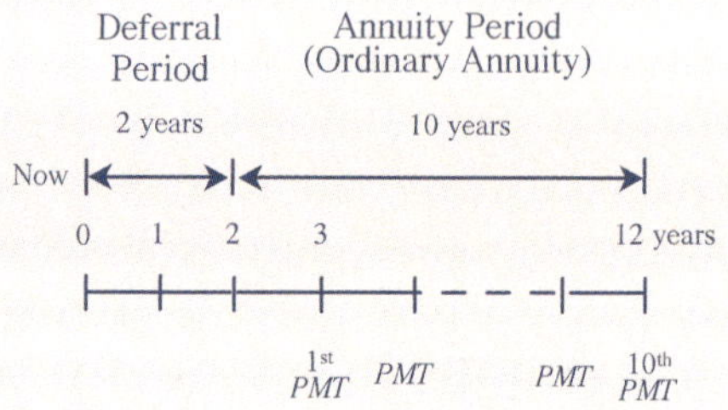

Deferral period: Since the payments start 3 years from now, the ordinary annuity term starts 2 years from now; i.e., one payment interval before the first periodic payment. Therefore the deferral period is 2 years.

Annuity period: 10 years

n = 1 payment/year × 10 years = 10 annual payments

Number of payments during the annuity term:

n = number of payments per year × number of years

= 1 × 10 = 10

(ii) $1000 is deposited at the beginning of each year for 10 years and the first payment is made 2 years from now.

Type of Annuity (based on the periodic payment date): The payments are made at the beginning of each payment period and the annuity is deferred. Therefore, it is a deferred annuity due.

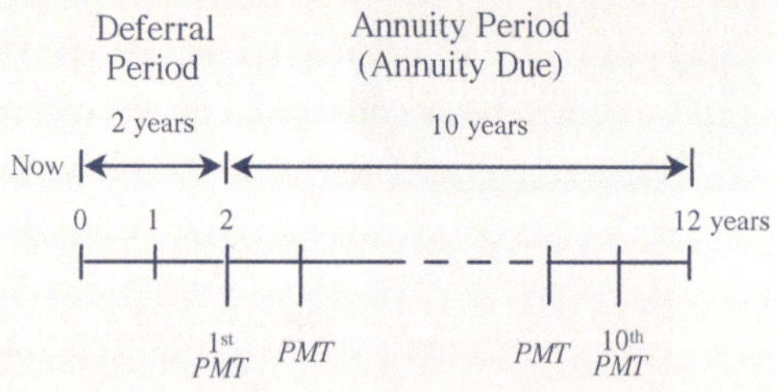

Deferral period: Since the payments start 2 years from now, the annuity due term starts 2 years from now. Therefore the deferral period is 2 years.

Annuity period: 10 years.

n = 1 payment/year × 10 years = 10 annual payments

Number of payments during the annuity term:

n = number of payments per year × number of years

= 1 × 10 = 10

(iii) $200,000 is invested in a savings account today and payments of $5000 are withdrawn at the end of every six months for 15 years. The first amount is withdrawn 5 years from now.

Type of Annuity (based on the periodic payment date): The withdrawals are at the end of each withdrawal period and the annuity is deferred. Therefore, it is an ordinary deferred annuity.

Deferral period: Since the withdrawal starts 5 years from now, the ordinary annuity term starts 4 years and 6 months from now; i.e., one payment interval before the first periodic payment. Therefore the deferral period is 4 years and 6 months.

Annuity period: 15 years.

Solution *continued*

Number of payments during the annuity term:

n = number of payments per year × number of years

$= 2 \times 15 = 30$

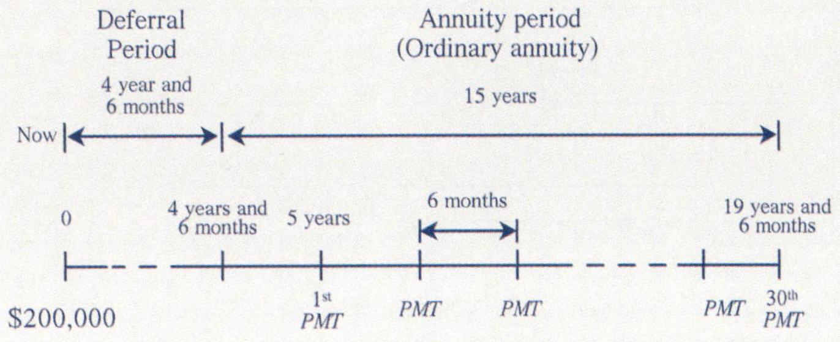

n = 2 payments/year × 15 years
= 30 semi-annual payments

(iv) $100,000 is invested in a retirement fund today giving you payments of $1000 at the beginning of every month for 8 years. You will receive the first payment 2 years from now.

Type of Annuity (based on the periodic payment date): The payments are made at the beginning of each payment period and the annuity is deferred. Therefore, it is a deferred annuity due.

Deferral period: Since the payments start 2 years from now, the annuity due term starts 2 years from now. Therefore the deferral period is 2 years.

Annuity period: 8 years.

Number of payments during the annuity term:

n = number of payments per year × number of years

$= 12 \times 8 = 96$

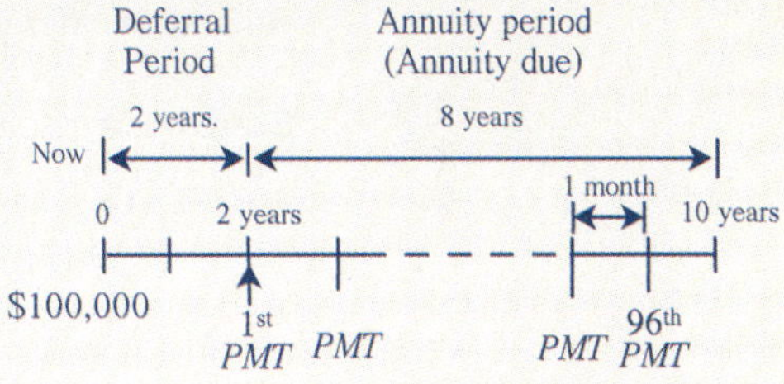

n = 12 payments/year × 8 years
= 96 monthly payments

Calculating the Future Value and Present Value of a Deferred Annuity

The future value of a deferred annuity (FV_{Def}) is the accumulated value of the stream of payments at the end of the annuity period. This is the same procedure as calculating the future value of any annuity that you have learned in Chapter 10.

The present value of a deferred annuity (PV_{Def}) is the discounted value of the stream of payments at the beginning of the deferral period. This follows a two-step procedure and the following examples will illustrate these calculations.

Example 11.1(b) **Calculating the Present Value of an Ordinary Simple Deferred Annuity**

What amount should you invest now if you want to receive payments of $1000 at the end of each year for 10 years with the receipt of the first payment in 3 years? Assume that money earns 5% compounded annually.

Solution

This is an ordinary simple deferred annuity as:

- Payments are made at the end of each payment period (annually)
- Compounding Period (annually) = Payment Period (annually)
- Since the payments start in 3 years, the ordinary annuity term starts in 2 years; i.e., one payment interval before the first periodic payment. Therefore the deferral period is 2 year

Solution continued

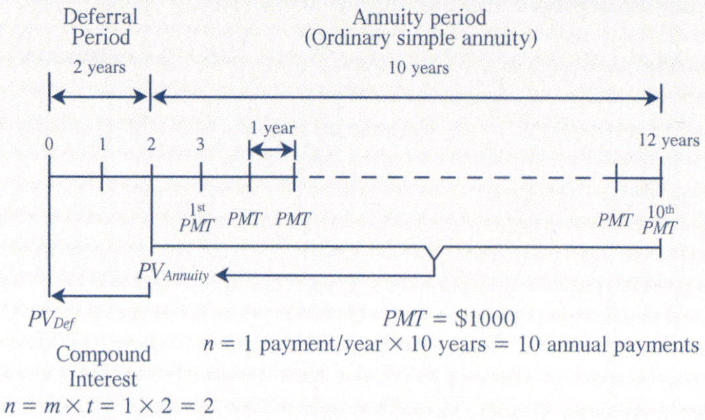

$$j = 0.05, \quad m = 1, \quad i = \frac{j}{m} = 0.05$$

As you can see in the time line diagram, there is a deferral period of 2 years followed by an annuity period for 10 years. We are required to find the present value of the deferred annuity (PV_{Def}).

Step 1: Calculate the present value of the ordinary simple annuity ($PV_{Annuity}$)

$$PV_{Annuity} = PMT\left[\frac{1-(1+i)^{-n}}{i}\right]$$

$$= 1000\left[\frac{1-(1+0.05)^{-10}}{0.05}\right] = \$7721.734929...$$

Step 2: Calculate the present value of this amount at the beginning of the deferral period (PV_{Def})

$$PV_{Def} = PV_{Annuity}\,(1+i)^{-n}$$

$$= 7721.734929...(1+0.05)^{-2} = \$7003.841206...$$

Therefore, you should invest $7003.84 in the fund now.

Do not CLR TVM as I/Y, P/Y, and C/Y remain the same.

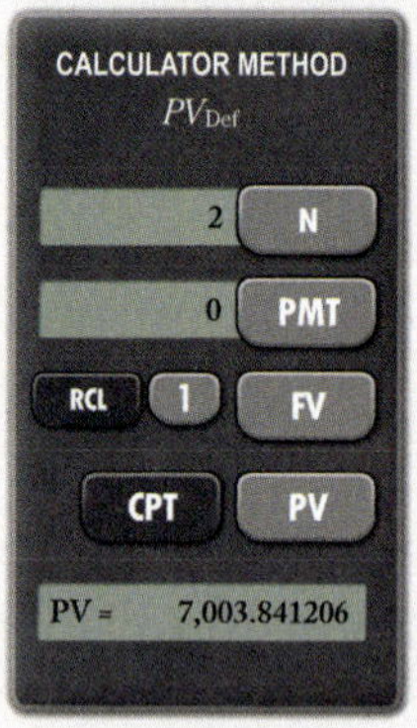

Example 11.1(c)

Calculating the Present Value of a General Deferred Annuity Due

Calculate the amount of money an investment banker would have to deposit in an investment fund that will provide him $1000 at the beginning of each month for 11 years. He receives his first payment in 2 years and the interest rate is 6% compounded semi-annually.

Solution

This is a general deferred annuity due as:

- Payments are made at the beginning of each payment period (monthly)
- Compounding period (semi-annually) ≠ payment period (monthly)
- Since the payments start in 2 years, the annuity due term starts in 2 years. Therefore the deferral period is 2 years.

Solution continued

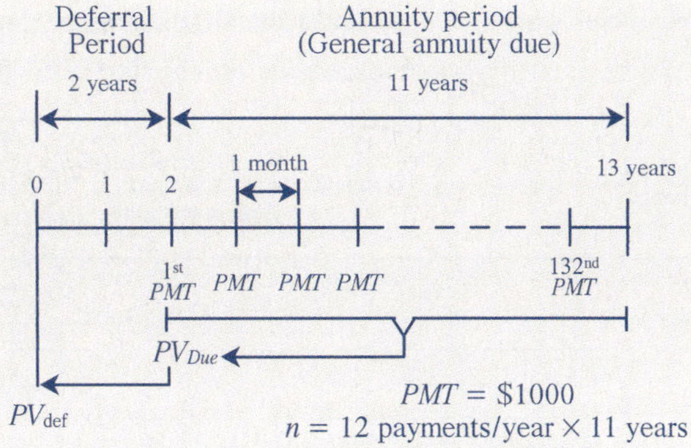

$PMT = \$1000$

$n = 12$ payments/year $\times$ 11 years

$= 132$ monthly payments

Compound Interest

$n = m \times t = 2 \times 2 = 4$

$$j = 0.06, \quad m = 2, \quad i = \frac{j}{m} = 0.03$$

We are required to calculate the present value of the deferral period (PV_{Def}).

Step 1: Calculate the present value of the annuity (PV_{Due})

$$c = \frac{\textit{Number of compounding periods per year}}{\textit{Number of payments per year}}$$

$$= \frac{2}{12} = \frac{1}{6}$$

$$i_2 = (1 + i)^c - 1 = (1+0.03)^{1/6} - 1 = 0.004938...$$

$$PV_{Due} = PMT\left[\frac{1-(1+i_2)^{-n}}{i}\right](1+i_2)$$

$$= 1000\left[\frac{1-(1+0.004938...)^{-132}}{0.004938...}\right](1 + 0.004938...)$$

$$= \$97{,}288.006312...$$

Step 2: Calculate the present value of this amount at the beginning of the deferral period (PV_{Def})

$$PV_{Def} = PV_{Due}(1 + i)^{-n}$$

$$= 97{,}288.006312...\ (1+0.03)^{-4} = \$86{,}439.13353...$$

Or

$$PV_{Def} = PV_{Due}(1 + i_2)^{-n}$$

$$= 97{,}288.006312...\ (1+0.004938...)^{-24} = \$86{,}439.13353...$$

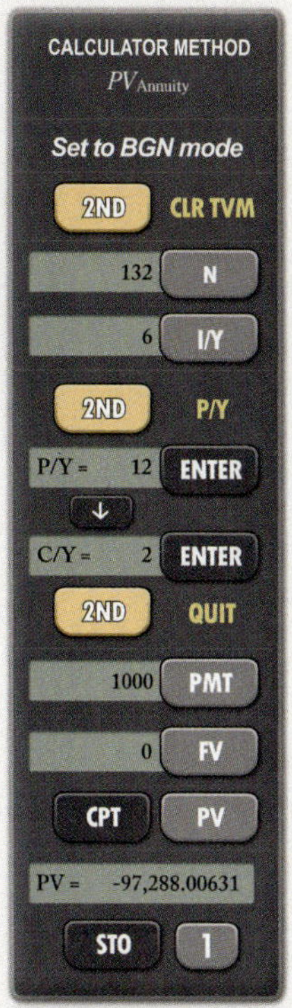

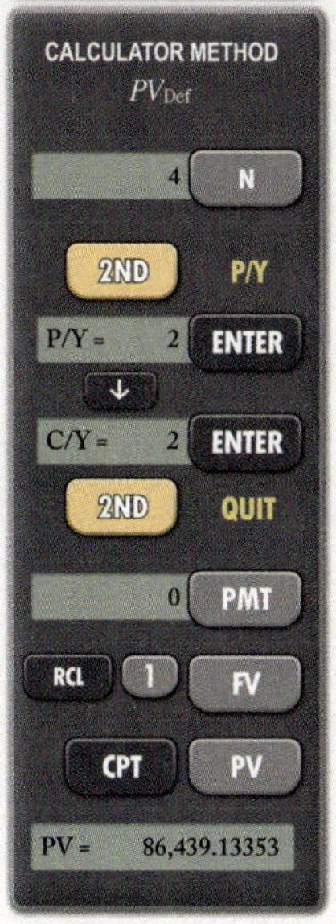

Therefore, the investment banker would have to deposit \$86,439.13 in the investment fund.

Example 11.1(d)

Calculating the Periodic Payments of an Ordinary General Deferred Annuity

The owner of a business borrowed \$7500 to purchase a new machine for his factory. The interest rate charged on the loan is 4% compounded semi-annually and he is required to settle the loan by making equal monthly payments for 5 years, with the first payment to be made in 1 year and 1 month. Calculate the size of the monthly payments that are required to settle the loan.

Solution

This is an ordinary general deferred annuity as:

- Payments are made at the end of each payment period (monthly)
- Compounding period (semi-annually) $\neq$ payment period (monthly)

Solution *continued*

- Since the payments start in 1 years and 1 month, the ordinary annuity term starts in 1 year; i.e., one payment interval before the first periodic payment. Therefore the deferral period is 1 year.

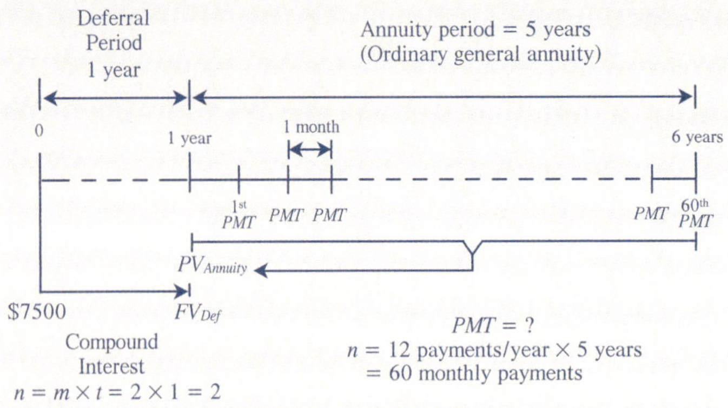

$$j = 0.04, \quad m = 2, \quad i = \frac{j}{m} = 0.02$$

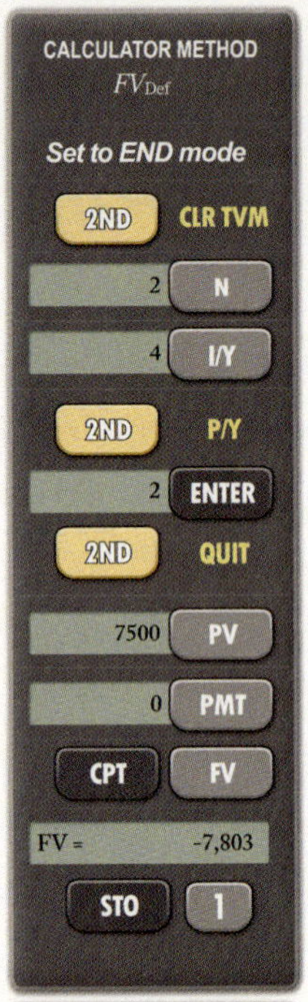

Step 1: Calculate the future value of the investment at the end of the deferral period (FV_{Def})

$$FV_{Def} = PV_{Def}(1 + i)^n = 7500(1 + 0.02)^2 = \$7803.00$$

This amount becomes the present value for the ordinary general deferred annuity ($PV_{Annuity}$).

$$c = \frac{\textit{Number of compounding periods per year}}{\textit{Number of payments per year}} = \frac{2}{12} = \frac{1}{6}$$

$$i_2 = (1 + i)^c - 1 = (1 + 0.02)^{1/6} - 1 = 0.003305...$$

We then use the PV formula for ordinary general annuity to solve for PMT:

$$PV = PMT\left[\frac{1 - (1 + i_2)^{-n}}{i_2}\right]$$

$$7803 = PMT\left[\frac{1 - (1 + 0.003305...)^{-60}}{0.003305...}\right]$$ Solving for PMT, we obtain,

$$PMT = \$143.588188...$$

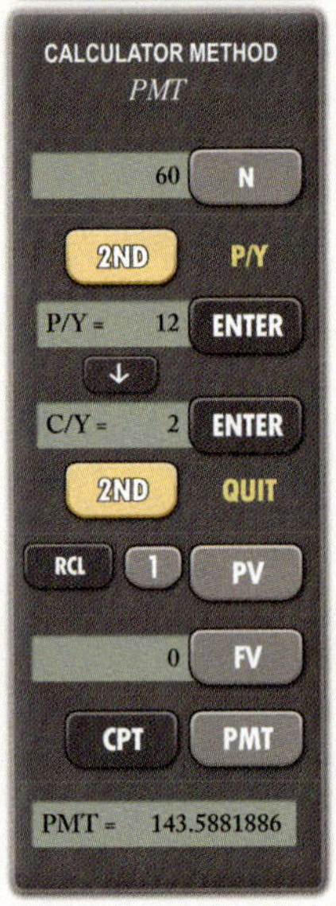

Therefore, the size of the monthly payments that is required to settle the loan is \$143.60.

Example 11.1(e) **Calculating the Number of Payments and Term of a General Deferred Annuity Due**

Neelima Glassware Corporation invested their annual net profits of \$500,000 in a fixed deposit at 8% compounded quarterly. They want to withdraw \$90,000 at the beginning of every year, with the first withdrawal made in 3 years. Calculate the time period of the annuity. Round your answer up to the nearest payment period.

Solution

This is a general deferred annuity due as:

- Payments are made at the beginning of each payment period (annually)
- Compounding period (quarterly) ≠ payment period (annually)
- Since the withdrawals start in 3 years, the annuity due term starts in 3 years. Therefore the deferral period is 3 years.

Solution continued

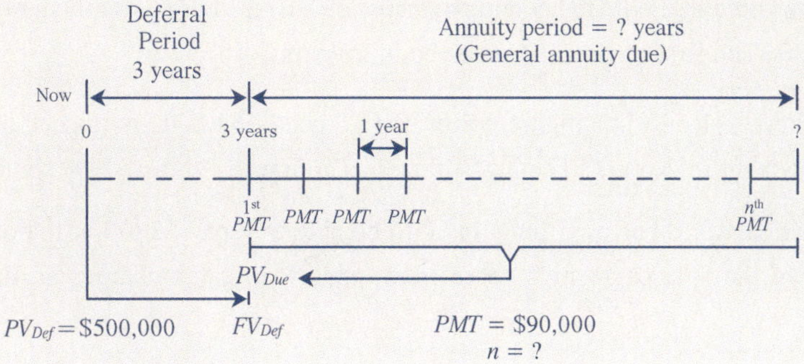

$n = m \times t = 4 \times 3 = 12$

$j = 0.08, \quad m = 4, \quad i = \frac{j}{m} = 0.02$

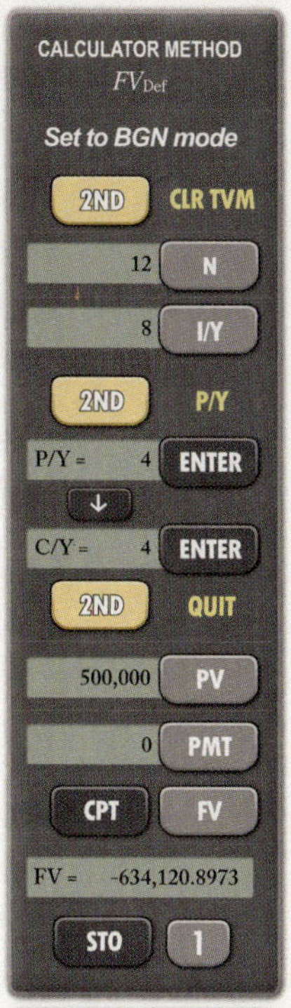

Step 1: Calculate the future value of the investment at the end of the deferral period (FV_{Def})

$$FV_{Def} = PV_{Def}(1 + i)^n$$

$$= 500{,}000\,(1 + 0.02)^{12} = \$634{,}120.897281...$$

This amount becomes the present value for the general annuity due (PV_{Due}).

$$c = \frac{\textit{Number of compounding periods per year}}{\textit{Number of payments per year}} = \frac{4}{1}$$

$$i_2 = (1 + i)^c - 1 = (1+0.02)^4 - 1 = 0.082432...$$

We then use the PV_{Due} formula for this general annuity due to solve for n:

$$n = -\frac{\ln\left[1 - \frac{i \times PV_{due}}{PMT(1+i)}\right]}{\ln(1+i)}$$

$$= -\frac{\ln\left[1 - \frac{0.082432... \times 634{,}120.897281...}{90{,}000(1 + 0.082432...)}\right]}{\ln(1 + 0.082432...)} = 9.709541...$$

$= 10$ payments (Rounded up to the nearest payment period)

$$t = \frac{n}{\textit{Number of payments per year}} = \frac{10}{1}$$

$= 10$ years

Therefore, the time period of the annuity is 10 years.

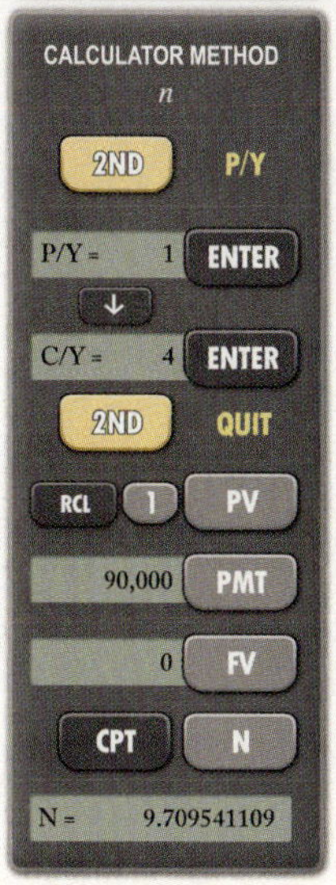

11.1 | Exercises

Identify the type of annuity (based on the periodic payment date), deferral period, annuity period, and number of payments in Problems 1 and 2:

1. Investments:
   a. \$500 is deposited in a savings account at the end of each month for 3 years and the first deposit is made in 5 months.
   b. \$500 is deposited in a savings account at the beginning of every 6 months for 5 years and 6 months and the first deposit is made in 2 years.
2. Payments:
   a. A certain amount is deposited in an RRSP that pays \$2000 at the end of every month for 10 years. The first payment is received in 7 years.

b. A certain amount is deposited in a GIC today and payments of $10,000 are withdrawn at the beginning of every quarter for 5 years. The first payment is received in 2 years.

3. How much would a business have to invest in a high-growth fund to receive $10,000 at the end of every quarter for 5 years, receiving the first payment in 2 years? The investment has an interest rate of 12% compounded quarterly.

4. What amount would a company have to borrow from a bank to be able to repay $2800 at the end of every month for 10 years, with a receipt of the first payment 2 years from now, if the bank charges an interest rate of 6% compounded monthly?

5. Keira is planning to retire in 7 years and would like to receive $3000 from her RRSP at the end of every month for 10 years during her retirement. She would like to receive her first periodic payment on the day she retires. How much would she have to invest in an RRSP that has an interest rate of 8% compounded quarterly?

6. Tasty Plantations Inc. wants to purchase a deferred annuity that would provide the company annuity payments of $20,000 at the end of every 6 months for 7 years. Calculate the purchase price of the deferred annuity if the period of deferment is 2 years and the interest rate is 6% compounded monthly.

7. Calculate the amount of money an investment banker would have to deposit in an investment fund that would provide him $1000 at the beginning of every month for 10 years if his payments were deferred by 3 years and 6 months and the interest rate is 6% compounded monthly.

8. A restaurant owner wants to invest in GICs that have an interest rate of 3.25% compounded semi-annually. Calculate the amount he should invest in order to receive annuity payments of $2000 at the beginning of every 6 months for a period of 5 years. He wants his annuity to begin in 2 years and 6 months.

9. On the birth of their first child, Cecilia and her husband invested their savings in a bank that was offering them an interest rate of 9% compounded quarterly. How much money should they have invested to be able to make annual withdrawals of $10,000 from the investment for 5 years starting from their child's 18th birthday?

10. Jemi purchased a deferred annuity with his 2010 earnings. If it pays him $1200 at the beginning of every month for 5 years and the payment period is deferred by 1 year, calculate the purchase price of the deferred annuity. Assume an interest rate of 8% compounded semi-annually.

11. For how long will Yuan receive payments from an annuity that he purchased for $10,000 that pays $800 at the end of every quarter. He will receive his first payment in 3 years and the interest rate is 8% compounded monthly.

12. How long will it take Ardiana to settle a $280,000 mortgage on her home if she makes equal month-end payments of $1500, making her first payment in 6 months? The interest rate on the mortgage is 3.45% compounded semi-annually.

13. Russ Inc. invested its annual net profits of $25,000 into a fixed deposit at 8% compounded quarterly. The company withdrew $2500 at the beginning of every 6 months, with the first withdrawal being made in 2 years. How long did the invested money last?

14. Samantha deposited her sales commission of $15,500 in an investment that was growing at 7% compounded monthly. If she wanted to withdraw $2500 at the beginning of every quarter, with the first withdrawal being made in 4 years, how long will her invested money last?

15. Jehona took an $8000 loan to purchase equipment for her hair salon. If the interest rate charged on the loan is 11% compounded quarterly, what month-end payments of equal amounts will settle the loan in 5 years if she made her first payment in 1 year and 4 months?

16. A small business invested its profits of $20,850 in an annuity that pays equal amounts at the end of every quarter for 5 years, receiving the first payment in 2 years. Calculate the size of the payments if the annuity has an interest rate of 8% compounded monthly.

17. A software company took a loan of \$85,000 from a bank and was required to pay equal repayment amounts at the beginning of every month for 10 years, with the first payment being made in 1 year. Calculate the size of the monthly payments if the interest rate charged is 11% compounded semi-annually.

18. Amanda obtained a student loan of \$55,000 for her 2-year MBA program. The loan agreement stated that she would have to make equal repayments at the beginning of each month to clear the loan over 10 years after she graduates. Calculate the size of the monthly payments if the interest rate on the loan is 6% compounded quarterly.

• 19. Leigha invested \$35,000 in a retirement fund and withdrew equal amounts at the end of each month for 20 years. She made her first withdrawal 5 years after she made the initial investment. Calculate the size of the withdrawals if the fund was earning 9.5% compounded quarterly during the deferral period and 8% compounded quarterly during the annuity period.

• 20. 5 years ago, a bank offered an interest rate of 4% compounded semi-annually on an investment of \$20,000. Now, a month before the first withdrawal will be made, the rate will be changing to 4% compounded quarterly. Calculate the size of the equal withdrawals at the end of each month that would ensure that the investment lasts for 10 years.

11.2 | Perpetuity

A perpetuity is an annuity in which the periodic payments begin on a fixed date and continue indefinitely. Therefore, it is not possible to calculate its future value. However, there is a definite present value for a perpetuity.

When 'n' is large,

$$(1+i)^{-n} = (1+i)^{-\infty} = \frac{1}{(1+i)^{\infty}} = \frac{1}{\infty} = 0$$

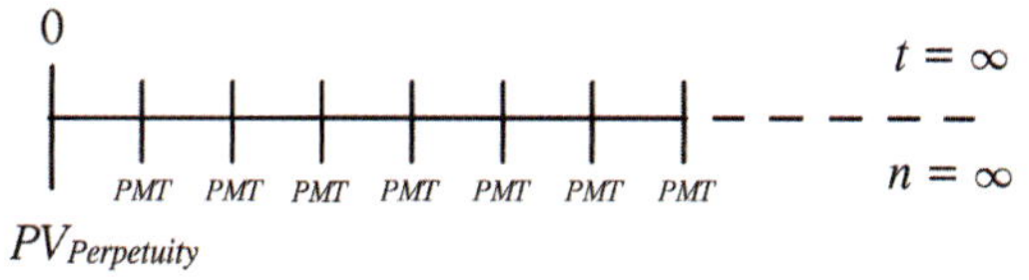

The present value of a perpetuity is calculated as follows:

As the number of payments, 'n', in a perpetuity is large (infinity), the factor $(1 + i)^{-n}$ in the PV formula of an ordinary annuity approaches 0.

$$PV = PMT\left[\frac{1-(1+i)^{-n}}{i}\right] = PMT\left[\frac{1-(1+i)^{-\infty}}{i}\right] = PMT\left[\frac{1-(0)}{i}\right] = \frac{PMT}{i}$$

Thus, the formula for the present value of an ordinary perpetuity can be expressed as follows:

Formula 11.2(a) **Present Value of an Ordinary Perpetuity**

$$PV_{Perpetuity} = \frac{PMT}{i}$$

If the periodic payment in a perpetuity is at the beginning of the payment period then it is a perpetuity due. The factor $(1 + i)^{-n}$ in the PV formula of an annuity due approaches 0.

$$PV_{Due} = PMT\left[\frac{1-(1+i)^{-n}}{i}\right](1+i) = PMT\left[\frac{1-(0)}{i}\right](1+i) = \left[\frac{PMT}{i}\right](1+i)$$

Thus, the present value of a perpetuity due can be expressed as follows:

Formula 11.2(b)

Present Value of a Perpetuity Due

$$PV_{Perpetuity\ Due} = \frac{PMT}{i}(1 + i)$$

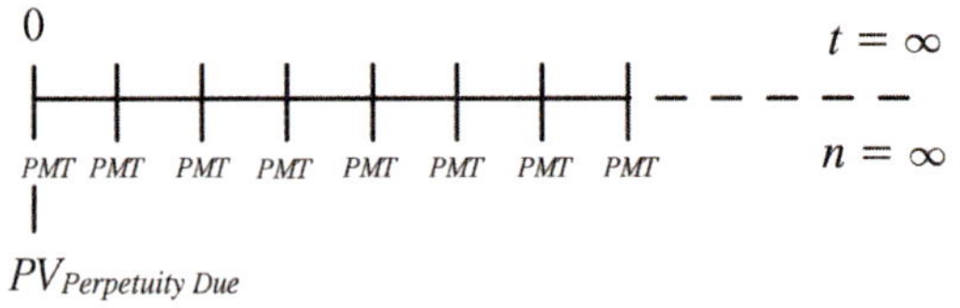

In the case of an ordinary general perpetuity (or a general perpetuity due), where the compounding period is not equal to the payment period, we would carry out the same procedure by first finding the equivalent periodic interest rate, 'i_2', and substituting this in place of 'i' in the $PV_{Perpetuity}$ formula.

A few examples of perpetuities are:

- Continuous interest payments from a lump sum of money invested at a fixed interest rate.
- A scholarship to students paid from an endowment fund on a perpetual basis.
- A charity fund established to provide regular payments indefinitely to needy children.

Example 11.2(a)

Calculating the Present Value of an Ordinary Simple Perpetuity

A college wants to provide students with a perpetual scholarship of $10,000 at the end of every 3 months. How large should their endowment fund be if invested at 8% compounded quarterly?

Solution

This is an ordinary simple perpetuity as:

- Payments are made at the end of each payment period (quarterly)
- Compounding period (quarterly) = payment period (quarterly)

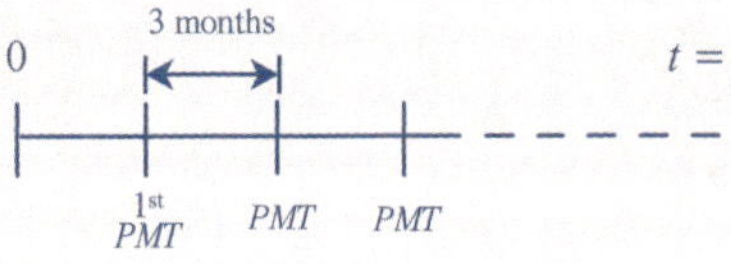

$PMT = \$10,000$

$j = 0.08, \quad m = 4, \quad i = \frac{j}{m} = 0.02$

Endowment Amount = PV =?

$$PV_{Perpetuity} = \frac{PMT}{i} = \frac{10,000}{0.02} = \$500,000.00$$

The endowment fund required is $500,000.00.

To use the financial calculator to solve perpetuity problems, assume the time period, 't', to be a very large number. This will result in a very large number for 'n'.

For example, assume t = 1000 years. This will give n = 1000 × 4 = 4000. Enter N = 4000 in the calculator.

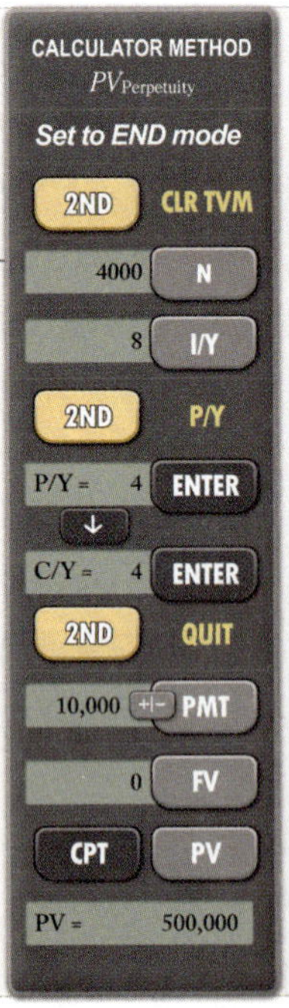

Example 11.2(b)

Calculating the Present Value of a General Perpetuity Due

Green Splash Publishers Inc. wants to invest a lump sum amount in a fund that will provide the company with $5000 at the beginning of every month in perpetuity to help pay for its employees' monthly salaries. How much should be invested in a fund that provides an interest rate of 8% compounded quarterly?

Solution

This is a general perpetuity due as:

- Payments are made at the beginning of each payment period (monthly)
- Compounding period (quarterly) ≠ payment period (monthly)

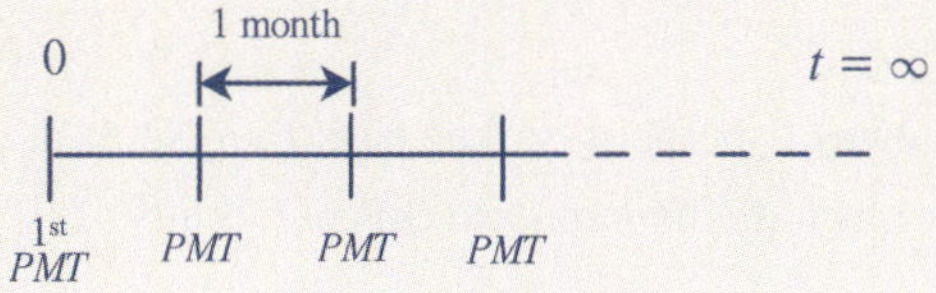

$$PMT = \$5000$$

$$j = 0.08, \quad m = 4, \quad i = \frac{j}{m} = 0.02$$

$$c = \frac{\textit{Number of compounding periods per year}}{\textit{Number of payments per year}} = \frac{4}{12}$$

$$i_2 = (1 + i)^c - 1 = (1 + 0.02)^{4/12} - 1 = 0.006622...$$

$$PV_{Perpetuity\ Due} = \frac{PMT}{i_2}(1 + i_2) = \frac{5000}{0.006622...}(1 + 0.006622...)$$

$$= \$759{,}977.997240...$$

Therefore, they should invest $759,978.00 in the fund.

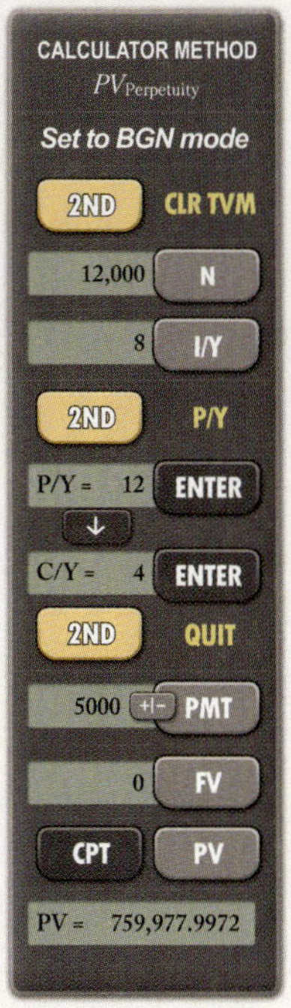

Example 11.2(c)

Calculating the Periodic Payment of an Ordinary General Perpetuity

A large telecommunication business purchases a perpetual bond at $500,000 that earns interest of 12% compounded monthly. Calculate the end-of-quarter payments that will be received from the bond.

Solution

This is an ordinary general perpetuity as:

- Payments are made at the end of each payment period (quarterly).
- Compounding period (monthly) ≠ payment period (quarterly)

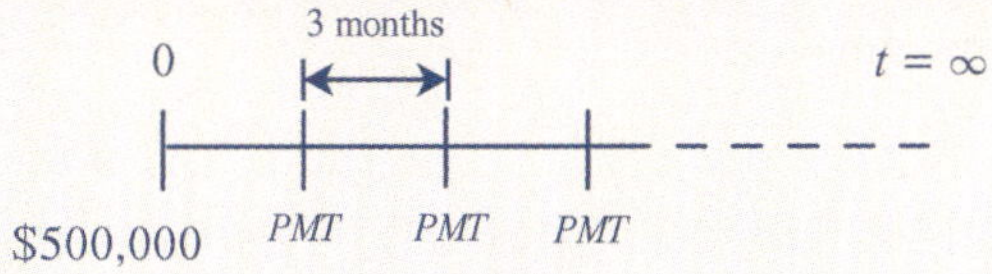

$$PMT = ?$$

$$j = 0.12, \quad m = 12, \quad i = \frac{j}{m} = 0.01$$

$$c = \frac{\textit{Number of compounding periods per year}}{\textit{Number of payments per year}} = \frac{12}{4}$$

$$i_2 = (1 + i)^c - 1 = (1.01)^{12/4} - 1 = 0.030301$$

Rearranging Formula 11.2(a), we obtain,

$$PMT = PV \times i_2 = 500{,}000.00\ (0.030301) = \$15{,}150.50$$

Therefore, the end-of-quarter payments will be $15,150.50.

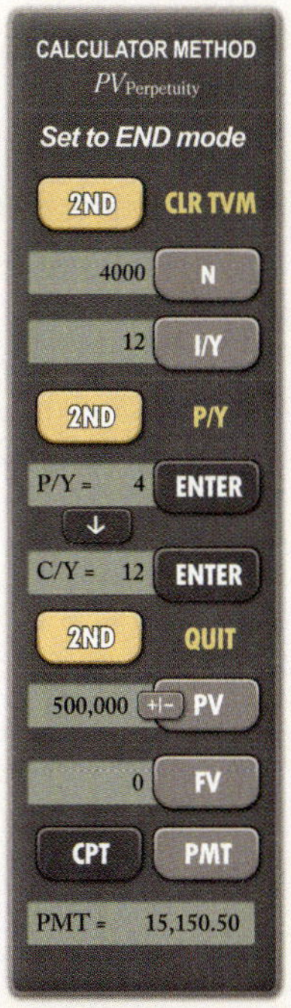

11.2 | Exercises

1. A college wants to provide students with a perpetual scholarship of $5000 at the end of every 3 months. How large should their endowment fund be if money can earn 12% compounded quarterly?

2. Ayes Inc., an e-learning company, wants to create a fund that pays $500 at the end of every month in perpetuity. If money earns 6% compounded monthly, calculate the initial investment into this fund?

3. How much money is required to fund a perpetuity that pays $1000 at the end of every 3 months and that earns 6% compounded semi-annually?

4. Henry, a retired businessman, owns a perpetuity that pays him $200 at the end of every month and earns 8% compounded quarterly. For how much did he purchase this perpetuity?

5. If Webcom Inc. pays dividends of $2.50 per share at the beginning of each quarter, calculate the market price per share assuming that money earns 5% compounded quarterly.s

6. A college was raising funds for a $5000 scholarship that it wanted to provide to its first semester students at the beginning of every 6 months. If money is worth 3.5% compounded semi-annually, how much money should the college raise for this endowment fund?

7. Alba was receiving rental payments of $3000 at the beginning of each month from the tenants of her commercial property. What would be the value of her property in the market if she wants to sell it, assuming money earns 9% compounded semi-annually?

8. A condominium was leased for $1200 per month with payments being made at the beginning of each month. Calculate the market price of the condominium, assuming that money is worth 4% compounded quarterly.

9. What is the size of the scholarship payments that students at a college will receive at the end of every 6 months if $700,000 is invested in an endowment fund that is earning 12% compounded semi-annually?

10. Roger runs a successful publishing business and invests his 2011 profits of $400,000 in a bank at 2% compounded monthly. How much money can he withdraw from this account at the end of every month in perpetuity?

11. If the market value of a telecommunications share is $280.50, calculate the end-of-month dividends that it should be able to pay in perpetuity if money is worth 6% compounded quarterly.

12. Calculate the end-of-month rent Ruben should charge for a condo that he purchased for $135,000. Assume money is worth 8% compounded semi-annually.

13. Anna purchased a perpetuity that was paying her $12,500 at the end of every 6 months and had an interest rate of 8% compounded semi-annually. By how much would this perpetuity be cheaper for Anna if it had an interest rate of 8% compounded quarterly instead of 8% compounded semi-annually.

14. A College endowment fund provides year-end scholarships of $7500 at 2.85% compounded semi-annually. If the fund was setup to earn 2.85% compounded monthly instead, how much less money would be required to start the fund?

15. If money could earn 4.55% compounded monthly instead of 4.55% compounded semi-annually, how much less would be the investment to start a perpetual scholarship that pays $11,500 at the beginning of every 6 months?

16. If the money was invested at 6% compounded annually rather than 6% compounded quarterly, how much more of an investment would be required to pay $1000 at the beginning of every 3 months in a perpetual scholarship?

• 17. Calculate the purchase price of a perpetuity that provides month-end payments of $1000, with the first payment received in 3 years. The interest on the perpetuity is 2.25% compounded quarterly.

• 18. Yara purchased a perpetuity that paid her $3000 at the end of every quarter, with the first payment received in 5 years. If the perpetuity had an interest rate of 4% compounded semi-annually, calculate its purchase price.

11.3 | Constant-Growth Annuity

A constant-growth annuity is an annuity where the periodic payment amount (*PMT*) increases by a constant rate ($g\%$) over the preceding payment amount.

Consider an example where you plan to deposit regular payments into your RRSP at the end of every month for 3 years, starting with an initial investment of \$100, and increasing the amount by 2% every month.

1st payment would be:	$PMT_1 = \$100.00$
2nd payment:	$PMT_2 = 100 + (2\% \text{ of } 100) = \$102.00$
This is the same as:	$PMT_2 = PMT + g(PMT) = PMT(1 + g)$
3rd payment:	$PMT_3 = 102 + (2\% \text{ of } 102) = \$104.04$
This is the same as:	$PMT_3 = PMT_2(1 + g) = PMT(1 + g)(1 + g) = PMT(1 + g)^2$

Notice that each payment amount increases by a factor of $(1+g)$, in relation to the previous payment.

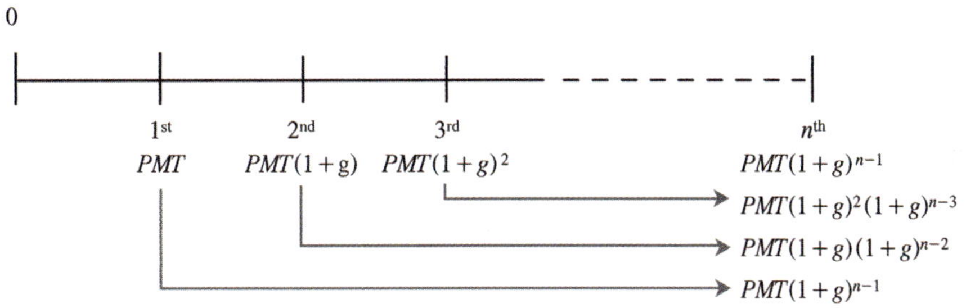

To calculate the future value of these payments at the end of the period:

$$FV_{\text{at the End of the Period}} = FV_{1^{st}\,PMT} + FV_{2^{nd}\,PMT} + FV_{3^{rd}\,PMT} \cdots + FV_{n^{th}\,PMT}$$

$$FV = PMT(1 + i)^{n-1} + PMT(1 + g)(1 + i)^{n-2} + PMT(1 + g)^2(1 + i)^{n-3} \ldots + PMT(1 + g)^{n-1}$$

This is a geometric series [first term $= PMT\,(1 + i)^{n-1}$, common ratio $= (1 + g)(1 + i)^{-1}$, number of terms $= n$] and the sum of this will be reduced to the following formula:

Formula 11.3(a)

Future Value of an Ordinary Simple Constant-Growth Annuity

$$FV = PMT\left[\frac{(1 + i)^n - (1 + g)^n}{(i - g)}\right]$$

Notice that if 'g' is zero (i.e., there is no growth in the payment), the formula reduces back to the 'FV' of an ordinary annuity

$$FV = PMT\left[\frac{(1 + i)^n - 1}{i}\right]$$

Similarly, the present value for a constant growth annuity is calculated by the following formula:

Formula 11.3(b)

Present Value of an Ordinary Simple Constant-Growth Annuity

$$PV = PMT\left[\frac{1 - (1 + g)^n(1 + i)^{-n}}{(i - g)}\right]$$

Notice that if 'g' is zero (i.e., there is no growth in the payment), the formula reduces back to the 'PV' of an ordinary annuity

$$PV = PMT\left[\frac{1 - (1 + i)^{-n}}{i}\right]$$

Example 11.3(a)

Calculating the Future Value of an Ordinary Simple Constant-Growth Annuity

A business made end-of-month investments in a high-growth fund starting at \$500 and increasing it by 1.5% per month thereafter for 15 years. If the fund has an interest rate of 12% compounded monthly, calculate the accumulated amount in the fund at the end of the period.

Solution

This is an ordinary simple constant-growth annuity as:

- Payments are made at the end of the payment period (monthly)
- Compounding period (monthly) = payment period (monthly)
- Constant growth rate is 1.5%

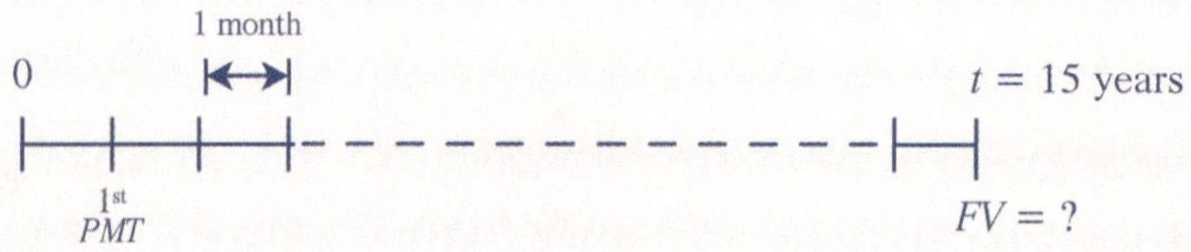

$$1^{st}\ PMT = \$500$$

$$n = 12 \text{ payments/year} \times 15 \text{ years} = 180 \text{ monthly payments}$$

$$j = 0.12, \quad m = 12, \quad i = \frac{j}{m} = 0.01, \quad g = 0.015$$

Using Formula 11.3(a),

$$FV = PMT\left[\frac{(1+i)^n - (1+g)^n}{(i-g)}\right]$$

$$= 500\left[\frac{(1+0.01)^{180} - (1+0.015)^{180}}{0.01 - 0.015}\right]$$

$$= 500\,[1717.713143...] = \$858{,}856.57$$

Therefore, the accumulated value in the fund at the end of the period would be \$858,856.57.

There is no pre-programmed formula in the Texas Instruments BAII Plus financial calculator to solve constant growth annuity problems.

Example 11.3(b)

Calculating the Present Value of an Ordinary Simple Constant-Growth Annuity

Abel purchased a 10-year annuity that has an interest rate of 5% compounded semi-annually and which will provide him payments at the end of every 6 months. If the first payment received is \$1000 and it increases by 2% thereafter every 6 months, how much did he pay for the annuity?

Solution

This is an ordinary simple constant-growth annuity as:

- Payments are made at the end of each payment period (semi-annually)
- Compounding period (semi-annually) = payment period (semi-annually)
- Constant growth rate is 2%

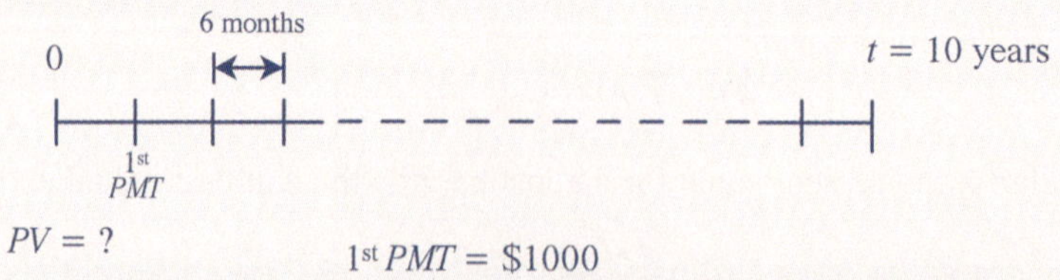

$$1^{st}\ PMT = \$1000$$

$$n = 2 \text{ payments/year} \times 10 \text{ years} = 20 \text{ semi-annual payments}$$

$$j = 0.05, \quad m = 2, \quad i = \frac{j}{m} = 0.025, \quad g = 0.02$$

Using Formula 11.3 (b),

$$PV = PMT\left[\frac{1 - (1+g)^n (1+i)^{-n}}{(i-g)}\right]$$

$$= 1000\left[\frac{1 - (1+0.02)^{20}(1+0.025)^{-20}}{0.025 - 0.02}\right]$$

$$= 1000\,[18.633896...] = \$18{,}633.89632...$$

Therefore, he paid \$18,633.90 for the annuity.

Example 11.3(c) **Calculating the Size of the Initial Payment of an Ordinary Simple Constant-Growth Annuity**

Addae made contributions growing at 2.25% at the end of every 3 months to his RRSP that was earning an interest rate of 8% compounded quarterly. In 30 years if his RRSP savings had accumulated to \$147,034.45, what was his initial investment?

Solution

This is an ordinary simple constant-growth annuity where:

- Payments are made at the end of each payment period (quarterly)
- Compounding period (quarterly) = payment period (quarterly)
- Constant growth rate is 2.25%

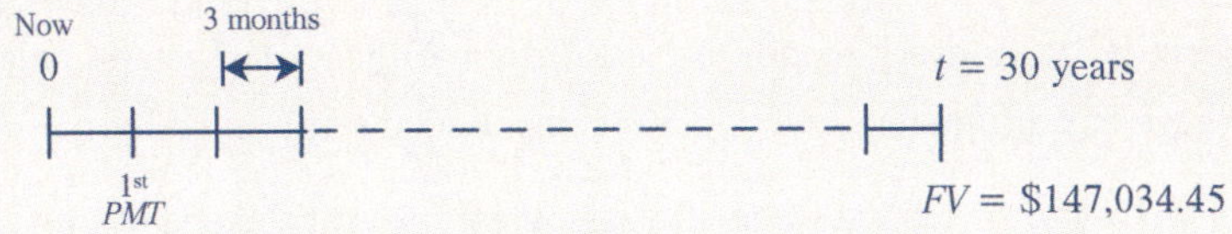

1st $PMT = ?$

$n = 4$ payments/year $\times$ 30 years = 120 quarterly payments

$$j = 0.08, \quad m = 4, \quad i = \frac{j}{m} = 0.02, \quad g = 0.0225$$

$$FV = PMT\left[\frac{(1+i)^n - (1+g)^n}{(i-g)}\right]$$

$$147{,}034.45 = PMT\left[\frac{(1+0.02)^{120} - (1+0.0225)^{120}}{0.02 - 0.0225}\right]$$ Solving for PMT, we obtain,

$PMT = \$99.999997...$

Therefore, his initial investment was \$100.00.

11.3 | Exercises

1. Investments were made at the end of every 6 months for 5 years in a fund that had an interest rate of 5% compounded semi-annually.
   a. If the investment amount was \$1000, calculate the accumulated amount in the fund.
   b. If the starting investment amount was \$1000 and it was increased by 1% thereafter every 6 months, calculate the accumulated amount in the fund.
2. An amount of \$850 was invested in a savings account at the end of every 3 months for 10 years. The interest rate on the account was 8% compounded quarterly.
   a. Calculate the accumulated amount in the account.
   b. After the 1st investment of \$850, if the amount was increased by 1% thereafter every 3 months for the time period, calculate the accumulated amount in the account.
3. Harold Petrochemicals made its first deposit for \$1,000 into an investment fund, increasing the size of the payments thereafter by 2% every month. If the deposits are made at the end of every month for 5 years and the investment fund had an interest rate of 6% compounded semi-annually, calculate the accumulated value in the fund at the end of the annuity term.
4. Micro-Fibres Inc. deposited \$10,000 at the end of the first year and increased this amount by 3% every year for the next 10 years in an overseas investment fund that had an interest rate of 12% compounded semi-annually. Calculate the accumulated amount in the fund at the end of the term.

5. Calculate the purchase price of a 5-year annuity that provides end-of-quarter payments that start at $2800 and grow by 2% every quarter. Assume money earns 6% compounded quarterly.

6. Janet secured a job that is paying her $35,000 per annum. Calculate the discounted value of her income stream assuming that her income grows by 5% every year, she works for 40 years, and money earns 4% compounded annually.

7. The city of Oshawa wants to accumulate $2,000,000 in a savings account by the end of 10 years. It will be making deposits at the end of every 3 months and will increase the deposit amount by 3% every 3 months. If the account earns 6% compounded semi-annually, what is size of the city's first deposit?

8. The Gupta family makes month-end payments to repay their mortgage of $825,000. If they plan to increase their payment by 1.2% every month to clear their mortgage in 7 years, calculate the size of their first payment. The mortgage has an interest rate of 3.5% compounded semi-annually.

9. Peter wishes to save $50,000 in 10 years. If he saves at the end of every year and increases the savings amount by 6% every year, calculate his first year-end deposit. Assume money earns 4.8% compounded monthly.

10. Lucy wants to save $60,000 in 4 years. If she makes a deposit at the end of every month and increases the savings amount by 2% every month, calculate her first month-end deposit. Assume money earns 4% compounded quarterly.

11. You wish to receive payments at the end of every year for the next 5 years, starting at $5000 per year with a 6% increment every year. If money is worth 6% compounded semi-annually, how much should you invest now?

12. You wish to receive increasing month-end payments with a 3% growth-rate per month for the next 2 years, starting at $750 per month. If money is worth 4.2% compounded semi-annually, how much should you invest now?

11 | Review Exercises

Answers to odd-numbered problems are available at the end of the textbook

1. How much would a vegetable oil business have to invest in a high-growth fund to receive $50,000 at the end of every quarter for 7 years, with the first payment being received in 4 years and 3 months? Money is worth 6% compounded quarterly.

2. An investment firm will receive $120,000 at the end of every month for 4 years with the first payment received in 2 years. For how much did it purchase this deferred perpetuity if money is worth 9.5% compounded monthly?

3. Ivan purchased a deferred annuity with his 2010 earnings. If it will pay $800 at the beginning of every quarter for 8 years and the payment period is deferred by 2 years, calculate the purchase price of the deferred annuity. Assume an interest rate of 7.5% compounded semi-annually.

4. Armery Inc. purchased a deferred annuity which pays $50,000 at the beginning of every quarter for 5 years, the payment period being deferred by 3 years.Calculate the expected purchase price for the annuity if money is worth 6% compounded monthly.

5. Tashoido Inc. invested its annual net profit of $60,000 in a fixed deposit at 6% compounded annually. If the company wants to withdraw $2000 at the beginning of every month starting 2 years from now, how long will the invested money last?

6. Pickles Inc. sold a plant and invested the proceeds of $200,000 into an investment earning interest at 8% compounded quarterly. If the company wants to withdraw $5000 at the beginning of every month starting 1 year from now, how long will the investment last?

7. A tool-die shop obtained a loan of $120,000 from a bank. The shop is required to pay equal repayment amounts at the beginning of every month for 8 years starting 18 months from now. Calculate the size of the monthly payments if the interest rate charged is 8% compounded semi-annually.

8. The Mitchell family is planning on taking on a $400,000 mortgage. The mortgage would be accumulating interest at a rate of 3.5% compounded quarterly and would have a term of 20 years. What would be the size of their beginning-of-month payments if the bank allows them to defer payments by 9 months?

9. What would be the size of the scholarship payments that students at a college would receive at the end of every quarter in perpetuity if $1,000,000 is invested in an endowment fund that is earning 3% compounded quarterly?

10. A perpetuity earning 6% compounded monthly is started with a $100,000 investment. What is the size of the periodic withdrawals taken from the investment at the end every month in perpetuity?

11. A perpetuity that is earning 7% compounded quarterly is to pay $30,000 at the end of every quarter. How much less money would be required to fund the perpetuity if the money could be invested to earn 7% compounded monthly instead of 7% compounded quarterly?

12. Nikia started a fund earning 3% compounded monthly, which would pay out $500 at the end of every month. How much less money is required to set up the fund if the interest rate was 3% compounded semi-annually, instead of 3% compounded monthly?

13. How much more should a college raise for their endowment fund to provide scholarships of $7500 at the beginning of every 6 months if the money were invested at 8.5% compounded semi-annually rather than 8.5% compounded monthly?

14. A perpetuity that is earning 6% compounded quarterly is to pay $10,000 at the end of every year. How much less money would be required to fund the perpetuity if the money could only earn 6% compounded monthly, instead of 6% compounded quarterly?

15. Petreas Fine Leather has made its first deposit of $1000 at the end of the month into an investment fund, and the company plans to increase the payments thereafter by 0.5% every month. If the deposits are made at the end of every month for 25 years and if the investment fund has an interest rate of 11% compounded semi-annually, calculate the accumulated value in the fund at the end of the annuity term.

16. At the end of last month, Elmough Bed & Breakfast decided to invest $500 monthly into an investment fund earning 6% compounded monthly. It plans on continuing these deposits on a regular monthly basis, increasing the deposit amount by 0.75% each time. If these payments continue for 15 years, what would be the accumulated value of the fund at the end of the term?

17. Calculate the purchase price of a 7-year annuity that provides end-of-quarter payments that start at $2800 and grow by 2% every quarter. Assume money earns 6% compounded quarterly.

18. Calculate the purchase price of a 10-year annuity that provides end-of-month payments starting at $500, growing by 1% every month. Assume money earns 5% compounded quarterly.

19. The Gauche Institute makes month-end payments to repay its outstanding loans of $825,000. If it plans to increase the payment by 1% every month to clear the loan in 7 years, calculate the size of the first payment. The loan has an interest rate of 5.5% compounded annually.

20. Cleverson Industries took a $50,000 loan, which it is repaying with increasing month-end payments, growing by 0.5% every month. If it plans on settling the loan in 5 years and is being charged interest of 12% compounded quarterly, what should be the size of the first payment?

11 | Self-Test Exercises

Answers to all problems are available at the end of the textbook

1. You received 60 annuity payments of $1000 each at the end of every month, with the first payment received in 3 years and 1 month. The interest rate for the deferral period was 4% compounded monthly, and 5.4% compounded monthly for the annuity period. Calculate the present value of this deferred annuity.

2. If you invested $350,000 in a business that would pay you monthly payments at the beginning of every month for 25 years, receiving the first payment in 5 years, calculate the size of the periodic payments. Assume that the interest rate is 6% compounded quarterly throughout the period.

3. A deferred annuity with a present value of $25,000 will pay $500 at the end of every month, and the payments are deferred by 4 years. If the interest rate is 3.6% compounded monthly, calculate the term of the annuity.

4. Ben has $150,000 in his RRSP which earns 4% compounded semi-annually. How much more money could he withdraw at the end of every month for a 10-year period if the annuity period is deferred by 5 years instead of 3 years.

5. A perpetual scholarship fund is to be setup to pay $10,000 at the end of every month. How much more money would be required to fund the scholarship if the money invested were to earn 4.5% compounded semi-annually instead of 4.5% compounded monthly?

6. If money earns 6% compounded annually, how much more money would be required to fund an ordinary perpetuity paying $1000 every year than to fund an annuity paying $1000 at the end of every year for 30 years?

7. A college alumnus donated $150,000 to start an annual perpetual scholarship for the best student in his college's business program. If the fund earns 5% compounded semi-annually, what will be the amount of scholarship award?

8. James wants to retire in 5 years and has started to save for his retirement with month-end contributions into a fund for 5 years which earns 6.8% compounded semi-annually. His initial contribution was $1000. The contribution will be increased by 2% each month. Calculate his retirement fund at the end of his last contribution.

9. Nadia wanted to convert her RRSP into an annuity for 10 years, so that she would be able to withdraw money at the end of every year, with an increasing withdrawal of 10% annually. If the first withdrawal amount was $5000, what amount should she have now if money earns 5.4% compounded quarterly?

10. Andrew has $40,000 in his RESP account and wants to withdraw annually from this account, with withdrawals increasing at 6% annually to pay for his higher education for the next 5 years. If money earns 4.8% compounded monthly, how much would be his first withdrawal?

CASE 11

Financial Planning for a Secure Future

Elijah and his wife, Carol, had their first child on Elijah's 30th birthday. They decided that it was time to meet their financial advisor, Cheng, and request that he create a sound financial plan for their future.

Cheng commenced his analysis by understanding their current situation. Through a few questions, he gathered the following information: Elijah had a stable job as a college professor and had plans to retire at the age of 65. He would like to receive a pension amount of $36,000 every year when he retires. Both of them would also like to create a fund that would support their child through his university education.

Recently, Elijah received a lump sum amount of $50,000 from the will of a wealthy uncle who had recently died. At the end of the discussion, Elijah also added that he had a vision of donating some money to his college when he retires. His hope is that the college would create an endowment fund that would provide a suitable scholarship for the college's business students.

With this information, Cheng, created the following financial plan for Elijah:

1. Make month-end deposits into an RESP starting at $50 and increasing the deposits by 1.25% every month for 14 years. 17 years from now, your son will be able to withdraw money at the beginning of every year from the RESP for his university education and increase his withdrawals by 2% every year (to cover for any inflation in the economy) for 5 years. During the first 17 years, your money will be growing at 9% compounded monthly, and thereafter, we will move the RESP to a fund that earns 10% compounded annually for the next 5 years.
2. Save the lump sum amount of $50,000 in an RRSP at 6% compounded quarterly. When you are 65 years old, withdraw one-fourth of the accumulated amount and donate it to your college to create the endowment fund.
3. Convert the balance amount in the RRSP to an annuity paying $36,000 annually.

Elijah and Carol were excited that they had a financial plan in place for their future. However, they needed a few clarifications and sent Cheng an email with their questions. Assist Cheng in providing Elijah with answers to the following questions:

a. What would be our son's first withdrawal amount for his 5-year university education?

b. How long would we receive our pension amount?

c. What would be the scholarship that students receive at the beginning of every six months in perpetuity if the college creates an endowment fund on my 65th birthday, and the fund earns 8% compounded quarterly?

11 | Summary of Notation and Formulas

NOTATION

$g\%$ = Constant growth rate

PMT = Periodic payment of the annuity

n = Number of payments during the term of an annuity

FV = Accumulated value or future value of an annuity

FV_{Due} = Future value of an annuity due

FV_{Def} = Future value of a deffered annuity

$PV_{Perpetuity}$ = Present value of an ordinary perpetuity

i = Interest rate per conversion period (periodic interest rate)

j = Nominal interest rate

t = Time period

PV = Discounted value or present value of an annuity

PV_{Due} = Present value of an annuity due

PV_{Def} = Present value of a deffered annuity

$PV_{Perpetuity\ Due}$ = Present value of a perpetuity due

FORMULAS

Present Value of an ordinary perpetuity | 11.2 (a)

$$PV_{Perpetuity} = \frac{PMT}{i}$$

Present Value of a perpetuity due | 11.2 (b)

$$PV_{Perpetuity\ Due} = \frac{PMT}{i}(1 + i)$$

Future Value of an ordinary simple constant-growth annuity | 11.3 (a)

$$FV = PMT\left[\frac{(1 + i)^n - (1 + g)^n}{(i - g)}\right]$$

Present Value of an ordinary simple constant-growth annuity | 11.3 (b)

$$PV = PMT\left[\frac{1 - (1 + g)^n(1 + i)^{-n}}{(i - g)}\right]$$

People borrow money from financial institutions for various reasons. Perhaps one of the largest amounts that one may ever borrow would be for the purchase of a property. The process of repaying a compound interest bearing loan by periodic payments over a period of time is called amortization. A mortgage is a claim on the purchased property by a financial institution lending the money at a specified interest rate for a period of time. In this chapter, we will use many of the terms and procedures that we learned in the previous chapters dealing with compound interest and annuities to examine applications involving amortization of loans and mortgages.

12 Amortization of Loans and Mortgages

LEARNING OBJECTIVES

- Understand the concept of amortization of loans.
- Construct an amortization schedule.
- Calculate the principal balance.
- Calculate the final payment.
- Calculate the interest portion, principal portion, and principal balance after any payment.
- Construct a partial amortization schedule.
- Understand the concept and types of mortgages.
- Calculate mortgage payments for the initial term and renewal term.
- Understand the concept of qualifying for a mortgage and the different options available to prepay a mortgage, and the effect of prepayment on the amortization period.
- Generate a mortgage schedule using Microsoft Excel.

CHAPTER OUTLINE

12.1 | Amortization of Loans

The **amortization of a loan** is the gradual reduction in the loan amount through periodic repayments, usually of equal amounts, over a period of time. Each repayment amount is first used to pay off the interest charged during that period and the rest of the repayment amount is used to reduce a portion of the principal of the loan. Therefore, after every repayment, the interest for the next period is calculated on the reduced principal. Some examples of loans that are amortized include a student loan, a car loan, and a mortgage on property.

Amortization
Amortization is the process of repaying a loan through periodic payments. The time set to repay the loan is called the amortization period.

Amortization of loans is primarily considered as an *ordinary annuity* because loan repayments are generally made at the end of the payment period.

Therefore, if the compounding period is equal to the payment period, the present value of a loan (which is the principal) is calculated by the ordinary simple annuity Formula 10.2(b):

$$PV = PMT\left[\frac{1-(1+i)^{-n}}{i}\right]$$

If the compounding period is not equal to the payment period, the present value of the loan is calculated by substituting the equivalent periodic interest rate per payment period (i_2) for 'i' in the above formula, which gives:

$$PV = PMT\left[\frac{1-(1+i_2)^{-n}}{i_2}\right]$$

The equivalent periodic interest rate per payment period (i_2) is calculated using Formula 10.3(a) and Formula 10.3(b), as follows:

$$c = \frac{\textit{Number of compounding periods per year}}{\textit{Number of payments per year}} \qquad \text{From Formula 10.3(a)}$$

$$i_2 = (1+i)^c - 1 \qquad \text{From Formula 10.3(b)}$$

Note that most of the notations and formulas in this section make use of those from the compound interest and annuity chapters.

At the beginning of the amortization schedule, a larger portion of the periodic payment goes towards the interest portion. However, later on in the schedule, a larger portion of the periodic payment goes towards the principal portion.

Amortization Schedule

An amortization schedule is a detailed table that breaks down each loan repayment amount into its interest portion and principal portion. It also shows the amount of principal balance after each payment is made.

Amortization schedules are created and used by financial institutions to provide customers with the exact amount of the loan that is outstanding after each payment. Amortization schedules are most frequently used for mortgages.

An amortization schedule typically contains the following information:

- Payment number (or payment date)
- Payment amount (*PMT*)
- Interest portion of the payment amount (*INT*)
- Principal portion of the payment amount (*PRN*)
- Principal balance after each payment (*BAL*)

Constructing an Amortization Schedule

Table 12.1(a) and the steps that follow illustrate the construction of a typical amortization schedule:

Table 12.1(a)

Payment Number	Amount Paid (Periodic Payment) PMT (\$)	Interest Portion (Previous Balance) INT (\$)	Principal Portion ($PMT - INT$) PRN (\$)	Principal Balance (Previous Balance − PRN) BAL (\$)
0	–	–	–	Loan amount: PV
1	PMT	INT_1 $(= PV \times i)$	PRN_1 $(= PMT - INT_1)$	BAL_1 $(= PV - PRN_1)$
2	PMT	INT_2 $(= BAL_1 \times i)$	PRN_2 $(= PMT - INT_2)$	BAL_2 $(= BAL_1 - PRN_2)$
3	PMT	INT_3 $(= BAL_2 \times i)$	PRN_3 $(= PMT - INT_3)$	BAL_3 $(= BAL_2 - PRN_3)$
.	.	.	.	.
.	.	.	.	.
$n-1$	PMT	$INT_{(n-1)}$ $(= BAL_{(n-2)} \times i)$	$PRN_{(n-1)}$ $(= PMT - INT_{(n-1)})$	$BAL_{(n-1)}$ $(= BAL_{(n-2)} - PRN_{(n-1)})$
n	PMT_n $(= BAL_{(n-1)} + BAL_{(n-1)} \times i)$	INT_n $(= BAL_{(n-1)} \times i)$	PRN_n $(= BAL_{(n-1)})$	0
Totals:	Total Amount Paid	Total Interest Portion	Total Principal Portion	

When the periodic payments, *PMT*, are rounded, the last payment amount will be different from the *PMT*.

Step 1: Calculate the periodic interest rate (i).

Step 2: Enter '0' as the first payment number in the first row and enter the original loan amount, PV, as the principal balance in this row.

Step 3: Enter the periodic payment, PMT, in a new row against its respective payment number. The periodic payment amount is generally a rounded amount. Therefore, the final payment will be different from the other periodic payments as it will carry the difference in rounding amount. The calculation for the final payment amount is explained in Step 8.

Step 4: Enter the interest portion, INT, of the payment in the 3rd column. This is the previous principal balance multiplied by the periodic interest rate.

Step 5: Enter the principal portion, PRN, of the payment in the 4th column. This is the difference between the periodic payment amount and the interest portion.

Step 6: Enter the principal balance, BAL, in the 5th column. This is the difference between the previous principal balance and the principal portion.

Step 7: Construct the remaining rows of the amortization schedule by performing the above calculations until the final payment number, where the principal balance will be nil (i.e., zero).

Step 8: The final payment amount is calculated by adding the previous principal balance and the interest charged on the previous principal balance.

Step 9: The last row contains all the totals and can be used to cross-check if the calculations are correct.

$$\textit{Total Principal Portion} = \textit{Original loan amount}$$

$$\textit{Total Amount Paid} = \textit{Total Interest Portion} + \textit{Total Principal Portion}$$

Example 12.1(a)

Constructing an Amortization Schedule for an Ordinary Simple Annuity

Shiela received a loan of $7500 from a bank to purchase furniture for her small business. She obtained the loan at an interest rate of 9% compounded quarterly for 1 year. Calculate the size of her end-of-quarter payments and construct an amortization schedule for her loan.

Solution

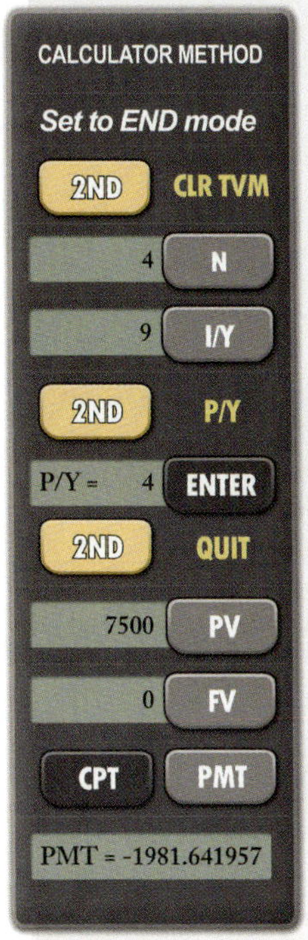

The loan is in the form of an ordinary simple annuity as:

- Payments are made at the end of each payment period (quarterly)
- Compounding period (quarterly) = payment period (quarterly)

Using Formula 10.2(b),

$$PV = PMT\left[\frac{1-(1+i)^{-n}}{i}\right]$$

Substituting, $$7500 = PMT\left[\frac{1-(1+0.0225)^{-4}}{0.0225}\right]$$

Cross-multiplying and solving,

$$PMT = \$1981.641957...$$

Therefore, the size of her end-of-quarter payments was $1981.64 (rounded to the nearest cent).

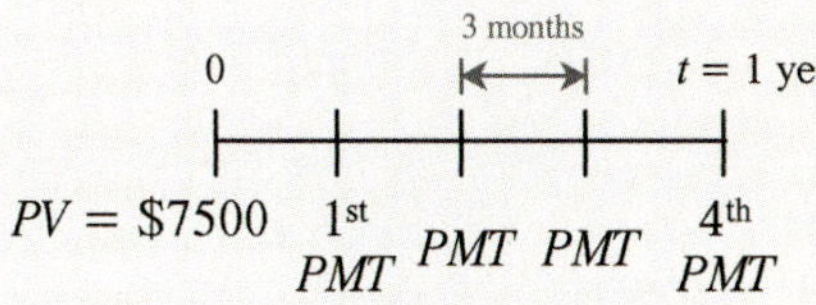

$PMT = ?$

$n = 4$ payments/year × 1 year = 4 quarterly payments

$j = 0.09,\ m = 4,\ i = \frac{j}{m} = 0.0225$ per quarter

Constructing an amortization schedule:

Payment Number	Amount Paid (Periodic Payment) *PMT* ($)	Interest Portion (Previous Balance) *INT* ($)	Principal Portion (*PMT* – *INT*) *PRN* ($)	Principal Balance (Previous Balance – *PRN*) *BAL* ($)
0	–	–	–	$7500.00
1	$1981.64	$168.75 (=7500.00 × 0.0225)	$1812.89 (=1981.64 – 168.75)	5687.11 (7500.00 – 1812.89)
2	1981.64	127.96 (=5687.11 × 0.0225)	1853.68 (=1981.64 – 127.96)	3833.43 (5687.11 – 1853.68)
3	1981.64	86.25 (=3833.43 × 0.0225)	1895.39 (=1981.64 – 86.25)	1938.04 (3833.43 – 1895.39)
4	1981.65 (=1938.04 + 1938.04 × 0.0225)	43.61 (=1938.04 × 0.0225)	1938.04	$0
Total	$7926.57	$426.57	$7500.00	

We can cross-check the above totals:

Total Principal Portion = *Original loan amount* = $7500.00

Total Amount Paid = *Total Interest Portion* + *Total Principal Portion*

= $426.57 + $7500.00

= $7926.57

Note: There may be situations when the amounts calculated may vary by a few cents from the answer obtained using the financial calculator. This is due to rounding of each step to the nearest cent in the amortization schedule.

Example 12.1(b)

Constructing an Amortization Schedule for an Ordinary General Annuity

A furniture manufacturer received a loan of $12,450 at 12% compounded monthly to purchase equipment for his factory. If he has to repay $3000 at the end of every 3 months, construct an amortization schedule providing details of his repayment.

Solution

This loan is in the form of an ordinary general annuity as:

- Payments are made at the end of each payment period (quarterly)
- Compounding period (monthly) ≠ payment period (quarterly)

Solution continued

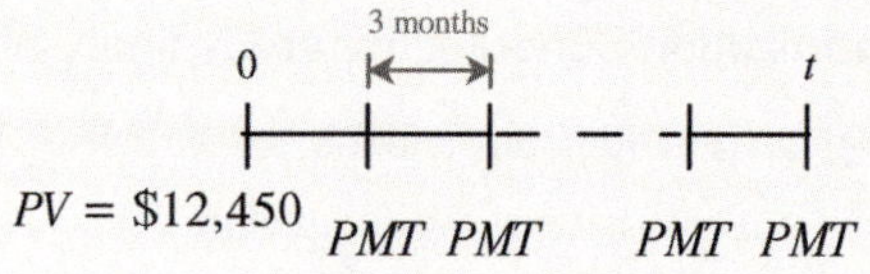

$$PMT = \$3000$$

$$j = 0.12,\ m = 12,\ i = \frac{j}{m} = 0.01 \text{ per month}$$

From Formula 10.3(a), $c = \dfrac{\textit{Number of compounding periods per year}}{\textit{Number of payments per year}} = \dfrac{12}{4}$

From Formula 10.3(b), $i_2 = (1 + i)^c - 1$

Substituting, $= (1 + 0.01)^{12/4} - 1$

Simplifying, $= 0.030301$ per quarter

In this problem, we have been given a specific rounded payment amount of $3000.00 that has to be made at the end of every 3 months. Therefore, the last payment amount will be different from this amount. The following amortization schedule will illustrate this:

Payment Number	Amount Paid (Periodic Payment) *PMT* ($)	Interest Portion (Previous Balance) *INT* ($)	Principal Portion (*PMT* − *INT*) *PRN* ($)	Principal Balance (Previous Balance − *PRN*) *BAL* ($)
0	–	–	–	$12,450.00
1	$3000.00	$377.25 (=12,450.00 × 0.030301)	$2622.75 (=3000.00 − 377.25)	9827.25 (=12,450.00 − 2622.75)
2	3000.00	297.78 (=9827.25 × 0.030301)	2702.22 (=3000.00 − 297.78)	7125.03 (=9827.25 − 2702.22)
3	3000.00	215.90 (=7125.03 × 0.030301)	2784.10 (=3000.00 − 215.90)	4340.93 (=7125.03 − 2784.10)
4	3000.00	131.53 (=4340.93 × 0.030301)	2868.47 (=3000.00 − 131.53)	1472.46 (=4340.93 − 2868.47)
5	1517.08 (=1472.46+1472.46 × 030301)	44.62 (=1472.46 × 0.030301)	1472.46	$0
Totals	$13,517.08	$1067.08	$12,450.00	

We can cross-check the above totals:

Total Principal Portion = *Original loan amount* = $12,450.00

Total Amount Paid = *Total Interest Portion* + *Total Principal Portion*

= $1067.08 + $12,450.00

= $13,517.08

Calculating the Principal Balance

It may be necessary to know the principal balance at an earlier time than the end of the loan period in order to settle the loan earlier or make a partial repayment. This may be done by creating an amortization schedule and finding the principal balance at the required date or by directly using any of the following three methods:

Method 1: Prospective Method (considering payments that are yet to be made)

The principal balance at any given date (focal date) can be calculated by finding the present value of all the outstanding payments on that focal date. This method is also known as the Present Value approach.

Since the periodic payments are usually rounded, it is necessary to calculate the exact number of remaining payments.

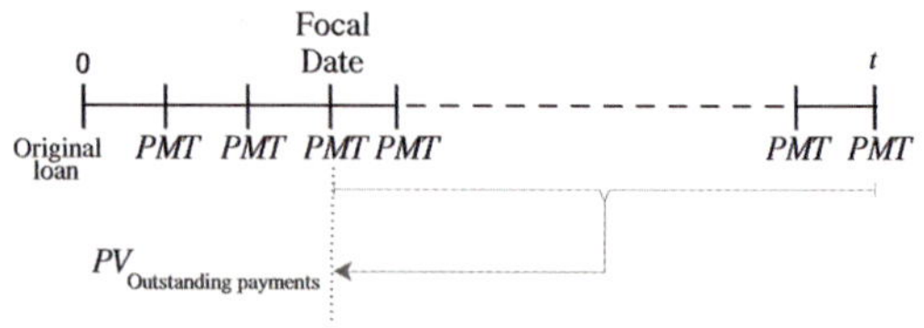

To do this, first calculate the exact number of periodic payments using the rounded periodic amount. Then subtract the number of payments made from this to determine the exact number of remaining payments and use this to calculate the present value on that focal date.

$$BAL_{\text{Focal Date}} = PV_{\text{Outstanding Payments on the Focal Date}}$$

Method 2: Retrospective Method (considering payments that have already been made)

The principal balance at a given date (focal date) can also be calculated by deducting the future value of all the payments that have been made until the focal date from the future value of the original loan amount on the focal date. This method is also aknow as the Future Value approach.

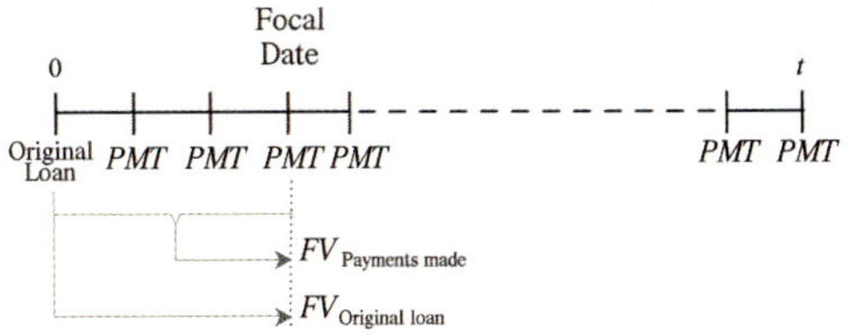

$$BAL_{\text{Focal Date}} = FV_{\text{Original Loan}} - FV_{\text{Payments Made until the Focal Date}}$$

Method 3: Using the Amortization Worksheet in a Financial Calculator

Financial calculators have an amortization worksheet that can be used to quickly find the values of the amortization schedule. First, compute the value of PMT using the calculator then follow these instructions to find the values of the amortization schedule using the calculator's amortization worksheet:

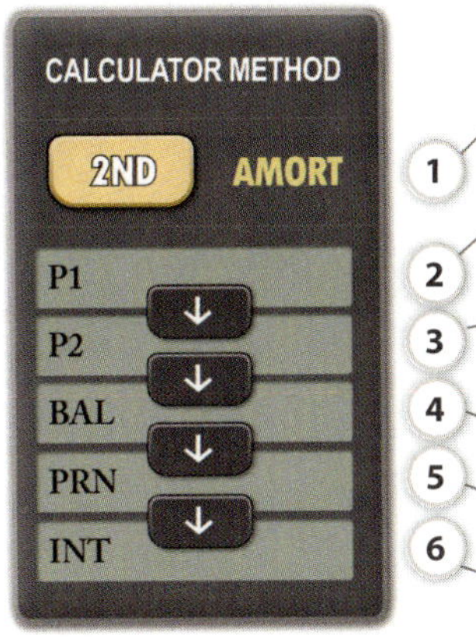

1. Press **2ND** then **AMORT** (secondary function of the **PV key**) to open the amortization worksheet.
2. ***P1*** is the payment number of the period from when you want to start viewing the schedule. To set a payment number for ***P1***, enter the number and press the **ENTER key**.
3. ***P2*** is the payment number of the period up to when you want to end viewing the schedule. To set a payment number for ***P2***, enter the number and press the **ENTER key**.
4. ***BAL*** displays the principal balance after the payment in period ***P2***.
5. ***PRN*** displays the total principal paid from periods ***P1*** to ***P2***.*
6. ***INT*** displays the total interest paid from periods ***P1*** to ***P2***. *

** To obtain the principal portion and interest portion of a particular payment number, set P1 and P2 to that payment number. For example, when P1 = 5 and P2 = 5, PRN displays the principal portion of the 5th payment and INT displays the interest portion of the 5th payment. BAL displays the principal balance after the 5th payment.*

Example 12.1(c) **Calculating the Principal Balance when the Periodic Payments are Equal**

Samantha received a loan of $25,000 at 4% compounded quarterly. If the loan is amortized over 10 years with payments (rounded up to the next dollar) made at the end of every 3 months, what was the balance on her loan after 1 year?

Solution

Calculating the payment amount, PMT:

This loan is in the form of an ordinary simple annuity as:

- Payments are made at the end of each payment period (quarterly)
- Compounding period (quarterly) = payment period (quarterly)

Solution continued

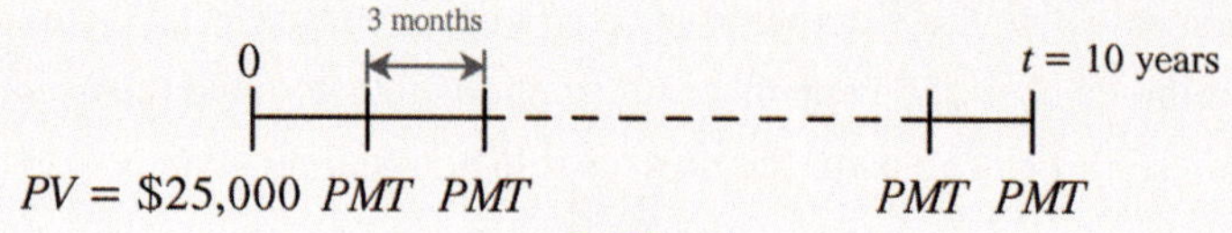

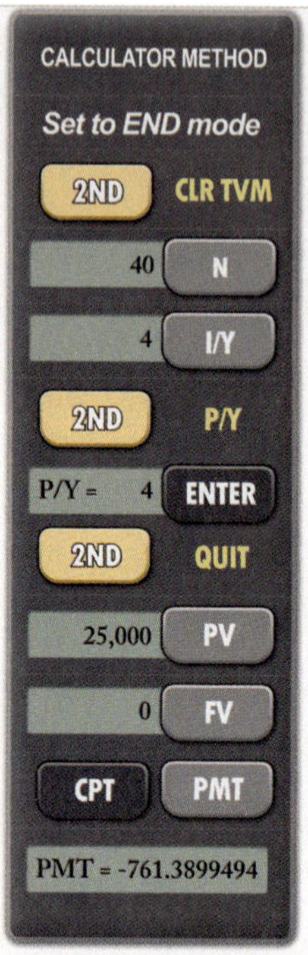

$$PMT = ?$$

$$n = 4 \text{ payments/year} \times 10 \text{ years}$$
$$= 40 \text{ quarterly payments}$$

$$j = 0.04,\ m = 4,\ i = \frac{j}{m} = 0.01 \text{ per quarter}$$

Using Formula 10.2(b), $PV = PMT\left[\frac{1-(1+i)^{-n}}{i}\right]$

Substituting, $25{,}000 = PMT\left[\frac{1-(1+0.01)^{-40}}{0.01}\right]$

Cross-multiplying and solving,

$$PMT = \$761.389949...$$
$$= \$762.00 \text{ (rounded up to the next dollar)}$$

Calculating the principal balance after 1 year:

Method 1: Prospective Method

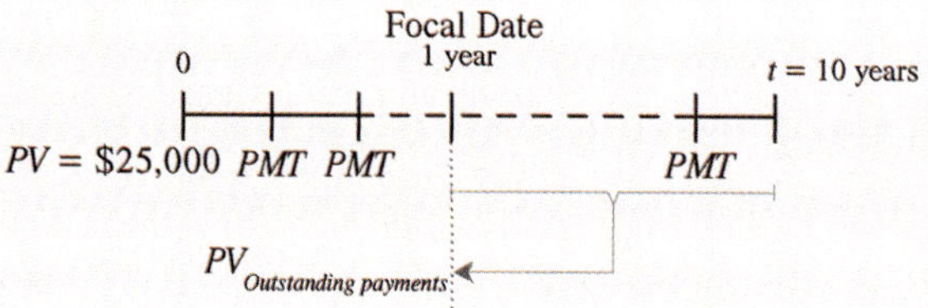

As the size of the periodic payment has been rounded up, we need to recalculate the number of payments.

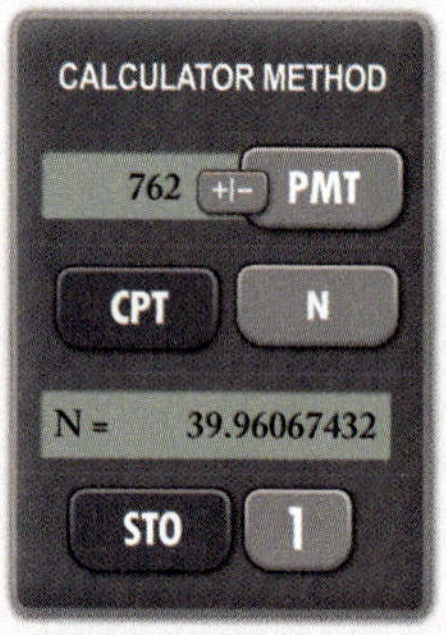

Using Formula 10.7(b), $n = -\frac{\ln\left(1 - \frac{i \times PV}{PMT}\right)}{\ln(1+i)}$

$$= -\frac{\ln\left(1 - \frac{0.01 \times 25{,}000}{762}\right)}{\ln(1+0.01)}$$

$$= 39.960674...$$

$$BAL_{\text{Focal Date}} = PV_{\text{Outstanding Payments on the Focal Date}}$$

After 1 year, 4 out of 39.960674... payments were made.

Therefore, there would have been 35.960674... payments remaining.

$$BAL_{\text{1 year}} = PV_{\text{Remaining 35.960674... Payments}}$$

Using Formula 10.2(b),

$$PV = PMT\left[\frac{1-(1+i)^{-n}}{i}\right]$$

Where 'n' is the number of remaining payments, which is 35.960674... payments.

Substituting and solving,

$$PV_{\text{Remaining 35.960674... Payments}} = 762\left[\frac{1-(1+0.01)^{-35.960674...}}{0.01}\right]$$

$$= \$22{,}921.07469...$$

Therefore, the principal balance on the loan after 1 year was \$22,921.07.

Solution *continued*

Method 2: Retrospective Method

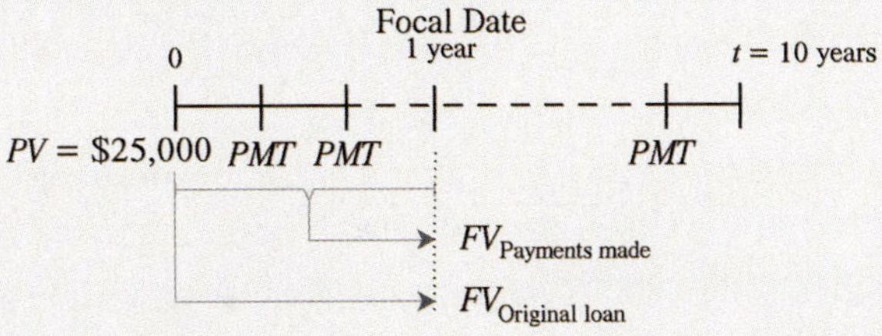

$$BAL_{Focal\ Date} = FV_{Original\ Loan} - FV_{Payments\ Made\ until\ the\ Focal\ Date}$$

In the retrospective method, we can calculate the outstanding principal by computing 'FV' using the financial calculator, as shown below.

It is not necessary to re-enter I/Y, P/Y, and PV as they have not changed and have not been cleared (by CLR TVM).

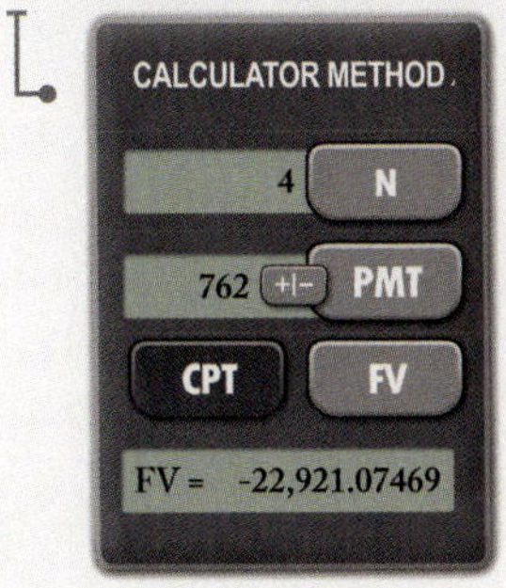

Using Formula 9.1(a) and Formula 10.2(a),

$$BAL = PV(1+i)^n - PMT\left[\frac{(1+i)^n - 1}{i}\right]$$

$$= 25{,}000(1+0.01)^4 - 762\left[\frac{(1+0.01)^4 - 1}{0.01}\right]$$

$$= 26{,}015.10025... - 3094.025562...$$

$$= \$22{,}921.07469...$$

Therefore, the principal balance on the loan after 1 year was $22,921.07.

Method 3: Using the Amortization Worksheet in the Financial Calculator

First re-enter the rounded value for *PMT* as −762 in the TVM worksheet. After 1 year, 4 payments were made. Therefore, we need to find the value of the principal balance at the end of the 4th payment as illustrated below:

1. **Enter 4** for ***P1*** as this is the payment number of the period from when you want to start viewing the schedule.
2. **Enter 4** for ***P2*** also as you want to view the schedule only for this payment number.
3. This displays the principal balance after the 4th payment.

Example 12.1(d) **Calculating the Principal Balance at a Given Focal Date when the Periodic Payment is Given**

Andrew received a student loan of $45,000 at 6% compounded monthly. If he has to repay $500 at the end of every month, what will be his principal balance at the end of 2 years?

Solution

Method 1: Prospective Method

The loan is in the form of an ordinary simple annuity as:

- Payments are made at the end of each payment period (monthly)
- Compounding period (monthly) = payment period (monthly)

$$i = \frac{j}{m} = \frac{0.06}{12} = 0.005$$

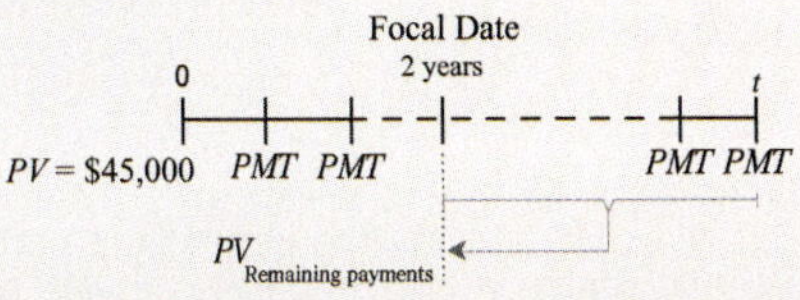

We need to find the number of payments, '*n*'.

Solution continued

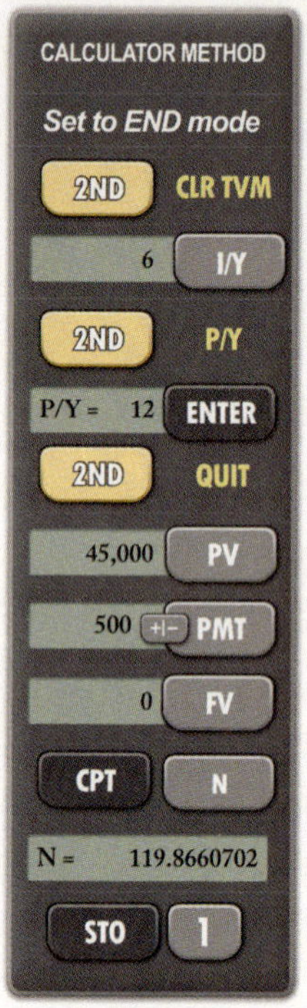

From Formula 10.7(b),
$$n = -\frac{\ln\left(1 - \frac{i \times PV}{PMT}\right)}{\ln(1+i)}$$

Substituting and solving,
$$n = -\frac{\ln\left(1 - \frac{0.005 \times 45{,}000}{500}\right)}{\ln(1+0.005)}$$
$$= 119.866070\text{... payments}$$

After 2 years, he would have made 24 payments out of 119.866070... payments. Therefore, there would have been 95.866070... payments remaining.

Using Formula 10.2(b),
$$PV = PMT\left[\frac{1-(1+i)^{-n}}{i}\right]$$

Where 'n' is the number of remaining payments.
$$PV_{Outstanding\ Payments} = 500\left[\frac{1-(1+0.005)^{-95.866070...}}{0.005}\right]$$
$$= \$38{,}006.21231...$$

Therefore, the principal balance on the loan after 2 years was $38,006.21.

Note: The prospective method of finding the principal balance becomes lengthy as we need to find the exact number of remaining payments to find the 'PV' of all the remaining payments.

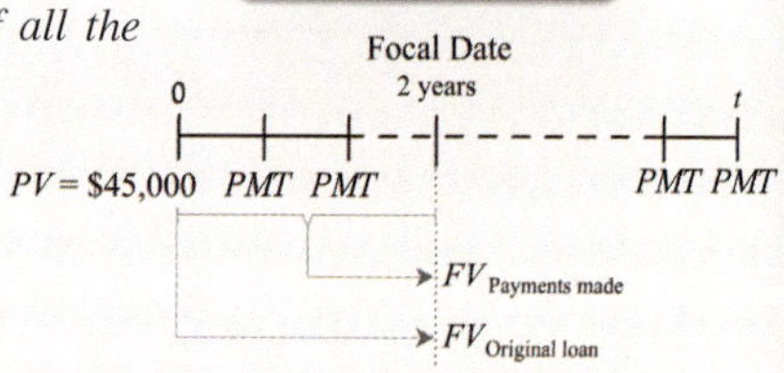

Method 2: Retrospective Method

$$BAL_{Focal\ Date} = FV_{Original\ Loan} - FV_{Payments\ Made\ until\ the\ Focal\ Date}$$

Using Formula 9.1(a) and Formula 10.2(a),
$$Principal\ Balance = PV(1+i)^n - PMT\left[\frac{(1+i)^n - 1}{i}\right]$$

Substituting and solving,
$$= 45{,}000(1+0.005)^{24} - 500\left[\frac{(1+0.005)^{24}-1}{0.005}\right]$$
$$= 50{,}722.18993... - 12{,}715.97762...$$
$$= \$38{,}006.21231...$$

Therefore, the principal balance on the loan after 2 years was $38,006.21.

It is not necessary to re-enter I/Y, P/Y, and PV as they have not changed and have not been cleared (by CLR TVM).

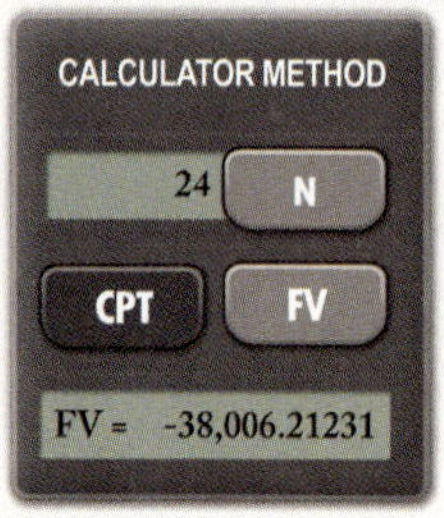

Calculating the Final Payment

The final payment can be calculated using any of the following methods:

Method 1: Direct Method

From Table 12.1(a), we know that the final payment is the sum of the principal balance before the final payment and the interest charged on that principal balance.

$$Final\ Payment\ Amount = Principal\ Balance_{Before\ Final\ Payment} + Principal\ Balance_{Before\ Final\ Payment} \times i$$
$$= Principal\ Balance_{Before\ Final\ Payment}(1+i)$$

Method 2: Overpayment Method

By rounding 'n' up to a whole number, the calculator assumes that the final payment is the same amount as all of the other payments. Thus, when you calculate the future value, the result will represent the overpayment that resulted from the final payment being larger than it should be. To find the correct amount for the final payment, subtract the amount of overpayment from the regular payment amount as shown:

$$PMT_{Final} = PMT - Overpayment$$

Example 12.1(e)

Calculating the Final Payment

A businessman receives a loan of $750,000 to purchase a software business. The interest on the loan is 12% compounded quarterly, and he is required to make payments of $50,000 at the end of every 6 months to repay the loan. What was the final payment on the loan?

Solution

This loan is in the form of an ordinary general annuity as:

- Payments are made at the end of each payment period (semi-annually)
- Compounding period (quarterly) ≠ payment period (semi-annually)

$$i = \frac{j}{m} = \frac{0.12}{4} = 0.03 \text{ per quarter}$$

From Formula 10.3(a), $c = \dfrac{\textit{Number of compounding periods per year}}{\textit{Number of payments per year}}$

$$= \frac{4}{2} = 2$$

From Formula 10.3(b), $i_2 = (1 + i)^c - 1$

Substituting, $= (1 + 0.03)^2 - 1$

Simplifying, $= 0.0609$ per half year

We need to find the number of payments, 'n'.

From Formula 10.7(b),

$$n = -\frac{\ln\left(1 - \dfrac{i \times PV}{PMT}\right)}{\ln(1 + i)}$$

Substituting and solving,

$$= -\frac{\ln\left(1 - \dfrac{0.0609 \times 750{,}000}{50{,}000}\right)}{\ln(1 + 0.0609)} = 41.402402...$$

CALCULATOR METHOD

Set to END mode

2ND CLR TVM

12 I/Y

2ND P/Y

P/Y = 2 ENTER

↓

C/Y = 4 ENTER

2ND QUIT

750,000 PV

50,000 +/- PMT

0 FV

CPT N

N = 41.40240266

Therefore, there will be more than 41 payments. 41 payments will be of $50,000 each and the 42nd payment (final payment) will be of a different amount.

Method 1: Direct Method

Using the retrospective method to find the principal balance after 41 payments are made:

$$\textit{Principal Balance}_{\textit{Focal Date}} = FV_{\textit{Original Loan}} - FV_{\textit{Payments Made until the Focal Date}}$$

Using Formula 9.1(a) and Formula 10.2(a),

$$\textit{Principal Balance} = PV(1+i)^n - PMT\left[\frac{(1+i)^n - 1}{i}\right]$$

Substituting and solving,

$$= 750{,}000(1+0.0609)^{41} - 50{,}000\left[\frac{(1+0.0609)^{41} - 1}{0.0609}\right]$$

$$= 8{,}466{,}690.593... - 8{,}447{,}389.812... = \$19{,}300.78124...$$

CALCULATOR METHOD

2ND AMORT

P1 = 41 ENTER

↓

P2 = 41 ENTER

↓

BAL = 19,300.7812

It is not necessary to re-enter I/Y, P/Y, and PV as they have not changed and have not been cleared (by CLR TVM).

CALCULATOR METHOD

41 N

CPT FV

FV = -19,300.78124

$$\textit{Final Payment Amount} = \textit{Principal Balance}_{\textit{Before Final Payment}}(1 + i)$$

Substituting and solving, $= 19{,}300.78124...(1 + 0.0609) = \$20{,}476.19882...$

Method 2: Overpayment Method

$$\textit{Final Payment Amount} = PMT - \textit{Overpayment}$$

$$= 50{,}000.00 - \$29{,}523.80118...$$

$$= \$20{,}476.19882...$$

CALCULATOR METHOD

42 N

CPT FV

FV = 29,523.80118

Therefore, the final payment was $20,476.20.

Calculating Interest Portion and Principal Portion of the Payment

In addition to finding the principal balance at a given time, it may be necessary to find the interest portion and principal portion of a payment at any given time. The interest portion at any given time is calculated on the previous principal balance. The principal portion can then be determined by subtracting the calculated interest portion from the payment amount of the loan.

Example 12.1(f)

Calculating Interest Portion and Principal Portion of the Payment

Clear Circuits Inc., an electrical contracting company, receives a loan of $130,000 at 6% compounded monthly to purchase some heavy equipment. Clear Circuits must make payments of $5000 at the end of every month to settle the loan. Calculate the interest portion and principal portion of their 19th payment.

Solution

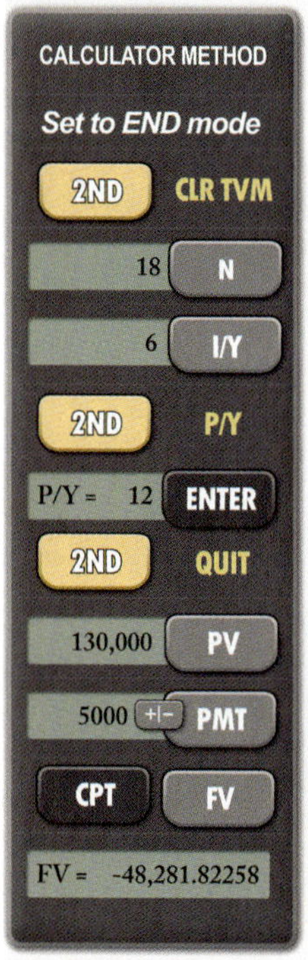

This loan is in the form of an ordinary simple annuity as:

- Payments are made at the end of each payment period (monthly)
- Compounding period (monthly) = payment period (monthly)

$$i = \frac{j}{m} = \frac{0.06}{12} = 0.005$$

The **interest portion** of a payment is calculated on the previous principal balance.

Therefore, to calculate the interest portion of the 19th payment, we need to calculate the principal balance after 18 payments.

Using the retrospective method,

$$Principal\ Balance_{18^{th}\ payment} = FV_{Original\ loan} - FV_{Payments\ made\ until\ the\ focal\ date}$$

Using Formula 9.1(a) and Formula 10.2(a),

$$Principal\ Balance_{18^{th}\ payment} = PV(1+i)^n - PMT\left[\frac{(1+i)^n - 1}{i}\right]$$

$$= 130{,}000(1+0.005)^{18} - 5000\left[\frac{(1+0.005)^{18} - 1}{0.005}\right]$$

$$= 142{,}210.76 - 93{,}928.94 = \$48{,}281.82$$

$$Interest\ Portion_{19^{th}\ payment} = 48{,}281.82 \times i = 48{,}281.82 \times 0.005 = \$241.41$$

The **principal portion** of the 19th payment = *Payment Amount* − *Interest Portion*

= 5000.00 − 241.41 = $4758.59

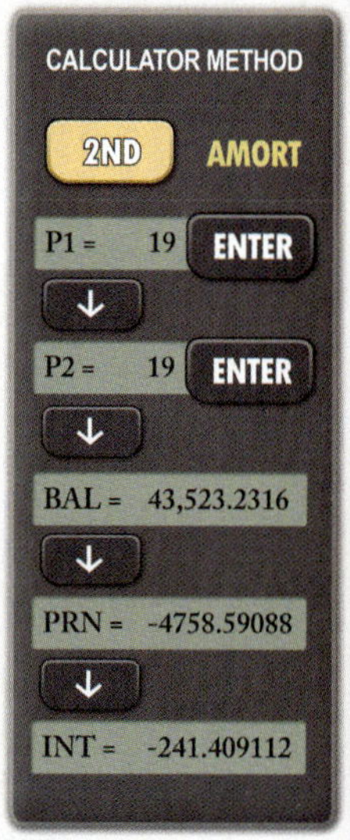

Therefore, the interest portion and principal portion of the 19th payment are $241.41 and $4758.59, respectively.

Constructing a Partial Amortization Schedule

There may be instances when it is necessary to determine the amortization details of a portion of the schedule for example, the last five payments or the first five payments or the interest portion and principal portion of a particular payment. It is for this reason that we find all the payment details and create a partial amortization schedule.

Example 12.1(g)

Constructing a Partial Amortization Schedule

Following the scenario given in Example 12.1(f), construct a partial amortization schedule showing details of the (i) 19th and 20th payments, (ii) first two payments, and (iii) last two payments. Calculate the total payment made, interest paid, and principal paid to settle the loan and construct a partial amortization schedule showing the totals.

Solution

(i) Amortization schedule of the 19th and 20th payments

Amortization details of the 19th payment:

$INT = \$241.41$ From Example 12.1(f)

$PRN = \$4758.59$ From Example 12.1(f)

$$BAL_{19th\ payment} = BAL_{18th\ Payment} - PRN_{19th\ Payment}$$
$$= 48{,}281.82 - 4758.59 = \$43{,}523.23$$

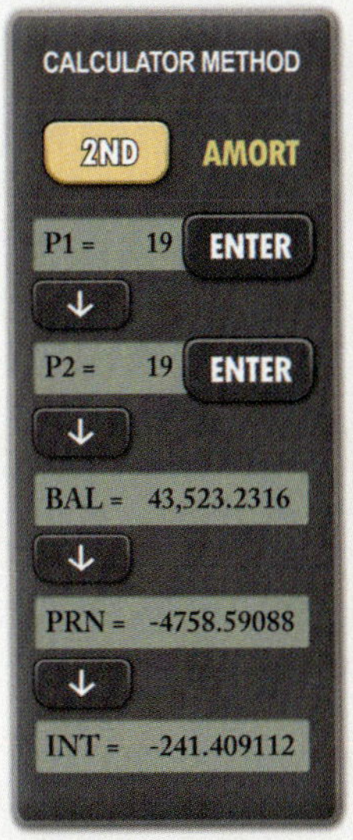

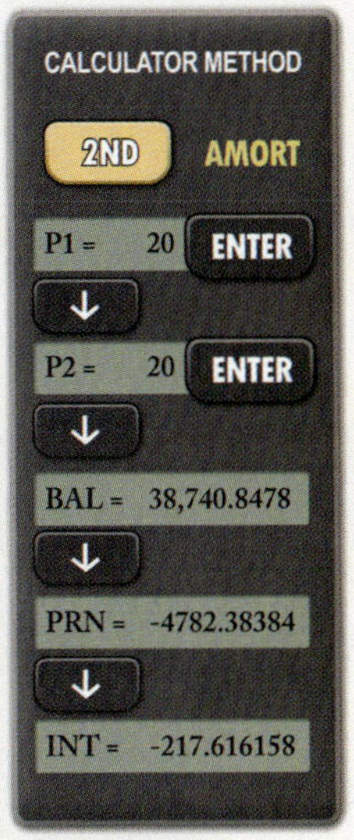

Amortization details of the 20th payment:

$$INT_{20th\ Payment} = BAL_{19th\ Payment} \times i$$
$$= 43{,}523.23 \times 0.005 = \$217.62$$

$$PRN_{20th\ Payment} = PMT - INT_{20th\ Payment}$$
$$= 5000.00 - 217.62 = \$4782.38$$

$$BAL_{20th\ Payment} = BAL_{19th\ Payment} - PRN_{20th\ Payment}$$
$$= 43{,}523.23 - 4782.38 = \$38{,}740.85$$

Using the above amortization details, we construct the partial amortization schedule of the 19th and 20th payments as shown below:

Payment Number	Amount Paid (Periodic Payment) *PMT* ($)	Interest Portion (Previous Balance) *INT* ($)	Principal Portion (*PMT* − *INT*) *PRN* ($)	Principal Balance (*Previous Balance* − *PRN*) *BAL* ($)
19	$5000.00	$241.41	$4758.59	$43,523.23
20	$5000.00	$217.62	$4782.38	$38,740.85

(ii) Amortization schedule of the first two payments

Amortization details of the 1st payment:

$$INT_{1st\ Payment} = Original\ Loan\ Amount \times i$$
$$= 130{,}000.00 \times 0.005 = \$650.00$$

$$PRN_{1st\ Payment} = PMT - INT_{1st\ Payment}$$
$$= 5000.00 - 650.00 = \$4350.00$$

$$BAL_{\text{1st Payment}} = Original\ Loan\ Amount - PRN_{1st\ Payment}$$
$$= 130{,}000.00 - 4350.00 = \$125{,}650.00$$

The principal balance at the beginning (payment number 0) is the original loan amount.

Amortization details of the 2nd payment:

$$INT_{2nd\ Payment} = \text{PRN}_{1st\ Payment} \times i$$
$$= 125{,}650.00 \times 0.005 = \$628.25$$

$$PRN_{2nd\ Payment} = PMT - INT_{2nd\ Payment}$$
$$= 5000.00 - 628.25 = \$4371.75$$

$$BAL_{2nd\ Payment} = BAL_{1st\ Payment} - PRN_{2nd\ Payment}$$
$$= 125{,}650.00 - 4371.75 = \$121{,}278.25$$

Solution *continued*

Using the amortization details on the previous page, we construct the partial amortization schedule of the first two payments as shown below:

Payment Number	Amount Paid (*Periodic Payment*) *PMT* ($)	Interest portion (*Previous Balance*) *INT* ($)	Principal portion (*PMT* − *INT*) *PRN* ($)	Principal Balance (*Previous Balance* − *PRN*) *BAL* ($)
0	–	–	–	$130,000.00
1	$5000.00	$650.00	$4350.00	$125,650.00
2	$5000.00	$628.25	$4371.75	$121,278.25

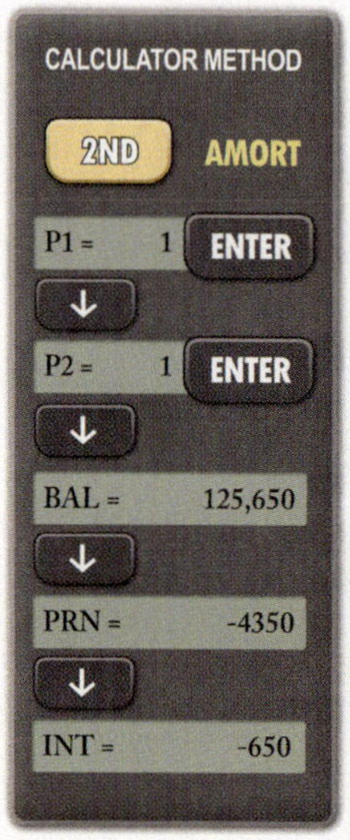

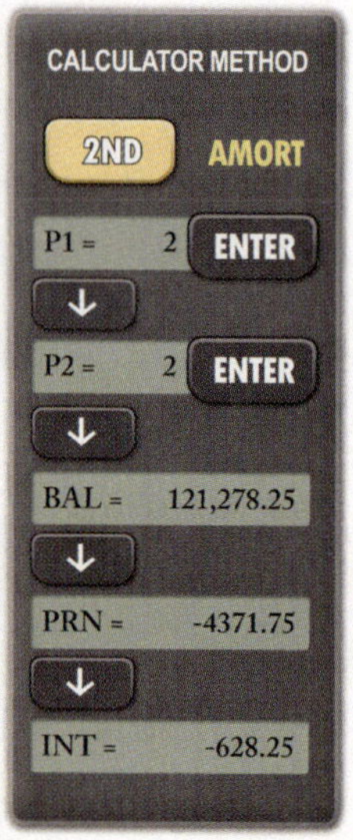

(iii) ***Amortization details of the last two payments:***

We need to find the number of payments, 'n'.

From Formula 10.7(a),

$$n = -\frac{\ln\left(1 - \frac{i \times PV}{PMT}\right)}{\ln(1+i)}$$

Substituting and solving,
$$= -\frac{\ln\left(1 - \frac{0.005 \times 130{,}000}{5000}\right)}{\ln(1+0.005)}$$

$$= 27.921986...$$

Rounding upwards, $n = 28$ payments

We need to find the payment details of the 27th and 28th payments.

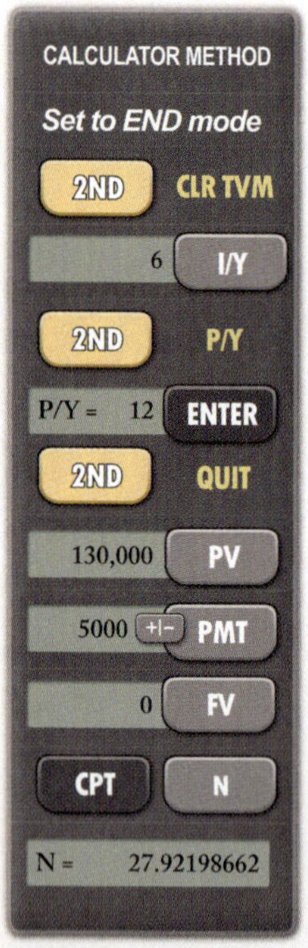

Amortization details of the 27th payment:

To calculate the amortization details of the 27th payment, we need to determine the principal balance after the 26th payment.

Using the retrospective method,

$$BAL_{26th\ Payment} = FV_{Original\ Loan} - FV_{Payments\ Made\ until\ the\ 26th\ Payment}$$

Using Formula 9.1(a) and Formula 10.2(a),

$$BAL_{26^{th}\ Payment} = PV(1+i)^n - PMT\left[\frac{(1+i)^n - 1}{i}\right]$$

$$= 130{,}000(1+0.005)^{26} - 5000\left[\frac{(1+0.005)^{26} - 1}{0.005}\right]$$

$$= 147{,}999.74 - 138{,}459.55 = \$9540.19$$

$$INT_{27^{th}\ Payment} = PRN_{26^{th}\ Payment} \times i = 9540.19 \times 0.005 = \$47.70$$

Solution *continued*

$$PRN_{27^{th}\ Payment} = PMT - INT_{27^{th}\ Payment} = 5000.00 - 47.70 = \$4952.30$$

$$BAL_{27^{th}\ Payment} = BAL_{26^{th}\ Payment} - PRN_{27^{th}\ Payment}$$
$$= 9540.19 - 4952.30 = \$4587.89$$

Amortization details of the 28th payment (last payment):

$$INT_{28^{th}\ Payment} = BAL_{27^{th}\ Payment} \times i$$
$$= 4587.89 \times 0.005 = \$22.94$$

$$PRN_{28^{th}\ Payment} = BAL_{27^{th}\ Payment} = \$4587.89$$

$$PMT_{28^{th}\ Payment} = INT_{28^{th}\ Payment} + PRN_{28^{th}\ Payment}$$
$$= 22.94 + 4587.89 = \$4610.83$$

$$BAL_{28^{th}\ Payment} = 0$$

Payment Number	Amount Paid (Periodic Payment) *PMT* ($)	Interest Portion (*Previous Balance*) *INT* ($)	Principal Portion (*PMT* − *INT*) *PRN* ($)	Principal Balance (*Previous Balance* − *PRN*) *BAL* ($)
27	$5000.00	$47.70	$4952.30	$4587.89
28	$4610.83	$22.94	$4587.89	$0

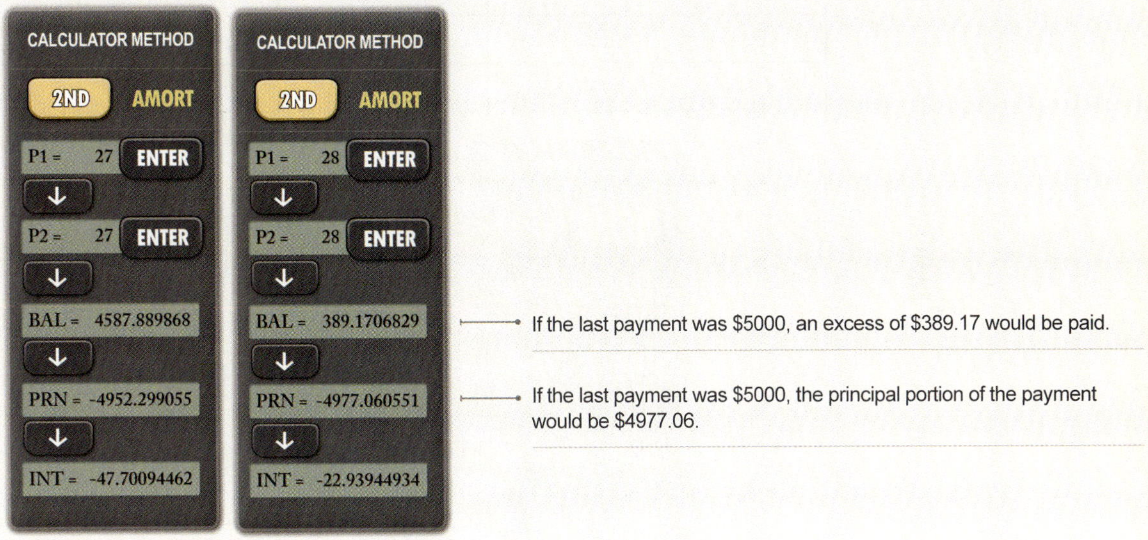

Using the above amortization details, we construct the partial amortization schedule of the last two payments as shown below:

Total payment made, interest paid, and principal repaid to clear the loan:

$$\textit{Total Payment Made} = (n-1)PMT + \textit{Final Payment}$$
$$= (27 \times 5000) + 4610.83$$
$$= \$139{,}610.83$$

The company should have repaid $130,000.00 of the principal (to clear the loan).

$$\textit{Total Interest Paid} = \textit{Total Payment Made} - \textit{Total Principal Paid}$$
$$= 139{,}610.83 - 130{,}000.00$$
$$= \$9610.83$$

Solution *continued*

Using the amortization details calculated in (i), (ii), and (iii), and the totals of *PMT*, principal paid, and interest paid, we construct the partial amortization schedule as shown below:

Payment Number	Amount Paid (*Periodic Payment*) *PMT* ($)	Interest Portion (*Previous Balance*) *INT* ($)	Principal Portion (*PMT* − *INT*) *PRN* ($)	Principal Balance (*Previous Balance* − *PRN*) *BAL* ($)
0	–	–	–	$130,000.00
1	$5000.00	$650.00	$4350.00	125,650.00
2	5000.00	628.25	4371.75	121,278.25
.	.	.	.	.
.	.	.	.	.
19	$5000.00	$241.41	$4758.59	$43,523.23
20	5000.00	217.62	4782.38	38,740.85
.	.	.	.	.
.	.	.	.	.
27	5000.00	47.70	4952.30	4587.89
28	4610.83	22.94	4587.89	0.00
Totals	$139,610.83	$9,610.83	$130,000	–

CALCULATOR METHOD

2ND AMORT

P1 = 1 ENTER

↓

P2 = 28 ENTER

↓

BAL = -389.1706829 — If the last payment was $5000, an excess of $389.17 would be paid.

↓

PRN = -130,389.1707 — If the last payment was $5000, the total principal paid would be $130,389.17.

↓

INT = -9610.829317

12.1 | Exercises

1. A loan of $35,560 at 5.5% compounded quarterly is to be repaid with payments at the end of every 3 months. Calculate the size of the periodic payment and the total interest paid if the loan was settled in 5 years.

2. Mercy received a loan of $80,000 at 2.75% compounded semi-annually to purchase office furniture. If she made equal payments at the end of every 6 months to pay off the loan, calculate the size of the periodic payments and the total interest paid if the loan was settled in 5 years.

3. Alberto received a loan of $10,000 at 4% compounded quarterly from a credit union to use as working capital for his business. He had to make end-of-quarter payments for a period of 1 year to settle the loan.
   a. Calculate the size of his payments.
   b. What is the total interest paid during the period?
   c. Construct an amortization schedule for his loan.

4. Aiden and Abbey received a small business loan of $81,500 at 9% compounded semi-annually to start a software business. They received the loan for 2 years and had to make payments at the end of every 6 months to settle the loan.
   a. Calculate the size of their payments.
   b. What was the total interest paid during the period?
   c. Construct an amortization schedule for their loan.

5. General Computers Inc. purchased a large server for $750,400. They paid 40% of the value as a down-payment and received a loan for the balance at 7.54% compounded annually. If the loan was for 5 years and they had to make year-end payments to settle the loan,
   a. Calculate the size of their payments.
   b. What was the total amount paid to settle the loan?
   c. Construct an amortization schedule for their loan.

6. A realtor purchased a property for $350,000. He paid 10% of this value as a down-payment and received a mortgage for the balance at 2.34% compounded semi-annually for 3 years. If he had to make payments at the end of every 6 months towards the mortgage,
   a. Calculate the size of his payments.
   b. How much did the building cost him, including the interest paid on the loan?
   c. Construct an amortization schedule for his loan.

7. Chang received a loan of $7500 at 8.25% compounded monthly which was amortized over 7 years with payments being made monthly. What was the principal balance on his loan after 3 years?

8. Betsy and Prince secured a loan of $645,000 at 11% compounded semi-annually to expand a garment factory. If their loan was amortized over 20 years and they made payments every 6 months, calculate the balance on their loan after 12 years.

9. Rex owed the bank $40,000 and made payments of $300 every month to settle the loan. If he received this loan at 5.56% compounded monthly, what was the balance on his loan at the end of 10 years?

10. Sheng-Li and Tai took a $5000 vacation loan from a bank at 7% compounded monthly for their honeymoon to Hawaii. If they had to make monthly payments of $100, what will be the balance on their loan at the end of 5 years?

11. For Problem 9, calculate the size of the final payment.

12. For Problem 10, calculate the size of the final payment.

13. For Problem 9, calculate the interest portion and principal portion of the 100th payment.

14. For Problem 10, calculate the interest portion and principal portion of the 50th payment.

15. Usman had to make payments of $600 every 3 months to settle a $10,850 loan that he received at 4.50% compounded quarterly.
    a. What was the time period of the loan?
    b. What was the interest portion and principal portion of the 12th payment?
    c. Construct a partial amortization schedule showing details of the first two payments, last two payments, total payment made, and total interest paid.

16. Alexandria renovated her kitchen for $13,860. She paid 15% of this amount as a down payment and financed the rest at 5% compounded monthly. She paid $250 every month to settle the loan.
    a. How long did it take for her to settle the loan?
    b. What was the interest portion and principal portion of the 40th payment?
    c. Construct a partial amortization schedule showing details of her first two payments, last two payments, total payment made, and total interest paid.

17. A design studio received a loan of $4850 at 6% compounded monthly to purchase a camera. If they settled the loan in $1\frac{1}{2}$ years by making quarterly payments, construct the amortization schedule for the loan.

18. Martha purchased a car for $38,000. She paid 20% of the value of the car as a down payment and received a loan for the balance from her bank at 3.6% compounded monthly. If she made semi-annual payments to settle the loan in 3 years, calculate the size of her periodic payments and construct an amortization schedule for the loan.

19. A loan of $100,000 at 5% compounded quarterly was amortized over 10 years with monthly payments. What is the size of the periodic payments and the principal balance at the end of 7 years?

20. A student loan of $11,200 received at 6% compounded semi-annualy was amortized over 5 years. If repayments are made at the end of every month, calculate the size of the payment and balance at the end of 4 years and 6 months.

21. A loan of $420,000 at 2.8% compounded semi-annually was to be settled with monthly payments of $20,000. What will be the balance on the loan at the end of 1 year?

22. A wealthy businessman purchased a hotel for $2,850,000. He made a down payment of $500,000 and received a loan for the balance at 4.35% compounded semi-annually. If he made monthly payments of $15,000 to settle the loan, what was the balance on the loan at the end of 15 years?

23. For Problem 21, calculate the size of the final payment.

24. For Problem 22, calculate the size of the final payment.

25. For Problem 21, calculate the interest portion and principal portion of the 20th payment.

26. For Problem 22, calculate the interest portion and principal portion of the 100th payment.

27. Joseph spent $280,000 to purchase machinery for his factory. He received a loan for the entire amount at 12.5% compounded semi-annually and made monthly payments of $3000 to settle the loan.
    a. What was the time period of the loan?
    b. What was the interest portion and principal portion of the 50th payment?
    c. What was the total amount of interest and principal paid by the end of 3 years?

28. Dennis, a successful technology entrepreneur, purchased a private yacht for $860,000. He paid 25% of the cost of the yacht as a down payment and financed the rest at 9.5% compounded monthly. He paid $35,000 every 6 months to settle the loan.
    a. How long did it take for him to settle the loan?
    b. What was the interest portion and principal portion of the 10th payment?
    c. What was the total amount of interest and principal paid by the end of 5 years?

29. For Problem 27, construct a partial amortization schedule showing details of the first two payments, last two payments, total payment made, and the interest paid.

30. For Problem 28, construct a partial amortization schedule showing details of the first two payments, last two payments, total payment made, and the interest paid.

12.2 | Mortgages

A **mortgage** is a loan that is issued by a financial lending institution to a borrower, to purchase real estate (business or residential property) at a specific interest rate for a specific time period. As the principal amount of mortgages is high, the borrower (mortgagor) generally provides the lender (mortgagee) with legal claim over the property (called collateral), as per the mortgage contract, until the mortgage loan has been completely amortized.

The **amortization period** is the number of years it takes to completely repay a mortgage. Mortgages can have varying amortization periods and they generally do not exceed 30 years. A shorter amortization period would mean that the borrower would repay the mortgage sooner, so the mortgage payments would be larger and the total amount of interest on the mortgage would be less. Longer amortization periods spread the repayment across several years and allow for smaller mortgage payments, but also result in more interest over the total life of the mortgage.

The **mortgage term** is the amount of time for which the mortgage contract is in effect. It usually varies from 6 months to 10 years. Mortgage terms are generally negotiated several times during the amortization period. Choosing a mortgage term depends on the borrower's expectation of how interest rates may fluctuate in the future. A shorter term is good if the interest rate goes down by the time the borrower renews his or her mortgage, however, a longer term is better if the interest rate goes up, as the borrower will still be paying the older, lower rate.

Types of Mortgages

Lenders offer two types of mortgages: fixed rate and variable rate mortgages.

Fixed rate mortgages have a fixed interest rate for a specific period of time (mortgage term). When the term expires, the lender may renew the term for another fixed period depending on the market interest rate.

Variable rate mortgages have rates that are dependent on changes in the market, such as the change in the Bank of Canada's prime lending rate. Mortgages with variable interest rates are also referred to as floating rate mortgages.

Sample Mortgage Rates (as of April 2011)

	Closed	Open
Fixed	3.50%	6.50%*
Variable	3.00%	3.80%

** Open Fixed rate mortgage rates are generally only offered for 6-month to 1-year terms*

Fixed or variable rate mortgages can be open or closed.

An **Open Mortgage** allows the borrowers to prepay any amount at any time, close the entire mortgage, or transfer from one lender to another without being charged an additional fee or penalty. Open mortgage rates are generally higher than closed mortgage rates.

A **Closed Mortgage** is for a specific term and borrowers would have to pay a penalty for prepaying a large amount, closing the loan, or transferring to another lender.

Calculating Mortgage Payments and Principal Balance

The Canadian law states that fixed mortgage rates must only be compounded semi-annually or annually. Also, the compounding must be at the end of the compounding period and not at the beginning of the period. Payments are generally paid monthly. However, lenders may also agree to receive payments semi-monthly, bi-weekly, or even weekly.

As the compounding frequency (annually or semi-annually) is usually different from the payment period (monthly), mortgages in Canada usually form an ordinary general annuity.

Example 12.2(a)

Calculating Mortgage Payments for the First Term and Renewal Term

A $250,000 mortgage for a house was issued with an amortization period of 25 years and payments had to be made monthly. If the interest rate on the mortgage was 5.4% compounded semi-annually for a fixed term of 3 years, calculate the:

(i) Size of the monthly payment.

(ii) Principal balance at the end of the 3-year term.

(iii) Size of the monthly payment if the mortgage is renewed for another 3-year term at 6.4% compounded semi-annually.

Solution

These mortgage payments represent an ordinary general annuity.

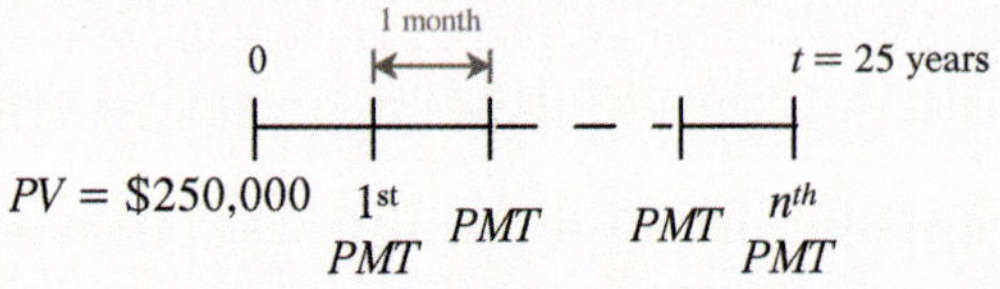

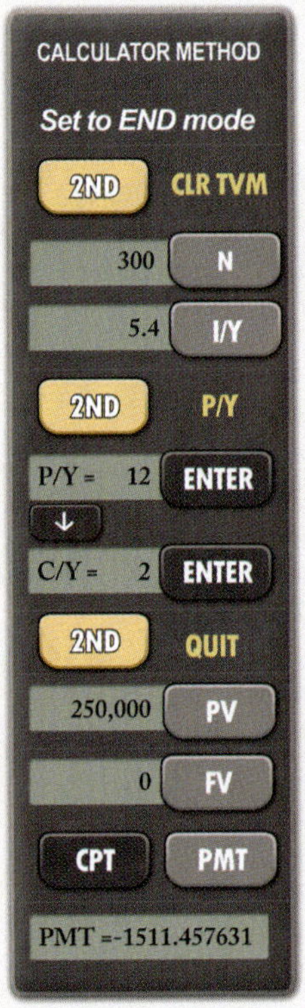

$$PMT = ?$$

$$n = 12 \text{ payments/year} \times 25 \text{ year} = 300 \text{ monthly payments}$$

$$j = 0.054,\ m = 2,\ i = \frac{j}{m} = 0.027 \text{ per half-year}$$

From Formula 10.3(a),

$$c = \frac{\textit{Number of compounding periods per year}}{\textit{Number of payments per year}} = \frac{2}{12}$$

From Formula 10.3(b),

$$i_2 = (1 + i)^c - 1$$

Substituting, $= (1 + 0.027)^{2/12} - 1$

Simplifying, $= 0.004450\ldots$ per month

(i) Size of the monthly payment.

Using Formula 10.2(b), $PV = PMT\left[\frac{1-(1+i)^{-n}}{i}\right]$

Substituting, $250{,}000 = PMT\left[\frac{1-(1+0.004450\ldots)^{-300}}{0.004450\ldots}\right]$

Simplifying, $PMT = \$1511.457631\ldots$

Therefore, the monthly payment amount was $1511.46.

It is not necessary to re-enter *I/Y*, *P/Y*, *C/Y*, and *PV* as they have not changed and have not been cleared (by CLR TVM).

(ii) Principal balance at the end of the 3-year term.

Number of payments made by the end of the 3-year term:

$$\textit{Number of Payments} = \textit{Payments Per Year} \times \textit{Number of Years} = 12 \times 3 = 36 \text{ payments}$$

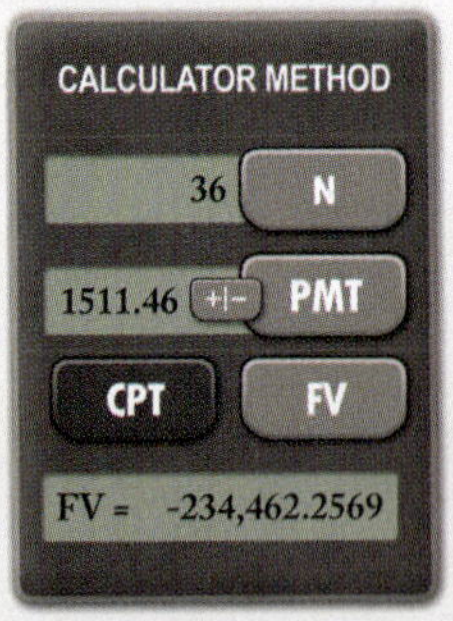

Using the retrospective method, calculate the principal balance at the end of 36 payments:

$$\textit{Principal Balance}_{36^{th}\ payment} = FV_{\textit{Original Loan}} - FV_{\textit{Payments Made until the Focal Date}}$$

Using Formula 9.1(a) and Formula 10.2(a),

$$\textit{Principal Balance}_{36^{th}\ payment} = PV(1+i)^n - PMT\left[\frac{(1+i)^n - 1}{i}\right]$$

$$= 250{,}000(1+0.004450\ldots)^{36} - 1511.46\left[\frac{(1+0.004450\ldots)^{36} - 1}{0.004450\ldots}\right]$$

$$= 293{,}334.1795 - 58{,}871.92267 = \$234{,}462.26$$

Therefore, the principal balance at the end of the 3-year term was $234,462.26.

Solution *continued*

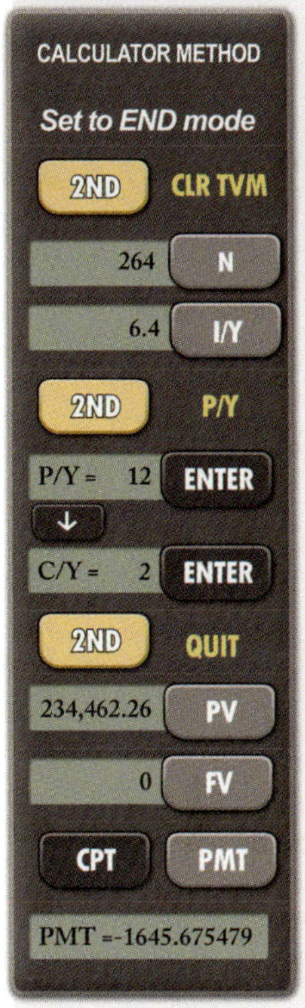

(iii) Size of the monthly payment if the mortgage is renewed for another 3-year term at 6.4% compounded semi-annually.

The renewed term will have a new periodic payment as the interest rate has changed.

$$\textit{Amortization Period} = 25 \text{ years} - 3 \text{ years} = 22 \text{ years}$$

$$\textit{Principal} = \textit{Principal Balance}_{\textit{3-year term}}$$

From the calculation in (b). $= \$234{,}462.26$

$$n = 12 \text{ payments per year} \times 22 \text{ years} = 264 \text{ payments}$$

$$j = 0.064,\ m = 2,\ i = \frac{j}{m} = 0.032 \text{ per half year}$$

From Formula 10.3(a), $c = \dfrac{\textit{Number of compounding periods per year}}{\textit{Number of payments per year}} = \dfrac{2}{12}$

From Formula 10.3(b), $i_2 = (1 + i)^c - 1$

Substituting, $= (1 + 0.032)^{2/12} - 1$

Simplifying, $= 0.005263\ldots$ per month

Using Formula 10.2(b), $PV = PMT\left[\dfrac{1-(1+i)^{-n}}{i}\right]$

Substituting, $234{,}462.26 = PMT\left[\dfrac{1-(1+0.005263\ldots)^{-264}}{0.005263\ldots}\right]$

Simplifying, $PMT = \$1645.675479\ldots$

Therefore, the monthly payment amount if the mortgage is renewed for another 3-year term at 6.4% compounded semi-annually would be \$1645.68.

Example 12.2(b) Calculations when Payments are Rounded Up

Kimberly received a \$60,000 mortgage amortized over 4 years. She negotiated a fixed interest rate of 4% compounded semi-annually for the term. Payments had to be made on a monthly basis.

(i) Calculate the size of the monthly payments if they are rounded up to the next \$100.

(ii) Calculate the size of the final payment on the mortgage.

Solution

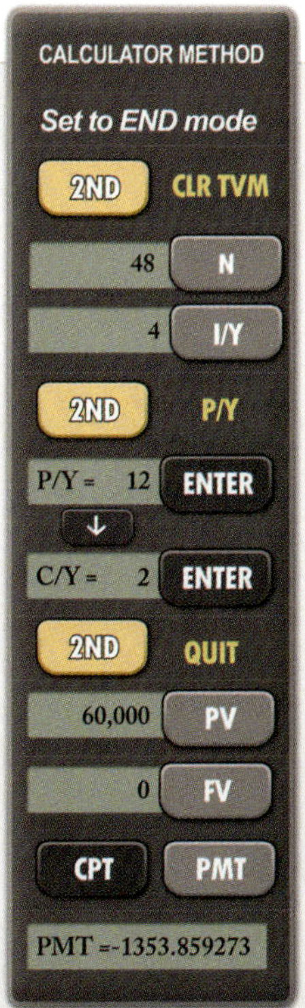

These mortgage payments represent an ordinary general annuity.

(i) Size of the monthly payments, rounded up to the next \$100.

$$n = 12 \text{ payments per year} \times 4 \text{ years} = 48 \text{ payments}$$

$$j = 0.04,\ m = 2,\ i = \frac{j}{m} = 0.02 \text{ per half year}$$

From Formula 10.3(a), $c = \dfrac{\textit{Number of compounding periods per year}}{\textit{Number of payments per year}}$

$= \dfrac{2}{12}$

From Formula 10.3(b), $i_2 = (1 + i)^c - 1$

Substituting, $= (1 + 0.02)^{2/12} - 1$

Simplifying, $= 0.003305\ldots$ per month

Using Formula 10.2(b), $PV = PMT\left[\dfrac{1-(1+i)^{-n}}{i}\right]$

Substituting, $60{,}000 = PMT\left[\dfrac{1-(1+0.003305\ldots)^{-48}}{0.003305\ldots}\right]$

Simplifying, $PMT = \$1353.859273\ldots$

Therefore, rounding up to the next \$100, the monthly payments are of \$1400.00

Solution continued

(ii) Size of the final payment on the mortgage.

By rounding the mortgage payments up to the next \$100, the mortgage payments are higher, so there will be fewer than 48 payments required to settle the mortgage.

We need to calculate the number of payments left to amortize the mortgage.

CALCULATOR METHOD: 1400 +/- PMT; CPT N; N = 46.29066668

From Formula 10.7(b), $n = -\dfrac{\ln\left(1 - \dfrac{i \times PV}{PMT}\right)}{\ln(1+i)}$

Substituting and solving, $n = -\dfrac{\ln\left(1 - \dfrac{0.003305... \times 60{,}000}{1400.00}\right)}{\ln(1+0.003305...)} = 46.290666...$ payments

Therefore, the number of payments has reduced from 60 payments to 47 payments by rounding the mortgage payment up to the next \$100.

We need to calculate the size of the final payment.

Method 1: Direct Method

We know that the final payment amount $= BAL_{n-1}(1 + i)$

Using the retrospective method to find the principal balance after 46 payments are made:

CALCULATOR METHOD: 46 N; CPT FV; FV = -406.0673873

$$Principal\ Balance_{46} = FV_{Original\ Loan} - FV_{Payments\ Made\ until\ the\ 46^{th}\ Payment}$$

$$= PV(1+i)^n - PMT\left[\frac{(1+i)^n - 1}{i}\right]$$

$$= 60{,}000(1+0.003305...)^{46} - 1400\left[\frac{(1+0.003305...)^{46} - 1}{0.003305...}\right]$$

$$= 69{,}837.05235 - 69{,}430.98496 = \$406.067390...$$

$$Final\ Payment\ Amount = BAL_{n-1}(1 + i)$$

Substituting and solving, $= 406.07(1 + 0.003305...) = \$407.412422...$

CALCULATOR METHOD: 47 N; CPT FV; FV = 992.5901984

Method 2: Overpayment Method

$$Final\ Payment\ Amount = PMT - Overpayment$$

$$= 1400.00 - \$992.5901984...$$

$$= \$407.409801...$$

Therefore, the size of the final payment on the mortgage was \$407.41.

Qualifying for a Mortgage

Before planning to purchase a new house, it is important that the buyer finds out if he or she qualifies for a mortgage to purchase the house.

There are two parameters that need to be calculated to determine how much mortgage the borrower can afford.

1. **Gross Debt Service Ratio (GDS)** measures the borrower's costs of owning the new house (such as mortgage payments, taxes, costs of utilities, etc.). Generally, this amount should not be more than 32% of the gross monthly income.

   For example, if your gross monthly income is \$5000, you should not be spending more than \$1600 in monthly housing expenses.

2. **Total Debt Service Ratio (TDS)** measures the borrower's total debt obligations (such as housing costs, personal loans, car payments, credit card bills, etc.). Generally, this should not be more than 40% of your gross monthly income.

Apart from the above two qualifiers for getting approved for a mortgage, most lenders look at the following factors when determining whether you qualify for a mortgage loan:

- Annual income
- Debts
- Employment history
- Credit history
- Value of the property interested to purchase
- Size of the down payment

Lenders are also required to pay an amount towards the cost of the house as down payment. The down payment is generally 20% of the value of the house. If the borrower does not have the 20% down payment amount and if they are a first-time home buyer, the federal government of Canada provides them with two options:

1. **Canadian Mortgage and Housing Corporation (CMHC)** 5% down payment option: CMHC operates Canada's Housing Insurance Fund, which assists borrowers who cannot afford the entire down payment by insuring the property for 95% of its value, thereby providing the buyer with an option to pay only 5% of the amount. There is a fee to insure the property, which may also be included in the mortgage.
2. **Retirement Savings Plan (RSP) Home Buyer's Plan:** This plan provides first-time home buyers with the option to withdraw up to $20,000 from their RSP for the purchase of the house. They are required to repay the amount withdrawn within 15 years.

Prepaying a Mortgage[1]

When a mortgage is paid off completely, the borrower can allocate more money towards other priorities, like buying a vacation property, upgrading or improving an existing home, saving up for children's education, etc.

A mortgage can be closed sooner if the borrower pays an extra amount over the periodic payment towards the mortgage, and this is known as prepaying a mortgage. Some popular prepayment methods are listed below:

- **Increased frequency of payments**: Borrowers have an option to pay half their monthly payment on a bi-weekly basis or even a quarter of their monthly payment on a weekly basis. These changes will help the borrower clear the mortgage sooner.
- **Increased periodic payment amount**: Lenders may allow borrowers to increase their payments by up to 100% of their periodic payments. In fact, by simply increasing the periodic payment by 10 to 15%, the borrower can save significant costs and can clear the mortgage sooner.
- **Making a lump-sum payment**: Lenders may permit the borrower to make a lump-sum payment of 15% of the original mortgage amount every year.
- **Combination of methods**: Lenders offer a situation where borrowers can take advantage of all the above strategies at the same time; i.e., switching to a higher frequency of payments, increasing the size of the periodic payment, and making a lump-sum payment every year. Savings are considerate in this case.
- **Reducing the amortization period**: Most mortgages are issued out for a 25-year period; however, the borrower has the option to choose a shorter period with increased periodic payments to clear the mortgage sooner.

1 Source: TD Bank Mortgages http://www.tdcanadatrust.com/mortgages/index.jsp

Example 12.2(c)

Calculating the Effect of a Prepayment or an Increase in the Payment on the Amortization Period

Andy and Hailey received a 25-year mortgage of $200,000 from a bank to purchase a condominium. They negotiated a fixed interest rate of 3.6% compounded semi-annually for a 5-year term. Their mortgage contract also stated that they could prepay 10% of the original principal every year without an interest penalty. By how much did their amortization period shorten, if:

(i) They made a prepayment of $15,000 at the end of the first year of the mortgage?

(ii) They increased their periodic payment by 15% starting from the 13th payment?

Solution

These mortgage payments represent an ordinary general annuity.

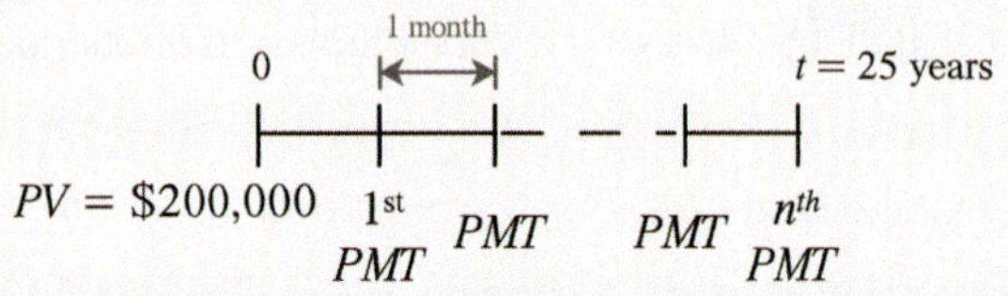

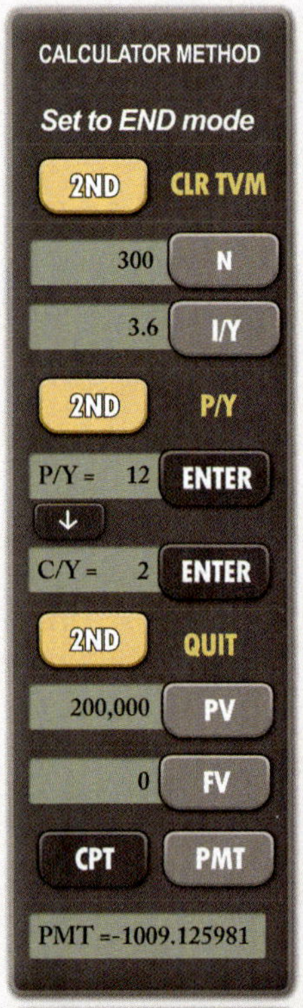

$$PMT = ?$$

$$n = 12 \text{ payments/year} \times 25 \text{ year}$$
$$= 300 \text{ monthly payments}$$

$$j = 0.036,\ m = 2,\ i = \frac{j}{m} = 0.018 \text{ per half year}$$

From Formula 10.3(a), $c = \dfrac{\textit{Number of compounding periods per year}}{\textit{Number of payments per year}} = \dfrac{2}{12}$

From Formula 10.3(b), $i_2 = (1 + i)^c - 1$

Substituting, $= (1 + 0.018)^{2/12} - 1$

Simplifying, $= 0.002977...$ per month

Monthly payment amount:

Using Formula 10.2(b),

$$PV = PMT\left[\frac{1-(1+i)^{-n}}{i}\right]$$

Substituting, $200{,}000 = PMT\left[\dfrac{1-(1+0.002977...)^{-300}}{0.002977...}\right]$

Simplifying, $PMT = \$1009.125981...$

Therefore, the monthly payment amount was $1009.13

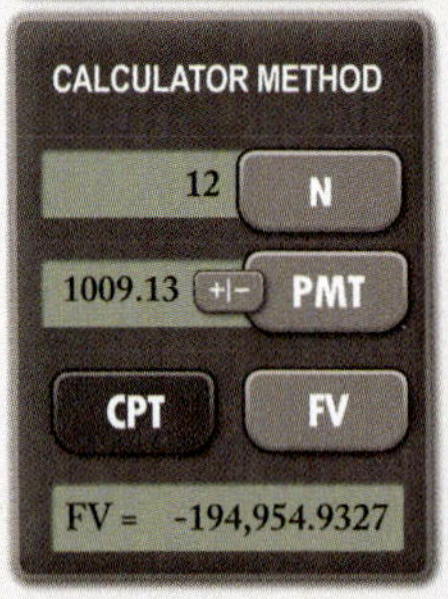

(i) They made a prepayment of $15,000 at the end of the first year of the mortgage.

$$\textit{Principal Balance}_{12^{th}\ Payment} = FV_{Original\ Loan} - FV_{Payments\ Made\ until\ the\ 12^{th}\ Payment}$$

Using Formula 9.1(a) and Formula 10.2(a),

$$\textit{Principal Balance}_{12^{th}\ Payment} = PV(1+i)^n - PMT\left[\frac{(1+i)^n - 1}{i}\right]$$

$$= 200{,}000\,(1+0.002977...)^{12} - 1009.13\left[\frac{(1+0.002977...)^{12} - 1}{0.002977...}\right]$$

$$= 207{,}264.80 - 12{,}309.86725... = \$194{,}954.9327$$

As they made a prepayment of $15,000 at this time,

$\textit{Principal Balance}_{12^{th}\ Payment}$ will reduce by $15,000.00.

$$\textit{New Principal Balance}_{12^{th}\ Payment} = 194{,}954.93 - 15{,}000.00$$
$$= \$179{,}954.93$$

Calculating the new number of payments, 'n':

Solution *continued*

From Formula 10.7(b), $n = -\dfrac{\ln\left(1 - \dfrac{i \times PV}{PMT}\right)}{\ln(1+i)}$

Substituting and solving, $n = -\dfrac{\ln\left(1 - \dfrac{0.002977... \times 179{,}954.93}{1009.13}\right)}{\ln(1 + 0.002977...)} = 254.657225...$

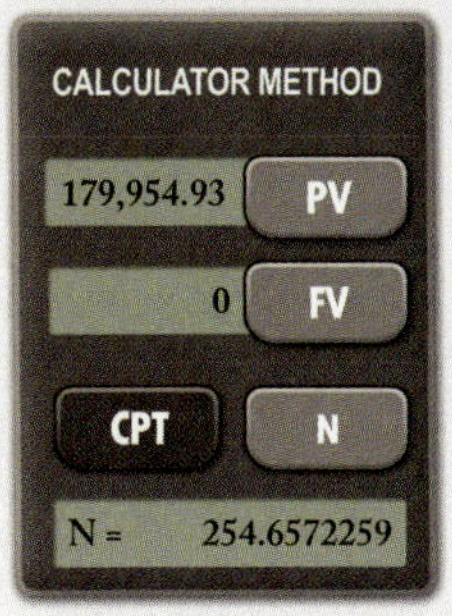

Therefore, the number of payments reduced from 288 payments (12 payments per year × 24 years) to 255 payments.

$$\text{Time Period} = \frac{\textit{Number of Payments}}{\textit{Payments Per Year}} = \frac{255}{12} \text{ years}$$

$= 21.25$ years $= 21$ years and (0.25×12) months

$= 21$ years and 3 months

Therefore, by making the prepayment of $15,000 at the end of the first year, their amortization period was shortened by: 24 years − 21 years and 3 months = 2 years and 9 months.

(ii) They increased their periodic payment by 15% starting from the 13th payment.

From the calculation in (a), we know that $\textit{Principal Balance}_{12^{th}\ Payment} = \$194{,}954.93$

New monthly payment, $PMT = 1009.13 \times 1.15 = \$1160.50$

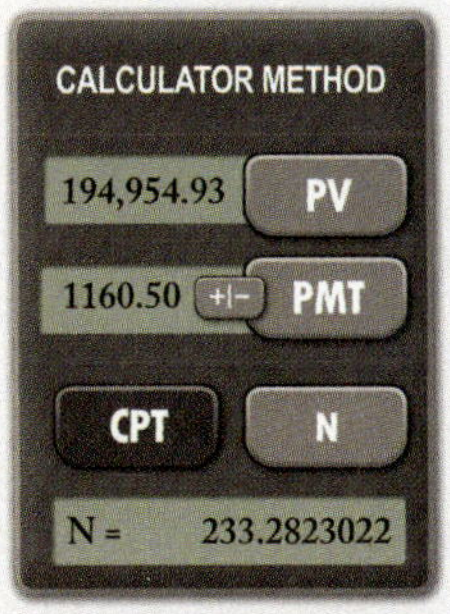

Calculating the new number of payments, '*n*':

From Formula 10.7(b), $n = -\dfrac{\ln\left(1 - \dfrac{i \times PV}{PMT}\right)}{\ln(1+i)}$

Substituting and solving, $n = -\dfrac{\ln\left(1 - \dfrac{0.002977... \times 194{,}954.93}{1160.50}\right)}{\ln(1 + 0.002977...)}$

$= 233.282302...$

Therefore, the number of payments reduced from 288 payments (12 payments per year × 24 years) to 234 payments.

$$\text{Time Period} = \frac{\textit{Number of Payments}}{\textit{Payments Per Year}} = \frac{234}{12}$$

$= 19.5$ years $= 19$ years and (0.5×12) months

$= 19$ years and 6 months

Therefore, by increasing their periodic payment by 15% starting from the 13th payment, their amortization period was shortened by: 24 years − 19 years and 6 months = 4 years and 6 months.

Generating a Mortgage Schedule using Microsoft Excel

Microsoft Excel has a Mortgage Loan Calculator template that helps you generate a complete mortgage schedule very easily. The use of this is shown in the following example:

Example 12.2(d)

Generating a Mortgage Schedule using Microsoft Excel

Kathleen purchased her first home for $350,000 and paid 25% of the value as a down payment. She received a mortgage for the balance amount with a term of 30 years and interest of 2.5% compounded semi-annually. The property tax rate for the house was 1.5% p.a. Assume that the interest rate and property tax rate remained constant throughout the period of the mortgage.

(i) Generate a mortgage schedule using Microsoft Excel.

(ii) What is the principal balance on the mortgage at the end of 3 years?

(iii) If she made a prepayment of $59,000 in the 120th month, by how long did the time period of the mortgage shorten assuming that the size of her monthly payments did not change?

Solution (i) Follow these instructions to generate the required mortgage schedule.

Open a Microsoft Excel. Click on New and run a search for Mortgage Loan Calculator in the New Workbook that pops up.

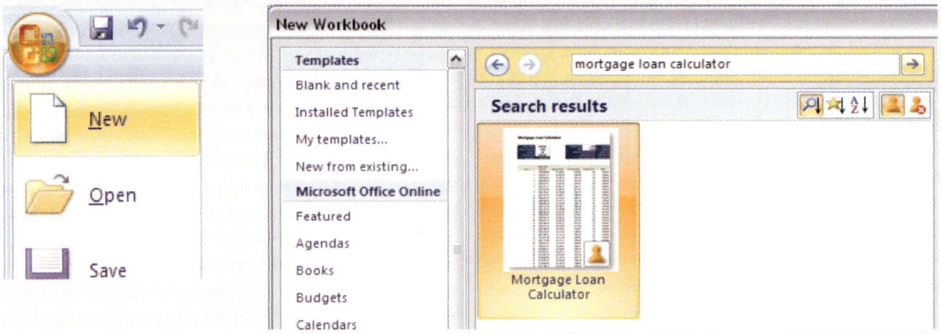

Select Mortgage Loan Calculator and enter the provided data from the problem into the table. The mortgage schedule will automatically be generated below the Mortgage Loan Calculator.

Mortgage Loan Calculator

Home Value:	$350,000
Rate of Interest:	2.50%
Months:	360
Loan Amount:	$262,500
Payment*:	$1,037.19

Property Tax:	1.50%	$437.50
PMI:	0.00%	$0.00
Total Monthly Payment:		$1,474.69
Total Payments:		$530,889.25
Total Interest Paid:		$110,889.25

(ii) Principal balance on the mortgage at the end of 3 years:

From the generated mortgage schedule, principal balance at the end of 3 years (36 months) = $244,189.57

(iii) Unhide column 'H', and under the Extra Payment column, enter $59,000 for the 120th month.

Time	Beginning Balance	Interest Due	Principal Due	Property Tax	PMI	Extra Payment	Principal Paid	Ending Balance	Payment Made
120	$196,360.64	$409.08	$628.11	437.5	$0.00	59000	$59,628.11	$136,732.53	$60,474.69

By doing this, you will notice that the time period of the mortgage reduced to 300 months from 360 months.

Therefore, the time period reduced by 60 months $= \frac{60}{12} = 5$ years.

12.2 | Exercises

1. Amanda purchased a town house for $320,000. She made a down payment of 10% of the value of the house and received a mortgage for the rest of the amount at 3.5% compounded semi-annually for 25 years. The interest rate was fixed for a 5-year period.
   a. Calculate the monthly payment amount.
   b. Calculate the principal balance at the end of the 5-year term.
   c. Calculate the monthly payment amount if the mortgage was renewed for another 5-year fixed term at 3.7% compounded semi-annually.

2. The Drew family purchased a villa on the outskirts of the city for $1,250,000. They made a down payment of 20% of the value and received a mortgage for the rest of the amount at 2.25% compounded semi-annually for 30 years. The interest rate was fixed for a 3-year period.
   a. Calculate the monthly payment amount.
   b. Calculate the principal balance at the end of the 3-year term.
   c. Calculate the size of the monthly payment if the mortgage is renewed for a 5-year fixed term at 2.5% compounded semi-annually.

3. A $100,000 mortgage was amortized over 10 years by monthly repayments. If the interest rate on the mortgage was fixed at 5.5% compounded semi-annually for the entire period.
   a. Calculate the size of the payments if they are rounded up to the next $100.
   b. Calculate the size of the final payment.

4. Henry received a mortgage of $80,000 that was amortized over 3 years and fixed at an interest rate of 2.75% compounded semi-annually. Calculate:
   a. The size of the monthly payments if they are rounded up to the next $500.
   b. The size of his final payment.

5. A mortgage for a condominium had a principal balance of $44,910 that had to be amortized over the remaining period of 4 years. The interest rate was fixed at 4.5% compounded semi-annually and payments were made monthly.
   a. Calculate the size of the monthly payments if they are rounded up to the next $50.
   b. If the monthly payments were set at $1200, by how much would the time period of the mortgage shorten? What is the size of the final payment?

6. Bradley had 5 years left to clear the mortgage on his house. The balance on the mortgage was $12,545.50 and the interest rate was fixed at 3.45% compounded semi-annually for the remaining 5 years. If his payments were made monthly.
   a. Calculate the size of the monthly payments if they are rounded up to the next $50.
   b. If the monthly payments were set at $300, by how much would the time period of the mortgage shorten? What is the size of the final payment?

7. Alexis received a mortgage of $150,000 at a variable interest rate of 4.5% compounded semi-annually for 10 years. At the end of 5 years, the interest rate changed to 5.2% compounded semi-annually and remained the same for the rest of the term. Calculate:
   a. The size of her monthly payments, rounded up to the next $10, during the first 5 years.
   b. The balance on the mortgage at the end of 5 years.
   c. The size of her monthly payments, rounded up to the next $10, during the last 5 years. What was the size of the final payment?

8. A mortgage of $105,400 was to be amortized over 7 years. The interest rate was a variable closed rate of 2.35% compounded semi-annually. Three years after the mortgage was issued, the Bank of Canada increased its prime lending rate. Therefore, the variable interest rate on the mortgage increased to 2.85% compounded semi-annually and remained the same for the rest of the term. Calculate:
   a. The size of the monthly payments, rounded up to the next $10, during the first 3 years of the mortgage.
   b. The balance on the mortgage at the end of 3 years.
   c. The size of the monthly payments, rounded up to the next $10, during the last 4 years. What was the size of the final payment?

9. Ashi planned to take a mortgage to purchase a house but could only afford to pay a maximum amount of $1550 every month as mortgage payments. The variable open interest rate offered by her bank was 4.5% compounded semi-annually on mortgages amortized over 25 years. Calculate the maximum mortgage amount she will receive.

10. Aden and his fiancée were planning to purchase an apartment in Toronto. They could afford to pay a maximum amount of \$1000 every month as mortgage payments. Their mortgage agent was offering them a variable open interest rate of 2.5% compounded semi-annually amortized over 20 years. Calculate the maximum mortgage amount they will receive.

11. Earl received a 30-year mortgage of \$250,000 to purchase a house. The interest rate was fixed at 4.5% compounded semi-annually for the first 5 years and he was allowed to make prepayments of 20% of the original principal every year without any penalty. By how much did his amortization period shorten, if he made a prepayment of \$40,000 at the end of the 4th year of the mortgage?

12. Munroe received a sales bonus of \$30,000 and used this amount as his 30th mortgage payment. If his mortgage of \$180,000 was for 25 years at 3.5% compounded semi-annually, calculate the reduction in the time period that he attained by making the lump sum payment. Assume that the mortgage contract does not charge him a penalty for making this lump sum payment.

13. In Problem 11, by how much would his amortization period have shortened if he had increased his periodic payment by 15% instead of making the lump sum payment at the end of the 4th year?

14. In Problem 12, by how much would his amortization period have shortened if he had increased his periodic payment by 15% from his 30th payment onwards, instead of making the lump sum payment?

12 | Review Exercises

Answers to odd-numbered problems are available at the end of the textbook

1. Aiden received a loan of \$17,500 at 5.25% compounded quarterly to purchase a printer for his office. If he made equal payments at the end of every 3 months to settle the loan, calculate the size of his periodic payments and the total interest paid if he settled the loan in 3 years. Construct a partial amortization schedule showing details of the first two payments and the last two payments for his loan.

2. Sturdy Metals Inc. received a loan of \$800,000 from the Small Business Banking Association to purchase additional factory space. They received their loan at 7.75% compounded monthly and had to make equal month-end payments for 20 years to amortize the loan. What was the size of their periodic payment and how much did they pay in interest over the period of the loan? Construct a partial amortization schedule showing details of the first two payments and the last two payments of the loan.

3. If \$500 were paid every month to amortize a \$16,850 student loan that was issued at 4.45% compounded quarterly, calculate the balance on the loan at the end of 2 years and 7 months and the size of the final payment.

4. Henry could afford to pay only \$1400 a month towards repayment of his student loan of \$50,000 that he received at 8.55% compounded semi-annually. If he made these payments, what was the balance on his loan at the end of 2 years and what was his final payment to clear the loan?

5. For Problem 3, calculate the interest portion and principal portion of the 30th payment.

6. For Problem 4, calculate the interest portion and principal portion of the 40th payment.

7. For Problem 3, construct a partial amortization schedule showing details of the first two payments, last two payments, total payment made, and total interest paid.

8. For Problem 4, construct a partial amortization schedule showing details of the first three payments, last three payments, total payment made, and total interest paid.

9. A Calgary based mining company received a loan of $1,250,000 at 4.55% compounded semi-annually to purchase an industrial boiler. They paid off the loan in 5 years by making annual payments. Construct an amortization schedule providing details of their loan payments.

10. Cranes Limited took a loan of $450,000 at 4% compounded monthly from their bank to train all their employees on new safety measures. If they made semi-annual payments to amortize the loan in 4 years, construct the amortization schedule for their loan.

11. Abha purchased a new line of clothing for her designer boutique for $12,680. She paid 20% of this amount as a down payment and took a loan for the balance at 11% compounded monthly. If she amortized this loan over 5 years by making semi-annual payments, calculate the size of her payments and the principal balance at the end of 2 years.

12. Adapt Developers, a leading construction development company in Vancouver, purchased land for $1,000,000 in the city. They paid 35% of this amount as a down payment and received a loan for the balance at 10.45% compounded semi-annually. If their loan was amortized over 10 years by making payments every 3 months, calculate the size of the payments and the principal outstanding at the end of 7 years.

13. In Problem 11, calculate the size of her final payment and the interest portion and principal portion of her 5th payment.

14. In Problem 12, calculate the size of the final payment and the interest portion and principal portion of the 18th payment.

15. Maada and his wife purchased a house for $447,000 in Toronto. They made a down payment of 20% of the value of the house and received a mortgage at 3.85% compounded semi-annually for the balance for 20 years. The interest rate was fixed for a period of 5 years. Calculate:
    a. The monthly payment amount.
    b. The principal balance at the end of the 5-year term.
    c. The monthly payment amount if the mortgage was renewed for another 5-year fixed term at 4.25% compounded semi-annually.

16. Grace recently graduated from college and purchased an apartment for $210,000 in London. She paid 10% of this amount as a down payment and received a mortgage for the rest of the amount for 30 years. If the interest rate on the mortgage was fixed at 4.5% compounded semi-annually for the first 5 years, calculate:
    a. The monthly payment amount.
    b. The principal balance at the end of the 5-year term.
    c. The monthly payment amount if the mortgage was renewed for another 5-year fixed term at 5.05% compounded semi-annually.

17. A $25,000 mortgage was amortized over 3 years by monthly repayments. If the interest rate on the mortgage was fixed at 3.28% compounded semi-annually for the entire period, calculate,
    a. The size of the payments if they are rounded up to the next $100.
    b. The size of the final payment.

18. Bernard took a mortgage to purchase a parking spot in his condominium for $40,000. The mortgage was amortized over 4 years at 4.5% compounded semi-annually for the entire period. Calculate:
    a. The size of the monthly payments if they are rounded up to the next $100.
    b. The size of the final payment.

19. Patricia and her husband were planning to purchase an apartment in British Columbia. They could afford to pay $800 every month towards mortgage payments. Their mortgage broker was offering them a variable open interest rate of 3.75% compounded semi-annually amortized over 25 years. Calculate the maximum mortgage amount they can afford.

20. Nikita received a mortgage to purchase a town-house and paid $1200 every month as mortgage payments. The variable open interest rate on the mortgage was 2.85% compounded semi-annually and it was amortized over 25 years. What was the mortgage amount she received?

12 | Self-Test Exercises

Answers to all problems are available at the end of the textbook

1. An automobile financing company was offering loans of $20,000 at 1.2% compounded monthly to purchase a specific model of their cars. If Alana received this loan and purchased the car, how much would she have to pay every month to amortize the loan in 10 years? Construct a partial amortization schedule showing details of the first two payments and the last two payments of the loan.

2. If Amy can pay only $350 a month towards her student loan of $18,400 that she received at 7.45% compounded quarterly, what would be the balance on the loan at the end of 4 years and what would be her final payment to settle the entire amount?

3. In Problem 2, calculate the interest portion and principal portion of the 50th payment.

4. In Problem 2, construct a partial amortization schedule showing details of the first three payments, last three payments, total payment made, and total interest paid.

5. Hair & Care, a salon in Edmonton, purchased chairs for $25,000. They paid 10% of this amount as a down payment and received a loan for the rest at 8.25% compounded semi-annually. Their loan was amortized over 5 years by making monthly payments. Calculate the size of the payments and the principal outstanding at the end of 3 years.

6. In Problem 5, calculate the size of her final payment and the interest portion and principal portion of her 12th payment.

7. Thema just qualified to receive a mortgage from her bank at 3.5% compounded semi-annually for a 5-year term. She purchased an apartment worth $220,000 and paid 10% as a down payment. If the amortization term for the mortgage was 25 years, and she was required to make monthly payments, calculate her:
   a. Monthly payment amount.
   b. Principal balance at the end of the 5-year term.
   c. Monthly payment amount if the mortgage was renewed for another 5-year fixed term at 4.5% compounded semi-annually.

8. Martin received a mortgage to purchase a locker in his condominium for $4000. The mortgage was amortized over 2 years at 3.26% compounded semi-annually for the entire period. Calculate the,
   a. Size of the monthly payments if they are rounded up to the next $10.
   b. Size of the final payment.

9. Natalie received her sales commission of $15,000 and used this amount as her 15th mortgage payment. If her mortgage of $250,000 was for 30 years at 2.88% compounded semi-annually, calculate the reduction in the time period by making the lump sum payment. Assume that the mortgage contract does not charge her a penalty for making this lump sum payment.

10. In Problem 9, by how much would her amortization period have decreased if she had increased her periodic payment by 25% from her 15th payment onwards instead of making the lump sum payment?

CASE 12
Financing a Growing Business

Jane, Georgia, and Melody started a cupcake business in their final year in college, registering the company as 'Sugary Bites'. They needed measuring cups, mixers, a food processor, and other baking equipment to prepare for production. This equipment cost a total of $1500, which the entrepreneurs financed through a loan from a bank at 12.5% compounded monthly, amortized over 2 years. Within a week they started making cupcakes in Melody's family kitchen and delivering them to their college cafeteria.

Within two months, Sugary Bites cupcakes were the talk of the college campus and the bakery business was making modest profits. After graduating, the three budding entrepreneurs decided to expand their operation. They rented a retail store in the city and added 10 new cupcake flavours to their product line. They also hired an assistant to run the store and a delivery person to handle personal orders.

After 2 years of successfully managing Sugary Bites, they saved $21,600 to use as a down payment to purchase a small shop where they could make their cupcakes, and a delivery truck to deliver them. They identified a $180,000 commercial property and secured a mortgage for 90% of its value to purchase it. The interest rate on the mortgage was 3.4% compounded semi-annually for a fixed term of 5 years. They also purchased a delivery truck for the business at a cost of $18,500 and financed 80% of it at 7% compounded quarterly. They made monthly payments of $300 towards this loan.

Answer the following questions related to each of their debts:

Startup Loan

a. What were their monthly payments to settle this loan?

b. What was the principal balance on the loan after 1 year?

c. Construct an amortization schedule for this loan.

Mortgage

d. Calculate the size of their monthly payments rounded to the nearest $10.

e. By how much would their amortization period have shortened if they had made a prepayment of $30,000 at the end of the 3rd year of the mortgage and increased their periodic payment by 30% starting from the 40th payment?

f. Using the information in (ii), generate a mortgage schedule using Microsoft Excel.

Delivery Truck Loan

g. How long would it take to settle this loan with the regular monthly payments of $300?

h. On their 50th payment, what will be the interest portion and what will be the principal portion?

i. Construct a partial amortization schedule showing details of the first two payments, last two payments, total payment made, and the total interest paid towards this loan.

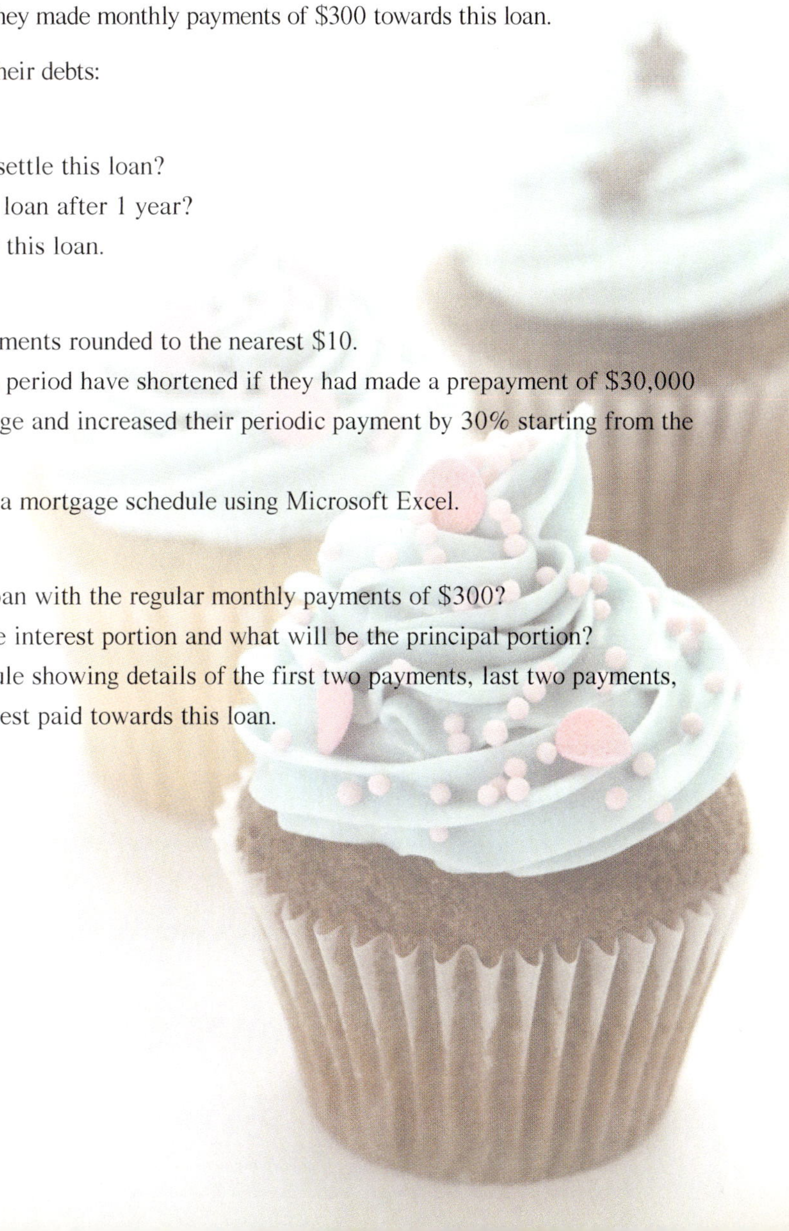

12 | Summary of Notation

PMT = Periodic payment

INT = Interest portion of a payment

PRN = Principal portion of a payment

BAL = Principal balance

You are probably familiar with the term 'bonds' as it commonly appears in newspapers and on television. Bonds are issued by governments or corporations as a method of raising money for new projects that they undertake or to expand their facilities. Canada Savings Bond (CSB) is an example of a bond that is issued by the federal government and sold to investors through financial institutions. Bonds are usually sold in the money market by investment dealers. In this chapter, we will study the terms and calculations that are necessary in determining the price of a bond, the rate of return expected by investors, etc. The calculations are based on the topics that you have learned in previous chapters.

13 Bonds and Sinking Funds

LEARNING OBJECTIVES

- Understand bond terminology.
- Calculate the purchase price of a bond on an interest payment date.
- Calculate the purchase price of a bond between interest payment dates.
- Use the quoted price of a bond in calculations.
- Construct a schedule of bond payments.
- Calculate the yield.
- Perform sinking fund calculations and construct a sinking fund schedule.

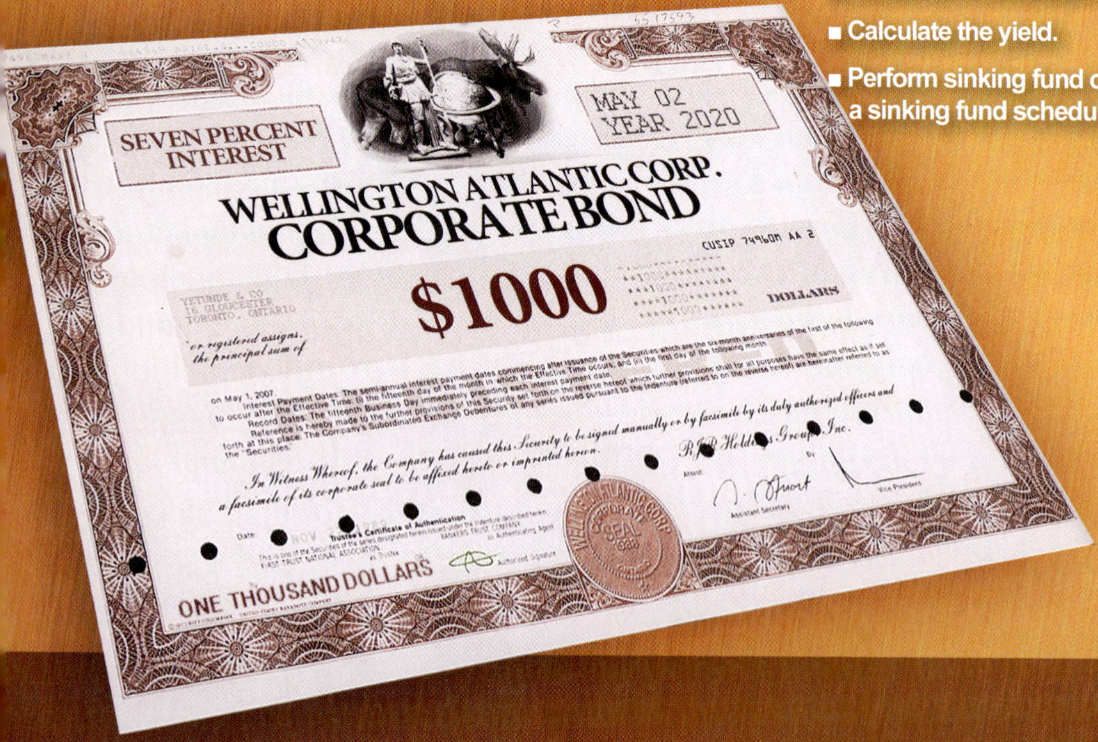

CHAPTER OUTLINE

13.1 | Bonds

Bonds
A bond is a certificate or contract that promises to repay a loan with interest payments periodically, and principal repayment on maturity.

When a government agency or a corporation borrows money from people for a long-term, they issue a printed contract or certificate to the lender promising to repay the loan with periodic interest payments, with the principal to be repaid upon maturity. This certificate or contract is called a *bond* or *debenture*. Therefore, a bond is like a loan where the borrower of the money is the **issuer** of the bond, the lender of the money is the **holder** of the bond, the interest rate is called the **coupon rate**, and the interest payments paid by the issuer to the holder are called **coupons**.

Since a bond is generally secured (by some underlying asset), the risk of default is low; whereas, a debenture is unsecured, and therefore, the risk of default is high. This is why debentures generally have a higher rate of return than bonds. However, the term 'bond' is often used to refer to both secured and unsecured debts.

For example, the Bank of Canada and Provincial Governments issue bonds that are unsecured but are considered very safe because they are backed by good credibility and are guaranteed by the Federal or Provincial Governments.

Bond Terminology

- **Face Value** of the bond: the value that is assigned to the bond by the issuer. It is the amount that is repaid to the bond holder at the end of the debt period. Common face values are $1000, $5000, $10,000, $25,000, or more. Interest payments (coupons) made to the holder are calculated on the face value of the bond. The face value of the bond is also called the **principal**, **redemption value**, **par value** or the **denomination** of the bond.

- **Coupon rate**: the interest rate of the bond. The coupon rate is used to calculate the interest payments (coupons) on a bond. This rate is assigned by the issuer of the bond and is fixed for the entire time period of the bond. It is generally compounded semi-annually with interest being paid at the end of each six-month period. The coupon rate is also called the bond rate or contract rate.

- **Maturity date**: the date when the debt period ends. It is the date when the issuer repays the principal and the final interest payment to the holder of the bond.

- **Purchase price**: the price that the holder pays to purchase a bond. The face value that is repaid on maturity and the periodic interest payments (coupons) usually remain fixed. However, the price of a bond fluctuates in the market depending on various market conditions that are explained in the next section. Although a bond has a specific face value and coupon rate assigned by the issuer, the price at which it is actually purchased in the market may not be the face value of the bond. A bond could be sold at its face value (at par), above its face value (above par), or below its face value (below par) depending on various market conditions, such as the market interest rate for a similar type of bond (called the bond's yield rate) and the credit-worthiness (trustworthiness to repay debt) of the issuer.

Bond purchased at par:
Purchase price = Face Value

Bond purchased at premium:
Purchase price > Face Value

Bond purchased at discount:
Purchase price < Face Value

- **Yield rate**: the rate of return that the bond will provide the holder by the maturity of the bond. The price of the bond in the market depends on this rate. This rate is also called **Yield to Maturity (YTM)**, **Yield**, or **Yield%**.

Bonds trade at par when their coupon rate is the same as the market rate of interest.

- **If the yield rate of the bond is the same as its coupon rate**, it signifies that the bond is providing the same rate of return as an investment in the market that has similar risk. Such a bond is said to be selling at par.
- **If the yield rate of the bond is higher than its coupon rate**, it signifies that the bond is providing a lower rate of return than an investment in the market that has similar risk. Therefore, the bond will not be in demand in the market and it will be traded at a price that is lower than its face value. Such a bond is said to be selling below par or at a **discount**. The amount of discount on the bond is the difference between its face value and purchase price.
- **If the yield rate of the bond is lower than its coupon rate**, it signifies that the bond is providing a higher rate of return than an investment in the market that has similar risk. Therefore, the bond will be in demand in the market and it will be traded at a price that is higher than its face value. Such a bond is said to be selling above par or at a **premium**. The amount of premium on the bond is the difference between its purchase price and face value.

The holder of the bond will receive periodic interest payments throughout the life of the bond and the Redemption Value of the bond when it is redeemed.

- **Redemption of bonds:** the repayment of the face value of the bond by the issuer of the bond to its holder. Bonds are usually redeemed at the time of maturity. However, they can also be redeemed before the maturity date for a value higher than the face value (redemption at premium) or less than the face value (redemption at discount). In this chapter, we only deal with bonds that are redeemed at par and at the time of maturity.

Example 13.1(a) **Understanding Bond Terminology**

The Bank of Canada issues a $1000 bond on January 01, 2010 that was paying a 10% coupon rate every 6 months for 10 years. What is the face value, coupon rate, and maturity date of the bond? Will the bond be sold at par, premium, or discount if its yield rate is:

(i) 10% compounded semi-annually

(ii) 20% compounded semi-annually

(iii) 5% compounded semi-annually

Solution

The face value of the bond is $1000, coupon rate is 10% compounded semi-annually and maturity date is January 01, 2020.

(i) Yield rate: 10% compounded semi-annually. As the yield rate is the same as the coupon rate, the bond is providing the same rate of return as any other investment of similar risk. Therefore, the bond will be sold at par.

(ii) Yield rate: 20% compounded semi-annually. As the yield rate is higher than the coupon rate, the bond is providing a lower rate of return than any other investment of similar risk. Therefore, the bond will be sold at a discount.

(iii) Yield rate: 5% compounded semi-annually. As the yield rate is lower than the coupon rate, the bond is providing a higher rate of return than any other investment of similar risk. Therefore, the bond will be sold at a premium.

Calculating the Purchase Price of a Bond

As described earlier, bonds can be purchased and sold on any date prior to its maturity date. It can be sold either on an interest payment date (i.e., a date when interest on the bond is to be paid) or a date between interest payments. The procedure for determining the purchase price of a bond differs depending on whether it is purchased on an interest payment date or between interest payment dates.

Purchase Price on an Interest Payment Date

Assume that interest on the bond is paid semi-annually and that it is sold on an interest payment date (shown as 'Purchase date' in the line-diagrams below).

The purchase price of the bond on the interest payment date is the sum of the present value of all the remaining interest payments on the bond (PV_{PMT}) on this date, and the present value of the face value of the bond ($PV_{Face\ Value}$) on this date discounted at the bond's yield rate, 'i'. This is illustrated below:

PV_{PMT} on the date the bond is sold:

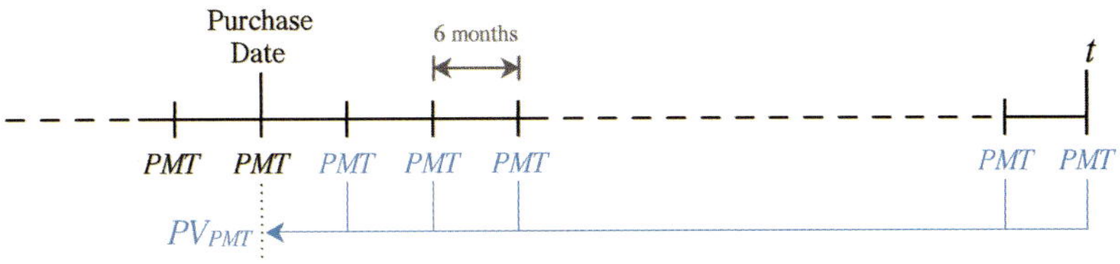

$PV_{Face\ Value}$ on the date the bond is sold:

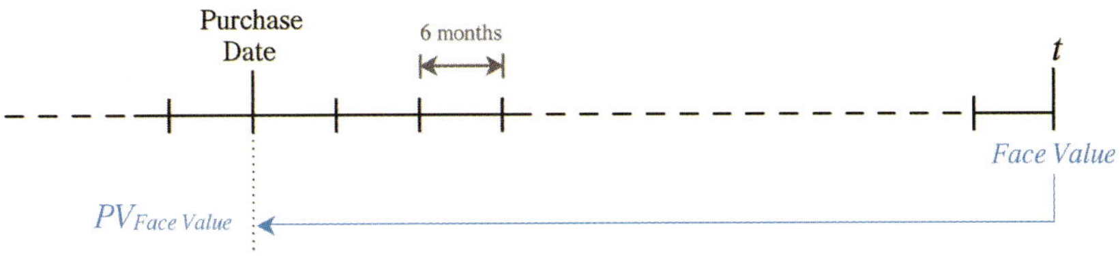

Therefore, the formula for the purchase price of a bond on an interest payment date is given by:

Formula 13.1(a)

Purchase Price of a Bond

$$Purchase\ Price = PV_{PMT} + PV_{Face\ Value}$$

Note: Interest payment on the date of purchase (which is an interest payment date) goes to the seller of the bond and not the buyer. Interest payments to the buyer starts only on the first interest payment date after the purchase.

Notation

- b = periodic coupon rate. It is used to calculate the periodic interest payment (coupon).

  Where $b = \frac{j}{m}$ (From Formula 9.1(d) for the periodic interest rate)

- i = yield rate

  Where $i = \frac{j}{m}$ (From Formula 9.1(d) for the periodic interest rate)

- FV = Face Value of the bond.

- PMT = Periodic interest payment (coupon) of a bond.

  Periodic interest payment on the bond = Face value × periodic coupon rate

Formula 13.1(b)

Periodic Interest Payment of a Bond

$$PMT = FV \times b$$

Example 13.1(b) Calculating the Purchase Price of a Bond at Different Yield Rates

A bond has a face value of $1000, coupon rate of 10% payable semi-annually, and will mature in 6 years.

(i) Calculate the purchase price when the yield is 10% compounded semi-annually.

(ii) Calculate the purchase price and discount when the yield is 12% compounded semi-annually.

(iii) Calculate the purchase price and premium when the yield is 8% compounded semi-annually.

Solution

Using the financial calculator, you can either compute '*PV*' seperately and add the answers together, or you can complete the entire calculation in one step as shown here.

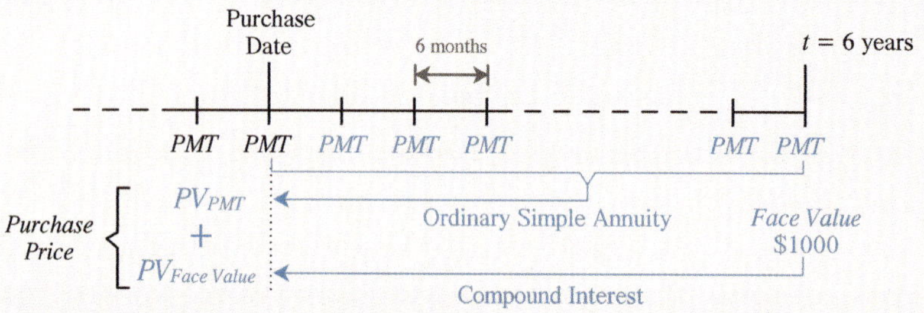

CALCULATOR METHOD

Set to END mode

2ND CLR TVM
12 N
10 I/Y
2ND P/Y
P/Y = 2 ENTER
↓
C/Y = 2 ENTER
2ND QUIT
50 PMT
1000 FV
CPT PV
PV = -1000

Face value, $FV = \$1000.00$, $n = 2 \times 6 = 12$,

Coupon rate, $b = \dfrac{j}{m} = \dfrac{0.10}{2} = 0.05$ per half-year

Using Formula 13.1(b), $PMT = FV \times b$

$= 1000.00 \times 0.05 = \$50.00$

(i) Bond purchased when the yield is equal to the coupon rate:

Yield, $i = \dfrac{j}{m} = \dfrac{0.10}{2} = 0.05$ per half-year

Using the Ordinary Simple Annuity Formula 10.2(b),

$$PV = PMT\left[\frac{1-(1+i)^{-n}}{i}\right]$$

$$PV_{PMT} = 50\left[\frac{1-(1+0.05)^{-12}}{0.05}\right]$$

$= 50[8.863251...]$

$= \$443.162581...$

Using the Compound Interest Formula 9.1(b),

$$PV = FV(1+i)^{-n}$$

$PV_{Face\ value} = 1000(1+0.05)^{-12}$

$= 1000(0.556837)$

$= \$556.837418...$

Using Formula 13.1(a), *Purchase Price* $= PV_{PMT} + PV_{Face\ Value}$

$= 443.162581... + 556.837418... = \$1000.00$

Therefore, the purchase price of the bond when the yield is the same as the coupon rate is $1000.00. As the purchase price is the same as the face value, the bond is sold at par.

(ii) Bond purchased when the yield is higher than the coupon rate:

Yield, $i = \dfrac{j}{m} = \dfrac{0.12}{2} = 0.06$ per half-year

It is not necessary to re-enter N, P/Y, C/Y, PMT, and FV as they have not changed and have not been cleared (by CLR TVM).

CALCULATOR METHOD

12 I/Y
CPT PV
PV = -916.1615606

$$PV_{PMT} = 50\left[\frac{1-(1+0.06)^{-12}}{0.06}\right]$$

$= 50[8.383843...]$

$= \$419.192197...$

$PV_{Face\ Value} = 1000(1+0.06)^{-12}$

$= 1000(0.496969...)$

$= \$496.969363...$

Using Formula 13.1(a), *Purchase Price* $= PV_{PMT} + PV_{Face\ Value}$

$= 419.192197... + 496.969363...$

$= \$916.161560...$

Solution *continued*

Therefore, the purchase price of the bond when the yield is higher than the coupon rate is \$916.16. As the purchase price is less than the face value of \$1000.00, the bond is sold below par or at a discount.

$$Discount = Face\ Value - Purchase\ Price$$
$$= 1000.00 - 916.16 = \$83.84$$

Therefore, the discount on the bond is \$83.84.

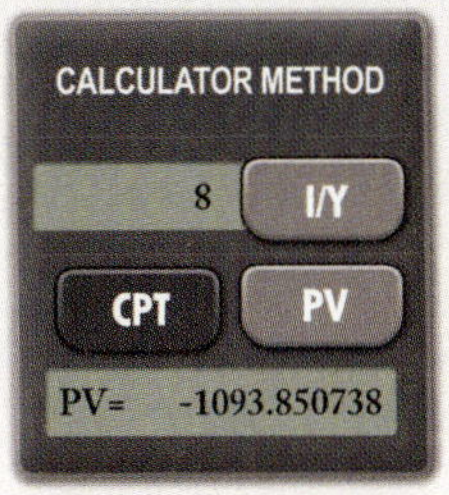

(iii) Bond purchased when the yield is less than the coupon rate:

$$\text{Yield, } i = \frac{j}{m} = \frac{0.08}{2} = 0.04 \text{ per half-year}$$

Using Formula 13.1(a), $Purchase\ Price = PV_{PMT} + PV_{Face\ Value}$

$$= 469.253688... + 624.597049...$$
$$= \$1093.850738...$$

Therefore, the purchase price of the bond is \$1093.85. As the purchase price is higher than the face value, the bond is sold above par or at a premium.

$$Premium = Principal - Face\ Value$$
$$= 1093.85 - 1000.00 = \$93.85$$

Therefore, the premium on the bond is \$93.85.

Example 13.1(c)

Calculating the Purchase Price of a Bond when the Yield Rate is at a Different Compounding Frequency than the Bond's Coupon Rate

If a \$25,000 bond that carries a 4.6% coupon payable semi-annually is purchased 5 years before maturity, calculate the purchase price and discount on the bond. The yield at the time of purchase was 5% compounded annually.

Solution

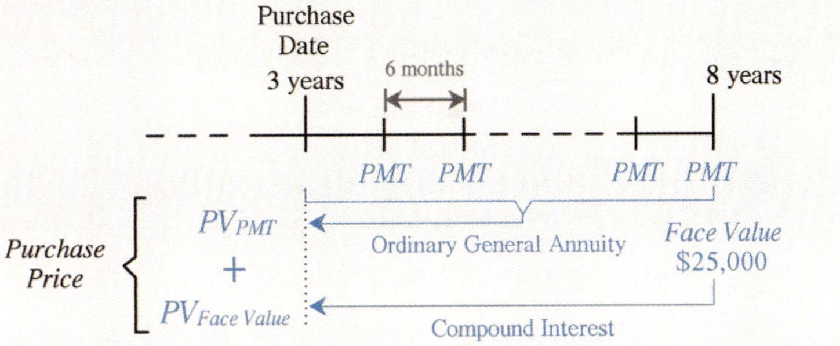

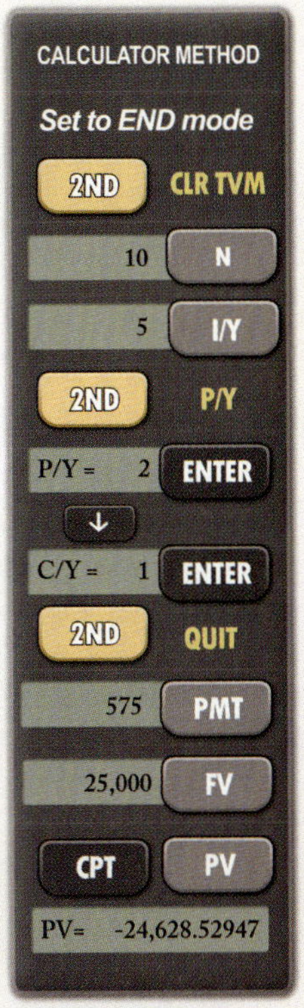

$FV = \$25{,}000.00$

$n = 2 \times 5 = 10$ ($t = 5$ since there are 5 years left on the bond)

$$\text{Coupon rate, } b = \frac{j}{m} = \frac{0.046}{2} = 0.023 \text{ per half-year}$$

Using Formula 13.1(b), $PMT = FV \times b = 25{,}000.00 \times 0.023 = \$575.00$

Since the yield is compounded annually and the coupon rate is compounded semi-annually, PV_{PMT} is calculated using the ordinary general annuity formula.

$$\text{Using Formula 10.3(a), } c = \frac{Number\ of\ compounding\ periods\ per\ year}{Number\ of\ payments\ per\ year} = \frac{1}{2}$$

Using Formula 10.3(b), $i_2 = (1 + i)^c - 1$

$$= (1 + 0.05)^{1/2} - 1$$
$$= 1.024695... - 1$$
$$= 0.024695... \text{ per half-year}$$

Solution continued

$$PV_{PMT} = 575\left[\frac{1-(1+0.024695...)^{-10}}{0.024695...}\right]$$
$$= 575(8.765870...)$$
$$= \$5040.375307...$$

$$PV_{Face\ Value} = 25{,}000(1 + 0.024695...)^{-10}$$
$$= 25{,}000(0.783526...)$$
$$= \$19{,}588.15416...$$

$$Purchase\ Price = PV_{PMT} + PV_{Face\ Value} = 5040.375307... + 19{,}588.15416... = \$24{,}628.52947...$$

Therefore, the purchase price of the bond is $24,628.53. The bond is sold below par or at a discount.

$$Discount = Face\ Value - Purchase\ Price$$
$$= 25{,}000.00 - 24{,}628.53 = \$371.47$$

Therefore, the discount on the bond is $371.47.

Example 13.1(d)

Gain or Loss while Buying and Selling Bonds

A $20,000 bond had a 6% coupon rate payable semi-annually and would mature on June 01, 2020. Suzanne purchased it on June 01, 2010 when the interest rate in the market was 7% compounded semi-annually. On June 01, 2014, she sold the bond when the interest rate in the market was 5% compounded semi-annually.

(i) What was the purchase price of the bond?

(ii) What was the selling price of the bond?

(iii) How much did she make or lose on this investment?

Solution

Face value, $FV = \$20{,}000.00$

Coupon rate, $b = \frac{j}{m} = \frac{0.06}{2} = 0.03$ per half-year

Using Formula 13.1(b), $PMT = FV \times b = 20{,}000.00 \times 0.03 = \$600.00$

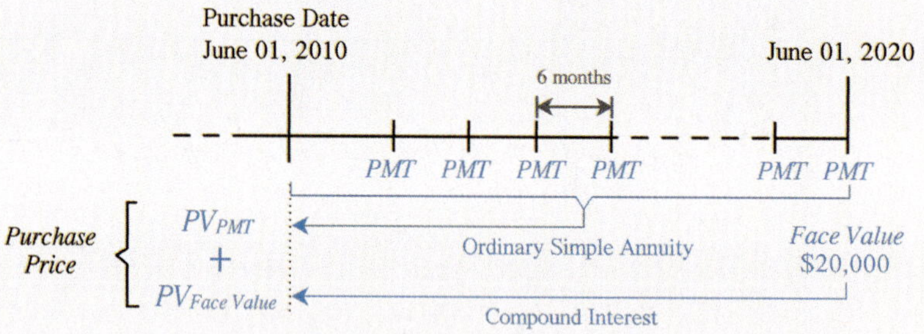

CALCULATOR METHOD

Set to END mode

2ND CLR TVM

20 N

7 I/Y

2ND P/Y

P/Y = 2 ENTER

↓

C/Y = 2 ENTER

2ND QUIT

600 PMT

20,000 FV

CPT PV

PV= -18,578.75967

(i) Purchase price of the bond when yield was 7% compounded semi-annually:

$$n = 2 \times 10 = 20$$

$$\text{Yield, } i = \frac{j}{m} = \frac{0.07}{2} = 0.035 \text{ per half-year}$$

Using Formula 13.1(a),

$$Purchase\ Price = PV_{PMT} + PV_{Face\ Value}$$
$$= 600\left[\frac{1-(1+0.035)^{-20}}{0.035}\right] + 20{,}000(1+0.035)^{-20}$$
$$= 8527.441981... + 10{,}051.31769... = \$18{,}578.75967...$$

Therefore, she purchased the bond for $18,578.76.

Solution *continued*

(ii) Selling price of the bond when yield was 5% compounded semi-annually:

$n = 2 \times 6 = 12$ ($t = 6$ since there are 6 years left on the bond)

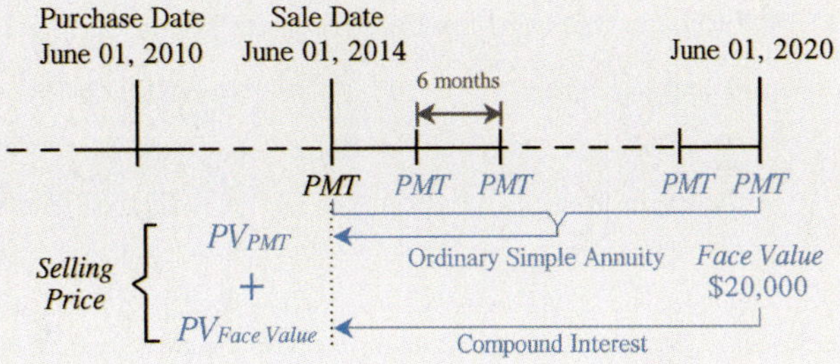

$$\text{Yield, } i = \frac{j}{m} = \frac{0.05}{2} = 0.025 \text{ per half-year}$$

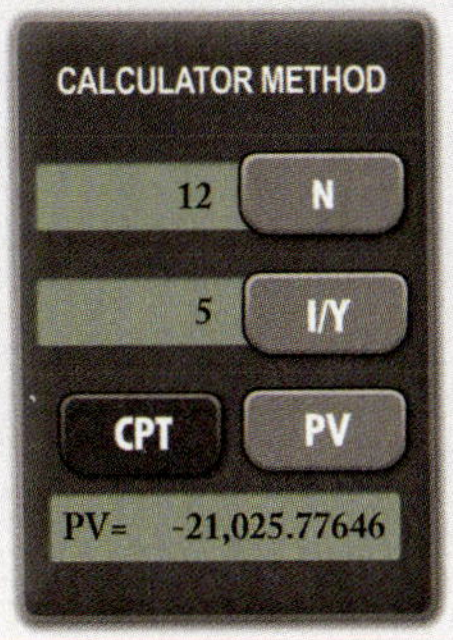

Using Formula 13.1(a),

$$\textit{Selling Price} = PV_{PMT} + PV_{Face\ Value}$$

$$= 600\left[\frac{1-(1+0.025)^{-12}}{0.025}\right] + 20{,}000(1+0.025)^{-12}$$

$$= 6154.658759... + 14{,}871.1177...$$

$$= \$21{,}025.77646...$$

Therefore, she sold the bond for $21,025.78.

(iii) Gain on the investment = 21,025.78 − 18,578.76 = $2447.02

Purchase Price Between Interest Payment Dates

In the previous section, we learned to calculate the purchase price of a bond when the bond is sold on an interest payment date. However, bonds are commonly sold on any date, and the date could be between interest payment dates. In this section, we will learn to calculate the purchase price of a bond when it is sold between interest payment dates.

The purchase price between interest payment dates is the sum of the purchase price on the previous interest payment date plus the **accrued interest**, which is the portion of the coupon payment (prorated *PMT*) for the period of time between the previous interest payment date and the purchase date.

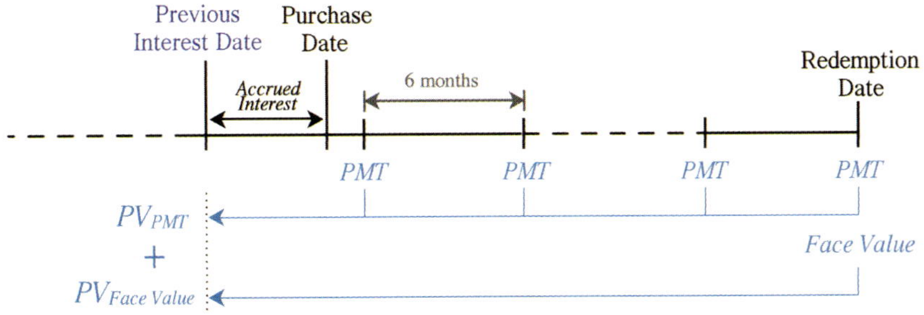

$$\textbf{\textit{Purchase Price}} = \underbrace{PV_{PMT} + PV_{Face\ value}}_{\text{At the previous interest date}} + \textit{Accrued Interest}$$

Example 13.1(e) **Calculating the Purchase Price of a Bond when it is Sold Between Interest Payment Dates**

The Province of British Columbia issued a $1000 bond with a coupon rate of 10% and redeemable on January 01, 2015. If Henry wanted to purchase this bond on April 16, 2008 when the yield was 7% compounded semi-annually, calculate the purchase price of the bond.

Solution

Step 1: Identifying Interest Payment Dates

Redemption date: January 01, 2015

As the redemption date is January 01, semi-annual interest payment dates would be January 01 and July 01 of every year.

Purchase date: April 16, 2008

Previous interest payment date: January 01, 2008

Next interest payment date: July 01, 2008

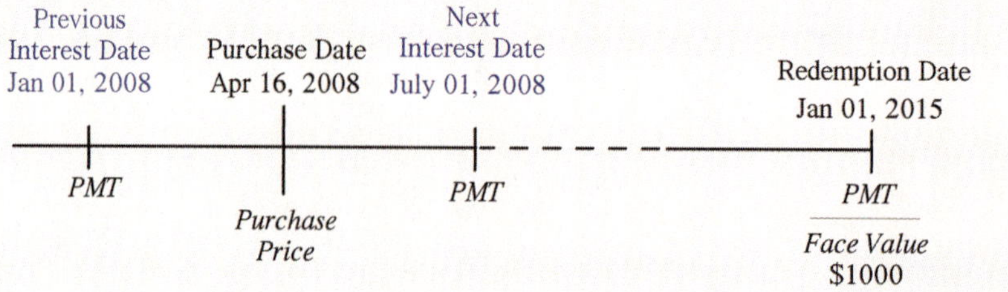

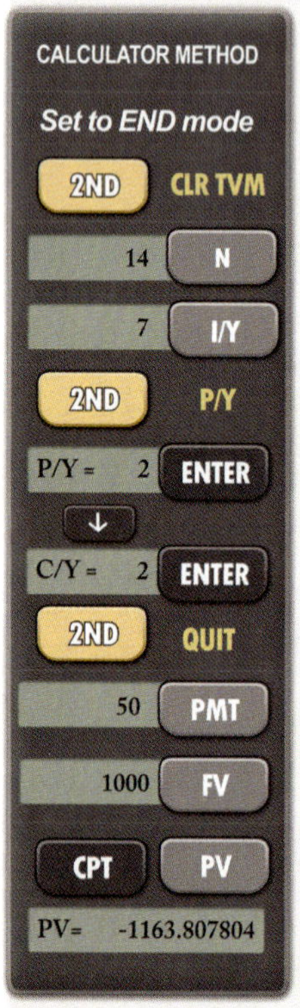

Step 2: Calculating Purchase Price on Previous Interest Payment Date

Time period from previous interest date to redemption date = January 01, 2008 to January 01, 2015 = 7 years

$$\text{Coupon rate, } b = \frac{j}{m} = \frac{0.10}{2} = 0.05 \text{ per half-year}$$

Using Formula 13.1(b), $PMT = FV \times b = 1000.00 \times 0.05 = \$50.00$

$$\text{Yield, } i = \frac{j}{m} = \frac{0.07}{2} = 0.035 \text{ per half-year}$$

$$n = 2 \times 7 = 14$$

Using Formula 13.1(a),

$$Purchase\ Price = PV_{PMT} + PV_{Face\ Value}$$

$$Purchase\ Price_{\text{January 01, 2008}} = 50\left[\frac{1-(1+0.035)^{-14}}{0.035}\right] + 1000(1+0.035)^{-14}$$

$$= 546.026013... + 617.781790... = \$1163.807804...$$

Step 3: Calculating Accrued Interest for the Time Period Between the Previous Interest Date and the Purchase Date

We now need to calculate the amount of interest that has accrued for the time period between the previous interest date and the purchase date.

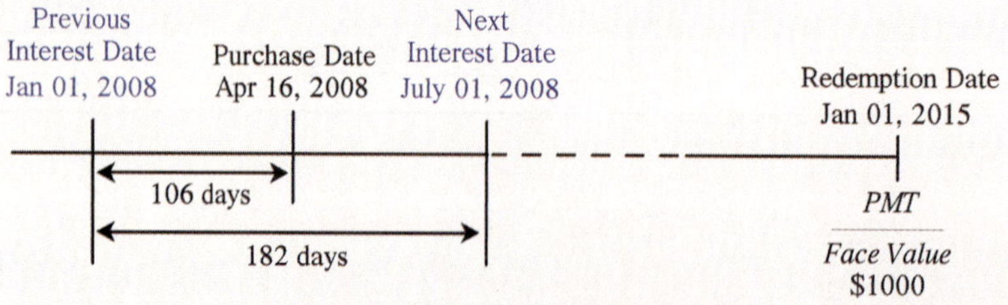

Assume 't' to be the fractional time period from the previous interest date to purchase date.

$$t = \frac{\text{Previous interest date to purchase date}}{\text{Previous interest date to next interest date}}$$

$$= \frac{\text{January 01, 2008 to April 16, 2008}}{\text{January 01, 2008 to July 01, 2008}}$$

$$= \frac{106}{182}$$

Interest amount accrued during this time $= PMT \times t = 50 \times \frac{106}{182} = \$29.120879...$

Solution *continued*

Step 4: Calculating Purchase Price

$$\left(\textit{Purchase Price of the Bond}\right) = \left(\textit{Purchase Price on the Previous Interest Date}\right) + \left(\textit{Accrued Interest for Time Period between the Previous Interest Date and the Purchase Date}\right)$$

$$= \$1163.807804... + \$29.120879... = 1192.928683...$$

Therefore, the purchase price of the bond is \$1192.93.

Note: The seller of the bond receives the accrued interest until the date of purchase of the bond which is why the accrued interest up to the purchase date is added to the purchase price of the bond.

Example 13.1(f)

Calculating the Purchase Price of a Bond When the Periods are Provided

A publicly traded company issued \$1000 bonds with 8% coupons that are paid semi-annually. An investor purchased the bond 8 years and 8 months before its redemption date. Calculate the purchase price of the bond if the yield was 12% compounded semi-annually.

Solution

Step 1: Identifying Interest Payment Dates

Interest payment dates are every 6 months.

Purchase date: 8 years and 8 months before redemption

Previous interest date: 9 years before redemption

Next interest date: 8 years 6 months before redemption

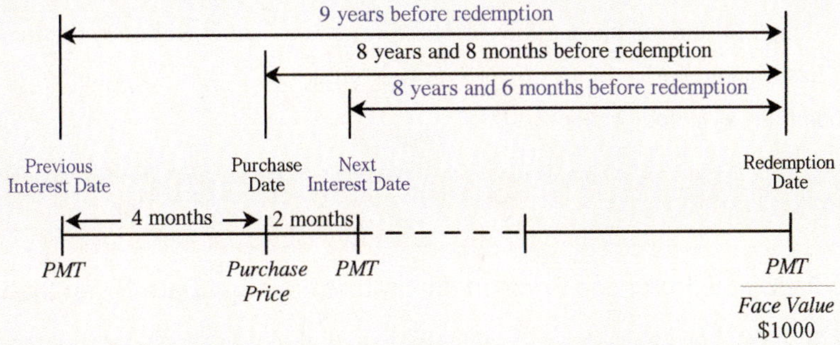

Step 2: Calculating Purchase Price on Previous Interest Date

Time period from previous interest date to redemption date = 9 years

Coupon rate, $b = \frac{j}{m} = \frac{0.08}{2} = 0.04$ per half-year

Using Formula 13.1(b),

$$PMT = FV \times b = 1000.00 \times 0.04 = \$40.00$$

$$\text{Yield, } i = \frac{j}{m} = \frac{0.12}{2} = 0.06 \text{ per half-year}$$

$$n = 2 \times 9 = 18$$

Using Formula 13.1(a),

$$\textit{Purchase Price} = PV_{PMT} + PV_{\textit{Face Value}}$$

$$= 40\left[\frac{1-(1+0.06)^{-18}}{0.06}\right] + 1000(1+0.06)^{-18}$$

$$= 433.104139... + 350.343791... = \$783.447930...$$

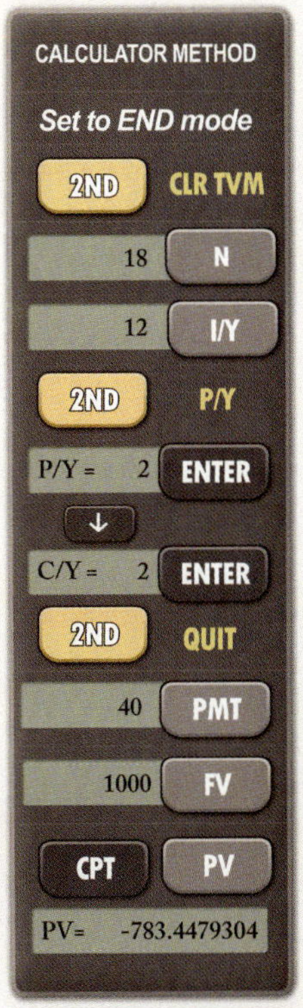

Solution continued

Step 3: Calculating the Accrued Interest for the Time Period between the Previous Interest Date and the Purchase Date

$$t = \frac{\textit{Previous interest date to purchase date}}{\textit{Previous interest date to next interest date}}$$

$$= \frac{[9 \text{ Years}] \text{ to } [8 \text{ Years and } 8 \text{ Months}]}{[9 \text{ Years}] \text{ to } [8 \text{ Years and } 6 \text{ Months}]}$$

$$= \frac{4 \text{ months}}{6 \text{ months}}$$

$$\textit{Accrued Interest} = PMT \times t = 40 \times \frac{4}{6} = \$26.666666...$$

Step 4: Calculating Purchase Price

$$\left(\begin{matrix}\textit{Purchase Price} \\ \textit{of the Bond}\end{matrix}\right) = \left(\begin{matrix}\textit{Purchase Price on the} \\ \textit{Previous Interest Date}\end{matrix}\right) + \left(\begin{matrix}\textit{Accrued Interest for Time Period} \\ \textit{between the Previous Interest} \\ \textit{Date and the Purchase Date}\end{matrix}\right)$$

$$= \$783.447930... + \$26.666666...$$

$$= \$810.114597...$$

Therefore, the purchase price of the bond is $810.11.

Quoted Price of a Bond

Quoted price of a bond is the price at which the bond is selling in the market. The daily bond prices in the market are quoted as a percentage of their face value.

For example, if a bond has a quote of 108.5 (or $108.5 or 108.5%) in the market, it means that the bond has a quoted price of 108.5% of its face value. So if the face value of the bond is $1000, then the bond has a quoted price of $1085.

Note: The quoted price of a bond is the price of the bond on the previous interest payment date. It does not include the accrued interest amount.

Example 13.1(g)

Calculating the Purchase Price on an Interest Payment Date Given the Quoted Price

A $5000, 4% bond payable semi-annually is purchased 5 years before maturity. Calculate the purchase price and discount on the bond if the quoted price on the date of purchase was 98.5.

Solution

The quoted price of the bond = 98.5% (5000) = 0.985(5000) = $4925.00

Since the purchase date is on an interest payment date, the quoted price is the purchase price of the bond.

$$\textit{Discount} = \textit{Face Value} - \textit{Purchase Price} = 5000 - 4925 = \$75.00$$

Therefore, the purchase price of the bond is $4925.00 and the discount is $75.00.

Example 13.1(h)

Calculating the Purchase Price between Interest Payment Dates Given the Quoted Price

A $10,000 bond with a coupon rate of 6% was redeemable on March 01, 2013. If it was purchased on February 16, 2007 when the quote was 102.5, calculate the purchase price of the bond.

Solution

Step 1: Identifying interest payment dates

Redemption date:	March 01, 2013
Interest dates:	March 01 and September 01 every year
Purchase date:	February 16, 2007

Solution continued

Previous interest date: September 01, 2006

Next interest date: March 01, 2007

Step 2: Calculating the purchase price on the previous interest payment date

The quoted price does not include the accrued interest from the previous interest payment date to the purchase date. It is the purchase price on the previous interest payment date.

Therefore, purchase price on the previous interest payment date:

Quoted price of the bond = 1.025 × 10,000.00 = $10,250.00

Step 3: Calculating the accrued interest for the time period between the previous interest date and the purchase date

$$t = \frac{\textit{Previous interest date to purchase date}}{\textit{Previous interest date to next interest date}}$$

$$= \frac{\text{September 01, 2006 to February 16, 2007}}{\text{September 01, 2006 to March 01, 2007}} = \frac{168}{181}$$

$$\text{Coupon rate, } b = \frac{j}{m} = \frac{0.06}{2} = 0.03 \text{ per half-year}$$

Using Formula 13.1(b), $PMT = FV \times b = 10{,}000.00 \times 0.03 = \$300.00$

Interest amount accrued during this time $= PMT \times t = 300 \times \frac{168}{181} = \$278.453038...$

Step 4: Calculating purchase price

$$\left(\begin{array}{c}\textit{Purchase Price}\\ \textit{of the Bond}\end{array}\right) = \left(\begin{array}{c}\textit{Purchase Price on the}\\ \textit{Previous Interest Date}\end{array}\right) + \left(\begin{array}{c}\textit{Accrued Interest for Time Period}\\ \textit{between the Previous Interest Date}\\ \textit{and the Purchase Date}\end{array}\right)$$

$$= 10{,}250.00 + \$278.453039... = \$10{,}528.453039...$$

Therefore, the purchase price of the bond is $10,528.45.

Constructing a Bond Schedule

While constructing a bond schedule, it is necessary to show how these payments are recorded using accepted accounting practices.

When a bond is purchased at par, there are no difficulties in recording the payments as the entire interest is recorded as interest revenue earned. However, when a bond is purchased at a premium, a large sum is paid out at the time of purchase, but at the time of maturity, a small sum is returned, which results in a capital loss. Similarly, when a bond is purchased at a discount, a small sum will be paid at the time of purchase, but at the time of maturity, a large sum is returned, which results in a capital gain. To prevent a capital gain or loss, it is an accepted accounting practice to make a proportionate deduction from each interest payment or addition to each interest payment to ensure that the principal on maturity is unaffected.

These calculations are made on the **bong schedule** that illustrates the **amortization of premium** or **accumulation of discount**.

The following 2 examples illustrate the construction of amortization schedules showing the amortization of premium and the accumulation of discount on a bond.

Example 13.1(i) **Constructing a Bond Schedule Illustrating the Amortization of Premium**

A $1000, bond with a coupon rate of 10% payable semi-annually is redeemable in 2 years and was purchased when the yield was 8% compounded semi-annually. Construct the bond schedule showing the amortization of premium.

Solution

Coupon rate, $b = \frac{j}{m} = \frac{0.10}{2} = 0.05$ per half-year

Using Formula 13.2 (b),

$$PMT = FV \times b = 1000.00 \times 0.05 = \$50.00$$

$$\text{Yield, } i = \frac{j}{m} = \frac{0.08}{2} = 0.04 \text{ per half-year}$$

$$n = 2 \times 2 = 4$$

Using Formula 13.1(a),

$$Purchase\ Price = PV_{PMT} + PV_{Face\ Value}$$

$$= 50\left[\frac{1-(1+0.04)^{-4}}{0.04}\right] + 1000(1+0.04)^{-4}$$

$$= 181.494761... + 854.804191... = \$1036.30$$

$$Premium = Purchase\ Price - Face\ Value$$

$$= 1036.30 - 1000.00$$

$$= \$36.30$$

CALCULATOR METHOD

Set to END mode

2ND CLR TVM

4 N

8 I/Y

2ND P/Y

P/Y = 2 ENTER

↓

C/Y = 2 ENTER

2ND QUIT

50 PMT

1000 FV

CPT PV

PV= -1036.298952

Schedule Showing the Amortization of Premium

Period	Interest Received ($FV \times b$)	Interest on BV ($BV \times i$)	Premium Amortized	Book Value (BV)	Unamortized Premium
0	–	–	–	$1036.30	$36.30
1	$50.00	$41.45	$8.55	1027.75	27.75
2	50.00	41.11	8.89	1018.86	18.86
3	50.00	40.75	9.25	1009.61	9.61
4	50.00	40.39	9.61	1000.00	0.00
Total	$200.00	$163.70	$36.30	–	–

Constructing the Amortization Schedule

- The purchase price of the bond is entered as the initial Book Value *(BV)* in the first row.
- Unamortized premium is the remaining premium that is required to be amortized.
- Interest received is calculated using $FV \times b$.
- Interest on the book value is calculated using $BV \times i$.
- Premium amortized is the difference between the interest received and interest on the book value.
- Book value decreases by the amount of premium amortized.

Bonds are recorded on a company's balance sheet at its face value plus or minus any unamortized premium or discount. This is called the book value of the bond and may differ from the market value of the bond.

This continues for each period until the book value is equal to the face value of the bond.

At the end of each period,

- Interest received is recorded as cash received.
- Interest on Book Value is recorded as interest earned.
- Premium on the bonds is amortized.
- Book value of bond is reduced by the premium amortized.

Example 13.1(j)

Constructing a Bond Schedule Illustrating the Accumulation of Discount on a Bond

A \$1000 bond carries an 8% coupon and is redeemable in 2 years. It is purchased when the yield to maturity was 10% compounded semi-annually. Construct the bond schedule showing the accumulation of discount.

Solution

Coupon rate, $b = \frac{j}{m} = \frac{0.08}{2} = 0.04$ per half-year

Using Formula 13.2 (b), Bond periodic payment,

$$PMT = FV \times b = 1000.00 \times 0.04 = \$40.00$$

$$\text{Yield, } i = \frac{j}{m} = \frac{0.1}{2} = 0.05 \text{ per half-year}$$

$$n = 2 \times 2 = 4$$

Using Formula 13.1(a),

$$\textit{Purchase Price} = PV_{PMT} + PV_{\textit{Face Value}}$$

$$= 40\left[\frac{1-(1+0.05)^{-4}}{0.05}\right] + 1000(1+0.05)^{-4}$$

$$= 141.838020... + 822.702474... = \$964.540495...$$

$$\textit{Discount} = \textit{Face Value} - \textit{Purchase Price} = 1000.00 - 964.54 = \$35.46$$

CALCULATOR METHOD

Set to END mode

- 2ND CLR TVM
- 4 N
- 10 I/Y
- 2ND P/Y
- P/Y = 2 ENTER
- ↓
- C/Y = 2 ENTER
- 2ND QUIT
- 40 PMT
- 1000 FV
- CPT PV
- PV= -964.540495

Schedule Showing the Accumulation of Discount

Period	Interest Received $(FV \times b)$	Interest on BV $(BV \times i)$	Accumulated Discount	Book Value (BV)	Discount to be Accumulated
0	–	–	–	964.54	35.46
1	40.00	48.23	8.23	972.77	27.23
2	40.00	48.64	8.64	981.41	18.59
3	40.00	49.07	9.07	990.48	9.52
4	40.00	49.52	9.52	1000.00	0.00
Total	160.00	195.46	35.46	–	–

Construction of the Amortization Schedule

- The purchase price of the bond is entered as the initial Book Value in the first row.
- Un-accumulated discount is the remaining discount that is required to be accumulated.
- Interest received is calculated using $FV \times b$.
- Interest on the book value is calculated using $BV \times i$.
- Discount accumulated will be the difference between the interest on book value and interest received.
- Book value will increase by the amount of discount accumulated.

This continues for each period until the book value is equal to the face value of the bond.

At the end of each period,

- Interest received is recorded as cash received
- Interest on Book Value is recorded as interest earned
- Discount on the bond is accumulated
- Book value of bonds is increased by the discount accumulated

Calculating the Yield

The yield can be calculated using Formula 13.2(b) ($PMT = FV \times b$) by substituting different values for 'i' to ensure that the left side of the equation equals the right side of the equation. However, the simplest method for solving 'i', is to work these problems on your financial calculator. Both methods to solve for yield are shown in the following examples.

Example 13.1(k)

Calculating the Yield

A 5-year bond has a face value of $10,000 and coupon rate of 12% payable semi-annually. If it is purchased at 96.4, calculate the yield of the bond.

Solution

$FV = \$10{,}000,\ b = \dfrac{0.12}{2} = 0.06,$

Using Formula 13.1(b),

$$PMT = FV \times b = 0.06 \times 10{,}000 = \$600.00$$

$$n = 2 \times 5 = 10$$

$$\begin{aligned} \textit{Purchase Price} &= 96.4\%(10{,}000) \\ &= 0.964(10{,}000) \\ &= \$9640.00 \end{aligned}$$

Using Formula 13.1(a),

$$\textit{Purchase Price} = PV_{PMT} + PV_{\textit{Face Value}}$$

$$9640 = 600\left[\frac{1-(1+i)^{-10}}{i}\right] + 10{,}000(1+i)^{-n}$$

By the method of trial and error, you will find $i = 13.00\%$.

The easier way to get an accurate answer is to use the financial calculator, as shown.

CALCULATOR METHOD

Set to END mode

2ND CLR TVM

10 N

2ND P/Y

P/Y = 2 ENTER

↓

C/Y = 2 ENTER

2ND QUIT

9640 +/- PV

600 PMT

10,000 FV

CPT I/Y

I/Y= 13.00159105

13.1 | Exercises

Assume that the coupon rate is payable semi-annually, unless otherwise stated.

1. Abigail purchased a $1000 bond that was paying a 3% coupon rate and had 5 more years to mature. How much did she pay for the bond if the yield at the time of purchase was 2.5% compounded semi-annually? What was the discount or premium on the bond?

2. Mark purchased a $5000 bond that had a coupon rate of 5% payable semi-annually and maturity of 10 years. He sold the bond, after holding it for 2 years, when the market interest rate was 7% compounded semi-annually. How much did he receive for the bond and what was the discount or premium on the bond at the time of sale?

3. The Province of Nova Scotia issued a $25,000, 4.5% bond with maturity in 10 years. What is the issue price and premium or discount of the bond if the yield to maturity at the time of issue was 3% compounded semi-annually?

4. Waterloo Power Corporation released $10,000 bonds having a coupon rate of 6% and interest paid semi-annually and maturity of 7 years. What is the issue price, and premium or discount of the bond, if at the time of issue the yield was 8% compounded semi-annually?

5. A $10,000 bond that is redeemable in 10 years had 3.5% coupons paid semi-annually and was purchased 3 years before maturity. What was the purchase price, and the discount or premium, on the bond if the yield was 3.5% compounded quarterly at the time of the purchase?

6. Sarena purchased a $5000, 5% bond when it had 5 years to maturity and the yield to maturity was 4.50% compounded monthly. What was her discount or premium on the bond?

7. A $1000 bond had a coupon rate of 5% with interest paid semi-annually. Ria purchased this bond when there were 5 years left to maturity and when the market interest rate was 6% compounded semi-annually. She held the bond for 2 years then sold it when the market interest rate was 4% compounded semi-annually. Calculate her gain or loss on this investment.

8. A municipality required immediate funding so they issued a $5000 bond paying a 4% coupon rate. When the yield was 3.5% compounded semi-annually, the bond had 7 years left to maturity and an investor purchased it. However, 3 years later, the investor required money and sold the bond. If the yield at the time of the sale was 5% compounded semi-annually, how much did the investor gain or lose on this investment?

9. A bond that has a face value of $10,000 and coupon rate of 4.65% payable semi-annually was redeemable on July 01, 2020. Calculate the purchase price of the bond on September 10, 2015 when the yield was 5.50% compounded semi-annually.

10. Martha purchased a $1000 bond on November 19, 2011 when the yield to maturity was 4% compounded semi-annually. Calculate the discount or premium on the bond if it had a coupon rate of 5% payable semi-annually and a maturity date of December 31, 2015.

11. A $5000, 3.5% bond was purchased 4 years and 3 months before its redemption date when the yield was 4% compounded semi-annually. Calculate the purchase price of the bond and its discount or premium.

12. How much did Harry pay for a $1000 bond that was paying a 7% coupon rate if he purchased it 6 years and 2 months before its maturity date. The yield at the time of purchase was 5% compounded semi-annually.

13. Five $10,000 bonds at a coupon rate of 6.5% were redeemable on January 01, 2019. If they were purchased on October 17, 2015 when the quote was 96.1, calculate the amount spent to purchase the bonds and the total discount or total premium on the purchase.

14. A $5000 bond carries a 7% coupon and was redeemable on June 01, 2010. If it was purchased at 98.15 on March 03, 2008, calculate the purchase price of the bond.

15. A $1000 bond that has a coupon rate of 4% payable semi-annually and maturity of 4 years was purchased when the yield was 3% compounded semi-annually. Construct the bond schedule showing the amortization of the premium.

16. Rachel purchased a $5000 bond at a coupon rate of 7.5% payable semi-annually and redeemable in 4 years. If the yield at the time of purchase was 7% compounded semi-annually, construct the bond schedule showing the amortization of the premium.

17. A $10,000 bond at a coupon rate of 10% payable semi-annually is purchased for 98.50, three years before maturity. Construct the bond schedule showing the accumulation of discount if money is worth 10.60% compounded semi–annually.

18. The ministry of transportation issued $5000 bonds at 7% coupon rate payable semi-annually. 3 years before maturity, the bond was purchased when the quoted price was 96.5. Construct the bond schedule showing the accumulation of discount if money is worth 8.34% compounded semi-annually.

19. A 10-year, $1000 bond paying an 8.5% coupon rate was purchased at 99.1. Calculate the yield at the time of purchase of the bond.

20. What is the yield to maturity on a $25,000, 5-year, 6% bond that was purchased at 103.4?

13.2 | Sinking Funds

A *sinking fund* is an interest-earning fund that is established to make periodic deposits for the purpose of retiring debts.

A sinking fund is an interest-earning fund that is set up by a corporation or government to periodically deposit money into it so that the accumulated funds will be available at a future date to repay the principal of a large debt at the time of its maturity. These funds are generally set up to assure investors, (who have purchased bonds or debentures from the corporation or government) that provisions have been made to ensure repayment of their principal amount at the time of maturity of their bonds or debentures.

Sinking funds can also be used to prematurely clear a portion of the debt.

For example, if a business receives \$1 million by issuing 10-year bonds to the public, on the date of maturity of the bond, they would have to repay the entire principal to the holders of the bond. As the principal amount is large, the business may establish a sinking fund to deposit money into periodically, until it accumulates to \$1 million by the maturity date of the bonds. This amount can then be used to repay the principal amount to the bond holders.

Sinking Fund Calculations and Constructing a Sinking Fund Schedule

As a sinking fund is generally a series of equal deposits made at regular intervals for a fixed period of time, it is treated as an annuity. Payments into the fund can be made at the end of the period (ordinary annuity) or at the beginning of the period (annuity due).

A sinking fund schedule provides details of the payment number, periodic payment into the fund, interest earned during the period, increase in the fund, and the fund balance.

Example 13.2(a)

Ordinary Simple Annuity Sinking Fund Calculations and Sinking Fund Schedule

Acapac Industries established a sinking fund in order to accumulate \$10,000 by depositing equal amounts of money at the end of every 6 months for 2 years. If the fund was earning interest at 4% compounded semi-annually, calculate the following and construct a sinking fund schedule to illustrate details of the fund:

(i) Size of the periodic sinking fund deposit.

(ii) Total amount deposited in the fund over the time period.

(iii) Total interest earned on the sinking fund deposits.

(iv) Sinking fund balance at the end of the 2nd payment period.

(v) Interest earned in the 3rd payment period.

(vi) Amount by which the sinking fund increased in the 3rd payment period.

Solution

(i) This sinking fund is an ordinary simple annuity.

$$FV = \$10{,}000$$

$$t = 2 \text{ years}$$

$$n = 2 \text{ deposits per year} \times 2 \text{ years} = 4 \text{ semi-annual deposits}$$

$$i = \frac{j}{m} = \frac{0.04}{2} = 0.02$$

Using Formula 10.2(a), $FV = PMT\left[\frac{(1+i)^n - 1}{i}\right]$

$$10{,}000 = PMT\left[\frac{(1+0.02)^4 - 1}{0.02}\right]$$

CALCULATOR METHOD

Set to END mode

2ND CLR TVM

4 N

4 I/Y

2ND P/Y

P/Y = 2 ENTER

↓

C/Y = 2 ENTER

2ND QUIT

0 PV

10,000 FV

CPT PMT

PMT= -2426.237527

Solution continued

$$10{,}000 = PMT\,[4.121608...]$$

Rearranging and solving, $PMT = \$2426.237527...$

Therefore, the periodic sinking fund deposit was $2426.24.

(ii) Total amount deposited in the fund over the time period $= n \times PMT$

$$= \$2426.24 \times 4$$

$$= \$9704.96 \text{ semi-annual deposits}$$

Therefore, $9704.96 was deposited over 2 years in the sinking fund.

(iii) Total interest earned on the sinking fund deposits $= FV - n \times PMT$

$$= 10{,}000 - 9704.96 = \$295.04$$

(iv) The sinking fund balance at the end of any given period is the future value of the periodic deposits made until the end of that period.

CALCULATOR METHOD

2 N

2426.24 +/- PMT

CPT FV

FV= 4901.0048

At the end of the 2nd payment period, $n = 2$. Let the Future Value at the end of the 2nd period be FV_2.

Using Formula 10.2(a), $$FV = PMT\left[\frac{(1+i)^n - 1}{i}\right]$$

$$FV_2 = 2426.24\left[\frac{(1+0.02)^2 - 1}{0.02}\right]$$

$$= 2426.24\,[2.02] = \$4901.0048$$

Therefore, the sinking fund balance at the end of the 2nd payment period was $4901.00.

(v) Interest that is earned in any period is on the amount that is available in the fund at the beginning of that period, which is the same as the amount that is available at the end of the previous period.

To calculate the interest earned in the 3rd period, we need to determine the fund balance at the end of the 2nd period.

From (iv), we know that the fund balance at the end of the 2nd period $= FV_2 = \$4901.00$.

Interest on this amount is $= i \times FV_2 = 0.02 \times 4901.00 = \$98.02$

Therefore, $98.02 was the interest earned by the fund in the 3rd payment period.

(vi) The amount by which the sinking fund increased in a period is the interest earned during that period plus the deposit made in that period.

$$\left(\begin{array}{c}\textit{Amount by which the Sinking Fund}\\ \textit{Increased in the 3}^{rd}\textit{ Period}\end{array}\right) = \left(\begin{array}{c}\textit{Interest Earned}\\ \textit{in the 3}^{rd}\textit{ Period}\end{array}\right) + PMT$$

$$= (4901.00 \times 0.02) + 2426.24$$

$$= \$2524.26$$

Therefore, the amount by which the sinking fund increased in the 3rd payment period is $2524.26.

Sinking fund schedule

Payment Period	Payment (*PMT*)	Interest Earned	Increase in the Fund	Fund Balance
0	–	–	–	0.00
1	2426.24	0.00	2426.24	2426.24
2	2426.24	48.52	2474.76	4901.00
3	2426.24	98.02	2524.26	7425.26
4	2426.24	148.51	2574.75	10,000.01*
Total	9704.96	295.05	10,000.01	

Solution continued

** Due to the rounding of amounts in each step, there is a minor rounding error of +$0.01 in the fund balance.*

In the above sinking fund schedule:

Interest Earned = $i \times$ *Previous Fund Balance*

Increase in the Fund = *PMT* + *Interest earned*

Fund Balance = *Previous Fund Balance* + *Increase in the Fund*

Example 13.2(b)

Simple Annuity Due Sinking Fund Calculations and Sinking Fund Schedule

In the previous Example 13.2(a), answer all parts of the problem assuming that Acapac Industries made deposits at the beginning of every 6 months instead of at the end of each period.

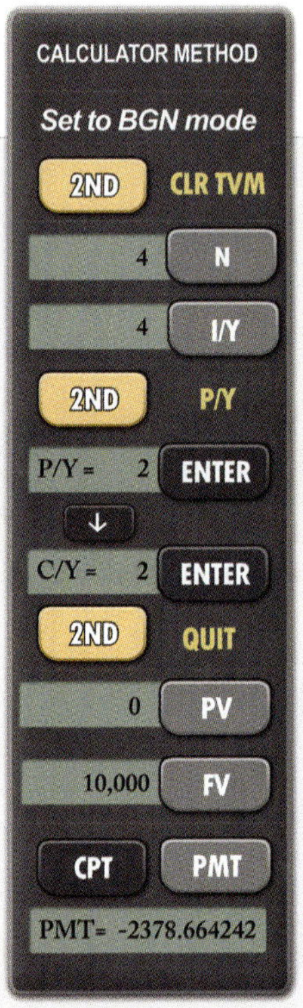

Solution

(i) Calculating the size of the periodic sinking fund deposit:

This sinking fund is a simple annuity due.

$FV = \$10,000$

$t = 2$ years

$n = 2$ deposits per year $\times$ 2 years = 4 semi-annual deposits

$$i = \frac{j}{m} = \frac{0.04}{2} = 0.02$$

Using Formula 10.4(a),

$$FV_{Due} = PMT\left[\frac{(1+i)^n - 1}{i}\right](1 + i)$$

$$10{,}000 = PMT\left[\frac{(1+0.02)^4 - 1}{0.02}\right](1 + 0.02)$$

$$10{,}000 = PMT\,[4.121608...] \times 1.02$$

Rearranging and solving, $PMT = \$2378.664242...$

Therefore, the periodic sinking fund deposit was $2378.66.

(ii) Calculating the total amount deposited in the fund over the time period:

Total amount deposited in the fund over the time period = $2378.66 × 4 semi-annual deposits
= $9514.64

Therefore, $9514.64 was deposited over 2 years in the sinking fund.

(iii) Calculating the total interest earned on the sinking fund deposits:

Total interest earned on the sinking fund deposits = $10,000 − $9514.64= $485.36

(iv) Calculating the sinking fund balance at the end of the 2nd payment period:

Sinking fund balance at the end of any given period is the future value of the periodic deposits made till the end of that period.

At the end of the 2nd payment period, $n = 2$. Let the Future Value at the end of the 2nd period be FV_2

Using Formula 10.4(a),

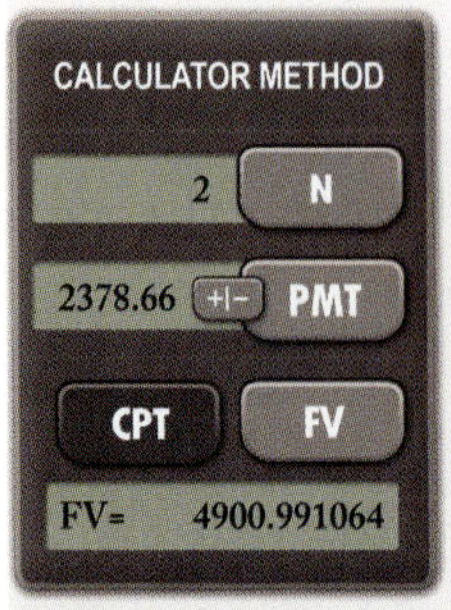

$$FV = PMT\left[\frac{(1+i)^n - 1}{i}\right](1 + i)$$

$$FV_2 = 2378.66\left[\frac{(1+0.02)^2 - 1}{0.02}\right](1 + 0.02)$$

$$= 2378.66\,[2.0604]$$

$$= \$4900.991064$$

Therefore, the sinking fund balance at the end of the 2nd payment period was $4900.99.

Solution continued

(v) Calculating the interest earned in the 3rd payment period:

The interest for a period is not only calculated on the fund balance of the previous period, but also on the periodic deposit, as the deposit is made at the beginning of the period.

$$\text{Therefore, } \left(\begin{array}{c}\textit{Interest Earned for the}\\ \textit{3}^{rd}\textit{ Payment Period}\end{array}\right) = i \times \left(\begin{array}{c}\textit{2}^{nd}\textit{ Period}\\ \textit{Fund Balance}\end{array} + \textit{Periodic Deposit}\right)$$

From (iv), we know that the fund balance at the end of the 2nd period = \$4900.99

$$\left(\begin{array}{c}\textit{Interest Earned for the}\\ \textit{3}^{rd}\textit{ Payment Period}\end{array}\right) = 0.02(4900.99 + 2378.66) = \$145.59$$

Therefore, \$145.59 is the interest earned by the fund in the 3rd payment period.

(vi) Calculating the amount by which the sinking fund increased in the 3rd payment period:

The amount by which the sinking fund increased in a period is the interest earned during that period plus the deposit made in that period.

$$\left(\begin{array}{c}\textit{Amount by which the sinking fund}\\ \textit{increased in the 3}^{rd}\textit{ period}\end{array}\right) = \left(\begin{array}{c}\textit{Interest Earned for the}\\ \textit{3}^{rd}\textit{ Payment Period}\end{array}\right) + \textit{Deposit Made}$$

$$= 145.59 + 2378.66 = \$2524.25$$

Therefore, the amount by which the sinking fund increased in the 3rd payment period was \$2524.25.

Sinking Fund Schedule

Payment Period	Payment (*PMT*)	Interest Earned	Increase in the Fund	Fund Balance
0	–	–	–	0.00
1	2378.66	47.57	2426.23	2426.23
2	2378.66	96.10	2474.76	4900.99
3	2378.66	145.59	2524.25	7425.24
4	2378.66	196.08	2574.74	9999.98*
Total	9514.64	485.34	9999.98	

***PMT* is made at the beginning of the interval.**
Interest Earned, Increase in the Fund, and Fund Balance are at the end of the interval.

* *Due to the rounding of amounts in each step, there is a minor rounding error of −\$0.02 in the fund balance.*

In the sinking fund schedule:

- Interest for the period is based not only on the fund balance of the previous period but also on the payment deposited. This is because the deposit is made at the beginning of the period and will earn interest during the period.
- Therefore, *Interest Earned* = $i \times$ (*Previous Fund Balance* + *PMT*)
- *Increase in the Fund* = *PMT* + *Interest earned*
- *Fund Balance* = *Increase in the Fund* + *Previous Fund Balance*

Calculating the Periodic Cost and Book Value of a Debt and Constructing a Partial Sinking Fund Schedule

When a company issues a bond and sets up a sinking fund, they make the following two periodic payments till the maturity of the bond:

- Periodic interest payments to the bond holder
- Periodic deposits made into the sinking fund

The **periodic cost** of this debt for any period is the sum of the above two payments for that period.

The **book value** of the debt at any time is the difference between the principal amount of the debt and the sinking fund balance at that time.

The **sinking fund schedule** shows the progress of accumulation of the fund by periodic payments into the sinking fund. It is similar to the amortization schedule showing the repayment of a loan by periodic payments.

At the time of maturity, the accumulated value in the sinking fund is the amount that is returned to the bond holder.

Example 13.2(c)

Calculating the Periodic Cost, Book Value of the Debt and Constructing a Partial Sinking Fund Schedule

A social networking company wanted to raise $100,000 and issued twenty $5000 bonds paying 10% coupon rate payable semi-annually for 5 years. They set up a sinking fund to repay the debt at the end of 5 years and made deposits at the end of every 6 months into the fund. If the sinking fund was earning 6.5% compounded semi-annually:

(i) Calculate the periodic cost of the debt.

(ii) Calculate the book value of the debt after 3 years.

(iii) Construct a partial sinking fund schedule showing details of the first two and last two payments and the totals of the schedule.

Solution

(i) $$\left(\begin{matrix}\textit{Periodic Cost}\\ \textit{of the Debt}\end{matrix}\right) = \left(\begin{matrix}\textit{Periodic Interest}\\ \textit{Payment of the Bond}\end{matrix}\right) + \left(\begin{matrix}\textit{Periodic Deposit into}\\ \textit{the Sinking Fund}\end{matrix}\right)$$

$$= PMT_{\textit{Interest Payment on the Bond}} + PMT_{\textit{Sinking Fund}}$$

Calculating periodic interest payment of the bond:

$FV = \$100{,}000$

$$b = \frac{j}{m} = \frac{0.10}{2} = 0.05$$

Using Formula 13.1(b),

$$PMT_{\textit{Interest Payment on the Bond}} = FV \times b$$
$$= 100{,}000.00 \times 0.05$$
$$= \$5000.00$$

Calculating sinking fund periodic deposit:

This sinking fund is an ordinary simple annuity.

$FV = \$100{,}000,\ t = 5$ years

$n = 2$ deposits per year $\times$ 5 years $= 10$ semi-annual deposits

$$i = \frac{j}{m} = \frac{0.065}{2} = 0.0325$$

Using Formula 10.2(a),

$$FV = PMT\left[\frac{(1+i)^n - 1}{i}\right]$$

$$100{,}000 = PMT\left[\frac{(1+0.0325)^{10} - 1}{0.0325}\right]$$

$$100{,}000 = PMT\,[11.596747...]$$

Rearranging and solving, $PMT_{\textit{Sinking Fund}} = \$8623.107239...$

The periodic cost of the debt $= PMT_{\textit{Interest Payment on the Bond}} + PMT_{\textit{Sinking Fund}}$

$$= 5000.00 + 8623.11 = \$13{,}623.11$$

Therefore, the periodic cost of the debt is $13,623.11.

CALCULATOR METHOD

Set to END mode

2ND CLR TVM
10 N
6.5 I/Y
2ND P/Y
P/Y = 2 ENTER
↓
C/Y = 2 ENTER
2ND QUIT
0 PV
100,000 FV
CPT PMT
PMT = -8623.107239

Solution continued

(ii) $\left(\begin{matrix}\textit{Book Value of the}\\ \textit{Debt after 3 years}\end{matrix}\right) = \left(\begin{matrix}\textit{Principal Amount}\\ \textit{of the Debt}\end{matrix}\right) - \left(\begin{matrix}\textit{Sinking Fund Balance at}\\ \textit{the End of 3 years}\end{matrix}\right)$

The sinking fund balance at the end of 3 years is the Future value of the sinking fund at the end of 3 years.

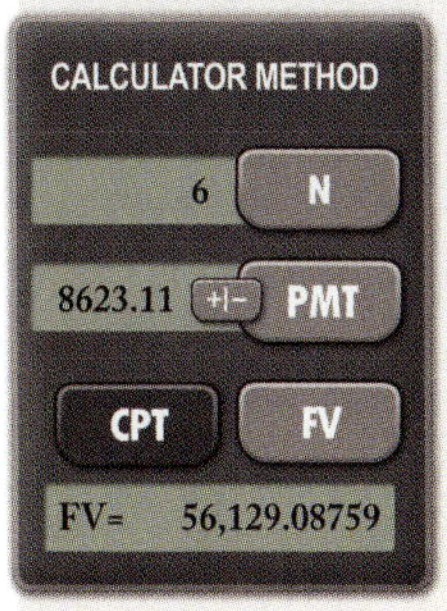

$t = 3$ years

$n = 2$ deposits per year $\times$ 3 years $= 6$ semi-annual deposits

$i = 0.0325$

Using Formula 10.2(a), $FV = PMT\left[\frac{(1+i)^n - 1}{i}\right]$

$$= 8623.11\left[\frac{(1+0.0325)^6 - 1}{0.0325}\right] = 56{,}129.08759...$$

$\left(\begin{matrix}\textit{Book Value of the}\\ \textit{Debt after 3 years}\end{matrix}\right) = \$100{,}000 - 56{,}129.09 = \$43{,}870.91$

Therefore, the book value of the debt after 3 years is $43,870.91.

(iii) Construct a partial amortization schedule showing the first two and last two payments.

Partial Sinking Fund Schedule:

Payment Period	Payment (*PMT*)	Interest Earned	Increase in the Fund	Fund Balance	Book Value
0	–	–	–	0.00	100,000.00
1	8623.11	0.00	8623.11	8623.11	91,376.89 (a)
2	8623.11	280.25 (b)	8903.36 (c)	17,526.47 (d)	82,473.53
–	–	–	–	–	–
8	–	–	–	77,363.24 (e)	22,636.76
9	8623.11	2514.31	11,137.42	88,500.65	11,499.35
10	8623.11	2876.27	11,499.38	100,000.03	0
Total	86,231.10	13,768.94	100,000.03		

In the above partial sinking fund schedule,

(a) $\textit{Book Value}_{\text{Payment 1}} = \textit{Principal} - \textit{Fund Balance}_{\textit{Payment 1}}$

$= 100{,}000.00 - 8623.11$

$= \$91{,}376.89$

(b) $\textit{Interest Earned}_{\textit{Payment 2}} = i \times \textit{Fund Balance}_{\textit{Payment 1}}$

$= 0.0325 \times 8623.11 = \$280.25$

(c) $\textit{Increase in the Fund}_{\textit{Payment 2}} = \textit{PMT}_{\textit{Payment 2}} + \textit{Interest Earned}_{\textit{Payment 2}}$

$= 8623.11 + 280.25 = \$8903.36$

(d) $\textit{Fund balance}_{\textit{Payment 2}} = \textit{Fund Balance}_{\textit{Payment 1}} + \textit{Increase in the Fund}_{\textit{Payment 2}}$

$= 8623.11 + 8903.36 = \$17{,}526.47$

(e) $\textit{Fund balance}_{\textit{Payment 8}} = \textit{Future Value}_{\textit{8 Payments}}$

Using Formula 10.2(a),

$$FV = PMT\left[\frac{(1+i)^n - 1}{i}\right] = 8623.11\left[\frac{(1+0.0325)^8 - 1}{0.0325}\right] = 77{,}363.2357... = \$77{,}363.24$$

13.2 | Exercises

1. A $10,000 bond was cleared in 4 years by setting up a sinking fund that was earning 5.5% compounded semi-annually. If deposits were made to the fund at the end of every 6 months, calculate the size of the periodic payments deposited and the total interest earned in the fund?

2. Rasheed Furnishings issued bonds worth $500,000 to expand their factory. They established a sinking fund to retire this debt in 3 years and made deposits into it at the end of every 6 months. If the fund was earning 7% compounded semi-annually, calculate the size of the periodic payment deposited into the fund and the total interest earned in the fund.

3. For Problem 1, construct a sinking fund schedule illustrating the details of the fund for 4 years.

4. For Problem 2, construct a sinking fund schedule illustrating the details of the fund for 3 years.

5. Victoria Appliances sold bonds for $500,000 that were redeemable in 5 years. They established a sinking fund that was earning 8% compounded semi-annually to pay back the principal of the bonds on maturity. Deposits were being made to the fund at the end of every 6 months.
   a. Calculate the size of the periodic sinking fund deposit.
   b. Calculate the total amount deposited in the fund over the time period.
   c. Calculate the total interest earned on the sinking fund deposits.
   d. Calculate the sinking fund balance at the end of the 6th payment period.
   e. Calculate the interest earned in the 7th payment period.
   f. Calculate the amount by which the sinking fund increased in the 7th payment period.
   g. Construct a partial sinking fund schedule to illustrate details of the last 2 payments.

6. A company issued bonds for $850,000 and established a sinking fund to retire the debt in 15 years. They made deposits at the end of every 6 months into the fund and the fund was earning 3.55% compounded semi-annually.
   a. Calculate the size of the periodic sinking fund deposit.
   b. Calculate the total amount deposited in the fund over the time period.
   c. Calculate the total interest earned on the sinking fund deposits.
   d. Calculate the sinking fund balance at the end of the 11th payment period.
   e. Calculate the interest earned in the 11th payment period.
   f. Calculate the amount by which the sinking fund increased in the 12th payment period.
   g. Construct a partial sinking fund schedule to illustrate details of the last 2 payments.

7. A company sold $100,000 bonds and set up a sinking fund that was earning 8% compounded semi-annually to retire the bonds in 4 years. If they made equal deposits into the fund at the beginning of every 6 months, calculate the size of the periodic payments deposited and the total interest earned in the fund?

8. Williams Software borrowed $1,250,000 through a bond issue to purchase new servers for their company. It established a sinking fund to retire this debt in 3 years and made deposits into it at the beginning of every 6 months. The fund earned 9.5% compounded semi-annually during the period. Calculate the size of the periodic payment deposited into the fund and the total interest earned in the fund.

9. In Problem 7, construct a sinking fund schedule illustrating the details of the fund.

10. In Problem 8, construct a sinking fund schedule illustrating the details of the fund.

11. A bank in Toronto issued bonds for $750,000 that were redeemable in 10 years. They established a sinking fund that was earning 3.5% compounded semi-annually to retire this debt on maturity and made equal deposits at the beginning of every 6 months into the fund.
    a. Calculate the size of their periodic deposits.
    b. Calculate the total amount deposited in the fund over the time period.
    c. Calculate the total interest earned in the fund.
    d. Calculate the fund balance at the end of the 19th payment period.
    e. Calculate the interest earned in the 19th payment period.
    f. Calculate the amount by which the sinking fund increased in the 12th payment period .
    g. Construct a partial sinking fund schedule to illustrate details of the first 2 payments.

12. A company borrowed $280,000 and set up a sinking fund to retire the debt in 6 years. They made equal deposits at the beginning of every 6 months into the fund and the fund was earning 8.55% compounded semi-annually.
    a. Calculate the size of the deposits made into the fund.
    b. Calculate the total amount deposited in the fund.
    c. Calculate the total interest earned in the fund.
    d. Calculate the sinking fund balance at the end of the 4th payment period.
    e. Calculate the interest earned in the 5th payment period.
    f. Calculate the amount by which the sinking fund increased in the 7th payment period.
    g. Construct a partial sinking fund schedule to illustrate details of the first 2 payments.

13. To raise $5,000,000 to expand into new markets, a very successful laptop manufacturer issued bonds in the market with a coupon rate of 7%, paying interest semi-annually, and redeemable in 20 years. They established a sinking fund to retire this debt on maturity and made equal deposits into the fund at the end of every 6 months. If the fund was earning 4% compounded semi-annually, calculate the periodic cost of the debt and the book value of the debt after 10 years.

14. Wynter Tires Inc. issued $300,000 worth of 5% bonds to purchase new equipment for their showroom. They planned to retire this debt in 10 years on maturity by setting up a sinking fund and making equal deposits into it at the end of every 6 months. If the fund was earning 4% compounded semi-annually, calculate the periodic cost of the debt and the book value of the debt after 5 years.

15. For Problem 13, construct a partial amortization schedule illustrating the first three payments, last three payments, and totals of the schedule.

16. For Problem 14, construct a partial amortization schedule illustrating the first two payments, last two payments, and totals of the schedule.

17. $100,000 bonds were issued at a coupon rate of 5% payable semi-annually and redeemable in 3 years. To retire this bond, a sinking fund was established, where equal deposits were made at the end of every 6 months. The fund was earning 4.5% compounded annually. What were the periodic cost of the debt and the book value of the debt after 2 years?

18. Demarco Electronics took a loan of $345,500 from a bank to purchase testing equipment to improve the quality of their electric meters. They set up a sinking fund to retire the debt in 4 years and made equal payments at the end of every 6 months to this fund. If the loan was received at 6% compounded semi-annually and the sinking fund was earning 5% compounded annually, calculate the periodic cost of the debt and the book value of the debt in 3 years.

19. For Problem 17, construct a sinking fund schedule illustrating details.

20. For Problem 18, construct a sinking fund schedule illustrating details.

13 | Review Exercises

Answers to odd-numbered problems are available at the end of the textbook

Assume that the coupon rate is payable semi-annually, unless otherwise stated.

1. Edgar purchased a $5000 bond that had a coupon rate of 5.50% payable semi-annually and was redeemable in 7 years. What was his purchase price for the bond if the yield to maturity at the time of purchase was 6.25% compounded semi-annually? What was the discount or premium on the bond?

2. A company invested $150,000 in bonds that were issued by another company. The bonds were paying a 11% coupon rate and were redeemable in 10 years. Five years after purchasing the bond, they required money urgently so they sold the bonds in the market when the yield was 9.5% compounded semi-annually. How much did they sell the bond for and what was the discount or premium on the bond at the time of sale?

3. What was the purchase price, and the discount or premium, on a $1000 bond with a coupon rate of 8.5% payable semi-annually if the yield at the time of issue was 8% compounded quarterly and the bond was redeemable in 5 years?

4. Heather purchased a $10,000 bond that had 4% coupons and 10 years to maturity. If the yield at the time of purchase was 5% compounded semi-annually, calculate the purchase price of the bond and the discount or premium at the time of purchase.

5. Anna and her husband invested their savings of $50,000 in bonds that were paying a 10% coupon rate and were redeemable in 10 years. The yield at the time of their purchase was 9% compounded semi-annually. They held the bond for 4 years and sold when the yield was 10% compounded semi-annually. Calculate their gain or loss on this investment.

6. The Province of Ontario issued $5000 bonds with a 9% coupon rate. An investor purchased ten of these bonds when the yield was 8.5% compounded semi-annually and there were 6 years left to maturity. However, after 4 years, the investor sold all the bonds in the market when the yield was 7% compounded semi-annually. How much did she gain or lose on this investment?

7. A $25,000 bond paying a 12.5% coupon rate was redeemable on August 01, 2015. What was its purchase price, and its premium or discount, on October 18, 2011 when the yield was 8% compounded semi-annually?

8. Calculate the discount or premium on a $5000 bond with a 4% coupon rate if it was redeemable on December 31, 2020 and was purchased on February 23, 2018 when the yield was 5% compounded semi-annually.

9. A $10,000 bond paying a 7% coupon rate was purchased 5 years and 1 month before its redemption date. If the yield on the date of purchase was 8% compounded semi-annually, calculate the purchase price on the bond and its discount or premium.

10. Bruno purchased a $5000 bond 8 months before its maturity. Calculate the purchase price on the bond if it was a 4.5% coupon bond and the yield at the time of purchase was 3.5% compounded semi-annually.

11. A $5000 bond at 9% coupon rate was redeemable on June 01, 2016. It was purchased on September 27, 2014 when the quote was 104.7. Calculate the purchase price and the discount or premium on the purchase of the bonds.

12. Simon purchased a $20,000 bond at a coupon rate of 10.5% payable semi-annually that was redeemable on August 01, 2020. If he purchased it at 97.5 on April 15, 2015, calculate the purchase price of the bond.

13. Sarah purchased a $1000 bond that had a coupon rate 6.5% payable semi-annually and was redeemable in 4 years. If the yield at the time of purchase was 5.5% compounded semi-annually, construct a bond schedule showing the amortization of the premium.

14. The ministry of education raised money to build a new high school by issuing $20,000 bonds at a coupon rate of 8% payable semi-annually. Three years before maturity, the bonds were purchased at 98.5. Construct the bond schedule showing the accumulation of discount.

15. A $5000, 9.5% bond was purchased at 98.2, five years before maturity. Calculate the yield at the time of purchase of the bond.

16. What is the yield on a $10,000, 10-year, 7.5% bond that was purchased at 101.5?

17. Sigmond Inc. issued bonds for $100,000 that were redeemable in 4 years. They established a sinking fund that was earning 12% compounded semi-annually to repay the principal of the bonds on maturity. If deposits were being made to the fund at the end of every 6 months, calculate the following:
    (i) Calculate the size of the periodic sinking fund deposit.
    (ii) Calculate the total amount deposited in the fund over the time period.
    (iii) Calculate the total interest earned on the sinking fund deposits.
    (iv) Calculate the sinking fund balance at the end of the 5th payment period.
    (v) Calculate the interest earned in the 6th payment period.
    (vi) Calculate the amount by which the sinking fund increased in the 6th payment period.
    (vii) Construct a sinking fund schedule to illustrate details of the fund.

18. A company borrowed $680,000 and set up a sinking fund to retire the debt in 3 years. They made deposits at the end of every 6 months into the fund and the fund was earning 8.5% compounded semi-annually.
    (i) Calculate the size of the periodic sinking fund deposit.
    (ii) Calculate the total amount deposited in the fund over the time period.
    (iii) Calculate the total interest earned on the sinking fund deposits.
    (iv) Calculate the sinking fund balance at the end of the 36rd payment period.
    (v) Calculate the interest earned in the 4th payment period.
    (vi) Calculate the amount by which the sinking fund increased in the 5th payment period.
    (vii) Construct a sinking fund schedule to illustrate details of the fund.

19. Woldridge Brothers Inc. issued $2,000,000 bonds in the market at a coupon rate of 12% payable semi-annually and redeemable in 20 years. They established a sinking fund to retire the debt on maturity and made equal deposits into the fund every 6 months. If the fund was earning 10.5% compounded semi-annually, calculate the periodic cost of the debt and the book value of the debt at the end of 15 years.

20. Agatha Investments, a leading investment banking firm in Toronto, issued bonds for $250,000 at 9.5% coupon rate payable semi-annually to expand their operations. They set up a sinking fund to retire this debt in 10 years on maturity by making equal deposits into it at the beginning of every 6 months. If the fund was earning 8% compounded semi-annually, calculate the periodic cost of the debt and the book value of the debt at the end of 7 years.

13 | Self-Test Exercises

Answers to all problems are available at the end of the textbook

Assume that the coupon rate is payable semi-annually unless otherwise stated.

1. Calculate the discount or premium on a $5000 bond at a coupon rate of 6% payable semi-annually if the yield at the time of purchase was 7% compounded semi-annually and the bond was redeemable in 10 years?

2. Sally purchased a $10,000 bond at a coupon rate of 8% payable semi-annually and was redeemable in 5 years. How much did she pay, and what was the premium or discount, for the bond if the yield at the time of purchase was 7% compounded monthly?

3. A company issues a $20,000 bond at a coupon rate of 7.5% payable semi-annually. Juan purchased this bond 10 years before maturity when the yield was 7% compounded semi-annually and sold it 2 years later when the bond's market yield was 8% compounded semi-annually. Calculate his loss or gain on this investment.

4. A $1000 bond paying a 6.5% coupon rate was redeemable on May 01, 2014. What was its purchase price, and premium or discount, on July 23, 2012 when the yield was 9% compounded semi-annually?

5. Marcelo purchased a $25,000 bond at a coupon rate of 3.5% payable semi-annually, 5 years and 1 month before its date of maturity. If the yield on the date of purchase was 4% compounded semi-annually, calculate the purchase price on the bond and its discount or premium.

6. A $10,000 bond with a 7.5% coupon rate is redeemable on October 01, 2015. It was purchased on September 18, 2010 when the quote was 103.8, calculate the purchase price and premium or discount on the purchase of the bond.

7. A company issued a $5000 bond at 8% coupon rate and redeemable in 4 years. If the yield at the time of issue was 7.50% compounded semi-annually, construct the bond schedule showing the amortization of the premium.

8. A $25,000 bond at a coupon rate of 4.75% payable semi-annually was purchased at 99.5, eight years before maturity. Calculate the yield of the bond.

9. A company issued bonds worth $750,500 and set up a sinking fund to retire the debt in 15 years. They made deposits at the end of every 6 months into the fund and the fund was earning 9% compounded semi-annually. Calculate the total amount deposited in the fund over the time period and the amount by which the sinking fund increased in the 25th payment period. Construct a sinking fund schedule to illustrate details of the last 2 deposits.

10. Irene Travels issued $100,000, 7.25% bonds in the market that were redeemable in 5 years. They established a sinking fund to retire the debt on maturity and made equal deposits into the fund every 6 months. If the fund was earning 9% compounded semi-annually, calculate the periodic cost of the debt and the book value of the debt at the end of 4 years.

CASE 13

Raising Money Through Bonds

Seth, a college business student, recently learned that bonds could be categorized as either investment grade bonds or junk bonds. Investment grade bonds are issued by established, low-risk companies whereas junk bonds are issued by high-risk companies.

Intrigued by the concept of junk bonds, Seth followed a company called Holdings Software Developers Inc. (HSD) - a high-risk company that issued junk bonds. The company had a low credit rating in the market and their bonds were considered very risky investments, which is why they would have to offer high interest payments to the holders of the bond. Although these bonds were junk bonds, surprisingly, there were many wealthy people who purchased their bonds, selling them shortly afterwards for a quick return on their investment.

In one particular case, HSD required $1,000,000 for an expansion project and raised the money by issuing $5000 bonds that were redeemable in 10 years. The bonds were rated as junk bonds and offered an 11% coupon paid semi-annually.

HSD had wanted to increase the rating of their bond by gaining the confidence of their investors, so they created a 10-year sinking fund to ensure that enough money would be available at the time of maturity of the bonds. The fund was growing at 2.5% compounded monthly and they made equal deposits into the fund at the end of every 6 months.

a. What was the discount on the bond at the time of issue if its yield was 14% compounded semi-annually?
b. What was the premium on the bond at the time of issue if the yield was 9% compounded quarterly?
c. If an investor purchased a bond at the time of issue at a yield of 14% compounded semi-annually, and sold it 2 years later when the market required a yield of only 13% compounded semi-annually, how much would the investor gain or lose on this investment?
d. What was the purchase price of the bond if an investor wanted to purchase it 6 years and 2 months before its redemption date and have the bond yield 12.5% compounded semi-annually?
e. If the bond was purchased 7 years before maturity for 103.4, what was its yield?
f. 2 years before maturity, an investor purchased the bond at a yield of 15% compounded semi-annually. Construct a bond schedule for the investor showing the amortization of discount.
g. What was the size of their periodic sinking fund deposit and what was the total interest earned during the period?
h. Construct a sinking fund schedule illustrating details of the fund.

13 | Summary of Notations and Formulas

NOTATION

b = Coupon rate

FV = Face value of the bond

PMT = Bond Payment

i = Yield or market rate of interest

FORMULAS

Purchase Price of a Bond | 13.1 (a)

$$Purchase\ Price = PV_{PMT} + PV_{Face\ Value}$$

Periodic Interest Payment of a Bond | 13.1 (b)

$$PMT = FV \times b$$

Investment is the purchase or creation of assets using financial resources with the objective of making gains in the future. Investors and business owners expect high returns on the money they invest. When various options and alternatives are available, it is necessary to assess, evaluate, and compare them to make the best investment decision. In this chapter, we will learn four different evaluation techniques. These are all based on concepts we learned.

14 Analyzing Business Investments

LEARNING OBJECTIVES

- Understand the different methods of comparing investments or evaluating the feasibility of investing in projects.
- Compare the discounted cash inflows of different investments.

CHAPTER OUTLINE

14.1 | Introduction

Individuals and businesses invest money to obtain future benefits. For example, individuals may invest money to benefit from its returns during their retirement, use these returns to purchase a property, or finance a child's education. Similarly, businesses make investments for the long-term to benefit from returns in the future. For example, businesses may invest in:

Investments are expenditures with determinable future benefits.

- Machinery to increase productivity.
- Training and development for their employees to improve performance.
- Equipment upgrades to improve product/service quality.
- Software to automate operations.
- Advertising to improve brand awareness.
- New business acquisition to expand their product offering or to own a larger market share.

The main consideration in making investment decisions will include the following:

1. The required and affordable amount
2. The waiting period to receive benefits from the investment
3. The expected profit or the required rate of return from the investment
4. The other available investment options and a comparison of benefits
5. The required time period to pay back the investment

In this chapter, we will focus on investments that result in monetary gains over a period of time. These are referred to as **capital investments**, the word 'capital' implying that the investments generate returns in the long-term. In accounting terms, such investments would be regarded as capital ***assets*** on the balance sheet (long-term) and not ***expenses*** on the income statement (short-term).

Capital investments are investments that generate monetary returns in the long-term.

As these investments are often large, it is important for business managers to carefully analyze their decision to invest. Utilizing the concept of time value of money (money growing over time when it is invested at an interest rate) there are different methods of comparing investments or evaluating the feasibility of investing in projects. We will look at the following four methods:

1. Discounted Cash Flow (DCF)
2. Net Present Value (NPV)
3. Internal Rate of Return (IRR)
4. Payback Period

14.2 | Discounted Cash Flow (DCF)

Discounted cash flow (DCF) is when all the expected future cash inflows are discounted to a particular date.

In the Discounted Cash Flow (DCF) method, all of the expected future cash flows from investing in a project are discounted to determine their present value on a particular date (focal date), which is then used to evaluate the investment option.

$$PV_{All\ Cash\ Flows} = PV_{Cash\ Flow\ 1} + PV_{Cash\ Flow\ 2} + PV_{Cash\ Flow\ 3} \cdots$$

If the present value of all cash flows is greater than the cost of investing in a project, then the project may be considered a good investment option. The discounted cash inflows of different investment options are compared on a particular focal date and the one with the highest discounted cash flows is accepted.

Cost of capital is the required rate of return that a business expects from investing in a project.

The rate of return used to calculate the present value of cash flows is the **required rate of return** that the business expects from investing in this project. This required rate of return is generally the **cost of capital,** which is the opportunity cost of investing; i.e., the rate of return that the business would otherwise earn when the amount is invested in another investment that has the same level of risk as this project.

Example 14.2(a) Calculating the Discounted Cash Flow (DCF) of a Project

A marketing company is evaluating a $25,000 marketing project devised by one of its interns. The project will generate a return of $15,000 in the 1st year, $10,000 in the 2nd year and $7,000 in the 3rd year. The company's required rate of return (cost of capital) is 10%. Calculate the discounted cash flow and determine whether this is a worth while investment.

If the compounding period is not provided, assume it to be an annually compounding interest rate.

Solution

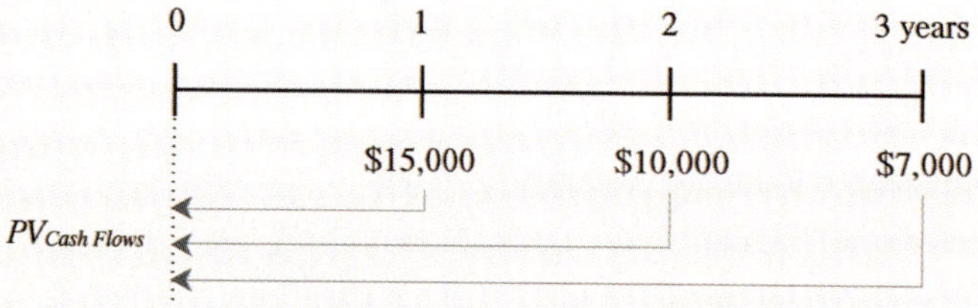

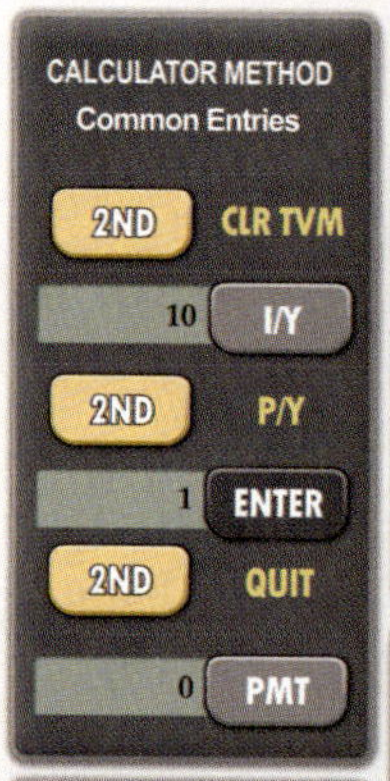

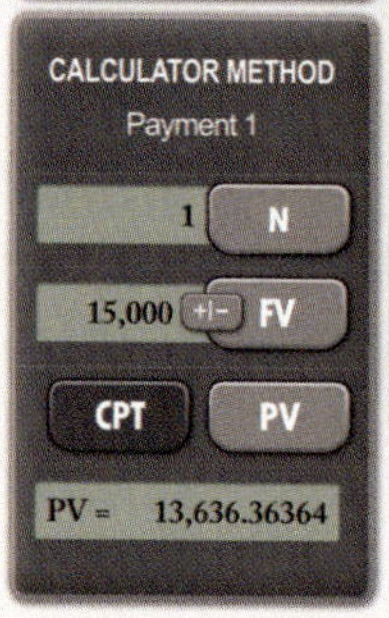

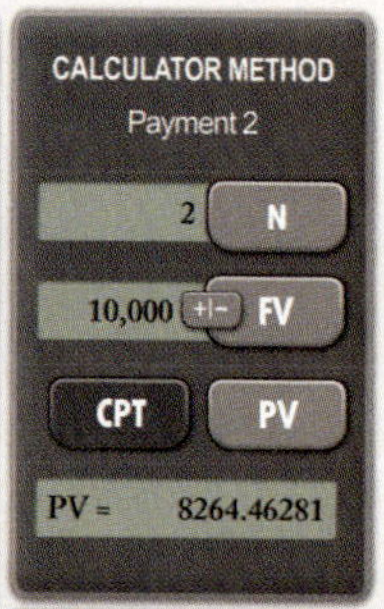

$$j = 0.10, \quad m = 1, \quad i = \frac{j}{m} = \frac{0.10}{1} = 0.10$$

Using Formula 9.1(b), $PV = FV(1 + i)^{-n}$

Present Value of cash flows:

$$\begin{aligned} PV_{\text{All Cash Flows}} &= 15{,}000(1 + 0.10)^{-1} \\ &\quad + 10{,}000(1 + 0.10)^{-2} \\ &\quad + 7000(1 + 0.10)^{-3} \\ &= 13{,}636.363636... \\ &\quad + 8264.462809... \\ &\quad + 5259.203606... \\ &= 27{,}160.06005... = \$27{,}160.03 \end{aligned}$$

The discounted cash flows of $27,160.03 are greater than the initial $25,000 cost for the project. Therefore, this is a worthwhile investment.

Example 14.2(b) Comparing Two Investment Options Using the DCF Method

The CEO of a software development company has to choose between investing in either Project A or Project B. Project A will provide the company returns of $60,000 in the 1st year and $60,000 in the 2nd year. Project B will provide $12,850 in the 1st year and $120,500 in the 2nd year. Which option should he choose if the company's required rate of return (cost of capital) is 16%? Assume that either project would require the same initial investment.

Solution

Project A

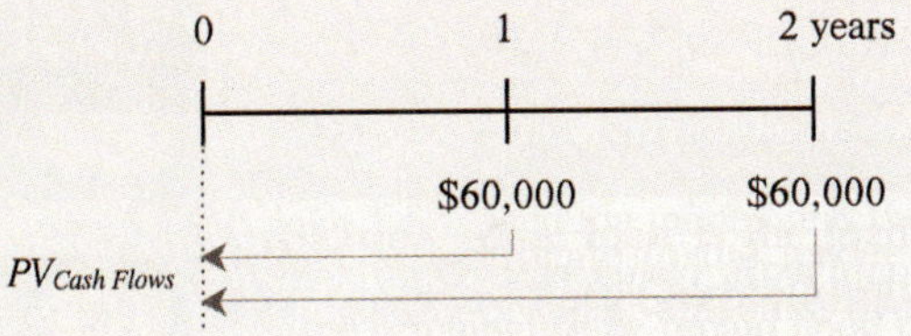

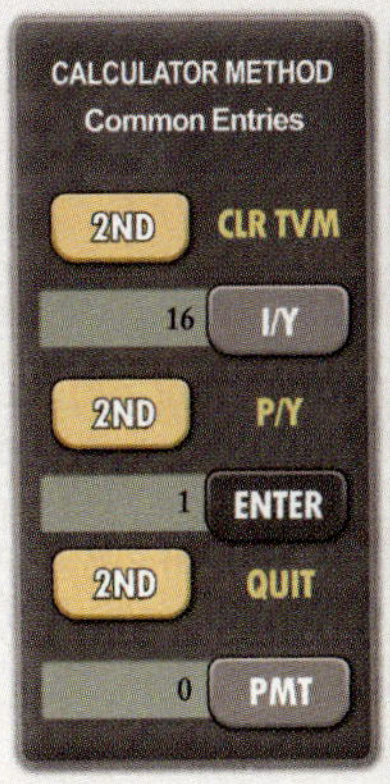

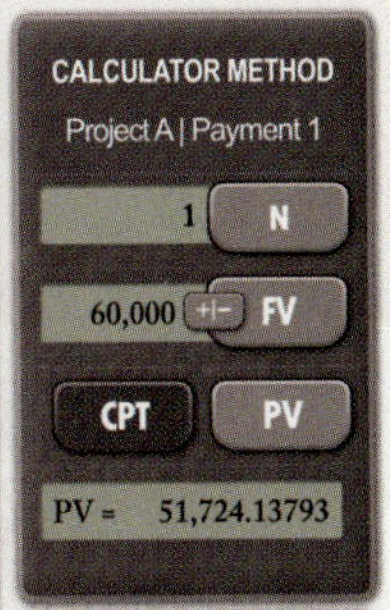

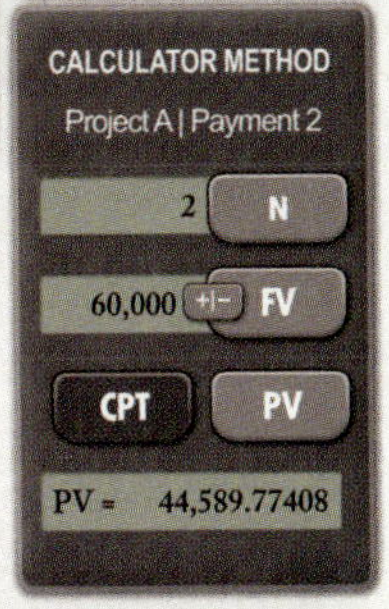

$j = 0.16, \quad m = 1, \quad i = \frac{j}{m} = \frac{0.16}{1} = 0.16$

Using Formula 9.1(b), $PV = FV(1 + i)^{-n}$

Present Value of cash flows from Project A:

$$
\begin{aligned}
PV_{Cash\ Flows} &= 60{,}000(1 + 0.16)^{-1} + 60{,}000(1 + 0.16)^{-2} \\
&= 51{,}724.13793... + 44{,}589.77408... \\
&= 96{,}313.91201... = \$96{,}313.91
\end{aligned}
$$

Project B

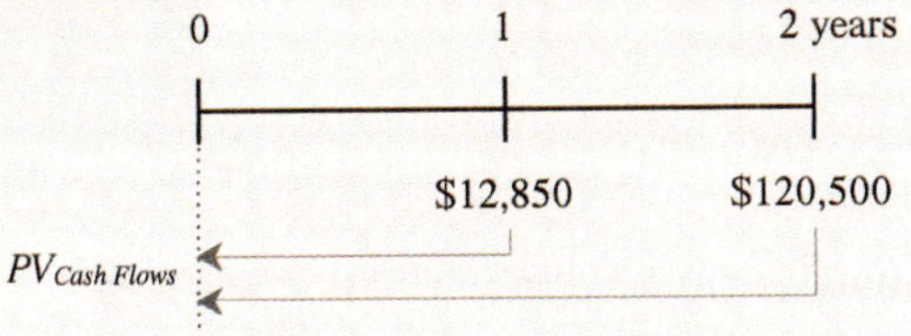

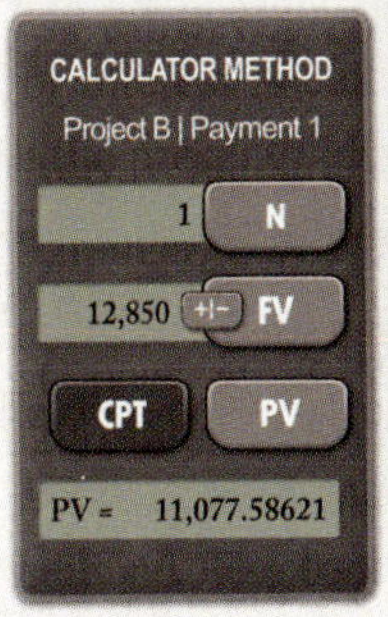

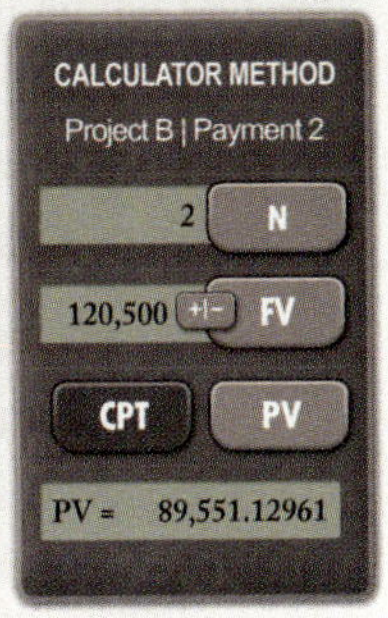

$j = 0.16, \quad m = 1, \quad i = \frac{j}{m} = \frac{0.16}{1} = 0.16$

Present Value of cash flows from Project B:

$$
\begin{aligned}
PV_{Cash\ Flows} &= 12{,}850(1 + 0.16)^{-1} + 120{,}500(1 + 0.16)^{-2} \\
&= 11{,}077.58621... + 89{,}551.12961... \\
&= 100{,}628.7158... = \$100{,}628.72
\end{aligned}
$$

Project B has a higher discounted cash flow than Project A.
Therefore, he should choose Project B.

Example 14.2(c) Evaluating an Investment Decision Using the DCF Method

Rombus Industries found out that if they purchase an automatic machine for $28,570, their profit would increase by $14,000 in the 1st year, $10,000 in the 2nd year, and $8000 in the 3rd year. At the end of the 3 years, the machine would have a salvage value (value at the end of its useful life) of $5000. Using the *Discounted Cash Flow* method, find out whether purchasing this machine is a sound investment decision if the required rate of return for the company is 20%.

Solution

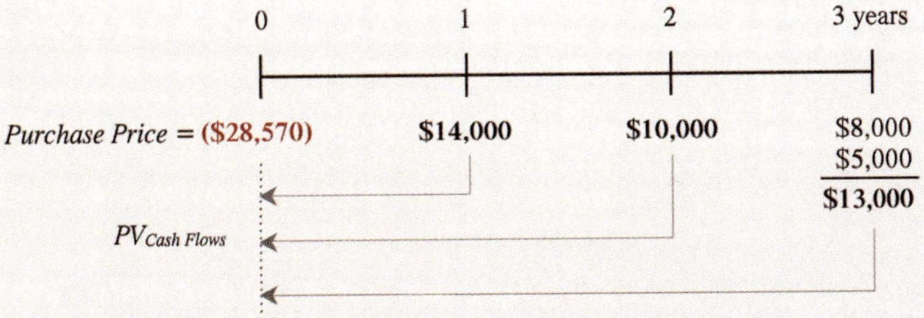

$j = 0.20, \quad m = 1, \quad i = \frac{j}{m} = \frac{0.20}{1} = 0.20$

Solution *continued*

Using the rearranged Formula 9.1(b), $PV = FV(1+i)^{-n}$

PV of cash flows including the salvage value at the end:

$$\begin{aligned} PV_{Cash\ Flows} &= 14{,}000(1+0.20)^{-1} \\ &\quad + 10{,}000(1+0.20)^{-2} \\ &\quad + 13{,}000(1+0.20)^{-3} \\ &= 11{,}666.666666... \\ &\quad + 6944.444444... \\ &\quad + 7523.148148... \\ &= 26{,}134.25926... = \$26{,}134.26 \end{aligned}$$

The PV of all returns, including the PV of the salvage value of the machine, is less than the purchase price of the machine.

Therefore, purchasing the machine would not be a sound investment decision.

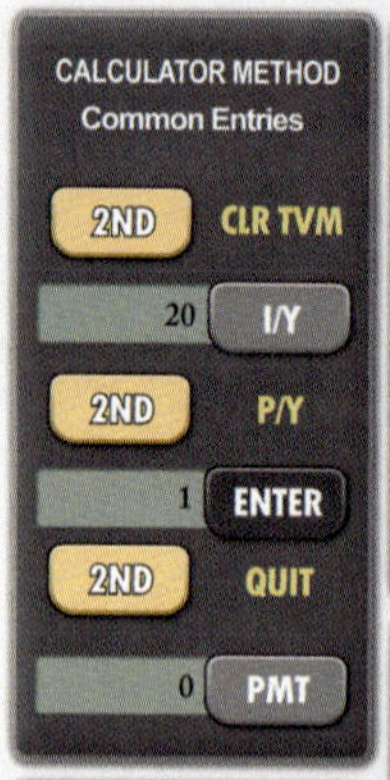

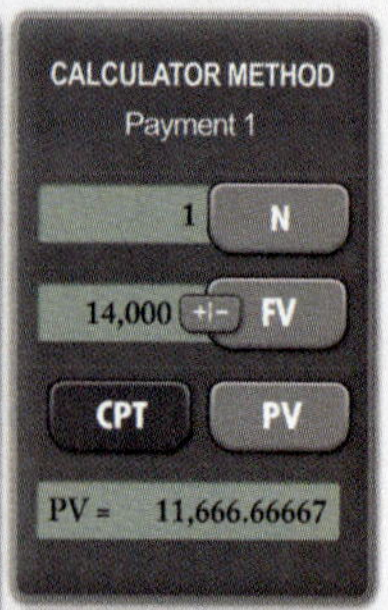

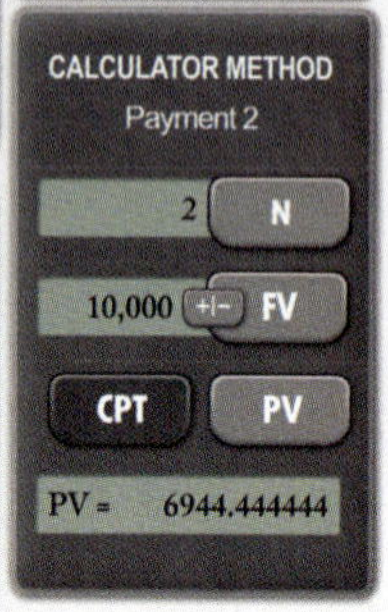

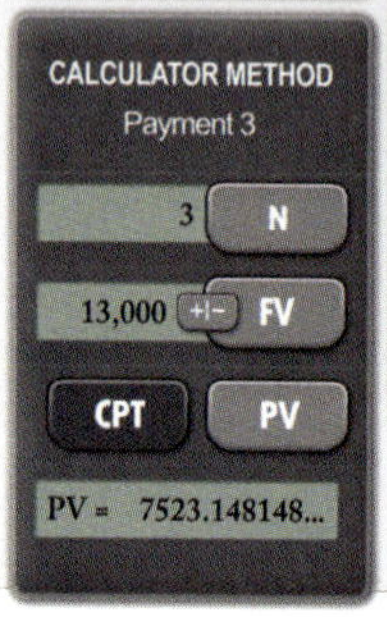

Example 14.2(d) **Evaluating Lease vs. Buy Option Using the DCF Method**

A salesman approached Meghan at a car showroom and offered her two financing options for a car that she liked:

- Lease option: Pay lease amounts of \$330 at the beginning of every month for 4 years. At the end of 4 years, purchase the car for \$15,000.
- Buy option: Purchase the car immediately for \$25,000.

Which option should she choose if money is worth 9% compounded monthly?

Solution

Lease Option

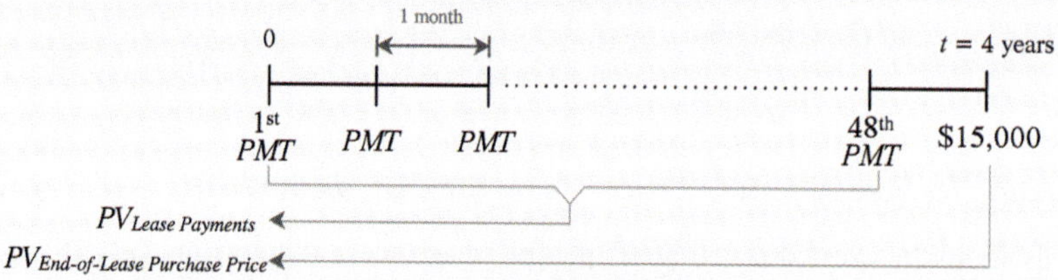

$$PMT = \$330$$

$$\begin{aligned} n &= 12 \text{ payments/year} \times 4 \text{ years} \\ &= 48 \text{ monthly payments} \end{aligned}$$

$$j = 0.09, \quad m = 12, \quad i = \frac{j}{m} = \frac{0.09}{12} = 0.0075 \text{ per month}$$

The lease payments form a simple annuity due.

Using Formula 10.4(b), $PV_{Due} = PMT\left[\frac{1-(1+i)^{-n}}{i}\right](1+i)$

$$\begin{aligned} PV_{Lease\ Payments} &= 330\left[\frac{1-(1+0.0075)^{-48}}{0.0075}\right](1+0.0075) \\ &= \$13{,}360.43536... \end{aligned}$$

Using Formula 9.1(b), $PV = FV(1+i)^{-n}$

$$PV_{End\text{-}of\text{-}Lease\ Purchase\ Price} = 15{,}000(1+0.0075)^{-48} = \$10{,}479.21204...$$

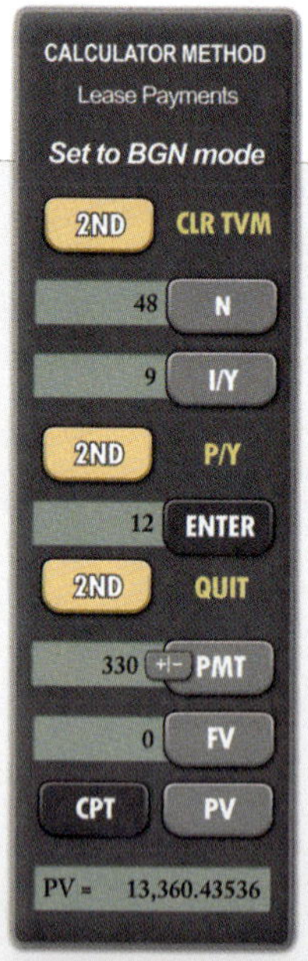

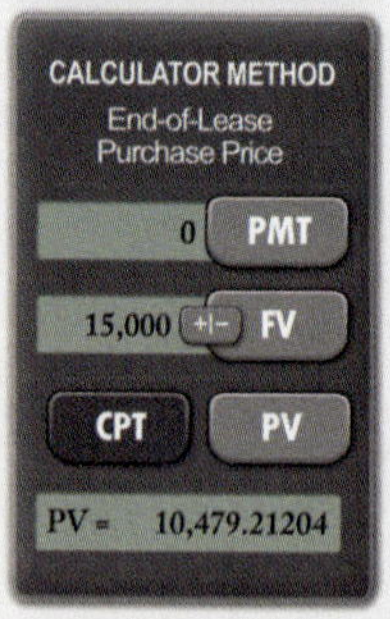

Solution continued

Therefore,

$$PV_{(Lease\ payments\ +\ End\text{-}of\text{-}Lease\ Purchase\ Price)} = 13{,}360.43536... + 10{,}479.21204...$$
$$= 23{,}839.6474... = \$23{,}839.65$$

Buy Option

The *PV* of the lease option is less than the buy option of purchasing it for $25,000.

Therefore, Meghan should choose the lease option.

14.2 | Exercises

1. Should a company invest $50,000 today in order to receive future cash flows of $10,000 in the 1st year, $20,000 in the 2nd year, and $30,000 in the 3rd year if their cost of capital is 10%?

2. John is assessing an investment in which he would have to spend $50,000 today in order to receive future cash flows of $30,000 in the 1st year, $20,000 in the 2nd year, and $10,000 in the 3rd year. Does this investment meet John's required rate of return of 10%?

3. A company is deciding between two marketing campaigns:
   - Campaign A will generate revenues of $120,000 in the 1st year and $30,000 in the 2nd year.
   - Campaign B will generate revenues of $40,000 in the 1st year and $120,000 in the 2nd year.

   Which option should they choose if the company's required rate of return is 20%?

4. A young investor is deciding between two investment options with equal costs.
   - Option 1 will provide returns of $30,000 in the 2nd year and $5000 in the 4th year.
   - Option 2 will provide returns of $20,000 in the 2nd year and $26,000 in the 4th year.

   Determine which option should the investor choose if his cost of capital is 12%.

5. A delivery service feels they could increase their profits by purchasing a new truck for $40,000. This should lead to increased profits of $20,000 in the 1st year, $15,000 in the 2nd year, and $5000 in the 3rd year. They could sell the truck at the end of 3 years for $15,000. Using the *discounted cash flow* method, find out whether purchasing this truck is a sound investment decision if the required rate of return for the company is 22% compounded annually.

6. A municipal government feels that they could reduce road maintenance costs by applying a special coating on the road. This project will cost $700,000 and is expected to reduce their costs by $200,000 in the 1st year, $300,000 in the 2nd year, and $400,000 in the 3rd year. If the government's required rate of return is 6% compounded annually, should they make this investment?

7. Amy was offered two options for a car she was purchasing:
   - Lease option: Pay lease amounts of $400 at the beginning of every month for 5 years. At the end of 5 years, purchase the car for $15,000.
   - Buy option: Purchase the car immediately for $25,000.

   Which option should she choose if money is worth 8% compounded monthly?

8. William is deciding between purchasing a new recreational vehicle for $120,000 or taking advantage of the financing option that requires him to pay amounts of $1600 at the beginning of every month for 8 years. At the end of 8 years, he could purchase the vehicle for $20,000. Which option should he choose if money is worth 11% compounded monthly?

9. Amanda was on a work contract in Canada for 5 years and was not sure if she had to rent an apartment or purchase an apartment and sell it when she leaves in 5 years. The total cost of the apartment she likes is $165,000 and other

costs would include maintenance and property tax payments of $500 to be made at the beginning of each month. She estimated that at the end of 5 years, she could sell the apartment for 10% more than what she had paid for it. However, renting the apartment would cost her $1000, to be paid at the beginning of each month for the entire period. Should she purchase the apartment or rent if money is worth:

a. 6% compounded monthly?

b. 5% compounded monthly?

10. Harris was evaluating the benefit of purchasing or leasing a colour laser printing machine for his office. The cost of the machine is $20,000 and he can sell it at the end of 5 years for $4500. He would also have to spend $1000 at the beginning of every month for supplies. However, if he leases it, he would only have to pay $1290 at the beginning of every month for the entire period and this amount would include supplies too.. Which option should he choose if money is worth:

    a. 3% compounded monthly.

    b. 4% compounded monthly.

14.3 | Net Present Value (NPV)

Net present value is a method of evaluating the feasibility of an investment decision by determining the difference between the Present Value of all cash inflows (returns) and the Present Value of all cash outflows (investments).

Formula 14.3 **Net Present Value**

$$NPV = PV_{Cash\ Inflows} - PV_{Cash\ Outflows}$$

Therefore,

Net present value (NPV) is the difference between the present value of cash inflows and the present value of all cash outflows.

$PV_{Cash\ Inflows} > PV_{Cash\ Outflows}$, NPV is greater than zero

$PV_{Cash\ Inflows} < PV_{Cash\ Outflows}$, NPV is less than zero

$PV_{Cash\ Inflows} = PV_{Cash\ Outflows}$, NPV is zero

To calculate the NPV of a project, a business must first determine their **required rate of return**. The required rate of return is used in discounting a project's cash flows in NPV calculations, which inform business decision-makers as to whether projects will produce an acceptable return.

If $NPV \geq 0$, Project is acceptable

If $NPV < 0$, Project should be rejected

When comparing different investment projects the project with the highest NPV should be chosen.

Example 14.3(a) **Evaluating Investment Decisions when Cash Flows are Capital Investments**

Blue Dreams Resort's senior management team is evaluating a project which will require an $80,000 investment. Based on their analysis, the project will generate future cash flows of $15,000 in the 1st year, $30,000 in the 2nd year, $45,000 in the 3rd year, and $25,000 in the 4th year. Given that the company requires a 10% rate of return on all of their investments, should they accept this project?

Solution This project can be evaluated by calculating its *NPV*.

Method 1

$$NPV = PV_{\text{Cash inflows}} - PV_{\text{Cash outflows}}$$

Cash inflows

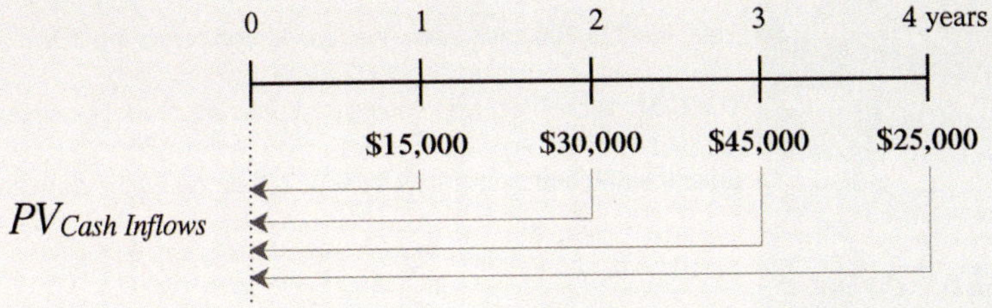

$$PV_{\textit{Cash Inflows}} = 15{,}000(1+0.10)^{-1} + 30{,}000(1+0.10)^{-2} + 45{,}000(1+0.10)^{-3} + 25{,}000(1+0.10)^{-4}$$

$$= 13{,}636.363636... + 24{,}793.388429... + 33{,}809.166040... + 17{,}075.336384...$$

$$= 89{,}314.25449... = \$89{,}314.25$$

Cash outflows

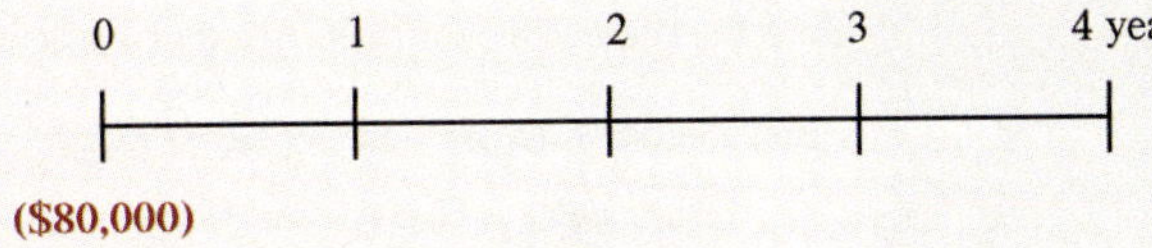

$$PV_{\textit{Cash Outflows}} = \$80{,}000$$

$$NPV = \$89{,}314.25 - \$80{,}000$$

$$= \$9314.25$$

$$NPV > 0$$

The *NPV* of the project is greater than zero; therefore, the company should accept this project.

Method 2

As shown on the next page, rather than seperately calculating the Present Value of all cash inflows and the Present Value of the cash outflows, we can calculate only cash inflows less cash outflows for every period (the Net Cash Flow) and calculate the Present Value of those amounts, to determine the Net Present Value. Most financial calculators require this format for evaluating the Net Present Value.

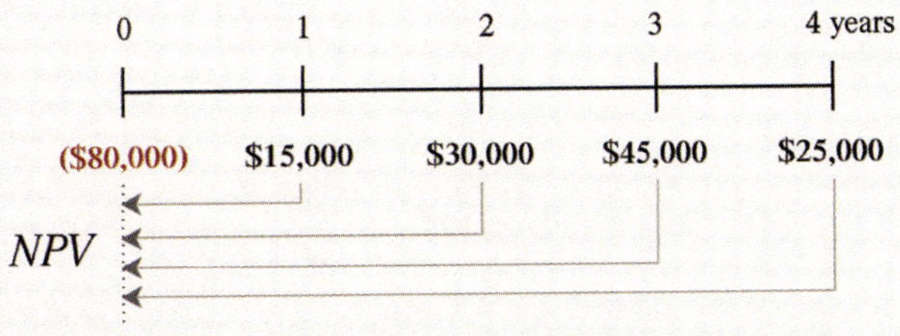

$$NPV = -80{,}000 + 15{,}000(1+0.10)^{-1} + 30{,}000(1+0.10)^{-2} + 45{,}000(1+0.10)^{-3} + 25{,}000(1+0.10)^{-4}$$

$$NPV = -80{,}000 + 13{,}636.363636... + 24{,}793.388429... + 33{,}809.166040... + 17{,}075.336384...$$

$$= \$9{,}314.25$$

$$NPV > 0$$

The *NPV* of the project is greater than zero; therefore, the company should accept this project.

Solution *continued*

CALCULATOR METHOD

CF	**Press CF** to open the Cash Flow Worksheet.
2ND CLR WORK	**Press 2ND** then **CLR WORK** *(secondary function of the CE|C button)* to clear previous work.
CFo = 80,000 +/- ENTER ↓	Enter the initial cash outflow (a negative value) of \$80,000, then **press** the **down arrow**.
C01 = 15,000 ENTER ↓	Enter the **\$15,000** cash inflow for year 1, then **press** the **down arrow**.
F01 = 1 ENTER ↓	The ***C01*** is only received once (i.e., it does not repeat for several years)
C02 = 30,000 ENTER ↓	Enter the **\$30,000** cash inflow for year 2, then **press** the **down arrow**.
F02 = 1 ENTER ↓	
C03 = 45,000 ENTER ↓	Enter the **\$45,000** cash inflow for year 3, then **press** the **down arrow**.
F03 = 1 ENTER ↓	
C04 = 25,000 ENTER ↓	Enter the **\$25,000** cash inflow for year 4, then **press** the **down arrow**.
F04 = 1 ENTER	Press **NPV**.
NPV	Enter the interest rate (discount rate for cash flows).
I = 10 ENTER ↓	**Press** the ***down arrow*** then press ***CPT*** to compute the value for ***NPV***.
NPV = 0 CPT	
NPV = 9314.254491	

Example 14.3(b)

Evaluating Investment Decisions when Cash flows are Capital Investments

The operations team at Hairpin Engineering Inc. was evaluating the feasibility of the following two projects that were required:

- Milling Project: Investment of \$260,000 in an automatic milling machine that would reduce wastage by \$180,000 in the 1st year and \$120,000 in the 2nd year.
- Grinding Project: Investment of \$120,860 in an automatic grinding machine that would reduce wastage by \$85,000 in the 1st year and \$116,000 in the 2nd year.

Are the projects feasible investments if their cost of capital is 12% compounded annually?

Solution

The reduction of wastage would be cash saved for the business and is considered a cash inflow.

Milling Project

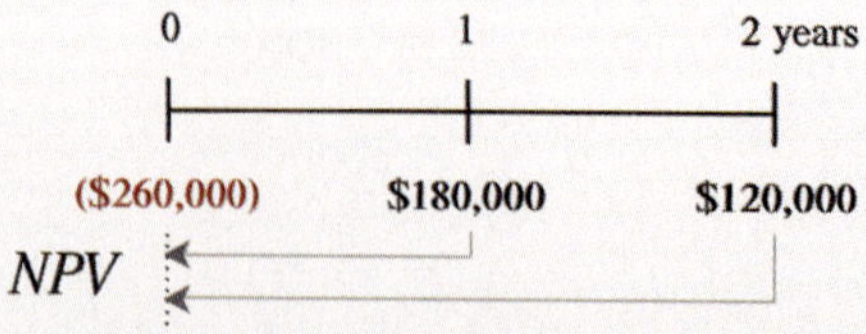

$$NPV_{Milling} = -260{,}000 + 180{,}000(1+0.12)^{-(1\times1)} + 120{,}000(1+0.12)^{-(1\times2)}$$

$$= -260{,}000.00 + 160{,}714.2857 + 95{,}663.26531$$

$$= -3622.44898... = -\$3622.45$$

$NPV_{Milling}$ is negative; therefore, it is not feasible.

CALCULATOR METHOD
Milling Project

- CF
- 2ND CLR WORK
- CFo = 260,000 +/- ENTER ↓
- C01 = 180,000 ENTER ↓
- F01 = 1 ENTER ↓
- C02 = 120,000 ENTER ↓
- F02 = 1 ENTER
- NPV
- I = 12 ENTER ↓
- NPV = 0 CPT
- NPV = -3622.44898

Solution *continued*

Grinding Project

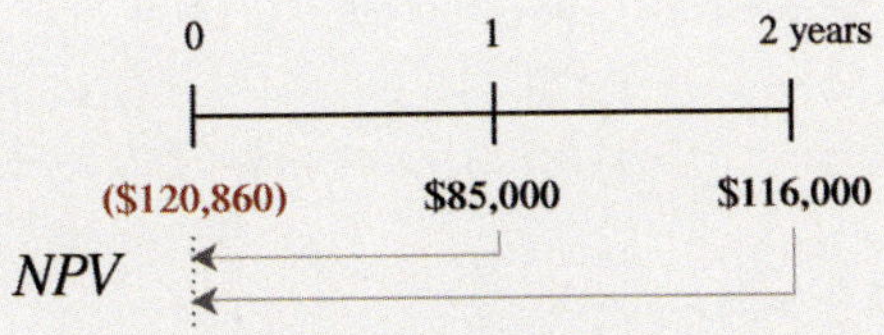

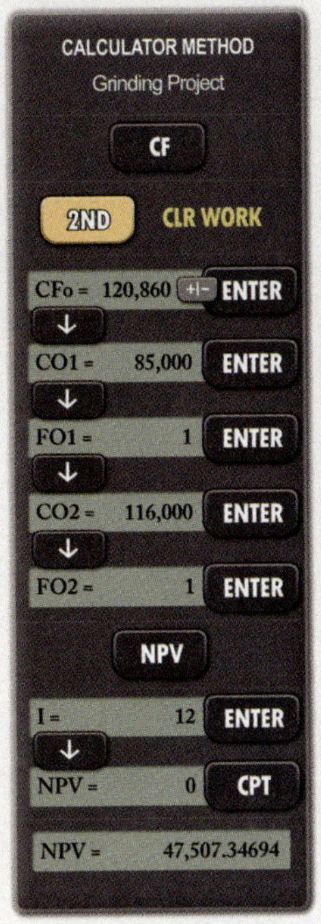

$$NPV_{Grinding} = -120{,}860 + 85{,}000(1 + 0.12)^{-(1\times1)} + 116{,}000(1 + 0.12)^{-(1\times2)}$$

$$= -120{,}860.00 + 75{,}892.85714... + 92{,}474.4898...$$

$$= 47{,}507.34694... = \$47{,}507.35$$

$NPV_{Grinding}$ is positive; therefore, they should choose Project Grinding.

Example 14.3(c)

Evaluating an Investment Decision when Cash Flows Form an Annuity

Martin was evaluating the feasibility of constructing a factory. He would require an initial investment of $1,470,000 followed by two more investments of $1,200,000 and $950,000 at the beginning of the 1st and 2nd years, respectively. The factory would start generating annual net income of $380,000 from year 2 onwards. He planned to sell the factory at the end of 8 years for $4,000,000. Is his plan profitable if his cost of capital is 15%?

Solution

Method 1

$$NPV = PV_{Cash\ Inflows} - PV_{Cash\ Outflows}$$

Cash inflows

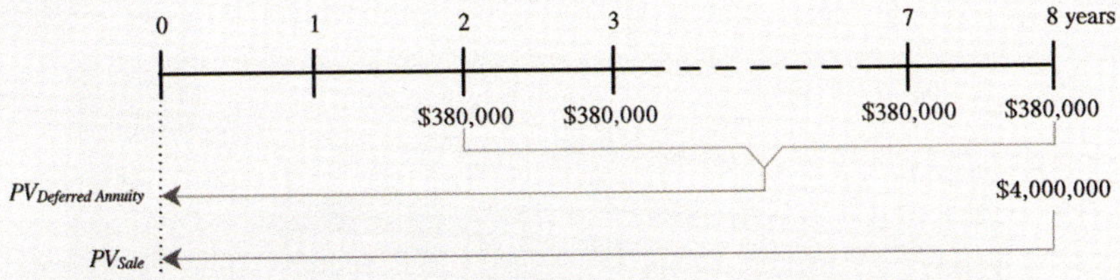

The Present Value of Cash inflows at the focal date can be calculated using the different approaches discussed in the Compound Interest and Annuities chapters. Let us consider the $380,000 annual net income from year 2 to year 8 as an ordinary deferred annuity (deferral period of one year), and the $4,000,000 single payment as shown on the line diagram.

$$PV_{Deferred\ Annuity} = 380{,}000\left[\frac{1-(1+0.15)^{-7}}{0.15}\right](1+0.15)^{-1}$$

$$= \$1{,}374{,}747.390314...$$

$$PV_{Sale} = 4{,}000{,}000(1+0.15)^{-8}$$

$$= \$1{,}307{,}607.095384...$$

Solution continued

$$PV_{Cash\ Inflows} = PV_{Deferred\ Annuity} + PV_{Sale}$$
$$= 1{,}374{,}747.390314... + 1{,}307{,}607.095384...$$
$$= 2{,}682{,}354.486...$$

Cash outflows

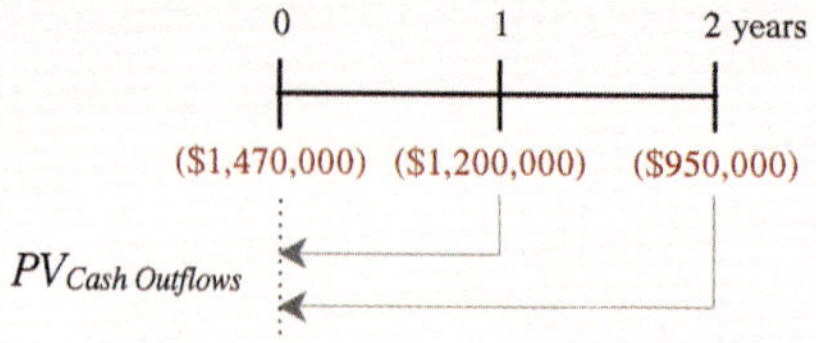

$$PV_{Cash\ Outflows} = 1{,}470{,}000 + 1{,}200{,}000(1+0.15)^{-1} + 950{,}000(1+0.15)^{-2}$$
$$= 1{,}470{,}000 + \$1{,}043{,}478.260869... + \$718{,}336.483931...$$
$$= \$3{,}231{,}814.745...$$
$$NPV = PV_{Cash\ Inflows} - PV_{Cash\ Outflows}$$
$$= 2{,}682{,}354.496... - 3{,}231{,}814.745...$$
$$= -549{,}460.2591... = -\$549{,}460.26$$

As the *NPV* is negative, this project would not cover Martin's cost of capital, and thus, would not be profitable for him.

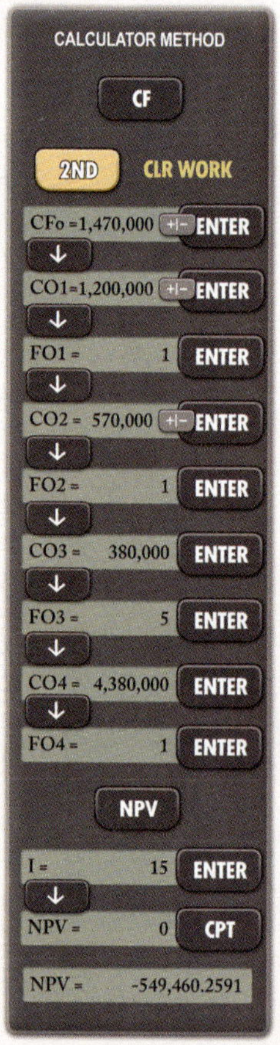

Method 2

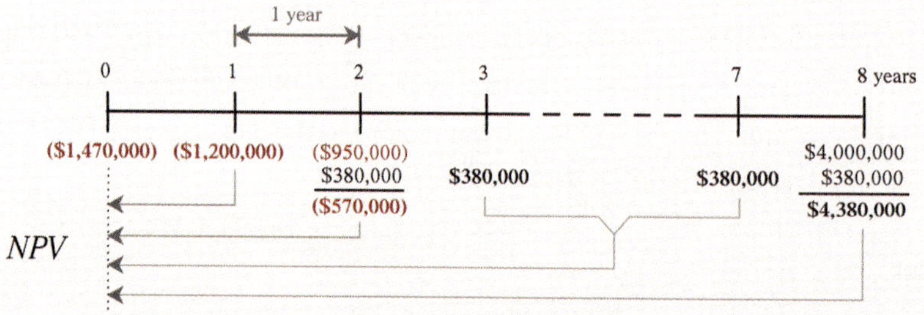

The net cash flow for each period must be calculated by subtracting all of the cash outflows from all of the cash inflows for each period.

When using the Texas Instruments BAII Plus Financial Calculator, a cash flow amount must be entered for every period.

If no cash flow exists for a particular period, enter 0 for that CF and 1 for the F0.

If more than one cash flow exists in a specific period, enter the net cash flow for that period.

14.3 | *Exercises*

1. Martha's hair salon is considering buying air-time for a television commercial to spread the word about their services and get clients during non-peak hours. Alternatively, they could invest in a cheaper newspaper ad campaign. They forecasted the following cash flows for the two options:
   - Television: Investment of $7500 today would increase profits by $6000 in the 1st year and $5000 in the 2nd year.

- Newspaper: Investment of $1000 today would increase profits by $1500 in the 1st year and $1050 in the 2nd year.

Which of these investments is better, and by how much, if its cost of capital is 20%?

2. A printing shop is evaluating the following two investments to improve their process.
   - Automate their printing press: Investment of $35,000 would increase profits by $40,000 in the 1st year and $20,000 in the 2nd year.
   - Purchase an automatic printing press: Investment of $150,000 would increase profits by $70,000 in the 1st year and $120,000 in the 2nd year.

   Which of these investments is better, and by how much, if their cost of capital is 18%?

3. The municipality of a city was evaluating the feasibility of purchasing a fleet of trucks for a total investment of $4,250,000. They forecasted that this purchase would generate profits of $880,500, $900,000, and $750,000, in the 1st, 2nd, and 3rd years, respectively. At the end of the 3rd year, they would sell the trucks for $3,000,000. Is this investment economical for them if their cost of capital is:

   a. 11% b. 12% c. 13%

   What is the NPV of the investment in each case?

4. The project manager of a steel manufacturing factory in Hamilton put forth a proposal to the senior management for the purchase of a specialized machine that costs $2,500,000. She forecasted that it would increase their profits through improved productivity by $1,200,000, $1,150,000, and $960,400, in the 1st, 2nd, and 3rd years, respectively. At the end of the 3rd year the machine would have a salvage value of $500,000. Is this investment economical for them if its cost of capital is:

   a. 15% b. 20% c. 25%

   What is the NPV of the investment in each case?

5. Harold purchased two trucks for his warehouse for a total of $65,000. This investment saved him $13,500 in truck rental charges every year (from the 1st year) for 10 years. At the end of the 10th year, he sold both the trucks for a total of $10,000. Was his investment in purchasing the trucks profitable if his cost of capital is 16%? What was the Net Present Value of the investment?

6. Gabrielle was spending a lot of money on outsourcing her printing jobs to a local printer. To save costs, she purchased a $18,500 colour laser printing machine for her office. This investment saved her $3250 every year (from the 1st year) for 8 years. At the end of the 8th year, she sold the printer machine for $2500. Was her purchase profitable if her cost of capital is 12%? What was the Net Present Value of the investment?

• 7. Samuel Semiconductors plan to invest $1,500,000 in the 1st year on a research project and $1,650,000 in the 2nd year. They forecast that they would start making a net income of $640,000 from the 3rd year onwards for 10 years, at the end of which, they would sell the project for $2,500,000. Is this project feasible? What is the Net Present Value of the project if their cost of capital is 18%? (Hint: there is no initial outlay for this project).

• 8. Coupix Inc. was developing a complex mobile application that required an investment of $1,200,000 in the 1st year and $1,350,000 in the 2nd year. The application started generating revenues of $1,000,000 from the 3rd year onwards for 3 years, at the end of which Coupix sold the application to a competitor for $3,500,000. What is the Net Present Value of the development if their cost of capital of 20%? (Hint: there is no initial outlay in this project).

• 9. Madrid Developers was evaluating the feasibility of constructing an amusement park. Construction would require an initial outlay of $3,230,000, then $1,600,000 in the 2nd year, and $450,000 in the 3rd year. Net income from the 2nd year onwards is expected to be $900,000 every year for 9 years. It would finally sell the park for $10,850,000 at the end of the 10th year. Is this plan profitable if the expected rate of return is 20% compounded annually? What is the Net Present Value of the development?

- 10. Microhaul Inc. is planning on building a private transportation network in London, Ontario. Construction would require an initial outlay of $1,230,000, then $250,000 in the 2nd year, and $150,000 in the 3rd year. Net income from the 2nd year onwards is expected to be $600,000 every year for 7 years. It had plans to sell the system to the government for $2,000,000 at the end of the 8th year. What is the Net Present Value of this plan at a cost of capital of 8% compounded annually?

14.4 | Internal Rate of Return (IRR)

The **Internal Rate of Return** (*IRR*) is the effective (annually compounding) rate of return for an investment. The *IRR* is the discount rate at which the *NPV* of an investment is zero; that is, the *IRR* is the rate of return that makes the present value of all cash inflows equal to the present value of all cash outflows ($PV_{Cash\ Inflows} = PV_{Cash\ Outflows}$). It is also called the **Return on Investment** (*ROI*).

As described earlier, the rate of return used to calculate the *NPV* is the **required rate of return** that the business expects from investing in this project. This required rate of return is generally the **cost of capital** (*i*), which is the opportunity cost of investing; i.e., the rate of return the business would otherwise earn when the amount is invested in another investment that has the same risk level as this project.

Projects are accepted if the internal rate of return is greater than or equal to the cost of capital (i) and projects are rejected if the IRR is less than the cost of capital (i).

In summary,

If $NPV = 0$, $IRR = i$, Project is acceptable

If $NPV > 0$, $IRR > i$, Project is acceptable

If $NPV < 0$, $IRR < i$, Project should be rejected

The higher a project's *IRR*, the more profitable the project (relative to the initial investment). As such, the *IRR* can be used to rank projects that a business is considering. When comparing investment projects, the project that has the highest *IRR* should be accepted.

Solving for a project's *IRR* using algebra alone is difficult and it can be computed only by trial and error. Using a financial calculator (such as the Texas Instruments BAII Plus) automates this trial and error process, and it becomes much more feasible to compute the *IRR* for several projects. We will be focusing on this approach in the following example.

Example 14.4 Calculating IRR for a Project

A company developed a product that required investments of $60,000 each year for the first three years. The sale of the product generated a profit of $35,000 in the 4th year and yearly profits of $40,000 for the next 9 years, at the end of which, the patent on the product was sold for $55,000.

a. Calculate the internal rate of return of this project.

b. If the company's required rate of return (cost of capital) is 14%, was it feasible for them to undertake this project?

Solution

The internal rate of return can be algebraically calculated by trial and error. This is a time consuming process, especially if we want to arrive at an accurate answer. However, a financial calculator can be used to accurately calculate the internal rate of return.

Solution continued

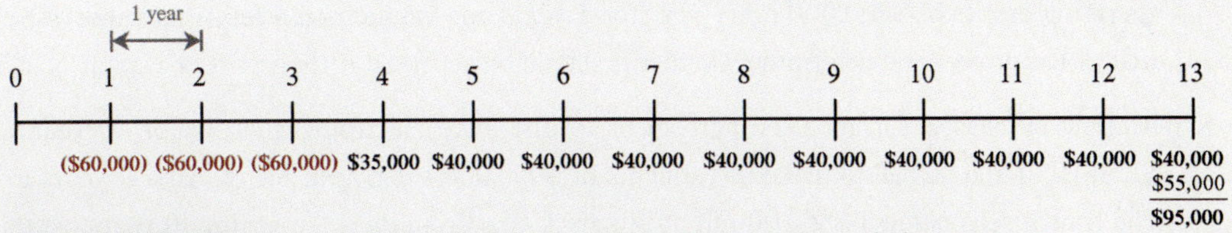

The *NPV* can also be calculated on your financial calculator as shown below.

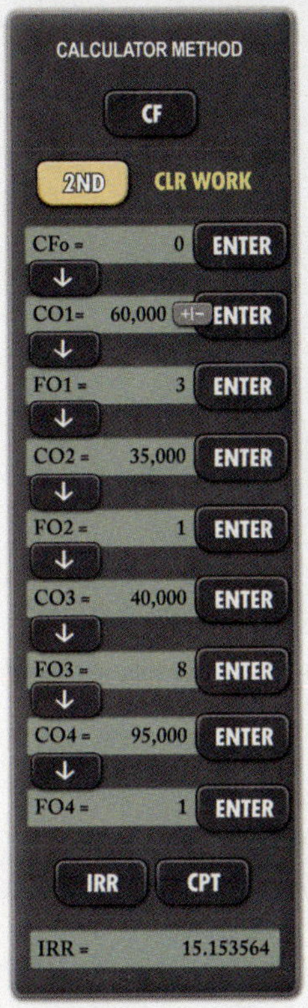

Press CF to open the Cash Flow Worksheet.

Press 2ND then **CLR WORK** (secondary function of the CE|C key) to clear previous work.

Enter 0 (there is no initial cash flow).

Enter the **$60,000** cash outflow (as a **negative** value).

Enter the number of cash flows for CO1. The $60,000 payment will be made **3** times.

Enter the **$35,000** cash inflow.

Enter the number of cash flows for CO2 (one cash flow)

Enter the **$40,000** cash inflow.

Enter the number of cash flows for CO3. There are **8** years in which the total inflow is $40,000.

Enter the total cash inflow of **$95,000** in the final year.

Enter the number of cash flows for CO4 (one cash flow)

Press IRR and **CPT** to compute the internal rate of return.

The *NPV* of the project is greater than zero; therefore, the company should accept this project.

a. Therefore, the internal rate of return for this project is 15.15%.

b. The IRR of 15.15% is higher than the company's cost of capital of 14%. It was therefore feasible for them to undertake this project.

14.4 | Exercises

1. Calculate the internal rate of return on a project that requires an initial investment of $35,000 and additional investments of $5000 in the 1st, 2nd, and 3rd years. It will generate $20,000 every year in profits from the 4th year onwards for 10 years at the end of which it will have no terminal value.

2. A research project would require an initial investment of $50,000 and additional investments of $850,000 every year from the 1st year onwards for 5 years. It would generate cost savings of $1,200,000 every year for the business from the 6th year onwards for 12 years. Calculate the IRR of the project.

3. Cheng was evaluating the feasibility of a project that has an initial investment of $200,000 and subsequent investments of $180,000 every year in the 1st and 2nd years. From the 3rd year onwards, it will generate cost savings of $250,000 every year for 7 years. If the project has a terminal value of $100,000, calculate its IRR. Should the project be accepted if the company's cost of capital is 30%?

4. Umar and Ali were planning to commence a project. They required $250,000 as an initial investment and $110,000 as subsequent investments in the 1st, 2nd, and 3rd year. From the 4th year onwards, the project would generate

operating profits of $400,000 every year for 5 years and would have a terminal value of $200,000. Calculate the IRR of the project and determine whether it should be accepted if their cost of capital is 30%?

5. Andrew purchased a franchisee agreement to distribute electronic gadgets for 10 years. The agreement costs $1,500,000 and he had to make investments of $950,000 every year for the first 2 years to set up his showroom. The franchise generated $850,000 in profits each year from the 1st year, for 10 years. At the end of the 10th year, he sold the furniture in his showroom for $20,000. Calculate the IRR of this investment. Should he have proceeded with this plan if his cost of capital was 25%?

6. Production Co. hired a management consulting firm to execute a new project launch. The consulting firm charged the company $180,000 as an initial appraisal fee, and $750,000 every year for the first 2 years to support the execution of the launch. Through the launch, Production Co. had profits of $450,000 every year from the 1st year, onwards for 10 years. If the project had no terminal value, calculate the IRR of this consulting engagement. If the company's required rate of return is 40%, was it worthwhile for them to hire this consulting firm?

7. Calculate the IRR of Harold's investment in Problem 5 of Exercise 14.3. Was it higher than his cost of capital?

8. Calculate the IRR of Gabrielle's investment in Problem 6 of Exercise 14.3. Was it higher than her cost of capital?

9. Calculate the IRR of Madrid Developers's project in Problem 9 of Exercise 14.3. Was it higher than its cost of capital?

10. Calculate the IRR of Microhaul Inc.'s construction project in Problem 10 of Exercise 14.3. Was it higher than its cost of capital?

14.5 | Payback Period

The payback period is the length of time required for an investment to break even, where the cash inflows reach the amount of the inital cash outlay.

The payback period is calculated as the ratio of the project's cost to its the annual cash inflows. For example, if a project costs $275,000 and it produces regular annual cash inflows of $50,000, then,

$$Payback\ Period = \frac{275,000}{50,000} = 5.5 \text{ years} = 5 \text{ years and } 6 \text{ months}$$

We can also find this value using a table (which is necessary if cash flows are not the same from year to year). The first two columns in the table show cash inflows (positive) and outflows (negative). The third column, Net Cash Flows, shows the difference between cash inflows and cash outflows for every year. The Cumulative Cash Flow column represents the total Net Cash Flows for the current year and all previous years. Once the Cumulative Cash Flow reaches zero, the project has reached its payback period.

	Cash Outflow	Cash Inflow	Net Cash Flows	Cumulative Cash Flow
Year 1	($275,000)	$50,000	($225,000)	($225,000)
Year 2	–	50,000	50,000	(175,000)
Year 3	–	50,000	50,000	(125,000)
Year 4	–	50,000	50,000	(75,000)
Year 5	–	50,000	50,000	(25,000)
Year 6	–	50,000	50,000	25,000

The cumulative cash flow shows that the company will break even in year 6 (it only needs $25,000 in year 6 to break even, which it will exceed).

$$Payment\ Period = \left(5 + \frac{25,000}{50,000}\right) = \left(5 + \frac{1}{2}\right) \text{ years}$$

$$= 5 \text{ years and 6 months}$$

The Payback Period Method ignores the time value of money and also ignores any benefits that occur after the payback period. Despite these deficiencies, the method is often used due for its simplicity.

Investors and businesses often employ a 'Payback Rule', which requires that all projects that are undertaken must not have a payback period exceeding a certain amount of time, such as 5 years. If the investment costs are recovered sooner, then the additional cash inflows can be reinvested into other projects. For this reason, investments with shorter payback periods may be considered less risky.

Example 14.5(a) **Evaluating Invesment Decisions using a Payback Rule**

Stewart Bradley Inc. is evaluating a project which will require a $40,000 investment. Based on analysis, the project will generate future cash flows of $7,000 in year 1, $15,000 in year 2, $22,000 in year 3, and $10,000 in year 4. Should the company accept the project if it has a payback rule of 3 years?

Solution

	Cash Outflow	Cash Inflow	Net Cash Flows	Cumulative Cash Flow
Year 1	($40,000)	$7,000	($33,000)	($33,000)
Year 2	–	15,000	15,000	(18,000)
Year 3	–	22,000	22,000	4000
Year 4	–	10,000	10,000	14,000

The cumulative cash flow shows that the company will break even in year 3 (it only needs $18,000 in year 3 to break even, which it will exceed).

$$Payment\ Period = \left(2 + \frac{18,000}{22,000}\right) = \left(2 + \frac{9}{11}\right) \text{ years}$$

$$= 2 \text{ years and 10 months (rounded up to the next month)}$$

The payback period is below the payback rule; therefore, the company should accept the project.

Example 14.5(b) **Evaluating Invesment Decisions using a Payback Rule**

A software company invested $120,000 to purchase a product from a competitor, and invested an additional $100,000 every year for the next 2 years to convert the product into a new service offering. When the service entered the market, it generated yearly profits of $60,000 from the 4th year, for the next 8 years, at the end of which, the underlying technology was sold for $800,000.

a. Calculate this project's payback period.

b. Does this satisfy the company's payback rule of 7 years?

Solution

	Cash Outflow	Cash Inflow	Net Cash Flows	Cumulative Cash Flow
Year 1	($120,000)	–	($120,000)	($120,000)
Year 2	(100,000)	–	(100,000)	(220,000)
Year 3	(100,000)	–	(100,000)	(320,000)
Year 4	–	$60,000	60,000	(260,000)
Year 5	–	60,000	60,000	(200,000)
Year 6	–	60,000	60,000	(140,000)
Year 7	–	60,000	60,000	(80,000)
Year 8	–	60,000	60,000	(20,000)
Year 9	–	60,000	60,000	40,000

The cumulative cash flow shows that the company will break even in year 9. Only $20,000 is needed to break even in year 9, but there are cash inflows of $60,000.

$$\textit{Payment Period} = \left(8 + \frac{20,000}{60,000}\right) = \left(8 + \frac{1}{3}\right) \text{ years}$$

$$= 8 \text{ years and } 4 \text{ months}$$

The payback period exceeds 7 years; therefore, it does not satisfy the company's payback rule.

14.5 | Exercises

1. KFX Corporation is considering a $40,000 investment which will provide cash inflows of $5000, $20,000, $25,000, and $45,000 in the 2nd, 3rd, 4th, and 5th years, respectively. The company has a payback rule of 4 years. What is the payback period and should the company undertake the investment?

2. Kabab Co. is considering a $260,000 investment which will provide cash inflows of $100,000, $150,000, and $200,000 in the 2nd, 3rd, and 4th years, respectively. The company has a payback rule of 3 years. What is the payback period and should the company undertake the investment?

3. In 2011, a distributor of fishing and camping equipment paid $225,000 to sponsor an event that was scheduled to take place in 3 years. They also paid $175,000 in 2012 and $100,000 in 2013 towards the sponsorship of the event. The sponsorship increased the company's brand awareness, leading to increased profits of $120,000 every year from 2013 onwards for 5 years. What is the payback period of the sponsorship and does it satisfy the distributor's payback rule of 6 years?

4. A movie studio invested $60 million to produce a film. This budget was exhausted in the 1st year, before the film was completed. It cost an additional $15 million in the 2nd year to complete the film. The film earned $40 million in the 3rd year, $25 million in the 4th year, and went on to earn $3 million every year for 5 years. Calculate the payback period on the film project and determine whether this satisfies the studio's 8-year payback rule.

• 5. Richard purchased a business for $200,000, borrowing from a family member to finance the purchase. The business generated profits of $50,000 every year from the 1st year. From the 2nd year onwards, Richard withdrew a salary of $45,000 per annum. In the 4th year, he spent $20,000 to renovate his showroom to attract more customers. This increased his profits to $130,000 every year starting from the 5th year. What was the payback period on the business? Does this meet his payback rule of $4\frac{1}{2}$ years?

- 6. Clara operates a specialized financial services business in Toronto. She's currently considering purchasing an exclusive service agreement from a rival for $120,000, but would like to ensure that the investment would meet her payback rule of 5 years. The service agreement would guarantee earnings of $30,000 per year, but would also require her to pay $15,000 for a regulatory audit every other year (starting from the 1st year). What is the payback period on this investment, and does it satisfy Clara's payback rule?

14 | Review Exercises

Answers to odd-numbered problems are available at the end of the textbook

1. An investment of $500,000 will generate cost savings of $100,000 every year for the first 6 years and $45,000 for the next 4 years. If there is no terminal value for the project, calculate its IRR.

2. An investment of $180,000 will generate operating profits of $50,000 every year for the first 2 years and $30,000 every year for the next 5 years. If the project has a terminal value of $5000, calculate its IRR.

3. A pharmaceutical company is developing a new pill that requires an initial investment of $1,550,000 and subsequent investments of $600,000 every year for 3 years. They anticipate that it will generate profits of $750,000, $1,000,000 and $1,250,000 in the 4th, 5th, and 6th years, respectively, at the end of which, the patents on the pill can be sold to a competing firm for $3,000,000. What is the IRR of this project? Is it feasible if the company's cost of capital is 15%?

4. The development of a new robotic machine required an initial investment of $780,000 and subsequent investments of $560,000 every year for 4 years. The team forecasted cost savings of $1,150,000, $1,200,000, and $1,610,000 in the 5th, 6th, and 7th years, respectively, at the end of which the machine would have a salvage value of $540,000. Calculate the IRR of this project and would it be feasible if the company's cost of capital is 10%?

5. Hydra Corp. is assessing an investment which would require $300,000 today and would provide future cash flows of $200,000 in the 1st year, $120,000 in the 2nd year, and $25,000 in the 3rd year. What is the IRR of the investment and does it meet the company's IRR of 10% if it has no terminal value?

6. Massey is assessing an investment in which she would have to pay $20,000 today to receive future cash flows of $15,000 in 1st year, $5000 in the 2nd year, and $10,000 in the third year. If the investment has no terminal value, what is its IRR and does it meet Massey's IRR of 20%?

7. Gabriel is deciding between purchasing a truck for $80,000 or taking advantage of another option where he pays $5000 immediately and then $10,000 at the end of every year for 10 years. At the end of 10 years, he would have to pay $15,000 to own the truck. Using the discounted cash flow method, calculate which option is cheaper, and by how much, if money is worth 7% compounded annually?

8. A new car model is selling for $19,000 but also has a financing option available which requires payments of $230 at the beginning of every month for 4 years, at the end of which, there is an option to purchase the vehicle for $10,000. Which option would be cheaper, and by how much, if money is worth 5% compounded monthly?

9. Louise, a senior manager at Tulip Waters LLP., is evaluating a proposal for the purchase of an automatic machine that costs $3,000,000. She forecasts that it would increase profits by $600,000, $1,800,000, and $2,200,000, in the 1st, 2nd, and 3rd years, respectively. At the end of the 3rd year the machine would have a salvage value of $500,000. Is this investment economical for them if their cost of capital is:

   a. 15% b. 20% c. 26%

   What is the NPV of the investment in each case?

10. A roof tiler is considering the purchase of the new machine at a cost of $20,000. This will enable him to save $6000, $12,000, and $11,000 in the 1st, 2nd, and 3rd years, respectively. He could sell the machine at a scrap value of $500 at the end of the 3rd year. Is this investment economical for him if his cost of capital is:

    a. 15% b. 20% c. 22%

    What is the NPV of the investment in each case?

11. In an attempt to save on their electricity bill, Mr. and Mrs. Gloucester spent $7000 to install solar panels on the roof of their home. This saved them $1000 every year (from the 1st year) for 12 years. At the end of the 12th year, they spent $500 to uninstall the panels and throw them away. Was this installation worthwhile if their cost of capital was 16%? What was the NPV of the installation?

12. Bluestine Inc. opened a sales office at a cost of $1,100,000. The office generated consistent profits of $300,000 every year (from the 1st year) for 5 years, at the end of the which, the office was forced to pay a $200,000 fine and close immediately. Calculate the net present value of the venture if the company's cost of capital was 7%?

13. A provincial government spent $960,000 to lay the foundation for a new set of toll roads. It spent an additional $4,350,000 in the 1st year, and $2,200,000 in the 2nd year, to construct the roads. The province then spent $2,400,000 in the 3rd year to finalize the project. The toll roads generated a consistent return of $700,000 every year from the 3rd year onwards, for 10 years. There are plans to privatize the system at the end of the 12th year by selling the network of toll roads for $5,000,000. What is the net present value of this investment for the government if their cost of capital was 2.5%?

14. Two friends started a company to build a product, spending $30,000 in their 1st year to build a prototype, and $90,000 in the 2nd year to scale it to their target market. They were able to generate $10,000 in revenues every year from the 2nd year, for 4 years, at the end of which they sold the company to a larger company, for $140,000. Calculate the IRR of project and determine whether it was profitable if the company's cost of capital is 15.5%.

15. A family bakery was established with an investment of $60,000. In its 1st year, they broke even. During its 2nd year, it required an additional $12,000 investment to survive. From its 3rd year onwards, the business generated consistent profits of $25,000, for 4 years, at the end of which it was sold for $35,000. Calculate the IRR of the investment in the business and determine whether it was profitable at a cost of capital of 20%.

16. A consulting firm offered a large factory the following proposal for their consulting services:

    - A payment of $60,000 to be made immediately for a thorough analysis of the current situation.
    - After analysis, payments of $300,000 to be made every year from the 1st year for 3 years to develop and implement a cost savings strategy.

    The consulting firm guarantees $310,000 in annual cost savings for 6 years from the 4th year. If the project had no terminal value, calculate the IRR of this consulting engagement. If the factory's required rate of return is 18%, was it feasible for them to hire this consulting firm?

17. A farmer purchased a machine for $60,000 in the hopes of increasing the productivity of his farm. The machine had a positive impact resulting in increased profits of $20,000 every year from the 2nd year onwards, for 6 years. In the 3rd year, the machine required repairs costing $8000. What is the payback period of the machine? Does it satisfy the farmer's 4-year payback rule?

18. Heartlife Finance lent $40,000 to a businesswoman to start a new business. The business did not earn any revenues in its 1st year and required an additional $20,000 investment from Heartlife Finance to continue operating into the 2nd year. From the 2nd year onwards, however, the business was able to generate profits of $25,000 for 7 consecutive years. Being a relatively small financier, Heartlife uses a 3-year payback rule on all of their small business investments. What is the payback period of this investment and does it satisfy the payback rule?

19. Hillary wanted to grow a small orchard on a property she owned in Niagara. She spent $20,000 in the 1st year to plant the trees and $6000 per year for the next 4 years to grow the trees. The orchard generated profits of $12,000 per year from the 5th year onwards. What is the payback period on the orchard and would it have satisfied a 7-year payback rule.

20. A large corporation purchased a start-up company for $600,000. The start-up generated profits of $120,000 in the 1st year, $80,000 in the 2nd year, and $75,000 in the 3rd year. In the 3rd year, the parent corporation invested $135,000 in a change initiative to transform the start-up into a high performer. They were successful in increasing profits to $200,000 per year from the 4th year onwards. What is the payback period on the investment in the start-up company and would it have satisfied a 6-year payback rule.

14 | Self-Test Exercises

Answers to all problems are available at the end of the textbook

1. A young investor is deciding between two investment options with equal costs.
   - Option 1 will provide returns of $40,000 in the 2nd year and $11,000 in the 5th year.
   - Option 2 will provide returns of $15,000 in the 2nd year and $40,000 in the 5th year.

   Determine which option is better, and by how much, if his cost of capital is 10%.

2. A fast-food restaurant chain would like to introduce a new chilled desert to their menu, but will need to invest in ice-cream machines for all of its restaurants. This upgrade will cost $200,000 and is expected to generate earnings of $125,000, $70,000, and $60,000, in the 1st, 2nd, and 3rd years, respectively. What is the IRR of this investment? Should they make this investment if their required rate of return is 15%?

3. A cell-phone manufacturer is evaluating the following two investments to improve their process.
   - Upgrade plastic molder: Investment of $75,000 would increase profits by $60,000 in the 1st year and $45,000 in the 2nd year.
   - Upgrade conveyer system: Investment of $320,000 would increase profits by $200,000 in the 1st year and $250,000 in the 2nd year.

   Which of these investments is better, and what is its IRR?

4. A senior member in a research organization had the opportunity to undertake a patent development project, but had to justify its economic viability. The project would require salaries and other expenses in the amount of $650,000, $725,000, and $550,000, in the 1st, 2nd, and 3rd years, respectively. The patent would then be marketed to various companies, generating annual royalties of $800,000 from the 4th year, onwards for 4 years, at the end of which, the royalty rights would be sold to a major manufacturer for $300,000. What is the IRR of this development project? If the research organization has a cost of capital of 18%, would this project be acceptable?

5. A software development project would require investments of $400,000 every year for 4 years. It would generate profits of $620,000 from the 5th year for 6 years. If the project has no terminal value, calculate its IRR.

6. Flock Investments Corp. purchased a trading license, which would allow them to provide a financial product to major Canadian banks for the next 12 years. It costs the company $450,000 to purchase the license and they had to allow for a regulator to investigate their firm during the first two years at their own cost of $10,000 per year. The agreement gave them profits of $180,000 every year from the 1st year, for 12 years. At the end of 12 years, they sold the license to another company for $500,000. What was Flock's IRR and did this investment satisfy the company's required rate of return of 30%?

7. Jason is considering a $50,000 investment which will provide cash inflows of $6000, $25,000, $30,000, and $55,000 in the 2nd, 3rd, 4th, and 5th years, respectively. What is the payback period and should Jacques undertake the investment if his payback rule is 3 years?

8. Holdon Ltd. purchased a small paragliding business for $300,000. The business is expected to provide revenues of $250,000 every year, starting from the 1st year, and has annual expenses of $120,000, as well as special licensing fees of $10,000 every year. What is the payback period on this investment and does it meet the company's 2-year payback rule?

CASE 14

Lease or Finance Option

Henry graduated from college and found a job as an online marketing specialist in a social networking company. Within a year, he saved $2000 and decided to buy a new car. He narrowed down on the car he wanted to buy but was not sure if he should lease it or buy it by financing the amount from a bank.

A car salesman at the showroom gave him the following tables illustrating the comparison of the lease vs. finance option for the car he liked.

Description	Leasing the car	Financing the car
List Price	$21,500.00	$21,500.00
Additional Purchase Costs*	$1,817.00	$1,817.00
13% HST	–	$3031.21
Net Price	$23,317.00	$26,348.21
Down payment	$2000.00	$2000.00
Term in months	48	48
APR**	4.75%	5.25%
Monthly payments	$250.00 + 13% HST = $282.50 (month-beginning payments)	$562.13 (month-end payments)
Residual value***	$12,453.56+ 13% HST = $14,072.52	N/A

**Additional purchase costs include freight & PDI, Air Conditioner Tax, Tire Tax, and registration fees .*

*** The Annual Percentage Rate (APR) is the effective interest rate or annually compounding interest rate.*

**** This is the amount he would have to pay to own the car at the end of the lease period.*

Assume that money is worth 5.50% compounded annually.

a. Which option would be economically better for Henry?

b. Which option would be economically better if the residual value was $15,500 for the lease option instead of $14,072.52?

c. Which option would be economically better if the monthly lease payments were $205.00 instead of $250.00 and the residual value was $15,500?

d. Calculate the new Annual Percentage Rate (APR) with the new monthly lease payments and residual value in (c).

14 | Summary of Notation and Formulas

NOTATION

DCF: Discounted Cash Flow

NPV: Net Present Value

IRR: Internal Rate of Return

FORMULAS

Net Present Value | 14.2

$$NPV = PV_{Cash\ Inflows} - PV_{Cash\ Outflows}$$

Answer Key

Chapter 1

Exercises 1.1

1. i. a) 5,000,000 + 200,000 + 40,000 + 9000 + 300 + 40 + 6
   b) Five million, two hundred forty-nine thousand, three hundred forty-six
   ii. a) 90,000,000 + 5,000,000 + 200,000 + 70,000 + 5000 + 300 + 80 + 5
   b) Ninety-five million, two hundred seventy-five thousand, three hundred eighty-five
   iii. a) 1,000,000,000 + 100,000,000 + 40,000,000 + 6,000,000 + 40,000 + 5000 + 700 + 80 + 7
   b) One billion, one hundred forty-six million, forty-five thousand, seven hundred eighty-seven
   iv. a) 200 + 90 + 7 + 0.50
   b) Two hundred ninety-seven point five zero

3. a) 65,244.34 b)12,452,832
   c) 125,000 d) 500,000,000

5. a) 89,613,522.13 b) 16,217,567
   c) 500,000 d) 750,000,000,000

7. a) 1650 b) 10,000 c) $26,000 d) $900

9. a) 132.1 b) 3 c) 85.43 d) 34.99

11. i. a) 6% b) 5.6%
   ii. a) 30% b) 29.9%
   iii. a) 75% b) 75.3%
   iv. a) 116% b) 115.8%

13. a) 5.57% b) 29.88% c) 75.25% d) 115.80%

15. a) 1800 b) 690 c) 1890
   d) 190 e) 500 f) 610

17. a) 1700 b) 700 c) 1900
   d) 100 e) 400 f) 600

19. a) 4800 b) 23,500 c) 7000
   d) 9 e) 20 f) 5

21. $0.03

23. 56%, 35%, 2%, 7%

Exercises 1.2

1. a) Prime: { 2, 3, 5, 7 }; Composite: { 4, 6, 8, 9 }
   b) Prime: { 17, 19, 23 }; Composite: { 15, 16, 18, 20, 21, 22, 24, 25, 26, 27}
   c) Prime: { 37, 41 }; Composite: { 33, 34, 35, 36, 38, 39, 40}
   d) Prime: { 47, 53}; Composite: { 45, 46, 48, 49, 50, 51, 52, 54, 55, 56, 57}

3. a) 2, 3 b) 2, 7 c) 2, 3 d) 5, 13

5. a) 15 b) 24 c) 36 d) 60

7. a) 14 b) 33 c) 60 d) 42

9. i. a) { 1, 2, 3, 4, 6, 9, 12, 18, 36}; and { 1, 2, 3, 4, 6, 7,12, 14, 21, 28, 42, 84 } b) { 1, 2, 3, 4, 6, 12} c) 12
   ii. a) { 1, 2, 3, 4, 6, 8, 12, 16, 24, 48 } and { 1, 2, 4, 5, 8, 10, 16, 20, 32, 40, 80, 160 }
   b) { 1, 2, 4, 8, 16 } c) 16
   iii. a) { 1, 2, 4, 19, 38, 76 }; and { 1, 2, 3, 6, 19, 38, 57, 1 14}; and { 1, 2, 4, 8, 19, 38, 76, 152};
   b) { 1, 2, 19, 38 } c) 38
   iv. a) { 1, 2, 3, 4, 6, 8, 12, 16, 24, 32, 48, 96 }; and { 1, 2, 3, 4, 6, 8, 9, 12, 16, 18, 24, 36, 48, 72, 144 }; and { 1, 2, 3, 4, 6, 8, 9, 12, 18, 24, 27, 36, 54, 72, 108, 216 };
   b) { 1, 2, 3, 4, 6, 8, 12, 24 }; c) 24

Exercises 1.3

1. a) $\frac{3}{2}$ b) $\frac{51}{4}$ c) $\frac{38}{5}$ d) $\frac{29}{3}$

3. a) $1\frac{5}{7}$ b) $2\frac{1}{8}$ c) $3\frac{4}{9}$ d) $2\frac{4}{5}$

5. a) 8, 18 b) 5, 21 c) 11, 30 d) 15, 30

7. a) $\frac{20}{3}$ b) $\frac{26}{3}$ c) $\frac{34}{5}$ d) $\frac{1}{4}$

9. a) $\frac{8}{7}$ b) $\frac{16}{39}$

11. a) $\frac{85}{12}$ b) $\frac{29}{18}$ c) $\frac{27}{20}$

13. a) $\frac{571}{35}$ b) $\frac{50}{39}$ c) $\frac{13}{9}$

15. a) $\frac{925}{74}$ b) $\frac{92}{45}$ c) $\frac{19}{18}$

17. a) 4 b) $\frac{4}{3}$ c) $\frac{5}{21}$

19. $13\frac{13}{24}$ kg

21. $5\frac{5}{6}$ years

23. $376\frac{1}{5}$ km

25. $3\frac{1}{2}$ km

Exercises 1.4

1. a) −99 b) 20

3. a) 4 b) −32

5. a) 110 b) 11

7. a) 208 b) −192

9. 29

11. 2

13. -6

15. 16

17. 158

19. a) $\frac{1}{16}$ b) $\frac{125}{27}$

c) 248,832

d) $\frac{1}{1,419,857}$

21. a) 4514.79
b) 1535.00

23. a) 2498.97
b) 1763.27

25. a) 16,911.28
b) 37,618.52

27. a) 5619.82
b) 1968.84

29. a) 17,581.16
b) 3545.30

Exercises 1.5

1. a) 22 b) 52.50

3. 37.125 hours per week

5. 117

7. 56.67

9. a) \$103.79
b) \$112.50

11. \$216.86

Review Exercises 1

1. a) 6.29 b) 2.32
c) 7.31 d) 1846.15

3. a) \$42.59 b) \$74.96
c) \$91.69 d) \$498.42

5. a) 660 b) 576
c) 990

7. a) 5 b) 2 c) 25

9. $24\frac{29}{60}$ hours

11. $7\frac{11}{12}$ hours

13. a) 76 b) 4

15. a) 90,691.77
b) 43,278.27

17. \$5150

19. \$26.05

Self-Test Exercises 1

1. \$1220.70

2. 79,000

3. a) 72 b) 80 c) 576

4. a) 4 b) 7 c) 12

5. $44\frac{7}{24}$ cm

6. 6

7. a) 2 b) 1

8. a) 52,141.33
b) 2856.13

9. \$38,962.50

10. \$23.57

Chapter 2

Exercises 2.1

1. a) $7xy, -4y$ b) $-y, 3$
c) $9xy, -6y$

3. a) 5; 5, −3 b) 1; −2, 3
c) 7; −2, −2 d) −4; 8

5. a) $11x^2 + 17x$
b) $y - 7y^2$
c) $3x + 3y^2$

7. a) $\frac{8}{5}$ b) $\frac{3}{2}$ c) 4

9. a) $-75x - 3$ b) -38

11. a) $-5x + 7$ b) $2x - 4$

13. a) $10(3x - y - 9)$
b) $-2(7y + 72)$

15. a) $-7y^2 - 12y + 6$
b) $4x + 25$
c) $24x^2 - 70x + 11$

17. a) $-x - y$
b) $5x - 3y + 1$ c) $\frac{x^2}{2y}$

19. a) $\frac{3(x+3)}{2}$
b) $\frac{3(x-5)}{8}$ c) $\frac{15y}{16}$

21. a) $\frac{23}{9}$ b) 24
c) 30 d) 22

23. a) 30 b) 56
c) −18 d) 6750

25. a) $12A, -7A; 4B, -B$
b) $6x, -5x; 8y, -3y; 7$
c) $-2x, 8x, -12x, 5y, 7y$
d) $6xy^2, 2xy^2; 2x^2y, 3x^2y; -4x^2, 2x^2; 4$

27. a) 24 b) 65

29. a) $3y(2x^2 - x - 3)$
b) $3(5y + 1)(y - 1)$
c) $b(6a - 5c) + 7ac$

31. a) $3y(2x - 3z)$
b) $2x^2(5x - 2)$
c) $-40y(3y + 1)$

33. a) $(5x + 3)(y + 2)$
b) $(4y - x)(x - 5)$
c) $(y + 5)(x - 2)$

35. a) $(x - y)(x + 1)$
b) $(2x + 3y)(x + 1)$

Exercises 2.2

1. a) $2x - 3$ b) $\frac{2x}{5}$
c) $3x + 25$ d) $6(3 + x)$

3. a) $x + 6 = 10$
b) $6x = 72$
c) $\frac{x}{5} = 4$
d) $\frac{2}{3}(x) = 12$

5. a) $x = 4$ b) $x = 12$
c) $x = 20$ d) $x = 18$

7. a) $x = 30$ b) $x = 18$
c) $x = -17$ d) $x = 6$

9. a) $x = \frac{7}{5}$ b) $x = 2$
c) $x = \frac{-3}{20}$

11. a) $x = 4$ b) $x = \frac{13}{11}$
c) $x = 1.72$

13. a) $x = -\frac{11}{5}$
b) $x = \frac{13}{3}$ c) $x = \frac{7}{17}$

15. $x = 52.60$

17. a) $y = 11$ b) $x = -5$

19. a) $x = 16$ b) $y = 42$

21. 5

23. 9, 16

25. \$175, \$325

27. \$10, \$7

29. $A = (x + 4)(x + 3)$, 182 m^2

Exercises 2.3

1. a) 609 b) 729 c) 256
d) −255 e) 1,000,000
f) 81

3. a) $\frac{3125}{32}$
b) −10,000,000
c) 400 d) 59,049
e) 104,976 f) 3

5. a) 25 b) 36 c) 4 d) 9
e) 27 f) 1,953,125

7. a) $20x^3$ b) x^6 c) x^{17}
d) x^4 e) x^6 f) x^6

9. a) $\left(\frac{x}{y}\right)^7$ b) $\left(\frac{x}{y}\right)^5$
c) $-x^7$ d) y^6
e) x^4y^8 f) x^2

11. a) x^{14} b) x^4 c) x^5
d) $3x^2$ e) x^2 f) $-x^2$

Exercises 2.4

1. a) $\log_{10}100{,}000 = 5$
b) $\log_2 64 = 6$
c) $\log_3 9 = 2$
d) $\log_4 1024 = 5$
e) $\log_6 7776 = 5$
f) $\log_9 6561 = 4$

3. a) $10^2 = 100$ b) $2^5 = 32$
c) $3^6 = 729$ d) $4^3 = 64$
e) $5^4 = 625$ f) $6^3 = 216$

5. a) 7.7187 b) 5.0370
c) 3.2958 d) 2.3076
e) 0.0050 f) −0.3930

7. a) 1.62 b) 2.33
c) 8.83 d) 5.53

9. a) $\ln 3 - \ln 7$
b) $\ln 4 + \ln 9$
c) $\ln A + \ln B - \ln C$
d) $\ln X - \ln Y - \ln Z$
e) $\ln 3x - \ln 2yz$

11. a) $\ln 40$ b) $\ln 5$
c) $\ln 675$ d) $\ln\left(\frac{32}{9}\right)$
e) $\ln\left(\frac{a^3b^2}{c^5}\right)$

13. a) $\ln 25$ b) $\ln 216$
c) $\ln\left(\frac{a}{b}\right)^5$
d) $\ln (a \times b)^4$
e) $\ln\left(\frac{81}{2}\right)$

15. a) 0.07 b) 0.52
c) 42.33 d) 31.00

Exercises 2.5

1. a) $L = \frac{N}{(1-d)}$
b) $C = S - M$
c) $E = S - P - C$
d) $r = \frac{C}{2\pi}$
e) $r = \frac{\left(\frac{S}{P} - 1\right)}{t}$

3. a) $a = \frac{b}{b+c}$
$c = \frac{b - ab}{a}$

b) $a = bc + c,\ b = \frac{a - c}{c}$

5. a) 3 b) 2000
c) 0.133333...

7. a) 70 m, 300 m^2
b) 50.27 cm, 201.06 cm^2

9. a) 19 cm, 15 cm^2
b) 32 cm, 42 cm^2

11. a) 42,400 cm^2, 480,000 cm^3
b) 5026.55 cm^2, 33,510.32 cm^3
c) 791.68 cm^2, 1696.46 cm^3

13. 1866.67 cm^3

Review Exercises 2

1. a) 12 b) –12
c) –32 d) 10

3. a) $2x(3x - 2)$, 2
b) $3y^2(y - 4)$, –72
c) $7x(y + 2x)$, 28
d) $3x(3x^2 - 2x + 1)$, 198

5. a) $12+3x$ b) $x - 5$
c) $(3+x)x$ d) $10x+15$

7. a) $5x + 17 = 42; x = 5$
b) $\frac{x}{15} = 45; x = 675$
c) $x - 10 = 10; x = 20$
d) $3(4x) = 36; x = 3$

9. a) 3 b) 18 c) –9 d) 2

11. a) 17 b) 72 c) 16
d) 5 e) $\frac{3}{2}$ f) 16

13. a) $3x^7$ b) x^4 c) $\frac{x^8}{4y^7}$
d) $2x^2$ e) $\frac{8x^9}{y^6}$ f) x^{14}

15. a) 26.25 b) 1691.63
c) 7.00 d) 28.36
e) 55.48 f) 8.97

17. a) 5.98 cm b) 898 cm^3

19. $h = \frac{3V}{\pi r^2}$; 35.99 cm

Self-Test Exercises 2

1. a) $x^2 + 2x - 3$, 5
b) $-x^2 - 6x + 10$, 19
c) $-19x^2 - 5y^2 - 7xy$, –15
d) $10x - 15y - 6x + 4y + 7$, 4

2. a) 96 b) 30
c) –56 d) 14

3. a) $3x - 25$ b) $x + 18$
c) $2x - 6$ d) $\frac{x}{3}$

4. a) 15 b) 5 c) 2 d) 5

5. a) 4 b) 18
c) $-\frac{4}{7}$ d) $\frac{14}{3}$

6. a) –128 b) –121
c) –1000 d) 3
e) 6 f) 3125

7. a) $9x^6$ b) $16x^4y^6$
c) $4y^2$ d) $\frac{1}{x^2}$
e) $\frac{y^2}{x^6}$ f) 1

8. a) 15.45 b) 3.17
c) 7.75 d) 13.33
e) 102.70 f) 4.00

9. a) 0.01 b) 0.01

10. a) $t = \frac{1}{r}(\frac{S}{P} - 1)$
b) 2

Chapter 3

Exercises 3.1

1. a) 0.8, $\frac{4}{5}$ b) 25%, $\frac{1}{4}$
c) 150%, 1.5 d) $\frac{13}{200}$, 0.065 e) 4.8%, $\frac{6}{125}$
f) 8%, 0.08 g) 0.106, $\frac{53}{500}$ h) 225%, $\frac{9}{4}$
i) 0.25%, 0.0025
j) –0.26, $-\frac{13}{50}$
k) –15%, $-\frac{3}{20}$
l) –58.33%, –0.5833

3. a) 70 b) 100 c) 52
d) 0.1875 e) 0.5 km
f) \$55

5. a) 45.45% b) 111.11%
c) 14% d) \$186.00
e) 130 f) \$16.50
g) \$2200.00 h) \$0.27

7. \$700,000.00

9. \$315,723.08

11. 13.00%

13. \$89,400.00

15. \$45.00

17. \$1,153,153.15

19. a) 36,750
b) 33,846,154

21. \$450

23. Tudor

Exercises 3.2

1. a) 306 b) \$9.00
c) \$11,250.00
d) 680.00 kg
e) \$530.00 f) 7.38
g) 75% h. 25.00%

3. \$2110.00

5. \$280,000.00

7. \$30.53

9. 20%

11. 10.34%

13. 13.33%

15. 11.86%

17. 22.22%

19. –13.51%, –21.56%, 32.16%

21. 16.67%

23. 4.76%

25. 25% less

27. 4.17%

29. \$468,000.00

Exercises 3.3

1. \$5000.00, \$2500.00, \$2307.69, \$1153.85

3. \$20,800.00, \$1733.33

5. \$37,440.00, \$1560.00

7. \$3843.75

9. \$1484.98

11. \$11,250.00

13. \$5820.00

15. \$2875.88, 4.76%

17. \$48,400.00

19. \$1820.00

21. \$60,000.00

23. 4.5%

25. \$1160.00

27. \$1260.00

Exercises 3.4

1. \$1170.00, \$10,170.00, \$10,395.00

3. \$30.33

5. \$3569.50

7. \$2800.00

9. \$25,350.00

11. \$6.00

13. \$7.00

15. \$2306.25, \$1845.00

Review Exercises 3

1. a) 2765
b) 30,722,223

3. a) 33.33% b) 22.54%

5. \$180,200.00

7. 5.80%

9. 13.04%

11. \$3022.50

13. 12.25%

15. \$2830.00, 6.29%

17. \$5041.54

19. \$2385.10

Self-Test Exercises 3

1. \$71,080.80

2. a) 60% b) \$500, 25%

3. \$150.54

4. a) –7.67% , –16.61%
b) 23.01%

5. 4% depreciation

6. \$3166.67, \$1583.33, \$1461.54, \$730.77

7. \$2191.18

8. \$45,250.00

9. \$915.46

10. \$47,294.00

Chapter 4

Exercises 4.1

1. a) 1.25 : 1 : 2
b) 7.2 : 1 : 1.80
c) 1 : 5 : 6.67

3. a) Not equal b) Equal
c) Not equal
d) Equal

5. a) 2 : 13 b) 4 : 35
c) 1 : 16

7. 1 : 10

9. 500 km/hr

11. 11 : 20 : 10

13. a) 12 : 2 : 1 : 4
b) 48 : 8 : 3 : 16

15. Susan: \$53.33, Robert: \$66.67

17. Amanda: \$1500, Fredrick: \$2400, Ronald: \$600

19. Andrew: \$1600, Brookes: \$2400

21. $11,250.00

23. 15 : 20 : 24

25. A's

Exercises 4.2

1. a) 10 **b)** 0.70 **c)** 0.61 **d)** 2.625

3. 234 litres

5. $254.55

7. 4.96 km

9. Telecommunication: $4360, Technology: $3270

11. a) $4565 **b)** $67,500, $22,500 **c)** $60,000, $90,000, $30,000

13. $865.38

15. $1306.67

17. $881.67

19. 5 : 9 : 15

21. $20,769.23

23. $15,000, $25,000, $20,000

25. 12 : 9 : 16

27. a) 33 **b)** 5 : 3

29. 325

Exercises 4.3

1. a) £120.74 **b)** US$2920.28 **c)** C$5136.50 **d)** C$16.41

3. a) C$1579.47 **b)** C$38.52

5. C$102.48

7. Yes, C$58.85

9. C$1027.27

11. C$5043.26

13. 5.00%

15. a) C$ appreciated **b)** C$ depreciated **c)** C$ appreciated

17. USA

19. C$1.0351

21. C$893.05

23. C$16,756.90

25. C$1262.63, No

Review Exercises 4

1. $46,350

3. $1000, $2500**5.** $1057.69

7. 4 : 6 : 3

9. 6 : 7 : 8

11. Gina, $0.75 per hour

13. $1093.75, $2333.33, $1822.92

15. 5.00%.

17. 18

19. C$2015.12

Self-Test Exercises 4

1. C$1.03854

2. $25,000

3. C$1027.37

4. $2125

5. 431.25 cm

6. 25 : 30 : 42

7. $208.33

8. C$42.75

9. C$637.59

10. Yes, C$3.78

Chapter 5

Exercises 5.2

1. a) $1875, $1500 **b)** $230, 12% **c)** 54%, $432 **d)** 2%, $490

3. a) 28.00%, $388.80, $151.20 **b)** $1970.19, 38.58%, $1210.19 **c)** $2768.09, 9.25%, $256.09 **d)** 17.94%, $215.26

5. $16.50, $93.50

7. $871.51, $91.51

9. $121,333.33, $103,133.33

11. 8.00%

13. $221.76, $58.24

15. 31.85%

17. $1028.85, $171.15

19. Orillia, 2.21%

21. Vendor A

23. Yes

Exercises 5.3

1. a) January 11, January31 **b)** April 4, April 29 **c)** May 10, May 30 **d)** September 10, October 15 **e)** August 10, August 30 **f)** March 10, March 25 **g)** July 26, August 15

3. a) $20,090.00 **b)** $20,090.00 **c)** $20,295.00 **d)** $20,500.00

5. $39,999.44

7. $469.54

9. $480.96

11. a) $2461.17 **b)** $451.12

13. $3071.25

15. a) $12,416.00 **b)** $12,416.00 **c)** $12,800.00

17. a) $918.00 **b)** $918.00 **c)** No discount

19. $2945.00

21. a) $12,450.72 **b)** $7301.71 **c)** $22,301.71

Exercises 5.4

1. a) $630.00, $1830.00, 52.50%, 34.43% **b)** $885.75, $22.50, 10.72%, 9.68% **c)** $1225.25, $320.50, 26.16%, 20.73% **d)** $10,455.00, 448.75, 19.13%, 16.06% **e)** $2926.83, $600.00, $3526.83, 7.01% **f)** $3538.87, $426.25, $3965.12, 12.04% **g)** $3049.50, $1674.10, 40.93%, 29.04% **h)** $9.00, $4.50, 138.46%, 58.06% **i)** $1000.00, $1100.00, $21.50, 9.09% **j)** $410.00, $430.50, $12.30, 4.76%

3. 6.95%, 6.50%

5. $600.94

7. $20,750.00, $4250.00, 25.76%

9. $243.00, $36.00

11. $120.00, $1080.00

13. $7.69, $2.31

15. 16.67%

17. 66.67%

19. The second computer

21. $2405.00

Exercises 5.5

1. a) $14.25, 28.08%, 21.92%, 8.46%, $59.50 **b)** $254.00, 10.43%, 9.45%, $39.75, 14.17% **c)** $211.25, $38.75, $250.00, 18.34%, $237.50 **d)** $2128.88, $101.12, $2230.00, 4.53%, $2174.25 **e)** $193.95, 42.49%, 29.82%, $22.77, $627.68 **f)** $491.50, $591.75, 20.40%, 16.94%, 1.86% **g)** $958.60, $72.15, $1030.75, 7.53%, 8.78%

3. $160.00

5. $3333.33, $2333.33

7. $120.00, 15.00%

9. $440.00, $308.00

11. $1087.50, $652.50

13. 30.00%

15. 13.57%

Exercises 5.6

1. a) $1000.00, $1150.00, 115.00%, 53.49%, $1612.50, $312.50 **b)** $800.50, $1700.75, 88.92%, 47.07%, $1105.49, $4.74 **c)** $2.44, $18.19, $0.26, 13.41%, $17.19, $1.18 **d)** $509.06, $169.69, $93.19, 33.33%, $593.91, $8.35 **e)** $3899.00, $515.75, 16.84%, 14.41%, 8.24%, $140.25 **f)** $21.50, $11.50, 56.58%, 36.13%, 21.00%, $47.00

3. $140.00, $2737.00, –$343.00

5. a) $96.00 **b)** $91.20, +$3.20

7. +$50.00

9. +$28.00
11. a) $777.60, Profit: $86.40 **b)** 20%
13. $4080.00, $6.00 per torch
15. $33.00

Review Exercises 5

1. $16.94, $1.19
3. $9486.00, $2914.00
5. 2.03%
7. $286.88, 68.13%
9. a) $42,750.00 **b)** $44,100.00 **c)** $45,000.00
11. a) $106,702.63 **b)** $54,434.52 **c)** $179,434.52
13. $84.00, 28.57%, $18.00
15. $2.22, $1.78
17. $45.00, $36.00
19. a) $177.87 **b)** –$6.88 **c)** 16.13%

Self-Test Exercises 5

1. a) $2100.00 **b)** 48.70%
2. a) Ajax **b)** 2.78%
3. a) $1960.00 **b)** $2940.00
4. a) $557.18 **b)** 25.71% **c)** $192.82
5. a) $18,054.00 **b)** $9027.00 **c)** No discount
6. $431.47
7. a) $65,897.44 **b)** $63,866.98 **c)** $63,866.98
8. Loss: $54.54
9. Loss: $10,312.50
10. $450.00, 25.93%
11. 66.67%
12. a) 9.24% **b)** 23.08%

Chapter 6

Exercise 6.1

1.

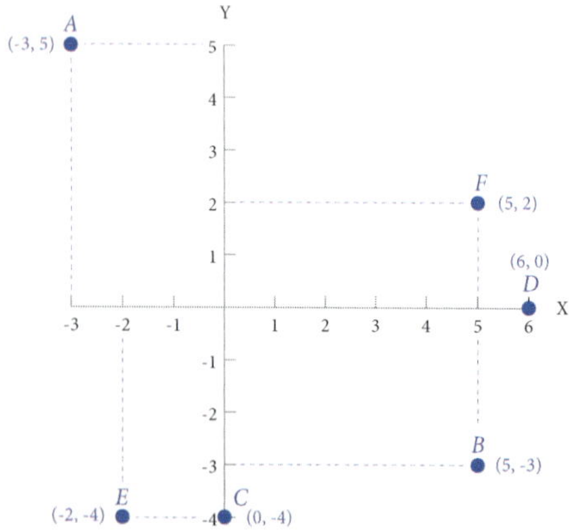

3. a) Second quadrant **b)** Fourth quadrant **c)** First quadrant **d)** X-axis **e)** Third quadrant **f)** Y-axis

5. a) 2 units

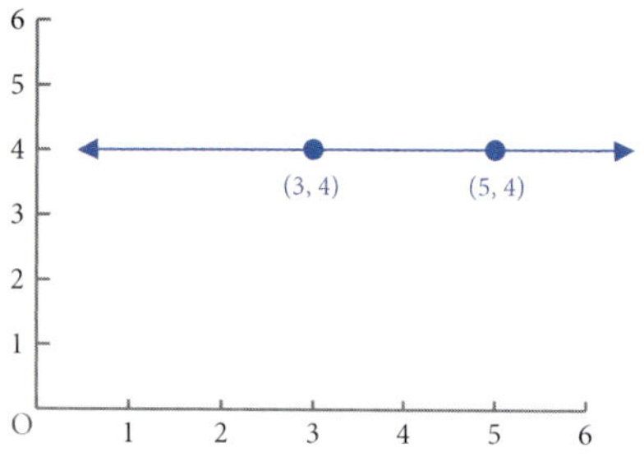

b) 9 units

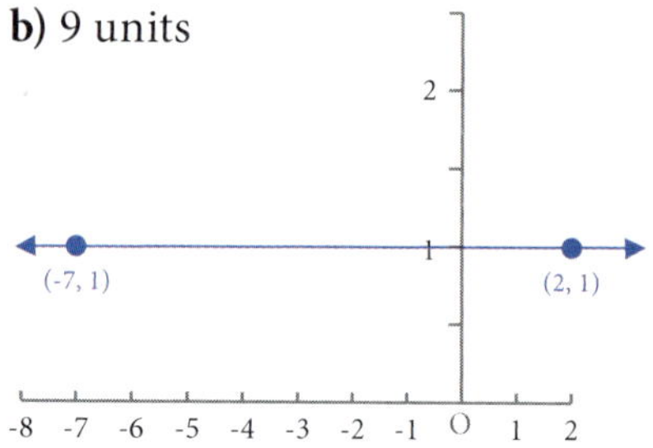

c) 5 units

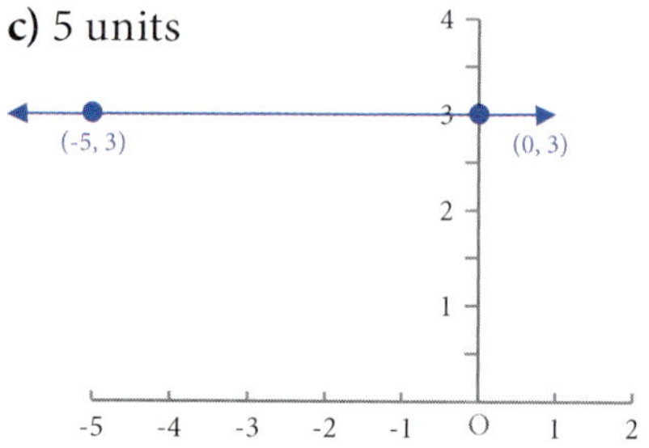

d) 8 units

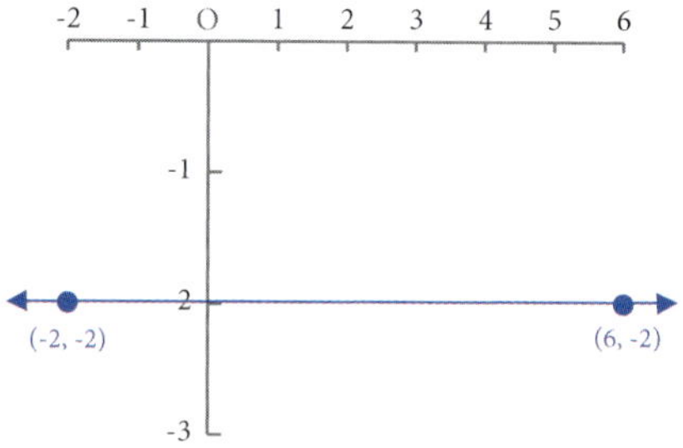

7. (–3, –1)
9. (1, 12) and (1, –2)

Exercise 6.2

1. a) (3, 4) **b)** (–6, 10) **c)** (0, 6) **d)** (9, 0) **e)** (15, –4) **f)** (6, 2)

3. a)

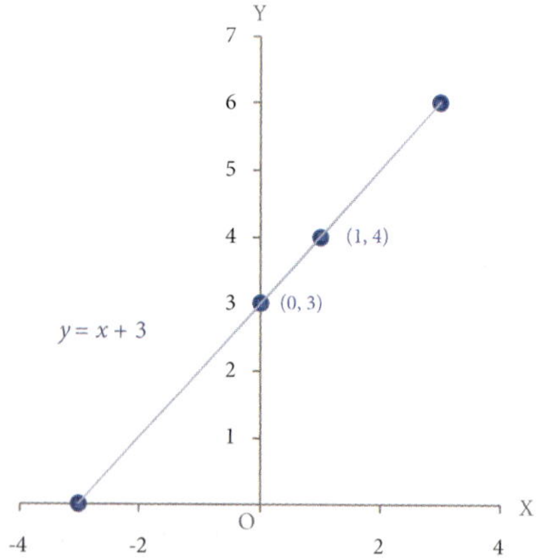

b)

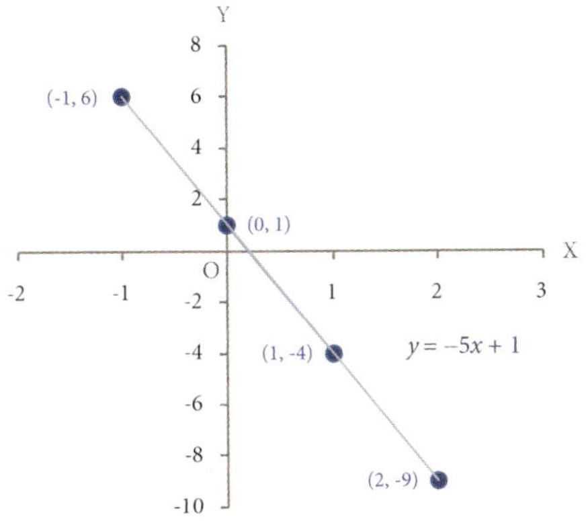

c)

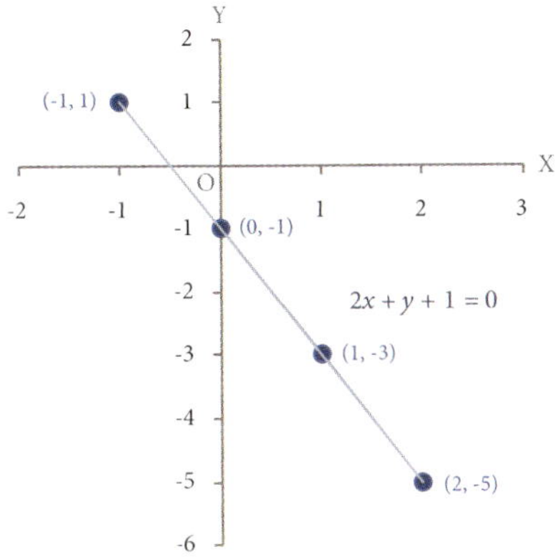

d)

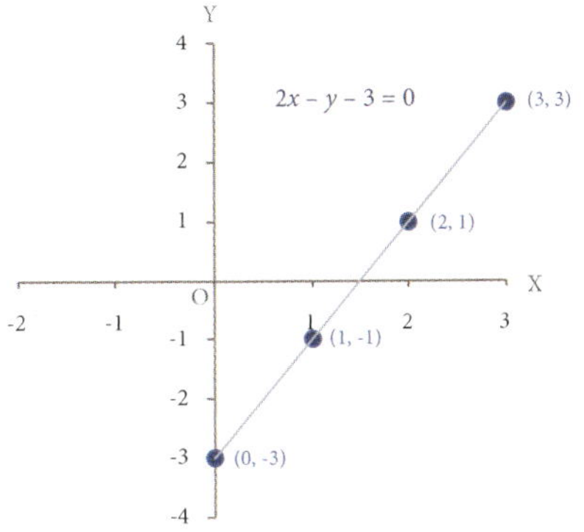

5. a) x-intercept: $-\frac{2}{3}$, y-intercept: -2

b) x-intercept: 7, y-intercept: 7

c) x-intercept: -2, y-intercept: 4

7. Positive

9. a) Slope = $\frac{2}{3}$, y-intercept = -6

b) Slope = $\frac{4}{7}$, y-intercept = 3

11. a) $y = 2$ **b)** $y = x - 2$

13. a) $y = x + 4$ **b)** $y = 2x$ **c)** $y = \frac{5}{4}x - 5$

15. a) 0 **b)** $\frac{-5}{8}$

17. $y = 2$

19. $y = 7$

21. $5x + 3y - 15 = 0$

Exercise 6.3

1. a) (1, 1) **b)** No solution **c)** Infinitely many solutions

3. a) Independent **b)** Independent **c)** Dependent

5. a) Consistent **b)** Inconsistent **c)** Consistent

7. 4

9. a) (-2, 1) **b)** Infinitely many solutions **c)** No solution

Exercise 6.4

1. a) $(2, -2)$ **b)** $\left(\frac{54}{11}, \frac{37}{11}\right)$ **c)** $(3, -3)$

3. a) $(2, 1)$ **b)** $(6, -1)$ **c)** $(1, 2)$

5. a) $(9, 2)$ **b)** $(2, 3)$ **c)** $(-1, -2)$

7. a) $(1, -2)$ **b)** $(2, 4)$ **c)** $(3, -2)$

9. a) $(-3, -1)$ **b)** $(3, 4)$ **c)** $(3, -2)$

11. a) $(10, 6)$ **b)** $(15, 12)$ **c)** $\left(\frac{9}{7}, \frac{27}{7}\right)$

13. a) $(1, 3)$ **b)** $(3, -2)$ **c)** $(2, 1)$

15. $12.

17. 60 years and 32 years

19. $y = 15x + 5$; y-intercept: 5, Slope: 15

21. a) $13,500.00 **b)** $25,500.00

Review Exercises 6

1. a) Fourth quadrant **b)** Second quadrant **c)** X-axis **d)** Fourth quadrant **e)** X-axis **f)** Y-axis

3.

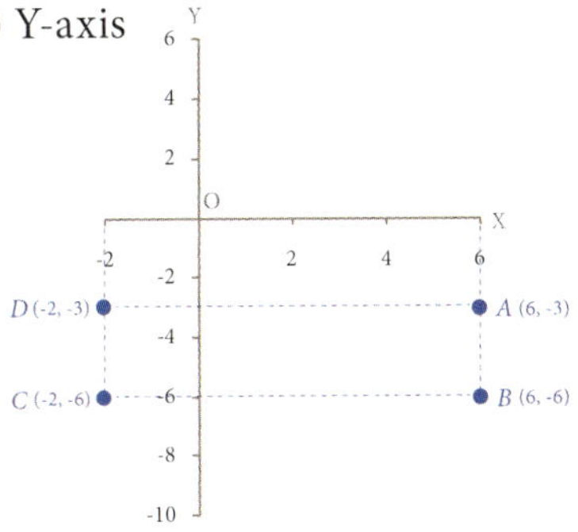

Rectangle; Area = 24; Perimeter = 22

5. a)

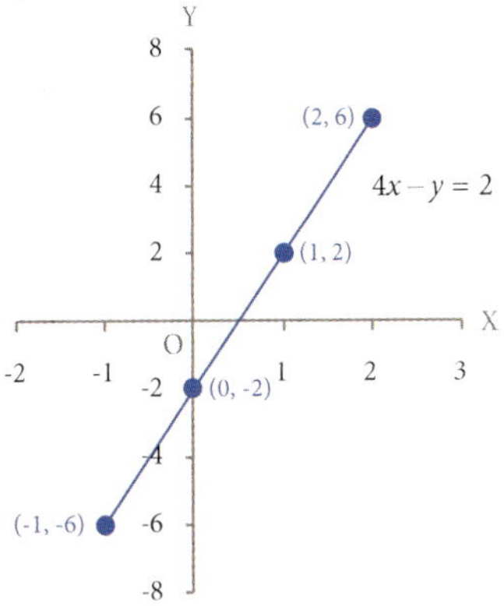

b)

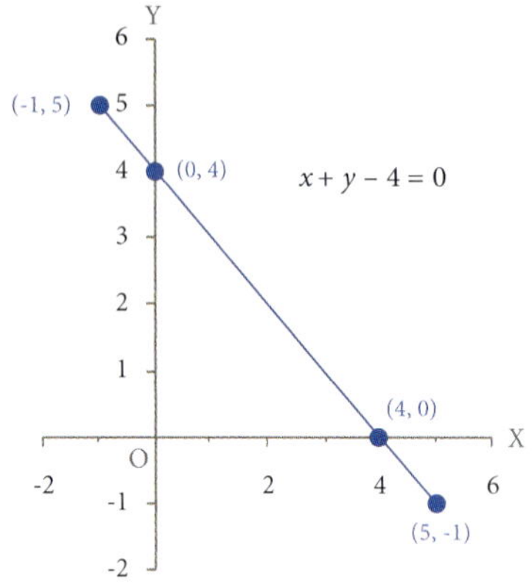

c)

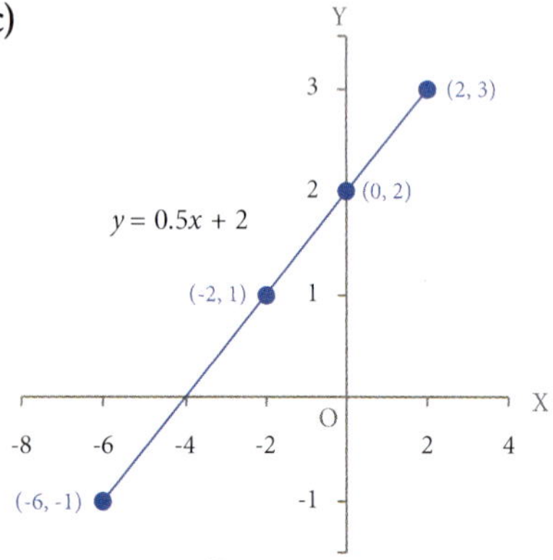

7. a)

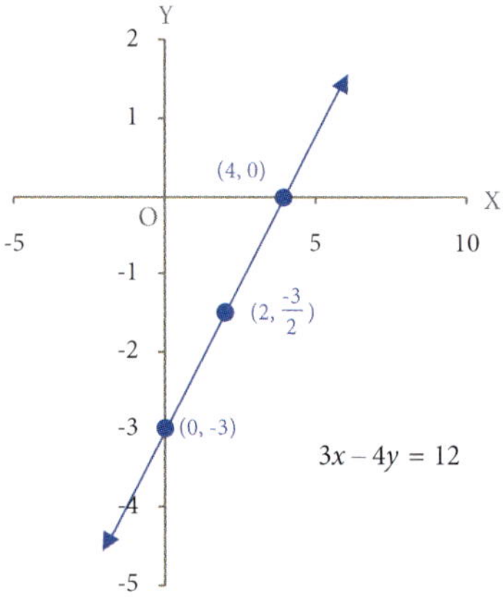

b)

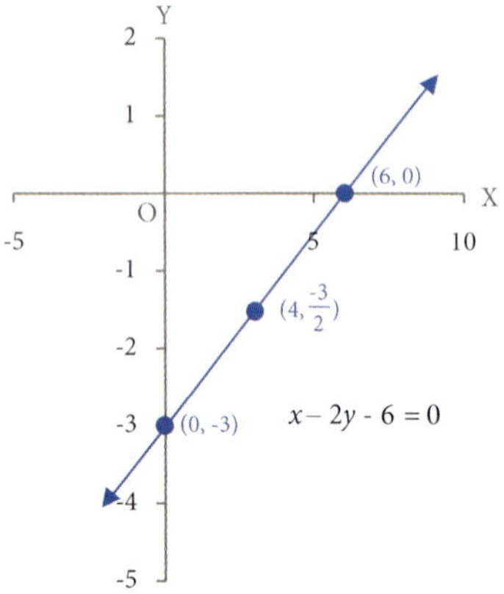

c)

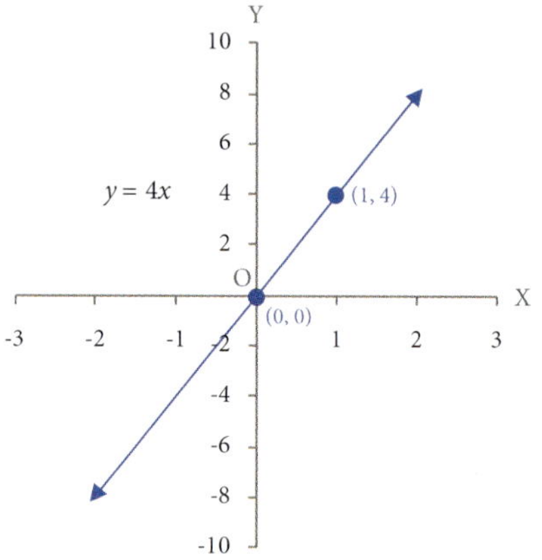

9. a)

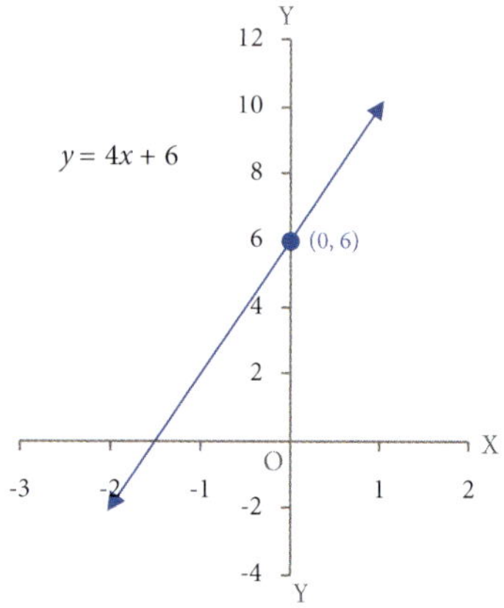

b)

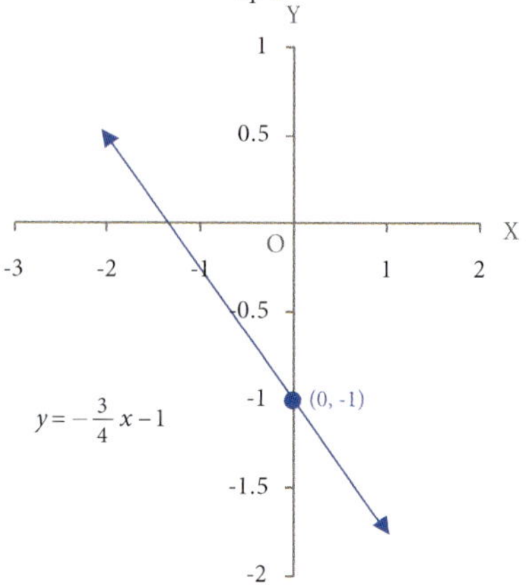

c)

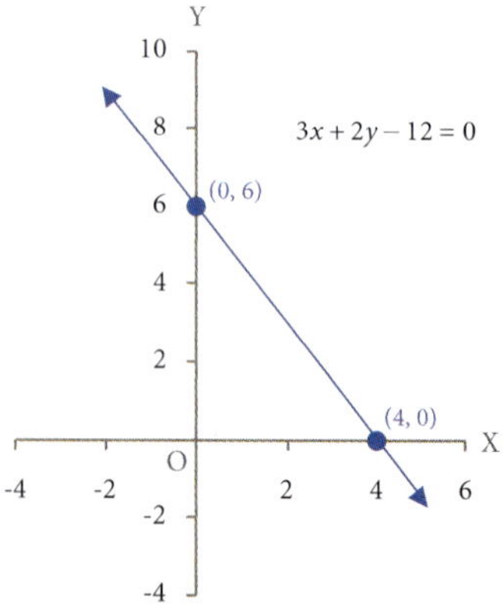

11. a) $y = \frac{3}{4}x - \frac{1}{4}$ **b)** $y = \frac{-4}{3}x + \frac{8}{3}$ **c)** $y = 3x - 5$

13. a) (2, −5) **b)** (6, 2) **c)** (2, 1)

15. a) (4, 1) **b)** $\left(\frac{52}{19}, -\frac{70}{19}\right)$ **c)** (1, 1)

17. a) (2, 1) **b)** (−4, −2) **c)** (3, 0)

19. $y = -3$; Equation of the line: $y = 2x - 1$

Self-Test Exercises 6

1. $(-3, -1)$; 40 square units

2. Slope: $\frac{2}{3}$, y-intercept: 2

3. $5y + 4x - 9 = 0$

4. a) $x + 2y + 8 = 0$
b) $2x - 3y - 6 = 0$

5. a)

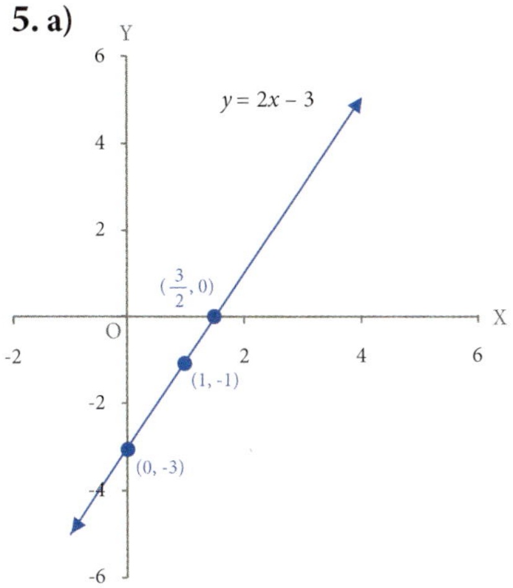

x-intercept: $\frac{1}{4}$, y-intercept: -3
Another point on the line: $(1, -1)$

b)

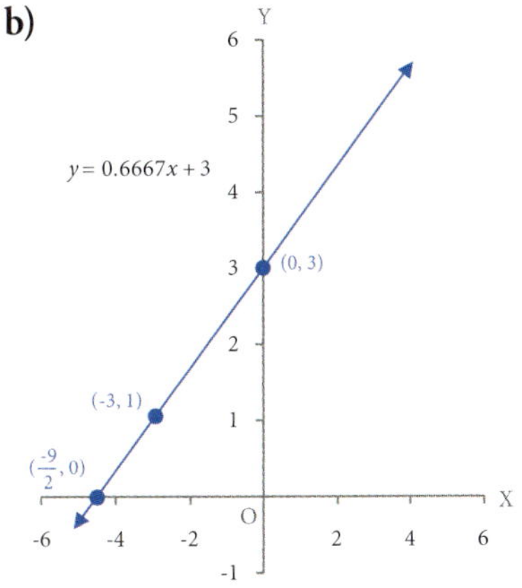

x-intercept: $-\frac{9}{2}$,
y-intercept: 3
Another point on the line: $(-3, 1)$

6. $3x - 2y + 12 = 0$

7. a) Infinitely many solutions
b) $\left(-\frac{25}{11}, \frac{2}{11}\right)$

8. a) $\left(\frac{15}{7}, -\frac{18}{7}\right)$ **b)** $(-4, 4)$

9. a) $\left(-\frac{3}{2}, -\frac{3}{2}\right)$ **b)** $\left(-\frac{17}{31}, \frac{128}{31}\right)$

10. $B = -1$; Equation of the line: $y = -8x - 6$

Chapter 7

Exercises 7.1

1.a) 100, \$300, \$1300 **b)** \$70, \$14,000, \$22,000 **c)** \$61, \$3782, \$9672 **d)** \$2300, \$2250, \$4550 **e)** \$58, 250, \$14,500 **f)** \$8500, \$317, 500

3. 800 units

5. \$180.00, \$639,000.00

7. \$7560, \$90.00

9. \$81,400, \$296,000

11. \$57.47

Exercises 7.2

1. 760

3. a) 5140 **b)** Loss: \$3000 **c)** 5807, 96.78%

5. a) 127 **b)** 495

7. a) 240 **b)** 492

Exercises 7.3

1. a) \$22.50, \$22,500, \$65,000, 1000 **b)** \$78,500, \$90,000, \$174,000, \$5500 **c)** \$30, \$45, \$23,940, \$9810 **d)** \$77,800, \$41.67, \$202,500, \$140,300

3. \$520, 86

5. \$11,010.00

7. a) \$8.71 **b)** \$19.29 **c)** \$1350.05

9. \$60,750, 2250, \$90,000.00

11. \$15,815.00

Exercises 7.4

1. 800

3. 760

5. a) 5140 **b)** \$3000.00 **c)** 96.78%

7. a) 127 **b)** 495

9. \$520.00, 86

11. \$11,010.00

Exercises 7.5

1. 800

3. 760

5. a) 5140 **b)** \$3000.00 **c)** 96.78%

7. a) 127 **b)** 495

9. \$520.00, 86

11. \$11,010.00

Review Exercises 7

1. a) 491 **b)** \$2250.00 **c)** 673

3. a) 950 **b)** \$184,875.00 **c)** 6950

5. a) \$13,000.00, 200 **b)** 333 **c)** \$7350.00

7. a) \$5.00, 40.00% **b)** 13,600 **c)** \$30,000.00

9. a) \$270.00 **b)** 400 **c)** 66.67%

11. a) \$60,000.00 **b)** 8500 **c)** 7200

13. a) 35.00% **b)** 96 **c)** 346

15. a) 640 **b)** \$50,000.00 **c)** 914

17. a) \$6.40, 40.00% **b)** 9600.00 **c)** \$1600.00

19. a) \$15,000.00
b) \$9000.00
c) \$60,000,000.00

Self-Test Exercises 7

1. a) 5000 **b)** 7500

2. a) 69.44% **b)** \$95,000.00

3. a) 18,000 **b)** \$75,000.00

4. a) –\$150,000.00 **b)** 3554

5. a) \$625,000.00 **b)** \$262,500.00

6. a) \$280.00
b) \$8,503,367.35, \$109.59

7. a) 90 **b)** 633

8. a) \$38.75 **b)** \$6.25 **c)** \$1800.00

9. a) 625 **b)** \$126,000.00 **c)** 853

10. \$21,156.00, 1763, \$60,000.00

Chapter 8

Exercises 8.2

1. a) $\frac{49}{365}$ years **b)** $\frac{279}{365}$ years
c) $\frac{132}{365}$ years **d)** $\frac{378}{365}$ years

3. a) \$10.96 **b)** \$48.22 **c)** \$855.77 **d)** \$25.20

5. \$312.50

7. \$37.81

9. \$372.60

11. \$32.88

13. \$443.84

15. 0.85% per month

17. \$225, \$172.50

19. \$235.33

21. \$43.60 more

Exercises 8.3

1. a) \$12,542.96 **b)** 1.19%
c) \$3976.15 **d)** 0.55%
e) December 24, 2010
f) September 12, 2008

3. \$6653.65

5. 201 days

7. 7.60%

9. $8960.00

11. $460.00; $60.00

13. 1 year and 2 months

15. $701.37, $20,701.37

17. Interest: $97.34; Maturity amount: $6887.59

19. 102 months

21. $3644.56, $39.94

23. $10,058.42; $10,308.42

25. $2553.33

Exercises 8.4

1. $37,975.00

3. $2627.02

5. $6118.55

7. $2198.72

9. $2141.68

11. Option (b)

13. $6051.81 (Focal date: 12 months)

15. $1027.50

Exercises 8.5

1. Option(a); $338.75

3. $235.52

5. $8999.21

7. $10,000.00

9. $9832.84

11. $4972.11

13. a) $988.66 **b)** $992.55 **c)** 3.19%

15. $4991.79, $8.21

17. $10,040.56

Review Exercises 8

1. 504 days

3. $4477.53, $252.53

5. $19,489.79

7. 41.67 months

9. $4560.00

11. $3035.78 (Focal date: now)

13. $6041.80 (Focal date: payment date)

15. $7527.00

17. $1718.38

19. $1325.35

Self-Test Exercises 8

1. $192.50

2. 0.47%

3. $277.17

4. $54.95

5. $4768.12

6. $1951.39

7. $2109.06

8. $191.77

9. 2.00%

10. a) $24,511.12 **b)** $24,735.03; $223.91 **c)** 3.70%

11. $25,184.02

Chapter 9

Exercises 9.1

1. a) $m = 2$, $i = 2.5\%$, $t = 2$ years, $n = 4$

b) $m = 4$, $i = 2.85\%$, $t = 1$ year and 6 months, $n = 6$

c) $j = 8.4\%$, $m = 12$, $t = 1$ year and 7 months, $n = 19$

d) $j = 7.3\%$, $m = 365$, $t = \frac{120}{365}$ years, $n = 120$

3. 26.4%

5. Semi-annually

7. 12

9. Quarterly

11. 16

13. 2%

Exercises 9.2

1. a) $i = 2.555\%$, $n = 11$, $FV = \$1319.85$

b) $j = 4.65\%$, $n = 9$, $FV = \$3939.72$

c) $m = 12$, $n = 7.2$, $FV = \$17{,}133.94$

d) $t = 11$ years and 3 months, $i = 6.57\%$, $FV = \$19{,}744.88$

3. $9891.34; $1441.34

5. $27,968.83; $2968.83

7. a) $17,068.86 **b)** $17,410.24, $341.38

9. $1114.61

11. Option (b)

13. $1715.61

15. Option (a), $95.69

17. $2697.41

19. $4000 today

21. $13,221.18

23. $2762.25

Exercises 9.3

1. a) $PV = \$4984.62$, $i = 2.69\%$, $n = 10$

b) $PV = \$8597.29$, $j = 5.82\%$, $n = 43$

c) $PV = \$12{,}000.00$, $m = 12$, $n = 84$

d) $PV = \$7500.00$, $t = 2$ years and 3 months, $i = 7.42\%$

3. $21,647.77

5. $223,826.60

7. $17,738.06

9. $14,825.40

11. $409,062.31

13. $319.45

15. Any option, as both yield almost the same result

17. $20,063.18

19. First option

21. $6451.69

Exercises 9.4

1. a) $3561.16 **b)** $1740.32

3. a) $4326.34 **b)** $7159.43

5. $33,365.24

7. $12,190.18

9. $15,034.63

11. $1501.09

13. $105,944.25

15. $666,532.39

17. $7582.86

Exercises 9.5

1. 6.99%, 1.75%

3. 3.70%, 0.92%

5. 10.02%

7. 4.63%, 6.95%

9. 5.46%, 10.73%

11. 2.41%

Exercises 9.6

1. 1 year and 11 months

3. 10 years and 1 month

5. a) 11 years and 7 months **b)** 14 years and 1 month

7. 30 years and 2 months

9. 5 years and 11 months

11. 4 years and 3 months

Exercises 9.7

1. a) 4.04% **b)** 4.06% **c)** 4.07%

3. 8.43%

5. 2.18%

7. b

9. 23.14%

11. Bank of Sarnia

13. 4.86%

15. Credit card company

Exercises 9.8

1. a) 6.94% **b)** 6.08% **c)** 7.92%

3. 8.09%

5. 6.21%

7. 3.24%

9. Any

11. 1.5% p.m

Review Exercises 9

1. $459,448.89, $259,448.89

3. $35,919.80

5. $91.92

7. $8075.66, $3924.34

9. $173,857.71

11. 8.70%, 8.85%

13. 1.61%, 3.21%

15. 10 years and 5 months

17. Any

19. 2.69%

21. 6.39%

Self-Test Exercises 9

1. $671,345.81, $90,445.81

2. $34,136.09

3. $2971.99

4. $23374.94

5. Nil
6. $10,241.88
7. $7719.15
8. 6.89%
9. 5 years and 7 months
10. 3.83%
11. $135,605.89

Chapter 10

Exercises 10.1

1. Ordinary simple annuity; 23
3. Ordinary general annuity; 180
5. Simple annuity due; 8
7. General annuity due; 41
9. General annuity due; 72; ordinary general annuity; 24

Exercises 10.2

1. a) $3488.50
b) $488.50
3. $1270.50
5. $394.60
7. $77,217.35
9. $29,806.22
11. $27,149.53
13. $171,673.43; $207,500.00; $35,826.57
15. Increase by $13.41
17. $172,657.10
19. $572.03
21. $7039.73; $1650.63

Exercises 10.3

1. $6797.02
3. a) $32,565.41
b) $32,833.56
5. $49,030.59
7. $13,259.80, $13,255.34, $13,248.74
9. a) $6400.42
b) $6791.71
11. $49,452.95
13. $9115.89
15. $12,680.33; $1189.67
17. $421,236.83; $818.59
19. $46,111.88

Exercises 10.4

1. $54,604.07
3. $10,503.13; $9000.00; $1503.13
5. $306,687.73
7. $50,387.68
9. $8877.58
11. $4376.40
13. $62,284.85
15. $18,278.54

Exercises 10.5

1. $28,706.93
3. $19,885.39
5. $34,497.75
7. $171,216.35
9. $38,900.61; decrease by $174.60
11. $146,698.06
13.a) Purchase Option
b) Lease Option

Exercises 10.6

1. $1909.24
3. $435.63
5. $193.73
7. $391.00
9. $109.68
11. $1229.40
13. $601.54
15. $1285.65

Exercises 10.7

1. 7 payments
3. 9 withdrawals of $150 each
5. 3 years and 2 months
7. 2 years and 2 months
9. $330.40; 6 years and 11 months

Exercises 10.8

1. 15.09%
3. 7.07%
5. 7.33%; 7.54%
7. 4.69%
9. a) 8.26%
b) 14.19%

Review Exercises 10

1. $2498.93
3. $78,941.69
5. $14,747.69; $4747.69
7. $167,543.03
9. $228,596.35
11. $14,289.05; $4289.05
13. $640.20
15. $548.24
17. $10.31
19. $17,634.43
21. $23,206.11
23. 4 years and 10 months
25. 5 years and 10 months
27. 8.87%; 0.74%
29. 24.13%

Self-Test Exercises 10

1. $14,819.19
2. Option (a)
3. Option (a)
4. $198,594.46
5. 7 years and 4 months
6. 29
7. $416.41
8. a) $11,453.21
b) $158,128.40
9. 10 years
10. $38,988.14, $6011.86
11. $534,395.07, $259,200, $275,195.07
12. $11,540.40
13. $0.52
14. 4 years and 2 months
15. 3.13%, $1324.36

Chapter 11

Exercises 11.1

1. a) Ordinary deferred annuity, 4 months, 3 years, 36
b) Deferred annuity due, 2 years, 5 years and 6 months, 11
3. $120,967.49
5. $143.291.95
7. $73,415.59
9. $8498.44
11. 4 years and 9 months (the last payment will be less than $800)
13. 8 years (the last payment will be less than $2500)
15. $198.75
17. $1278.72
19. $462.68

Exercises 11.2

1. $166,666.67
3. $67,162.97
5. $202.50
7. $410,435.81
9. $42,000.00
11. $1.40
13. $3094.06
15. $4770.51
17. $499,549.69

Exercises 11.3

1. a) $11,203.38
b) $11,697.49
3. $128,614.69
5. $57,832.31
7. $20,757.70
9. $3099.42
11. $23,524.95

Review Exercises 11

1. $895,467.91
3. $16,851.31
5. 3 years and 1 month (the last withdrawal will be less than $2000)
7. $1886.93
9. $7500.00
11. $9961.22
13. $3099.27
15. $2,542,515.73
17. $82,604.34
19. $7786.66

Self-Test Exercises 11

1. $46,554.48
2. $3013.67
3. 5 years and 4 months (the last payment will be less than $500)
4. $140.76
5. $24,891.84
6. $2901.84
7. $7593.75
8. $130,724.69
9. $57,573.27
10. $8219.50

Chapter 12

Exercises 12.1

1. $2045.79; $5355.80

3. a) $2562.81
b) $251.24
c) Amortization Schedule:

#	Amount Paid	Interest Portion	Principal Portion	Principal Balance
0				$10,000.00
1	$2562.81	$100.00	$2462.81	7537.19
2	2562.81	75.37	2487.44	5049.75
3	2562.81	50.50	2512.31	2537.44
4	2562.81	25.37	2537.44	0.00

5. a) $111,401.72
b) $557,008.60
c) Amortization Schedule:

#	Amount Paid	Interest Portion	Principal Portion	Principal Balance
0				$450,240.00
1	$111,401.72	$33,948.10	$77,453.62	372,786.38
2	111,401.72	28,108.09	83,293.63	289,492.75
3	111,401.72	21,827.75	89,573.97	199,918.78
4	111,401.72	15,073.88	96,327.84	103,590.94
5	111,401.70	7810.76	103,590.94	0.00

7. $4,803.66

9. $21,650.54

11. $15.97

13. $118.79; $181.21

15. a) 5 years and 3 months
b) $59.48, $540.52
c) Partial Amortization Schedule:

#	Amount Paid	Interest Portion	Principal Portion	Principal Balance
0				$10,850.00
1	$600.00	$122.06	$477.94	10,372.06
2	600.00	116.69	483.31	9888.75
...	.	.	.	.
20	600.00	8.87	591.13	197.28
21	199.50	2.22	197.28	0.00
Total	**$12,199.50**	**$1,349.50**	**$10,850.00**	

17. Amortization Schedule:

#	Amount Paid	Interest Portion	Principal Portion	Principal Balance
0				$4850.00
1	$851.52	$73.11	$778.41	4071.59
2	851.52	61.38	790.14	3281.45
3	851.52	49.47	802.05	2479.40
4	851.52	37.38	814.14	1665.26
5	851.52	25.10	826.42	838.84
6	851.49	12.65	838.84	0.00

19. $1059.64; $35,367.14

21. $188,756.33

23. $11,080.34

25. $118.00; $19,882.00

27. a) 24 years and 5 months
b) $2,743.22; $256.78
c) $101,238.76; $6761.24

29. Partial Amortization Schedule:

PMT #	Amount Paid	Interest Portion	Principal Portion	Principal Balance
				$280,000.00
1	$3000.00	$2843.49	$156.51	279,843.49
2	3000.00	2841.90	158.10	279,685.39
...	.	.	.	.
292	3000.00	38.62	2961.38	841.09
293	849.63	8.54	841.09	0.00
Total	**$876,849.63**	**$596,849.63**	**$280,000.00**	

Exercises 12.2

1. a) $1437.90
b) $248,486.35
c) $1,463.15

3. a) $1100.00
b) $479.91

5. a) $1050.00
b) 6 months; $445.97

7. a) $1560.00
b) $82,744.20
c) $1570.00; $1363.22

9. $280,049.82

11. 7 years and 1 month

13. 5 years and 7 months

Review Exercises 12

1. $1585.72; $1528.64;
Partial Amortization Schedule:

PMT #	Amount Paid	Interest Portion	Principal Portion	Principal Balance
0				$17,500.00
1	$1585.72	$229.69	$1356.03	$16,143.97
2	1585.72	211.89	1373.83	14,770.14
...	.	.	.	.
11	1585.72	40.82	1544.90	1565.18
12	1585.72	20.54	1565.18	0.00

3. $2500.29; $28.38

5. $12.84; $487.16

7. Partial Amortization Schedule:

PMT #	Amount Paid	Interest Portion	Principal Portion	Principal Balance
0				$16,850.00
1	$500.00	$62.26	$437.74	$16,412.26
2	500.00	60.64	$439.36	$15,972.89
...	.	.	.	.
36	500.00	1.94	$498.06	$28.28
37	28.38	$0.10	$28.28	0.00
Total	**$18,028.38**	**$1178.38**	**$16,850.00**	

9. Amortization Schedule:

PMT #	Amount Paid	Interest Portion	Principal Portion	Principal Balance
0				$1,250,000.00
1	$285,547.43	$57,521.95	$228,025.48	1,021,974.52
2	285,547.43	47,028.78	238,518.66	783,455.87
3	285,547.43	36,052.73	249,494.70	533,961.16
4	285,547.43	24,571.59	260,975.84	272,985.31
5	285,547.43	12,562.12	272,985.31	0 .00

11. $1354.03; $6736.83

13. $1354.03; $379.12, $974.91

15. **a)** $2133.12 **b)** $291,938.85 **c)** $2,190.71

17. **a)** $800.00 **b)** $560.23

19. $156,080.51

Self-Test Exercises 12

1. $176.95;
Partial Amortization Schedule:

PMT #	Amount Paid	Interest Portion	Principal Portion	Principal Balance
0	–	–	–	$200,000.00
1	$176.95	$20.00	$156.95	19,843.05
2	176.95	19.84	157.11	19,685.94
...	.	.	.	.
119	176.95	0.35	176.60	176.75
120	176.93	0.18	176.75	0.00

2. $5,236.56; $261.39

3. $30.35; $319.65

4. Partial Amortization Schedule:

PMT #	Amount Paid	Interest Portion	Principal Portion	Principal Balance
0				$18,400.00
1	$350.00	$113.53	$236.47	18,163.53
2	350.00	112.07	237.93	17,925.60
3	350.00	110.60	239.40	17,686.21
...	.	.	.	.
62	350.00	5.86	344.14	606.05
63	350.00	3.74	346.26	259.79
64	261.39	1.60	259.79	0.00
Total	**$22,311.39**	**$3911.39**	**$18,400.00**	

5. $457.42; $10,102.57

6. $457.59; $128.61, $328.81

7. **a)** $988.56 **b)** $170,834.05 **c)** $1,076.95

8. **a)** $180.00 **b)** $170.52

9. 2 years and 7 months

10. 7 years and 11 months

Chapter 13

Exercises 13.1

1. $1023.36; premium = $23.36

3. $28,219.12; premium = $3219.12

5. $9995.68; discount = $4.32

7. gain $70.66

9. $9722.51

11. $4941.72; discount = $58.28

13. $49,012.65; discount = $987.35

15. Bond schedule:

PMT #	Interest Received	Interest on BV	Amortized Premium	Book Value	Unamortized Premium
0	–	–	–	$1037.43	$37.43
1	$20.00	$15.56	$4.44	1032.99	32.99
2	20.00	15.49	4.51	1028.48	28.48
3	20.00	15.43	4.57	1023.91	23.91
4	20.00	15.36	4.64	1019.27	19.27
5	20.00	15.29	4.71	1014.56	14.56
6	20.00	15.22	4.78	1009.78	9.78
7	20.00	15.15	4.85	1004.93	4.93
8	20.00	15.07	4.93	1000.00	0.00
Total	**$160.00**	**$122.57**	**$37.43**		

17. Bond schedule:

PMT #	Interest Received	Interest on BV	Accumulated Discount	Book Value	Discount to be Accumulated
0	–	–	–	$9850.00	$150.00
1	$500.00	$522.05	$22.05	9872.05	127.95
2	500.00	523.22	23.22	9895.27	104.73
3	500.00	524.45	24.45	9919.72	80.28
4	500.00	525.75	25.75	9945.47	54.53
5	500.00	527.11	27.11	9972.58	27.42
6	500.00	528.55	28.55	10,001.13	−1.13
Total	**$3000.00**	**$3151.13**	**$151.13**		

19. 8.64% compounded semi-annually

Exercises 13.2

1. $1134.58; $923.36

3. Sinking fund schedule:

PMT #	Payment	Interest Earned	Increase in the Fund	Fund Balance
0	–	–	–	$0.00
1	$1134.58	$0.00	$1134.58	1134.58
2	1134.58	$31.20	1165.78	2300.36
3	1134.58	63.26	1197.84	3498.20
4	1134.58	96.20	1230.78	4728.98
5	1134.58	130.05	1264.63	5993.61
6	1134.58	164.82	1299.40	7293.01
7	1134.58	200.56	1335.14	8628.15
8	1134.58	237.27	1371.85	10,000.00
Total	**$9076.64**	**$923.36**	**$10,000.00**	

5. a) $41,645.47 **b)** $416,454.70 **c)** $83,545.30 **d)** $276,233.38 **e)** $11,049.34 **f)** $52,694.81

g) Partial sinking fund schedule:

PMT #	Payment	Interest Earned	Increase in the Fund	Fund Balance
9	41,645.47	15,349.23	56,994.70	440,725.48
10	41,645.47	17,629.02	59,274.49	499,999.97

7. $10,435.37; $16,517.04

9. Sinking fund schedule:

PMT #	Payment	Interest Earned	Increase in the Fund	Fund Balance
0	–	–	–	$0.00
1	$10,435.37	$417.41	$10,852.78	10,582.78
2	10,435.37	851.53	11,286.90	22,139.68
3	10,435.37	1303.00	11,738.37	33,878.05
4	10,435.37	1772.54	12,207.91	46,085.96
5	10,435.37	2260.85	12,696.22	58,782.18
6	10,435.37	2768.70	13,204.07	71,986.25
7	10,435.37	3296.87	13,732.24	85,718.49
8	10,435.37	3846.15	14,281.52	100,000.01
Total	**$83,482.96**	**$16,517.05**	**$100,000.01**	

11. a) $31,099.18 **b)** $621,983.60 **c)** $128,016.40 **d)** $706,001.49 **e)** $11,598.30 **f)** $37,752.52

g) Partial sinking fund schedule:

PMT #	Payment	Interest Earned	Increase in the Fund	Fund Balance
1	$31,099.18	$544.24	$31,643.42	$31,643.42
2	31,099.18	1098.00	32,197.18	63,840.60

13. $257,778.74; $2,988,694.34

15. Partial sinking fund schedule:

PMT #	Payment	Interest Earned	Increase in the Fund	Fund Balance	Book Values
0	–	–	–	$0.00	$5,000,000
1	$82,778.74	$0.00	$82,778.74	82,778.74	4,917,221.26
2	82,778.74	$1655.57	84,434.31	167,213.05	4,832,786.95
3	82,778.74	3344.26	86,123.00	253,336.05	4,746,663.95
...	.	.	.		.
37	.	.	.	4,472,887.51	527,112.49
38	82,778.74	89,457.75	172,236.49	4,645,121.00	354,876.00
39	82,778.74	92,902.48	175,681.22	4,820,805.22	179,194.78
40	82,778.74	96,416.10	179,194.84	5,000,000.00	0.00
Total	**$3,311,149.60**	**$1,688,850.46**	**$5,000,000.00**		

17. $18,263.28; $34,810.85

19. Sinking fund schedule:

PMT #	Payment	Interest Earned	Increase in the Fund	Fund Balance	Book Values
0	–	–	–	$0.00	$100,000.00
1	$15,763.28	$0.00	$15,763.28	15,763.28	84,236.72
2	15,763.28	350.77	16,114.05	31,877.33	68,122.67
3	15,763.28	709.35	16,472.63	48,3349.96	51,650.04
4	15,763.28	1075.90	16,839.18	65,189.14	34,810.86
5	15,763.28	1450.62	17,213.90	82,403.04	17,596.96
6	15,763.28	1833.67	17,596.95	99,999.99	0.01
Total	**$94,579.68**	**$5420.31**	**$99,999.99**		

Review Exercises 13

1. $4789.99; discount = $210.01

3. $1017.00; premium = $17.00

5. Loss $3251.98

7. $29,449.53; premium = $4449.53

9. $9853.64; discount = $146.36

11. $5380.08; premium = $380.08

13. Bond schedule:

PMT #	Interest Received	Interest on BV	Premium Amortized	Book Value	Unamortized Premium
0	–	–	–	$1035.47	$35.47
1	$32.50	$28.48	$4.02	1031.45	31.45
2	32.50	28.36	4.14	1027.31	27.31
3	32.50	28.25	4.25	1023.06	23.06
4	32.50	28.13	4.37	1018.69	18.69
5	32.50	28.01	4.49	1014.20	14.20
6	32.50	27.89	4.61	1009.59	9.59
7	32.50	27.76	4.74	1004.85	4.85
8	32.50	27.64	4.86	1000.00	0.00
Total	**$260.00**	**$224.52**	**$35.48**		

15. 9.97%

17. (i) $10,103.59 (ii) $80,828.72 (iii) $19,171.28 (iv) $56,954.88 (v) $3417.29 (vi) $13,520.88
(vii) Sinking fund schedule:

PMT #	Payment	Interest Earned	Increase in the Fund	Fund Balance
0	–	–	–	$0.00
1	$10,103.59	$0.00	$10,103.59	10,103.59
2	10,103.59	606.22	$10,709.81	20,813.40
3	10,103.59	1248.80	11,352.39	32,165.79
4	10,103.59	1929.95	12,033.54	44,199.33
5	10,103.59	2651.96	12,755.55	56,954.88
6	10,103.59	3417.29	13,520.88	70,475.76
7	10,103.59	4228.55	14,332.14	84,807.90
8	10,103.59	5088.47	15,192.06	99,999.96
Total	**$80,828.72**	**$19,171.24**	**$99,999.96**	

19. $135,572.74; $919,829.94

Self-Test Exercises 13

1. discount = $355.31
2. $10,372.08; premium = $372.08
3. loss $1293.23
4. $969.82; premium = $30.18
5. 24,752.91; discount = $247.09
6. $10,728.36; premium = $728.36
7. Bond schedule:

PMT #	Interest Received	Interest on BV	Premium Amortized	Book Value	Unamortized Premium
0	–	–	–	$5085.03	$85.03
1	$200.00	$190.69	$9.31	5075.72	75.72
2	200.00	190.34	9.66	5066.06	66.06
3	200.00	189.98	10.02	5056.04	56.04
4	200.00	189.60	10.40	5045.64	45.64
5	200.00	189.21	10.79	5034.85	34.85
6	200.00	188.81	11.19	5023.66	23.66
7	200.00	188.39	11.61	5012.05	12.05
8	200.00	187.95	12.05	5000.00	0.00
Total	**$1600.00**	**$1514.97**	**$85.03**		

8. 4.83%

9. $369,055.50; $35,380.29
Partial sinking fund schedule:

PMT #	Payment	Interest Earned	Increase in the Fund	Fund Balance
28				664,217.89
29	12,301.85	29,889.81	42,191.66	706,409.55
30	12,301.85	31,788.43	44,090.28	750,499.83
Total	**$369,055.50**	**$381,444.32**	**$750,499.83**	

10. $11,762.88; $23,666.57

Chapter 14

Exercises 14.2

1. No
3. Campaign A
5. No
7. Buy option
9. a) Rent **b)** Purchase

Exercises 14.3

1. Newspaper; $6.95
3. a) Yes; $15,671.11, **b)** No; – $77,188.87
c) No; – $167,026.34
5. Yes; $2515.41
7. No; –$47,488.94
9. Yes; $174,032.67

Exercises 14.4

1. 21.16%
3. 28.55%; No
5. 27.36%; Yes
7. 16.99%; Yes
9. 20.74%; Yes

Exercises 14.5

1. 3 years and 8 months; Yes
3. 6 years and 2 months; No
5. 5 years and 10 months; No

Review Exercises 14

1. 10.87%
3. 13.63%; No
5. 9.94%; No
7. Purchase; $2861.05
9. a) Yes; $658,091.56 **b)** Yes; $312,500.00
c) No; –$40,276.43
11. No; –$1887.12
13. $22,485.04
15. 15.01%; No
17. 4 years and 5 months; No
19. 7 years and 8 months; No

Self-Test Exercises 14

1. Option 1; $2654.44
2. 15.37%; Yes
3. Upgrade plastic molder; 27.18%
4. 17.95%; No
5. 18.97%
6. 38.99%; Yes
7. 3 years and 8 months; No
8. 2 years and 6 months; No

Glossary

Algebra a branch of mathematics that deals with different relations and operations by using letters and symbols to represent numbers, values, etc.

Algebraic expression consists of one or more terms with a combination of variables, numbers, and operation signs. Equations and formulas are formed using algebraic expressions.

Algebraic term a number, variable, or a combination of numbers and variables, which forms a part of an expression.

Amortization the process of repaying a loan through periodic payments.

Amortization period the time taken to repay a loan.

Amortization schedule a table showing the reduction of a loan's principal balance from period to period, including the payment size, the interest portion, and the principal portion for each period.

Amount of interest the amount charged for using a principal amount for a period of time.

Amount of markup (also known as margin or gross profit) the difference between the selling price and the cost of merchandise.

Annual salary the salary that an employee receives for his or her service over the period of a year.

Annuity a series of payments (usually in equal amounts) made at regular intervals for a fixed period of time.

Annuity due an annuity where payments are made at the beginning of each payment period.

Base (B) the number that represents the whole (100%) quantity or value; used in percentage calculations.

Base salary + commission when an employee receives a commission on the sales made, in addition to his/her base salary.

BEDMAS the acronym for the order of arithmetic operations: Bracket, Exponent, Division, Multiplication, Addition, and Subtraction.

Bi-weekly pay period when an employee is paid once every two weeks.

Binomial a polynomial with 2 terms.

Bond an (often transferrable) contract that promises regular payments over time, as well as a larger lump-sum payment at the end of the contract's term. These contracts are generally sold to investors with the promise of a return on their investment.

Break-even point the point at which the total sales or total revenue equals the total costs. At the break-even point, there are no profits made or no losses incurred.

Break-even price the selling price of an item, which includes only the cost and overhead expenses. When a product is sold at the break-even price, neith is profit made nor loss incurred.

Cash-inflow when money is received.

Cash-outflow when money is paid out.

Cash discount the amount of discount on the net price (invoice amount) offered by a seller to a buyer to encourage early payment of an invoice.

Coefficient the number factor in front of the variable(s) of an algebraic term.

Collateral the legal claim that a lender holds over a borrower's property, assigned in a lending agreement, which grants the lender the right to take the property if the borrower has shown an inability to pay the debt.

Commercial paper similar to T-bills, except that it is issued by large corporations rather than by governments.

Commission a percentage of sales for a given pay period that is given to an employee as part of his/her salary.

Common logarithms the logarithm of a number to the base 10; referred to by the symbol 'log'.

Complex fraction a fraction in which one or more fractions are found in the numerator or denominator.

Composite number a whole number that has at least one factor other than 1 and the number itself.

Compounding frequency the number of times interest is compounded every year.

Compounding period the time interval between two successive interest dates.

Compound interest a procedure where interest is added to the principal at the end of each compounding period to earn interest in the subsequent compounding period.

Constant-growth annuity an annuity where the periodic payment amount increases by a constant rate over the preceding payment amount.

Constant a letter used in an algebraic expression that only represents a single number.

Contribution Margin per unit the amount remaining from the selling price per unit after deducting the variable costs per unit.

Contribution Ratio the ratio of the contribution margin to the selling price per unit; expressed as a percentage.

Cost the amount paid for an item after trade discounts and cash discounts have both been deducted.

Cost of capital the cost of spending money in a business (either through direct interest charges on borrowed money, or relative opportunity costs through profits lost from alternative projects), expressed as compounded rate.

Deferred annuity an annuity in which the first periodic payment is made after a certain interval of time, known as the deferred period.

Deferred annuity due a deferred annuity where periodic payments are made at the beginning of each payment period.

Demand loan a loan that becomes payable when it is demanded by the lender who issues the loan.

Discounted Cash Flow a method of valuing an investment by discounting all future cash inflows and outflows, to their present value.

Effective interest rate the annually compounding interest rate.

End-of-Month dating (EOM) a cash payment term where the credit period and discount period start from the end of the month in which the invoice is dated.

Equivalent algebraic equations equations with the same solutions.

Equivalent fraction the resulting fraction when both the numerator and denominator of a fraction are either multiplied by the same number or divided by the same number.

Equivalent interest rates nominal interest rates with different compounding periods that result in the same future value of a given principal for any fixed period of time.

Equivalent ratio the resulting ratio when all the terms of the ratio are multiplied by the same number or divided by the same number.

Exchange rate (also called the foreign exchange rate or forex rate) used to convert currencies between countries.

Exponents mathematical notation for representing the product of a repeated number. For example, $2 \times 2 \times 2 \times 2 \times 2$ is represented as 2^5 using exponents.

Face Value the amount that is to be transferred from the issuer to the holder of a promissory note; the redemption value of the note.

Factors of a number whole numbers that can divide the number with no remainder.

Fixed Costs costs that remain the same irrespective of how many items are produced and sold.

Fraction a rational number written as one integer divided by another non-zero integer.

Fractional exponent when the exponent of a term is a fraction.

Future value the accumulated value of a payment or a series of payments.

General annuity due an annuity due where the compounding period and the payment period are not the same.

Goods and Services Tax (GST) sales taxes that are levied by the federal government. The federal GST rate for all provinces and territories in Canada is 5%.

Graduated commission when an employee's commission increases gradually with increased sales.

Graduated piecework rate when the rate per unit increases above a pre-determined output level.

Gross pay the total amount of earnings before any deductions are made.

Guaranteed Investment Certificate (GIC) investment where the investor is guaranteed to receive the full principal investment plus interest at the end of the specified time period.

Harmonized Sales Tax (HST) a single tax which combines the GST and PST. In British Columbia, New Brunswick, Newfoundland, Nova Scotia, and Ontario, HST is collected by Canada Revenue Agency, which then remits the appropriate amounts to the participating provinces.

Highest Common Factor (HCF) the largest common number that divides two or more numbers with no remainder.

Hourly wages when employees are paid on an hour-by-hour basis.

Improper fraction a fraction in which the absolute value of the numerator is greater than the absolute value of the denominator.

Interest a fee paid by borrowers to lenders for using money temporarily.

Interest bearing promissory note a promissory note where the face value is the amount of loan that must be repaid with the interest calculated based on the interest rate specified on the note.

Internal Rate of Return (IRR) the annually compounding rate at which an investment produces a gain.

Least or Lowest Common Denominator (LCD) the smallest whole number that is divisible by each of two or more fractions' denominators.

Least or Lowest Common Multiple (LCM) the smallest multiple that is common to two or more whole numbers.

Like terms two or more algebraic terms that have the same variables and exponents.

Linear equation a first degree algebraic equation with one or two variables which produces a straight line when plotted on a graph.

List price (also known as the manufacturer's suggested retail price or MSRP) the price of a merchandise item before discounts have been applied.

Markdown the amount by which the selling price of a product is reduced to determine the sale price or reduced selling price.

Markup the amount that a business adds to the cost of the product to arrive at the selling price of the product.

Maturity value the accumulated value of a principal amount that is invested or borrowed at an interest rate for a period of time.

Merchandising a process that involves the buying and selling of goods (merchandise) from a manufacturer to the final sale of those goods to consumers.

Mill rate the amount of property tax per thousand dollars of property value.

Mixed number a number consisting of both a whole number and a fraction, which are written side-by-side and imply that the whole number and proper fraction are added together.

Monomial an algebraic expression that only has one term.

Mortgage a loan issued by a financial lending institution to a borrower for the purpose of purchasing real-estate property, generally with the lender holding a legal claim over the property until the loan has been repaid.

Monthly pay period when an employee is paid once a month.

Multiples of a number whole numbers that can be divided by the number with no remainder.

Natural logarithms the logarithm of a number to the base 'e', where e = 2.718282...; referred to by the symbol 'ln'

Net Income the difference between the total revenue collected and the total costs incurred in a business.

Net loss when the total revenue is less than the total costs.

Net pay the actual payment that an employee receives after all payroll deductions.

Net Present Value the present value of all future cash inflows less the present value of all future cash outflows. This represents the total gain of an investment over its life, taking the time value of money into account.

Net price the price of a merchandise item after deducting all discounts.

Net profit when the total revenue of a business exceeds its total costs.

Nominal interest rate the quoted or stated interest rate per annum on which the compound interest calculation is based for a given compounding period.

Non-interest bearing promissory note a promissory note where the face value is the maturity value of the note.

Operating profit also known as profit, is the amount of desired profit necessary to stay in the business.

Ordinary annuity an annuity where payments are made at the end of each payment period.

Ordinary dating cash payment terms where the credit period and the discount period start on the invoice date.

Ordinary deferred annuity a deferred annuity where periodic payments are made at the end of each payment period.

Ordinary general annuity an ordinary annuity where the compounding period and the payment period are not the same.

Ordinary simple annuity an ordinary annuity where the compounding period and the payment period are the same.

Overhead expenses (also known as operating expenses) expenses that are necessary to operate the business.

Overtime factor used to calculate the overtime rate of pay for an employee.

Overtime rate the hourly rate of pay for working overtime.

Payment interval (or payment period) the time between two successive payments.

Pay period how often payments are made to an employee. They could be monthly, semi-monthly, bi-weekly, or weekly.

Payback period the length of time required for an investment's cash inflows to match and/or cross its cash outflows (ignoringing the time value of money).

Payroll a record that employers maintain to register employees' names, the types of payment, and the amount of payment made towards them.

Payroll deductions deductions from the employees' salary to pay towards taxes, the employees' pension, savings, etc.

Percent used to express a quantity out of 100 units and is represented by the symbol %.

Percent change the percentage by which a quantity increases or decreases from its initial value.

Periodic interest rate the interest rate for a given compounding period.

Perpetuity an annuity where the periodic payments begin on a fixed date and continue indefinitely.

Perpetuity due a perpetuity where periodic payments are made at the beginning of the payment period.

Piecework rate when employment is based on the number of units produced or task completed (output), employees' gross pay is calculated based on an agreed flat rate called piecework rate for each item or task completed.

Place value the value of a digit in a number based on its place or position.

Polynomial an algebraic expression that has two or more terms.

Portion (P) a part of the whole quantity or value (portion of the base); used in percentage calculations.

Present value the discounted value or principal amount of a payment or a series of payments.

Prime number a whole number that has no factors other than 1 and the number itself.

Principal the amount of money borrowed or invested at the beginning of a period.

Pro-ration sharing or allocating quantities, usually amounts, on a proportionate basis.

Promissory note a written promise to repay a borrowed amount of money to a lender on an agreed date.

Proper fraction a fraction in which the absolute value of the numerator is less than the absolute value of the denominator.

Property tax the amount the owner of a property is required to pay the municipal government and is generally calculated as a percentage of the value of the property that is being assessed.

Proportions when two sets of ratios are equal, we say that they are proportionate to each other.

Provincial Sales Tax (PST) the sales tax levied by Canadian provinces. No PST is levied in Alberta, the Northwest Territories, Nunavut, or the Yukon. In Prince Edward Island and Quebec, PST is applied to the combined cost and GST.

Quoted price of a bond a number above or below 100 which represents the discount or premium applicable to a bond's face value.

Rate (R) the percentage relationship between base and portion.

Rate of markdown markdown expressed as a percentage of selling price.

Rate of markup markup expressed as a percentage of cost or selling price.

Ratio a comparison or relationship between two or more quantities.

Receipt-of-Goods dating (ROG) cash payment terms where the credit period and discount period start from the date of receipt of goods.

Redemption in the case of bonds, repayment of the face value and the end of coupon payments.

Savings account a convenience account, where the interest is often calculated on the daily balance and posted monthly.

Selling price the price at which merchandise is sold to customers.

Semi-monthly pay period when an employee is paid 2 payments per month.

Simple annuity due an annuity due where the compounding period and the payment period are the same.

Simple arithmetic average (also called arithmetic mean or mean) the sum of all the values of the terms divided by the number of terms.

Simple interest rate the rate at which a principal amount is borrowed or invested.

Sinking fund an interest-earning fund that is built up over time with periodic deposits, so that the accumulated funds may later be withdrawn to make large payments to settle debts (such as the repayment of a bond's face value).

Straight commission when an employee is paid a percentage of the sales for the pay period as salary.

Straight piecework rate when a certain amount of pay per unit of output is given regardless of the output quantity.

Taxes fees that federal, provincial, or municipal governments charge organizations and individuals on income and property.

Term deposits (also known as fixed deposits or time deposits) investments where money is invested for a fixed period of time.

Term of an annuity the time from the beginning of the first payment interval to the end of the last payment interval.

Time period the period of time for which the principal amount is borrowed or invested during which interest is charged or earned.

Time value of money money grows with time when it is invested or borrowed at a particular interest rate.

Total costs the sum of the fixed costs and the total variable costs of a business.

Total Revenue the amount of money received or brought into the business from the sale of merchandise.

Total Variable Costs costs that vary directly with the number of units of items produced.

Trade discount the discount offered on the list price.

Treasury bill (also known as a T-bill) is a written agreement or contract issued to investors for a short term; issued by the federal government on every other Tuesday through major financial institutions as their agents.

Trinomial a polynomial with 3 terms.

Unlike terms two or more algebraic terms that have different variables or the same variables with different exponents.

Variable when a certain letter represents various numbers it is called a variable; i.e., a variable is used to represent a value that can change in an algebraic expression.

Variable Cost per unit the cost of producing one unit of merchandise.

Weekly pay period when an employee is paid every week.

Weighted arithmetic mean a method of calculating an average for a set of values, where each value is given a weight which determines its contribution to the final average.

Workweek the number of working hours in a week.

Yield to Maturity (YTM) indicates the internal rate of return of an investment to the end of its term. As an interest rate, indicates the periodically compounding rate of growth of the investment.

Index

D

E

F

G

H

I